Praise for Donald Shoup and the hardcover edition of
The High Cost of Free Parking

"Donald Shoup is a professor of urban planning at the University of California, Los Angeles, whose work on the pricing of parking spaces and whether more spaces are good for cities has led to a revolution in ideas about relieving congestion."
— *New York Times*

"This is an extraordinary book. An appropriate descriptive subtitle would be 'Everything you really wanted to know about parking but were afraid to ask!'"
—*Journal of Urban Design*

"A landmark in the annals of urban planning. This important book deserves a prominent spot on any planner's bookshelf. It's brilliant."
— Robert Cervero, Professor of City and Regional Planning, University of California, Berkeley

"Imagine an entire book on the length and breadth of parking by an author as facile as James Michener with the insight of Jane Jacobs and the passion of Lewis Mumford and you have Donald Shoup on the subject of parking. This book is destined to become a planning classic."
— Martin Wachs, FAICP, Professor Emeritus of City and Regional Planning and Civil and Environmental Engineering, University of California, Berkeley

"Parking rock star"
— *Wall Street Journal*

"Urban planners and economists should be embarrassed about how little thought we have given to off-street parking requirements. Shoup shows how parking standards have fundamentally shaped our built environment, usually for the worse."
— José A. Gómez-Ibáñez, Derek C. Bok Professor of Urban Planning and Public Policy, Harvard University

"The Jane Jacobs of parking policy"
— *Greater Greater Washington*

"This meticulously researched book is a must-read for all policymakers, community groups, planners, and citizens. Donald Shoup tackles head on the 100-year addiction to car travel and does so with enough humor and wit to hold the hope that a cure could lie ahead."
— Anne Vernez Moudon, Professor of Architecture, Urban Design, and Planning, University of Washington

"Godfather of parking reform"
— *Terrapass*

"The master of parking research"
— *Gainesville Sun*

"Convinced that urbanism can emerge in the backwash of sprawl, Shoup contends that if big boxes, malls and even strip malls were allowed to reduce their parking and replace excess spaces with something more useful, suburbanites might embark on the greatest land reclamation scheme this side of the Netherlands. He envisions apartment buildings and townhouses sprouting on the edges of mall parking lots and thereby creating nearly fully formed neighborhoods in place of vacant asphalt."
— *In Transition*

"Shoup engages with his deceptively weighty topic in a clear and progressive manner accessible to anyone from amateur parking enthusiasts to planning professionals."
— *Planning Theory and Practice*

"[Shoup] provides a wealth of resources, information, and ammunition for those seeking to change parking regulation, planning, and design paradigms."
— *Journal of Planning Literature*

"Shoup's accomplishment in this book is impressive. He brings to light an often-dismissed topic — parking — that has enormous impact on the urban form. I can't think of any other topic in all my reading about urban areas that has been so ignored and yet has such a demonstrated potential for improving urban life."
— *Book Notes*

"Parking god"
— *LAist*

"The hands-down favorite for Top Books status, *The High Cost of Free Parking*, despite its epic length, undoubtedly deserves high praise. Donald Shoup, FAICP, an urban planning professor at UCLA, presents a tour de force on free parking, a dubious fact of city life planners have taken for granted for years, and which Shoup has studied for decades."
— *Planetizen*

"This book should be required reading for anyone who cares about this nation's cities. Shoup helps us understand how we can use the billions we are spending to store motor vehicles in ways that can solve our parking problems and build healthy communities."
— Michael S. Dukakis, former Governor of Massachusetts; Distinguished Professor of Political Science, Northeastern University

The High Cost of Free Parking

By
Donald C. Shoup

American Planning Association
Planners Press

Making Great Communities Happen

Chicago | Washington, D.C.

To Pat

Contents

Tables

Figures

Acknowledgements

This book has been long in the writing, and I have accumulated many intellectual debts. First, I want to thank my wife Pat, who is the best editor a husband ever had. She has read and reread all the many versions of the manuscript, and contributed many ideas as well as unfailing encouragement. And these are the least of her contributions to my life.

I am also indebted to the Ph.D. students I have worked with at UCLA. Don Pickrell and Richard Willson both wrote their dissertations on employer-paid parking, and I gratefully acknowledge all they have taught me. Mary Jane Breinholt, Jeffrey Brown, Daniel Chatman, Gregg Doyle, Daniel Hess, Hiro Iseki, Eugene Kim, David King, Jianling Lee, Lewison Lem, Michael Manville, William Pitkin, Lisa Schweitzer, and Paul Sorensen have read all or parts of the book manuscript with keenly critical eyes and have made many important contributions.

I also want to thank many colleagues who have commented on the manuscript and given valuable advice. I have learned much from Daniel Benson, Kiran Bhatt, Leland Burns, Robert Cervero, Randall Crane, Elizabeth Deakin, Renee Fortier, William Francis, José Gómez-Ibáñez, Peter Gordon, Genevieve Giuliano, Paul Helmle, Thomas Higgins, Stanley Hoffman, Robin Liggett, Anastasia Loukaitou-Sideris, Frank Mittelbach, Joseph Morton, Vinit Mukija, John Pucher, Nicholas Pyle, Margaret Richardson, Frank Shoup, Richard Steinman, Mark Stocki, Peter Valk, Martin Wachs, Melvin Webber, and Joel Woodhull.

The California Air Resources Board, Lincoln Institute of Land Policy, University of California Transportation Center, United States Department of Transportation, and United States Environmental Protection Agency provided invaluable funding for my research on parking. I confess, however, that I may sometimes have used their funds in ways they did not intend. New planning students arrive at UCLA every year and most of them are required to take my course on Public Research Allocation. Invariably, some of them are superb writers, and their essays are a pleasure to read. I have used much of my research funding to hire these accomplished writers as editors of my manuscript, which has taken many years to straighten out. If you find anything easy to understand in this book, you can thank, as I do, Ellison Alegre, Heather Barnett, Aaron Bernardin,

Matthew Benjamin, Jennifer Bruno, Eric Carlson, Joy Chen, Francisco Contreras, T. H. Culhane, Daniel Dermitzel, Amy Ford, Simon Fraser, Jeanne Gilbert, Kay Gilbert, Leslie Goldenberg, Mark Hansen, Tania Hayes, Susan Herre, Kathleen Hiyaki, Kevin Holliday, Mimi Holt, Jeffrey Jones, Douglas Kolozsvari, Danny Krouk, Cheol-ho Lee, Trent Lethco, Christopher Lock, Bravishwar Mallavarapu, Douglas Miller, Andrew Mondschein, Eric Morris, Jeremy Nelson, Todd Nelson, Virginia Parks, Thomas Rice, Rafael Ruiz, Michael Sabel, Yuji Sakaguchi, Charles Sciammas, Gian-Claudia Sciara, Alexander Smith, Manuel Soto, Seth Stark, Florian Urban, Joseph Vardner, Kylee Williams, and Matthew Zisman. Easy reading is hard writing, and my student editors have spent many hours helping me say what I mean. It has been a joy to work with them, and I hope they have learned as much from me as I have from them.

Several chapters in the book have been adapted from articles that were previously published in *Access, Journal of the American Planning Association, Journal of Planning Education and Research, Journal of Regional Science and Urban Economics, Journal of Transportation and Statistics, Transport Policy, Transportation, Transportation Quarterly, Transportation Research, Transportation Research Record,* and *Traffic Quarterly.* The editors at these journals have often suggested substantial improvements. I am especially grateful to the editor of *Access,* Melvin Webber, who has set a high standard for excellence in writing about transportation policy in the United States.

Finally, I would like to thank my editor at the American Planning Association, James Hecimovich, for his encouragement, enthusiasm, and wise advice in converting my manuscript into a book. And thanks to Jim's editorial assistant, Rhonda Smith, for her impeccable copyediting of the many figures, tables, and references in the book.

It is a testament to our profession's integrity that although I have severely criticized current planning practices, and been less than kind to some of the APA's own publications, the APA is not only open to this criticism but also willing to publish it. I have strongly condemned the way planners deal with parking, but what I offer is an indictment of strategy and tactics, not motives. Whatever our differences, I am sure that those I criticize share with me the goal of improving city life. How to go about this task is the enduring question of our profession, and I hope this book will start a dialogue that brings us to a better answer. After all, that is why we are city planners.

Preface

A Progress Report on Parking Reforms

All of us, if we are reasonably comfortable, healthy and safe, owe immense debts to the past. There is no way, of course, to repay the past. We can only repay those debts by making gifts to the future.

—*JANE JACOBS*

Who would have predicted that a 750-page book on parking could be popular enough to reprint as a paperback? One sign that *The High Cost of Free Parking* has attracted a following is a Facebook group for the book with about a thousand members, called the Shoupistas. Although the group sounds radical, the members support market-rate prices for parking, which sounds conservative. Because of this widespread interest across the political spectrum, the American Planning Association is publishing this paperback edition to make the book more affordable, especially for students who are the next generation of city planners.

When the hardback edition was published in 2005, the reviews were, with one unimportant exception, very good.[1] More important than good reviews, several cities have adopted the policies proposed in the book, and the paperback edition offers an opportunity to report on progress made in parking reforms during the past six years. In this preface I will discuss reforms that have taken place in relation to the three basic policies recommended in the book: (1) set the right price for curb parking, (2) return the parking revenue to pay for local public services, and (3) remove minimum parking requirements. (The Afterword on pages 683–709 presents more information about these reforms.)

I hope the progress reported here will convince readers that my policy proposals are not theoretical and idealistic but are instead practical and realistic. The good news about our decades of bad planning for parking is that the damage we have done will be far cheaper to repair than to ignore.

1. SET THE RIGHT PRICE FOR CURB PARKING

Cities should set the right price for curb parking because the wrong prices produce such bad results. Where curb parking is underpriced and overcrowded, a surprising share of traffic can be cruising in search of a place to park. Sixteen studies conducted between 1927 and 2001 found that, on average, 30 percent of the cars in congested traffic were cruising for parking (see Chapter 11). New studies continue to find that many drivers cruise for curb parking like hawks looking for prey. For example, when researchers interviewed drivers who were stopped at traffic signals in New York City, they found that 28 percent of the drivers on one street in Manhattan and 45 percent on a street in Brooklyn were cruising for curb parking.[2]

In another study, observers found the average time to find a curb space on 15 blocks in the Upper West Side of Manhattan was 3.1 minutes and the average cruising distance was 0.37 miles. These findings were used to estimate that cruising for underpriced parking on these 15 blocks alone creates about 366,000 excess vehicle miles of travel and produces 325 tons of CO_2 per year.[3]

Performance Parking Prices

Free curb parking in a congested city gives a small, temporary benefit to a few drivers who happen to be lucky on a particular day, but it creates large social costs for everyone else every day. To manage curb parking and avoid the problems caused by cruising, some cities have begun to adjust their curb parking prices by location and time of day to produce an 85 percent occupancy rate for curb parking, which corresponds to one vacant space on a block with eight curb spaces. The price is too high if many spaces are vacant and too low if no spaces are vacant. But if one or two spaces are vacant on a block and drivers can reliably find open curb spaces at their destinations, the price is just right. We can call this the Goldilocks principle of parking prices.

Although cruising may seem to be an inevitable consequence of living in a crowded city, some drivers believe they have good "parking karma," an uncanny ability to find a curb space when they arrive at a destination. Given the laws of probability, some drivers will be luckier than others in finding a parking spot, and they may interpret this luck as a rare gift rather than pure chance. Setting the right parking prices can give all drivers the gift of good parking karma.

Some cities refer to the policy of setting prices to produce one or two open curb spaces on every block as *performance pricing*. It can improve performance in three ways. First, curb parking will perform more efficiently. If all but one or two curb spaces are occupied on every block, parking will be well used but also remain readily available for drivers who want to park. Second, the transportation system will perform more efficiently because cruising for curb parking will not congest traffic, waste fuel, pollute the air, and waste drivers' time. Third, the economy will perform more efficiently. In business districts, drivers will park, buy something, and leave promptly, allowing other customers to use the spaces.

SFpark. With a grant from the U.S. Department of Transportation, San Francisco has embarked on an ambitious program, called SF*park*, to get the prices of curb parking right. The city is installing meters that can charge variable prices and sensors that can report the occupancy of each space in real time. The city will thus have information on curb occupancy rates and the ability to adjust curb parking prices in response to the occupancy rates. The city intends to adjust prices once a month, by not more than 50¢ an hour. By nudging prices up or down in a trial-and-error process, the city will seek a structure of prices that vary by time and location throughout the city, yielding one or two open spaces on every block.[4]

The central idea of SF*park* is that you cannot set the right price for curb parking without observing the occupancy. The goal is to set the lowest price that will yield one or two open spaces on every block. Figure P-1 shows that nudging up the price on crowded Block A by enough to shift only one car to less crowded Block B can significantly improve the performance of the transportation system. This shift will eliminate cruising on Block A and take advantage of the empty spaces on Block B. Even if all the curb spaces are occupied on all the nearby blocks, shifting only one car per block from a curb space to nearby off-street parking can also eliminate cruising. Small changes in parking prices and location choices can lead to big improvements in transportation efficiency.

Beyond managing the curb parking supply, SF*park* can depoliticize parking by stating a clear principle for setting the prices for curb spaces: the

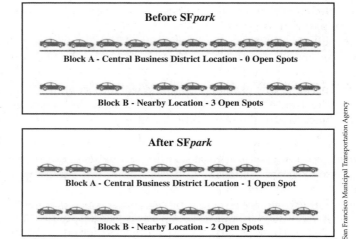

Figure P-1. Performance prices create open spaces on every block.

lowest prices the city can charge without creating a parking shortage. Because San Francisco has set a policy goal for how curb parking should perform, the demand for parking will set the prices.

Performance parking programs do not rely on complex models to set prices; they rely only on paying attention to the results. After shifting from a revenue goal to an outcome goal for the parking system and choosing the occupancy rate to indicate the desired outcome, the city council will no longer have to vote on parking prices. If too many curb spaces are vacant, the price will go down, and if no curb spaces are vacant, the price will go up. Wanting more money will no longer justify raising prices. Relying on the power of an impersonal rule to set prices makes an end run around the politics of parking.

In preparing for SF*park*, San Francisco conducted a census of its parking spaces and found 281,000 on-street spaces, which make up 58 percent of all publicly available parking in the city. San Francisco has one on-street parking space for every three people in the city, but only 9 percent of those spaces are metered.[5] Expanding SF*park* into areas that have a shortage of curb parking can greatly improve management of this valuable asset and also yield substantial revenue for local public investments.

Several other cities—including Los Angeles, New York, Seattle, and Washington, D.C.—have adopted similar performance parking policies. The Afterword explains their programs.

Opposition to SFpark. Drivers who cruise in search of free curb parking pay with time instead of money, and their cruising congests traffic, pollutes the air, and wastes fuel. In contrast, drivers who pay money for performance-priced curb parking provide funds to improve public services. Nevertheless, some people oppose charging anything for curb parking. One group in San Francisco, the Act Now to Stop War and End Racism (ANSWER) Coalition, has strongly but unsuccessfully tried to block SF*park*. One flyer proclaimed:

> Stop the parking meter hike! Make the rich pay, not the workers! Don't squeeze workers and small business. This is a tax on the people! It's time to organize and defeat the parking meter robbery![6]

The ANSWER Coalition opposes foreign wars for oil but supports free parking at home, and this sort of confusion is common in debates about parking policy. Thinking about parking seems to take place in the reptilian cortex, the most primitive part of the brain responsible for making snap decisions about urgent fight-or-flight choices, such as how to avoid being eaten.[7] The brain's reptilian cortex is said to govern instinctive behavior involved in aggression, dominance, territoriality, and ritual display—all important factors in cruising for parking and debating about parking policies.

The ANSWER Coalition's criticism of SF*park* is misguided. Thirty percent of households in San Francisco don't own a car, and the city uses all the parking meter revenue to subsidize public transit. Many poor people ride buses that are mired in traffic congested by richer drivers who are cruising for underpriced curb parking.[8]

Drivers who don't want to pay for parking often push poor people out in front of them like human shields, claiming that charging for parking will hurt the poor. Free curb parking limits the revenue available to pay for public services, and poor people are less able to replace public services with private purchases the way richer people can. The poorest people cannot afford cars, but they can benefit from public services—such as public transportation—that are financed by parking revenues. Using curb parking revenue to pay for local public services is much fairer than keeping curb parking free and requiring ample off-street parking (see pp. 530–539).

Some opposition to performance parking prices may be due to unfamiliarity, and only experience will change minds. Once drivers have become accustomed to performance prices and see that prices can decline as well as increase, they may come to value the ready availability of curb parking. What seems indefensible for a current generation may become indispensable for future generations. Familiarity breeds acceptability and, as Thomas Paine wrote, "Time makes more converts than reason."

New Technology for Performance Pricing

Setting an occupancy goal is easier than achieving it. How can a city adjust parking prices to yield one or two open curb spaces on every block? Fortunately, the technology used to charge for parking and measure occupancy has advanced rapidly in recent years. This new technology enables cities not only to set different prices at different times of day but also to measure the resulting occupancy of curb spaces.

Occupancy sensors are one promising new technology (see Figure P-2).[9] These sensors are about the size of a hockey puck and are placed in every curb space, either on the surface of the street or a few inches beneath it. They sense changes in the earth's magnetic field when a ton of metal is parked above and send this information to a central database. San Francisco will use the data from sensors to adjust parking prices once a month to reach the occupancy goal.[10]

The technology for charging variable prices has also advanced. Most multispace meters can charge variable prices through the day, and these prices can be remotely updated without touching the meters. Multispace parking meters on the UCLA campus charge four different prices during

Figure P-2. Occupancy sensor

a day, and the price of parking is not printed anywhere on the meter. When drivers touch a button on the meter, the digital display shows the price of parking at that time (see Figure P-3). For example, during peak hours the price of parking at the center of campus is $3 for the first hour and $4 for the second hour. Is this too much to charge for parking at a university? You cannot answer this question without looking at the results. The right price of curb parking is like Supreme Court Justice Potter Stewart's definition of pornography: "I know it when I see it."

Figure P-3. Variable parking prices

UCLA has not installed occupancy sensors, but I took photographs of eight parking spaces governed by the meter in Figure P-3 every four minutes for an hour and calculated the occupancy rate. In effect, I was the occupancy sensor. The goal of having one or two vacant spaces was met 87 percent of the time, and the average occupancy rate was 83 percent (see Figure P-4). I am *not* saying that $3 an hour is the right price for curb parking. I am saying that $3 an hour was the right price *at that time, at that place.* The combination of high-tech meters and occupancy sensors will allow cities to charge the right prices for curb parking everywhere.

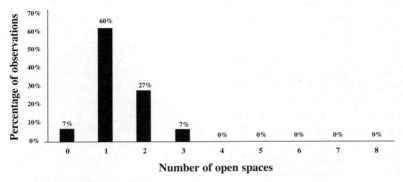

Figure P-4. Parking is well used but readily available.

Should the price of parking be lower? Then all the spaces will often be full and drivers will have to cruise for parking. This cruising will waste fuel, pollute the air, congest traffic, and increase carbon emissions. Should the price of parking be higher? Then more spaces will remain vacant because fewer drivers will pay to park in them. In business districts the stores will lose customers, the city will lose sales tax revenue, employees will lose jobs, and the economy will suffer. So other than aiming for one or two open spaces on every block, can anyone recommend a better principle for setting the price of curb parking?

Miniaturization is another technology that allows even single-space meters to offer sophisticated features such as variable prices, remote updates, payment by credit card, and solar power (see Figure P-5).[11] Drivers who pay by credit card can pay for more time than they expect to use, and, upon returning, reinsert the credit card to deduct the unused time before the card is charged.[12] This arrangement has two advantages. First, it reduces uncertainty. Drivers no longer have to guess how much to pay, worry that they have guessed wrong, or rush back to the meter to avoid getting a ticket. Second, drivers pay only for the time they use.

The increasingly common option of paying for parking by mobile phone also offers drivers the ability to pay only for the time parked, with no worry about returning before a meter has expired (see pp. 389–390). Paying for curb parking can thus be as convenient and worry

Figure P-5. Smart meter

IPS Group Inc., San Diego

free as paying for other services where the charge depends on the time used, such as long-distance telephone calls. If cities remove time limits at meters and give drivers the option to use credit cards at meters or pay by mobile phone, performance prices may become more acceptable, because they give drivers greater convenience.

Because occupancy sensors and parking meters provide real-time information for every parking space, the city has real-time information about the number of occupied but unpaid-for spaces on every block, enabling enforcement officers to focus on areas with high violation rates. Paying at a parking meter is like taking out an insurance policy against getting a parking ticket. It is a gamble, and a higher probability of being ticketed for overtime parking will encourage drivers to pay the meter rather than risk a ticket.

These two new technologies—occupancy sensors and remotely configured, variably priced parking meters—may change parking and transportation as profoundly as the invention of the cash register in the 19th century changed retail commerce. They can unlock the immense value of land now devoted to free parking and bring transportation into the market economy.

If the Price Is Right, Customers Will Come

Often when I present a proposal for performance parking prices in a city, someone in the audience vehemently says something like "If this city operates the parking meters in the evening, I will never drive downtown to eat in a restaurant again." This threat to boycott downtown restaurants would be a convincing argument if many curb spaces remained empty after the meters began operating in the evening. But this threat ignores the key argument for performance prices: *If the meters are priced right, cars will fill most of the curb spaces, leaving only one or two vacant spaces on each block.* If most curb spaces are filled, parking meters can't be chasing all the customers away.

Meters *will* chase away some drivers, but the curb spaces these drivers would have occupied will then become available to customers who are willing to pay for parking if they can easily find a convenient curb space on the block they want to visit. Because the curb spaces will remain almost fully occupied, merchants shouldn't be alarmed that performance prices will harm their businesses. And who is likely to leave a bigger tip in a restaurant? Drivers who are willing to pay for parking if they can always find open curb spaces at their destinations? Or drivers who will come only if they can park free after they circle the block a few times to find free parking?

The benefits do not stop with bigger tips. Whenever I am in a restaurant, I usually ask the waiters where they park. If the meters cease operating at 6 p.m. in the area, waiters often tell me they try to arrive shortly before 6 p.m. so they can find a meter and park free for the whole evening. But the curb spaces these waiters use are then not available for potential restaurant customers. If cities instead charge performance prices for curb parking and run the meters as late as needed to manage demand, waiters can park off-street or farther away in cheaper curb spots, making the most convenient spots available for more restaurant customers, who can leave more tips for the waiters.

Both common sense and empirical research suggest that performance-priced curb parking will motivate more people to carpool, because carpoolers can share the cost of parking while a solo driver pays the full cost (see p. 362). Waiters who park free at the curb will probably be solo drivers, but diners who pay to park may arrive with two, three, or four customers in a car. Further, performance prices will promote faster turnover because drivers will pay as long as they park. If a curb space turns over twice during the evening, each space can deliver two groups of diners to a restaurant rather than one waiter (see pp. 363–366). For both reasons—higher-occupancy vehicles and faster turnover—performance prices for curb parking will attract more customers to a business district. With more customers, the restaurants can expand and hire more waiters and pay more in sales taxes. Charging performance prices to manage curb parking can thus benefit many people, including even those who don't live in the metered areas.

A further advantage of performance prices is that they will decline when demand declines during a recession. The price of curb parking will automatically fall to keep the customers coming. The cheaper curb parking will help businesses survive and prevent job losses. But if curb parking prices remain high during a recession, curb spaces will be underoccupied, stores will lose customers, and more people will lose jobs.

If cities eliminate cruising by charging performance prices for curb parking, where will the cruising cars go? Because drivers will no longer have to arrive at their destinations 5 to 10 minutes early to search for a curb space, their vehicle trips will be 5 to 10 minutes shorter. The reduction in traffic will come not from fewer vehicle trips but from shorter vehicle trips.

Everybody wants something for nothing, but we should not promote free parking as a principle for transportation pricing and public finance. Using performance prices to manage curb parking can produce a host of benefits for businesses, neighborhoods, cities, transportation, and the environment. Parking wants to be paid for.

2. RETURN PARKING REVENUE TO PAY FOR LOCAL PUBLIC SERVICES

Drivers want to park free, and that will never change. What can change, however, is that people can want to *charge* for curb parking. The simplest way to convince people to charge for curb parking in their neighborhood is to dedicate the resulting revenue to paying for added public services in the neighborhood, such as repairing sidewalks, planting street trees, and putting utility wires underground. That is, the city can offer each neighborhood a *package* that includes both performance-priced curb parking *and* the added public services financed by the meters. Performance pricing will improve the parking and the revenue will improve the neighborhood. The people who live and work and own property in the neighborhood will see the meter money at work, and the package will be much more popular than meters alone.

Local Politics

Old Pasadena, a historic business district in Pasadena, California, is the leading example of a battered area that dramatically improved after the city used parking meter revenue to finance added public services (see Chapter 16). Spending more than $1 million a year of meter money on new public services helped convert what had been a commercial skid row into one of the most popular tourist destinations in Southern California. The success has even accelerated in recent years. In 2010, Marilyn Buchanan, a prominent business leader in Old Pasadena, said about the use of meter revenue:

Our public-private parking management situation works because of the knowledge we [the Old Pasadena business community] bring to it. . . . We have the passion for Old Pasadena and the business sense to recognize long-term good. Money is still a very personal issue and you can't just take our money and throw it into the general fund. Our money belongs here in Old Pasadena and we know how to put it to good use. Not selfish use but use for the good of the community which in the end of course helps us, the business people.[13]

If all parking revenue disappears into a city's general fund, business leaders and residents probably won't campaign for meters, even with all the sophisticated hardware now available to charge performance prices. Dedicating the revenue to paying for local public services can be the political software necessary to create local support for performance prices. If meter money stays in the neighborhood, it will probably be spent on things the residents value highly. And if new public spending in a neighborhood is financed by new revenue generated in that neighborhood, residents in the rest of the city will probably find this spending more acceptable.

Some people seem to think that parking meter revenue should go neither into the general fund nor back to the neighborhood but instead into a trust fund for motorists—for example, to build off-street parking garages. But if each neighborhood's parking meter revenue goes into a trust fund for the neighborhood and the money can be spent for the neighborhood's highest priorities, such as cleaner and safer sidewalks, residents may soon realize that subsidizing cars is not the best use of their trust fund.

Redwood City

In 2005, Redwood City, California, south of San Francisco, adopted legislation establishing a performance parking policy and returning the meter revenue to the metered district. The city council set a performance goal for curb parking—a target occupancy rate of 85 percent—and gave city staff the responsibility for adjusting prices to achieve the target occupancy. The council thus set parking *policy*, not parking *prices*. The council also dedicated the meter revenue to pay for public improvements in the metered zone. Once the merchants understood that the revenue would remain in the metered district, they strongly backed the proposal, and the members of the city council voted for it unanimously.

REDWOOD CITY'S PERFORMANCE PARKING ORDINANCE

To accomplish the goal of managing the supply of parking and to make it reasonably available when and where needed, a target occupancy rate of eighty-five percent (85%) is hereby established.

The Parking Manager shall survey the average occupancy for each parking area in the Downtown Meter Zone that has parking meters. Based on the survey results, the Parking Manager shall adjust the rates up or down in twenty-five cent ($0.25) intervals to seek to achieve the target occupancy rate.

Revenues generated from on-street and off-street parking within the Downtown Meter Zone boundaries shall be accounted for separately from other City funds and may be used only . . . within or for the benefit of the Downtown Core Meter Zone.

Sections 20.120 and 20.121 of the Redwood City Municipal Code

---

When Redwood City began to charge performance prices for curb parking, it also removed the time restrictions at meters, and this has been the program's most popular feature.[14] Because curb parking prices are higher than the adjacent off-street prices, most drivers who want to park for a long time naturally choose the off-street spaces.

Removing time limits for curb parking is especially important if meters operate in the evening. Having a one-hour time limit can make the curb spaces almost useless for people who want to dine in a restaurant or go to a movie. In 2009, desperate for new revenue, Los Angeles extended the hours of meter operation to 8 p.m. in business districts but left many of the one-hour time limits in place. As a result, many spaces remain empty in the evening and most revenue is from tickets for overtime parking. The time limits harm the adjacent businesses by making it difficult for restaurant or theater patrons to park and by irritating customers who get tickets. If customers have convenient curb parking, businesses will prosper and the city will receive more sales tax revenue, so removing time limits and pricing curb spaces to yield one or two vacancies in each block can help everyone.

The Afterword reports on the programs in several other cities—including Austin, Texas; St. Louis, Missouri; Ventura, California; and Washington, D.C.—that earmark the revenue from curb parking to pay for public services in the metered districts.

3. REMOVE MINIMUM PARKING REQUIREMENTS

Reform is not only adopting good policies but also repealing bad policies. Charging performance prices for curb parking and dedicating the revenue to pay for local public services are two good policies that cities can adopt. In contrast, requiring all buildings to provide ample parking is a bad policy that cities can repeal.

In Greek mythology, a cornucopia always overflowed with whatever its owner wanted. Chapters 1 to 10 show how the prohibition against buildings without ample parking does give us all the free parking we want, but that this cornucopian parking distorts transportation choices, debases urban design, damages the economy, and degrades the environment. Like alcohol prohibition in the 1920s, minimum parking requirements do more harm than good and should be repealed.

Some cities have begun to remove minimum parking requirements, at least in their downtowns, for two reasons. First, parking requirements prevent infill redevelopment on small lots, where fitting both a new building and the required parking is difficult and expensive. Second, parking requirements prevent new uses for many older buildings that lack the parking spaces required for the new uses (see pp. 97–101 and 153–156).

A search of newspaper articles about minimum parking requirements found 129 reports of cities that have removed off-street parking requirements in their downtowns since 2005. Although newspaper articles do not represent what all cities are doing, the articles include many comments on *why* cities are beginning to change their policies. At least in downtown business districts, some elected officials have been convinced that parking requirements put the brakes on what they want to happen and accelerate what they want to prevent. Some of the reasons given for removing parking requirements are "to promote the creation of downtown apartments" (Greenfield, Massachusetts), "to see more affordable housing" (Miami), "to meet the needs of smaller businesses" (Muskegon, Michigan), "to give business owners more flexibility while creating a vibrant downtown" (Sandpoint, Idaho), and "to prevent ugly, auto-oriented townhouses" (Seattle).

According to these quotes, cities remove parking requirements to prevent bad results and to produce good ones. The logical corollary is that parking requirements produce bad results and prevent good ones.[15] Removing a minimum parking requirement is not the same, however, as restricting parking or putting the city on a parking diet. Rather, minimum parking requirements force-feed the city with parking spaces, and removing a parking requirement simply stops this force-feeding. Businesses will be free to provide as much parking as they like.

An Example from Downtown Los Angeles

Many older downtowns have some wonderful buildings in terrible condition. Minimum parking requirements make restoring these historic buildings difficult or impossible, because they rarely have all the parking spaces cities require for new uses. Spring Street in Los Angeles, once known as the Wall Street of the West, is a prime example. It has the nation's largest collection of intact office buildings built between 1900 and 1930. Starting in the 1960s, the city's urban renewal program moved most office uses a few blocks west to Bunker Hill and left many splendid Art Deco and Beaux Arts buildings on Spring Street vacant except for retail uses on the ground floor.

In 1999, Los Angeles adopted its Adaptive Reuse Ordinance (ARO), which allows the conversion of economically distressed or historically significant office buildings into new residential units—with no new parking spaces (Figure P-6). Before 1999, the city required two parking spaces per condominium unit in downtown Los Angeles; in effect, the city had determined that no housing was better than any housing without all the required parking spaces.[16] Michael Manville studied the results of the ARO and found that many good things can happen when a city removes its parking requirements.[17]

Developers used the ARO to convert 56 historic office buildings into at least 7,300 new housing units between 1999 and 2008. All the office buildings had been vacant for at least five years, and many had been vacant much longer. By contrast, only 4,300 housing units were added in downtown between 1970 and 2000.[18]

Skeptics doubted that banks would finance developers who wanted to convert office buildings into residential condominiums without two parking spaces each, but the skeptics were proved wrong. Developers provided, on average, only 1.3 spaces per unit, with 0.9 spaces on-site and 0.4 off-site in nearby lots or garages. Had the ARO not been adopted, the city would have required two *on-site* spaces for every unit, or more than twice as many as developers did provide. Manville noted, "The ability to supply parking off-site helped developers simultaneously satisfy lenders, minimize development costs, and maximize the potential of an old building."[19] Deregulating both the *quantity* and the *location* of parking for the new housing was a key factor in restoring and converting the 56 office buildings Manville studied. Manville concluded that removing the parking requirements "led to both *more* housing and a greater *variety* of housing. Not only were more units built, but these units were constructed in buildings and neighborhoods that had long been stagnant and underused. Further, almost half of these buildings unbundled some or all of the parking from rent, allowing them to target an underserved demographic—people without cars."[20]

The ARO also exempts the converted office buildings from other planning requirements, such as density and height limits for residential uses, so the exemption from parking requirements isn't the sole reason for the conversions. Nevertheless, if the city hadn't removed the parking requirements these conversions couldn't have occurred, and the conversion boom shows that there is a residential market for people who don't own two cars. These results strongly suggest that until the ARO was adopted, minimum parking requirements had been preventing the restoration and conversion of many obsolete office buildings into housing.

The ARO also produced other benefits. It allowed the preservation of many historic buildings that had been vacant for years and might have been demolished if minimum parking requirements had remained in place. Historic buildings are a scarce resource in any city, and the evidence shows that parking requirements stood in the way of preserving these buildings. The ARO applied only to downtown when it was adopted in 1999, but the benefits were so quickly apparent that it was extended citywide in 2003.

The ARO preserved not only individual historic buildings but also a historic neighborhood. The Spring Street Financial District was listed in the National Register of Historic Places in 1979, but by then, the *Los Angeles Times* reported, it had become "a neighborhood of hoodlums, derelicts

Figure P-6. Office building in Los Angeles converted to residential use without adding on-site parking spaces.

and winos—a neighborhood of echoing buildings full of absolutely nothing above the ground floor."[21] If empty office buildings blight a neighborhood, preserving and converting them to residential use can help restore a neighborhood. The benefits of removing off-street parking requirements do not stop with historic preservation. The conversion projects created many jobs, and the government receives higher property tax revenue on the converted buildings.

Los Angeles's ARO shows the good results of removing off-street parking requirements. We usually can't see things that don't happen or count things that don't occur, but the beautifully restored buildings on Spring Street show us some wonderful things that parking requirements had been preventing in Los Angeles and are now preventing in many other cities.

An Example from Silicon Valley

Cities are removing or reducing off-street parking requirements in their downtowns, but most people live and work outside downtown. In the suburbs, cities often require more space for cars than for people. Figure P-7 shows the relationship between buildings and the required parking at a few land uses in San Jose, California.[22] The area required for parking at a restaurant, for example, is more than eight times larger than the dining area in the restaurant itself. Even if the required parking is used only intermittently, as at an auction house, the city requires the parking lots to be big enough to meet the peak demand for free parking.[23]

High parking requirements help to explain the parking-dominated landscape in many parts of San Jose and the rest of Silicon Valley. The top picture in Figure P-8 shows an example of the parking-disoriented development. Developers rarely provide more parking than cities require (see pp. 89–92), so the buildings in the picture are probably as big as they can be, given the number of parking spaces surrounding them. Many of the spaces, especially the ones at the periphery of the parking lots and adjacent to the streets, remain vacant almost all the time. So what would happen if

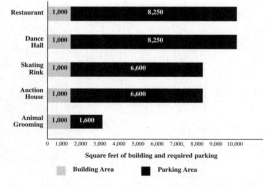

Figure P-7. San Jose's minimum parking requirements

San Jose removed off-street parking requirements, charged performance prices for on-street parking, and returned the resulting revenue to the metered neighborhoods? Property owners might decide their land was more valuable for housing than for vacant parking spaces.

Everyone in Silicon Valley complains about high housing prices, long commutes, traffic jams, air pollution, and the difficulty of attracting employees. Building housing on the periphery of parking lots would help to solve all these problems. The bottom picture in Figure P-8 suggests what might happen without minimum parking requirements. If apartment buildings were built next to the sidewalks, anyone walking, biking, or driving by would see what looks like a real city. The smartest way to travel is to be near your destination already, and this job-adjacent housing would give commuters out-of-car experiences while walking to work.

Stuart Cohen, Transportation and Land Use Coalition

Figure P-8. Parking lots in Silicon Valley before and after liner buildings

Liner Buildings

New urbanists refer to buildings that mask a parking lot
or garage from the street as
liner buildings. Figure P-9
shows one of the liner buildings inserted in the bottom
picture in Figure P-8.[24] The
term *liner* suggests that the
wrapping is a superficial
way to hide what is inside,
but in this case the wrapping
would probably be far more

Figure P-9. Liner building

valuable than the parking spaces it would replace. Parking is probably
the least profitable use of this peripheral land since almost any other use
would yield far more revenue. In parking, as in everything else, there
are opportunity costs.

The land is already assembled, and the housing could be built without
new parking because the existing spaces could be shared between office
buildings and apartments. To avoid a parking shortage, the owner
would probably have to unbundle the cost of parking from the rent for
both apartments and offices, so car owners would pay only for the parking spaces they use (see Chapter 20). Some residents who work in a
nearby office building may find they could easily live with only one car,
and they would appreciate the freedom to rent an apartment without
paying for two parking spaces.

If cities remove off-street parking requirements, they will have to
charge performance prices for the curb spaces to prevent spillover, but
this will produce another great benefit: All the money paid for curb
parking will become a new revenue stream to pay for local public services. Curb parking will become too valuable not to meter.

Removing the parking requirements for both housing and offices can
produce a cascade of benefits: shorter commutes, less traffic, a healthier
economy, a cleaner environment, and more affordable housing. And the
benefits don't stop there. If we reform our misguided planning for parking, the money now spent on cars and fuel will become available for
other things. Cars and fuel are often imported, but we cannot import
apartment buildings. Shifting spending from cars, fuel, and parking to
housing construction will increase the demand for labor in a host of professions, such as architects, carpenters, electricians, engineers, garden-
ers, glaziers, laborers, lawyers, locksmiths, painters, plumbers, real
estate agents, roofers, surveyors, and even urban planners. Importing

less oil and hiring all these people to build infill development will boost the whole economy.

The five-story apartment buildings shown in Figure P-8 are not the only option for liner buildings. Courtyard apartments, row houses, office buildings, stores, restaurants, or even single-family houses might be the best use for the land on the periphery of a parking lot. Liner buildings can create the atmosphere of a city, not a parking lot. If cities stop requiring off-street parking, vast suburban parking lots can evolve into real communities.

It is easy to see the bad results caused by parking requirements— asphalt everywhere and a lack of life on the streets. But it is hard to see the good results that parking requirements *prevent*. Photoshop can suggest, however, what cities might look like without parking requirements. The upside of the mess we have made is that we have an accidental land bank readily available for job-adjacent housing. This land is now locked up in required parking, but if cities remove their unwise parking requirements we can reclaim land on a scale that will rival the Netherlands.

A QUIET REVOLUTION IN PARKING POLICIES

Academic research has repeatedly shown that minimum parking requirements inflict widespread damage on cities, the economy, and the environment. But this research has had little influence on planning practice. Most city planners continue to set minimum parking requirements as though nothing has happened. The profession's commitment to minimum parking requirements seems to be a classic example of *groupthink*, which Yale professor of psychology Irving Janis defined as "a mode of thinking that people engage in when they are deeply involved in a cohesive in-group, when the members' striving for unanimity overrides their motivation to realistically appraise alternative courses of action."[25] The process of setting minimum parking requirements displays most of the symptoms of defective decision making that Janis identified with groupthink: incomplete survey of alternatives; incomplete survey of objectives; failure to examine risks of preferred choice; poor information search; and selective bias in processing information at hand.[26] Unfortunately, academic research on parking has had little effect on practitioners' groupthinking, even though the research shows that a central part of the practice does so much harm.

Requiring Peter to pay for Paul's parking, and Paul to pay for Peter's parking, was a bad idea. People should pay for their own parking, just as they pay for their own cars and their own gasoline. The planning profession has given cities bad advice about parking requirements, which have misshaped our cities to fit the car—almost without planners' noticing.[27] Parking requirements hide the cost of parking, but they cannot make it go away, and free parking usually means fully subsidized parking. At the very least, parking requirements should carry strong warning labels about all the dangerous side effects.

Suppose cities required all fast-food restaurants to include french fries with every hamburger. The fries would appear free, but they would have a high cost in money and health. Those who don't eat the fries pay higher prices for their hamburgers but receive no benefit. Those who do eat the fries they wouldn't have ordered separately are also worse off, because they eat unhealthy food they wouldn't otherwise buy. Even those who would order the fries if they weren't included free are no better off, because the price of a hamburger would increase to cover the cost of the fries. How are minimum parking requirements different? Minimum parking requirements force people who are too poor to own cars to pay for parking spaces they don't use, and they encourage others to buy more cars and drive them more than they would if they had to pay separately for parking. I am not saying that there should be no parking. I am saying that parking should be supplied in a fair market.

Despite institutional inertia in the practice of planning for parking, reforms are sprouting. Paradigm shifts in urban planning are often barely noticeable while they are happening, and after they have happened it is hard to tell that anything has changed. But shifts happen. Planners simply begin to understand cities in a new way and can scarcely remember a time when they understood cities differently. The incremental reforms now under way suggest that off-street parking requirements will not quickly disappear but will gradually erode. Cities may slowly shift from minimum parking requirements to performance parking prices without explicitly acknowledging that planning for parking had ever gone wrong. Eventually, however, planners may recognize that minimum parking requirements were a poisoned chalice, providing ample free parking while hiding the many costs. Our ample free parking comes at the expense of our cities' future.

All parking is political, and the prospects for parking reform depend on what the political context allows. Diverse interests from across the political spectrum can for different reasons support a shift from minimum parking requirements to performance parking prices. Liberals will see that it increases public spending. Conservatives will see that it reduces government regulation. Environmentalists will see that it reduces energy consumption, air pollution, and carbon emissions. Business leaders will see that it unburdens enterprise. New urbanists will see that it enables people to live at high density without being overrun by cars. Libertarians will see that it increases the opportunities for individual choice. Developers will see that it reduces building costs. Neighborhood activists will see that it devolves public decisions to the local level. Local elected officials will see that it reduces traffic congestion, encourages infill redevelopment, and pays for local public services without raising taxes. The current system of planning for parking does such widespread harm that the right reforms can benefit almost everyone.

But all these people also want to park free. They may not have an ideological or professional interest in free parking, but they do have a *personal* interest in it. This personal interest in free parking helps explain the popularity of minimum parking requirements. But the right use of parking meter revenue can also create a countervailing personal interest in *charging* for curb parking. Cities can create the necessary political support for performance parking prices by dedicating the meter revenue to pay for enhanced public services on the metered streets (see Chapters 16 and 17).

Both Jane Jacobs and Robert Moses might have agreed that charging performance prices for curb parking and using the revenue to improve the metered neighborhoods are good public policy. Jane Jacobs loved lively neighborhoods, and Robert Moses mastered the art of using tolls to finance public investments. Combining the best of both Jacobs and Moses can guide cities off the hard path of minimum parking requirements onto the soft path of performance parking prices.

In this book I focus on how performance parking policies can repair the damage minimum parking requirements have done to American cities, but the same policies are also appropriate for developing countries that do not yet have high levels of automobile ownership. Even countries with low automobile ownership have chaotic parking problems, as suggested by this description of Mexico City:

> Cars dominate nearly every square inch of Mexico City's public space. Vehicle owners double- and triple-park on the streets, to say nothing of curbs, sidewalks, gardens, alleys, boulevards and bike paths.[28]

Crowded cities in India also have problems with sacred cars, although only 14 percent of households in India own a car, and ownership is concentrated among the relatively rich.[29]

Many big cities in poor countries have such a high density of people that even a low rate of car ownership per household leads to a high density of cars. If these cities adopt performance prices for curb parking and use the revenue to pay for local public services, never before will so many poor people receive so much public benefit paid for by so few rich people. Even drivers will benefit because performance prices will help solve the two most difficult problems of owning a car in these cities: traffic congestion and parking shortages.

Market prices can manage the demand for parking spaces. If cities continue to offer free curb parking and require ample off-street parking, it won't be because performance prices don't work but because planners and politicians choose not to change course. There is a way, but we need the will. We can make great gifts to the future by reforming our misguided planning for free parking. In both sprawling rich cities and crowded poor cities, charging performance prices for curb parking, spending the revenue on local public services, and removing off-street parking requirements can do a world of good.

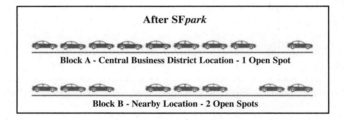

PREFACE NOTES

1. Twenty-four reviews of the book are available at http://its.ucla.edu/shoup/BookReviews.pdf.

2. Schaller (2006, 1, 15) and Transportation Alternatives (2007, 1).

3. Transportation Alternatives (2008, 10). Another way to learn about cruising is to ask drivers how much time they spend hunting for parking spaces. A survey of 9,000 drivers in the United Kingdom in 2010 found that British drivers reported spending an average of 25 minutes per day, or 152 hours per year, cruising for parking (Macrae 2010). That adds up to 11 months for someone who drives over the course of 50 years. Londoners lost the most time cruising, an average of 182 hours a year, or 54 weeks in 50 years.

4. Also with a grant from the U.S. DOT, Los Angeles will establish a similar program, called ExpressPark (Groves 2010). Berkeley, California, is establishing a program of "dynamic parking pricing" in two neighborhoods. In Los Angeles, occupancy sensors send information on curb vacancies to an iPhone app, Parker, which provides a real-time map showing nearby city blocks with more than four, more than two, or less than two vacant curb spaces, as well as blocks with "rock star" parking—the closest blocks with the most open spaces. The app also shows information about meter time limits, meter prices, and whether meters take credit cards or coins.

5. The census did not include off-street residential parking spaces. The data are available at http://sfpark.org/2010/04/05/parkingcensus.

6. The ANSWER Coalition's website is www.answercoalition.org/national/index.html.

7. See, for example, Raskin (2007).

8. Even rich people who complain about paying for parking may shift to public transit. Consider this instance in Beverly Hills: "Glen Rosten, 60, a retired real estate investor in Beverly Hills, took the bus to shop at Cartier on Rodeo Drive on Friday. 'You hate to get ripped off for parking, especially if you're going to spend the money you generally spend in Beverly Hills,' said Rosten after buying new sunglasses for about $1,000. 'The parking wouldn't break me,' he said. 'It's just the principle. If I'm going to spend $1,000 for sunglasses, I shouldn't have to pay for parking'" (Hennessy-Fisk and Abdollah 2007).

9. Barry (2010).

10. SF*park* has an excellent website that describes the program, including a short video that shows how the program works: http://sfpark.org.

11. Pierce (2010). Multispace meters also offer a new twist: pay by license plate number. Drivers enter their license plate numbers at the pay station when paying for parking. They do not need to remember their space numbers or return to their cars to display receipts. Parking enforcement officers use vehicle-mounted license-plate-recognition cameras that communicate with the payment database to check whether drivers have paid or whether they have permits for residential parking districts.

12. The payment system has two forms: (1) start–duration, in which the driver inserts the credit card to pay for a fixed time in advance and reinserts the card when leaving to receive a rebate for unused time, or (2) start–stop, in which the driver inserts the credit card to start paying and reinserts the card when leaving to stop paying. Payment by cell phone can have the same start–duration and start–stop options.

13. Salzman (2010, 27).

14. In a *Wall Street Journal* article about Redwood City's program, Conor Dougherty (2007) wrote, "In the past, Cheryl Angeles has had to jump up in the middle of a coloring treatment, foil in her hair and a black-plastic cape around her neck, to pop more quarters in the meter. Twice the self-storage company regional manager got $25 parking tickets when she didn't make it in time. Now that the time limits have been removed, she can pay once and return when the appointment is over."

15. Many other newspaper articles illustrate how off-street parking requirements affect the layout and restrict the use of buildings. Consider, for example, this report about the design of the $25 million Holocaust Memorial Museum in Illinois: "The number of seats in the main lecture hall of the museum, originally set at 293, has been reduced to 270 to meet parking requirements" ("Holocaust Museum makes modifications to site plan," *Pioneer Press*, December 1, 2005). Consider also this report about a restaurant in Florida: "Town planning staffers have recommended approval of the site plan changes, but tagged several conditions onto their recommendations. Chief among them are the requirements to reduce the restaurant area by 1,500 square feet to match the parking available during the day" ("Guanabanas seeks Jupiter's permission to become full-fledged restaurant," *Jupiter Courier*, December 4, 2005).

16. Behdad (2006) explains the history of the ARO. For conversion of an office building to residential use under the ARO, Section 12.222-A, 26(h)(3) of the Los Angeles Municipal Code requires that "the number of parking spaces shall be the same as the number of parking spaces that existed on the site on June 3, 1999."

17. Manville (2010).

18. Manville (2010, 12).

19. Manville (2010, 17).

20. Manville (2010, 26).

21. Dreyfuss (1982).

22. The average size of an off-street parking space is assumed to be 330 square feet, including the access aisles needed for circulation in the parking lot or structure. San Jose requires 25 parking spaces per 1,000 square feet of dining area in a restaurant, so the parking lot is 8,250 square feet for every 1,000 square feet of dining area (25 spaces x 330 square feet).

23. See Table 20-190 in the San Jose Municipal Code.

24. The apartment buildings inserted on the periphery of the parking lot are copied from downtown Los Angeles.

25. Janis (1982, 9). Other definitions of groupthink emphasize conformity and uncritical acceptance of a perceived majority point of view; the lack of creativity or individual responsibility in making decisions; the search for consensus without critically testing, analyzing, and evaluating ideas; the desire to minimize conflict; and making decisions without weighing all the facts, especially those contradicting the majority opinion.

26. Janis (1982, 175).

27. A survey of land-use plans in 30 cities and counties in North Carolina found that only two included any discussion of off-street parking requirements. Rodriguez et al. (2004, 7) explain that minimum parking requirements "lie at the intersection between land use and transportation planning, and as such are rarely included explicitly in either type of plan."

28. Dickerson (2004).

29. The Centre for Science and Environment (2009) explains how parking reforms in New Delhi can reduce traffic congestion, air pollution, and energy consumption; save drivers' time and fuel; and improve both neighborhood businesses and the environment. Barter (2010) studied parking policies in 14 Asian cities and recommends many promising policy reforms. The Institute for Transportation and Development Policy has also recently published two excellent reports on parking reforms in the United States (Weinberger, Kaehny, and Rufo 2010) and in Europe (Kodransky and Hermann 2011).

1

The Twenty-first Century Parking Problem

You don't know what you've got till it's gone. They paved paradise and put up a parking lot.

— *JONI MITCHELL*

Children first learn about free parking when they play Monopoly. The chance of landing on free parking is low, about the same as the chance of going to jail. Monopoly misleads its players on this score, however, because parking is free for 99 percent of all automobile trips in the U.S.[1] This book will argue that another kind of deception is also at play on the Monopoly board because in the real world, there is no such thing as "free" parking. The cost of parking is hidden in higher prices for everything else. In addition to the monetary cost, which is enormous, free parking imposes many other hidden costs on cities, the economy, and the environment.

Why is most parking free to the driver? When only the rich owned cars at the beginning of the twentieth century, motorists simply parked their new cars at the curb where they had formerly tethered their horses and carriages. But when car ownership grew rapidly during the 1910s and 1920s, the parking problem developed. Curb parking remained free (the parking meter was not invented until 1935), but there were no longer enough spaces for everyone to park whenever and wherever they wanted. Drivers circled in vain looking for a vacant curb space, and their cars congested traffic. In the 1930s, cities began to require off-street parking in their zoning ordinances to deal with the parking shortage, and the results were miraculous. One delighted mayor reported:

> We consider zoning for parking our greatest advance…. It is working out exceptionally well, far better than we had expected. In brief, it calls for all new buildings to make a provision for parking space required for its own uses.[2]

This sounds like a good idea. In one sense, it *was* a good idea. Requiring all new buildings provide ample on-site parking did solve one problem—the shortage of free curb parking—but the solution soon created new problems. Urban planners began to assume that most people would travel everywhere by car, park on-site while they worked, shopped, or dined, and then drive on to their next destination. Cities began to require each site to provide its own parking lot big enough to satisfy the expected peak demand for free parking, and most commercial buildings are now required to provide a parking lot bigger than the building itself. The required parking lot at a restaurant, for example, usually occupies at least three times as much land as the restaurant itself. Off-street parking requirements encourage everyone to drive wherever they go because they know they can usually park free when they get there: 87 percent of all trips in the U.S. are now made by personal motor vehicles, and only 1.5 percent by public transit.[3]

If drivers don't pay for parking, who does? Everyone does, even if they don't drive. Initially the developer pays for the required parking, but soon the tenants do, and then their customers, and so on, until the cost of parking has diffused everywhere in the economy. When we shop in a store, eat in a restaurant, or see a movie, we pay for parking indirectly because its cost is included in the prices of merchandise, meals, and theater tickets. We unknowingly support our cars with almost every commercial transaction we make because a small share of the money changing hands pays for parking. Residents pay for parking through higher prices for housing. Businesses pay for parking through higher rents for their premises. Shoppers pay for parking through higher prices for everything they buy. We don't pay for parking in our role as motorists, but in all our other roles—as consumers, investors, workers, residents, and taxpayers—we pay a high price. Even people who don't own a car have to pay for "free" parking.

Off-street parking requirements collectivize the cost of parking because they allow everyone to park free at everyone else's expense. When the cost of parking is hidden in the prices of other goods and services, no one can pay less for parking by using less of it. Bundling the cost of parking into higher prices for everything else skews travel choices toward cars and away from public transit, cycling, and walking. Off-street parking requirements thus change the way we build our cities, the way we travel, and how much energy we consume. All the required parking spaces use up land, spread the city out, and increase travel distances. Free parking also reduces the price of driving wherever we want to go, so the increased travel distances combined with the reduced price of driving make cars the obvious choice for most trips. Because highway transportation accounts for half of U.S. oil consumption, which is a quarter of the world's oil production, American motor vehicles now consume one-eighth of the world's oil. Free parking helps to explain this extreme automobile dependence, rapid urban sprawl, and extravagant energy use.[4]

Parking affects both transportation and land use, but its effects are often overlooked or misunderstood. Many people see urban problems—congestion, pollution, decay, and sprawl—but even the most ferocious critics of cars often fail to connect these problems with parking policies. Consider the apocalyptic titles of these jeremiads against the car: *Autokind vs. Mankind, Car Mania, Dead End, The Pavers and the Paved*, and *Road to Ruin*.[5] Off-street parking requirements contribute to the automobile-and-asphalt dominance the authors criticize, but none of the books even mentions parking. Parking is a blind spot in most studies of automobile transportation. Whether polemical or analytical, most books about cars and cities ignore the role that parking plays in both transportation and land use.

Journalists occasionally write about parking, usually with a critical tone. Here is *New York Times* columnist David Brooks's description of a shopper's trip to the mall in suburban Sprinkler City:

> He steps out into the parking lot and is momentarily blinded by sun bouncing off the hardtop. The parking lot is so massive that he can barely see the Wal-Mart, the Bed Bath & Beyond, or the area-code-sized Old Navy glistening through the heat there on the other side. This mall is…so vast that shoppers have to drive from store to store, cutting diagonally through the infinity of empty parking spaces in between…there are archipelagoes of them—one massive parking lot after another surrounded by huge boxes that often have racing stripes around the middle to break the monotony of the windowless exterior walls.[6]

Brooks describes a scene that is all too real, and many people concerned about sprawl decry the expanses of land used by big-box retail. But few people realize that cities *require* the developers of these "dark Satanic malls" to provide the massive parking lots that remain nearly empty much of the time.[7]

Because I want to call attention to our mistaken parking policies, I toyed with alarmist titles like *Aparkalypse Now* or *Parkageddon*. I eventually settled on the more sober *The High Cost of Free Parking* because this oxymoron captures the conflict between free parking and its hidden cost. In this book I show that "free" parking distorts transportation choices, debases urban design, damages the economy, and degrades the environment. I argue that American cities have made devastating mistakes with their parking policies, and I propose reforms designed to undo the damage caused by nearly a century of bad planning.

THE CAR EXPLOSION

Coming to grips with the parking problem is essential because the rest of the world is poised to repeat America's mistakes. America adopted the car much faster and to a far greater extent than other nations, and many factors help to explain this phenomenon—abundant land, rapid population growth, low fuel prices, and high incomes, among others. Abundant free parking also contributes to our high demand for cars because it greatly reduces the cost of car ownership. And because we own so many cars, we need lots of land to park them. We can speculate about the amount of land the whole world will need for parking if other nations ever acquire as many cars as Americans owned at the end of the twentieth century.

The first American gasoline car was sold in February 1896.[8] By 2000, Americans owned 771 motor vehicles per 1,000 persons. Figure 1-1 shows the U.S. vehicle-ownership rates (motor vehicles per 1,000 persons) from 1900 to 2000. Apart from dips during the Depression, World War II, and the early 1990s, ownership rose rapidly. Fifteen other nations' vehicle-ownership rates in 2000 are placed in the graph beside the year in which the U.S. had the same rate. In 2000, France had the same vehicle-ownership rate as the U.S. in 1972, Denmark the same as the U.S. in 1961, and China the same as the U.S. in 1912.[9]

China is now the world's fourth-largest market for new cars (after the U.S., Japan, and Germany), but the U.S. still *added* more than twice as many vehicles during the 1990s (29 million) as China owned in 2000 (13 million). Other nations are, however, gaining on the U.S. Since 1950 the vehicle population has grown more than twice as fast outside the U.S. as inside (see Figure 1-2).[10] And yet, taken together, in 2000 the world outside the U.S. owned only 89 vehicles per 1,000 persons—the U.S. rate in 1920. But just as the U.S. vehicle-ownership rate doubled in the five years after 1920, rapid growth may also occur soon in other countries.

The 6.1 billion people on earth in 2000 owned 735 million vehicles. Imagine what would happen if all the countries on earth ever achieve the

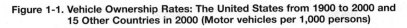

Figure 1-1. Vehicle Ownership Rates: The United States from 1900 to 2000 and 15 Other Countries in 2000 (Motor vehicles per 1,000 persons)

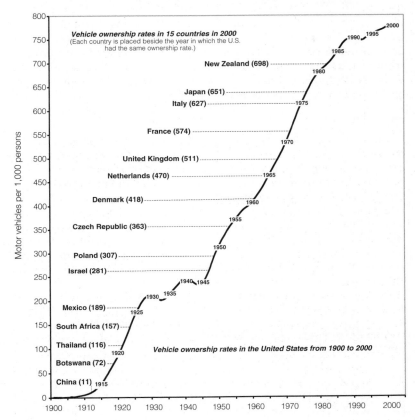

Source: Tables H-1 and H-2 in Appendix H.

same vehicle-ownership rate as the U.S. in 2000: there would be 4.7 billion vehicles even if the human population does not increase.[11] A parking lot big enough to hold 4.7 *billion* cars would occupy an area about the size of England or Greece.[12] If there are four parking spaces per car (one at home, and three more at other destinations), 4.7 billion cars would require 19 billion parking spaces, which amounts to a parking lot about the size of France or Spain.[13] More cars would also require more land for roads, gas stations, used car dealers, automobile graveyards, and tire dumps.

Figure 1-2. Number of Motor Vehicles on Earth

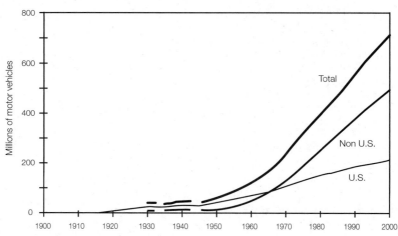

Source: Table H-1 in Appendix H.

If the past trends in vehicle ownership continue, the world will have more than 4.7 billion cars well before the end of the twenty-first century. Even if the vehicle population grows by only 2 percent a year, it will increase from 735 million in 2000 to 5 billion in 2100. Can the world supply all the fuel needed to power 5 billion cars? Will humans be able to breathe the fumes coming out of 5 billion exhaust pipes? And where will 5 billion cars park?

These questions are not meant to sound alarmist. A simple projection is often a poor forecast because technology and policy can change. For example, horse-drawn carriages befouled cities a century ago. In New York City in 1900, horses deposited 2.5 million pounds of manure on the streets every day.[14] Projected growth in transportation demand made a public health disaster seem inevitable, but then the horseless carriage solved that problem. Now, horseless carriages create their own problems, but new solutions will arrive. Improved technology will increase fuel efficiency and reduce pollution emissions, but technology alone is unlikely to solve the parking problem. Regardless of how fuel efficient our cars are or how little pollution they emit, we will always need somewhere to park them, and the average car spends about 95 percent of its life parked.[15]

This book proposes new policies to solve our parking problems. After all, we don't want to see France or Spain paved for a parking lot. Before proposing any solutions, however, I will first explain what I believe creates most parking problems: *the treatment of curb parking as a commons.*

THE "COMMONS" PROBLEM

Free curb parking presents a classic "commons" problem. Land that belongs to the community, and is freely available to everyone without charge, is called a commons. City life requires common ownership of much land (such as streets, sidewalks, and parks), but the neglect and mismanagement of common property can create serious problems. Aristotle observed:

> What is common to the greatest number has the least care bestowed upon it. Every one thinks chiefly of his own, hardly at all of the common interest.[16]

The archetypical commons problem occurs on village land that is freely available to all members of a community for grazing their animals. This open-access arrangement works well in a small community with plenty of grass to go around. But when the community grows, so does the number of animals, and eventually, although it may take a while to notice it, the land is overrun and overgrazed. Harvard economist Thomas Schelling describes the problem:

> The commons has come to serve as a paradigm for situations in which people so impinge on each other in pursuing their own interests that collectively they might be better off if they could be restrained, but no one gains individually by self-restraint. Common pasture in a village of England or Colonial New England was not only common property of the villagers but unrestrictedly available to their animals. The more cattle (or sheep or whatever) that were put to graze on the common, the less forage there was for each animal—and more of it got trampled—but as long as there was any profit in grazing one's animal on the common, villagers were motivated to do so.[17]

Free curb parking is an asphalt commons: just as cattle compete in their search for scarce grass, drivers compete in their search for scarce curb parking spaces. Drivers waste time and fuel, congest traffic, and pollute the air while cruising for curb parking, and after finding a space they have no incentive to economize on how long they park.

Where many people want to use a scarce public resource, self-restraint does not produce any individual reward. Free curb parking thus presents the perfect commons problem—no one owns it, and everyone can use it. In his famous essay on the "tragedy of the commons," Garrett Hardin used curb parking to illustrate the problem he was describing:

> During the Christmas shopping season the parking meters downtown were covered with plastic bags that bore tags reading: "Do not open until after Christmas. Free parking courtesy of the mayor and city council." In other

words, facing the prospect of an increased demand for already scarce space, the city fathers reinstituted the system of the commons.[18]

Some cities continue to gift wrap their parking meters in December, and they give motorists a commons problem for Christmas. Although voters may thank their mayor and city council for free parking at the time of peak demand, vacant spaces become even harder to find. Drivers circle the block searching for a curb space, and when they find one they occupy it longer than they would if they paid to park. What makes sense for an individual driver is bad for the community as a whole.

Although urban planners have not ignored the commons problem created by free curb parking, they have misdiagnosed it. Planners have identified the source of the problem not as the city's failure to charge market prices for curb parking, but as the market's failure to supply enough off-street parking. Cities therefore require ample on-site parking for all new buildings. The logic behind this policy is simple: development may increase the demand for parking, but cities can require developers to provide enough on-site spaces to satisfy this new demand. If a new building increases the demand for parking by 100 spaces, for example, cities can require it to provide 100 new spaces so that competition for the scarce curb parking doesn't increase. Curb parking remains a commons, and cities require enough off-street parking to satisfy the increased demand.

A major flaw in this solution, however, is the way planners estimate demand: they do not estimate it as a function of price. Instead, they make the unstated (perhaps even unconscious) assumption that all parking is free. They estimate the demand for *free* parking and then require enough spaces to meet this demand. In effect, urban planners treat free parking as an entitlement, and they consider the resulting demand for free parking a "need" that must be met. Off-street parking requirements create an abundance of parking spaces, driving the market price of parking to zero, which explains why drivers can park free for 99 percent of their trips. Off-street parking requirements are a fertility drug for cars.

Most markets depend on prices to allocate resources—so much so that it's hard to imagine they could operate in any other way. Nevertheless, cities have tried to manage parking almost entirely without prices. To see the absurdity of this policy, look at it from a new perspective. Cities require off-street parking because the market supposedly fails to provide enough of it. But the market fails to provide many things at a price everyone can afford. For instance, it fails to provide affordable housing for many families. Advocates for affordable housing usually find themselves in an uphill battle, but without a second thought cities have imposed requirements to ensure affordable parking. Rather than charge fair-market prices for on-street parking, cities insist on ample off-street parking for every land use. As a result, most of us drive almost everywhere we go.

SKEWED TRAVEL CHOICES

Every transport system has three elements: vehicles, rights-of-way, and terminal capacity. Rail transport, for example, has trains, tracks, and stations. Sea transport has ships, oceans, and seaports. Air transport has planes, the sky, and airports. Automobile transport has cars, roads, and parking spaces. Two aspects of its terminal capacity set automobile transport apart from all other transport systems. First, automobile transport requires enormous terminal capacity—it is land-hungry—because there are so many cars and several parking spaces for each one. Second, motorists park free for 99 percent of their trips because off-street parking requirements remove the cost of automobile terminal capacity from the transport sector and shift it everywhere else in the economy. Free parking helps explain the enormous demand for automobile terminal capacity. By shifting the cost of parking from drivers to everyone else, off-street parking requirements provide a huge subsidy to motorists, and thus increase the demand for cars, parking spaces, and vehicle travel.

For a typical trip *to* work, the cost of parking *at* work (if drivers pay for it) is over half the total out-of-pocket cost of automobile commuting.[19] But most drivers do *not* pay for parking, or at least not in their role as drivers. Because a cost-recovery price for parking is such a large share of the total cost of automobile travel, "free" parking seriously skews travel choices toward solo driving and away from other forms of travel that require less terminal capacity: public transit, carpooling, bicycling, and—the extreme case—walking, which requires shoes and sidewalks, but no terminal capacity at all. Free parking gives the largest subsidy per mile to the shortest vehicle trips—the ones that, without a parking subsidy, we would most likely make by walking, cycling, or public transport. Free parking is an invitation to drive wherever we go.

CURES THAT KILL

Most people know that cities require off-street parking spaces for every building, but few people—even those in the planning profession—have examined how these requirements affect cities. To see how parking requirements harm cities, consider how a popular medical practice once poisoned millions of patients.

An Analogy: Lead Poisoning

From antiquity until the twentieth century, physicians prescribed lead as medicine to treat all manner of ailments. One eighteenth-century medical treatise stated:

> When the reader has perused the following treatise he will be inclined to think that this metal [lead] is one of the most efficacious remedies for the cure of most diseases which require the assistance of surgery.[20]

Doctors recommended "lead therapy" as a cure for abscesses, burns, cancer, contusions, gout, gunshot wounds, inflammation, itch, piles, rheumatism, ruptures, sprains, stiffness of the joints, and ulcers. Lead was useful in treating some of these ailments because it is toxic to microorganisms and therefore has local antiseptic properties. But physicians did not understand that lead is toxic to humans, and the medical misuse of lead killed many patients.[21] Although lead poisoning—a byproduct of lead therapy—went largely unnoticed until the late nineteenth century, a few early critics, like Benjamin Franklin, recognized the harm. Because he was a printer, Franklin had much contact with lead, and he wrote to a friend in 1786:

> The Opinion of this mischievous Effect from Lead is at least above Sixty Years old; and you will observe with Concern how long a useful Truth may be known, and exist, before it is generally receiv'd and practis'd on.[22]

Despite Franklin's warning, physicians continued to prescribe lead as a medicine until the twentieth century. They did so for understandable reasons: when the medical problem went away, the success could easily be attributed to lead therapy. But when the treatment did not work, or—worse—when it slowly killed the patient, the precise cause was less apparent; the patient was sick to begin with, and any number of factors could have been at play. The lead therapy sometimes produced a local antiseptic benefit and did help to cure one medical problem, but often did so at a high cost to the whole person.[23]

Off-street parking requirements are similar. They produce a local benefit—ample free parking—while harming the whole city. Free parking increases the demand for cars, and more cars increase traffic congestion, air pollution, and energy consumption. More traffic congestion in turn spurs the search for more local remedies, such as street widenings, more freeways, and even higher parking requirements. Off-street parking requirements quietly create citywide problems that are far worse than the local ones they are meant to solve.

Although parking requirements resemble lead therapy in producing a local benefit while harming the whole system, the comparison goes only so far. Lead poisoning kills people, after all, and parking requirements do not. But this should not cheer us. Physicians continued to recommend lead as medicine until the twentieth century, even as their patients regularly died from the treatment. If physicians were so slow to recognize the evidence of lead therapy's lethal effects, planners may take even longer to recognize the more subtle systemic harm from parking requirements, no matter how strong the evidence.

Lead therapy and parking requirements are not the only professional practices that evolved into conventional wisdom without good theory or careful research. Medical practice was astonishingly primitive as recently as a century ago. Writing in 1981, Lewis Thomas (Chancellor of the Memorial Sloan-Kettering Cancer Center in New York) described a leading medical text that was published in 1896. The book presents a picture of medical practice *circa* 1900 that eerily resembles planning for parking today. Here is Thomas's dismaying description of the book:

> The public expectation then, as now, was that the doctor would *do something*. There was no disease for which a treatment was not recommended.... Every other page contains a new, complex treatment always recommended with the admonition that the procedure be learned by rote (since it rarely made any intrinsic sense) and be performed precisely as described. Acute poliomyelitis had to be treated by subcutaneous injections of strychnine; the application of leeches; the administration of belladonna and purgative doses of mercury; the layering of thick ointments containing mercury and iodine over the affected limbs; faradic stimulation of the muscles; ice-cold shower baths over the spine; and cupping [bleeding].... All of this has the appearance of institutionalized folly, the piecing together of a huge structure of nonsensical and dangerous therapy, and indeed it was. The pieces were thought up and put together almost like thin air, but perhaps not quite. Empiricism made a small contribution, just enough in the case of each to launch it into fashion.[24]

This description of precise, disciplined folly bears a depressing similarity to contemporary parking policy. Every land use has a parking requirement that is learned by rote. A gas station must provide 1.5 parking spaces per fuel nozzle, and a mausoleum must provide 10 parking spaces per maximum number of interments in a one-hour period.[25] Why? Nobody knows. The requirements rarely make any intrinsic sense, but parking spaces must be provided exactly as required. Empiricism makes a small contribution, just enough in the case of each requirement to launch it into the zoning code. Medicine is a much older profession than urban planning, and perhaps planning for parking is at the same stage of intellectual development that medicine was in 1900. Planners are under tremendous pressure to *do something* about parking, and, just as doctors did a century ago, they have erected "a huge structure of nonsensical and dangerous therapy" in response. Off-street parking requirements do not solve transportation problems, but make them worse.

Poleodomogenic Catastrophes

Parking requirements are now firmly entrenched in planning practice, but experience suggests that future planners may regret them. Urban planners of the 1950s and 1960s hurled themselves into implementing some truly bad ideas. High-rise public housing projects were once state-of-the-art, but many cities have since demolished them. Urban renewal (which Jane Jacobs compared to bloodletting) was once the best hope of downtowns, but most cities have now abandoned it in favor of historic preservation. Similarly, some cities have shifted from minimum parking requirements to parking caps, and other cities may follow. We do eventually recognize our mistakes, and we may some day condemn off-street parking requirements just as we now condemn the urban renewal disasters of the twentieth century.[26]

The problems caused by parking requirements resemble iatrogenic illnesses in medicine. *Iatrogenic* illness (illness caused by a physician) is a combination of the Greek *iatros* (physician) + *genic* (generated). Medical history is filled with iatrogenic illnesses, including lead poisoning. Catastrophes caused by city planners can be called *poleodomogenic*, a combination of the Greek *poleodomos* (city planner) + *genic*. Poleodomogenic catastrophes like slum clearance and urban renewal happen because city planners sometimes mistake Pandora's box for a toolkit. In *The Reflective Practitioner: How Professionals Think in Action*, MIT planning professor Donald Schön described:

> the counterintuitive consequences, the harmful side effects, and the unwanted by-products of implemented plans. Plans designed to solve problems either failed to solve them or created problems worse than the problems they had been designed to solve.[27]

This lament about planning resembles what Lewis Thomas said about medicine:

> The tendency in medicine to try something, anything, to "try it out," persists. Perhaps the profession will outgrow its vulnerability to fads and fancies as the scientific base for diagnosis and treatment steadily matures, but the long record of well-intentioned folly is both an embarrassment and a warning.[28]

I believe planners will eventually admit that off-street parking requirements are a well-intentioned folly similar to lead therapy—a poison prescribed as a cure. Parking is desirable in most locations, but you can have too much of a good thing. The principle that "the dose makes the poison" applies perfectly to parking.[29] By prescribing massive overdoses of parking spaces, planners are poisoning the city. This sounds harsh, but it is a criticism of current practice, not of individual planners. Physicians who prescribed lead therapy were following the professional doctrine of their time, just as planners who require massive overdoses of parking are following the professional doctrine of our time. Planning for parking has caused severe adverse reactions, and if a policy is judged by its consequences, off-street parking requirements are a catastrophe. I hope the analogy with lead poisoning will provoke those who advocate parking requirements to explain their reasoning and defend their methods, but reform of even the worst practice can be a slow process (as Ben Franklin predicted), and parking requirements are unlikely to be an exception.

Professionally induced disasters are not unique to urban planning and medicine, of course. Before the *Titanic* sank, shipbuilders underestimated the need for lifeboats. Before the *Challenger* exploded, engineers underestimated the ambient temperature necessary for safely launching the space shuttle, and before the *Columbia* burned up, they underestimated the damage caused by shreds of foam striking the shuttle's wings. Sometimes dramatic disasters like these must occur to stimulate reforms in a profession, but—like lead poisoning—the harmful consequences of parking requirements are insidious. Nevertheless, they confront us everywhere: automobile dependency, traffic congestion, energy waste, air pollution, and perhaps even global climate change. Although not the sole cause of these problems, parking requirements intensify them.

THE TWENTY-FIRST CENTURY PARKING SOLUTION

If parking requirements do more harm than good, how should cities plan for parking in the twenty-first century? In this book I analyze the parking problem, criticize current planning practice, and propose reforms. To foreshadow my arguments, I will summarize the three main parts of the book. Parts I and II analyze the parking problem, while Part III proposes solutions.

Part I examines our current approach to planning for parking. Urban planners set minimum parking requirements for every land use, but the requirements often seem pulled out of thin air or based on studies that are poorly conceived (e.g., samples taken at times of peak demand at sites where parking is free) and limited (e.g. the typical sample size is statistically inadequate). In turn, these faulty standards and policies are

Figure 1-3. Parking is desirable, but you can have too much of a good thing.

perpetuated as they are copied from one city to the next. The many significant costs related to current parking policies (e.g., increased housing prices, unjust subsidies for cars, distorted transportation choices, sprawl, social inequity, and economic and environmental degradation) are not a consideration. Beyond their quantitative flaws, parking requirements are also divorced from any qualitative criteria: they ignore what the results *look* like.

Part II shows that cities inadvertently create the economic incentive to cruise for curb parking when they charge too low a price for it. Research at six sites showed that an average of 30 percent of the cars in congested traffic were cruising for parking. Cruising increases vehicle travel without adding either vehicles *or* real travel. The aggregate consequences of all this cruising—congested traffic, wasted time, squandered fuel, and polluted air—are staggering.

Part III offers new solutions to the parking problem. It explains how a well-functioning market with prices that vary by the time of day and day of the week can balance a variable demand for curb parking with the fixed supply of curb spaces. If cities charge market prices for curb parking, drivers will usually be able to find an available space near their destination. Market-priced curb parking will therefore save time, reduce congestion, conserve energy, improve air quality, and produce public revenue. The real barrier to charging for curb parking is political, not technological. I argue that cities can overcome this political barrier by returning all meter revenue to the neighborhoods that generate it. Where nonresidents pay for most curb parking, using the revenue to pay for neighborhood public services can persuade residents to support charging market prices for their curb parking spaces. And if cities charge market prices for curb parking, spillover will no longer be a problem, so they can remove their off-street parking requirements. These three reforms—charge fair-market prices for curb parking, return the resulting revenue to the neighborhoods that generate it, and remove the zoning requirements for off-street parking—can align our individual incentives with our collective interests and produce enormous benefits at almost no cost. All these benefits will result from subsidizing people and places, not parking and cars.

In sum, this book offers not just a critique of free parking, but it also suggests how planners can frame an argument—economic, social, environmental, and aesthetic—about new ways to plan for parking that are sensible, effective, and fair.

CHAPTER 1 NOTES

1. The 1990 Nationwide Personal Transportation Survey asked respondents, Did you pay for parking during any part of this trip? for all automobile trips made on the previous day (see Appendix B). Respondents reported that they parked free for 99 percent of their trips. Most drivers probably feel that they pay for parking on more than 1 percent of their own trips, and many do. Drivers who live in older and more compact cities undoubtedly pay for parking more frequently than do those who live in sprawling suburbs. Americans make 235 billion vehicle trips a year, so if they pay to park on 1 percent of these trips, they pay for parking more than 2 billion times a year, but they also park free 233 billion times a year.

2. Mogren and Smith (1952, 27).

3. The 2001 National Household Travel Survey found that 87 percent of trips of less than 50 miles were made by personal vehicle. Of the rest, 1.5 percent were by public transit, 1.7 percent by school bus, 8.6 percent by walking, and 1.7 percent by other modes (United States Department of Transportation 2003a, 21 and 25).

4. See Davis and Diegel (2002, Tables 1.4, 1.13, and 2.5) for the data on energy consumption for transportation in the U.S. The U.S. consumed 25.9 percent of total world oil consumption in 2001 (Table 1.4). Transportation accounted for 67.3 percent of U.S. oil consumption (Table 1.13), and road transportation accounted for 75.5 percent of U.S. oil consumption for transportation (Table 2.5). Therefore, U.S. road transportation accounted for 13.2 percent of world oil consumption (25.9% x 67.3% x 75.5%). Road transportation refers to travel by cars, trucks, motorcycles, and buses. In 2001 the U.S. imported $104 billion worth of petroleum, which accounted for 8 percent of total imports and 29 percent of the balance of trade deficit (U.S. Census Bureau 2002a, Exhibits 1, 6, and 9).

5. See Schneider (1971), Wolf (1996), Buel (1973), Kelly (1971), and Mowbray (1969). The word "parking" does not appear in the index of any of these books. Academic writers also fail to analyze how parking affects transportation and cities. Consider two recent texts by distinguished scholars of transportation and urban planning: *Essays in Transportation Economics and Policy* by Gómez-Ibáñez, Tye, and Winston (1999), and *Urban Land Use Planning* by Kaiser, Godschalk, and Chapin (1995); parking does not appear in the index of either of these books.

6. Brooks (2002, 19 and 24).

7. William Blake (1757-1827) was referring to an earlier land-use problem (smoky factories during the Industrial Revolution) when he asked "And was Jerusalem builded here / Among these dark Satanic mills?"

8. Flink (1976, 15) reports that Charles and Frank Duryea made the first sale.

9. Appendix H shows the data on human and vehicle populations from 1900 to 2000. The high rank of New Zealand in vehicle ownership can be explained by its low population density (a population of 4 million in a country 10 percent larger than the United Kingdom) and a large supply of second-hand cars from Japan; both Japan and New Zealand drive on the left, and Japan's strict vehicle-inspection program strongly encourages the export of cars after only a few years.

10. The data for the total number of vehicles in the rest of world are available only in selected years before 1946 (1930, 1935, and 1937-1940). Although the U.S. owned half of all the world's vehicles in 1965, it owned only 30 percent in 2000.

11. The 6.079 billion persons on earth in 2000 owned 735 million vehicles. If 6.079 billion persons owned 771 vehicles per 1,000 persons (the U.S. rate in 2000), they would own 4.7 billion vehicles—over six times the actual number of vehicles on earth in 2000.

12. Not all motor vehicles are cars, but vehicles other than cars—such as trucks—occupy even larger parking spaces, so estimating the space required to park 4.7 billion cars will underestimate the space required to park 4.7 billion vehicles. A typical parking lot holds about 130 cars per acre (335 square feet per car); this is equivalent to 83,200 cars per square mile (130 cars per acre x 640 acres per square mile). At this density, 4.7 billion parked cars would occupy 56,000 square miles (4.7 billion cars ÷ 83,200 cars per square mile). England and Greece each occupy 51,000 square miles.

13. See Chapter 7 for the ratio of parking spaces to cars. The area of France is 212,000 square miles and the area of Spain is 192,000 square miles. Another way to imagine the area needed to park 4.7 billion cars is to look at a parking lot big enough to hold 100 cars. Forty-seven million of these 100-car lots would be needed to park 4.7 billion cars.

14. Flink (1976, 34).

15. Increases in fuel prices will spur increases in fuel efficiency, and increases in parking prices will spur increases in parking efficiency. Automated garages, for example, reduce the space needed for parking because they typically store twice as many cars in the same volume as a conventional garage (see Appendix A). Other changes, such as car-sharing arrangements, may also reduce the share of the time that cars are parked. See Appendix B for the average time a car is parked.

16. Aristotle (*Politics*, Book II, Chapter 3). A century earlier, the Athenian historian Thucydides made a similar observation: "[The Peloponnesians] spend a small fraction of [their time] considering any public matter and the greater part acting on domestic interests; each thinks that his own negligence does no harm and it is someone else's business to use foresight on his behalf, so that when the same notion is entertained by everyone separately it goes unobserved that common interests are being destroyed collectively" (Thucydides, Book 1, Section 141, p. 69). Ronald Lipp (2001, 92) comments that the human tendency to neglect common interests is so fundamental that a literature search would find early statements of the problem in many cultures.

17. Schelling (1978, 111-113).

18. Hardin (1977, 21). Garrett Hardin was a professor of human ecology at the University of California at Santa Barbara and the author of many books and articles on biology, ecology, and ethics. Hardin (1977, 27) also used parking meters as an example of social arrangements that encourage responsible behavior: "To keep downtown shoppers temperate in their use of parking space we introduce parking meters for short periods, and traffic fines for longer ones. We need not actually forbid a citizen to park as long as he wants to; we need merely make it increasingly expensive for him to do so. Not prohibition, but carefully biased options are what we offer him." Most parking meters, however, are in the central business district and curb parking is free almost everywhere else.

19. Chapter 7 shows that for a typical commute trip, the driver's total variable cost of automobile commuting (operating cost plus parking cost) is $2.32 a day if the employer pays for parking, but $8.09 a day if the driver pays for it. Free parking at work therefore subsidizes 71 percent of the total variable cost of automobile commuting.

20. Goulard (1784, 2).

21. In her research on the medical history of lead, Jane Lin-Fu (1992) describes lead poisoning as the only preventable man-made disease that was allowed to remain pandemic for centuries.

22. Letter to Benjamin Vaughn on July 31, 1786. Reprinted in Goodman (1945, 556). Available online at www.ledizolv.com/LearnAbout/LeadHazards/benfranklin.asp. See also McCord (1953, 398). Lead was added to gasoline (and thus to urban air pollution) through most of the twentieth century, showing that Franklin was correct in warning about how long a useful truth may be known before it is acted on. Lead additives to gasoline improved automobile performance but polluted the air that drivers (and everyone else) breathed.

23. Lead was used for many purposes where its immediate benefits were appreciated but its long-term harm was unrecognized. The Romans wore lead oxide as a cosmetic, prepared food in lead pots, stored wine in lead vessels (lead tastes sweet, and improved the wine's flavor), and drank water delivered in lead pipes (the word "plumber" comes from the Latin word for lead, *plumbum*). Lead poisoning may even have contributed to the decline of the Roman Empire. University of Michigan environmental chemist Jerome Nriagu (1983) argues that the aristocrats' diets were unusually rich in lead, and that this helps explain why only one of Rome's original aristocratic families had any surviving members by the second century AD. Although many people must have died of lead poisoning throughout history, diagnosis is difficult long after their deaths. Nevertheless, the famous case of Ludwig von Beethoven's hair provides startling evidence. Beethoven suffered from many painful medical problems during his life: kidney stones, hepatitis, rheumatism, skin disorders, and deafness. When he died in 1827, admirers snipped locks of hair from his corpse and revered them as relics. Analysis of several strands of this hair in 1995 showed massive lead toxicity in Beethoven's body at his death, more than 40 times the normal presence of lead (Martin 2000, 235). Lead poisoning may have caused, or at least exacerbated, his many illnesses. The source of the lead in Beethoven's body is unknown, but it could have come from cookware or tableware that contained lead, from wine that was "plumbed" to lessen its bitterness, or from lead therapy.

24. Thomas (1981, 40). Lewis Thomas, M.D., served as dean of the New York University School of Medicine and president and chancellor of the Memorial Sloan-Kettering Cancer Center. When Thomas went to medical school in the 1930s, his father (also a physician) gave him the textbook (*Therapeutics of Infancy and Childhood*) with the advice that although the book was out of date, there were things in it that might be useful. When the younger Thomas looked through the book while he was a medical student, he found it bewildering and irrelevant to medicine in the 1930s, but as he grew older, the book fascinated him as a historical document that showed the state of the medical profession in 1900. The book's distinguished author (Dr. Abraham Jacobi) was one of the major figures of his time in academic medicine, and his popular textbook ran through several editions.

25. See Table 3-4 in Chapter 3.

26. Consider also these 180-degree turns in transportation planning. In the 1950s, many cities created one-way street systems to speed traffic through downtowns, and in the 1990s converted them back to two-way streets to calm traffic. Similarly, in the 1950s, many cities eliminated on-street parking in downtowns to speed traffic and provided off-street parking lots instead. In the 1990s, a common strategy was to redevelop off-street parking lots to increase downtown density and to restore on-street parking to calm the traffic flow and to buffer pedestrians from moving vehicles.

27. Schön (1983, 206). Similarly, Berkeley planning professor Michael Teitz (2000, 304) refers to "the disasters of public housing and urban renewal in the 1950s and 1960s.... It may be fair to say, however, that planners did learn from these errors."

28. Thomas (1981, 42). Similarly, Reyner Banham, Paul Barker, Peter Hall and Cedric Price (1969, 435-436) wrote, "planning tends to lurch from one fashion to another, with sudden revulsion setting in after equally sudden acceptance.... Planning is always in thrall to some outmoded rule of thumb."

29. The sixteenth century Swiss physician Paracelsus (1493-1541) wrote, "Dosis facit venenum" (The dose makes the poison). No substance is inherently poisonous, but too much of anything in the system can be poisonous.

I

Planning for Free Parking

Paul had noticed already that in Los Angeles automobiles were a race apart, almost alive. The city was full of their hotels and beauty shops, their restaurants and nursing homes—immense, expensive structures where they could be parked or polished, fed or cured of their injuries. They spoke, and had pets—stuffed dogs and monkeys looked out of their rear windows, toys and good-luck charms hung above their dashboards, and fur tails waved from their aerials. Their horns sang in varied voices...few people were visible. The automobiles outnumbered them ten to one. Paul imagined a tale in which it would be gradually revealed that these automobiles were the real inhabitants of the city, a secret master race which only kept human beings for its own greater convenience, or as pets.

—ALISON LURIE, *The Nowhere City*

2

Unnatural Selection

What I tell you three times is true.

—*LEWIS CARROLL*

In the beginning the earth was without parking. The planner said, Let there be parking, and there was parking. And the planner saw that it was good. And the planner then said, Let there be off-street parking for each land use, according to its kind. And developers provided off-street parking for each land use according to its kind. And again the planner saw that it was good. And the planner said to cars, Be fruitful, and multiply, and replenish the earth, and subdue it, and have dominion over every living thing that moves upon the earth. And the planner saw everything he had made, and, behold, it was *not* good.

THE GENESIS OF PARKING REQUIREMENTS

Why do planners require off-street parking for every kind of land use? Because if on-street parking is free and developers fail to provide enough off-street parking, competition for the scarce curb spaces will congest local traffic. Angry citizens will then ask urban planners and elected officials, Why did you let this happen? To avoid these spillover parking problems, most cities require developers to supply at least enough on-site parking to accommodate all the cars that will be drawn to each site. A typical municipal ordinance states the goal of parking requirements:

> In connection with the use of each lot, sufficient off-street parking space shall be provided to meet the demand created by all activities on the lot.[1]

This goal sounds reasonable, but how many parking spaces are enough "to meet the demand created by all activities on the lot"? If curb parking is free and the city wants to prevent spillover, developers must supply at least enough on-site spaces to satisfy the demand for *free* parking.

This chapter shows that urban planners do not conduct site-specific analyses to establish parking requirements. Instead, they usually (1) refer to national surveys of the peak parking occupancy observed at suburban sites with ample free parking and no public transit, or (2) copy other cities' requirements. As a result, cities require so much parking that drivers park free for 99 percent of their trips.[2] With free parking available almost everywhere, almost everyone can go almost anywhere without resorting to public transportation, carpooling, biking, or their own two feet.

HUDDLED MASSES YEARNING TO PARK FREE

Drivers obviously need to park somewhere, and they don't want to pay for it. Our yearning to park free helps explain why off-street parking requirements spread rapidly after planners invented them. A 1946 survey of 76 cities found that only 17 percent had parking requirements in their zoning ordinances. Five years later, 71 percent of these cities had parking requirements or were adopting them.[3] Other than zoning itself, few if any other planning practices have spread more rapidly. Parking requirements have not been imposed on an unwilling public, and they are not the product of a conspiracy by automobile makers; instead, parking requirements result from democratic decision making.

As early as 1944, the Los Angeles County Planning Commission concluded that cities should require each building to provide at least as much space for parking as there is floor area for stores or offices:

> While the parking requirements of a particular store or office building will vary, there may be an irreducible minimum requirement of parking space equal in area to the retail floor or business area.[4]

Similarly, in 1952 Edward Mogren and Wilbur Smith asserted in their book *Zoning and Traffic* that cities,

> need to base zoning requirements for off-street parking on *maximum possible* building usage and increased automobile travel rather than on normal building usage and present automobile travel factors.[5]

In 1991, after many years of experience with parking requirements, the American Planning Association's Planning Advisory Service (PAS) noted:

> It is widely accepted within the professional literature that a requirement for "excessive" amounts of parking yields only lower densities and larger impervious surface areas. Off-street parking can grow quickly and eat up a tremendous amount of land if it is not looked at critically.[6]

Off-street parking does eat up a tremendous amount of land, but minimum parking requirements lead planners and developers to think that parking is a problem only when there isn't enough of it. But too much parking is also a problem—it wastes money, degrades urban design, increases impervious surface area, and encourages overuse of cars.

PLANNING WITHOUT PRICES

Urban planners have diagnosed the parking problem in a way that makes it extremely expensive to solve. Believing that the problem is a parking shortage, planners require enough off-street spaces to satisfy the peak demand for *free* parking. When California Polytechnic University, Pomona, planning professor Richard Willson surveyed planning officials in 138 cities about how they set parking requirements, their most frequent response to the question, Why does your city have minimum parking requirements? was the tautological answer, To have an adequate number of spaces.[7] Adequate for what? The implicit answer is an adequate number of spaces to satisfy the demand for free parking.

Robert Weant and Herbert Levinson at the Eno Transportation Foundation explain that most cities require every land use to supply enough off-street spaces to meet the recurrent peak demand for parking:

> Most local governments, through their zoning ordinances, have a parking supply policy that requires land uses to provide sufficient off-street parking space to allow easy, convenient access to activities while maintaining free traffic flow. The objective is to provide enough parking space to accommodate recurrent peak-parking demands.... Parking demand is defined as the accumulation of vehicles parked at a given time as the result of activity at a given site.[8]

Similarly, PAS reports that off-street parking requirements should meet the peak parking demand without overflow:

> Most of the developments studied provided adequate parking spaces to meet the observed peak demand without overflow conditions. This was important

because in order to develop standards for parking space requirements, the peak demand had to be identified.[9]

Planners define parking demand as the peak parking occupancy observed at a site, without taking into account the price that drivers pay for parking. Cities then require each land use to supply at least enough parking spaces to accommodate this peak demand, without considering how much the required spaces cost to construct. The maximum observed demand thus becomes the minimum required supply. In effect, cities tell developers, no matter how great the cost, and no matter how small the benefit, you must supply ample on-site parking if you want to build in our town.

Parking spaces are an essential part of the transportation system, and they produce enormous benefits, but this does not mean that we need more parking spaces, or that parking should be free. Food also produces enormous benefits, but this does not mean that we need more food, or that food should be free. When planners set minimum parking requirements, they do not define demand and supply the way economists do. For example, economists do not define the demand for food as the peak quantity of food consumed at free buffets where overweight diners eat until the last bite has zero utility. Nor do economists, when asked for policy prescriptions, recommend that restaurants should be required to supply at least this quantity of free food no matter how much it costs. Yet planners *do* define parking demand as the peak number of spaces occupied at sites with free parking, and cities *do* require developers to supply at least this number of parking spaces, whatever the cost. Planning for parking is planning without prices.

Some developers voluntarily provide abundant free parking because they believe that the benefits outweigh the costs, but these voluntary choices of some developers do not justify requiring *all* developers to provide on-site parking. Some cities explicitly require *free* on-site parking, as in this specific plan ordinance in Los Angeles:

> For office and other commercial uses there shall be at least three parking spaces provided for each 1,000 square feet of gross floor area available *at no charge to all patrons and employees of those uses.*[10]

This ordinance applies to a stretch along Wilshire Boulevard that has the best bus service in Los Angeles. Some cities prohibit charges for required parking anywhere in the city. For example, Monterey Park, California, requires that "The parking of motor vehicles shall be without monetary charge when such parking is required in conjunction with a use or uses permitted by this [ordinance]."[11]

Parking requirements illustrate a common pattern in transportation policy: politicians and planners typically respond to shortages with physical rather than economic solutions. They build new roads rather than price existing ones, and they require off-street parking rather than price curb parking. But this leads to a new question: how much parking does each land use actually need?

PLANNING WITHOUT THEORY

Planning education provides no instruction on how practicing planners should set parking requirements, and textbooks offer no help. Consider the four editions of *Urban Land Use Planning* by F. Stuart Chapin and his coauthors.[12] This distinguished text is the bible of urban land-use planning, yet no edition mentions parking. Most texts in regional science, transportation planning, and urban economics also ignore parking.[13] I have asked many professors of urban planning if their departments offer any instruction on how planners set parking requirements, and the answer is always *no*. Perhaps planning students learn almost nothing about parking requirements because their professors know almost nothing to teach them. Somehow, the urban land use with the biggest footprint and a profound effect on the transportation system has been invisible to scholars in every discipline.

Because parking requirements are a major component of zoning ordinances, the failure to consider them in professional planning education is a serious weakness, especially in light of our reliance on cars for most transportation. In their book, *American Planning Law*, Norman Williams and John Taylor explain that zoning ordinances have three basic sets of regulations:

1. Permitted uses—such as residential, commercial, and industrial zones,
2. Permitted bulk—regulated by floor-area ratios, height limits, setbacks, and open-space requirements; and
3. Off-street parking requirements.[14]

The regulations for permitted uses and bulk tell developers and property owners what they can and cannot do on a specific site: you can build single-family houses but not apartment buildings, for example, and you cannot build within five feet of your property line, or more than 45 feet high. But parking requirements tell developers and property owners what they *must* do: you must provide four parking spaces per thousand square feet of floor area in an office building, for example, or three spaces per dwelling unit in an apartment house. Parking requirements thus impose costs on society to provide parking for cars, but planners do not estimate the subsidies for cars implicit in these parking requirements, or the effects on transportation and land use.

The regulations for permitted uses and bulk were firmly established before cities began to require off-street parking in the 1930s. University of Iowa professor of urban planning John Shaw points out that "the near-universal adoption of parking requirements represents the most substantial change to local zoning controls in the last 60 years."[15] Even Houston, which does not zone for permitted uses or bulk, requires off-street parking for every land use.[16] Parking requirements are a central feature of urban planning, and they profoundly affect transportation and cities, but planning education ignores them, perhaps exemplifying what MIT planning professor Donald Schön deplored as universities' commitment to "a view of knowledge that fosters selective inattention to professional competence."[17]

Despite their lack of professional training, practicing planners in every city must set the parking requirements for every land use. Zoning codes throughout the country contain thousands of different parking requirements—the Ten Thousand Commandments for off-street parking. Planners set parking requirements almost as if they were physicians prescribing drugs, but they have no theory, no training, and often no data to help them. No textbook explains the theory of parking requirements because there is none. Professors cannot teach their students how to set parking requirements because no one has carried out research on how to do it.

Without clairvoyance, how do practicing planners predict how much parking every land use needs? To find out, Richard Willson surveyed planning directors and senior planners, and asked, What sources of information do you normally use to set minimum parking requirements for workplaces? Forty-five percent of the respondents ranked "Survey nearby cities" as most important, and "Institute of Transportation Engineers handbooks" came in second place at 15 percent. More planners responded "Don't know" (5 percent) than responded that they commissioned parking studies (3 percent).[18] According to Robert Dunphy of the Urban Land Institute, "Local codes typically are based on either someone else's requirements or on the Institute of Transportation Engineers (ITE) parking data."[19] I will explore these two strategies—copy other cities, and consult ITE data—and the problems they cause.

FIRST STRATEGY: COPY OTHER CITIES

PAS has published a series of national surveys that planners consult to learn about other cities' parking requirements. These surveys tell how many parking spaces cities do require, not how many a city *should* require. Nevertheless, PAS has found that planners copy other cities' requirements because they have few alternatives.

Planning Advisory Service Surveys

PAS reports that its surveys of parking requirements are a natural response to a strong demand for information:

> [We] receive hundreds of requests each year about off-street parking require-
> ments for different land uses—*in fact, we receive more requests year after year on
> this topic than on any other*. Drafting off-street parking requirements is clearly
> one of the most important tasks of a planning agency. There is typically
> tremendous citizen concern about the availability of parking, its effect on the
> transportation network, and ultimately on the quality of life in a community.
> There are also, of course, significant effects on developers and their projects,
> often with serious cost implications.[20]

PAS has conducted five surveys of parking requirements since 1964, and the results suggest two main features of planning for parking. First, parking requirements are often copied from other cities. Second, they are often based on scant evidence—or none at all. We can use PAS's own words to summarize its main conclusions:

> The underlying assumptions used in drafting parking requirements are
> unknown.[21]
>
> Copying other cities' parking requirements may simply repeat someone
> else's mistakes.[22]
>
> For every land use whose parking demand planners know something about,
> at least a dozen remain mysteries.[23]
>
> Absurd twists of logic in the way the standards were drafted sometimes
> make it impossible to say which of two cities requires more parking for the
> same land use.[24]
>
> Many communities have created parking standards that require develop-
> ments to build parking spaces far in excess of demand.[25]

Clearly, PAS has doubts about how planners set parking requirements. PAS also elaborates on the problems caused by copying other cities' requirements:

Since the establishment of the principle that zoning ordinances may legally require the provision of off-street parking, ordinance drafters have been asking questions like: How many spaces should be provided for a drive-in restaurant?—or any other land use for that matter. The question is typically answered by relying upon what ordinances for other jurisdictions require. Two options are then open: first, to go through [other cities'] ordinances in the agency's files, and, second, to consult nationally published surveys. The implicit assumption is that other areas must know what they are doing (the ordinances were adopted, after all) and so it is a relatively safe bet to adopt a parking standard "close to the average." This may simply result in a repetition of someone else's mistakes.[26]

Why do planners copy other cities' requirements—without understanding how they were set in the first place—and risk repeating someone else's mistakes? PAS explains the strong temptation for planners to cut corners when they set parking requirements:

The planner who needs to present a numerical standard by the next planning commission meeting can't answer the original question [how many parking spaces should be provided?] by saying, "I don't really know."[27]

Planners have no special expertise to estimate parking demand, but they have to provide an answer. This dilemma explains planners' most frequent question to PAS every year: *how many parking spaces should we require?* Despite PAS's reservations about its own national surveys of parking requirements, planners do use them to copy other cities' requirements. Writing in *Transportation Planning*, Connecticut zoning administrator Carol Gould says:

Parking requirements in most zoning regulations are not founded on an empirical analysis of what any land use will require to meet patrons' needs, but appear to have been "handed down" from one community to another.[28]

As a result, most parking requirements amount to little more than a collective hunch. They are a perfect example of what Pietro Nivola termed "accidental urban policies" that have profound but commonly unrecognized effects on the design of cities.

Shopworn Planning Tools

APA's landmark *Growing Smart Legislative Guidebook: Model Statutes for Planning and the Management of Change* missed a tremendous opportunity to change this pattern of parking-requirement guesswork. The *Guidebook* was published in 2002 as the culmination of the APA's seven-year, $2.5-million "Growing Smart" project to offer reforms for outdated planning laws. Stuart Meck, the *Guidebook's* general editor, explains the goal:

> Our planning tools date from another era. They are shopworn and inadequate for the job at hand…. Reform of planning statutes is a serious contemporary concern that affects every state, region, and community in this nation. This 2002 edition of *Legislative Guidebook* will provide the means to address that subject by offering statutory options—many from contemporary planning practice and successful state experience—to aid legislators, state and local government officials, planners, and concerned citizens, confront and make reasoned, informed choices concerning just about any planning issue facing us today.[29]

The APA consulted virtually every relevant interest group in the country, and *Washington Post* journalist Neal Peirce reports, "The APA appears to have left no stone unturned in its effort to check out, to smooth, to perfect the array of planning tools it's publishing."[30] The 11-pound, 1,514-page *Guidebook* suggests reforms concerning just about any planning issue except one—parking requirements. The *Guidebook's* 72-page index has five pages for the words that start with 'P,' but parking is not one of them.[31]

Parking is a major part of both transportation and land use, and PAS receives more questions about parking requirements than any other topic. Nevertheless, the *Growing Smart Legislative Guidebook* ignores parking, as though urban planners had nothing to do with it. But planners have everything to do with parking, as Allan Jacobs (Berkeley professor of city planning and former director of the San Francisco City Planning Commission) explains:

> Automobile parking is a pervasive issue. Prepare a plan for an individual street or neighborhood, or for a central area, and parking is certain to be a major subject—a bone of contention—more time and energy consuming than housing.[32]

Similarly, University of Chicago law professor Richard Epstein says:

> Parking is in most communities one of the most difficult and politically explosive issues to deal with. Anyone who has ever witnessed the proceedings of a local planning commission knows how pitched the battles over parking can become.[33]

Given the importance of parking in urban planning, one might think the *Legislative Guidebook's* neglect is an aberration, but it is not. Parking does not appear in the index for any of these other books published by the APA, as if it were irrelevant to the issues discussed: *American City Planning since 1890; The Citizen's Guide to Planning; City Zoning: The Once and Future Frontier; Comprehensive City Planning: Introduction and Explanation; Growth Management Principles and Practices; Guidelines for Preparing Urban Plans; Making Places Special; Neighborhood Planning: A Guide for Citizens and Planners; Planning Small Town America; The Practice of Local Government Planning; Strategic Planning: Threats and Opportunities for Planners;* and *Zoning and the American Dream.*[34]

Even classics on zoning such as *The Zoning Game* and *The Zoning Game Revisited* do not mention parking or parking requirements.[35] Parking is not absent from all these planning texts by accident; because most planners and planning professors know so little about parking, they have little to say about it, if they even think of it. Planners are not alone in their neglect of parking; consider the 1,124-page *Land Development Handbook: Planning, Engineering, and Surveying*, a mammoth how-to guide for developers. Parking is not mentioned anywhere in the book.[36]

Some APA books do mention parking, of course, but often little is said. Consider the sole reference to parking in the 305-page *Small Town Planning Handbook*:

> Parking is always a challenge to the visual character of the town. Most com-munities have adequate parking spaces, but they are often scattered, incon-venient, and visually unappealing. The use of a well-crafted plan with easy access to business and visual screening with trees and other vegetation can help make parking areas fit in with the town's appearance.[37]

No one can disagree with this advice, but planners should recognize that parking spaces are scattered because parking requirements create this pattern. The parking supply is also visually unappealing because zoning requires enough spaces to satiate the peak demand for free parking, but largely ignores their design.

The Golden Rule

Urban planners receive almost no academic or professional guidance on how to set parking requirements. According to PAS, planners also have little time to analyze the requirements:

> Few communities have the staff time or financial resources to conduct a com-prehensive review of local parking standards on a regular basis. Many do not have the resources to even analyze standards for a few uses. Because of these

limitations, standards are sometimes transferred from code to code without being adapted to a city's specific parking needs.[38]

If planners do copy other cities' parking requirements in an unscientific process we might term "unnatural selection," the requirements of different cities should converge over time. Do they? We can use two surveys of parking requirements for office buildings in 117 Southern California cities to test this convergence hypothesis. Parking consultant Rex Link conducted the first survey in 1975, and I repeated it in 1993 to examine trends in the requirements (see Table A-2 in Appendix A). The two surveys suggest that planners set requirements close to the average of other cities. In 1975, the most frequent requirement for office buildings was 4 spaces per 1,000 square feet of floor area. By 1993, 65 percent of the cities that required fewer than 4 spaces in 1975 had increased their requirement, while none had reduced it; and 80 percent of the cities that required more than 4 spaces in 1975 had reduced their requirement, while none had increased it. This convergence doubled the share of cities that require 4 spaces per 1,000 square feet, from 27 percent in 1975 to 54 percent 1993.

Practitioners sometimes refer to 4 parking spaces per 1,000 square feet for office buildings as the "magic number" or "golden rule" of planning for parking. The Urban Land Institute, for example, says, "In an office park development, the provision of on-site parking for tenant and visitor cars is nearly as important as the building itself.... An allowance of four spaces per 1,000 square feet of net rentable space (or of one space per 250 net square feet) is an across the board ideal solution."[39] On the surface, this may seem reasonable, but 4 parking spaces occupy at least 1,200 square feet (including the area for ramps and access lanes). Therefore, the golden rule provides at least 20 percent more space for parked cars than for the office space where the drivers work—more space for *cars* than for *people*. Even senior executives rarely have offices much larger than the 300 square feet needed to park their cars, and many commuters occupy cubicles much smaller than their parking spaces. When planners follow the golden rule, cars rule the city.

SECOND STRATEGY: CONSULT ITE DATA

Planners' other common source of information about parking is the *Parking Generation* report published by the Institute of Transportation Engineers (ITE). In developing this report, transportation engineers survey the parking occupancy at various land uses, and for each one ITE reports a "parking generation rate" that relates the *peak parking occupancy* to a characteristic of the land use, such as the floor area or number of employees at a site. ITE's 1987 edition of *Parking Generation* describes the data used to estimate parking generation rates:

> A vast majority of the data…is derived from suburban developments with little or no significant transit ridership…. The ideal site for obtaining reliable parking generation data would…contain ample, convenient parking facilities for the exclusive use of the traffic generated by the site…. The objective of the survey is to count the number of vehicles parked at the time of peak parking demand.[40]

Half the 101 parking generation rates are based on four or fewer studies, and 22 percent are based on a single study.[41] Because drivers park free for 99 percent of automobile trips in the U.S., most survey sites probably offer free parking. Parking generation rates therefore measure the peak parking demand observed at a few suburban sites with ample free parking and no public transit. As a result, urban planners who use these parking generation rates to set minimum parking requirements are shaping a city where almost everyone will drive wherever they go and park free when they get there. In 2001, 87 percent of all trips in the U.S. were made by personal motor vehicle, 8.6 percent by walking, and only 1.5 percent by public transit.[42] We cannot significantly increase the share of all trips made by car unless we find a way to eliminate walking.

Problems with Parking Generation Rates

Parking Generation is a questionable resource for several reasons. First, free parking inflates the parking generation rates. Case studies have shown that employer-paid parking increases commuter parking demand by about a third when compared with driver-paid parking.[43] Second, the focus on suburban sites that lack public transit also inflates the parking generation rates because everyone is likely to drive to these sites; the rates therefore overstate parking demand in areas where more trips are made on foot or by public transit. Third, the focus on peak parking demand inflates the parking generation rates; and the peak demand for some uses may last only a few hours each year. *Parking Generation* raises more questions than it answers, and a close look at the methodology reveals serious flaws.

Figure 2-1 shows a typical page from the second edition of *Parking Generation*. It reports the peak number of parking spaces occupied on a weekday at a familiar land use—fast-food restaurants.[44] Each point in the plot represents one study (based on the observations at one site on one day). If parking occupancy was observed at one restaurant for five days, for example, this would account for five points in the plot.[45] Dividing the

Figure 2-1. ITE Parking Generation Rate for a Fast-Food Restaurant with Drive-in Window (Second Edition of *Parking Generation*, 1987)

Peak Parking Spaces Occupied vs: **1,000 Gross Square Feet Leasable Area**

On a: **Weekday**

PARKING GENERATION RATES

Average Rate	Range of Rates	Standard Deviation	Number of Studies	Average 1,000 GSF Leasable Area
9.95	3.55-15.92	3.41	18	3

DATA PLOT AND EQUATION

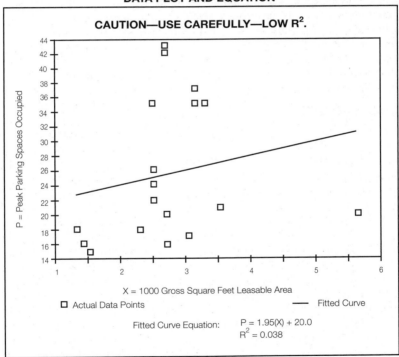

CAUTION—USE CAREFULLY—LOW R^2.

X = 1000 Gross Square Feet Leasable Area

□ Actual Data Points   — Fitted Curve

Fitted Curve Equation: P = 1.95(X) + 20.0
                                            R^2 = 0.038

Source: ITE (1987, 146).

peak parking occupancy observed in a study by the floor area of the restaurant gives the parking generation rate for the study. The parking generation rates in the 18 studies range between 3.55 and 15.92 spaces per 1,000 square feet of leasable floor area. Note that the largest restaurant generated one of the lowest peak parking occupancies, while a midsize one generated the highest. The near-zero R^2 of 0.038 for the fitted-curve (regression) equation at the bottom of the figure confirms the visual impression that parking demand is unrelated to floor area in this sample.[46] Nevertheless, ITE reports the sample's average parking generation rate— which planners normally interpret as *the* relationship between parking demand and floor area—as *precisely* 9.95 spaces per 1,000 square feet of floor area.

This precision is misleading. The equation below the plot suggests that a fast-food restaurant generates a peak parking occupancy of 20 spaces (the intercept) plus 1.95 spaces per 1,000 square feet of floor area (the coefficient). But the 95-percent confidence interval around the coefficient ranges from -3 to +7 spaces per 1,000 square feet.[47] Since this interval includes zero, the data do not show that parking demand is related to floor area. The *average* parking generation rate of 9.95 spaces per 1,000 square feet is due mainly to the intercept, which is independent of floor area, and the fitted curve is almost horizontal.[48] The data plot does contain the warning "Caution—Use Carefully—Low R^2," which is good advice, but how can planners carefully use a parking generation rate derived from data that show *no* relationship between parking demand and floor area?

Exaggerated Estimates of Parking Demand

Aside from the problem that many parking generation rates are statistically insignificant, they can seriously overestimate even the peak demand for free parking. Consider the results found by a well-known consultant, the Parsons Transportation Group, in a study of the peak parking occupancy at Home Depot stores. Parsons observed the parking occupancy at hourly intervals at 17 Home Depot stores on a Saturday, the busiest day of the week, and found "no correlation between the square footage of a store and its resultant peak parking demand."[49] Because all stores sell the same items in similar buildings, the sample is much more suitable than are most ITE samples for estimating parking generation, but peak parking occupancy was nevertheless unrelated to floor area. Because Parsons undertook the study for Home Depot, it had access to important data that ITE never considers—the sales revenue for each store. Not surprisingly, the peak parking occupancy at a store was related to its sales revenue: stores with higher sales had more cars in their parking lots. Parsons used the sales data at each store to predict its peak parking occupancy on the 5th-busiest day of the year, which was selected as the "design day" for the parking supply. Parsons explained:

> Choosing the 5th-busiest day as the design day would mean that some cus-
> tomers may not be able to find a parking space immediately *during the peak*
> *hour* of the busiest four or five days of the year; however, they should have no
> problem finding a parking space in the lot at any other time.[50]

Parsons used each store's sales revenue on both the study day and the day with the fifth-highest sales of the year to predict the store's peak park-ing occupancy on the 5th-busiest day. If, for example, the peak parking occupancy observed on the study day at a store was 200 spaces, and if the store's sales revenue on the 5th-busiest day of the year was 50 percent more than on the study day, Parsons estimated that the peak parking occupancy on the 5th-busiest day of the year at that store would be 300 spaces.[51] Table 2-1 shows the estimated peak parking occupancy at the 17 stores on the 5th-busiest day (see column 1); the average was 316 spaces (see last row).

Parsons compared its estimates of the peak parking occupancy at each store with estimates derived from *Parking Generation* data, using the park-ing generation rate based on floor area at a Hardware/Paint/Home Improvement Store. Columns 2 and 3 show the peak parking occupancy estimated from the parking generation rate and from the regression equa-tion for this land use. The average peak parking occupancy estimated from the ITE parking generation rate (420 spaces) is 33 percent higher than Parsons's estimate of 316 spaces. The peak parking occupancy esti-mated from the ITE regression equation (524 spaces) is 66 percent higher than Parsons's estimate.

Parsons then compared these estimates of peak parking occupancy with the number of parking spaces actually supplied at each store (column 4), and with the number of spaces that cities typically require for this type of land use at the rate of 5 spaces per 1,000 square feet of floor area (column 5). The average parking supply was 530 spaces per store, 67 percent more than Parsons had estimated as the peak parking occupancy on the 5th-busiest day of the year. Finally, the average municipal parking require-ment based on floor area was 639 spaces, more than double the estimated peak parking occupancy on the 5th-busiest day.[52]

Two findings from the Parsons study stand out. First, peak parking occupancy was unrelated to floor area at these Home Depots. Second, both the ITE guidelines and the cities' parking requirements led to an oversupply of parking at the busiest time of the year.

Table 2-1. Peak Parking Occupancy and Minimum Parking Requirements (at 17 Home Depot stores)

Store number	Peak occupancy estimated for the 5th-busiest day	ITE *Parking Generation* average rate	ITE *Parking Generation* regression equation	Parking spaces supplied	Parking spaces required at 5 per 1,000 sq.ft.
	(1)	(2)	(3)	(4)	(5)
1	502	430	539	540	654
2	347	445	562	462	676
3	426	428	536	443	651
4	433	427	535	648	650
5	383	430	539	703	654
6	287	433	543	594	658
7	290	447	566	489	680
8	269	379	460	439	576
9	310	426	533	461	647
10	274	427	534	539	649
11	292	428	535	570	650
12	267	428	536	459	650
13	373	330	387	532	501
14	238	433	543	528	658
15	243	430	539	565	653
16	233	436	548	568	662
17	210	386	472	462	587
Total	**5,377**	**7,143**	**8,908**	**9,002**	**10,855**
Average	**316**	**420**	**524**	**530**	**639**

Source: Parsons Transportation Group (2002, 12 and 19).

Note that *peak parking occupancy* is not the same thing as *parking demand*. Economists define parking demand as the relationship between the price of parking and the number of parked cars; they would call the peak parking occupancy observed at a site with free parking "the quantity of parking demanded at a zero price at the time of peak demand." Confusion results when ITE's parking generation rates (which refer to the peak parking occupancy at a zero price) are loosely referred to as "parking demand." Parking generation rates actually refer to the peak demand for *free* parking. To make the distinction between peak parking occupancy and parking demand clear, imagine a similar study of chocolate consumption. Dietitians observe a small, nonrandom sample of overindulgent people and measure the amount of chocolate they consume each day. All the chocolate is free—everyone can grab another piece of rich milk chocolate at any time, but they must pay for anything else they eat. The peak quantity of chocolate consumed by this sample does not measure "the demand for chocolate," just as parking generation rates do not measure "the demand for parking."

The estimated peak parking occupancy at Home Depot during the peak hour on the 5th-busiest day of the year was 2.5 spaces per 1,000 square feet, not 5 spaces per 1,000 square feet. Even if the parking supply were only 2.5 spaces per 1,000 square feet, the worst that would happen is that a few drivers would not immediately find a vacant space when they drove into the parking lot during the four or five busiest hours of the whole year. Some customers might react by choosing not to drive to Home Depot stores during the five peak hours of the year—a minor inconvenience—and the parking "shortage" would be solved.

Although ITE's parking generation rates are hardly scientific and can seriously overestimate even the peak demand for free parking, planners who consult *Parking Generation* act like frightened suppliants bowing before a powerful totem. ITE's stamp of authority relieves planners from the obligation to think for themselves because simple answers are right there in the book. ITE offers a precise, off-the-shelf number without addressing difficult public policy questions, although it does warn, "Users of this report should exercise extreme caution when utilizing data that is based on a small number of studies."[53] This sounds suspiciously like the Surgeon General's warning on a pack of cigarettes. Users have an obligation to be cautious, but planners nevertheless rely on ITE's parking generation rates to set the minimum requirements for their communities. For example, the median parking requirement for fast-food restaurants in the U.S. is 10 spaces per 1,000 square feet of floor area—almost identical to ITE's reported parking generation rate of 9.95 spaces per 1,000 square feet.[54] Because parking lots occupy about 330 square feet of land per parking space, a parking requirement of 10 spaces per 1,000 square feet of floor area leads to a parking lot over three times the size of the restaurant itself.[55] Planners expect minimum parking requirements to meet the peak demand for free parking, and parking generation rates predict this peak demand precisely! When ITE speaks, urban planners listen.

Planning on Uncertainty

Cities require parking spaces during the permit application process when planners, developers, and tenants know the least about the future demand for parking. The inevitable uncertainty about parking demand helps explain why cities often require more than enough spaces to meet the peak demand. An office building, for example, may first be used by a corporate headquarters with 300-square-foot offices for executives, and then by a telemarketing firm with 30-square-foot cubicles for sales personnel. Squeezing more workers into a building can greatly increase parking demand. In a survey of 57 employment centers, Robert Cervero found that the building occupancy rates ranged from 0.5 to 6 persons per 1,000 square feet (a ratio of 12 to 1).[56] In a similar survey of 33 low-rise office buildings, Gruen Associates found occupancies ranging from 1.6 to 17 persons per 1,000 square feet (a ratio of 11 to 1).[57] And in the Seattle region, a survey of 36 employment sites found densities ranging from 0.5 to 5.6 persons per 1,000 square feet (a ratio of 11 to 1).[58] Given this broad range of possible building occupancy, no one can accurately predict the demand for parking at an office building throughout its useful life.

ITE's format for presenting data helps explain why cities require too much parking in response to uncertainty. Figure 2-2 shows the report for nonconvention hotels in the second edition of *Parking Generation*. (The parking generation rates for the four observations have been added to the data plot.) Four observations may seem too few to estimate a parking generation rate, but half the ITE parking generation rates are based on four or fewer observations.

Given the variation in observed peak demand (ranging from 0.29 to 0.68 parking spaces per room), what is a planner to say when asked to set the parking requirement for a hotel? ITE reports that average peak parking occupancy is 0.52 spaces per room. Transportation engineer Steven Smith points out that if a city requires only enough parking spaces to satisfy the *average* parking generation rate, about half of all sites will have a peak parking demand higher than this average, and the required parking supply may be inadequate.[59]

To be safe in the case of a hotel, why not require 0.68 spaces per room, the highest demand observed? Maybe 0.75 spaces per room would appear less arbitrary. One space per room also seems plausible. PAS reports eight cities' parking requirements for hotels: two cities require 0.75 spaces per room, two require 0.9 spaces per room, and four require 1 space per room. When they set parking requirements, planners appear to take the arbitrary and uncertain estimate of the maximum parking demand and then revise it *upward* to set the minimum parking requirement.

As an analytical way to play it safe, Smith recommends that minimum parking requirements should meet the peak parking demand observed at the 85th percentile of all sites:

> Setting parking supply levels is a policy decision involving a degree of risk that the actual parking demand will be higher or lower (or perhaps both, over time) than the predicted demand.... [Figure 2-3] presents a different way of looking at the data in *Parking Generation*. It is a cumulative distribution of parking generation rates (peak parked cars per 1,000 GSF) for general office buildings between 100,000 and 200,000 GSF in size.... One way to look at the design level parking demand issue is to set the parking supply level at a certain percentile of the curve [in Figure 2-3]. A value of 85 percent will be used

Figure 2-2. ITE Parking Generation Rate for a Nonconvention Hotel (Second Edition of *Parking Generation*, 1987)

Peak Parking Spaces Occupied vs: **Rooms**
On a: **Weekday**

PARKING GENERATIONS RATES

Average Rate	Range of Rates	Standard Deviation	Number of Studies	Average Number of Rooms
0.52	0.29-0.68	*	4	188

DATA PLOT AND EQUATION

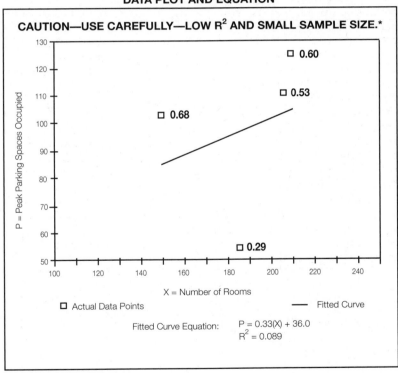

CAUTION—USE CAREFULLY—LOW R^2 AND SMALL SAMPLE SIZE.*

Fitted Curve Equation: $P = 0.33(X) + 36.0$
$R^2 = 0.089$

Source: ITE (1987, 44).

as an example. Assuming that the building being planned has the same general characteristics as the group of sites represented in the *Parking Generation* sample, one could then say that there is an 85 percent chance that the parking demand will be less than 3.1 spaces per 1,000 GSF.[60]

This reasoning helps explain why parking requirements often exceed the ITE parking generation rates, which represent the *average* peak demand for free parking. The 85th-percentile level of demand in Smith's sample (3.1 spaces per 1,000 square feet) is 24 percent above the average level (2.5 spaces per 1,000 square feet). But requiring enough parking to satisfy the 85th-percentile level of peak parking demand (regardless of how much the spaces cost) is unwise and impractical. Unwise because it leads to

Figure 2-3. Cumulative Distribution of Parking Generation for a General Office Building of 100,000–299,000 Gross Square Feet

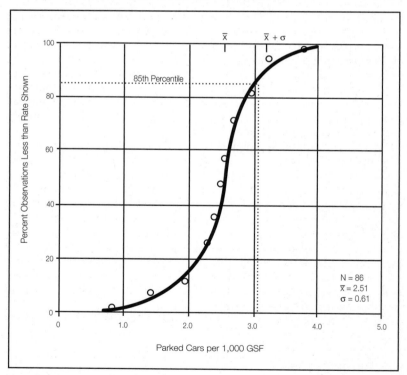

Source: Smith (1990, 27).

even more free parking than we now have and impractical because half of all parking generation rates are based on four or fewer observations (22 percent are based on only *one* observation).

In 2004, ITE published the third edition of *Parking Generation*, and Figure 2-4 shows its report of trip generation for a fast-food restaurant.[61] As was the case in the second edition in 1987, the data plot shows little if any relationship between floor area and the peak number of parked vehicles. The main change between 1987 and 2004 is the method of presenting the data. The peak period is identified as 12:00–1:00 p.m., and the peak parking occupancy is explicitly identified as "parking demand." The average peak parking occupancy of 9.90 parked vehicles per 1,000 square feet in 2004 is almost identical to the figure of 9.95 in 1987, but the deviation around this average increased in 2004. The peak parking occupancy in the sample of 46 study sites in 2004 ranged from 1.45 to 23.32 vehicles per 1,000 square feet. The largest restaurant had the second-lowest parking occupancy while a midsize one had the highest. The fitted-curve equation and the R^2 are not shown, but the 95 percent confidence interval around the *average* parking generation rate is reported as 8.51–11.29 vehicles per 1,000 square feet. Note that this confidence interval is *not* placed around the coefficient of floor area in a regression equation, which would test whether parking occupancy is related to floor area. When the regression equation is calculated for the data shown in the plot, the R^2 is 0.11, which means that variation in floor area explains only 11 percent of the variation in peak parking occupancy. A quick look at the plot also shows little relationship between floor area and parked vehicles.

The main innovation in the third edition is the added report of the 85th percentile of the parking generation rate: 14.81 vehicles per 1,000 square feet. What does this new information imply for minimum parking requirements? Well, one interpretation is that planners who want to ensure at least an 85 percent chance of always having enough spaces to satisfy the peak parking demand ever observed at fast-food restaurants in suburban sites with free parking should require at least 14.81 parking spaces per 1,000 square feet of floor area, although peak parking occupancy is unrelated to floor area in the sample.[62] Reporting the 85th-percentile value is the most important change between the second and third editions of *Parking Generation*, and it is sure to have adverse effects on transportation and land-use planning.

Prices can regulate parking demand (as they do for most other goods and services), but cities bypass the market and directly regulate the parking supply. Because planners and politicians want to avoid criticism for allowing development that later creates parking spillover, cities require an oversupply of parking spaces that often remain vacant. The desire to

Figure 2-4. ITE Parking Generation Rate for a Fast-Food Restaurant with Drive-Through Window (Third Edition of *Parking Generation*, 2004)

**Average Peak Period Parking Demand vs: 1,000 sq. ft. GFA
On a Weekday**

Statistic	Peak Periond Demand
Peak Period	12:00–1:00 p.m.
Number of Study Sites	46
Average Size of Study Site	3,400 sq. ft. GFA
Average Peak Period Parking Demand	9.90 vehicles per 1,000 sq. ft. GFA
Standard Deviation	4.81
Coefficient of Variation	49%
95% Confidence Interval	8.51–11.29 vehicles per 1,000 sq. ft. GFA
Range	1.45–23.32 vehicles per 1,000 sq. ft. GFA
85th Percentile	14.81 vehicles per 1,000 sq ft. GFA
33rd Percentile	7.46 vehicles per 1,000 sq ft. GFA

Weekday Peak Period
Parking Demand

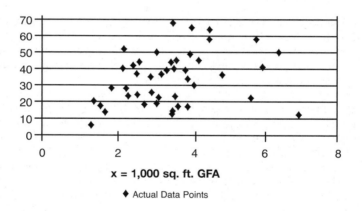

x = 1,000 sq. ft. GFA

♦ Actual Data Points

Source: ITE (2004, 288).

avoid criticism about not having enough free parking helps explain why planners seem to assume that every household owns at least two cars and everyone travels everywhere by car. Because these assumptions then determine the parking supply required for all new development, they have become self-fulfilling prophecies. Mistakes in planning for parking are literally cemented into the urban form. In 1961, British transportation economist D. H. Glassborow presciently observed, "The advantage of parking charges is that they can be abandoned if they do not work, but the cost of very expensive bulldozer work in cities would not be recoverable."[63]

To deal with the uncertainty in predicting the demand for parking, some cities allow developers to provide fewer parking spaces if they set aside land that can later be converted to parking if demand is higher than expected. Palo Alto, California, for example allows reductions of up to 50 percent in parking requirements if the difference is made up through a landscaped reserve. Not one of these landscaped reserves has subsequently been converted to parking.[64]

Problems with Trip Generation Rates

Parking demand at a site depends on vehicle trips *to* the site, and ITE publishes another report, *Trip Generation*, which shows the number of vehicle trips as a function of land use. For each land use it reports the "trip generation rate," which predicts the number of vehicle trips to and from a land use during a given period. The 1997 edition of *Trip Generation* describes the data used to estimate trip generation rates:

> This document is based on more than 3,750 trip generation studies submitted to the Institute by public agencies, developers, consulting firms, and associations.... Data were primarily collected at suburban localities with little or no transit service, nearby pedestrian amenities, or travel demand management (TDM) programs.[65]

As with the estimates of parking generation discussed earlier, ITE says nothing about the price of parking at the survey sites, and, as with the surveys of parking generation, most samples are small: half the 1,515 published trip generation rates are based on surveys at five or fewer sites, and 23 percent are based on surveys at only one site.[66] Trip generation rates thus measure the average number of vehicle trips observed at a few suburban sites with plentiful free parking but no public transit, pedestrian amenities, or TDM programs. Urban planners who rely on these trip generation rates to design the transportation system are planning cities for cars, not people.

Figure 2-5 shows the page for fast-food restaurants from the 1987 edition of *Trip Generation*.[67] It reports the number of vehicle trips to and from eight survey sites on a weekday.[68] Each of the eight studies is represented in the figure by a point showing the number of vehicle trips per day (on the vertical axis) and the floor area (on the horizontal axis) at a restaurant. Dividing the number of vehicle trips by the floor area gives the trip gen-

Figure 2-5. ITE Trip Generation Rate for a Fast-Food Restaurant with a Drive-Through Window (Fourth Edition of *Trip Generation*, 1987)

Average Vehicle Trip Ends vs: **1,000 Square Feet Gross Floor Area**
On a: **Weekday**

TRIP GENERATION RATES

Average Weekday Vehicle Trip Ends per 1,000 Square Feet Gross Floor Area				
Average Trip Rate	*Range of Rates*	*Standard Deviation*	*Number of Studies*	*Average 1,000 Square Feet GFA*
632.125	284.000–1359.500	*	8	3.0

DATA PLOT AND EQUATION

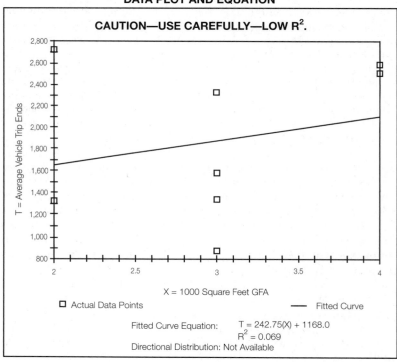

CAUTION—USE CAREFULLY—LOW R^2.

X = 1000 Square Feet GFA

☐ Actual Data Points   —— Fitted Curve

Fitted Curve Equation: T = 242.75(X) + 1168.0
R^2 = 0.069
Directional Distribution: Not Available

Source: ITE (1987, 1199).

eration rate for the restaurant, and the rates range between 284 and 1,360 vehicle trips per 1,000 square feet at the eight sites. A glance at the figure suggests that vehicle trips are unrelated to floor area in this sample, and the extremely low R^2 of 0.069 for the equation at the bottom of the figure confirms this impression.[69] Nevertheless, ITE reports the sample's *average* trip generation rate—which urban planners normally interpret as *the* relationship between floor area and vehicle trips—as *precisely* 632.125 trips per day per 1,000 square feet of floor area.[70] The trip generation rate looks accurate because it is so precise, but again the precision is misleading. Reporting the trip generation rate as 632 rather than 632.125 trips per 1,000 square feet would alter few transportation or land-use decisions, so the three-decimal-point precision serves no purpose other than to give the impression of accuracy.

The equation at the bottom of Figure 2-5 suggests that a fast-food restaurant generates 1,168 trips (the intercept) plus 242.75 trips per 1,000 square feet of floor area (the coefficient), but the 95-percent confidence interval around the coefficient ranges from -650 to +1,141 trips per 1,000 square feet.[71] Since this confidence interval contains zero, the data do not show that vehicle trips are related to floor area. Reporting an average trip generation rate implies that larger restaurants generate more vehicle trips, but the figure shows that the smallest restaurant generated the most trips, and a midsize one generated the fewest. Despite its precision, the average trip generation rate (632.125 vehicle trips per day per 1,000 square feet) is far too unreliable to use for transportation planning.

Suppose Figure 2-5 showed blood cholesterol level (on the vertical axis) as a function of the number of aspirin tablets per day taken by a sample of eight patients (on the horizontal axis). The data would not convince medical researchers that aspirin affected the outcome. When it comes to transportation, however, the data seem to convince many engineers and planners that each 1,000 square feet of a fast-food restaurant generates 632.125 vehicle trips a day. Parking and trip generation rates combine some basic insights and rough measurements with faulty statistical procedures and wrong economic interpretations. We need less precision—and more truth—in transportation planning.

Statistical Insignificance

Does size matter? According to the traditional rules of statistical inference, ITE data do not say much about how floor area affects either vehicle trips or parking demand at a fast-food restaurant, because the 95-percent confidence interval around the floor-area coefficient includes zero in both cases.[72] This is not to say that parking demand and vehicle trips are unrelated to a restaurant's size, because common sense suggests some corre-

Truth in Transportation Planning

How far is it from San Diego to San Francisco? An estimate of 632.125 miles is precise but not accurate. An estimate of somewhere between 400 and 500 miles is less precise but more accurate because the correct answer is 460 miles.

Nevertheless, if you had no idea how far it is from San Diego to San Francisco, whom would you believe: someone who confidently says 632.125 miles, or someone who tentatively says somewhere between 400 and 500 miles? Probably the one who says 632.125 miles because pre-cision creates the impression of certainty.

ITE's parking and trip generation rates illustrate a familiar problem with statistics used in transportation planning. Reporting data with extreme precision implies confidence in their accuracy, but transportation engineers and urban planners often report highly uncertain estimates as precise numbers. Placing unwarranted trust in the accuracy of these precise but uncertain data then leads to bad transportation and land-use policies.

---

lation. Nevertheless, the low R^2 shows that factors other than floor area (such as the price of parking, the density of the neighborhood, or the quality of the food) explain most of the variation in parking demand and vehicle trips at these restaurants. Size does not matter in these two samples of parking and trip generation, and it is misleading to publish precise *average* parking and trip generation rates based on floor area.

The breathtaking combination of extreme precision and statistical insignificance for the parking and trip generation rates for a fast-food restaurant raises an important question: how many parking and trip generation rates for other land uses are statistically insignificant? The 1987 edition of *Trip Generation* does not state a policy on statistical significance, but it does show the plots and equations for most land uses with more than two data points. Nevertheless, it fails to show them for some land uses with more than 10 data points. Consider the report of trip generation at recreational land uses. ITE reports 14 studies of trip generation at recreational land uses but says "No Plot or Equation Available—Insufficient Data."[73] The trip generation rates in the 14 studies range from a high of 296 to a low of 0.066 trips per acre on a weekday, a ratio of 4,500 to 1. Given this wide range, reporting the average trip generation rate as *precisely* 3.635 trips per acre is grossly misleading.

ITE first stated a policy regarding statistical significance in the 1991 edition of *Trip Generation*:

Best fit curves are shown in this report only when each of the following three conditions are met:
- The R^2 is greater than or equal to 0.25.
- The sample size is greater than or equal to 4.
- The number of trips increases as the size of the independent variable increases.[74]

The third criterion is notably unscientific. Suppose, for example, the R^2 is greater than 0.25 and the sample size is greater than 4, but vehicle trips *decrease* as floor area increases (the first two criteria are met but the third is not). In this case ITE would report the *average* trip generation rate (which implies that vehicle trips *increase* as floor area increases), but not the regression equation that casts doubt on this rate. The stated policy therefore conceals evidence that contradicts the presumed relationship.[75] In a more rigorous world, one would test the relationship between land use and vehicle trips, not simply assume it, and one would never conceal the results of a statistical test that casts doubt on the assumed relationship. Data on trip generation are closer to numerology than to statistics.

Figure 2-6 from the 1991 edition of *Trip Generation* shows how these three criteria affect the reported trip generation at a fast-food restaurant. It shows the same eight data points from the fourth edition, but it omits the regression equation, the R^2, and the warning "Caution—Use Carefully—Low R^2." The omitted R^2 remains 0.069 because the data are unchanged from the fourth edition, but the fifth edition is more cautious about needless precision: it truncates the average trip generation rate from 632.125 to 632.12 trips per 1,000 square feet.[76]

ITE revised its reporting policy in the 1997 edition of *Trip Generation.*[77] Under the new policy, regression equations are shown only if the R^2 is greater than or equal to 0.5, while the other two criteria remain the same (the sample size is 4 or more, and vehicle trips increase as the independent variable increases). Figure 2-7 shows the sixth edition's report of trip generation at a fast-food restaurant. (ITE does not explain why all eight study sites in the fourth and fifth editions were exactly 2, 3, or 4 thousand square feet, but none in the sixth edition matched these sizes.) The number of studies increased to 21, and the average trip generation rate fell to 496.12 trips per 1,000 square feet. The R^2 is below 0.5, but we are not told what it is. Since the fifth edition's rate was 632.12 trips per 1,000 square feet, anyone comparing the two editions might conclude that vehicle trips at fast-food restaurants declined 22 percent between 1991 and 1997. But since both the previous rate (632.12) and the new one (496.12) were derived from data that show almost no relation between floor area and vehicle trips, this decline was likely a spurious artifact of questionable

Figure 2-6. ITE Trip Generation Rate for a Fast-Food Restaurant with

Average Vehicle Trip Ends vs: **1,000 Square Feet Gross Floor Area**
On a: **Weekday**

Number of Studies: 8
Average 1000 Square Feet GFA: 3
Directional Distribution: 50% entering, 50% exiting

Trip Generation per 1000 Square Feet Gross Floor Area

Average Rate	Range of Rates	Standard Deviation
632.12	284.00-1359.50	266.29

DATA PLOT AND EQUATION

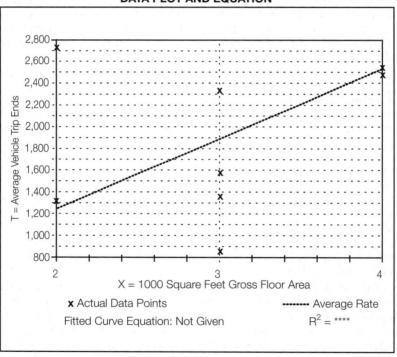

Source: ITE (1991, 1308).

data.[78] In 2003, ITE published the seventh edition of *Trip Generation,* but the page for fast-food restaurants on a weekday is identical to the one in the sixth edition (see Figure 2-7).[79]

The 1997 edition shows regression equations for only 34 percent of the 1,515 trip generation rates. Although 66 percent of the rates fail to meet at least one of the three significance criteria, ITE nevertheless published a precise rate for every land use no matter how small the sample or how unrelated vehicle trips are to floor area. Consider, for example, the report of trip generation at a fast-food restaurant with a drive-through window and no indoor seating, a new land use that was reported for the first time in the seventh edition in 2003 (see Figure 2-8). Two sites were surveyed, and the larger site generated fewer vehicle trips. Nevertheless, ITE reports the average trip generation rate at the two sites and plots a line suggesting that larger sites generate more vehicle trips. The precision defies common sense, but there it is: 153.85 vehicle trips per 1,000 square feet during the peak hour of adjacent street traffic on a weekday. Two observations were thus sufficient to launch this new land-use category, even though its precise trip generation rate and the plot are statistically absurd.[80]

Because trip generation rates are merely a stripped-down version of the gravity model for travel forecasting, their statistical insignificance is not surprising. Gravity models predict travel between origin and destination zones in terms of both zone characteristics and generalized travel cost, while trip generation rates predict the number of vehicle trips to and from one site solely as a function of floor area (or another variable), with no reference to cost. In the 1970s, Berkeley professor Daniel McFadden (who won the Nobel Prize in economics for his work on the theory and methods for analyzing discrete choice) revolutionized travel demand forecasting by shifting focus of the analysis from travel between zones to travel by individuals. As McFadden says, "Zones don't travel; people travel."[81] Similarly, land uses don't make vehicle trips; people make vehicle trips.

The transportation circumstances can vary greatly among different sites for the same land use (such as a fast-food restaurant), and floor area is only one among many factors (and may not even be the key factor) influencing the number of vehicle trips to and from each site. Although floor area alone cannot accurately predict the number of vehicle trips, urban planners and transportation engineers continue to report trip generation as a function of building size because they have always done so. But despite their precision, trip generation rates are unreliable estimates of the relationship between land use and transportation, with a meager theoretical basis. ITE's parking and trip generation rates are another example of what Michael Brooks (past president of both the American Planning Association and the Association of Collegiate Schools of Planning) refers

Figure 2-7. ITE Trip Generation Rate for a Fast-Food Restaurant with Drive-Through Window (Sixth Edition of *Trip Generation*, 1997)

Average Vehicle Trip Ends vs: **1,000 Square Feet Gross Floor Area**
On a: **Weekday**

Number of Studies: 21
Average 1000 Square Feet GFA: 3
Directional Distribution: 50% entering, 50% exiting

Trip Generation per 1000 Square Feet Gross Floor Area

Average Rate	Range of Rates	Standard Deviation
496.12	195.98-1132.92	242.52

DATA PLOT AND EQUATION

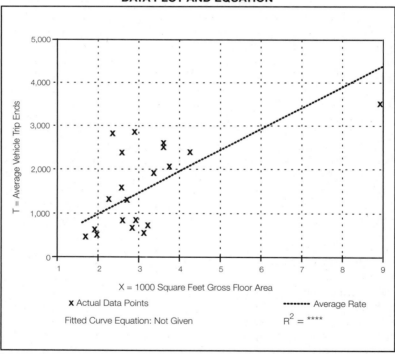

X = 1000 Square Feet Gross Floor Area

x Actual Data Points ┄┄┄┄ Average Rate

Fitted Curve Equation: Not Given $R^2 = ****$

Source: ITE (1997, 1401).

Figure 2-8. ITE Trip Generation Rate for a Fast-Food Restaurant with Drive-Through Window and No Indoor Seating (Seventh Edition of *Trip Generation*, 2003)

Average Vehicle Trip Ends vs: **1,000 Square Feet Gross Floor Area**
On a: **Weekday**
Peak Hour of Adjacent Street Traffic, One Hour Between 4 and 6 p.m.

Number of Studies: 2
Average 1000 Square Feet GFA: 0.35
Directional Distribution: 54% entering, 46% exiting

Trip Generation per 1000 Square Feet Gross Floor Area

Average Rate	Range of Rates	Standard Deviation
153.85	124.37-191.56	*

DATA PLOT AND EQUATION

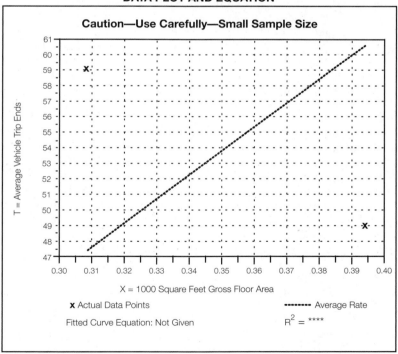

Source: ITE (2003, 1773)

to as "the unfortunate durability of many so-called sound planning principles that turn out to be based on little more than tradition."[82] Rather than being facts about the relationships between land use, parking demand, and vehicle trips, ITE's parking and trip generation data raise an important question: why are these relationships often statistically insignificant?

Significant Digits

ITE's convention of rounding every parking and trip generation rate to two digits after the decimal point blurs the distinction between precision and accuracy.[83] An estimate always has some associated uncertainty, and the number of significant digits used to express an estimate should reflect this uncertainty. The least significant digit in a number is the one farthest to the right, and the accuracy of any number is usually assumed to be ± 1 of the least significant digit, unless stated otherwise. In a typical engineering context, an estimate expressed with five significant digits appears to have been measured more accurately than an estimate expressed with only two significant digits. Because the number of significant digits used to express an estimate should be related to the associated uncertainty, ITE's automatic two-digits-after-the-decimal-point convention is inappropriate and unscientific. Accuracy is more important than digits-after-the-decimal-point consistency, and ITE should not report insignificant digits simply for the sake of uniformity.

If all users of *Parking Generation* and *Trip Generation* were well trained in statistics and traffic engineering, ITE's spurious precision would matter less, but the actual users are a broad and diverse group.[84] ITE itself says, "*Trip Generation* is an educational tool for planners, transportation professionals, zoning boards, and others who are interested in estimating the number of vehicle trips generated by a proposed development."[85] Many of these people are not trained in statistics and traffic engineering. Zoning boards are elected or appointed to their positions, perform their duties as volunteers, and rely heavily on references such as *Parking Generation* and *Trip Generation* for guidance. They probably will not realize that the reported rates are often statistically insignificant and refer only to suburban sites with ample free parking and no public transit.

Serious Consequences

Reporting statistically insignificant estimates with misleading precision creates serious problems because many people rely on ITE manuals to predict how urban development will affect parking and traffic. When estimating the impacts of development, for example, developers and cities sometimes battle fiercely over whether a precise trip generation rate is correct. Given the uncertainty involved, the debates are ludicrous.

Nevertheless, the burden of proof is shifted to developers who must pay for special studies to show that the actual trip generation may be less than reported in ITE manuals. Some zoning codes state that when a land use is not specifically included in the list of parking requirements in the zoning code, then the ITE parking generation rate for the land use is applied by default. As a result, *Parking Generation* directly governs many of the cities' parking requirements.[86] And because developers want their projects approved with a minimum of negotiation and delay, they usually provide all the required parking without protest.

Some cities even base zoning categories on trip generation rates. Consider this zoning ordinance in Beverly Hills, California:

> The intensity of use shall not exceed either sixteen (16) vehicle trips per hour, or 200 vehicle trips per day for each 1,000 gross square feet of floor area for uses as specified in the most recent edition of the Institute of Traffic Engineers' publication entitled "Trip Generation."[87]

The precise but uncertain ITE data thus govern which land uses the city will allow.

Supposedly scientific court testimony that lacks statistical or theoretical grounding is now commonly referred to as "junk science." To the extent that they are based on statistically insignificant results, parking and trip generation rates risk being lumped with junk science, although they are difficult to challenge once they have been incorporated into municipal codes. Planning is an inherently uncertain activity, but the legal system of land-use regulation makes it difficult to acknowledge uncertainty in planning decisions. Admitting the flimsy basis of the parking and trip generation rates would expose land-use decisions to countless lawsuits from developers, neighborhood groups, and property-rights advocates, all of whom could rightly question the legitimacy of the "science" used to establish parking requirements and could argue for either more or less parking. In addition, most people are not trained in statistics, and presenting a confidence interval rather than a precise estimate would probably create confusion. Finally, clients who have paid a lot of money for any research feel entitled to an aura of certainty about the results. This desire for certainty—or at least a facade of credibility—explains why transportation engineers, urban planners, developers, and elected officials rely on precise point estimates to report the highly uncertain parking and trip generation rates.

Using ITE's parking generation rates for planning purposes is even more inappropriate outside the U.S. than in it. In a study of parking generation for commercial developments in Singapore, Henry Fan and Soi Hoi Lam report, "In may cases, parking requirements of proposed developments in Asian cities are determined using rates developed for western cities."[88] When Fan and Lam studied the peak parking occupancy at 13 commercial sites in Singapore, they found the parking generation rates were only about one-quarter to one-third of those reported in *Parking Generation*.[89] Clearly, using ITE's data to set minimum parking requirements outside the U.S. can produce a gross oversupply of parking.

Derived Demand

Transportation lies at the intersection of demography and geography. People often want to be somewhere other than where they are, and the demand for travel is therefore derived from the demand for spatially separated activities.[90] Parking demand is also derived, but from what? The demand for parking at sites away from home is derived from the demand for vehicle travel to these sites, while the demand for parking at home is derived from car ownership, which is itself derived from the demand for the option to travel by car. In some specialized cases, such as with classic cars, the demand for parking comes from the demand for the cars themselves, not from the demand for travel, but few people view parking as an end in itself.

The derived demands for vehicle travel and parking differ in one key sense. The demand for vehicle travel depends on how far you are from where you want to be, while the demand for parking depends on how long you stay after you get there—the number of trip-end-hours, or parking duration. The relationship between vehicle trips *to* a site and parking duration *at* the site determines the "parking turnover rate" at each site.

Problems with Parking Turnover Rates

Dividing the daily number of cars driven to a site by the number of parking spaces at the site gives the parking turnover rate, which shows the average number of cars that successively occupy a parking space during the day. If 100 cars a day park at a site that has 20 spaces, for example, the turnover rate is 5 cars per space per day. If ITE parking and trip generation data are reliable, they should give a reliable estimate of the turnover rate for each land use. Do they?

Table 2-2 shows the trip generation rates (column 1) and the parking generation rates (column 2) for comparable land uses included in both *Trip Generation* and *Parking Generation*.[91] Column 3 shows the parking turnover rate. If each 1,000 square feet of floor area in a fast-food restaurant generates 316.1 vehicle-round-trips a day and has a peak parking occupancy of 10 parking spaces, for example, about 32 different cars occupy each parking space on an average weekday (316.1 ÷ 10).[92]

Table 2-2. Parking Turnover Rates

Land use	Trip generation (round trips/day)	Parking generation (parking spaces)	Parking turnover (round trip/space)
	(1)	(2)	(3) = (1)/(2)
Manufacturing	1.9	1.6	1.2
Research center	3.0	**1.8**	1.7
Furniture store	2.2	1.2	1.8
High-rise apartment	2.1	0.9	2.4
Residential condominium	3.0	1.1	2.7
Clinic	**11.9**	4.1	2.9
University	1.2	0.4	3.3
Hospital	5.9	1.8	3.3
Senior high school	0.7	0.2	3.6
Quality restaurant	47.8	12.5	3.8
Warehousing	2.4	0.5	4.9
Marina	1.5	**0.3**	5.8
Retirement community	1.7	0.3	6.1
Government office	**34.5**	3.8	9.0
Discount store	35.6	3.6	10.0
Hardware store	25.6	2.4	10.6
Supermarket	62.8	2.9	21.9
Tennis club	**16.5**	0.7	23.2
Fast Food w/ drive-thru	316.1	10.0	31.6
Fast Food w/o drive-thru	388.6	11.7	33.3
Bank w/ drive-in	145.6	4.2	34.4
Bank w/ walk-in only	95.0	**0.6**	150.8
Convenience market	443.5	1.4	314.6

Rates are per dwelling unit for condominiums, high-rise apartments, and retirement communities; per bed for hospitals; per berth for marinas; per student for high schools and universities; and per 1,000 square feet of floor area for all other land uses. All rates are for weekdays. Rates marked in bold are based on a single survey. Sources: Institute of Transportation Engineers (1987a, 1987b).

The data produce strange results. The parking turnover rate at a furniture store is only 1.8 cars a day for each space, implying slow trade. At a tennis club it is 23 cars a day, meaning fast play. At a convenience market it is 315 different cars a day in every space, suggesting frantic shoppers. The data also show another anomaly. A drive-in window should reduce parking demand because some customers don't park while they carry out their transactions. Nevertheless, the parking generation rate is seven times higher at a bank *with* a drive-in window than *without* one (4.2 versus 0.6 spaces per 1,000 square feet), which shows the opposite of what one would expect. The addition of a drive-in window at a bank surely cannot increase the peak parking demand by a factor of seven.[93]

Dividing one uncertain estimate by another compounds the uncertainty. Each parking or trip generation rate, taken alone, looks plausible, but the implicit parking turnover rates look suspicious. Do 23 different cars a day really occupy each parking space at a tennis club? Do 151 different cars a day occupy each parking space at a bank without a drive-in window? These bizarre turnover rates provide further evidence that either the parking generation rates or the trip generation rates—or both—are unreliable. They are unreliable in part because they are based on small samples (six of the table's 23 land uses have parking or trip generation rates that are based on a single survey). Further, the surveys of parking and trip generation for each land use are conducted at different places and at different times.[94] The unbelievable turnover rates also reveal a more serious problem: *the parking and trip generation rates are misleading guides to transportation and land-use planning.*

Planning for Sprawl

When ITE's parking and trip generation rates are used for urban planning, their statistical shortcomings create serious consequences. Most ITE samples are too small to draw statistically significant conclusions, and ITE's method of collecting data skews observations toward sites with high parking and trip generation rates. Larger samples might reduce the problem of statistical insignificance, but a more serious problem with the rates would remain: they measure the peak parking demand and the number of vehicle trips *at suburban sites with ample free parking*. Using these data to plan a city ultimately leads to more traffic, lower density, and greater sprawl.

  How do ITE's parking and trip generation rates influence transportation and land-use planning? Consider the six-step circular process of planning for free parking in the U.S. (See Figure 2-9.) In step 1, transportation engineers survey the peak parking demand at a few suburban sites with free parking but no transit service, and ITE publishes the results in *Parking Generation* with misleading precision. In step 2, urban planners consult *Parking Generation* to set minimum parking requirements, so the maximum observed parking demand becomes the minimum required parking supply. In step 3, developers provide all the parking that cities require, driving the price of most parking to zero, and the lower price of automobile travel increases the number of vehicle trips. In step 4, transportation engineers survey vehicle trips to and from suburban sites with free parking but no transit service, and ITE publishes the results in *Trip Generation* with misleading precision. In step 5, transportation planners consult *Trip Generation* as a guide to design the transportation system to bring cars to the free parking.[95] In step 6, cities reduce the allowable density so development won't generate more vehicle trips than nearby roads can carry. This lower density spreads activities farther apart, increases the cost of travel by bus, bicycle, and walking, and further increases both vehicle travel and parking demand. The loop is completed when transportation engineers again survey the peak parking demand at suburban sites with free parking but no transit service and—surprise!—find that more parking spaces are "needed." Misusing precise numbers to report uncertain data gives a veneer of rigor to this elaborate but unscientific practice, and the circular logic explains why planning for parking, transportation, and land use has gone subtly, incrementally wrong.[96]

ITE data do not *cause* this circular process, which began to distort planning for transportation and land use before the earliest editions of *Trip Generation* (1976) and *Parking Generation* (1985) were published. In 1965, economist Edgar Hoover described the circular planning process in words that still apply:

> In practice, the separation of highway-building programs from parking programs (they are in different and quite independent bureaucracies or authorities) introduces a still further pernicious element. We know the story of the man who took another piece of bread in order to finish his butter, then another piece of butter in order to finish his bread, and so on till he burst. Similarly, every provision of new freeways into a congested area heightens the observed demand and the public pressure for more parking facilities; every additional downtown parking garage heightens the demand for more new freeways to bring people to it; and so on back and forth indefinitely. Each of the two independent public authorities involved can argue persuasively that it is merely trying to keep up with an undeniably strong and growing demand.[97]

The only change since Hoover's observation in 1965 is that transportation engineers and urban planners now have precise parking and trip generation rates to quantify the "undeniably strong and growing demand" for parking and highways. Engineers and planners mutually reinforce each other when they gather and interpret data on parking and trip generation, and their interaction helps explain why planning for parking in the U.S. is really planning for *free* parking.

With roads, the planning strategy during the freeway-building era was to "predict and provide," which meant forecasting traffic and then building enough road space to accommodate it. Spiraling public costs greatly slowed most freeway programs by the 1970s, especially in California where the number of new freeway-miles opened fell from a peak of 342 in 1966 to only 66 in 1972 and just 17 in 1978, a 95 percent drop in 12 years.[98] With parking, in contrast, the planning strategy is to "predict and require." The results of the predict-and-require parking strategy are even more disastrous than those of the predict-and-provide road strategy,

Figure 2-9. Six-step Process of Planning for Free Parking

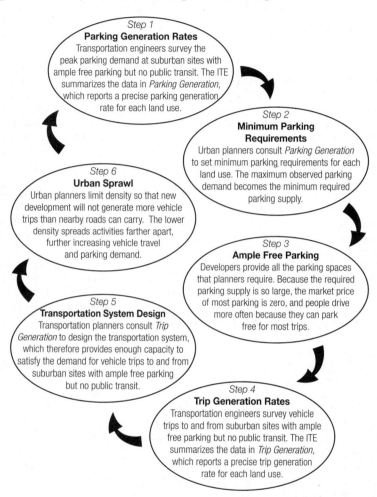

Step 1
Parking Generation Rates
Transportation engineers survey the peak parking demand at suburban sites with ample free parking but no public transit. The ITE summarizes the data in *Parking Generation*, which reports a precise parking generation rate for each land use.

Step 2
Minimum Parking Requirements
Urban planners consult *Parking Generation* to set minimum parking requirements for each land use. The maximum observed parking demand becomes the minimum required parking supply.

Step 3
Ample Free Parking
Developers provide all the parking spaces that planners require. Because the required parking supply is so large, the market price of most parking is zero, and people drive more often because they can park free for most trips.

Step 4
Trip Generation Rates
Transportation engineers survey vehicle trips to and from suburban sites with ample free parking but no public transit. The ITE summarizes the data in *Trip Generation*, which reports a precise trip generation rate for each land use.

Step 5
Transportation System Design
Transportation planners consult *Trip Generation* to design the transportation system, which therefore provides enough capacity to satisfy the demand for vehicle trips to and from suburban sites with ample free parking but no public transit.

Step 6
Urban Sprawl
Urban planners limit density so that new development will not generate more vehicle trips than nearby roads can carry. The lower density spreads activities farther apart, further increasing vehicle travel and parking demand.

because the cost of parking remains entirely hidden, and there is no budgetary limit on the planning process. Cities require parking without taking into account the price charged for it, the cost of constructing and maintaining it, or the wider consequences for transportation, land use, the economy, and the environment. Parking requirements also ignore the local context of development. Higher densities reduce automobile ownership in part because more places can be reached on foot, by bicycle, and by public transit, but cities rarely reduce the parking requirements for higher-density developments. The freeway-building era has ended, but the parking-building era is in full flower.

Suppose cities financed roads the same way they finance parking. Cities could require new buildings to pay for adding enough road capacity to handle all the additional vehicle trips generated. Each new building would pay for street widening and intersection flaring, for example, to meet the added demand for driving, so that traffic congestion would not increase. Like the cost of parking, the cost of roads would be shifted from drivers into higher prices for everything except driving. Would this be a good idea? No, because everyone but drivers would pay for the roads, and vehicle travel would increase. We cannot forecast traffic without considering how roads and parking will be financed, and when drivers don't pay for roads and parking directly, they will naturally "need" more of both.

Shifting the cost of roads away from drivers is unwise, but many local governments do just that. In new subdivisions, developers must pay the full cost for all the internal roads, and this cost is shifted to the landowners or homebuyers, not to motorists. Because any view of local streets from the air usually shows far more parked than moving cars, a large part of the developers' cost for streets is a subsidy for parking, not driving. Residents without a car pay just as much for the local roads as do those with multiple cars. In addition, a survey in California found that 59 percent of counties and 56 percent of cities impose "traffic impact fees" on new development to finance road improvements. Forty-two percent of the jurisdictions base their fees on a proposed project's number of vehicle trips per day, 34 percent on the project's size (square feet, number of dwelling units), and 23 percent on the number of peak-hour vehicle trips.[99] In Signal Hill, California, for example, the fee is $66 per daily vehicle trip generated by a development project, and the number of trips is calculated by multiplying the size of the project by its trip generation rate "as set forth in the most recent edition of the *Traffic Generation* manual of the Institute of Transportation Engineers."[100] The trip generation rate for a fast-food restaurant, for example, is 496.12 trips per 1,000 square feet (see Figure 2-7). Signal Hill's traffic impact fee is thus $32,744 per 1,000 square feet ($66 x 496.12), or $32.74 per square foot of restaurant space. Trip generation rates thus determine the city's tax rates. And, of course, the restaurant must also satisfy the city's parking requirements.

ITE naturally deplores any misuse of its parking and trip generation rates, and it warns users to be careful when the R^2 is low (although it has removed this warning from the plots in the most recent editions of *Parking*

Generation and *Trip Generation*). ITE also advises users to modify the trip generation rates in response to special circumstances:

> At specific sites, the user may want to modify the trip generation rates presented in this document to reflect the presence of public transportation service, ridesharing or other TDM measures, enhanced pedestrian and bicycle trip-making opportunities, or other special characteristics of the site or surrounding area.[101]

Nevertheless, ITE does not suggest *how* a user might modify the rates in response to any special characteristics of a site or its surrounding area, and does *not* include the price of parking on the list of special characteristics that might affect trip generation.[102] *Parking Generation* and *Trip Generation* are rough guides for predicting the peak parking occupancy and the number of vehicle trips at low-density, suburban, single-use sites with free parking and no alternatives to the car, but not elsewhere. Parking demand and vehicle trips probably vary less by land use than by the price of parking, urban density, and the availability of alternatives to the car, all factors ITE ignores.

A naive interpretation of the data in *Parking Generation* is that the peak demand for free parking *is* the demand for parking, and ITE itself seems to accept this. Another ITE publication, *Transportation and Land Development*, defines parking demand as:

> The number of parking spaces that are needed in a given area during a specific time period.... An available data source is ITE's *Parking Generation*, Second Edition. It contains parking demand characteristics from more than 60 different land uses.[103]

This definition reflects the way most drivers think about parking demand. Whenever a parking lot overflows, we naturally conclude that it fails to meet the demand, not that parking is too cheap. And when parking lots routinely overflow, we conclude that parking requirements should be increased, not that we should pay more to park. ITE data are easy to misuse because they seem reasonable even when they lack statistical significance.

Users of data should always ask themselves whether the data are appropriate for the intended purpose. Only users can misuse data, but ITE invites misuse of its data when it reports statistically insignificant estimates as precise numbers. This spurious precision has helped to establish parking requirements and trip generation rates as dogma in the planning profession.

Honest Mistakes

The upward biases in parking and trip generation data differ from the strategic misrepresentation in forecasts that overestimate the benefits of proposed transportation projects. Analysts who have studied the repeated errors in transportation forecasting typically conclude that the economic self-interest of the forecasters and their clients helps explain the outcomes. Writing in the *Journal of the American Planning Association*, Bent Flyvbjerg, Mette Holm, and Søren Buhl say:

> When a project goes forward, it creates work for engineers and construction firms, and many stakeholders make money. If these stakeholders are involved in or indirectly influence the forecasting process, then this may influence outcomes in ways that make it more likely that the project will be built. Having costs underestimated and benefits overestimated would be economically rational for such stakeholders because it would increase the likelihood of revenues and profits.[104]

Studying a sample of 258 transportation projects with a combined cost of $90 billion, they found that the forecasts used to decide whether to build the projects were systematically misleading. Roads, bridges, rail lines, and tunnels are all built to serve the public interest, of course, but they also serve the private interests of construction firms, labor unions, engineers, politicians, financiers, lawyers, and developers, all of whom want optimistic forecasts of the projects' benefits and costs.

Transportation economist Don Pickrell discovered similar errors when he compared the actual ridership with the forecast ridership for eight urban rail transit projects in the United States. He found that seven had actual ridership less than half the forecast ridership. Seven of the eight projects also cost much more than expected, with cost overruns ranging from 17 percent to more than 150 percent. He concluded that the source of these errors was not the difficulty of forecasting ridership and costs because almost every error steered the planning choice in the same direction: toward building rail transit. He also concluded that the federal grants for rail transit helped to explain the optimistic forecasts:

> The transit planning process has been reduced to a forum in which local officials use exaggerated forecasts to compete against their counterparts from other cities to obtain federal financing of projects they have already committed themselves to support, but realize cannot prevail in an unbiased comparison to plausible alternatives.[105]

Martin Wachs explains that planners' forecasts are not simply analytical studies because planners work for employers or clients who favor particular policies or programs for reasons of ideology, political commitments, or economic self-interest. Planners thus have divided loyalties when they forecast the results of proposed projects:

> Planners are constantly trapped between two competing models of their role. On the one hand, planners may see themselves as "scientists," who analyze data to discover the truth and to arrive at the best course of action. On the other hand, planners see themselves as "advocates," who use data and models to prove that a course of action preferred by a client or employer is the best choice in a given situation. These two roles inherently conflict with one another.[106]

These well-known problems with transportation forecasting raise an important question: does the systematic upward bias in the estimated parking and trip generation rates stem from any economic interest in the results? I think the answer is definitely *no*. Transportation engineers are trying to discover the truth, but the parking and trip generation rates are biased upward because they measure the peak parking occupancy and the number of vehicle trips observed at suburban sites with ample free parking and no public transit. The bias is real, but strategic misrepresentation is not the cause. The volunteer committees who assemble and edit *Parking Generation* and *Trip Generation* are dedicated to the profession of transportation engineering, and they have no personal stake in misstating the results. Mistakes are not being made to advance anyone's private interest.

The upward bias of the parking and trip generation studies is understandable. The desire to count the number of cars parked by visitors to a site explains why "the ideal site for obtaining reliable parking generation data would…contain ample, convenient parking facilities for the exclusive use of the traffic generated by the site."[107] The parking generation rates are biased to suburban sites with ample free parking because these are the only locations where parked cars can easily be attributed to each specific destination and where supply does not limit demand. The same applies to trip generation rates. A personal interview with every patron would be necessary to estimate the number of vehicle trips made by everyone who visits a downtown restaurant, for example, or to count the number of cars they have parked. Parking and trip generation cannot be observed easily in dense urban areas.

It is harder to condone neglect of traditional rules of statistical inference when reporting the precise parking and trip generation rates. Most samples are too small to find a statistically significant relation between land use and parking occupancy or vehicle trips. The unwillingness to reveal the statistical insignificance of most parking and trip generation rates may help explain the omission of standard statistical tests. Beyond the problem of suburban bias and statistical insignificance, ITE cannot control for the accuracy of the studies included in *Parking Generation* and *Trip Generation*. Anyone can submit a study, including students who conduct them as class exercises, so the data do not really qualify as scientific observations. If we accept the maxim that research results are only as good as their worst data source, parking and trip generation forecasts are severely compromised.

Precision without Accuracy

Estimates of parking and trip generation respond to a real demand for essential information about the consequences of land-use decisions. Citizens want to know how development will affect parking demand and traffic congestion in their neighborhoods. Developers want to know how many parking spaces to provide for employees and customers. Planners want to regulate development to prevent problems with parking and traffic. Politicians want to avoid complaints from unhappy parkers. These are all valid concerns, but reporting the parking and trip generation rates with needless precision creates both an illusion of knowledge and false confidence in the data. To unsophisticated users, these precise rates look like constants, similar to the boiling point of water or the speed of light. This spurious precision resembles what, in his 1974 Nobel Prize lecture, economist Friedrich Hayek referred to as the *pretense* of knowledge. He warned of,

> the long run dangers created in a much wider field by the uncritical acceptance of assertions which have the appearance of being scientific.... There will always be some who will pretend, and perhaps honestly believe, that they can do more to meet popular demands than is really in their power. It is often difficult enough for the expert, and certainly in many instances impossible for the layman, to distinguish between legitimate and illegitimate claims advanced in the name of science.[108]

When planners set parking requirements and engineers design the transportation system, they often treat parking and trip generation like physical laws and ITE data like scientific observations. But as another great economist, John von Neumann, said, "There's no sense being exact about something if you don't even know what you're talking about."[109] Parking and trip generation are poorly understood phenomena, and they both depend on many factors, especially on the price of parking. Like it or not, demand is a function of price, not a fixed number, and this does not cease to be true merely because we ignore it. (How much more pizza would you eat if it were free? A lot more than if you pay by the slice.) Estimating parking demand without considering prices is planning without economics. Most cities are planned on the unstated assumption that parking should be free—no matter how high the cost or how small the benefit.

FIVE EASY REFORMS

Because urban planners and transportation engineers think they know how land use affects parking and trip generation, they tend to resist new ideas about the relationships between transportation and land use. ITE's precise but misleading parking and trip generation rates have led, in practice, to planning requirements for ubiquitous free parking, which contributes to the automobile's dominance of our transportation system. What can be done to improve this situation? Here are five easy reforms:

1. ITE should state in the report for each parking and trip generation rate that it refers only to a suburban site with ample free parking and no public transit, pedestrian amenities, or TDM program.
2. ITE should show the regression equation and the R^2 for each parking and trip generation report, and state whether the coefficient of floor area (or other independent variable) in the equation is significantly different from zero.
3. ITE should report the confidence intervals for parking and trip generation rates, not simply the precise point estimates.
4. Urban planners should recognize that even if ITE data were accurate, they refer only to suburban sites with free parking and no transit service. Using these data to set off-street parking requirements will dictate a low-density, automobile-dominated urban form with free parking everywhere. If planners do not reduce parking requirements near transit stations, they are assuming that people will drive just as much as if transit did not exist.
5. Finally, the British counterpart to *Trip Generation* suggests some possible improvements. The "Trip Rate Information Computer System" (TRICS) gives full information about the characteristics of every surveyed site and its surroundings.[110] Users can thus estimate a trip generation rate based on sites comparable to the one under consideration. In addition to counts of *vehicles*, TRICS also includes counts of all the *people* (pedestrians, cyclists, public transport users, and car occupants) who arrive at and depart from a site. By including more than vehicle trips, TRICS takes a broader view of trans-

portation. When all modes are included, the person trip rates are often much higher than the *vehicle* trip rates.

With its narrow focus on counting cars at suburban sites with ample free parking, *Trip Generation* presents a precise but uncertain, skewed, and incomplete measure of the relationship between transportation and land use in the United States. Fortunately, ITE's Parking and Trip Generation Committees seek to improve each successive edition of *Parking Generation* and *Trip Generation*. In future editions, they should settle for less precision and strive for more accuracy.[111]

Both transportation engineers and urban planners should also ponder this warning from Lewis Mumford: "The right to have access to every building in the city by private motorcar, in an age when everyone possesses such a vehicle, is actually the right to destroy the city."[112] The dysfunctional interactions between transportation engineers and urban planners in producing and consuming data on parking and trip generation have severely damaged American cities. Reforms of *Parking Generation* and *Trip Generation* will reduce some of the widespread misunderstandings about parking and travel "demand," and will improve planning for transportation and land use. Being roughly right is better than being precisely wrong.

CONCLUSION: THE IMMACULATE
CONCEPTION OF PARKING DEMAND

The vision behind planning for parking is a drive-in utopia, and cities legislate this vision into reality for every new building, regardless of the cost. Off-street parking requirements that satisfy the peak demand for free parking are, in reality, *free* parking requirements. Urban planners may believe in the immaculate conception of parking demand, and economists may believe that market choices reveal consumer preferences for travel by car. But the demand for parking was not immaculately conceived, and it does not result from consumer preferences revealed in a fair market. Instead, planners and the market coupled long ago to produce today's swollen demand for cars and parking.

CHAPTER 2 NOTES

1. Buena Park, California, City Code Section 19.536.040. In its most recent survey of off-street parking requirements in U.S. cities, the Planning Advisory Service (2002, 7) says, "Most [cities] simply have statements such as 'The provisions of this chapter have been established to ensure that adequate off-street parking is provided to meet the parking needs of uses located within the city.'"

2. See Appendix B.

3. Mogren and Smith (1952, 29). The sample included the same 76 cities in both 1946 and 1951. When nonrespondents were removed from the 1951 survey, 81 percent of cities had or were adopting parking requirements; there were no nonrespondents in the 1946 survey.

4. "Business Districts," Los Angeles Regional Planning Commission, Los Angeles, California, 1944; quoted in Mogren and Smith (1952, 33). This "irreducible minimum" parking requirement of parking space equal in area to the retail floor or business area is approximately 3 parking spaces per 1,000 square feet of retail or office space. Only 16 years later, the Urban Land Institute reported, "Based on its long period of experimentation and experience in shopping center planning, the Community Builders' Council recommends a ratio of 3 square feet of parking area to 1 square foot of gross floor area" (Urban Land Institute 1960, 303); this amounts to 9 parking spaces per 1,000 square feet!

5. Mogren and Smith (1952, 37), italics in the original.

6. Planning Advisory Service (1991, 1).

7. Willson (2000, 18).

8. Weant and Levinson (1990, 35-37).

9. Planning Advisory Service (1991,3).

10. Section 6B(2) of the Park Mile Specific Plan (italics added), available online at www.lacity.org/pln/complan/specplan/pdf/parkmile.pdf.

11. Monterey Park City Code Section 21.40.330. Similarly, the zoning ordinance City of Rancho Mirage, California, states, "The use of parking facilities shall be without monetary charge when the parking is required in compliance with this chapter" (Section 17.26.030 of the Rancho Mirage Municipal Code). California is not the only state where required parking must be free. In the unincorporated parts of Spokane County, Washington, for example, "all required parking shall be made permanently free of charge to the customers of the use on the site and maintained for parking purposes only," and in Union Gap, Washington, "it shall be the responsibility of the owner and/or occupant of any main building or structure to provide, and thereafter maintain, the minimum free off-street facilities set forth in this chapter" (Washington State Department of Transportation 1999, 65). The requirement for *free* parking is the only reference to the price of parking I have seen in any city's zoning code.

12. The word "parking" does not appear in the index of Chapin (1957), Chapin (1965), Chapin and Kaiser (1979), or Kaiser, Godschalk, and Chapin (1995). Other texts on planning and zoning also fail to mention either parking or parking requirements; for example, parking does not appear in the index of Allmendinger, Prior and Raemaekers (2000), Cullingworth and Nadin (2002), Fabos (1985), Fischel (1985), Hall (2002), Nelson (1980), Patterson (1979), and So and Getzels (1988). The index of a book on urban planning typically skips from "Paris" to "participation." Bracketing the missing word parking more closely, Manual Castells (1983) skips from "Paris commune" to "Parti Communiste Français."

13. See, for example, Alonso (1964), Balchin, Isaac, and Chen (2000), Beckmann (1968), Bish and Nourse (1975), Catanese and Steiss (1970), Cheshire and Mills (1999), Creighton (1970), Darin-Drabkin (1977), Denman and Prodano (1972), Dickey (1983), DiPasquale and Wheaton (1996), Emerson (1975), Evans (1985), Fujita (1989), Fujita, Krugman, and

Venables (1999), Gómez-Ibáñez, Tye, and Winston (1999), Heilbrun (1987), Henderson (1985), Henderson and Ledebur (1972), Hirsch (1973, 1984), Isard (1956, 1960), Isard *et al.* (1998), Kneafsey (1975), McCarthy (2001), Meyer and Miller (2001), Mieszkowski and Straszheim (1979), Mills (1972), Muth (1969, 1975), Nagurney (2000), Nijkamp (1996), Papacostas and Prevedouros (1993), Richardson (1978, 1979), Sussman (2000), van Kooten (1993) and Weiner (1999). Hoover (1975), Netzer (1974) and Segal (1977) are rare and insightful exceptions. In most research on automobile transportation, the emphasis is on vehicles and roads. Some researchers do not consider parking to be a part of automobile transportation at all. In *Financing Transportation Networks*, for example, University of Minnesota transportation economist David Levinson (2002, 42-43) estimates the cost of automobile transportation, but excludes the costs of parking because "they are outside the strictly defined transportation sector."

14. Williams and Taylor (1986, 3). The bulk regulations create a "zoning envelope" that prescribes a building's outer measurements.

15. Shaw (1997a, 3).

16. Chapter 26, Article II of the Houston Code of Ordinances (Requirements for Parking Spaces) looks identical to the parking requirements of any other city. Houston requires 1.25 parking spaces for each efficiency apartment, for example, and 1.33 parking spaces for each one-bedroom apartment.

17. Schön (1983, vii).

18. Willson (2000, 118).

19. Dunphy (2000).

20. PAS (1991, 1), italics added. PAS explained that the chief reason for the 1991 survey was to reorganize the data, not to present any new analysis. "Perhaps the most compelling reason for the update of the 1971 report, however, was that it has been difficult to use for some because of the way it is organized. In this new report, standards are segregated by land use rather than by the amount of required parking, as in the case in the 1971 report. Within each land use category, we arranged the standards from those that require the least amount of parking to those that require the most" (PAS 1991, 1). The 2002 survey abandoned the arrangement of standards from those that require the least amount of parking to those that require the most. The American Society of Planning Officials (now the American Planning Association) established PAS in 1949 to conduct research and give advice on practical planning issues. The February 1999 issue of *Planning* magazine explains PAS's history and operations.

21. PAS (1964, 1)

22. PAS (1971, 1)

23. PAS (1983, 15)

24. PAS (1991, 1)

25. PAS (2002, 6)

26. PAS (1971, 1). Journalists sometimes refer to the practice of copying parking requirements. For example, when Des Moines, Iowa, was considering changes in its parking requirements in 2003, the *Des Moines Register* reported, "City officials are now researching how other cities use similar ordinances and will introduce their findings to the council in October. 'We're looking at what other cities are doing and what our parking requirements should be,' [City Manager] Henderson said" (Officials Consider Solutions to Parking Shortage, *Des Moines Register*, September 12, 2003).

27. PAS (1971, 1). When PAS published its latest report on parking standards in 2002, the APA's *Zoning News* noted, "The most popular method for determining off-street parking requirements may be to borrow from the ordinances of other communities. To a large degree, it's difficult to fault this approach. APA would not be publishing this report if it thought that borrowing standards from other cities—or at least having an awareness of the range of standards that exist—was an unacceptable approach. When APA's Planning Advisory Service (PAS) receives inquiries related to off-street parking standards, PAS provides subscribers with ordinances, studies, and guides such as this one" (Wittenberg 2003, 2).

28. Gould (2003, 11). Similarly, in *Planning* magazine, Wayne Swanson (1989, 14) writes, "Parking issues occupy an inordinate amount of planners' time.... New standards are often copied blindly from other locales. Even worse, the standards used may be based on the old-fashioned assumption that demand is paramount."

29. Meck (2002, *xxx-xxxi*).

30. Neal Peirce, "Landmark Planning Guide May Remake America's Future," *Washington Post*, February 13, 2002.

31. See Meck (2002, I-47 to I-52). The index skips from *Palm Beach County* v. *Wright* to *Pauly* v. *Kelly*. The *Guidebook* does mention parking occasionally, but usually only in a long list of routine items that planners should consider in certain circumstances. Parking is among the "Unnecessary Cost Generating Requirements" that may be reduced to make housing more affordable, for example; alas, the list also includes landscaping, reforestation, sidewalks, and stormwater drainage (Meck 2002, 4-82). The *Guidebook* also mentions that developers of affordable housing often seek a reduction in parking requirements, which suggests that providing the required parking increases the cost of housing (Meck 2002, 9-93).

32. Jacobs (1993, 305).

33. Epstein (2001, 3).

34. Scott (1995), Smith (1993), Weaver and Babcock (1979), Branch (1985), Nelson and Duncan (1995), Anderson (1995), Bunnell (2002), Jones (1990), Ford (1990), Hoch, Dalton, and So (2000), Bryson and Einsweiler (1988), and Haar and Kayden (1989).

35. Babcock (1966) and Babcock and Siemon (1985).

36. Dewberry and Champagne (2002).

37. Daniels, Keller, and Lapping (1995, 249).

38. Marya Morris (1989, 1).

39. Urban Land Institute (1982b, 54 and 56). Because a one-acre parking lot holds about 130 cars, a parking requirement of 4 spaces per 1,000 square feet means that an acre of parking is needed for each 32,500 square feet of floor area (4 x 32,500 ÷ 1,000 = 130).

40. ITE (1987a, vii-xv).

41. *Parking Generation* includes data for only 46 different land uses, but it reports more than one parking generation rate for some land uses. For example, it reports six parking generation rates for commercial airports (Land Use Code 021). Rates are reported for two bases (daily airplane movements and emplaning passengers) and for three time periods (weekday, Saturday, and Sunday).

42. The *2001 National Household Travel Survey* found that 87 percent of trips of less than 50 miles were made by personal vehicle. Of the rest, 1.5 percent were by public transit, 1.7 percent by school bus, 8.6 percent by walking, and 1.7 percent by other modes. Personal vehicles include cars, vans, SUVs, pickup trucks, recreational vehicles, and motorcycles. Ninety percent of trips greater than 50 miles were made by personal vehicle (United States Department of Transportation 2003a, 21 and 25).

43. Shoup (1997b) and PAS Report 532 (forthcoming).

44. Parking occupancy was surveyed at establishments like McDonald's, Dunkin Donuts, and Burger Chef.

45. It appears that eight restaurants were observed for one day, one restaurant was observed for two days, and two restaurants were observed for four days. We are not told the hour(s), the weekday, or the month when parking occupancy was observed. The 18 studies of parking occupancy at fast-food restaurants are an unusually large sample. In contrast, consider the report for Technical Colleges (Land Use 541). Parking occupancy was observed for one hour on one day at one site, and on this basis the parking generation rate for a technical college is reported as 0.82 parking spaces per student (ITE 1987a, 88). Parking occupancy was observed for only one or two hours for many of the studies in *Parking Generation*. Because only the *peak* occupancy at a site is needed to calculate the parking generation rate, the observer's main concern is to report the peak number of cars parked during the hour(s) of expected peak demand.

46. An R^2 of 0 shows complete lack of correlation between two variables, and one would expect some correlation by chance. The significance test for the regression equation shows there is a 42 percent chance of getting an R^2 of 0.038 or higher even if there were no relationship between floor area and peak parking occupancy. ITE (1987a, viii) divides the sum of all parking generation rates by the number of studies to calculate the unweighted average parking generation rate.

47. If the sample were random, this confidence interval would include the mean of the population in 95 out of every 100 similar samples from the same distribution. The confidence interval was calculated by re-estimating the regression equation from the 18 observations in the data plot.

48. For a restaurant in this sample, predicting a peak parking occupancy of 26 spaces (the average for the 18 sites), regardless of size, produces about the same average error as multiplying the parking generation rate times the floor area of each restaurant.

49. Parsons (2002, *iii*).

50. Parsons (2002, 6), emphasis in the original. Parsons (2002, *vii*) defined the design-day peak parking demand as "The largest number of parking spaces required to accommodate all the customers and employees that will want to park at the store at one time during the design day. This typically occurs between 11AM and 1PM on a Saturday." The peak sales day at most stores occurred in the spring (March or April). Observing the parking occupancy on Saturdays in March and April would seem like a more straightforward way to estimate the peak parking occupancy on the 5th-busiest day of the year.

51. This procedure assumes that the sales revenue per parked car was uniform throughout the year. If the spending per customer is higher on the days of peak sales revenue (which seems reasonable), this procedure will overestimate the peak parking occupancy on the 5th-busiest day.

52. Home Depot has subsequently requested large reductions on the parking requirements for its new stores. For example, in Harrison, Arkansas, the city's parking requirement for a new store was more than 900 spaces, and Home Depot requested a reduction to 544 spaces (*Harrison Daily Times*, November 30, 2003). The results for Home Depot show that, at least for a chain that can afford an expensive study of parking occupancy, developers do not provide more parking than cities require and often want to provide less.

53. ITE (1987a, vii).

54. The median parking requirement for a fast-food restaurant is 10 spaces per 1,000 square feet in the cities that base their requirements for fast-food restaurants on gross floor area (PAS 1991 and 2002). In 2002, PAS reports the parking requirements for fast-food restaurants in seven places: Provo, Utah; Lexana, Kansas; Shasta County, California; Columbia, Missouri; Blue Springs, Missouri; Glenville, New York; and Gresham, Oregon.

55. The average of 330 square feet per parking space includes the aisles needed for circulation within the parking lot.

56. Cervero (1988, 26).

57. Gruen Associates (1986, 11).

58. Kadesh and Peterson (1994, 61).

59. Smith (1990, 27) says, "Typically, the mean [parking] generation rate is above 45 percent and below 55 percent of the individual observations (the median would be the individual observations at which 50 percent of the observations are lower). The direct use of the mean or median generation rate may not be consistent with the program or policy objectives that a developer or public policy agency desires."

60. Smith (1990, 26). ITE's third edition of *Parking Generation*, published in 2004, includes this information on the 85th-percentile of peak parking demand.

61. ITE (2004, 288). ITE renumbered the land use code for a fast-food restaurant from 836 in the second edition to 934 in the third edition, but the land use is identical. A fast-food restaurant is identified as a limited-service eating establishment that does not provide table service. Patrons generally order food at a cash register and pay before they eat (ITE 2004, 285). I am grateful to ITE for providing pre-publication proofs of the third edition of *Parking Generation*.

62. ITE also shows the parking generation rate at the 33rd percentile of parking generation: 6.54 vehicles per 1,000 feet. Note the asymmetry between reporting the 85th and 33rd percentiles. Why not 67th and 33rd percentiles, or 85th and 15th percentiles?

63. Glassborow (1961, 32).

64. Forinash et al. (2004). Regarding Palo Alto's landscape reserve policy, the U.S. Environmental Protection Agency (2004, 23) reports that one apartment development "was granted a request to defer 22 of the 95 parking spaces required by city code, using the land instead for a family play lot, a barbeque area, and picnic benches, Nearly 15 years after construction, the landscape reserve has not been needed for parking, and the open space constitutes an important environmental and social benefit for the community."

65. ITE (1997, Volume 3, ix and 1).

66. This refers to the 1997 edition of *Trip Generation*. The corresponding figures for *Parking Generation* in 1987 were a median of four surveys, and 22 percent based on one survey.

67. The fourth edition of *Trip Generation* and the second edition of *Parking Generation* were both published in the same year (1987). That edition of *Parking Generation* reports a fast-food restaurant with a drive-in window as land use code 836, while that edition *Trip Generation* reports a fast-food restaurant with a drive-through window as land-use code 834, but they are the same land uses. In addition, *Parking Generation* refers to a bar/drinking place as land-use code 834, while *Trip Generation* has no land-use code 836. The first edition of *Parking Generation* in 1985 refers to a fast-food restaurant with a drive-in window as land-use code 883.

68. The eight studies for trip generation are for only three sizes of restaurant: 2,000 square feet, 3,000 square feet, and 4,000 square feet. In contrast, the 18 studies for parking generation come in many sizes, and no study has a floor area that is a multiple of 1,000 square feet (compare Figures 2-1 and 2-2). ITE does not explain the implausible clustering of trip-generation data points in 1,000-square-foot increments.

69. The significance test for the regression equation shows there is a 53 percent chance of getting an R^2 of 0.069 or higher even if there were no relationship between floor area and vehicle trips.

70. ITE (1987b, 9) divides the sum of all vehicle trips by the sum of all floor areas to calculate the weighted average trip generation rate.

71. The confidence intervals around the intercept and coefficient were calculated by re-estimating the regression equation from the eight observations in the data plot.

72. Statistical insignificance does not mean that floor area has no effect on vehicle trips or peak parking occupancy; rather, it means that floor area does not reliably predict either variable.

73. In the fourth edition of *Trip Generation*, Land Use 400 (Recreational) includes bowling alleys, zoos, sea worlds, lakes, pools, and regional parks (ITE 1987b, 537 and 538).

74. ITE (1991, I-8). ITE gives no explanation for showing the regression equation and the R^2 only when all three criteria are met.

75. In effect, ITE censors regression equations that cast doubt on the reported trip generation rates, either because there is not a strong relationship or the relationship is unexpected. Because ITE shows only the regression equations that "make sense," it gives users an impression of trip generation that is far more orderly than the data warrant.

76. Figure 2-6 (from the fifth edition) differs from Figure 2-5 (from the fourth edition) in two other respects. First, the directional distribution of vehicle trips was "not available" in 1987, but became "50% entering, 50% exiting" in 1991. Second, the standard deviation was not reported in 1987 but was reported as 266.29 in 1991.

77. ITE (1997, 19). In 2003, ITE published the seventh edition of *Trip Generation*, and the criteria for reporting the regression equation and the R^2 were unchanged from the sixth edition (ITE 2003, Vol. 1, 17).

78. The 1997 trip generation rate of 496.12 is 22 percent lower than the 1991 rate of 632.12. If the eight studies from the 1987 and 1991 editions are included among the 21 studies reported in the 1997 edition, the average trip generation rate for the 13 new studies must be well below 496.12 in order to reduce the average rate for the 21 studies to 496.12. Parking and trip generation rates are not the only uncertain estimates that are reported as inappropriately precise numbers, and Appendix F shows the disappointing lack of evidence behind other transportation statistics.

79. ITE (2003, Vol. 3, 1751). The only change in the seventh edition was to renumber the Land Use Code for fast-food restaurants to 934 (it had been 834 in previous editions).

80. ITE (2003, Vol. 3, 1773).

81. McFadden (2002, 4). Even the most sophisticated models have difficulty in incorporating the actual price of parking that drivers may face, because it can be a price per hour for some trips, and a flat price for other trips, and the price can vary by time of day.

82. Brooks (2002, 23).

83. The 1991 and 1997 editions of *Trip Generation* report all rates with two digits after the decimal point, but the 1987 edition reports with three digits after the decimal point. The 1976, 1979, and 1983 editions of *Trip Generation* report some rates with no digits after the decimal point, and other rates with one or two digits after the decimal point.

84. Even if everyone who refers to *Parking Generation* and *Trip Generation* were a statistician or engineer, that does not excuse the use of unjustified precision. Journalists do not casually break the rules of grammar and spelling just because most people might be able to figure out what they mean anyway. The burden of accuracy and clarity falls on the writer—it cannot be shifted to the reader, no matter who one supposes the reader to be.

85. ITE (1997, vol. 3, p. *ix*)

86. Planning Advisory Service (2002, 7).

87. Section 10-3.162(5) of the Beverly Hills Municipal Code. ITE changed its name from the Institute of Traffic Engineers to the Institute of Transportation Engineers in 1976.

88. Fan and Lam (1997, 238).

89. Fan and Lam (1997, 242). In his study of parking requirements for a cross-section of American, European, and Asian cities, Herbert Levinson (1984b) says, "Cities throughout the world view zoning for parking as a means of balancing parking space supply and demand." He notes that while India had only 2 percent as many cars per capita as the U.S., the city of Madras required 20 percent as many parking spaces per 1,000 square feet for office buildings and theaters as U.S. cities. Following ITE's guidelines for estimating parking generation rates, Al-Masaeid, Al-Omari, and Al-Harahsheh (1999) found that in Jordan the parking generation rate for apartment buildings was 0.6 parking spaces per dwelling unit, although the vehicle ownership rate in Jordan was only one vehicle per 15 persons; the parking generation rate was, as in the U.S., based on the peak parking occupancy observed at apartment buildings, with no consideration given to the price charged for parking or the cost of providing the parking spaces.

90. Mokhtarian and Salomon (2001) argue that people sometimes consider movement as an end in itself, and their travel demand is not derived solely from the desire for access to opportunities at other places. "Half the fun is getting there" is a familiar slogan that suggests this nonderived demand for travel, although most driving in congested traffic is much less fun than the eventual arrival. Walking and cycling, on the other hand, are often ends in themselves, rather than being derived from a demand for access to other sites.

91. The 1987 editions of *Trip Generation* and *Parking Generation* are used because they were the most recent reports published in the same year. Trip generation is expressed in *round trips*, or the number of cars that park at the site between arriving and leaving. The table shows all land uses included in both *Trip Generation* and *Parking Generation* with rates calculated in proportion to the same basis (dwelling units, beds, berths, students, or area). I assume that the trip generation rate predicts the number of vehicle trips to and from the site, and that the parking lot satisfies the parking generation rate.

92. Not all parking spaces are occupied 100 percent of the time, so the turnover rate in the spaces that *are* occupied will be higher.

93. The parking generation rate at a fast-food restaurant *without* a drive-through window (11.7 spaces per 1,000 square feet) is only slightly higher than the parking generation rate at a fast-food restaurant *with* a drive-through window (10 spaces per 1,000 square feet).

94. ITE does not identify the survey sites. Figure 2-1 does, however, show that parking generation at a fast-food restaurant was observed at sites ranging in size from a little over 1 to almost 6 thousand square feet, while Figure 2-4 shows that trip generation was observed at sites of exactly 2, 3, and 4 thousand square feet. The two scattergrams (the only data ITE provides) show no overlap between the two samples of restaurants observed for parking generation and trip generation.

95. Transportation planners often use the Urban Transportation Modeling System (UTMS) to predict modal flows on links in a network, and the first of the four major steps in the UTMS model is "trip generation." The four-step UTMS model is thus used to carry out step 5 of the six-step process of planning for free parking. Meyer and Miller (2001) explain the UTMS model.

96. As C. S. Lewis (1942, 65) wrote in *The Screwtape Letters*, "The safest road to Hell is the gradual one—the gentle slope, soft underfoot, without sudden turnings, without milestones, without signposts."

97. Hoover (1965, 188-189).

98. Taylor (2000, 210-211).

99. Lawler and Powers (1997).

100. Section 21.48.020 of the Signal Hill Municipal Code. The code is available online at www.ci.signal-hill.ca.us/homepage.php. The code should refer to *Trip* Generation rather than *Traffic* Generation.

101. ITE (1997, Volume 3, 1).

102. ITE is not alone in neglecting the price of parking. Consider *The Dimensions of Parking*, published by the Urban Land Institute and the National Parking Association. It contains an immense amount of useful information about parking, but the chapter on "Parking Demand" has only one reference to the price of parking: "Other factors being equal, if a garage has high fees, it will experience less-than-ideal patronage compared with competing facilities that charge lower rates" (Salzman and Keneipp 2000, 12).

103. Stover and Koepke (2002, 9-2 and 3).

104. Flyvbjerg, Holm, and Buhl (2002, 288).

105. Pickrell (1992, 169).

106. Wachs (1989, 476-477).

107. ITE (1987a, vii-xv). ITE does not report when the surveys were conducted. If a survey was conducted on a day with low demand, it will underestimate the peak occupancy on days with normal or high demand. On the other hand, if a survey was conducted on a day with high demand, it will overestimate the peak occupancy on days with normal or low demand.

108. Hayek (1974, 6-7).

109. Quoted in Gause and Weinberg (1989, *xv*).

110. The TRICS database is available online at www.trics.org/.

111. Reform will be slow, however. Most of my criticisms of *Parking Generation* and *Trip Generation* were previously published in the *Journal of Transportation and Statistics* (Shoup 2003a). Because I wanted to stimulate discussion among transportation engineers, I had previously submitted this article to *ITE Journal*. In her rejection letter, the managing editor wrote, "Adoption of the author's conclusions without input from the Trip Generation and Parking Generation Committees could harm current usage (and acceptance) of the Handbooks." The one referee's comment concluded, "I think the paper makes valid points that should be disseminated to the user community in *ITE Journal*; however, not at the expense of ITE." I responded to the editor saying that I would appreciate input from the Trip Generation and Parking Generation Committees before the manuscript was published elsewhere. Given the managing editor's earlier statement about the lack of input from the Trip Generation and Parking Generation Committees, I was surprised to receive her response: "Members of the Trip Generation and Parking Generation Committees reviewed your manuscript initially. Their comments were included in my [rejection] letter to you dated Nov. 21, 2000. Therefore, I will not be asking either committee to review your manuscript further." When the *Journal of Transportation and Statistics* later published the article, ITE was offered the opportunity to respond, and their comment suggests they see little need for change (Buttke and Arnold 2003). Nevertheless, a start toward reform was made in the seventh edition of *Trip Generation*. ITE (2003, Vol. 1, 6-7) says, "The regression equations found throughout the report have been modified to display only two digits after the decimal point instead of three. These changes were made to maintain consistency with the descriptive statistics provided for each plot and minimize the implied precision of the data."

112. Requiring every developer to provide at least enough parking spaces so that everyone can park free everywhere will help guarantee that everyone will have a car.

3

The Pseudoscience of Planning for Parking

I have been making believe.... I have fooled everyone so long that I thought I should never be found out...[but] how can I help being a humbug when all these people make me do things that everybody knows can't be done?

— THE WIZARD OF OZ

Cities require off-street parking for hundreds of different land uses, and urban planners must set a specific requirement for each one. How do they do it? Some copy the requirements from nearby cities, others consult *Parking Generation*, and a few conduct special studies or pull the requirements out of thin air. Regardless of the data source, however, planners must go through three steps to set the parking requirement for any land use:

1. Define the land use (such as a fast-food restaurant);
2. Choose the basis for the requirement (such as floor area); and
3. Specify how many spaces are required per unit of this basis (such as 10 spaces per 1,000 square feet of floor area).

THE THREE-STEP PROCESS

A close look at each of these three steps will show why most cities usually require more than enough spaces to satisfy the peak demand for free parking.

Step 1: Define the Land Use

The Planning Advisory Service (PAS) of the American Planning Association (APA) reports that cities require parking for at least 662 different land uses (see Appendix A). Because the requirements refer to the number of parking spaces for each land use, the first step in setting a parking requirement is to define the specific land use. Table 3-1 shows a few of the myriad uses for which cities require parking, such as convents, kennels, night clubs, and tea rooms.

Table 3-1. Selected Land Uses That Have Parking Requirements

Abattoir	Ice cream manufacturing	Rifle range
Batting cage	Junkyard	Sex novelty shop
Convent	Kennel	Tea room
Diet clinic	Landfill	Ultra-light flight park
Exterminator	Massage parlor	Veterinarian
Furrier	Night club	Wastewater treatment
Gas storage plant	Oil change shop	Zoo
Horse stable	Pet cemetery	

Source: Selected from the 662 land uses shown in PAS (2003).

Convents and night clubs clearly create different parking demands, but simply recognizing this difference does not tell planners how many parking spaces either one needs. Nevertheless, planners must set a requirement for every land use—from abattoirs to zoos. Developers and property owners need to know how many parking spaces they are legally obligated to provide for each use. Neighbors also want to know that proposed development will supply all the required parking, so that spillover will not occur. Even when planners do not have good data (or any data at all), they must set a minimum parking requirement for every conceivable land use in their city.

Step 2: Choose the Basis

After planners have defined the hundreds of possible land uses, they must then require parking spaces in proportion to one or more factors they believe will affect parking demand at each use. The most plausible basis for the requirement is the number of people (employees, customers, visitors, or residents) who will occupy the site, but this number is highly variable over time, and planners cannot predict it accurately. It is also difficult to enforce parking requirements based on the number of people at a site, as Norman Williams and John Taylor explain:

If a given establishment is found to have more employees than provided for in the parking area, the problem of enforcement resolves itself simply into the question of whether the zoning authorities will insist that a considerable number of employees be fired, which on the whole appears unlikely; and there is always the excuse that this is a temporary rush-order situation, as just before Christmas. For these reasons, parking requirements related to floor space, although a rather crude measure of need, may in fact be more sensible.[1]

Despite the problems of basing parking requirements on the number of people at a site, many cities do so. They also require parking spaces in proportion to many other factors that might predict parking demand. Table 3-2 shows a few of the 216 bases planners have chosen for parking requirements, such as the number of bassinettes (in a hospital), fuel nozzles (at a gas station), holes (at a golf course), nuns (in a convent), or reposing rooms (in a funeral parlor).

Table 3-2. Selected Bases for Parking Requirements

Amusement devices	Homeless children	Reposing rooms
Bassinettes	Interments in one hour	Service bays
Clergymen	Largest number of visitors	Tie-downs
Driving tees	Mechanics	Users
Examination beds	Nuns	Vehicles maintained
Fuel nozzles	Operator stations	Washing machines
Grease racks	Persons lawfully permitted in pool	

Source: Selected from the 216 bases for parking requirements shown in Appendix A.

But there is a problem with many bases for parking requirements: property owners can easily increase whatever is supposed to predict parking demand without getting a planning permit and thus without increasing the number of parking spaces. For example, a hospital may add bassinettes and a convent may take in additional nuns without notifying the city planning department. Similarly, where the parking requirement for a church is based on the fixed number of seats or the linear feet of permanent seating, churches can evade the limit by using folding chairs instead of seats attached to the floor. Some churches don't want to pay for parking spaces they use only on Sundays, so they have taken advantage of the folding-chair loophole, as the *New York Times* explains:

There is a stretch of Flushing, Queens, where Christians, Buddhists, Jews, Muslims and Hindus worship within blocks of one another without a hint of sectarian strife. When it comes to parking spaces, though, it is all-out war.

Every Sunday, a flood of cars descends on the neighborhood, thanks in large part to its dozens of newly built Korean churches. City law requires houses of worship to provide parking spaces for their parishioners if they have seating fixed to the floor, but many of the churches use folding chairs and are thus not covered by that rule. For years, residents have complained bitterly about that situation—and the ungodly noise, the crowds and the cars that often block their driveways.[2]

To avoid these problems cities usually require parking in proportion to something known when a building permit is granted, is difficult to change without another permit, and can be measured easily to verify compliance. For this reason, cities usually require parking in proportion to the built floor space at a site, even if this is a poor predictor of parking demand.[3]

The lack of theory and data helps explain the ad hoc nature of these bases for parking requirements. Put yourself in the shoes of a planner who must recommend the requirement for any land use. When I ask planning students how many spaces they would require for, say, a hospital, they typically answer with some variant of "I don't know, but I'd give it my best shot." This attitude shows the plucky spirit most planners bring to their profession, but it also invites confusion and waste. For example, if a planner guesses that the number of bassinettes in a hospital helps explain parking demand, that number gets factored into the parking requirement for hospitals, regardless of whether it actually affects parking demand (do babies drive?). Without theory or data, who can say whether bassinettes do or do *not* affect parking demand?

Even for the same land use, cities base parking requirements on many different factors. Table 3-3 shows the findings of a survey of 66 cities' parking requirements for funeral parlors, a land use that raises the awkward question of how many spaces to require per…per what? The cities required parking for funeral parlors in proportion to 14 different factors: chapels, dwelling units, employees, families on premises, funeral vehicles, parlor area, parlors, persons of design capacity, seats, seats in chapel, seats in largest chapel, square feet, square feet of seating area, and square feet of other areas. The 66 cities had 27 different requirements, and 20 cities had a requirement no other city had.[4] Each requirement, taken alone, may appear plausible, but collectively these requirements raise grave doubts about planning for parking.

Step 3: Specify the Number of Spaces

After planners have defined each land use and chosen the basis for each requirement, they must then decide how many spaces to require per unit

Table 3-3. Parking Requirements for the Afterlife

Parking spaces required for funeral parlors	Number of cities
1 per 100 sq. ft.	3
1 per 200 sq. ft.	1
1 per 250 sq. ft.	1
1 per 100 sq. ft. + 1 per dwelling unit	1
1 per 100 sq. ft. or 1 per 6 seats	1
1 per 5 seats or 1 per 35 sq. ft. seating area, + 1 per 400 sq. ft. other areas	1
1 per 3 seats	1
1 per 4 seats	1
5 + 1 per 5 seats in largest chapel	1
1 per 6 seats in chapel	1
1 per 3 seats + 1 per funeral vehicle	1
1 per 4 seats + 1 per funeral vehicle + 1 per employee	1
1 per 5 seats + 1 per funeral vehicle + 1 per dwelling unit	1
1 per 25 sq. ft. of parlor area	1
1 per 50 sq. ft. of parlor area	4
3 per parlor	2
4 per parlor	1
5 per parlor	3
15 + 5 per parlor over 3 parlors	1
5 per parlor or 1 per 4 seats	1
5 per parlor + 1 per funeral vehicle	2
8 per parlor + 1 per funeral vehicle	9
10 per parlor + 1 per funeral vehicle	4
5 per parlor + 1 per funeral vehicle + 1 per family on premises	1
5 minimum	1
30 minimum	1
1 per 4 persons of design capacity	1
No specific requirements	19
Total	**66**

Source: Planning Advisory Service (1971, 36).

of this basis. Planners try to estimate how many parking spaces every land use needs to meet the peak demand for *free* parking, not how many spaces drivers will demand at a price that covers the cost of the spaces. To suggest the problems in predicting need, Table 3-4 presents the requirements for several land uses. Planners typically require at least one parking space per person except at religious land uses (1 space per 10 nuns and 3 spaces per 4 clergymen). The requirements look simple when planners can link parking to people: 1 space per tennis player, 2 spaces per barber, and 3 spaces per beautician. But other requirements are dazzling in their combination of precision and inventiveness: 1 space per 2,500 gallons of water (for a swimming pool), 1.5 spaces per fuel nozzle (for a gas station), and 10 spaces per maximum number of interments in a one-hour period (for a mausoleum). When planners deal with difficult land uses,

Table 3-4. Pataphysical Parking Requirements

Land use	Parking requirement
Adult entertainment	1 space per patron, plus 1 space per employee on the largest working shift
Barber shop	2 spaces per barber
Beauty shop	3 spaces per beautician
Bicycle repair	3 spaces per 1,000 square feet
Bowling alley	1 space for each employee and employer, plus 5 spaces for each lane
Gas station	1.5 spaces per fuel nozzle
Health home	1 space per 3 beds and bassinettes, plus 1 space per 3 employees, plus 1 space per staff doctor
Heating supply	3.33 spaces for every 1,000 square feet of sales and office area, plus 2 spaces per 3 employees on the maximum shift, plus 1 space for every vehicle customarily used in operation of the use or stored on the premises
Heliport	1 space per 5 employees, plus 5 spaces per touchdown pad
Machinery sales	1 space per 500 square feet of enclosed sales/rental floor area, plus 1 space per 2,500 square feet of open sales/rental display lot area, plus 2 spaces per service bay, plus 1 space per employee, but never less than 5 spaces
Mausoleum	10 spaces per maximum number of interments in a one-hour period
Nunnery	1 space per 10 nuns
Rectory	3 spaces per 4 clergymen
Swimming pool	1 space per 2,500 gallons of water
Taxi stand	1 space for each employee on the largest shift, plus 1 space per taxi, plus sufficient spaces to accommodate the largest number of visitors that may be expected at any one time
Tennis court	1 space per player

Sources: Planning Advisory Service (1964, 1971, and 1991); Witheford and Kanaan (1972).

perhaps they simply close their eyes and tap the heels of their ruby slippers together three times to conjure up the parking requirements.

One parking space per person has become the norm for some land uses. In a survey of 57 of the largest suburban employment centers in the country, Berkeley planning professor Robert Cervero found an average of 3.85 parking spaces per 1,000 square feet of floor area, which was slightly more than one parking space per employee.[5] In his book *Edge City*, journalist Joel Garreau says the rule of thumb is that there must be one parking space for every worker, and as a result, office buildings must provide about 1.5 times as much space to park cars as there is office space for the drivers; he concludes that parking is "the pivot of urbanity and civilization at the approach of the twenty-first century."[6]

Parking requirements appear arbitrary and excessive even when planners have data that purport to predict parking demand. Chapter 2 showed that the ITE parking generation rates are intended to measure the peak demand for free parking at suburban sites without public transit, but many cities require even more spaces. The ITE parking generation rate for office buildings is 2.79 spaces per 1,000 square feet, for example.[7] Nevertheless, in a survey in nine Southeastern states, Stanley Polanis and Keith Price found that cities require an average of 3.7 spaces per 1,000 square feet of office space.[8] Another survey in California found that cities require an average of 3.8 spaces per 1,000 square feet.[9] In a similar survey in Iowa, Minnesota, and Wisconsin, John Shaw at Iowa State University found that cities require an average of 4 spaces per 1,000 square feet.[10] In these surveys, the parking requirements ranged from 33 percent to 43 percent greater than the parking generation rate as computed by ITE.

The generous supply of required parking often goes unused. In a survey of nine suburban office parks with 336 buildings, Gruen Associates found that the parking supply averaged 2.8 spaces per 1,000 square feet, and the peak parking occupancy was 1.4 spaces per 1,000 square feet.[11] Peak parking occupancy ranged from 28 to 61 percent of capacity and averaged only 47 percent of capacity even though 97 percent of all employees arrived by car. A survey by the Urban Land Institute (ULI) at eight suburban business parks in 1986 also found that the peak parking occupancy averaged only 47 percent, and the highest peak occupancy at any site was 61 percent.[12] Surveys in the Seattle region in 2002 found an average peak parking occupancy of only 63 percent of capacity at sites in the Seattle Central Business District (CBD), and 60 percent in the Bellevue CBD; in nine other areas, it ranged between 46 percent and 79 percent.[13] Another survey of 26 neighborhoods in Seattle in 2000 found that the peak occupancy rate for off-street parking was only 61 percent.[14] Surveys in Northwestern Connecticut conducted during the Christmas season found that the peak occupancy was only 36 percent of capacity at big-box retail stores, and 79 percent at shopping plazas.[15] ULI found that the peak parking occupancy at 43 percent of shopping centers in the U.S. was never more than 85 percent of capacity even during the busiest hour of the year.[16] If the goal is to satiate the demand for free parking, many cities have achieved their objective. Defying Malthus, the number of cars does *not* always increase to fill all the space provided.

Richard Willson conducted case studies of parking demand and supply at suburban office developments in 10 Southern California cities, and he found that the peak parking occupancy averaged only 56 percent of capacity.[17] He also discovered a paradox: the parking lots were half empty even at the time of peak parking demand, but they looked full because the most visible spaces are the first to be occupied:

> These results [the half-empty lots] contradict the impression of the sites as viewed from the street, because the most visible spaces are the most likely to be occupied. This observation suggests that parking utilization counts are essential to counteract any mistaken impressions about parking utilization held by planners, local decision makers, and the public. In these instances, for example, zoning codes required levels of parking almost twice the measured demand, even though parking was free to the motorist. The projects were required to devote land and capital to a substantial number of parking spaces that are normally not used, and thus resources were diverted from providing more building area, better design, and more landscaping or common areas.[18]

City officials, developers, lenders, leasing agents, and tenants all assumed that planners knew how many parking spaces each land use needs, but the oversupply of parking did create doubts:

> One developer described his growing concern about parking after he noticed that spaces in the top floor of the parking structures never had oil spots, indicating that they are seldom, if ever, used.[19]

Developers also reported that they did not supply more parking spaces than the city required.

Other experts on the role of parking in the development process agree with Willson's findings. ULI's Robert Dunphy says:

> In most cases you meet the local [parking] requirements and nobody really thinks about them after that. Developers who do think about the amount of parking needed run into the question of where parking requirements come from and what their rationale is. Often nobody knows.[20]

After seeing the results of Willson's study in Southern California, the Chicago Regional Transportation Authority commissioned similar case studies of parking demand and supply at office developments in 10 Chicago suburbs. These studies found that the average supply of employee parking was 3.6 spaces per 1,000 square feet, that peak parking occupancy was only 68 percent of capacity, and that developers did not supply more parking than required by the zoning.[21] These studies in Chicago and Southern California thus show that cities require parking spaces that are rarely used.

Parking garages are seldom built as freestanding commercial ventures because parking revenues cannot cover the cost. In a study of eight municipal parking agencies in the Middle Atlantic and New England states, Herbert Levinson found that their annual operating revenue per space ranged between 26 and 36 percent of the annual cost per new garage space:

> In most cities it has become clear that downtown parking can no longer pay its own way through parking revenues…. Parking fees are often insufficient to cover the debt service; frequently they are little more than what is required to meet day-to-day operating costs.[22]

Parking spaces are expensive and require large subsidies, but most cities prohibit property owners from using the required spaces for any purpose other than parking (such as for landscaping or as a storage or loading area), even when they turn out not to be needed for parking. No wonder most developers don't provide more parking than the city requires. Some people, of course, want even more parking spaces than the zoning requires, and some new mini-mansions come equipped with "garagemahals" for five or six cars.[23]

Minimum parking requirements appear to exceed the peak demand for free parking in other countries as well. In the United Kingdom, for example, the Department of the Environment, Transport, and the Regions commissioned a study of parking requirements in the Southeast of England. The parking supply exceeded the peak parking occupancy at 33 of the 37 suburban sites studied, and at seven of the nine town-center sites. The conclusion was:

> Demand levels for most land use categories are frequently over-estimated, resulting in parking provision well in excess even of peak time demand…. In the main, developers are required to provide minimum levels of parking on site, related to the gross floor area of the scheme…. Parking provision is frequently well in excess of full demand at peak periods. We can find no justification for such over-provision, which is both wasteful of valuable development land, and encourages profligate use of the car.[24]

These studies conducted throughout the U.S. and in the U.K. suggest that the minimum parking requirements in many zoning ordinances are excessive, in part because they are based on the assumption that parking should be free. Urban designer Dom Nozzi says:

> When we hear the claim that there is "not enough parking downtown," what we are really hearing is that there is "not enough *free* parking *a few feet* from where I want to go." To demand such an impossible supply of parking is to ask a downtown to compete with outlying suburbs on *suburban terms*, that is, asking for the impossible.[25]

William Whyte, one of America's most astute observers of city life, said that even too much parking is never enough:

> In cities most dominated by parking lots and parking garages a key civic issue is the lamentable lack of parking. Let me cite Dallas. It has the highest ratio of parking spaces to office space in the country. But studies continually call for more parking, and at moderate cost…. Supply has so conditioned demand that parking has become an end in itself, with people in a bondage to it more psychological than physical.[26]

To give an extreme example of this bondage, Montgomery County, Maryland, requires funeral parlors to provide 83 parking spaces per 1,000 square feet of floor area in the main chapel. This astonishingly high and weirdly precise requirement (exactly 83 parking spaces per 1,000 square feet!) means that the parking lot must be at least 25 times larger than the main chapel. One additional parking space must also be provided for each employee on the largest shift (the graveyard shift?) and for each vehicle used in connection with the business.[27]

CIRCULAR LOGIC

Circular logic is a crucial flaw in parking requirements. Planners observe the peak parking occupancy at suburban sites with free parking but no public transit, and then require at least enough spaces to meet this demand (see Figure 2-9). The parking demand at new land uses with free parking then confirms the prediction that all the required spaces are "needed." A 1982 ULI study, *Parking Requirements for Shopping Centers*, illustrates this problem. Parking has always been a key element in the design of shopping centers, and *Time* magazine enthusiastically described one of the first centers, Southdale, in the 1950s as a "pleasure dome with parking."[28] The high cost of all the parking spaces required for these pleasure domes justified an unusually thorough study—by far the most comprehensive ever conducted on parking for a single land use. ULI suspected that many cities' parking requirements were excessive, and it warned about the environmental and economic costs:

> The community, for example, should avoid the environmental consequences from an unnecessarily large pavement area; the consumer should not be burdened by higher indirect costs from an excessive number of parking spaces.[29]

Despite these good intentions, the study went on to repeat the fundamental errors made in setting minimum parking requirements. ULI gathered data on parking occupancy at 506 participating shopping centers in 41 states and six Canadian provinces. It also obtained detailed parking occupancy counts at 135 centers and daily counts for an entire year at 22 centers. From this survey, ULI estimated the number of parking spaces needed to satisfy the demand for free parking in the 20th busiest hour of the year:

> To provide adequate parking for a typical shopping center today, the number of spaces required is:
>
> > 4.0 spaces per 1,000 square feet of gross leasable area (GLA) for centers having a GLA of 25,000 to 400,000 square feet;
> >
> > from 4.0 to 5.0 spaces in a linear progression, with an average of 4.5 spaces per 1,000 square feet of GLA, for centers having from 400,000 to 600,000 square feet;
> >
> > 5.0 spaces per 1,000 square feet of GLA for centers having a GLA of over 600,000 square feet.
>
> The provision of parking based on these standards will serve patrons and employee needs at the 20th-busiest hour of the year, and allow a surplus during all but 19 hours of the remainder of the more than 3,000 hours during which a typical center is open annually. During 19 hours of each year, which are distributed over 10 peak shopping days, *some patrons will not be able to find vacant spaces when they first enter.*[30]

These recommendations appear sensible, but the study's methodology has serious flaws. First, parking occupancy was surveyed at sites where parking was free, so the study estimated the demand for *free* parking. Second, requiring enough spaces to satisfy the demand during the 20th-busiest hour of the year (the "design hour") means that the parking lot will be full only 20 hours a year, and many spaces will therefore be unused for more than 99 percent of the year.[31] An earlier ULI study of parking requirements for shopping centers chose the 10th-busiest hour as the design hour. In neither study was the design hour justified by estimating the resulting costs and benefits of parking to shoppers, merchants, developers, cities, or society. The only reference cited to justify using the design-hour criterion was a 15-year-old textbook by transportation engineers Martin Wohl and Brian Martin, who severely criticized the design-hour criterion on the grounds that (1) the parking supply influences parking demand and (2) the optimum parking supply cannot be chosen without examining the costs and benefits of the choice:

> While [it] may seem frustrating, and while use of simpler and more straight-forward concepts, such as…the thirtieth highest hour, may seem more practical to the 'real world' engineer, the fact remains that proper engineering design techniques require more detailed and more comprehensive analysis.[32]

Despite this admonition, planners set the parking requirements for new shopping centers to meet the demand for free parking observed at existing shopping centers at the 20th-busiest hour. Therefore, planners implicitly base parking requirements on the peak demand for *free* parking, without regard to either the cost of providing the parking or the price that drivers are willing to pay for it.

ULI published a second edition of *Parking Requirements for Shopping Centers* in 1999, and it repeated the methodology of the 1982 study with almost identical results.[33] The study again estimated the parking demand at the 20th-busiest hour—around 2 p.m. on the second Saturday before Christmas—but offered no justification for this choice.[34] The study did, however, provide additional information not included in the 1982 study. For example, 90 to 95 percent of all shoppers arrived by car at the "vast majority" of centers, but at 43 percent of the centers the parking lots were never more than 85 percent occupied even at the busiest hour of the year. Parking was generally oversupplied by 0.5 to 1 space per 1,000 square feet of gross leasable area:

> The parking supply is higher than parking demand by an average of almost a full space per 1,000 square feet of GLA for centers smaller than 600,000 square feet, and by about half a space for larger centers. *This suggests that parking supply is not constricting demand. Moreover, it suggests that building more parking spaces will not result in increased traffic volumes and, subsequently, in increased sales at centers.*[35]

Employees accounted for about 20 percent of parking demand during the peak period, which suggests that providing special employee transportation programs (such as off-site parking with shuttle buses) on the few days of the customers' peak parking demand could reduce a shopping center's annual peak parking demand—and the required parking supply—by 20 percent. This finding illustrates a crucial but often neglected aspect of parking requirements: if the peak parking demand occurs for only a few hours a year, reducing parking demand during this short time is far more cost-effective than increasing the year-round parking supply. Parking spaces that are occupied for only a few hours a year are a spectacularly bad investment, not only for developers but also for everyone else.

Only 2 percent of the centers charged for parking, and they validated it for customers. Only 1 percent charged employees for parking. This ubiquitous free parking is not surprising: if there are more than enough spaces to satisfy the peak demand at a zero price, why charge for them? Free parking thus leads to the "demand" that planners observe to set parking requirements, and the requirements then perpetuate the free parking. Once the pattern has been established, urban planners project past mistakes into the future, and planning for parking resembles progress along a Möbius strip.[36] (See Figure 3-1.)

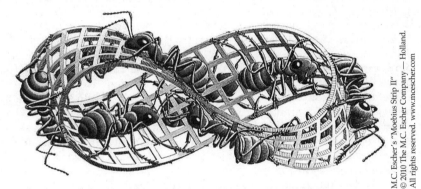

Figure 3-1. A Möbius strip with ants (as drawn by M.C. Escher)

ESTIMATING DEMAND WITHOUT PRICES

If urban planners do not consider prices when estimating the demand for parking, off-street parking requirements are perfectly circular and wholly unscientific. In foretelling the demand for parking, urban planners resemble the Wizard of Oz, deceived by his own tricks. After he was exposed as a fraud, the Wizard confessed:

> I have been making believe…. I have fooled everyone so long that I thought I should never be found out…[but] how can I help being a humbug when all these people make me do things that everybody knows can't be done?[37]

Planners cannot predict parking demand any better than the Wizard of Oz could give the Scarecrow brains or send Dorothy back to Kansas. When Dorothy accused the Wizard of being "a very bad man" for making promises he couldn't keep, he protested, "I'm really a very good man; but I'm a very bad Wizard, I must admit."[38] Urban planners are good people, but they cannot help being humbugs when they struggle to appear methodologically rigorous about parking requirements. In the 1939 film, the unmasked Wizard resembles a hapless urban planner trying to set parking requirements: he desperately twiddles knobs, wrenches levers, and—when his audience expresses doubt—roars, "Do you presume to question the Great Oz?... The Great Oz has spoken!"[39]

Urban planners get away with their wizardlike conduct because they produce a wonderful result: free parking. If only for parking, planners have produced the utopian life of the Emerald City:

> Each person was given freely by his neighbors whatever he required for his use, which is as much as anyone may reasonably require.... Each man and woman, no matter what he or she produced for the good of the community, was supplied by the neighbors with food and clothing and a house and furniture and ornaments and games.[40]

And, presumably, free parking. Dorothy and the Scarecrow marched down the yellow brick road to the Emerald City singing "We're off to see the Wizard...because of the wonderful things he does!"[41] Then it turns out that what he does is fraud and humbug.

Even the phrase "set a parking requirement" is humbug. The word "set" suggests the possession of special expertise or technical ability to calibrate a finely tuned instrument. But urban planners have no special expertise or technical ability to predict parking demand, and parking requirements are not finely tuned instruments. Planning for parking is a skill learned only on the job, and it is more a political than a professional activity. Perhaps planners merely "impose" parking requirements. At best, these requirements are the outcome of simple tinkering. Whenever a land use begins to create spillover parking, planners nudge up the off-street parking requirement until the problem goes away.

PROFESSIONAL CONFIDENCE TRICK

"Parking requirement" is a misleading term because it suggests that *buildings* require a certain number of parking spaces. Instead, *zoning* requires the parking spaces, some of which are rarely used. Parking that is not "up to code" sounds risky, like substandard electrical wiring or plumbing, but this is far from true. The only risk of "substandard" parking is perhaps not satisfying the peak demand for free parking.

Because planners are confused, parking requirements are often confusing. For example, when parking requirements are expressed as 1 space per 250 square feet or 1 space per 200 square feet, the difference is not obvious. When the same requirements are expressed as 4 and 5 spaces per 1,000 square feet, the difference becomes much clearer.[42] Nevertheless, planners often express high requirements with "1 space" in the numerator and the number of square feet in the denominator—such as 1 parking space per 50 square feet of floor area. Why? This may occur because the same requirement, phrased instead as 20 spaces per 1,000 square feet of floor area, sounds excessive. This 1-space-in-the-numerator method of expressing a parking requirement enables planners to hide—even from themselves—the large number of parking spaces they routinely require. Urban planners have pulled the wool over their own eyes, and they play a professional confidence trick on everyone—including themselves. When dealing with parking, planners often behave like the Scarecrow who, after the Wizard gave him a diploma rather than brains, blurted an impressive-sounding but gibberish version of the Pythagorean Theorem: "The sum of the square roots of any two sides of an isosceles triangle is equal to the square root of the remaining side."[43]

In urban planning, actions have symbolic value apart from their other consequences, as implied by the slogan: "The things we do show we care, even if they have no other effect." If citizens complain about parking problems, for example, an increase in the parking requirements for a specific land use—at fast-food restaurants, perhaps—can at no cost to the government demonstrate that the city is doing something about the problem, even if planners have no real evidence to show that fast-food restaurants "need" more parking. The costs are hidden, the action is politically useful, and planners can always provide an impressive-sounding rationale to require, say, 1 parking space for every 50 square feet of restaurant space. Few people will understand that the city is requiring parking lots that are six times larger than the restaurants they serve.[44]

PLANNERS IN DENIAL

Planners sometimes admit parking requirements are misguided but then say this is not a serious problem because developers, lenders, and tenants all demand even more parking spaces than the city requires. But parking requirements would be superfluous if everyone demanded more parking than cities require because developers would then provide the spaces of their own accord. The only empirical studies that have compared the parking supply with parking requirements found that developers usually supply only the parking that zoning requires.[45] Many developers want to provide more floor space or a different use for their building than their parking supply allows, so they obviously want to supply less parking than the zoning requires. Parking spaces are expensive, and developers do not provide them frivolously.

In my own experience as a member of a Design Review Board for the Los Angeles City Planning Department, I reviewed the plans for all development in Westwood between 1994 and 2003. I saw many projects where the parking requirements limited the floor space of a building, prevented changing its use, or disfigured its design. But I never saw a project with significantly more parking than the zoning requires. Consider a typical case: a 12-unit condominium with two two-bedroom units (2.25 required parking spaces apiece) and 10 three-bedroom units (3.25 required parking spaces apiece). Thirty-seven parking spaces were required, exactly the number supplied in the one level of underground parking. The submitted plans showed that the project had 60 square feet of parking for every 100 square feet of housing. The housing floor area was 38 percent less than allowed by the floor-area ratio in the zoning, which suggested that the parking requirement, not the floor-area ratio, limited the amount of housing.[46] As is typical of condominium projects in Westwood, the subterranean garage was excavated from lot line to lot line, so it was larger than the footprint of the building (which must be set back from the property line on all sides), and all landscaping was in a thin layer of soil above the garage.

A similar case is also instructive: a 19-unit building with 58 parking spaces (2.5 spaces per unit), exactly the number required by the zoning code. Because of the small site, two levels of underground parking were needed to satisfy the parking requirement. The small, two-level underground garage was very inefficient, with 520 square feet of garage floor area per parking space because the ramps, aisles, columns, stairs, and elevators occupied a high proportion of the area. The garage's construction cost was $80 per square foot, so the cost per space was $41,600 ($80 x 520), and the required parking added $104,000 to the cost of each apartment (2.5 x $41,600). With an average apartment size of 1,969 square feet, the required parking added $53 per square foot to the apartment's construction cost ($104,000 ÷ 1,969). The project provided 54 square feet of parking for every 100 square feet of housing. Again, all landscaping for the project was in a thin layer of soil above the garage.[47]

Members of other municipal planning boards report similar cases where cities require developers to sacrifice density, design, and economy to provide more parking. For example, Lawrence Solomon, former Vice-Chairman of the City of Toronto's Planning Board, wrote:

Without exception, every developer that came before us tried to supply less parking than the planners required, often providing detailed analyses showing that the city was demanding far more spaces than the development would ever need. The developers often obtained concessions in other areas, but never, as I recall, in obtaining exemptions from the parking requirements. I was typically the only vote in the developer's favor—neighborhood pressure for additional parking invariably persuaded the Board.[48]

To examine how parking requirements inflate the parking supply, consider what would happen if cities did *not* require off-street parking. The market would supply parking only when it is profitable (just as the market supplies gasoline only when it is profitable), and there would be fewer spaces. For example, some stores or restaurants might prefer to lose a few customers on the busiest days of the year rather than pay for parking spaces that are often empty. Parking spaces that remained empty for too many hours a day would likely be redeveloped for more productive uses, and the price of parking would increase.

If parking were less plentiful and more expensive, we would own fewer cars. But cities have required off-street parking since the middle of the last century, so car ownership, urban form, transportation infrastructure, and travel habits have adapted to ubiquitous free parking. Most sites now offer free parking, and almost everyone of driving age has a car. We have tailored our housing, employment, and shopping patterns to the plenitude of free parking, and parking demand is now far higher than it would be if zoning had never required off-street parking. An automobile-dependent city is also parking dependent, and by increasing our automobile dependency, off-street parking requirements have increased our parking dependency. The spread of asphalt parking lots may seem inevitable and unstoppable, like lava descending on a doomed city, but planners should recognize that off-street parking requirements are a cause of the problem.

Cities sometimes use high parking requirements as an indirect way to discourage specific land uses. If residents oppose fast-food restaurants, for example, a higher parking requirement can make it more difficult to build them. But this strategy creates even more problems because the fast-food restaurants that *do* get built have supersize parking lots that are asphalt eyesores, and residents dislike them even more. The right solution is to regulate the offending aspects of a land use, not simply to require more parking spaces that make that land use even more undesirable.

Because high parking requirements impose a high cost on development, they might be explained as an indirect way for cities to control growth and the associated traffic congestion. But if cities want to control traffic, high parking requirements have a serious unintended consequence. If all new development comes with free parking, the inevitable result is more vehicle trips and traffic congestion. Growth would scarcely be noticed if the new people came without cars. High parking requirements are thus a perverse way to control growth if the real goal is to limit traffic. Some cities require bicycle racks to encourage cycling, but most planners and elected officials do not seem to recognize that parking requirements will likewise encourage driving.

PAROCHIAL POLICIES

Planning for parking is almost entirely a municipal responsibility. Federal, state, and regional transportation plans rarely mention parking, although it is an essential and expensive part of the transportation system. As a result, parking policy is parochial. When higher levels of government do take note of the wider consequences of parking on transportation, the environment, and the economy, however, they tend to limit rather than require parking.[49] Oregon's Transportation Systems Plan, for example, requires local governments to amend their land-use and subdivision regulations to achieve a 10 percent reduction in the number of parking spaces per capita.[50] The Portland, Oregon, metropolitan government limits the minimum parking requirements that cities can impose. For example, a city's minimum parking requirement for general office buildings cannot exceed 2.7 spaces per 1,000 square feet. The metropolitan government also caps the maximum amount of parking that cities can allow.[51] If the site is transit- and pedestrian-accessible, for example, the maximum parking allowed is 3.4 spaces per 1,000 square feet. In the United Kingdom, the national government's transport policy guidelines for local planning specify, "plans should state maximum levels of parking for broad classes of development.... There should be no minimum standards for development, other than parking for disabled people."[52] These attempts to take state and regional concerns into account suggest that leaving parking policy entirely to local control produces too much parking.

Removing the requirements for off-street parking is not a "restraint" on off-street parking, because developers can still provide as much as the market will support. Some cities that remove the off-street parking requirements in their CBDs, however, switch directly to parking caps, which are a restraint. Fewer parking lots improve the appearance of the downtown, and new buildings give more reasons to visit it, but businesses are naturally concerned about having "enough" parking, and they may fear that restraining the parking supply will keep customers away. Does it? In a survey of research on whether parking restraint policies affect the economic vitality of urban centers, Ben Still and David

Simmonds concluded, "There is no clear evidence from aggregate statistical studies that parking [restraint] is clearly linked to retail or other sector economic vitality.... There is very little evidence of any sort available and certainly a lack of clear evidence regarding the wider effects from parking restraint policies."[53] If restraints on the parking supply really did limit economic vitality, one would expect to find some evidence, but there is none.

In many communities, sales taxes are an important source of local revenue, and planners are thus under pressure to do "whatever it takes" to attract retail sales. The competition for retail tax base puts cities in a race to offer plenty of free parking for all potential customers. From a regional perspective, this race is a zero-sum game because more parking everywhere cannot increase the total regional sales volume. The Portland Metro's regionwide limit on parking requirements is like a disarmament treaty among local governments: because of their desire to avoid "mutually assured destruction," cities agree not to compete with each other by trying to require more parking than everyone else. A city's cap on the amount of parking may also be interpreted as a disarmament treaty among developers: they cannot compete with each other by providing more parking. Where cities reduce their parking requirements, individual developers may be willing to provide less parking if they know that all other developers will do likewise; they will save money on construction costs and also reduce the vehicle traffic generated by their projects. Parking caps arise from a recognition of the many long-term connections between traffic, land use, and urban form, while minimum parking requirements are reactive responses to local and immediate concerns.[54]

MOBILITY VERSUS PROXIMITY

Mobility and proximity are two ways to improve accessibility—the ease of reaching destinations. In the U.S., mobility has come to mean mainly the ability to drive wherever you go and to park free when you get there. A problem with using off-street parking requirements to provide this mobility is that they reduce proximity. Abundant parking makes it easier and cheaper to drive, but pandemic parking lots spread activities farther apart, making cars more necessary. Off-street parking requirements increase mobility by car, but they also reduce mobility by walking, cycling, and public transit.[55] By reducing both propinquity and non-car mobility, the parking supply creates its own demand because a car is needed to get to most places. The increased vehicle travel also increases traffic congestion. If drivers have to fight their way through congested traffic while traveling between their free parking spaces, off-street parking requirements can both increase vehicle travel *and* reduce accessibility.

Transportation economists Jonathan Levine and Yaakov Garb explain how pursuing the goal of mobility can reduce accessibility:

> The derived nature of transportation demand implies that enhancement of mobility per se is not a reasonable goal for transportation policy.... "Mobility" is defined here as ease of movement; accessibility is defined as ease of reaching destinations. The concepts are related but readily distinguishable. Where destinations are close by, greater accessibility can be afforded even if mobility is constrained; where destinations are remote, mobility may be high without high-level accessibility.[56]

Similarly, Robert Cervero says, "Planning of the automobile city focuses on *saving time*. Planning for the accessible city, on the other hand, focuses on *time well spent*."[57]

Once implemented, parking requirements start a vicious cycle. Parking spaces and cars are complements, which means that free parking increases the demand for cars, and more cars in turn increase the demand for parking. Off-street parking requirements and cars therefore present a symbiotic relationship: the requirements lead to free parking, the free parking leads to more cars, and more cars then lead to even higher parking requirements. When 3 spaces per 1,000 square feet no longer satisfy the peak demand for free parking, a stronger dose of 4 spaces per 1,000 square feet can alleviate the problem, but not for long because cars increase in numbers to fill the new parking spaces. Every jab of the parking needle relieves the local symptoms, but ultimately worsens the real disease—too much land and capital devoted to parking and cars. Parking requirements are good for motorists in the short run but bad for cities in the long run.

SYSTEMWIDE EFFECTS OF PARKING REQUIREMENTS

Almost everyone in the U.S. now leads a lifestyle adapted to the car and ubiquitous free parking. As a result, the demand for parking is now higher than it would be if cities had never required on-site parking. Therefore, we cannot estimate how the whole *system* of parking requirements increases the parking supply simply by looking at the difference between the number of spaces that cities require and the number that developers now voluntarily provide because developers are responding to a level of demand that has already been inflated by the prevalence of free parking. The difference between the required and voluntary supplies of parking at each individual site therefore underestimates the systemwide effects of minimum parking requirements.

To see why the increase in the total parking supply is greater than the sum of its parts, consider two hypothetical cases for the development at one site: first, no parking requirements at this site alone, and second, no parking requirements anywhere. In the first case, only the individual site is exempt from parking requirements, and every other site in the city must provide all the required parking. In the second case, the city has never required on-site parking anywhere, and developers have always provided only the number of parking spaces they thought were worth the cost. Although the site is not subject to off-street parking requirements in either case, a developer will voluntarily provide more parking spaces in the first case—to compete with all the other buildings that offer plentiful free parking—than in the second case.

The two curves in Figure 3-2 illustrate the two cases. Both show how many parking spaces a developer will *voluntarily* provide as a function of the cost per space. If parking spaces cost less, the developer will provide more of them, so the curve slopes downward. A profit-maximizing developer will voluntarily provide some parking spaces, but the quantity will depend on the cost.

The VS curve is not a typical supply curve in a traditional economic demand-supply diagram. Instead, it shows the outcome of choices about the profit-maximizing number of parking spaces for a development, given both the cost of providing parking spaces and the expected demand for parking in the development. The greater the demand for parking, the more parking spaces the developer will voluntarily supply; the greater the cost of providing the parking spaces, the fewer parking spaces the developer will voluntarily supply. The downward-sloping VS curves can thus be thought of as the developer's own demand for parking spaces.

First consider the upper curve, VS_1, which shows the number of parking spaces a developer will *voluntarily* provide if the city requires at least 4 spaces per 1,000 square feet everywhere else. We can use this curve to examine how a prevailing requirement of 4 spaces per 1,000 square feet increases the parking supply at *this site*. Because the requirement applies at all other sites in the city, parking is free everywhere else, nearly everyone has a car, and everyone expects to park free wherever they go. This market environment increases the developer's willingness to provide on-site parking (depending on its cost), as shown by the upper curve, VS_1. Suppose the cost to provide parking at this site is $15,000 per space. In this case, the developer will voluntarily provide 3 spaces per 1,000 square feet (point A), which is 1 less than the city requires. The requirement therefore appears to increase the parking supply by only 1 space per 1,000 square feet.

Now consider the second case in which the city has *never* required parking anywhere. Most buildings would have fewer spaces, and urban den-

Figure 3-2. Voluntarily Provided Parking Spaces as a Function
of the Cost per Space

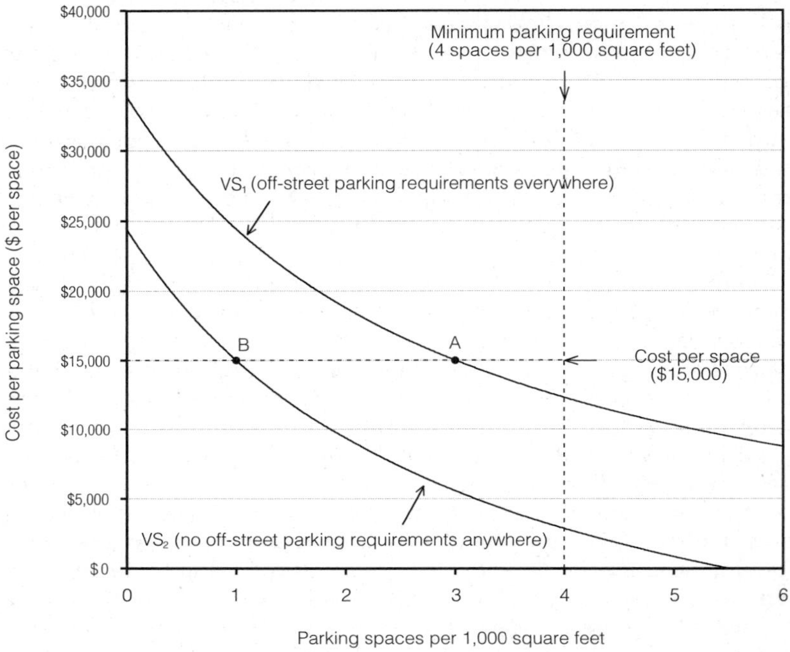

sity would be higher. With higher density, more travelers would ride public transit, cycle, and walk, and they would own fewer cars. This different
market environment reduces the developer's willingness to provide on-
site parking (which is not required), as shown by the lower curve, VS_2. In
this case, if the cost of parking is again $15,000 per space, the developer
will voluntarily provide only 1 space per 1,000 square feet (point B).

The individual developer's behavior *seems* to suggest that requiring 4
spaces per 1,000 square feet increases the parking supply by only 33 percent (from the voluntary 3 spaces to the required 4). But the parking
requirement had already altered urban form, increased the number of
cars, and oriented travel habits toward solo driving. As a result, the
requirement really increases the parking supply by 300 percent (from the
voluntary 1 space to the required 4) because the market would supply
only 1 space per 1,000 square feet if the city had never required off-street
parking.[58]

This hypothetical example illustrates two important points. First, we cannot estimate how parking requirements increase the parking supply without knowing how much it costs to provide parking spaces. If parking spaces are not expensive, parking requirements may not increase the parking supply at all because developers may voluntarily provide the required spaces. But if parking spaces are expensive, the requirements can greatly increase the supply. Second, we cannot look at the current behavior of individual developers to estimate how the whole system of requirements has increased the parking supply. An individual developer may voluntarily provide all the parking required at a site, but this decision is in part due to the free parking everywhere else. Therefore, the whole system of requirements increases the parking supply beyond what the market would provide, even if many developers voluntarily provide all the spaces required at their individual sites.

If a city removes its parking requirements, land use will not snap back to what it would have been if the city had never required off-street parking. Urban form is "path dependent," and cities that cease to require off-street parking may never resemble cities that never required it. The engineer's term for path dependency is "hysteresis," which refers to the failure of a property that has been changed by an external agent to return to its original value when the cause of the change is removed. Even if a city removes its parking requirements, most parking will remain free in the short run because the capital stock is long lived. In the long run, however, no cost is fixed, and nothing is free: without off-street parking requirements, the price of parking will rise toward the cost of providing parking spaces. Post-parking-requirement cities will become more compact and less automobile dependent over time. Automobile dependency resembles addiction to smoking, and free parking is like free cigarettes. More people would get into the habit of heavy smoking if cigarettes were free, and their addiction would be hard to break even if the subsidies for smoking were removed. Likewise, automobile dependency will also be a hard habit to break even if parking subsidies are removed. Cities will adjust slowly to the removal of parking requirements because new development will occur in the midst of a largely car-oriented society. Off-street parking requirements have cemented many planning mistakes into the built environment, and it will take decades for cities to recover from the damage.

PARKING SPACES REQUIRED FOR A CHANGE OF LAND USE

Parking requirements severely restrict the use of older buildings. For example, if a building has 2 parking spaces per 1,000 square feet of floor area, most cities will not allow it to be converted to a new use with a requirement of more than 2 spaces per 1,000 square feet unless more parking spaces are added or a variance is obtained. Adding new spaces to an older building is usually out of the question because there is simply no room. Older buildings are thus limited to uses for which the existing parking supply meets the current parking requirements.

The restrictions on building use become especially severe after a city increases its parking requirements. The new requirements do not apply retroactively to existing buildings in their current uses, but the parking supply becomes "nonconforming" at buildings that do not have enough spaces to meet the new requirements. Cities grant these nonconforming buildings a "grandfather" right to continue doing business in their current use with their existing parking supply, but they can require additional spaces to be added if the use changes.[59] (A grandfather clause in a statute exempts those already involved in a regulated activity or business from the new regulations established by the statute.) Parking requirements triggered by a change of use severely limit the possible occupants for older buildings and stunt the economic development of older areas.

Two Policies

Cities have two common policies about the number of parking spaces required when a building's use changes, and both limit the use of older buildings.[60] These two policies can be explained by examining the zoning ordinances of two California cities: Long Beach and San Diego. What happens when a building is converted to a new use that has a higher parking requirement than the existing use?

Parking Spaces Required When A Use Changes

A use with nonconforming parking may change to another use without adding parking [unless] the new use would require more parking than the existing use. Then, in order to establish the new use, the applicant must add parking equal to the difference between the parking requirement of the existing use and the new use (net change in parking intensity).

Long Beach, California,
Municipal Code Section 21.27.070C.

When a change of use is proposed to a use that requires the same or fewer off-street parking spaces than the previous use…no change in parking spaces is required…. When a change in use is proposed to a use that requires more off-street parking spaces than the previous use, parking shall be required as provided in this division for the new use.

San Diego, California,
Municipal Code Section 142.0510(d).

---

1. Long Beach requires adding enough parking spaces to meet the difference between the parking requirements for the existing and the new uses.
2. San Diego requires adding enough parking spaces to meet the parking requirement for the new use.

Table 3-5 illustrates these two cities' policies in the case of a 1,000-square-foot building that has no off-street parking spaces because it was built before the city required parking (column 1). In both cities, the current requirement for the building's existing, grandfathered use is 2 spaces per 1,000 square feet (column 2). Suppose the owner wants to establish a new use for this building. We can examine how many additional parking spaces each city requires when the current requirement (in column 3) for the new land use is 2 spaces per 1,000 square feet (Scenario A) or 3 spaces per 1,000 square feet (Scenario B).

In Scenario A, where 2 spaces are required for both new and existing uses, neither city requires more parking, and the requirement does not prevent changing the building's use. Next consider Scenario B, where 3 spaces are required for the new use. Long Beach requires 1 new space to meet the difference between the requirements for the new use (3 spaces) and the existing use (2 spaces). San Diego, however, requires 3 new spaces because the building must meet the requirement for the new use. Both policies hobble reuse, but San Diego's more stringent policy raises a higher barrier.

Zoning consultant Charles Reed recommends reducing the number of uses with different parking requirements to as few as possible, so that most new uses will have the same requirement as the old one.[61] This uniformity will make older buildings easier to reuse. Because most retail establishments lease their quarters and are prone to a high failure rate, securing loans to build or remodel a building may be difficult unless the space is adaptable to other uses at a low cost, without the need for additional parking spaces.

Table 3-5. Parking Spaces Required When a Building's Use Changes

| | Existing parking spaces | Spaces required | | Additional spaces required for a change of use | |
		Existing use	New use	Long Beach	San Diego
	(1)	(2)	(3)	(4)	(5)
A	0	2	2	0	0
B	0	2	3	1	3

For an existing building of 1,000 square feet.

The zoning codes in Long Beach and San Diego clearly state the number of parking spaces required when a land use changes, but some cities' zoning codes are vague or even silent on this issue, and many planners cannot explain their city's policy. Some cities appear to have an even more stringent policy: they require each new use to meet the city's current parking requirement for the new use, even if it is the same or lower than that for the existing grandfathered use. For example, suppose a building with no parking has an existing grandfathered use with a requirement of 3 spaces per 1,000 square feet. An owner who wants to convert the building to a new use with a requirement of only 2 spaces per 1,000 square feet must meet the requirement for the new use even though it is lower than that for the existing grandfathered use.

The change-of-use rules refer to buildings that have a grandfathered right to operate with the parking supply for the previous use. But a building that has been unoccupied for a specific time (one year in Long Beach, two in San Diego) loses its grandfathered rights and must meet the current parking requirement before any new use can be established. A building that has been vacant for more than a year or two can thus become extremely difficult to reuse. Someone who wants to reoccupy the building even in its previous use must provide all the parking spaces currently required for the use. This counterproductive policy works against revival: once an area has been neglected for a few years, parking requirements make adaptive reuse even more difficult, and older buildings must be adaptable to survive.

An Example

An example can explain how parking requirements prohibit many desirable land uses. Suppose an existing warehouse has no off-street parking because it was built before the city required any. The city now requires a warehouse to provide 1 space per 1,000 square feet. Although the building does not conform to the current requirement, it can continue to be used as a warehouse without providing the required parking because the use was established before the city imposed the current requirement. If the current occupant goes out of business, the building can be reused as a warehouse without providing the required parking because there is no change of use.

Suppose also that the parking requirement for a research laboratory is 3 spaces per 1,000 square feet. Because the requirement for a research laboratory is higher than for a warehouse, the warehouse cannot be converted into a research laboratory without providing more parking spaces or seeking a variance.[62] Long Beach requires 2 new spaces per 1,000 square feet, and San Diego requires 3. Parking lots have about 330 square feet per space, so 3 spaces per 1,000 square feet of a building's floor area produce a parking lot about the size of the building itself. Because adding new parking spaces to most older buildings is impractical, parking requirements in zoning ordinances can freeze buildings in their existing land uses or even prevent any feasible use.

In summary, off-street parking requirements have different meanings for new buildings and for existing buildings. For a new building, parking requirements determine the number of spaces that a developer must supply. For an existing building, parking requirements limit the uses that a city will allow. Given the haphazard methods planners use to set parking requirements, many important land-use decisions are made with no rational basis.

QUANTITY VERSUS QUALITY

Architects and urban designers have published several excellent guides to better design of parking lots and structures, including Mark Childs's *Parking Spaces*, Jim McCluskey's *Parking: A Handbook of Environmental Design*, Catherine Miller's *Carscape*, and Thomas Smith's *The Aesthetics of Parking*. But despite many good "parkitecture" proposals, most design is dismal because the sheer number of parking spaces required by zoning leaves little room or budget for anything other than asphalt lots and blank structures. PAS has published five surveys of cities' requirements for the *number* of parking spaces, but only one survey of cities' requirements for the *design* of parking spaces.[63] Andres Duany, Elizabeth Plater-Zyberk, and Jeff Speck explain the problems caused by zoning's fixation on numbers and ratios rather than on design:

> The problem with current development codes is not just their size…. They have no images, no diagrams, no recommended models, only numbers and words. Their authors, it seems, have no clear picture of what they want their communities to be…. Most zoning codes, focused on numbers and ratios rather than on physical form, can't tell the difference between a dingbat and a block of row houses, as they seem to be statistically identical.[64]

Planners focus almost exclusively on the ratio of parking spaces to floor area, and they neglect how all the required parking spaces affect urban design. Off-street parking requirements represent the triumph of quantity over quality in urban planning. Planners should stop requiring more parking *spaces* and start requiring better parking *design*.

Parking lots are often asphalt eyesores that interrupt the streetscape and expand the distances between destinations. Thomas Smith, in PAS Report No. 411, says:

Visually, parking lots and parking structures can be a mess. They are often too big, contain too much asphalt or concrete, and have little or no relationship to the buildings and activities around them. They are not inviting places for pedestrians, and they do not have the interest or attraction of other urban open spaces. The size and scale of parking lots and parking garages cause them to break up the links between buildings and destroy the continuity of some streetfronts.... All too often, however, planners give no attention to improving the appearance of parking lots.[65]

As a result, visitors must walk through a maze of vehicles in a desolate, oil-stained parking lot before finally arriving in a sparkling, marble-veneered lobby. And beyond being ugly themselves, the required parking spaces can disfigure the design of buildings they serve. Fitting both a building and the required parking onto the site can be difficult, and the building's design often must be compromised to accommodate the parking. Architects often complain about the need to shoehorn a building in after the parking requirement has been satisfied. Removing off-street parking requirements can therefore increase the potential for better design. Planners can then use zoning more creatively to improve the design of parking itself. To illustrate this potential, I will give four examples of how zoning for parking can significantly improve urban design:
1. Limit the number of parking spaces
2. Improve the appearance of residential garages
3. Improve the location of parking
4. Improve the design of parking structures

Off-Street Parking Limits

As Berkeley professor Allan Jacobs observed, often in city planning "it's not what you see that says it's a good job..., its what you don't see."[66] Carmel, California, provides a fine example of parking that you don't see. Carmel is famous for its attractive downtown, and zoning helps explain its unique pedestrian ambience. To achieve this ambience, the city *prohibits* off-street parking spaces anywhere in the central commercial district. The zoning ordinance states:

> On-site parking is prohibited in the central commercial (CC) land use district. This policy reduces the need for curb cuts in sidewalks and the interference with free pedestrian traffic flow that would result from an excessive number of driveways. This policy is intended to enhance the opportunities for creating intra-block courts and walkways between properties and buildings.[67]

Carmel does have parking requirements, but developers in the central commercial district must pay fees in lieu of the required spaces; that is, Carmel simultaneously requires *and* prohibits off-street parking, and it collects in-lieu fees for the required-but-prohibited spaces. The city then uses the revenue to finance shared public parking spaces on the periphery of the downtown.[68] The *absence* of off-street parking helps make the center of Carmel one of the best places in America to be a pedestrian, and people from all over the world come to stroll its sidewalks.

Most cities will probably not want to prohibit *all* off-street parking in their centers, but they can take the intermediate step of taxing or prohibiting *surface* parking.[69] Restricting off-street surface parking to improve pedestrian ambience accords with the views of Berkeley professor of architecture Christopher Alexander, who argued that too much land for parking degrades the environment. In *A Pattern Language*, Alexander says:

> When the density of cars passes a certain limit, and people experience the feeling that there are too many cars, what is really happening is that subconsciously they feel that the cars are overwhelming the environment, and that the environment is not a place for people.... The effect of the cars reaches far beyond the mere presence of the cars themselves. They create a maze of driveways, garage doors, asphalt and concrete surfaces, and building elements which people cannot use. When the density goes beyond the limit, we suspect that people feel the social potential of the environment has disappeared.[70]

Alexander speculates that no more than 9 percent of the land should be devoted to parking, and most pedestrians probably do feel the less parking, the better. Many other designers have also deplored the deadening effects of excessive surface parking, and the few who embraced the automobile tended to ignore the parking problems their designs would cause. Le Corbusier and Frank Lloyd Wright, for example, usually illustrated tall buildings surrounded by parks, while in reality they were surrounded by parking lots.[71] In describing the enormous influence of Corbusier's highrise fantasies, architect Moshe Safdie says:

> In the *City of Tomorrow* (1929), Le Corbusier wrote, "The center of the great city is like a funnel into which every street shoots its traffic..." and concluded that, "wide avenues must be driven through the centers of our towns," presaging countless downtown highway projects carved right out of the historic meeting places of busy streets, commerce, and civic institutions. "We must create vast and sheltered public parking places where cars can be left during working hours," he suggested, enthusiastically describing one of the most widespread and drastic influences on the shape of cities for years to come. It would take

the passing of a full generation before a new group of younger architects...
came to appreciate that the Modern movement had entirely overlooked what
had been a fundamental component of urban life: the pedestrian.[72]

Much damage has to be undone, and limits on off-street parking are one
way to start.

Garage Door Restrictions

In its residential areas, Carmel has another simple but effective zoning
ordinance that reduces the impact of parking on the streetscape. If a house
has a garage that faces the street, the garage door cannot be wider than
one car.[73] As a result, garage doors cannot dominate the fronts of houses,
and the city therefore appears to be designed for people rather than for
cars. Figure 3-3 shows some of the resulting facades. The one-car garage
doors contribute to, rather than mar, the overall design of houses and the
street.

Other cities also have zoning provisions to improve the residential
garagescape. Olympia, Washington, requires that garage sidewalls facing
the street should appear as habitable space, through the use of windows
or other design elements. Portland, Oregon, limits the length of the garage
wall facing the street to no more than 50 percent of the entire building

**Figure 3-3. Carmel, California, requires that garage doors do not exceed
one car width**

facade.[74] New Jersey requires cities to calculate the number of off-street parking spaces in a way that reduces the garage frontage. A one-car garage and driveway combination count as two parking spaces if the length of the driveway is at least 18 feet between the face of the garage door and the right-of-way.[75] Developers can thus satisfy a two-space requirement with a one-car garage and cut by half the street frontage required for garage doors.

Parking Location Requirements

Restrictions on the location of parking can also improve the street frontage. Consider how the zoning ordinance in SeaTac, Washington, prevents parking lots from degrading the urban design and pedestrian ambience of commercial districts:

> No parking shall be located between the building and the front property line. On corner lots, no parking shall be located between the building and either of the two (2) front property lines.[76]

This requirement puts on-site parking spaces either beside or behind buildings, rather than in front.

In his PAS Report on how to prepare zoning ordinances, Charles Lerable shows how the placement of parking lots can influence, for better or for worse, the pedestrian quality of the streetscape (see Figure 3-4). In the top panel, the parking is placed between the building and the sidewalk, a common pattern for mini-malls and strip shopping centers. The middle panel shows the parking beside buildings, which reduces the amount of frontage devoted to parking but still leaves gaps between buildings. The bottom panel shows the parking lots placed behind buildings, so that the only gap between shops is the access to the parking.

Urban historian Richard Longstreth has written extensively about how cars and parking transformed commercial space in Los Angeles in the first half of the twentieth century.[77] Longstreth does not mention off-street parking requirements (Los Angeles did not begin to require off-street parking for commercial buildings until 1946), but he explains that merchants placed a high value on sidewalk orientation even as they voluntarily began to provide parking spaces. For this reason, developers commonly placed parking behind buildings:

> Wilshire Boulevard set the standard for countless smaller retail precincts of the region during the 1930s and 1940s. Planned shopping centers developed during this period maintained a sense of street-front drama by adhering to the pattern of showing facades and offering rear parking. Such complexes were often conceived and operated more as an agglomeration of stores than as a

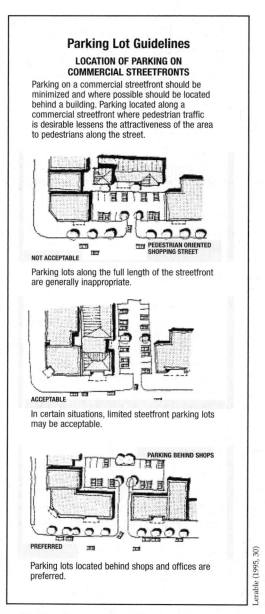

Parking Lot Guidelines

LOCATION OF PARKING ON COMMERCIAL STREETFRONTS

Parking on a commercial streetfront should be minimized and where possible should be located behind a building. Parking located along a commercial streetfront where pedestrian traffic is desirable lessens the attractiveness of the area to pedestrians along the street.

PEDESTRIAN ORIENTED SHOPPING STREET

NOT ACCEPTABLE

Parking lots along the full length of the streetfront are generally inappropriate.

ACCEPTABLE

In certain situations, limited steetfront parking lots may be acceptable.

PARKING BEHIND SHOPS

PREFERRED

Parking lots located behind shops and offices are preferred.

Lerable (1995, 30)

Figure 3-4. How parking lot placement can influence the pedestrian quality of streets

fully integrated facility. On the whole merchants showed a persistent reluctance to abandon their traditional sidewalk orientation. Food retailers whose supermarkets formed the anchor units of these centers were especially adamant on the matter.[78]

Los Angeles was not unique in this regard. University of Pennsylvania professor of urbanism Witold Rybczynski says that this rear-parking pattern was present in the earliest shopping centers that were developed as part of master-planned communities:

> Market Square [in Lake Forest, Illinois] and Country Club Plaza [in Kansas City, Missouri] consciously recalled small-town shopping districts in the intimate, almost domestic scale of their architecture and in their layouts—the stores faced the street and the parking lots were in the rear. This was not accidental. The developers of the shopping village were also the developers of the surrounding residential areas, and retail stores were designed to fit into the overall master plan.[79]

In outlying areas that were not part of a master plan, however, parking gradually migrated to the fronts of buildings. In 1937, Douglas Haskell observed in the *Architectural Record*, "Los Angeles appears to the casual view as a series of parking lots interspersed with buildings.... These parking lots are functionally as indispensable to the city as a car is to the citizen."[80] (The cars made the parking lots indispensable, and the parking lots, by spreading the city out, made the cars indispensable.) In 1951, two shopping center architects noted about Los Angeles, "A car has become as essential as a pair of shoes, with significant results upon business."[81] In his history of American roadside architecture, Chester Liebs says that strip developers started out by relying on curb parking, and then began setting buildings back a car length to provide perpendicular parking in front of the stores. They finally abandoned pedestrians to make life even more convenient for motorists; they paved vacant lots and put buildings at the rear of their property. "The long-standing tenet of Main Street commercial site planning—line the shops along the sidewalk with room for parking only at the curb—was finally cast aside."[82]

When parking is *behind* a building, pedestrians can see into the store windows as they walk by, and they can easily wander in. If parking is in *front* of a building, however, pedestrians cannot see what the store has to offer. Pedestrians must approach the store by walking through the parking lot, which is uninviting, even hazardous. If *all* parking is in front of buildings, few pedestrians have any reason to use the sidewalks. Duany,

Plater-Zyberk, and Speck say that placing the parking lot in front sends a rude message to the neighborhood:

> The presence of the parking lot in front of the building, in addition to damaging the pedestrian quality of the street, gives the signal that the store is oriented less toward its local neighbors than toward strangers driving by.[83]

With parking lots in front of every store, the important customers are drivers. Drawing pedestrians into a store is not an important goal because there are no pedestrians.

The location of residential parking can also be greatly improved. In Britain, the Department of the Environment's design guidelines recommend that off-street parking should not interrupt the street facades of housing and that cars should be parked either beside or behind residences. Moreover, off-street parking space should be designed for flexible uses so that it can be converted to a patio or garden if residents do not use it for parking.[84]

Cities would have continued adjusting to cars even without off-street parking requirements in zoning ordinances, but the advent of these requirements for a large parking supply at every site surely accelerated and exaggerated the migration of parking spaces from the rear to the front of buildings. Cities would be in much better shape today if urban planners had regulated the *location* rather than the *number* of off-street parking spaces during the last century.

Parking Structure Design Requirements

Drivers choose among parking spaces for their convenience, location, and price, not for their architectural style, urban design, or aesthetic fit into the neighborhood. Developers therefore often neglect the architecture of parking structures and instead make them as cheap as possible. For this reason, cities should regulate the design of parking structures to ensure that they do not disfigure the street. Only to the extent that the appearance of a parking structure increases the value of the residential or commercial building it serves will most developers voluntarily spend money to improve its design. Parking structures, even more than other buildings, need design review.

The blank walls of parking structures degrade the pedestrian ambience of a street, and the structures themselves are often ugly, although they needn't be if architects are given the chance to treat them like real buildings and not just a cheap way to store unneeded cars. Consider, for example, the new parking structure at the Milwaukee Art Museum, with its arches and clerestory windows; its architect, Santiago Calatrava, explained:

The parking lot is the place where 90 percent of the people arrive today. You have a right to expect quality from the earliest moment you enter the gate. I think any parking lot has the potential to be a place of welcoming, of gathering. We have to re-dignify such spaces.[85]

To improve the streetscape, some cities require parking structures to include retail space and architectural features facing the street. Consider this requirement in San Diego's CBD:

> All parking that is incidental and associated with a project shall be enclosed and architecturally integrated into the structure…. At least fifty percent (50%) of the street wall of any project or structured parking, excluding vehicular access areas, shall include street level [retail/commercial] uses.[86]

New Urbanist architect Peter Calthorpe has shown how parking structures with ground-floor retail can provide visual interest, safety, and shelter for pedestrians.[87] Some parking structures with street-level stores are so well designed that pedestrians don't even notice that they are parking structures, and the rent for the retail space exceeds the rent that would be earned by the same area of parking. Figure 3-5 shows two examples of parking structures that enhance rather than degrade the quality of life on the street.[88]

A step beyond including ground-floor retail is to "wrap" a parking structure with retail or other uses. This is particularly appropriate for transit-oriented developments, as ULI explains:

> In place of the typical suburban sea of surface parking, creative designers can wrap a parking structure with retail shops, eateries, residences, and services, such as dry cleaners. This mixed-use approach makes the parking structure more attractive as an urban place, allows people who park there to take care of errands, makes the walk to and from the parking lot more interesting, and creates a built-in clientele for the businesses.[89]

Some developers have shown how good parking design can greatly improve the appearance of a building, and Thomas Smith of PAS says many innovations in good parking design "have been pioneered by private developers without local requirements or incentives. A broader application of design improvements, however, will require local policies that are consistently applied."[90] Parking gives many people their first and last impression of a place, and planners can do much to improve these impressions. Cities should require better parking, not more parking. Planning for parking should become more of an art and less of a pseudoscience.

Figure 3-5. Parking Structures with Ground-Floor Uses

CONCLUSION: AN ELABORATE STRUCTURE
WITH NO FOUNDATION

Parking is the unstudied link between transportation and land use. Urban planners seem to assume parking requirements are a transportation issue, and transportation engineers must study them; after all, transportation engineers estimate the parking generation rates for each land use. Transportation engineers seem to assume parking requirements are a land-use issue and urban planners must study them; after all, urban planners set the parking requirements for each land use. As a result, no one is really responsible for off-street parking requirements.

Because off-street parking requirements produce free parking almost everywhere, they seem to work well, at least if free parking is the only goal. But all the required parking spaces disrupt the built fabric of the city, create underused parking lots everywhere, and degrade both the natural and the built environments. Even worse, parking requirements achieve this effect by hiding the cost of parking in higher prices for everything else. Admittedly, we all want to park free, but we also want to reduce traffic congestion, energy consumption, and air pollution. We also want affordable housing, efficient transportation, green space, good urban design, great cities, and a healthy economy. Unfortunately, ample free parking conflicts with all these other goals. If our real problem is too many cars rather than too few parking spaces, minimum parking requirements make everything much worse.

Off-street parking requirements are embedded in an elaborate structure of laws, permits, fees, variances, and political compromises. They have been incorporated into every city's zoning code and have been interpreted in many court cases.[91] These requirements have put the parking supply on automatic pilot: all new development routinely comes with abundant free parking, as if it were predestined, just as everything in the Emerald City looked green because everyone was required to wear green spectacles. Once planners set the requirements, they no longer have to think about the parking supply again. But these requirements do not emerge from strategic planning that considers urban design, land use, transportation, and the environment. Most planning for parking amounts to no more than a shopping list of requirements for every land use, and most research on parking amounts to little more than simple inventories. Off-street parking requirements are an elaborate structure with no foundation.

CHAPTER 3 NOTES

1. Williams and Taylor (1986, 4).

2. "Religious Rites Welcomed; Parking Rights are Thornier," *New York Times*, March 29, 2004. The controversy has led to a proposal to base the parking requirement for houses of worship on the maximum allowed occupancy of the largest room in the building, as determined by the Fire Department and the Department of Buildings. Orthodox Jews, who walk to synagogue on the Sabbath and holidays, have argued that they don't need any parking spaces.

3. In describing their study of parking requirements in Montgomery County, Maryland, for example, Steven Smith and Alexander Hekimian (1985, 36) say, "employee density is the most important variable in determining the peak parking demand for office buildings.... Serious difficulties exist, however, in predicting the total number of employees in advance (particularly for speculative multitenant buildings) and in assuring that those totals will not change significantly in the future. For those reasons, the study recommended a standard based on square footage."

4. An earlier survey by the Highway Research Board (1955, 20-22) found a similarly confusing array of parking requirements for funeral parlors. Almost every one of the 38 surveyed cities had a different requirement, and they had a few extra bases for the requirements not mentioned in the 1971 PAS report: assembly rooms, mortuaries, parlors for 100 or more persons, principal auditoriums, and slumber rooms. One city required a 30-foot setback for parking, and another city required 35 feet; rather than require the parking to be placed in back of the funeral parlors, the cities thus required it to be in front.

5. Cervero (1988).

6. Garreau (1991, 119). Parking must not only be ample but also convenient to satisfy some cities. Regarding a developer's request to put some spaces on the roof at a Lowe's home improvement store in Framingham, Massachusetts, for example, the Planning Board Vice Chairwoman expressed concern that many customers would "live park," meaning they would leave their cars running if they could not immediately find a parking space, rather than go all the way to the roof to find one. "The way people are," she said, "we know they'd drive through the front door if they could" (*MetroWest Daily News*, Framingham, Massachusetts, September 1, 2004).

7. ITE (1987a, 104).

8. Polanis and Price (1991, 32). The sample included 33 cities. The average parking requirement is 32 percent higher than the ITE parking generation rate.

9. See Appendix A. This parking requirement was for a 10,000-square-foot office building; the sample included 117 cities. The average parking requirement is 36 percent higher than the ITE parking generation rate.

10. Shaw (1997a, 37). This parking requirement was for a 10,000-square-foot office building; the sample included 71 cities. The average parking requirement is 43 percent higher than the ITE parking generation rate.

11. Gruen Associates (1986, pp. 4, 9, 14, and 30). The office parks were in the Philadelphia and San Francisco regions, and had an average occupancy rate of 87 percent. The average mode shares at the nine sites were 84.7 percent solo driver, 12.3 percent carpool/vanpool, 0.9 percent bike/motorcycle, 1.4 percent public transit, and 0.6 percent other. Eight of the nine parks reported that transit service was available within a five- to ten-minute walk of the site, but no firms in three of the parks encouraged transit use; 3 percent of the firms encouraged transit use in three of the parks; 42 percent of the firms encouraged transit use in one California park because of environmental protection regulations. Gruen's analysis of the parking data led to the conclusion that "a parking ratio of about 1.8 [spaces per 1,000 square feet] would provide an adequate number of parkwide space" to meet the peak demand for free parking (Gruen 1986, 15).

12. Transit Cooperative Research Program (2003b, 18-9). The average peak parking occupancy at the eight sites was 1.4 spaces per 1,000 square feet of occupied gross floor area.

13. Puget Sound Regional Council (2003, xi). Five earlier surveys between 1989 and 1999 found that the peak parking occupancy ranged between 73 percent and 80 percent of capacity in downtown Seattle, and between 56 percent and 64 percent in downtown Bellevue (Puget Sound Regional Council 2000, 6 and 28). Surveys at 36 employment sites in the Seattle region in 1991 found that the peak parking occupancy for office buildings was only 72 percent of capacity (Kadesh and Peterson 1994, 59).

14. Seattle Strategic Planning Office (2000, 14).

15. Gould (2003, 3). The surveys were conducted at 42 lots associated with 10 different land uses in 13 towns in Northwestern Connecticut.

16. Urban Land Institute (1999, 23).

17. Willson adjusted the observed parking occupancy upward to correspond with 95 percent building occupancy. For example, if the office-space occupancy was 50 percent, Willson multiplied the observed peak parking occupancy by 95/50 to estimate what the peak parking occupancy would be if the office-space occupancy were 95 percent.

18. Willson (1995, 32).

19. Willson (1995, 3)

20. Wormser (1997, 10).

21. Chicago Regional Transportation Authority (1998). It is sometimes assumed that chain stores demand more parking spaces than the zoning requires, but they often want to provide fewer. For a Wal-Mart SuperCenter in Michigan, for example, the parking requirement called for 1,016 spaces, but Wal-Mart applied for a variance to provide only 796 spaces, a 22 percent reduction ("Planning Commission Reviews Wal-Mart SuperCenter Site Plan," *Iosco County New-Herald*, September 9, 2003).

22. Levinson (1984a, 77). The average annual operating revenue was $373 per space, annual maintenance and operating costs were $246 per space, and annual debt service was $800 to $1,200 per new garage space. The average annual deficit therefore ranged from $673 to $1,073 per space. Levinson estimated that at 1983 cost levels, garage development expenses (land, construction, engineering, legal, and contingency costs) averaged $10,000 per space. He also assumed a 10 percent interest rate and a 30-year amortization period.

23. Car collectors require even more spaces. For example, Jay Leno uses three airplane hangers to store his collection of 80 cars and 60 motorcycles (Berg 2003, 42).

24. United Kingdom Department of the Environment, Transport, and the Regions (1998b, 5, 16, and 17). Blake (1999) summarizes the study.

25. Nozzi (2003, 50).

26. Whyte (1989, 54).

27. Section 59-E-3.7 of the Montgomery County Zoning Ordinance. Since there are at least 300 square feet per parking space in a parking lot, 83 parking spaces occupy at least 24,900 square feet. Perhaps 83 is a misprint for 8.3 parking spaces per 1,000 square feet, but it has been in the Montgomery County Zoning Ordinance for many years.

28. Hardwick (2004, 145). Southdale, designed by Victor Gruen, is in Edina, Minnesota.

29. Urban Land Institute (1982a, 12).

30. Urban Land Institute (1982a, 2). Italics added.

31. For example, the study found that the over half the spaces were vacant at least 40 percent of the time a shopping center is open for business (Urban Land Institute 1982a, 12). For shopping centers smaller than 600,000 square feet, the study found that the number of spaces required at the 20th-busiest hour is only 5 percent fewer than at the busiest hour (on the afternoon of the Saturday before Christmas). If the number of spaces required at the 20th-busiest hour is only 5 percent fewer than at the busiest hour, requiring enough spaces to satisfy the demand for parking during the 20th-busiest hour is almost the same as requiring them to satisfy the demand for free parking during the busiest hour of the year.

32. Wohl and Martin (1967, 176). Their critique of the design-hour criterion applied to all transportation facilities and was not specific to parking.

33. Urban Land Institute (1999).

34. Urban Land Institute (1999, 81). The 20th-busiest hour fell within this two-hour period at 69 percent of the shopping centers surveyed.

35. Urban Land Institute (1999, 25), italics added.

36. The Möbius strip is named after its inventor, August Möbius, a nineteenth century astronomer. If a belt-shaped loop is cut and rejoined after half a twist, one can travel along its entire surface without crossing an edge. M. C. Escher illustrated a Möbius strip with ants crawling endlessly along its surface.

37. Baum (1903, 147-148; 160-161).

38. Baum (1903, 152). No one should blame planners for dispensing the elixir of plenteous free parking because everyone wants to park free, and planners are under tremendous pressure to solve the problem of spillover. Nevertheless, planners can be faulted for their pretension to special skills in dealing with parking.

39. Langley, Ryerson, and Woolf (1989, 121).

40. Baum (1910). Baum wasn't always consistent, however. When Dorothy asked the Wizard to send her back to Kansas, he replied, "You have no right to expect me to send you back to Kansas unless you do something for me in return. In this country everyone must pay for everything he gets" (Baum 1903, 98). So perhaps the Wizard would have recommended charging for curb parking.

41. Langley, Ryerson, and Woolf (1989, 70).

42. The Parking Consultants Council (1992, 4) says, "In the past, parking ratios tended to be stated as one space for each xxx square feet. However, most groups in the industry now prefer to use a ratio stated as xx spaces per 1,000 square feet. It is simply easier for the average person to multiply than to divide." Putting the number of square feet in the denominator makes comparisons of parking requirements difficult and confusing. For example, in discussing how planning regulations affect land consumption, urban planning professors Emily Talen and Gerrit Knapp (2003, 354) say, "Parking requirements of one space per two [sic] 200 square feet (for cities) and one space per 250 square feet [for counties] of retail fall below the optimal parking requirement of one space per 300 square feet of retail area." But a requirement of one space per 200 square feet (5 spaces per 1,000 square feet) is 50 percent *above* a requirement of one space per 300 square feet (3.3 spaces per 1,000 square feet), not below it.

43. Langley, Ryerson, and Woolf (1989, 122). The Pythagorean Theorem states that the sum of the squares of the lengths of the two sides of a right triangle is equal to the square of the length of the hypotenuse.

44. If a parking space occupies 300 square feet (a conservative estimate), requiring one parking space per 50 square feet of dining area devotes six times more area to parking than to dining (300 ÷ 50). The parking requirement for a restaurant in Beverly Hills, California, for example, is 1 space per 45 square feet of dining area (see Chapter 9).

45. Willson (1995) and Chicago Regional Transportation Authority (1998).

46. The case was considered on February 19, 2003. In some cases a large building may have one or two extra parking spaces, but this is only because the design of the parking structure happens to produce them. For example, a second level of underground parking may be necessary to meet the parking requirement for a large building, and it may also provide a few more spaces than required.

47. The case was considered on June 8, 2003. The housing floor area is only 67 percent of the total allowed by the floor-area ratio in the zoning.

48. Personal communication from Lawrence Solomon on July 28, 2001.

49. Parking is an "intermodal facility" because it allows travelers to change travel modes—between driving and walking—and this intermodal quality has occasionally been used to justify federal subsidies for local parking structures. These subsidies are, however, more the result of pork barrel politics than of deliberate transportation policy.

50. Oregon Administrative Rules, section 660-012-0045. The rule is available online at http://arcweb.sos.state.or.us/banners/rules.htm. New Jersey mandates statewide parking requirements: cities cannot set minimum parking requirements either above or below the statewide standard. For example, the requirement for garden apartments is 1.8 spaces per one-bedroom apartment, 2 spaces per two-bedroom apartment, and 2.1 spaces per three-bedroom apartment (Table 4.4 of the New Jersey Residential Site Improvement Standards). Unfortunately, New Jersey's statewide requirements seem just as arbitrary as those in any local zoning code.

51. Section 3.07.210 of the Portland Metro code. The Urban Growth Management Functional Plan is available online at www.metro-region.org/library_docs/about/chap307.pdf.

52. United Kingdom Department of the Environment, Transport, and the Regions (1998a, paragraph 52).

53. Still and Simmonds (2000, 302 and 313).

54. A regionwide maximum for cities' minimum parking requirements is different from a cap on the number of parking spaces allowed. Another regional policy, therefore, would be a regionwide cap on the number of parking spaces each land use can provide. There is, however, probably as little analysis to justify specific parking caps as there is to justify the specific parking minimums, and the parking caps may, by default, become the parking minimums for many developments. Nevertheless, parking caps make far more sense than minimum parking requirements as a planning policy.

55. Forinash et al. (2004) explain how parking lots reduce the attractiveness of walking and biking by increasing the distances between activities and by creating unattractive routes. Free parking reduces the potential for public transit by attracting travelers to cars and by reducing the density of development.

56. Levine and Garb (2002, 179).

57. Cervero (1996, 19).

58. In this example the developer will voluntarily provide 4 spaces per 1,000 square feet only if parking spaces cost about $12,500 each in the first case, and about $2,500 each in the second case.

59. Santa Monica, California, has a typical grandfather clause for its parking requirements: "Any existing lawful use may continue so long as the number of off-street parking spaces provided for the use is not reduced below the requirements of this Part or below the number of off-street parking spaces required at the time the use was legally established, whichever is less" (Santa Monica Municipal Code Section 9.04.10.08.030b).

60. The change-of-use policies were identified in a survey of parking requirements in 117 Southern California cities (see Appendix A). When I telephoned the cities' planning departments, many planners simply did not know how to answer the question about the number of parking spaces required when a land use changes and could produce no written policy. Nevertheless, the logic of parking requirements forces cities to face this issue. Without a change-of-use policy, a developer could say that a new building will be used as, for example, a furniture store for which the city requires 1 space per 1,000 square feet, and then, without adding any parking, convert it into a restaurant for which the city requires 10 spaces per 1,000 square feet.

61. Reed (1984, 2).

62. Long Beach, California, requires 1 space per 1,000 square feet for warehouses and 3 spaces per 1,000 square feet for research laboratories.

63. Thomas Smith (1988) reports on zoning for the design of parking lots and structures.

64. Duany, Plater-Zyberk, and Speck (2000, 19 and 176).

65. Thomas Smith (1988, 2 and 5).

66. Adams (2003, 26).

67. Section 17.34.030A of the Carmel-by-the-Sea Municipal Code.

68. Chapter 9 explains the in-lieu parking fees in Carmel and other cities.

69. Vancouver, British Columbia, prohibits off-street surface parking in its regional town centers. Cervero (1998, 425) says the prohibition of surface parking and the high cost of structured and underground parking in the town centers have led some developers to orient their projects to take advantage of their proximity to public transit. Eran Feitelson and Orit Rotem (2004) propose taxing surface parking spaces to internalize their external costs.

70. Alexander, Ishikawa, and Silverstein (1977, 122).

71. In *The Radiant City*, Le Corbusier (1967) exalted the car in urban life but neglected to mention that cars need somewhere to park.

72. Safdie (1997, 18-19).

73. "On sites of less than 6,000 square feet, only a single-car width garage door shall face the street" (Section 17.24.120C of the Carmel-by-the Sea Municipal Code).

74. Jason Wittenberg (2002) discusses zoning requirements for the design of residential garages.

75. Section 5:21-4.14(d)(2) of the New Jersey Administrative Code (Residential Site Improvement Standards).

76. Section 15.13.110 A (4a) of the SeaTac Municipal Code. The City of SeaTac is adjacent to the Seattle-Tacoma International Airport in Washington.

77. See Longstreth (1992, 1997, and 1999).

78. Longstreth (1992, 152).

79. Rybczynski (1995, 205).

80. Haskell (1937, 19).

81. Hardwick (2004, 95).

82. Liebs (1985, 14).

83. Duany, Plater-Zyberk, and Speck (2000, 27). Not everyone is so critical. Consider this optimistic description of parking lots in *Learning from Las Vegas*: "The A&P parking lot is the current phase in the evolution of vast space since Versailles.... The parking lot is the *parterre* of the asphalt landscape. The patterns of parking lines give direction much as the paving patterns, curbs, borders, and *tapis vert* give direction in Versailles; grids of lamp posts substitute for obelisks, rows of urns, and statues as points of identity and continuity in the vast space" (Venturi, Scott Brown and Izenour 1986, 13).

84. Stubbs (2002, 217). In the U.S., cities often prohibit owners from converting off-street parking spaces to other uses. Los Angeles, for example, requires that off-street residential parking spaces must be covered, as in garages.

85. "Parking Garages Need their Share of Architectural Beauty Too," *Milwaukee Journal Sentinel*, October 27, 2002.

86. Chapter 10, Article 3, Division 19 of the San Diego Municipal Code, available online at http://clerkdoc.sannet.gov/legtrain/mc/MuniCodeChapter10/Ch10Art03Division19.1.

87. Calthorpe (1993, 112).

88. The structure on the left is in Beverly Hills and the structure on the right is in Westwood Village in Los Angeles.

89. Dunphy, Myerson, and Pawlukiewicz (2003, 11). An award-winning parking structure at 15th and Pearl Streets in Boulder, Colorado, for example, is wrapped with ground-floor retail and upper-floor offices (*New Urban News*, December 2003, 13). Other proposals about parking design are also promising. Neal Payton (1993) recommends several ways to improve parking architecture—hiding it (as with underground parking), decorating it (as with the structures in Figure 3-8), or screening it (landscaping can help). M. J. P. Smith (1988, 58 and 63) says that parked cars in any quantity are an affront to the eye. "Their 'inorganic,' roachlike glossiness might account for this.... Simply put, cars in motion *live*. Parked, however, they die. Robbed of its vitalizing motion, the car becomes, if only temporarily, a corpse; masses of cars a necropolis.... Where parked cars are concerned, a little visual hypocrisy is kinder than the wretched functional truth. If we must have these sepulchres, then by all means let them be whited ones." Masello (1988, 79) describes the high quality of the architectural design of early parking structures in New York City and says, "since style and expression no longer seem to be important to garage design, the best place for parking may indeed be underground." Berkeley professor of architecture and geography Paul Groth (1990, 137) suggests that in parking lots, "designers might use the automobiles themselves as units of design: we might point them toward Detroit, perhaps, or toward the Middle Eastern oil fields."

90. Thomas Smith (1988, 33).

91. Williams and Taylor (1986, 8) say that a 60-page legal decision on the constitutional validity of off-street parking requirements is the longest decision in American planning law.

4

An Analogy: Ancient Astronomy

No version of the system ever quite withstood the test of additional refined observations.

— THOMAS KUHN

Astronomers once believed the earth stood motionless at the center of the universe and everything else revolved around it. This geocentric theory accurately predicted the motion of all the stars as seen by someone on earth, but the planets seemed to wander aimlessly through the night sky—"planet" stems from the Greek for "wanderer." Ptolemy, a Greek astronomer who lived in Egypt during the second century A.D., devised an ingenious hypothesis to account for the planets' strange behavior. Harvard historian of astronomy Owen Gingerich describes the puzzle to be solved:

> The problem at hand, already posed by Plato to his students, was finding some explanation for the windings to and fro of the planets. We can take as a prototype the behavior of Mars. This ruddy and not very bright planet moves eastward throughout the zodiacal signs for months on end, but then it slows, comes to a stop against the background stars, brightens, and, now quite conspicuous, moves westward for several weeks before stopping, fading, and finally resuming its direct motion. How could this retrograde motion be accounted for?[1]

Ptolemy surmised that each planet orbited in an "epicycle," a small circle whose center (the epicenter) moved on the circumference of a larger circle (the deferent) whose center was slightly offset from the earth. While fundamentally wrong, this model explained (at least approximately) the observed motions of the planets, and it dominated scientific thinking for more than a thousand years. Even with this

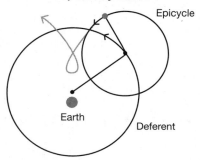

Figure 4-1. Ptolemy's model of planetary motion

Epicycle

Earth

Deferent

convoluted fix for the geocentric theory, however, astronomers could not accurately predict planetary motion. In describing the astronomers' dilemma, Princeton historian of science Thomas Kuhn said that even as the model grew increasingly complex, its predictions were never correct:

> Accuracy was invariably achieved at the price of complexity...and the increased complexity gave only a better approximation to planetary motion, not finality. No version of the system ever quite withstood the test of additional refined observations.[2]

Urban planners face a similar dilemma in predicting the demand for parking as a function of land use: their theory is based on false assumptions. The most obviously false assumption is that price does not affect demand. Planners fail to make the connection between parking prices and parking occupancy, and as a result they cannot accurately predict parking demand.

A PARALLEL UNIVERSE

Planners have made some progress in predicting the demand for parking as a function of land use, but it resembles the ancient astronomers' attempts to predict the motion of planets. Planners have devised increasingly complex rules and regulations, a patchwork of fixes. For example, over the years they have devised more requirements for more land uses. The Planning Advisory Service's first survey of parking requirements in 1964 reported requirements for 30 different land uses. Its second survey only seven years later reported 83 land uses. The third survey in 1991 reported 179 land uses, while the most recent survey in 2002 reported a staggering 662 land uses (ranging from abattoir to zoo).[3] The number of land uses with parking requirements more than doubled with each succeeding survey. Planners have also invented many pseudoscientific terms to describe poorly understood parking phenomena: *parkability, parking deficit, parking generation, parking intensity, parking ratio, peak parking factor, replacement parking, spillover parking,* and *underparked.*

The growing complexity extends far beyond more requirements for more land uses. Some cities allow shared parking for combinations of uses whose peak parking demands occur at different times.[4] Some cities allow valet and tandem parking to reduce the space needed for parked cars. All cities grant parking variances—the planner's version of epicycles—whenever administrative or political considerations call for them. This complexity stems more from confusion than from careful calculation, and it arouses the suspicion that planners have misdiagnosed the problem.

Simple answers to complex questions are often wrong. But in the case of parking requirements, we have wildly complex answers to a simple question: how many parking spaces do we need? The real estate market can supply as many parking spaces as drivers are willing to pay for, but cities impose a panoply of parking requirements for all land uses.

THE MUDDLE IS THE MESSAGE

Planners cannot even agree on whether to *require* or *restrict* off-street parking. Consider the diametrically opposed approaches in the Los Angeles and San Francisco Central Business Districts (CBDs): Los Angeles requires parking, while San Francisco restricts it. For a concert hall, Los Angeles requires, as a minimum, 50 times more parking spaces than San Francisco allows as the maximum.[5] This difference in planning helps to explain why downtown San Francisco is much more exciting and livable than downtown Los Angeles. The confusion about whether to require or restrict parking even occurs within the same city. London changed its parking policies in the 1960s in response to recommendations in the 1963 Buchanan Report, *Traffic in Towns*, which criticized minimum parking requirements:

> Present policies need re-examination to ensure that traffic difficulties are not being 'built in' by the provision of too much parking space in the wrong position, and that owners and developers are not being burdened with liabilities which are not really for them to carry.[6]

When London began to restrict off-street parking in the late 1960s, the new maximum number of parking spaces allowed was less than half the former minimum number of spaces required.[7]

Despite their ambivalence about whether to require or restrict parking, planners always regulate it. This behavior recalls a Soviet maxim: What is not required must be prohibited.[8] American cities put a floor under the parking supply to satisfy the peak demand for free parking, and then cap development density to limit vehicle trips. European cities, in contrast, often cap the number of parking spaces to avoid congesting the roads and combine this strategy with a floor on allowed development density to encourage walking, cycling, and public transport. That is, Americans require parking and limit density, while Europeans require density and limit parking. When combined with complaints about traffic congestion and calls for smart growth, the American policy looks exceptionally foolish.

A few American cities—Boston, New York, and San Francisco—do limit parking in their downtowns, but even these cities require parking every-where else. If parking caps *reduce* vehicle trips, parking requirements surely *increase* them. If we want to reduce traffic congestion, energy con-sumption, and air pollution, the simplest and most productive single reform of American zoning would be to declare that all the existing off-street parking requirements are maximums rather than minimums, with-out changing any of the numbers, just as the London Borough of Kensington and Chelsea did in 1995.[9] From that point we can let the mar-ket take care of parking, and let city planners take care of the many vital issues that really demand their attention.

Developers may worry that lenders will refuse to finance projects that have reduced parking, but in his Urban Land Institute guide to real estate development, Harvard planning professor Richard Peiser says, "lower parking requirements can save money, and lenders will still provide financing if all developers are subject to the same restrictions."[10] Lenders may be unwilling to finance an *individual* development that has reduced parking if all the competition has plentiful parking, but if *all* develop-ments must provide reduced parking, developers can save money with-out being put at a competitive disadvantage.

Planning consultant Victor Dover says, "Parking is a narcotic and ought to be a controlled substance. It is addictive, and one can never have enough."[11] Parking *is* highly controlled in the U.S., but not in the way Dover intended: most cities require parking rather than restrict it. Nevertheless, planners cannot agree on how many spaces they should require. To examine the variation in parking requirements, John Cook et al. surveyed 49 cities in the San Francisco Bay Area and calculated the number of parking spaces each city required for several building types.[12] The number of parking spaces required for a typical hospital, for exam-ple, ranged between 29 and 1,682 spaces; that is, for identical hospitals, the highest parking requirement was 58 times the lowest. The variation in requirements among the 49 cities was unrelated to the cities' population density or total population. Nothing appeared to explain the variation in parking requirements.[13]

When planners in the surveyed cities were asked how the city arrived at its requirements, 70 percent of the respondents did not know the answer or made a guess. Cook et al. concluded that planners give little thought to parking requirements:

> We found it surprising that few people with whom we spoke could identify the reasoning behind the policies they are charged with enforcing on a daily basis. This underscores the extent to which parking policies are given little attention by zoning and planning staff members.[14]

This confusion about parking requirements is widespread. After conducting a survey of the requirements in English cities, Simon Haworth and Ian Hilton commented on the wide variation in standards imposed by authorities for the same type of development:

> Not only are the standards numerically different, but they are frequently calculated by different authorities on different bases, commonly employment or floor area. Some use gross leasable area for shops, others retail sales area. With no agreement on the bases of standards and so much variation in their numerical values, problems and confusion are inevitable.[15]

An unsuspecting observer would never guess how groundless most parking requirements are. Each specific requirement—considered in isolation—may seem reasonable. Only by looking behind the pretentious facade can one see that the whole system of requirements is a house of cards. Describing other policy failures, MIT planning professor Donald Schön said:

> Some of the solutions advocated by professional experts were seen as having created problems as bad as or worse than those which they had been designed to solve.... The most promising solutions, painstakingly worked out and advocated by the experts, came to be seen as problematic. They were ineffective, they created new problems, and they were derived from theories which had been shown to be fragile and incomplete.[16]

Schön might as well be describing minimum parking requirements, which stem from the presumption that parking is a problem only when there isn't enough of it. Fragile and incomplete theory helps explain why most cities now require more space for cars than for people at restaurants, office buildings, and many other land uses. Whatever the problem, more parking always seems to be the default solution, but more parking, unfortunately, has become a problem in itself.

Planners are not the only people confused about parking policies, as shown by a recent European study. Representatives of business organizations in Athens, Como, Dresden, and Oslo were surveyed about their perceptions of urban mobility problems in their cities. The study concluded, "business representatives see urban transport as suffering from severe problems, in particular a lack of parking space, congestion, air pollution, and inadequacy of public transport."[17] The business representatives apparently saw no contradiction between providing more parking and solving the problems of congestion, air pollution, and the inadequacy of public transport.

By comparing planning for parking to ancient astronomy, I am criticizing parking requirements, not urban planners. The early astronomers were diligent scientists, but they made a mistake in thinking that the universe revolves around the earth. Similarly, most urban planners are dedicated public servants, but they make a mistake in thinking that cities revolve around parking. One big difference does separate the two professions: the astronomers' flawed theory did not harm anyone, but flawed parking requirements harm everyone. Parking requirements began as a solution but have become a problem.

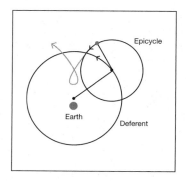

CHAPTER 4 NOTES

1. Gingerich (1993, 8).

2. Kuhn (1957, 74).

3. Planning Advisory Service (1964, 1971, 1991, 2002). The 1964 survey found 368 different requirements for 30 different land uses. Its second survey only seven years later found 609 different requirements for 83 different land uses. The 1991 survey found 648 different requirements for 179 land uses, but this greatly understates the growth in the number of different requirements after 1971. The 1964 and 1971 surveys reported every requirement found for each land use, but the 1991 and 2002 surveys reported only a selection of the many different requirements found for each land use. In 2002, PAS surveyed the parking requirements in only 15 cities, and a larger sample would undoubtedly have discovered many more land uses for which cities require parking.

4. Shared or joint-use parking refers to a situation in which two or more different land uses (an office building and a movie theater, for example) share a common parking supply. If the peak occupancies for the different uses occur at different times, a smaller parking supply can satisfy the peak demand for the shared uses than if the parking were supplied separately for each use. Cities allow shared parking only for a development where parkers are willing to walk to all uses from most points in the parking lot or structure. Cities usually require developers to provide an elaborate study to justify reducing the parking requirements for shared uses. In a survey of 204 cities and counties in Illinois, Talen and Knapp (2003) found that only 11 percent reduced parking requirements if the parking spaces are shared; that is, most cities do *not* reduce the parking requirements when different land uses share their parking spaces.

5. San Francisco allows as a maximum no more than 2 percent of the parking spaces that Los Angeles requires as a minimum. For a concert hall in the CBD, Los Angeles requires a minimum of 10 parking spaces per 1,000 square feet, with no maximum. San Francisco allows parking spaces equal to a maximum of 7 percent of building area (0.2 spaces per 1,000 square feet if a parking space occupies 350 square feet), with no minimum. For office buildings in the CBD, Los Angeles requires a minimum of 1 parking space per 1,000 square feet, with no maximum. San Francisco allows parking spaces equal to a maximum of 7 percent of building area, with no minimum. If some physicians prescribed bloodletting and others prescribed blood transfusion to treat the same disease, everybody would demand to know what is going on. But when city planners do essentially the same thing, nobody questions the contradiction.

6. United Kingdom Ministry of Transport (1963, 195).

7. Collins and Pharoah (1974, 477) show that, for offices in the central district in 1968, the *minimum* parking requirement was 1 space per 2,000 square feet; in 1969 the new *maximum* was 1 space per 5,000 to 12,000 square feet, depending on location. See also Thomson (1977, 280), Bayliss (1999, 27), and May (1975, 228).

8. Planners recommend either minimum parking requirements or maximum parking limits, but rarely consider the middle ground of laissez faire. As Vinit Mukija (2003, 9-10) says about changes in housing policies, reforms are often "based on doing the opposite of what is believed to have failed. There is no empirical evidence to substantiate that the opposite will work, or that it is the best and only alternative."

9. Stubbs (2002, 223). The land use plan of Kensington and Chelsea is available online at www.rbkc.gov.uk/planning/unitarydevelopmentplan/.

10. Peiser (2003, 224).

11. See "A Collection of Urban Design Quotes," available online at http://user.gru.net/domz/quaoes.htm.

12. Cook et al. (1997) found that the 49 cities based their parking requirement for hospitals on four factors—gross floor area, beds, doctors, and nonphysician employees—but different cities used different factors or different combinations of the factors. Cook et al. examined how parking requirements varied among cities by calculating how many parking spaces each city required for a prototypical hospital (336,430 gross square feet, 228 beds, 106 doctors, and 455 other employees). These measurements were taken from an actual hospital at 2425 Geary Boulevard in San Francisco. Different cities' parking requirements for the same land use also vary greatly in other regions. The Washington State Department of Transportation (1999, 27) reports that for a 100,000-square-foot manufacturing establishment with 50 employees, cities' parking requirements range from a low of 13 parking spaces (1 per 4 employees) to a high of 500 spaces (5 per 1,000 square feet); that is, for an identical manufacturing plant, the highest parking requirement was 38 times the lowest.

13. Cook et al. (1997, 26-27). Perhaps, as the Tin Woodman explained, "laws were never meant to be understood, and it is foolish to make the attempt."

14. Cook et al. (1997, 31).

15. Haworth and Hilton (1981, 87).

16. Schön (1983, 10).

17. Government Institute for Economic Research (2001, vi).

CHAPTER

5

A Great Planning Disaster

To know our disease, to discover what we suffer from, may itself be the only possible cure.

— *DANIEL BOORSTIN*

In his book *Great Planning Disasters*, Peter Hall defined a great planning disaster as a planning process that costs a lot of money and has gone seriously wrong. Urban renewal and high-rise public housing are classic examples.[1] But many things in life cost a lot of money and go seriously wrong, so how does a great *planning* disaster differ from a great moviemaking disaster, for example, or a great catering disaster? One major difference is that individual investors, producers, or caterers bear the cost of their disasters. With a great planning disaster, almost everyone loses something.

Few people now recognize parking requirements as a disaster because the costs are hidden and the harm is diffused. This chapter will show that parking requirements cause great harm: they subsidize cars, distort transportation choices, warp urban form, increase housing costs, burden low-income households, debase urban design, damage the economy, and degrade the environment. Chapters 6 and 7 will then show that off-street parking requirements also cost a lot of money, although this cost is hidden in higher prices for everything except parking itself. Off-street parking requirements thus have all the hallmarks of a great planning disaster.

Parking requirements seem like a minor matter, but even small disturbances to complex systems sometimes produce disastrous effects. Urban planners have not *caused* this disaster, of course, because off-street parking requirements result from the interplay of complicated political and market forces. Nevertheless, planners provide a veneer of professional language that serves to justify parking requirements, and in this way planners unintentionally *contribute* to the disaster.

BUNDLED PARKING AND THE DECISION TO DRIVE

Each person plays many different roles in life—tenant, homeowner, worker, consumer, investor, and motorist. We pay for parking in all these roles except, usually, as motorists. Because we pay for parking indirectly, its cost does not deter us from driving. Off-street parking requirements "externalize" the cost of parking by shifting it to everyone but the parker. Only when we pay for parking directly does its cost affect our decisions on whether to drive for particular trips.

To make this point clear, consider what would happen if cities required landlords to include the cost of electricity in the rent for housing. Although tenants would pay for electricity indirectly, it would appear free to them. They would buy and use refrigerators, air conditioners, and other appliances without thinking about the cost of electricity. Faulty regulation by the city—rather than bad behavior by landlords or tenants— would cause this profligate waste.

Suppose also that a shortage of electricity suddenly developed—with rolling blackouts and economic disruption. An obvious reform would be to separate the cost of electricity from the rent for housing. This *unbundling* would make residents aware of the cost of electricity, which would begin to influence their decisions about buying and using electric appliances. A further reform would be to vary the price of electricity by the time of day, so that residents would shift their consumption from peak periods when demand is high to off-peak periods when demand is low.

Cities do not, of course, require landlords to include the cost of electricity in the rent for housing. In reality, many building codes require an individual electric meter for each apartment (rather than one master meter for the whole building) to discourage waste. But cities *do* require an ample supply of parking spaces for every building, and this saves everyone the trouble of thinking about parking and its cost. Parking appears free because its cost is widely dispersed in slightly higher prices for everything else. Because we buy and use cars without thinking about the cost of parking, we congest traffic, waste fuel, and pollute the air more than we would if we each paid for our own parking. Everyone parks free at everyone else's expense, and we all enjoy our free parking, but our cars are choking our cities.

DISTORTED URBAN FORM

Although parking is a passive part of the transportation system, it strongly affects trip generation, mode choice, land use, urban design, and urban form. Even without parking requirements, cars would have reshaped cities during the past century, because they greatly reduce the time and monetary cost of travel. The lower cost of travel has reduced urban density and the demand for public transit. Reductions in transit service further increase the demand for cars, and the cycle continues. Parking requirements do not *cause* this cumulative process, but by ensuring that parking remains free they have exacerbated it (see Figure 5-1).

Charging drivers directly for the cost of their parking would have slowed the increase in vehicle ownership, but parking requirements have severed the link between the cost of providing a parking space and the price that drivers pay for it. Cities respond to increasing vehicle travel and declining density by increasing their parking requirements. When citizens then object to the resulting traffic congestion, cities respond by

Figure 5-1. Off-street Parking Requirements Accelerate Urban Sprawl

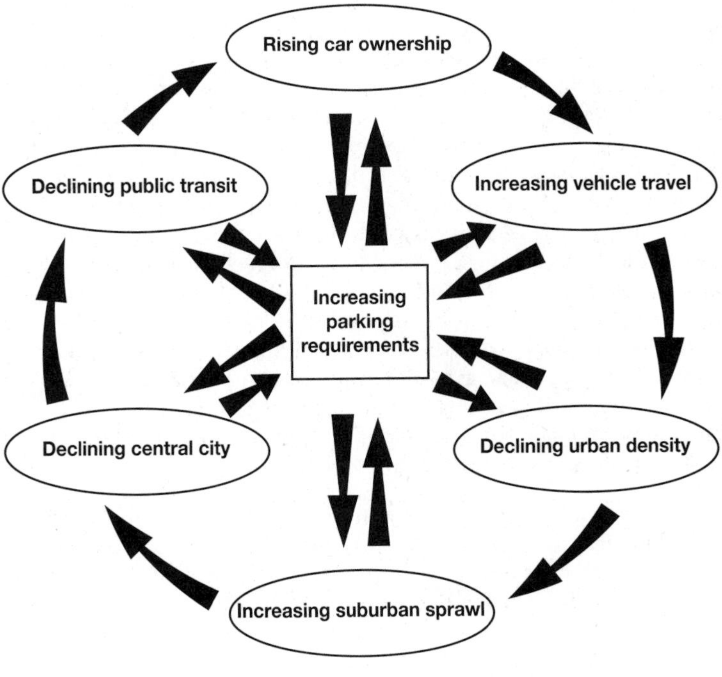

restricting development density and requiring even more on-site parking. The increased travel distances increase the need for cars for most trips, and the increased car ownership further inflames the opposition to charging for parking. Almost like a religion, parking requirements are expected to solve the problems they create. When establishing the requirements, neither planners nor politicians seem to realize that there is a price to pay. Beyond the high cost of providing the free parking, the requirements disfigure urban design and the free parking accelerates sprawl; that is, the city forces people to subsidize cars, and it then limits the density of people to limit the density of cars. Cars have replaced people as zoning's real concern, and free parking has become the arbiter of urban form, with serious consequences that extend far beyond parking itself. Off-street parking requirements produce the free parking that everyone wants, but this free parking helps explain why our cities sprawl on a scale fit more for cars than for people.

Off-street parking requirements help explain why Americans now make 87 percent of all their trips by personal motor vehicle.[2] If even most short trips are made by car, parking lots have to be everywhere. And with ubiquitous free parking, we have a cheap, convenient, direct, sedentary connection to almost every point in the city, so long as the roads aren't congested. Public transportation increases the number and variety of destinations that pedestrians can reach, but parking requirements reduce pedestrian access. No wonder we rarely walk anywhere.

Parking requirements create winners and losers: drivers win and everyone else loses. More accurately, people win in their role as drivers, and they lose in all their other roles. But people who don't own cars don't organize to change the system. Instead, most of them change their behavior to join the winners. More people buy cars, cities increase their parking requirements, and the system becomes ever more difficult to reform. Because cities sprawl faster and farther, cars become necessary for almost every errand. Even those who prefer a less automobile-dependent lifestyle find themselves in the motoring majority, driving everywhere, cursing congestion, staring at taillights, inhaling exhaust, and expecting to park free when they get wherever they are going.

Older cities have also been reshaped to satisfy the demand for free parking. William Whyte explained this process:

> In some American cities, so much of the center has been cleared to make way for parking that there is more parking than there is city. Some cities, such as Topeka, Kansas, have gone so far as to reach a tipping point. If they clear away any more of what's left, there would not be much reason to go there and park.[3]

The Topeka example is telling: by reducing a location's appeal, increasing the parking supply can reduce parking demand until supply and demand eventually come into equilibrium. In explaining the theory of New Urbanism, architects Andres Duany, Elizabeth Plater-Zyberk, and Jeff Speck also describe how providing too much parking damages older cities:

> There is a point at which a city can satisfy its parking needs. This situation can be found in many small, older American cities and is almost always the result of the same history: at mid-century, with automobile ownership on the rise, a charming old downtown with a wonderful pedestrian realm finds itself in need of more parking spaces. It tears down a few historic buildings and replaces them with surface parking lots, making the downtown both easier to park in and less pleasant to walk through. As more people drive, it tears down a few more buildings, with the same result. Eventually, what remains of the old downtown becomes unpleasant enough to undermine the desire to visit, and the demand for parking is easily satisfied by the supply.[4]

You don't go somewhere to park your car; you go there because you want to be there, and large parking lots in an area reduce the desire to be there.

Where parking requirements work as intended, they do "solve" the parking problem, but they also create many other problems. We not only pay for off-street parking, but we also have to *look* at it. In his book on parking as public space, Mark Childs illustrates this problem with a plan of downtown Albuquerque, New Mexico, which devotes more land to parking than to all other land uses combined (see Figure 5-2).[5] The long distances between widely spaced buildings encourage driving, while the need to dodge cars and avoid tripping over the wheel stops in parking lots make walking less enjoyable. A study in Buffalo, New York, also found that half the downtown is devoted to parking.[6] One of the authors explained, "If our master plan is to demolish all of downtown, then we're only halfway there. If you look very closely, there are still some buildings that are standing in the way of parking progress." Commenting on plans for expanding the downtown parking supply, a Buffalo City Council member said, "There will be lots of places to park. There just won't be a whole lot to do here." Another civic leader noted, "It should be very clear that downtown doesn't have a parking problem. It has a planning problem." And describing an aerial view of downtown Oakland, California, landscape architect Lawrence Halperin said, "At least half of this valuable area is devoted to streets and parking lots which intrude like cavities in the fabric of the city."[7]

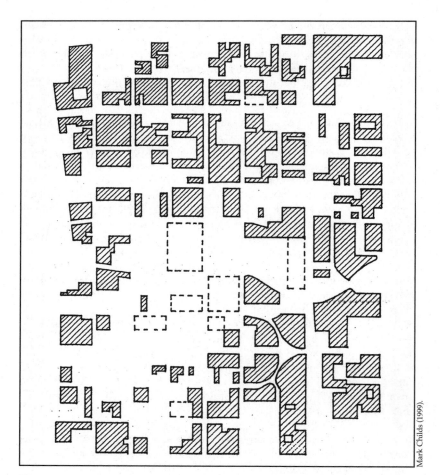

Mark Childs (1999).

Figure 5-2. This plan of downtown Albuquerque, New Mexico, shows surface parking lots as hatched areas and major parking garages as dashed boxes. On-street parking and small garages are not shown. The remainder of the plan (the white area) shows streets, sidewalks, and all the off-street area that is not devoted to parking.

Some insects, such as cicadas, periodically appear in such enormous numbers that enough survivors are left to breed and multiply even after all the potential predators have gorged themselves—an evolutionary strategy called *predator satiation*. Similarly, if planners require enough parking spaces, all potential drivers can park free even at the time of peak demand—a policy we can call *parking satiation*. Everyone can park free everywhere because parking requirements keep the parking supply high enough and zoning keeps the human density low enough.[8]

The parking requirements themselves reduce human density in two important ways. First, land that could have been used for housing is taken for parking instead. Second, the high cost of providing the required parking often restrains development to less floor area than the zoning otherwise allows. In their book, *American Planning Law*, Norman Williams and John Taylor explain that what gets developed is usually what the parking requirements will allow:

> In suburban areas and the outer parts of large cities, [parking] requirements (particularly for retail development) are often more restrictive than the bulk requirements (by floor area ratio or otherwise)… so in such areas it is the parking requirements which actually control the bulk of buildings used for retail purposes.[9]

In his *Guide to California Planning*, William Fulton also explains how parking squeezes out housing and alters land uses:

> Take the example of a high-density apartment project in an area that's already built-up. Let's say that the property is zoned for 30 apartment units per acre. Theoretically, building a 30-unit apartment building on a piece of land already zoned for such a project should be easy. However, most zoning ordinances require two off-street parking spaces per unit, plus additional parking spaces for guests or visitors (usually one space for every four units). Suddenly, the owner of a one-acre site must build not only 30 apartment units but also 68 parking spaces.

> This is a much harder task—probably meaning that the developer must forego surface parking and provide spaces within or underneath the apartment building itself. Furthermore, if the area in question has a three-story height limit, the only alternative is to provide underground spaces, which doubles their cost of construction.

> A developer boxed in by this kind of zoning envelope—and a substantial impact requirement, such as 2.25 parking spaces per unit—may discover that building the largest project permitted is just too expensive. In order to cut the cost of providing the parking the developer may have to reduce the size of the project.

> In this example, the project size is driven by the parking requirement, not by the allowable density or the setback requirements.[10]

Off-street parking requirements, Fulton says, mean that developers first have to build a parking lot, and then the city allows them to build something to finance the parking lot.

Fulton shows how parking requirements burden housing construction, and another example shows how they can also change land use. Consider a zone with a permitted floor-area ratio (FAR) of 1.0.[11] Suppose a developer wants to build a one-story restaurant with 1,000 square feet of floor area, and the parking requirement is 10 spaces per 1,000 square feet.[12] Because 10 parking spaces occupy at least 3,000 square feet, the restaurant requires a site of at least 4,000 square feet. The zoning allows a FAR of 1.0, but the parking requirement effectively limits the FAR to 0.25. With all the required parking, the restaurant occupies four times the land it would need without parking, even if everything on the site other than the restaurant itself is surface parking (i.e., there is no landscaping or outside dining). This heavy burden of providing the parking required for a restaurant can easily shift land into another use that happens to have a lower parking requirement.[13]

Table 5-1. An Example of How Parking Requirements Reduce Floor Area Ratios

	Dimension	Measurement	Formula
1.	Restaurant area	1,000 square feet	
2.	Allowed FAR	1.0	
3.	Parking requirement	10 spaces per 1,000 square feet	
4.	Required parking spaces	10 spaces	(3)x(1)
5.	Area per parking space	300 square feet per space	
6.	Total parking lot area	3,000 square feet	(5)x(4)
7.	Total site area	4,000 square feet	(1)+(6)
8.	Feasible FAR	0.25	(1)÷(7)

Many other commercial uses also end up with parking lots bigger than the buildings they serve. In *Edge City*, Joel Garreau says, for most land uses, developers must provide 50 percent more space for parking than for buildings and a developer's cheapest option is thus to "build a one-story building. Let it cover 40 percent of the ground. That leaves 60 percent of the land to be covered with a simple parking lot. No grass or trees or sidewalks…which explains why an awful lot of cheap development looks the way it does."[14] Garreau also says this parking-to-building ratio explains why many developments with surface parking have a FAR of only 0.4.

A study of the engineering plans for a sample of commercial developments in Olympia, Washington, found a similar result. The study measured the share of land covered by streets, sidewalks, parking, driveways, buildings, and landscaping. On average, parking and driveways occupied 53 percent of the land, while the commercial buildings themselves occupied only 26 percent. Parking and driveways therefore occupied twice as much land as the buildings they served.[15]

These examples show that off-street parking requirements produce smaller buildings, more parking spaces, and different land uses. They also create vast expanses of open space that are no amenity, as Todd Litman explains:

> In practice, paved surfaces provide few of the amenities that make lower densities desirable, such as privacy, noise reduction, aesthetics and access to greenspace. Thus, increased parking results in the worst of all worlds: lower density, automobile-oriented communities with degraded environments.[16]

In this worst of all worlds, shopping malls are giant parking lots with a few stores. But off-street parking requirements leave few alternatives for developing a successful group of stores *except* as a mall, megamall, minimall, or strip mall because no one is now allowed to build a street of shops of the sort that was common before cities began to require each building to provide its own parking. By hindering the development of any other retail uses, off-street parking requirements have helped "mallify" America. Only *inside* the better malls can we now find the dense, car-free villages that off-street parking requirements have made impossible everywhere else. Every effect has a cause, and off-street parking requirements are a major cause of modern urban form.

Perhaps the most surprising evidence that parking requirements limit density comes from the SmartCode, a model municipal zoning code authored by Duany Plater-Zyberk & Company. The SmartCode was crafted to improve urban design and is based on the principles and practices of New Urbanism. The SmartCode does not limit land-use intensity in the way conventional codes do, such as by limiting FARs or the number of dwelling units per acre. Instead, parking requirements limit intensity.[17] The only limit on the intensity of land use is that developers must provide all the parking spaces the SmartCode requires for the land use. In the city center, for example, the SmartCode requires 1 space per bedroom for a hotel, 2 spaces per 1,000 square feet of floor area for office buildings, and 3 spaces per 1,000 square feet for retail.[18] These parking requirements are the only limit on the allowed floor area, and they are not low for a city center (some cities do not require any parking in the center). Even at the fountainhead of New Urbanist thinking, parking requirements dictate density, and cars rule the city.

DEGRADED URBAN DESIGN

Architectural historian Colin Rowe gave us a succinct definition of an ideal city: "Out the front door, London; out the back door, Los Angeles." Turned around, this definition implies the opposite of an ideal city: out the front door, Los Angeles; out the back door, London. And what detracts from going out the front door—onto the street—in Los Angeles and many other American cities? Off-street parking requirements are part of the problem. Most of the streets we admire for their great urban design cannot be replicated with today's parking requirements. In his book on *Great Streets*, Allan Jacobs (Berkeley professor of city planning and former director of the San Francisco City Planning Commission) compares the physical qualities of what he considers the best streets in Europe and America. After careful examination of these streets, ranging from the Avenue Montaigne in Paris to Roslyn Place in Pittsburgh, he concludes:

> None of the great streets can be characterized as having an abundance of parking places, on street or off…. Auto parking in great amounts, to any contemporary standard, is not a characteristic of great streets. They seem to do well without "enough."[19]

Fortunately, many older areas were built before cities required off-street parking, and we can see the difference. San Francisco, for example, established its residential parking requirements in the 1960s, and the neighborhoods built since then compare unfavorably with older neighborhoods that have far less parking. (See Figure 5-3.) In a study done for the city's "Better Neighborhoods" program, the San Francisco Planning Department says:

> No great city is known for its abundant parking supply. If we had to rebuild a place like North Beach under today's parking requirements, as much as a third of the space where people live would be given up for parking. We would lose much of the street life—the shops and cafes, the vendors and the stoops—that make areas like North Beach vibrant and interesting. We don't build places like these today because we require so much parking. There are plenty of examples of the kinds of buildings our parking requirements result in. We just need to imagine a city composed entirely of these buildings, and ask ourselves if this is the kind of city we want in the future.[20]

Some buildings that meet today's parking requirements look quite strange if they are perched atop their parking structures. Consider the 500-foot office tower at 1100 Wilshire Boulevard in downtown Los Angeles: it has 21 floors of offices above 15 levels of parking. (See Figure 5-4.) The

San Francisco Planning Department

Figure 5-3. Street Scene in San Francisco

office building essentially begins on the 16th floor. Commuters could drive to parking level 15 and then walk up one flight of stairs to their offices. The building has remained empty since it was completed in 1986, however, in part because of its odd parking arrangement: the dizzying drive up or down 15 levels of ramped parking discourages most potential tenants.[21] Sadly, the building doesn't even need all this parking because it is located only three blocks from the city's busiest subway station (Metro Center at Seventh and Figueroa), where two rail transit lines meet, and three bus lines stop directly in front of the building. Perhaps this can be called transit-adjacent development with all the required parking.

The first concern in the design of many buildings has become parking, not architecture. Robert Dunphy, senior fellow of the Urban Land Institute, describes the results:

> Nowhere is the deadening effect of parking on urban vitality felt more than on the suburban shopping strip, where an excessive supply of parking perpetuates a pattern of development that generally is ugly, wasteful, auto dependent, and antithetical to creating a vibrant community. In addition, the conventional suburban mall design template of "a box in a sea of parking" creates transportation problems by precluding virtually any means of travel other than driving, even to nearby destinations.[22]

Donald C. Shoup

Figure 5-4. 1100 Wilshire Boulevard: 21 floors of offices above 15 levels of parking

The common practice of using parking generation rates as the basis for parking requirements is particularly inappropriate at land uses with short, sharp peaks in parking demand. The peak parking occupancy at a church, for example, may last for only a few hours each week. Using this peak demand to set a minimum parking requirement leaves many parking spaces empty almost all the time. The full cost of the parking lot is incurred to serve a few hours each week, so the cost per hour the parking spaces are occupied can be enormous.[23] Religious leaders advise, "Do not build the church for Easter Sunday," but planners ignore this advice for church parking requirements.

For buildings too small to support a garage, minimum parking requirements result in surface parking lots, and since the lots are private, they sit
empty and often padlocked when the businesses are closed, creating a
depressing aura. Even though they may be used only a few hours each
week, parking lots mar the landscape 24 hours every day. As Dunphy
says, "Parking truly is the big foot of urban land uses, since the amount
of land required for parking and circulation exceeds the building footprint."[24] Parking spaces in the city are like dark matter in the universe: we
tend not to see them, but somehow they add up to an enormous area that
deadens the urban environment, as journalist Whitney Gould observed:

> Developers and building owners treat [parking] spaces as leftovers: essential
> to have but not worth investing any money to design. Architecture schools
> don't spend much time on the subject. And the rest of us, who just want a
> place to park, take what we can get, preferably close to our destination. The
> results…are basically paved deserts.[25]

Parking requirements strongly affect what can be built, what it costs, and
how it looks. Many residential streets have become garagescapes—
appearing to be a place not where people live, but where cars are
parked—and the only obvious way to enter a building is with an electronic garage-door opener (see Figure 5-5).

In their examination of street form at the urban edge of the San Francisco
Bay Area from the 1920s to the 1990s, Michael Southworth and Peter
Owens describe the dramatic changes in the prominence of garages in the
residential landscape:

> The garage has grown in size and stature. Originally a small structure con-
> fined to the back corner of a lot and reached by a long narrow driveway or an
> alley, the garage has slowly migrated forward to a position of prominence next
> to the house and has expanded from one to two or even three bays. More
> recently, as lots have narrowed, the garage has moved out in front of the house
> and become a primary element of the streetscape. Simultaneously, the front
> porch has moved from its position of dominance on the residential street into
> obsolescence. In older urban edge neighborhoods the porch contributed both
> formally and functionally to a human street scale. It provided an intimate tran-
> sition space from the public to the private world and a safe place for social
> interaction among neighbors. As the garage has moved forward it has become
> the primary place of entry while the front porch has been reduced to a resid-
> ual symbolic form reserved for strangers and formal occasions. The porch
> often does not even retain direct sidewalk connection with the street. Finally,
> as lots have narrowed over the past decade, the front entry and porch have
> completely disappeared. Pedestrian access to the house is commonly by a nar-
> row alley along the garage to a side door.[26]

Southworth and Owens (1993)

Figure 5-5. From porchscape to garagescape

Houses with two- or more-car garages jutting in front are now called "snout houses" because the garage resembles a pig's snout poking onto the street.[27] These multiple-car thrust garages are the single greatest change in domestic architecture in the past several centuries, and they now dominate the facades of most new houses, flaunting the prominent role of cars and parking in American society.

Popular historic styles like courtyard housing cannot be replicated with today's parking requirements. Planners initially intended parking requirements to serve buildings, but architects now design buildings to serve the parking requirements. Form no longer follows function, fashion, or even finance. Instead, form follows parking requirements. And because function follows form, cities are now in thrall to their own parking requirements.

HIGHER HOUSING COSTS

Parking requirements bundle the cost of parking spaces into the cost of dwelling units, and therefore shift the cost of parking a car into the cost of renting or owning a home—making cars more affordable but housing more expensive. The higher the parking requirement, the higher the cost of housing. When the U.S. Census Bureau surveyed owners and managers of multifamily rental housing to learn which governmental regulations made their operations most difficult, parking requirements were cited more frequently than any other regulation except property taxes.[28]

Writing in *Urban Land*, parking consultant John Dorsett explains that the cost of parking is passed on to tenants and then to all customers:

> There are real costs associated with providing parking, and they can significantly affect real estate projects and even block their development. When shopping centers, office buildings, and hotels do not charge for parking, there is the popular misconception that it is free; however, someone must pay for the parking facility—as well as for the land under it and the lighting, insurance, security, and maintenance needed to keep it functioning—and that money must be recouped. There also are design, testing, and contracting fees, as well as financing costs, developer's costs, and surveying costs. On top of all that, owners of parking facilities often pay property, sales, and parking taxes.

> If these costs are not covered by parking fees, they are passed on to the facility owner and ultimately to the facility users. For example, to cover parking costs at a shopping center, the owner charges tenants higher rents and common area maintenance fees. In turn, the tenants charge consumers higher prices for their services and merchandise. Hotels indirectly bill the cost of parking to their guests as part of the cost of overhead. In short, just as there is no such thing as a free lunch, there is no free parking.[29]

Planners long ago noticed that parking requirements restrict housing construction. In 1935, Los Angeles began to require one off-street parking space per dwelling unit for multifamily housing, and a 1948 article in the *Journal of the American Institute of Planners* noted a surprising result: "In many cases, the number of garage spaces actually controlled the number of dwelling units which could be accommodated on a lot."[30] The 1935 zon-

Figure 5-6. Dingbats

ing ordinance required a garage building on the same lot as the main building, sufficient to accommodate one automobile for each apartment. Garages (covered parking) were required to insure that the space would remain available for cars. Planners suspected that if only surface parking were required, it could easily be converted to other uses, such as a garden, without a permit. Los Angeles still requires covered parking for residential uses, and this requirement surely contributed to the postwar epidemic of dingbats with off-street parking spaces that are covered but not out of sight (Figure 5-6). Journalist Mark Frauenfelder says of these dingbats: "You couldn't make an uglier building if you tried. Los Angeles is full of dingbats—boxy two-story apartments supported by stilts, with open stalls below for parking."[31] One can easily see a dramatic difference between apartment buildings built before and after 1935. Tall buildings on small sites are obviously pre-1935, while the later buildings are smaller. The better post-1935 apartment buildings have separate garages that take up a significant share of the land and are designed to match the architectural style of the apartment buildings (like salt and pepper shakers), but the humble dingbats simply perch directly above their "covered" parking spaces.

By restricting the supply of housing, parking requirements inevitably increase rents. It is difficult, however, to find data on how parking requirements increase the construction cost of housing. Because developers must provide the required parking to obtain a building permit, they don't usually calculate the cost of the parking separately, just as they don't separate out the cost of the walls or ceilings. The parking is an inescapable part of the building. Nevertheless, five studies that did separate the cost of parking from the cost of buildings show that parking requirements significantly raise housing prices, reduce land values, and encourage sprawl. The cost of structured parking sometimes exceeds the cost of the land for multifamily housing.[32]

Study 1: Apartments in Oakland

A study in Oakland, California, showed the effects of introducing a parking requirement where none existed before. In 1961, Oakland began to require one space per dwelling unit for apartment buildings. To examine the effects of this change, housing economist Brian Bertha collected data for 45 apartment projects developed in the four years before Oakland required parking and for 19 projects developed in the two years afterward.[33] Table 5-2 shows the changes in housing costs, housing density, housing investment, and land values after the requirement was adopted.

With the advent of parking requirements, the construction cost per apartment increased by 18 percent, and the number of apartments on a typical lot fell by 30 percent.[34] Bertha explains:

> The zoning change made prior densities impossible without underground garages. This increased the cost of development if the same density were to be achieved before and after the zoning change.... The developers interviewed stated that the increased pre-development land costs encouraged development of an apartment with a higher rent structure, and in order to be able to receive higher rents in the market, the developer tried offering the tenants larger units.[35]

Developers said that *adding* an apartment required another parking space but *enlarging* an apartment did not; they therefore built fewer but larger

Table 5-2. Effects of Introducing a Parking Requirement for Apartments (Oakland, California)

Variable	Before requirement	After requirement	Change Absolute	Percent
Construction cost ($/dwelling unit)	$6,613	$7,805	+$1,192	+18%
Housing density (dwelling units/acre)	77.5	54	-23.5	-30%
Housing investment ($/acre)	$513,000	$421,000	-$92,000	-18%
Land value ($/acre)	$217,000	$145,000	-$72,000	-33%

Source: Brian Bertha (1964, 113-120).

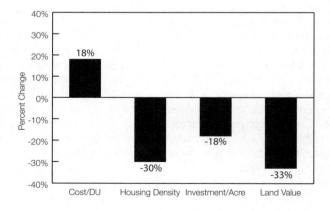

A Great Planning Disaster 145

apartments. Reluctant to build expensive underground garages, developers reduced the number of apartments and devoted more land to surface parking.

The parking requirements also triggered another effect. Because the required parking increased development costs and reduced feasible density, land values fell by 33 percent. The decline was greatest in the area that had the fewest parking spaces per unit before the zoning change because in this area the parking requirement reduced density and increased costs the most. Conversely, land values fell least in the area with the most parking spaces per unit before the zoning change.[36] Property tax revenues also fell because both land values and the construction of taxable improvements declined.[37]

Oakland's modest requirement of one parking space per apartment dramatically affected land use, but some cities have much higher requirements. In Los Angeles, for example, the Specific Plan for North Westwood Village requires 3.5 spaces per unit for apartments with more than four habitable rooms—and even a kitchen counts as a habitable room. Consider also the Park Mile Specific Plan on Wilshire Boulevard: "For dwelling units, there shall be at least two and one-half parking spaces for each dwelling regardless of the number of habitable rooms contained therein." If requiring one space per apartment in Oakland increased housing costs by 18 percent and reduced density by 30 percent, imagine how requiring 3.5 parking spaces per apartment must increase the cost and reduce the supply of housing in Los Angeles.

Study 2: Houses in San Francisco

Wenyu Jia and Martin Wachs at the University of California, Berkeley, studied the conflict between housing affordability and parking availability in San Francisco, where many working people cannot afford a house or apartment, and where finding a place to park is almost as difficult. To ease the parking problem, San Francisco requires one off-street parking space for each new dwelling unit, but this parking solution intensifies the housing problem.

Jia and Wachs found that single-family houses *without* off-street parking sold for an average of $348,000, while otherwise similar houses *with* an off-street space sold for $395,000. A parking space thus increased the price of a house by $47,000.[38] Only dwelling size and the number of bathrooms affected housing prices more. Because a one-car garage for a single-family house requires a curb cut that reduces the on-street parking supply by almost one space, the off-street parking requirement does little to increase the total supply; instead, it vacates the on-street space to provide access to the off-street space; that is, the off-street requirement converts public curb parking spaces into private off-street spaces. As Columbia University planning professor Moshe Adler says, "For people who have garages, street parking is almost private property. No one is permitted to block the entrance to a garage, and the effect of this privilege on other potential users is the same as if a garage were a privately owned parking spot on the street, at the entrance to the garage."[39] Because the curb cuts are not available for on-street parking, and because the off-street spaces are often unused during the weekdays when residents are at work, the required off-street parking spaces effectively reduce the available parking supply. To increase the curb parking supply, a few cities allow residents to purchase a driveway parking permit to park on the street in front of their own driveway, so the length of the curb cut becomes a reserved on-street parking space for the resident.[40]

Jia and Wachs also estimated how the required parking increased the income necessary to buy a house. The annual family income necessary to qualify for a mortgage was $67,000 for a house without parking, and $76,000 for one with parking. As a result, 24 percent more San Francisco households could afford to buy houses if they did not include the required on-site parking space. The parking requirement therefore significantly reduces housing affordability in San Francisco.

Study 3: Offices in Southern California

Richard Willson conducted case studies of parking demand and supply at suburban office projects in 10 Southern California cities and used the data to estimate how parking requirements affect land values and development density.[41] Land devoted to the required parking is not available as building area, open space, or for other productive uses. To examine how parking requirements affect development density, Willson created two scenarios based on the characteristics of the typical case study site: a four-story office building on a site of 190,000 square feet with surface parking (see Table 5-3). One scenario shows the project as built: a 95,000-square-foot building with 3.8 parking spaces per 1,000 square feet (column 2). The second scenario illustrates how much more building area the same site could accommodate if the parking requirement were reduced to 2.5 parking spaces per 1,000 square feet, which Willson estimated was more than sufficient to meet the peak demand for free parking (column 3). In both cases, 17 percent of the site was devoted to landscaping and setbacks.

The comparison shows that if there were no other constraint on density, reducing the parking requirement by 34 percent would allow a 42 percent increase in the size of the office building (see column 4). Willson then developed a pro-forma analysis to calculate the land values the project

Table 5-3. Effects of Reducing the Parking Requirement for Office Buildings (Southern California)

Characteristic (1)	As built (2)	Reduced parking (3)	Change Absolute (4)	Change Percent (5)
Parking requirement (spaces/1,000 square feet)	3.8	2.5	-1.3	-34%
Site size (square feet)	190,000	190,000	0	0%
Number of stories	4	4	0	0%
Building size (square feet)	95,000	135,000	40,000	42%
Number of parking spaces	361	338	-23	-6%
Parking lot area (@370 square feet/space)	133,570	125,060	-8,510	-6%
Percent of site devoted to parking	70%	66%	-4%	-6%
Floor-area ratio (building size/site size)	0.50	0.71	0.21	42%
Land value ($/square foot)	$11.00	$16.25	$5.25	48%
Project cost	$10,592,000	$14,496,000	$3,904,000	37%
Annual net operating income ($/year)	$1,042,000	$1,440,000	$398,000	38%
Project value (@ 9% capitalization rate)	$11,703,000	$16,005,000	$4,302,000	37%
Property tax revenue (@ 1% tax rate)	$117,030	$160,050	$43,020	37%

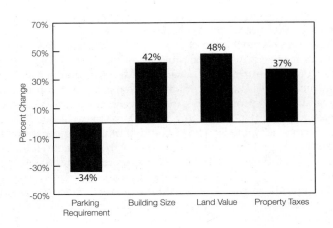

would support at the two parking ratios. Assuming the developer's goal is an investment return of 15 percent a year and the market rent for the office building is $1.60 a month per square foot, he estimated that reducing the parking requirement by 34 percent would increase land values by 48 percent and property tax revenues by 37 percent. Note the estimated effects of parking requirements on office buildings in Southern California in 1995 were almost identical to the effects observed for apartment buildings in Oakland 34 years earlier.[42]

Study 4: Apartments in Los Angeles

Although developers usually do not separate the cost of parking from the other costs of a building, a new apartment project on the UCLA campus does provide these two costs separately. The housing and the parking were planned as a single development (with the housing above the parking), but the Campus Housing Administration financed the apartments, and the Campus Parking Service financed the parking spaces, so the two separate costs were carefully calculated. Weyburn Terrace cost $148 million—$118 million for 848 apartments and $30 million for 1,430 parking spaces.[43] The mix of two-bedroom and efficiency (one-room) apartments on the 12.5-acre site provide 1,362 bedrooms for graduate students, with one parking space for each bedroom and 68 additional parking spaces for staff and visitors (see Table 5-4).[44]

The cost of the Weyburn Terrace housing was $139,000 per apartment, and the cost of the parking was $21,000 per space. Because there are 1.7 parking spaces per apartment, the parking therefore added $35,000 per apartment to the project's construction cost. The project provides 73 square feet of parking for every 100 square feet of housing, and the parking increased the cost of construction by 25 percent.

Although one parking space per bedroom seems more than enough for on-campus student housing, the project provides 21 percent fewer spaces than the zoning requires.[45] UCLA can provide less than the code-required parking because it is exempt from the city's regulations. A private developer would have to provide 1.5 spaces for each efficiency apartment, and 2.5 spaces for each two-bedroom apartment.[46] The right-hand column in the lower panel of Table 5-4 shows the cost of parking construction had the campus complied with the city's zoning. The project would provide 92 square feet of parking for every 100 square feet of housing. The required parking would cost $44,600 per apartment (greater than the land cost for a typical apartment) and would increase the cost of construction by 32 percent.[47]

**Table 5-4. Required Parking Increases the Cost of Housing
(Weyburn Terrace apartment project at UCLA)**

	Apartments		
1. Number of two-bedroom apartments	532		
2. Number of efficiency apartments	316		
3. Total number of apartments	848		(1)+(2)
4. Total number of bedrooms	1,362		2x(1)+(2)
5. Total square feet of housing	641,000		
6. Total cost of housing	$117,780.000		
7. Cost per apartment	$139,000		(6)/(3)
8. Cost per bedroom	$86,000		(6)/(4)
9. Cost per square foot of housing	$184		(6)/(5)

	Parking Spaces		
	Built by UCLA	Required by LA	
10. Number of parking spaces	1,430	1,804	2.5x(1)+1.5x(2)
11. Total square feet of parking	470,000	593,000	(10)x(12)
12. Square feet per parking space	329	329	(11)/(10)
13. Total cost of parking	$29,990,000	$37,834,000	
14. Cost per parking space	$21,000	$21,000	(13)/(10)
15. Cost per square foot of parking	$64	$64	(13)/(11)
16. Parking spaces per apartment	1.7	2.1	(10)/(3)
17. Parking spaces per bedroom	1.0	1.3	(10)/(4)
18. Parking cost per apartment	$35,000	$45,000	(13)/(3)
19. Parking cost per bedroom	$22,000	$28,000	(13)/(4)
20. Parking cost as % of housing cost	25%	32%	(13)/(6)
21. Parking sq. ft. as % of housing sq.ft.	73%	93%	(11)/(5)

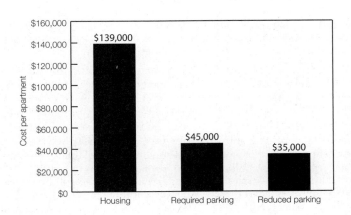

Study 5: Apartments in Palo Alto

Parking requirements dramatically increase the cost of low-income housing. A single room occupancy (SRO) apartment building developed by the nonprofit Palo Alto Housing Corporation in 1998 shows this effect. Alma Place, which was financed by the federal Low Income Housing Tax Credit Program, has 107 SRO units for very-low-income residents.[48] Palo Alto requires 1.25 parking spaces per unit for studio apartments; at this rate, the normal requirement for Alma Place would be 134 parking spaces, but the city allowed a reduction to only 72 spaces. In the resulting design, the first two levels of the five-story building are parking, while the top three levels are residential.[49] Because parking was a contentious issue, the planning commission report calculated the construction cost of the parking spaces and the dwelling units separately. Even with the reduced requirement, the parking spaces increased the construction cost of the building by 38 percent (see Table 5-5).

The construction cost of $32,000 per apartment is low because the units are small—only 260 square feet per apartment.[50] Because the parking spaces increased the building's total construction cost by 38 percent, they also increased the rents for the apartments. Many residents are too poor to own a car (the average income of residents is 33 percent of the area's median income), but the city rejected a proposal to unbundle the rent for parking spaces from the rent for apartments:

> To reduce rents and parking demand, the Palo Alto Housing Corporation requested permission to "unbundle" parking costs, by charging for them separately. A separate $100 per month parking rent could have reduced rents (currently $330 to $490 per month) by approximately $50 per month per unit. The proposal was turned down, however, out of concern over spill-over parking.[51]

Cars were more controversial than people in planning this project. One planning commissioner "stated his concern that the presence of a residential use may affect the long-term viability of the existing auto uses in the area."[52] (The new SRO apartments are right next to Palo Alto BMW! Because automobile dealers produce substantial sales tax revenue, while SRO housing requires a subsidy, cities have a clear fiscal incentive to favor automobile dealers over low-income housing.) The planning commission also considered several other parking proposals:

> The Commission asked the City Attorney's office to research the legality of a requirement that prospective SRO tenants be employed at jobs within walking distance of the site as a measure which would tend to reduce the likelihood of auto ownership among tenants.... Planning staff opposes this option since one purpose of locating housing on a site such as this is so that residents will have the ability, if they choose, to commute by public transit to jobs in other areas.[53]

**Table 5-5. Required Parking Increases the Cost of SRO Housing
(Alma Place in Palo Alto, California)**

1 Construction cost for 107 apartments	$3,420,000	
2 Construction cost for 72 parking spaces	$1,300,000	
3 Total construction cost	$4,720,000	(1)+(2)
4 Construction cost per apartment	$32,000	(1)/107
5 Construction cost per parking space	$18,100	(2)/72
6 Parking spaces per apartment	0.67	72/107
7 Parking cost per apartment	$12,100	(2)/107
8 Parking cost as % of housing cost	38%	(2)/(1)
9 Code-required parking spaces per apartment	1.25	
10 Code-required parking cost per apartment	$22,600	(9)x(5)
11 Savings per apartment from reduced parking	$10,500	(10)-(7)
12 Code-required parking cost as % of housing cost	71%	(10)/(4)

Source: Palo Alto Planning Commission (1995).

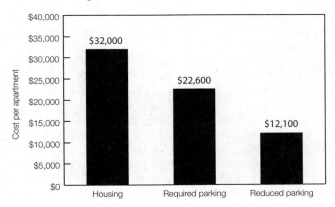

In case the reduced parking supply turned out to be insufficient to meet the residents' demand for free parking, the planning commission considered further proposals, such as a preference for tenants without cars, or a prohibition on renting to new tenants with cars.[54] When it came to dealing with parking, the planning commissioners appeared to consider almost everything except charging for it.

If Alma Place had complied with Palo Alto's normal requirement of 1.25 spaces per unit and all the required spaces had cost the same as the existing spaces ($18,100 apiece), the parking would have cost $22,600 per apartment (1.25 x $18,100). The reduced parking requirement for Alma Place thus saved $10,500 per apartment ($22,600 - $12,100) for units that cost only $32,000 apiece to build. Without the reduced parking requirement, the parking would have increased the cost of constructing the housing by 71 percent ($22,600 ÷ $32,000). Without doubt, off-street parking requirements significantly increase the cost of small apartments and can make development almost impossible without a large subsidy. A substantial share—or perhaps all—of the subsidies for low-income housing therefore goes to pay for the high cost of free parking.

Requiring a fixed number of parking spaces per dwelling unit disproportionately increases the cost of small apartments and makes them uneconomical. Although this policy clearly discourages small apartments, many cities require the same number of parking spaces regardless of dwelling-unit size. A survey in California's Silicon Valley, for example, found that half the cities have the same parking requirement for any size unit, whether a small studio or a five-bedroom penthouse.[55] As an alternative to this one-requirement-fits-all-apartments policy, Berkeley, California, requires 1 parking space per 1,000 gross square feet of floor area for buildings with 10 or more dwellings.[56] At this rate, the parking requirement for Alma Place would be only 40 spaces (1 x 39.6), not 134 spaces (1.25 x 107). Merely changing the base of the parking requirement from dwelling units to square feet can dramatically reduce the cost of small apartments.

Affordable Parking vs. Affordable Housing

Parking requirements increase the price of housing not only by adding to the cost of constructing the housing but also by restricting its supply. Parking requirements often reduce the number of dwelling units on a site below what the zoning allows because both the permitted dwelling units *and* the required parking spaces cannot be squeezed onto the same site. That is, the parking requirement, not the bulk limitation (such as the allowed number of dwelling units per acre or the FAR), is often zoning's limiting constraint on density. In the Oakland case study, for example, a parking requirement of only one space per dwelling unit reduced housing density by 30 percent, and most cities now have higher parking requirements. A survey of 18 cities in Southern California in 2003, for example, found that their parking requirements ranged between 1.25 and 3.25 spaces per apartment.[57] Cities don't prohibit the construction of apartments with only one bedroom or one bathroom, but they do prohibit the construction of apartments with only one parking space.

Because all new dwelling units (and all other new buildings) come bundled with their full complement of required parking spaces, residents tend to buy more cars. As a result, each dwelling unit produces a larger number of vehicle trips and vehicle miles travelled (VMT): in 2001, the national averages were 2,200 vehicle trips and 21,200 VMT per household per year.[58] Planners must then further restrict the density of dwelling units and of all other development to restrict the amount of traffic they generate. This traffic-induced downzoning further restricts the ability of land to provide housing and further increases housing prices.

If parking requirements substantially raise housing prices, building a small number of subsidized housing units—including all the required parking—will make only a small contribution to the supply of affordable housing. Reducing or removing off-street parking requirements, however, can increase the supply and reduce the price of *all* housing, without any subsidy.[59] Planners everywhere are concerned about housing costs and urban sprawl, but they have not attempted to evaluate how parking requirements affect either housing costs or urban density. The five case studies presented here show that parking requirements substantially increase development cost and reduce density. Scarce land and capital are shifted from housing for people to housing for cars. Zoning requires a home for every *car* but ignores homeless *people*. By increasing the cost of housing, parking requirements make the real homelessness problem even worse. People sleep in the streets, but cars park free in their ample off-street quarters. In city planning, free parking has become more important than affordable housing.

PARALYSIS BY PARKING REQUIREMENTS

The usual interpretation of a parking requirement is that it specifies the number of parking spaces that a new building must provide; that is, the land-use decision comes first, and the required parking depends on the use. This assumes, however, that an entirely new building is going up. For older buildings, which often cannot provide more on-site parking, the situation is reversed. Here the parking requirements limit the uses a city will allow because the building's use must conform to the available parking (see Chapter 3).

Suppose a furniture store occupies a building that has 1 parking space per 1,000 square feet. The furniture store goes out of business and a bicycle shop wants to move into the building. The parking requirement for a bike shop, however, is 3 spaces per 1,000 square feet of floor area.[60] Because the available parking does not meet the requirement for a bike shop, the shop cannot obtain an occupancy permit without providing more parking spaces (which it probably does not have the land or money to do) or seeking a variance (which can be both time consuming and costly to obtain, if it is granted at all). Most likely, then, the bike shop cannot use the building. Unless a new furniture store—or another use with a parking requirement of 1 space per 1,000 square feet—moves in, the building will remain vacant. Vacancy, of course, can lead to blight, which makes the neighborhood a less desirable place to open a business. Entrepreneurs therefore build new buildings in new areas, instead of reusing existing ones in established areas, and the result is disinvestment in older buildings and neighborhoods. According to New Urbanist architects Andres Duany, Elizabeth Plater-Zyberk, and Jeff Speck, parking requirements are "the single greatest killer of urbanism in the United States today."[61] The requirements drive businesses out of established areas, and—most infuriatingly—they do it for no logical reason. Why, after all, does a bicycle shop "need" three times more parking spaces than a furniture store? The answer is anyone's guess, but these nonsensical requirements distort the land market in wholly unintended ways.

To encourage infill development and reuse, a few cities exempt small commercial buildings from off-street parking requirements. In its Central Business District (CBD), for example, Manhattan Beach, California, requires parking only for buildings with a FAR that exceeds 1:1. Minneapolis and Chicago exempt the first 4,000 square feet of retail space on a lot from parking requirements.[62] Most cities, however, do not offer similar exemptions.

As one consultant wrote to me, "There are heartbreaking stories of people who are trying to make use of vacant buildings but are forbidden to do so by onerous parking requirements."[63] Journalists sometimes write about these heartbreaking stories. Consider the roadblocks parking requirements put in the way of opening Spud's, a proposed new restaurant in Berkeley, California (see sidebar).

Only the most hardhearted urban planner could fail to understand from this zoning story that off-street parking requirements can cause real suffering. The only unusual feature of this case is that someone tried to open a restaurant in an old building because he thought he had a legal arrangement with a church to provide the required parking, and it fell through. In the typical case, no one would even think of trying to open a new restaurant in an old building that lacks the required parking.

Parking requirements can freeze older buildings in their existing uses or even prevent any feasible use at all and therefore reduce the economic opportunities these buildings can offer to their neighborhoods. If a building does not satisfy the parking requirement for a new use, zoning will not allow it even if all other planning requirements are met. Parking requirements have become a moral imperative, and in planning disputes they are invoked in nonnegotiable terms, like sacred cows. All it takes to prohibit many possible new uses for an older building is to say there isn't enough parking. People who oppose a project for any reason can cite the lack of required parking as the reason for objecting to it, as though parking were the real issue. When a proposed new restaurant, for example, requests a variance to open without the required number of off-street parking spaces, protests often come from existing restaurants that want to stifle competition, even if the site is in a derelict part of town where every-

A Parking Requirement Nightmare

In 2003 and 2004, Andrew Beretvas was trying to open Spud's, a pizza-and-beer restaurant in Berkeley, California. He had found the perfect spot—a 1910 building with attractive architectural details and seating for up to 100 patrons. The southside neighborhood, which some saw as blighted or unfriendly to nighttime pedestrians, was enthusiastic about Beretvas's plan, but he found his proposal beset by restrictive parking and zoning regulations to the point where the entire project seemed endangered.

Beretvas was not the first entrepreneur to find the Berkeley zoning rules and ordinances unduly restrictive. Local real estate agent John Gordon told the *Berkeley Daily Planet* in 2004 that parking provisions in particular had led to empty storefronts. Gordon's sentiment was echoed by local merchants' association president Sam Dykes, who told the paper, "This isn't the first time rigid zoning ordinances have jeopardized South Berkeley business."

The specific city regulation in this instance is a parking requirement that must be met when a business files a change-of-use permit. The city required Spud's to provide 12 spaces on a lot that did not have room for any parking and that was in a neighborhood without a conspicuous parking problem.

The city did allow that Spud's could arrange to use spots on other properties within a 300-foot radius, so Beretvas negotiated a deal with Progressive Missionary Church, which was close enough and had an available lot. Unfortunately, under existing city law, such an arrangement with a nonprofit was illegal. The city changed that law, but then the church objected to serving alcohol in the restaurant, so Beretvas dropped alcohol from his plan. But Beretvas's woes did not end, as the city subsequently ruled that the church would also have to agree to a deed restriction that would ensure the ongoing availability of the parking spots. When the church did not consent to this condition, planners agreed to allow a clause whereby the church, should it choose, would need to provide only 30 days' notice before reclaiming the parking spots.

This condition did not sit well with Beretvas's partner Allan Cadgene. He feared that his investment would run too high a risk if the church could reclaim its parking spaces on short notice, opening up the possibility that the city would then revoke the restaurant's use permit. For a time, it seemed that Spud's would not open at all, for want of 12 possibly superfluous parking spaces.

Eventually, Beretvas found other sources of financing. After working through a number of other regulatory issues with the city, he did ultimately open the restaurant late in 2004. "This is the type of business we've wanted here," neighborhood association member Anne Healy told the *Daily Planet* early in 2004. "But the city just throws roadblocks up all the time."

For more on Beretvas's battle, see Matthew Artz, "South Berkeley Neighbors Dream of Fancy Pizza," *Berkeley Daily Planet*, February 13, 2004. See also "Spud's Pizza & Brew FAQ," available at www.spudspizza.com/ H08%20-%20Spud's%20FAQ.htm.

one else would welcome a new restaurant. The frequent references to parking requirements in planning disputes make it appear that everyone always insists on more parking, including even environmentalists who are no friends of the car.

Urban planners unwittingly make many land-use decisions by setting unreasonable parking requirements and in the process have created a disaster without noticing it. Parking requirements create especially severe problems in older commercial areas. For example, they have hindered rebuilding of Los Angeles's older retail corridors that were destroyed in the 1992 riots. Many blocks along these corridors had continuous storefronts on narrow lots, and the stores had no on-site parking because they were built before the city required it. After the original stores burned down, the narrow parcels made it difficult to build a new store *and* meet the current parking requirement.[64] As a result, many sites on these commercial corridors remain idle. Parking requirements also prohibit other commercial corridors from being revitalized because existing buildings cannot be rebuilt without providing the required on-site parking. What does manage to get built has parking lots that break up the street frontage. Corner mini-malls, for example, can provide all the required parking, but they also blight the landscape. In most areas this change-of-use impediment leads to gradual decay because commercial buildings obsolesce slowly, but the Los Angeles riots revealed this problem overnight. In effect, minimum parking requirements imply that *no* shopping is better than shopping without free parking. The result is tragic. Cities kill the chance of revitalizing older areas and drive development to greenfield sites that can easily be paved over for parking lots.

Parking requirements hamper the reuse even of buildings well served by public transit. Consider the case of a historic building on University Avenue in Saint Paul, Minnesota:

> Developers and the community had hoped to restore the old building as four floors of office space, but a shortage of parking with which to meet the city's minimum parking standards forced some floors to be used as storage. Location of the property on one of the region's busiest bus routes did not alter the parking minimums.[65]

Older buildings without on-site parking are often part of the historic fabric cities want to preserve, but parking requirements obstruct adaptive reuse. Even worse, the requirements often encourage demolition of older buildings—sometimes to make way for a parking lot. Parking requirements may also force an increase in the parking supply even at sites where land use does not change. Because all new uses must supply ample parking, all the existing uses face competitive pressure to provide more. Therefore, owners may try to add more parking spaces to a historic building by paving a garden or by making other inappropriate alterations. As an extreme example, Mormons believe that what is now a parking lot in Missouri was once the Garden of Eden.[66]

LIMITS ON HOMEOWNERSHIP

Parking requirements limit homeownership opportunities in older cities by restricting the conversion of rental units to owner occupancy. Many older apartment buildings have at most one parking space per dwelling unit, but they have a grandfathered right to their parking supply. Some cities, such as Los Angeles, require additional parking spaces if a building is converted to condominium ownership. Los Angeles, for example, requires 1.25 resident spaces per dwelling unit with three or fewer habitable rooms, and 1.5 parking spaces per unit with more than three habitable rooms. On top of these resident spaces, the city requires an additional 0.25 guest parking spaces per unit for buildings with 50 or fewer units, and 0.5 guest spaces per unit for buildings with more than 50 units.[67] Even if all other regulations are met, a building cannot be converted to owner occupancy unless it provides, at a minimum, 1.5 spaces per unit.

Because most older buildings—and especially historic ones—do not have 1.5 parking spaces per unit, they cannot be converted to owner occupancy. The owner's "solution" in some cases is to reduce the number of apartments to match the number of parking spaces available, either by combining small apartments to create fewer but larger ones or demolishing enough apartments and converting the land to parking. More commonly, developers tear the rental apartment house down and build a condominium with all the required parking. Although many apartment residents would prefer to own rather than rent their existing dwellings, parking requirements prohibit this opportunity and particularly discriminate against tenants who would like to own their apartment but not a car. If cities allowed the conversion of rental properties to owner occupancy without requiring more parking or exempted all properties built before a certain date—such as 1950—from parking requirements, many more central-city residents could own their own homes.

DAMAGE TO THE URBAN ECONOMY

Beyond discouraging the renovation and reuse of older buildings, parking requirements can also stunt the businesses that operate in these buildings. Suppose a restaurant meets the requirement of 1 space per 3 seats in the dining area. It becomes popular and wants to add tables on an outdoor terrace during the summer. The parking requirement, however, prohibits adding tables without adding new parking spaces—an impossible burden in many locations. The restaurant loses potential new customers, the public loses outdoor dining, workers lose jobs, and the city loses sales taxes, all because of an innocuous-seeming requirement.[68]

Parking requirements cause even more harm if cities require replacement parking when developers want to build on a surface parking lot. Consider the replacement parking requirement in the specific plan for Westwood Village in Los Angeles:

> If a project results in the removal of any parking spaces which existed at the time this Ordinance became effective and which do not serve an existing building or buildings, 50% of such parking spaces shall be replaced and shall be in addition to the number of spaces otherwise required for the project or for any existing building or building on any other lot or lots. Replacement parking shall be made available for public use.[69]

To see how this replacement requirement works, consider the case of a parking lot not required for any existing building; the owner has simply used the land as a parking lot until future development. A developer who wants to build a grocery store on this land must provide all the parking spaces required for the grocery store *and also replace 50 percent of the surface parking spaces already on the land*. With this replacement requirement, landowners "owe" the city half the parking spaces they have previously supplied voluntarily. The heavy burden of meeting this replacement requirement effectively freezes land as surface parking lots and discourages redevelopment.

The heavy restrictions that parking requirements put on land use suggest that removing them will make more urban land available for infill residential, commercial, and industrial development. Parking requirements hide the capacity of urban land to serve people, and unburdening cities from these requirements will reveal this hidden capacity. Many brownfield sites that are now difficult to redevelop may suddenly find economic uses if cities remove off-street parking requirements.

HARM TO THE CENTRAL BUSINESS DISTRICT

Off-street parking requirements especially harm the CBD. High density is a prime advantage of the CBD because it offers proximity to many social, cultural, and economic activities. The clustering of museums, theaters, restaurants, stores, and offices is what a downtown can offer but other areas cannot. But high density also implies a high cost of constructing new parking spaces. Richard Voith points out the conflict between high density and cheap parking in the CBD:

One defining feature of successful CBDs is their high density of economic, social, and cultural activities. This density gives CBDs a unique market niche that is difficult to replicate in other parts of the metropolitan area. Abundant, inexpensive parking would make the CBD more attractive if it had no other consequences; however, plentiful, low-cost parking may be at odds with the very aspect that makes a downtown area unique—high density.[70]

Because more people want to visit a more desirable CBD and parking spaces cost more to build in a dense area, the price of parking in a healthy CBD is bound to be higher than at suburban sites. Off-street parking requirements increase the supply and thus reduce the price of parking in the CBD, *but they also have other consequences.* They increase the cost of all development, reduce density by preempting land from other uses, and increase traffic both within the CBD and on the routes to it. Parking requirements thus reduce the CBD's attractiveness by undermining the essential features that make it attractive—high density and accessibility.

The success of a downtown depends on the ability to combine large amounts of capital and labor with small amounts of land. Because off-street parking requirements increase the cost of combining capital and labor with land, they reduce density.[71] And since density typically declines from the center of a city to its suburban edge, the same parking requirement imposes a higher cost on development in the center than at the periphery. Therefore, applying the same requirement everywhere in a city will shift development away from the center toward the periphery where providing the required parking is cheaper. Downtown parking requirements have accelerated the decentralization they were supposed to have prevented.

The economics of shared parking help to explain the appeal of a successful downtown. Everybody wants to park once and then walk around to shop, dine, and go to a movie or the theater. A dense downtown can provide this experience, but off-street parking requirements reduce density because each building has its own, unshared parking that is often unavailable to the general public. To maintain density in the CBD, a few cities limit rather than require parking spaces and limit the construction of stand-alone parking garages; New York, San Francisco, and Seattle are examples. Nevertheless, most cities still require parking spaces in the CBD and do not limit the construction of stand-alone garages; Dallas, Los Angeles, and Miami are examples.[72] These diametrically opposed parking policies strongly affect how the city center looks and functions. To see the results, consider the differences between Los Angeles and San Francisco in their parking regulations for a specific land use—concert halls.

Parking at Disney Hall

For a downtown concert hall, Los Angeles requires, as the minimum, *50 times* more parking spaces than San Francisco allows as the maximum. These different priorities help explain the very different parking arrangements for Louise Davies Hall (home of the San Francisco Symphony) and Disney Hall (home of the Los Angeles Philharmonic). San Francisco built Louise Davies Hall with no parking garage, while Los Angeles completed Disney Hall's 2,188-space, $110 million parking garage three years before it had raised the $274 million needed to start building the 2,265-seat Disney Hall itself.

Los Angeles County borrowed the money to finance the $50,000-per-space parking garage, with the debt to be repaid from the expected revenues. Because the garage was completed in 1996, but Disney Hall did not open until 2003, parking revenues fell far short of the debt payments for seven years. As a result, the county had to subsidize the garage from general revenues at a time when it was nearly bankrupt. In *The Reluctant Metropolis*, William Fulton relates the debacle of Los Angeles's parking-first policy: "The pauperized county government is forced to subsidize the [Disney Hall] parking garage even as it lays off employees."[73]

At a price of $3 for every 15 minutes with a maximum of $17 a day, or a flat rate of $8 after 5 p.m., Disney Hall's garage never fills even when Disney Hall is sold out, and it is almost empty for the rest of the year. The county's lease for the site specifies that Disney Hall must offer at least 128 concerts a year during the Winter season.[74] Why 128? The county needs enough concerts to generate enough parking revenue to pay the debt service on the garage. And how many concerts did Disney Hall schedule in its first Winter season? Exactly 128. The garage was intended to satisfy the parking demand for concerts at Disney Hall, but Disney Hall's concerts must now satisfy the financial demands of the parking garage. Because of minimum parking requirements, Disney Hall has a minimum concert requirement.

Concertgoers can drive to Disney Hall's six-level subterranean garage and take the "escalator cascade" directly to the foyer without ever stepping on a sidewalk in downtown Los Angeles. Many restaurants in downtown Los Angeles offer free parking for diners who attend a concert at Disney Hall, including free shuttle service to and from Disney Hall. It would be a great boost for downtown if more people ate there before or after a concert, and parked at the restaurants during the concert, but the zoning code specifies that every building must provide its own parking. No matter how well intentioned, off-street parking requirements harm rather than help the CBD by undermining its unique qualities.

The difference in parking policy helps explain why almost everyone prefers downtown San Francisco to downtown Los Angeles. After a concert or theater performance in San Francisco, people stream out onto bustling sidewalks where all the restaurants, bars, bookstores, and flower shops seem to be open and busy, and where it is a long walk to your parking space, if you even drove. In Los Angeles, the sidewalks are empty and threatening at night. Even a spectacular new concert hall does not help to create a vibrant downtown if every concertgoer drives straight into its underground garage and feels the sidewalks a block away are unsafe.

Disney Hall's architect, Frank Gehry, originally specified limestone for the building's exterior, but to save money it was clad in cheaper stainless steel. By diverting spending from architecture to cars, parking requirements make great design more difficult. Disney Hall is now compared to the Sydney Opera House or the Eiffel Tower as the city's icon, but it subtly shows the paramount importance of parking in Los Angeles.[75]

Too Many Parking Spaces?

Minimum parking requirements, with no maximum, imply that cities care only about having enough parking spaces and that there can never be *too many*. But as Jane Jacobs says:

> The main purpose of downtown streets is transaction, and this function can be swamped by the torrent of machine circulation. The more downtown is broken up and interspersed with parking lots and garages, the duller and deader it becomes in appearance, and there is nothing more repellant than a dead downtown.... In a panicky effort to combat the suburbs on their own terms, something downtown cannot do, we are sacrificing the fundamental strengths of downtown—its variety and choice, its bustle, its interest, its compactness, its compelling message that this is not a way-station, but the very intricate center of things. The only reason people come downtown or set up business downtown at all is because downtown packs so much into such a compact area.[76]

Because downtown packs so much into a small area, people are willing to visit it even if they have to ride public transit or pay for parking and then walk to get there. A successful downtown must be accessible, which means traffic and parking, but too much parking enfeebles a downtown. Fred Kent, president of Partners for Public Spaces, describes the difference in parking "requirements" for a great place and a dull place:

> Parking is important where the place isn't important. In a place like Faneuil Hall in Boston it's amazing how far people are willing to walk. In a dull place, you want a parking space right in front of where you're going.[77]

Kent also says minimum parking requirements "assure that a place will be uninteresting." Every downtown parking lot has a very high and very visible opportunity cost. Instead of a building teeming with activity, there is an expanse of asphalt with one employee manning a booth; where there could be something special, there is instead not much. Or as architecture and planning critic Jane Holtz Kay put it, "The more parking, the less place. The more place, the less parking." Where there are plenty of off-street parking spaces, "the pedestrian is now as likely to be ambushed by a car sliding from some underground garage as visually assaulted by gap-toothed parking lots and eerie garage facades."[78]

Parking lots are asphalt holes in the urban fabric. They make driving easier, but walking more difficult and less rewarding. Past some critical point, more parking spaces harm rather than help the CBD. To examine this issue, Table 5-6 is derived from transportation data that Jeffrey Kenworthy and Felix Laube provide for 44 world cities.[79] Columns 2 and 3 show the land area (in hectares) and number of parking spaces in each city's CBD, and column 4 shows the number of parking spaces per hectare. Los Angeles has the highest density of parking spaces in the world (263 per hectare), and the top nine cities are either American, Australian, or Canadian.

Many CBD parking spaces are in structures rather than in surface lots, but column 5 shows how much land they would occupy if they were all spread horizontally in a surface lot.[80] The 107,441 parking spaces in the Los Angeles CBD would cover 331 hectares of land, and this hypothetical parking lot would cover 81 percent of the CBD's 408 hectares (see column 6). The ratio of parking area to land area can be termed the "parking coverage" rate. In the next-highest city, Melbourne, the parking coverage rate is 76 percent. At the lower end, it is 18 percent in New York, 16 percent in London, and only 7 percent in Tokyo.

The density of parking depends on both the density of jobs and the number of parking spaces per job (jobs/hectare x parking spaces/job = parking spaces/hectare). Los Angeles tops the list because it is both denser than other car-oriented cities and more car-oriented than other dense cities. To illustrate this phenomenon, we can compare the Phoenix, San Francisco, and Los Angeles CBDs, all three of which are about the same size (approximately 400 hectares or 1,000 acres). (See Table 5-7.)

Why does Phoenix, which most people would consider the most auto-oriented of the three cities, have the lowest parking coverage rate, at 25 percent? Phoenix has the highest number of parking spaces per job, but by far the fewest number of jobs per hectare, and thus the fewest parking spaces per hectare. San Francisco, on the other hand, has the highest number of jobs per hectare, but by far the fewest number of parking spaces per

Table 5-6. Parking in the CBD

City	Land area (hectares)	Parking spaces	Parking spaces per hectare	Parking area (hectares)	Parking coverage	Employment (jobs)	Jobs per hectare	Parking spaces per job
(1)	(2)	(3)	(4) = (3)/(2)	(5) = (3)/325	(6) = (5)/(2)	(7)	(8)=(7)/(2)	(9)=(3)/(7)
1. Los Angeles	408	107,441	263	331	81%	206,474	506	0.52
2. Melbourne	172	42,601	248	131	76%	126,286	734	0.34
3. Adelaide	181	42,857	237	132	73%	73,868	408	0.58
4. Houston	392	72,797	186	224	57%	118,889	303	0.61
5. Detroit	362	65,639	181	202	56%	93,012	257	0.71
6. Washington	460	80,100	174	246	54%	316,723	689	0.25
7. Brisbane	117	19,895	170	61	52%	61,844	529	0.32
8. Calgary	298	45,260	152	139	47%	86,700	291	0.52
9. Portland	280	41,861	150	129	46%	103,872	371	0.40
10. Brussels	308	45,512	148	140	45%	144,906	470	0.31
11. Vancouver	337	46,053	137	142	42%	104,000	309	0.44
12. Edmonton	297	37,512	126	115	39%	63,200	213	0.59
13. Frankfurt	240	29,487	123	91	38%	119,735	499	0.25
14. Canberra	329	39,558	120	122	37%	22,521	68	1.76
15. Chicago	395	46,653	118	144	36%	363,794	921	0.13
16. Denver	636	67,757	107	208	33%	93,012	146	0.73
17. San Francisco	391	39,756	102	122	31%	291,036	744	0.14
18. Toronto	188	18,436	98	57	30%	174,267	927	0.11
19. Sydney	416	39,031	94	120	29%	175,620	422	0.22
20. San Diego	570	50,234	88	155	27%	72,964	128	0.69
21. Winnipeg	440	37,419	85	115	26%	68,593	156	0.55
22. Boston	868	73,604	85	226	26%	119,189	137	0.62
23. Ottawa	305	25,565	84	79	26%	111,031	364	0.23
24. Perth	759	63,000	83	194	26%	99,819	132	0.63
25. Phoenix	393	31,937	81	98	25%	35,267	90	0.91
26. Montreal	1,224	94,745	77	292	24%	273,203	223	0.35
27. Paris	2,333	172,000	74	529	23%	862,180	370	0.20
28. Munich	795	58,430	73	180	23%	219,518	276	0.27
29. Vienna	298	21,036	71	65	22%	112,770	378	0.19
30. Singapore	725	45,870	63	141	19%	280,000	386	0.16
31. Copenhagen	455	27,400	60	84	19%	122,770	270	0.22
32. Sacramento	462	27,677	60	85	18%	54,121	117	0.51
33. New York	2,331	138,148	59	425	18%	2,305,545	989	0.06
34. Hamburg	460	27,056	59	83	18%	152,590	332	0.18
35. Zurich	152	8,668	57	27	18%	63,410	417	0.14
36. Hong Kong	113	6,376	56	20	17%	193,520	1,713	0.03
37. Kuala Lumpur	1,625	86,030	53	265	16%	290,000	178	0.30
38. London	2,697	138,843	51	427	16%	1,142,781	424	0.12
39. Amsterdam	824	28,600	35	88	11%	80,722	98	0.35
40. Stockholm	424	13,050	31	40	9%	111,233	262	0.12
41. Seoul	2,117	59,758	28	184	9%	1,226,830	580	0.05
42. Bangkok	2,056	50,848	25	156	8%	271,944	132	0.19
43. Tokyo	4,208	98,755	23	304	7%	2,300,738	547	0.04
44. Manila	3,600	22,000	6	68	2%	815,400	227	0.03
Average	**828**	**53,074**	**100**	**163**	**31%**	**321,043**	**403**	**0.36**

Total parking area in column 5 is the surface parking area (in hectares) that all parking spaces in column 3 would occupy.
Each hectare of surface parking accommodates about 325 parked cars.
Source for CBD area and parking spaces: Kenworthy and Laube (1999, Chapter 3).

job, and its parking coverage rate is only slightly higher, at 31 percent. And what about Los Angeles? LA has more than five times as many jobs per hectare as Phoenix, and has more than three times as many parking spaces per job as San Francisco, so its parking coverage rate, 81 percent, is much higher than in either of these other cities.

Table 5-7. Land, Jobs, and Parking in Three CBDs

	Phoenix	San Francisco	Los Angeles
CBD area (hectares)	393	391	408
CBD parking spaces	31,937	39,756	107,441
CBD jobs	35,267	291,036	206,474
Jobs/hectare	90	744	506
Parking spaces/1,000 jobs	910	140	520
Parking spaces per hectare	81	102	263
Parking coverage rate	25%	31%	81%

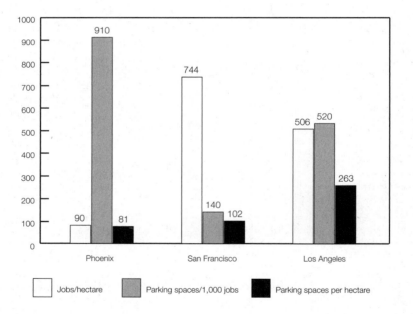

The Los Angeles CBD has more parking spaces per hectare than any other city because it is both dense *and* car-oriented. This car-oriented density creates something different from plain old sprawl. Los Angeles is dense and getting denser, but so long as its zoning assumes that almost every new person will also bring a car—and requires parking for that car—it will never develop the sort of vital core we associate with San Francisco. The need to house humans might push toward an increasingly dense center, but the zoning requirement to house cars pushes back, sending development outward. With off-street parking requirements, higher density simply brings more cars and more congestion, as well as increased disruptions in the urban fabric, with more money directed away from buildings and toward parking lots. Its unusual combination of both density *and* car orientation helps explain why Los Angeles has the worst traffic congestion in the U.S.[81] With off-street parking requirements, higher urban density always induces more cars, more congestion, and more air pollution. Higher density leads to a higher quality of life only in cities that restrict rather than require off-street parking, as in downtown San Francisco.

HARM TO LOW-INCOME FAMILIES

Off-street parking requirements especially harm low-income and renter families because they own fewer cars but still pay for parking indirectly, and the hidden costs of all the required parking consume a greater share of their income. Further, forcing all families to pay for "free" parking reduces the perceived price of owning a car and leads to increased vehicle ownership; the cost of supporting a car then consumes a greater share of household income for poorer families. Off-street parking requirements harm all families, but especially poor families.

Poor families receive fewer benefits from parking requirements because they own fewer cars. Let's look at the numbers. The *2001 Nationwide Household Travel Survey* found that only 73 percent of urban households with incomes less than $20,000 a year own a car, while 99 percent of households with incomes greater than $75,000 a year own a car; 39 percent of families with incomes greater than $100,000 a year own three or more cars.[82] The 2000 Census found that 22 percent of renter households do not own a car, and only 31 percent own more than one car; in contrast, only 5 percent of homeowners do not own a car, while 67 percent own more than one car.[83] The *1997 American Housing Survey* found that apartment residents own an average of one car per occupied apartment, slightly less than half the 2.1 cars per household for single-family homeowners.[84] Although 8 percent of all households in the U.S. do not own a car, they pay for parking in the form of higher prices for everything they buy.[85] Imposing hidden costs on the entire population to subsidize parking takes money from the poorest renters to subsidize richer homeowners.

Even though lower-income households own fewer cars, few cities reduce the parking requirements for low-income housing. Some cities deliberately set high parking requirements to exclude low-income housing. The United States District Court for the Northern District of Ohio found that Parma, a Cleveland suburb, required 2.5 parking spaces per dwelling unit in multifamily rental housing "with the purpose and effect of severely restricting low-income housing."[86]

> The effect of Parma's 2.5 parking space requirement has been to inhibit the construction of low-income housing in Parma. Because a higher parking space requirement requires a developer to use more land for an apartment development, it reduces the practicality of dense development and makes it less feasible for a developer to construct a housing project under low- or moderate-income HUD programs. Rigid enforcement of the 2.5 parking space requirement is one of the ways in which Parma has been able to keep all low-income housing out of the community.
>
> The record does not show that [the high parking requirement] was passed for the purpose of excluding minorities. Yet the effect…is to make the construction of low-income housing substantially more difficult and thereby preserve the all-white character of the City.[87]

Because different ethnic groups have different rates of car ownership, parking requirements affect these groups differently. Although 7 percent of White households, 13 percent of Asian households, 17 percent of Latino households, and 24 percent of Black households do not own a car, they all pay for required parking spaces through higher rents and higher prices for all goods and services.[88] While most cities do not require parking in order to restrict housing opportunities for minorities, even good intentions can produce bad results. The conclusion reached in a related court case describes planning for parking perfectly: "The arbitrary quality of thoughtlessness can be as disastrous and unfair to private rights and the public interest as the perversity of a willful scheme."[89]

Even where cities are eager to provide affordable housing, parking requirements make it more difficult, as shown in the case study of the Alma Place SRO apartment house in Palo Alto. Consider also the case of Casa Gloria in Los Angeles, a federally subsidized 46-unit apartment development that offers three-bedroom, two-bath apartments for $353 a month. Built in 1993 by an offshoot of the National Association for the Hispanic Elderly, the project cost $233,000 per apartment ($304,000 when adjusted for inflation to 2004), making it the most expensive affordable-housing project in California history. The city's requirement for two parking spaces per apartment contributed to this high cost, even though most residents are too poor and too old to own cars. Because of the difficult site, the required parking spaces were built underground, adding to the expense. A *Los Angeles Times* reporter who visited the project six months after it opened wrote, "The parking garage is nearly empty. The tenants do not have enough cars to fill it up."[90] Parking requirements for subsidized housing force developers to build fewer units or to charge higher rents, and a substantial part of the subsidy for low-income housing pays for parking spaces. If cities want to improve the availability and affordability of housing, they should not require more off-street parking than developers want to provide.

Some planners recognize the perversity of parking requirements and are attempting to reduce or eliminate them. Amit Ghosh, San Francisco's chief of comprehensive planning, says:

> Parking requirements are a huge obstacle to new affordable housing and transit-oriented development in San Francisco. Nonprofit developers estimate that they add 20 percent to the cost of each unit, and reduce the number of units that can be built on a site by 20 percent. We're forcing people to build parking that people cannot afford. We're letting parking drive not only our transportation policies, but jeopardize our housing policies, too. We want to get away from the situation where people are forced to pay for parking regardless of whether they have a car.[91]

Unfortunately, most urban planners seem unaware of these problems, and most American cities continue to require ample off-street parking for every land use, even low-income housing. A few cities do have inclusionary zoning ordinances that require some developments to set aside a small share of housing units for low-income households, but off-street parking requirements are the real inclusionary zoning, and they require housing for all cars, at the expense of housing for poor people.

PRICE DISCRIMINATION

Off-street parking requirements are not the only explanation for free parking, of course. Free parking at a store helps attract motorized shoppers who can choose among many alternative stores within easy driving distance, and who can buy in large quantities at one time (such as a whole week's groceries in one trip to the supermarket), making a long journey worthwhile. If stores bundle the cost of parking into the price of everything they sell, they "price discriminate" in favor of customers who drive. The economic motive to offer free parking for drivers rather than slightly lower prices for everyone is the presumption that charging for parking would reduce the number of customers who drive to the stores where they shop. Merchants don't need to offer an equivalent subsidy to the nondriving customers who have fewer shopping options.[92] Because drivers tend to be richer than nondrivers, the free parking discriminates against low-income households. Although off-street requirements do not motivate *all* free parking at stores, they do increase the parking supply and therefore favor drivers over those who ride public transit, cycle, or walk for shopping trips.

Even if free parking does increase total sales at a store, it may not guarantee a higher profit because free parking has a cost. Furthermore, the benefits of bundled parking are offset by the external costs of additional driving. Berkeley transportation economists Lawrence Lan and Adib Kanafani examine the economics of bundling the cost of parking into the price of merchandise at stores.[93] They say that *higher* parking prices are called for to deal with the external costs of driving and that free parking works directly counter to public policy. They also show that bundled parking can increase private profit (which is the motive to offer it), but when the external effects of traffic congestion are also considered, the bundled parking reduces social welfare.

Oxford University economist Robert Bacon developed a model showing that while bundled parking increases vehicle travel and traffic congestion, it may, perversely, not increase the total sales of shopping centers.[94] Free parking at one shopping center offers a competitive advantage only if other shopping centers charge for parking. If all shopping centers compete with each other by providing free parking, the free parking at each shopping center may not attract any more customers. Competition among shopping centers may thus increase the total parking supply and parking subsidy without increasing total sales. Because the frequency of automobile shopping trips depends on the price of parking, households may respond to free parking not by spending more at the shopping centers but by making more frequent trips and buying less on each trip. This outcome may not change any shopping center's share of total sales, but it does increase the number of vehicle trips in two ways. First, free parking leads to more frequent shopping trips with lower average purchases on each trip. Second, free parking diverts some shopping trips from walking, cycling, carpools, and public transit to solo driving. Together, these two factors can significantly increase traffic congestion. Given this collectively undesirable outcome, the appropriate planning regulation is to limit the number of parking spaces at shopping centers, not to require even more parking.

PRICES AND PREFERENCES

By reducing the cost of driving, off-street parking requirements increase the demand for cars and vehicle travel. They also encourage sprawl by increasing the cost of dense development. Parking requirements thus distort consumer choices for both transportation and land use. Our transportation and land-use choices do not accurately reveal our true preferences for cars and sprawl because the prices we pay for mobility and low density do not reflect their full costs.

Consider what would happen if the gasoline tax were doubled. Vehicle travel would decline, but this would not imply that our *preference* for driving had decreased. We would simply be responding to a higher *price* for driving. Similarly, vehicle travel would decline if parking prices rose to cover the cost of providing parking spaces.[95] If all homeowners and renters were given a fair choice between parking spaces and something else (such as another bedroom or a larger garden), some would choose fewer parking spaces, fewer cars, and a more liveable neighborhood. But off-street parking requirements deny us this choice, and they have helped to automobilize America beyond our natural desires; they hide the cost of parking in higher prices for everything else, and we respond accordingly. Consider an exactly equivalent system of subsidies for parking, financed by taxes on everything else. Rather than require off-street parking, cities could impose a sales tax on all goods and services, and use the revenue to reimburse motorists for all their parking expenses. The effects would resemble those produced by off-street parking requirements, but everyone would see that the tax-and-subsidize policy is indefensible, even grotesque.

Prices are the terms on which alternatives are offered to consumers, and consumers' choices accurately reveal their preferences only when prices accurately reflect the costs of these alternatives. In an efficient market, prices inform consumers about the cost of producing everything they buy, but transportation analysts commonly neglect parking prices when discussing whether drivers' choices reflect their preference for automobile travel. Consider Rutgers political scientist James Dunn's *Driving Forces: The Automobile, Its Enemies, and the Politics of Mobility*, published by the Brookings Institution. Commenting on the World Resources Institute's estimate that motorists receive a subsidy of $85 billion a year in free parking at shopping malls, factories, and offices, Dunn does not dispute the cost of the free parking, but instead says:

> Counting $85 billion in free parking as a subsidy is odd accounting, to say the least. The private owners of these parking lots paid to acquire, pave, light, and (increasingly) police them. No taxpayer dollars are involved.[96]

True, *taxpayers* don't pay for parking, but this misses the important point: *drivers* don't pay for it. Because off-street parking requirements hide the cost of parking in higher prices for everything else, solo driving appears much cheaper than it really is, and the result is massive overuse of both cars and parking. We take one or two tons of metal with us wherever we go and expect to park it as easily as we might leave a coat while we don't need it. We may burn a quart of gasoline to go for a fifth of gin, but we object to paying for parking at the liquor store.

People do pay for parking through higher prices for everything else. *Parking* is subsidized, not *people*, and we should not confuse the action with the actor. People park free in their role as motorists only because they pay for parking in all their other roles. People without cars also subsidize parking for people with cars, and this further skews choices toward cars and sprawl. Off-street parking requirements do not, by themselves, explain the popularity of cars and sprawl because both of these phenomena began before cities first required off-street parking in the 1930s. Most transportation historians agree that cars became popular because they offered great advantages compared with public transit, which was often viewed as a corrupt and unresponsive monopoly. In addition, growing traffic congestion reduced the speed of trams and buses, and therefore reduced the quality and increased the cost of public transportation; this had the perverse effect of further increasing the advantages of cars. What historians have not noticed, however, is that parking requirements—and the ubiquitous free parking they produce—have skewed our transportation and housing choices toward more cars and lower density.[97]

In *The Car and the City*, urban historian Sam Bass Warner says the car is a new form of public transportation. "It is a special kind of public transportation: the public provides the road, and, to use it, you must bring the car."[98] Cars do share the same right-of-way with buses, but not the same terminal capacity, which Warner neglects. Who provides the parking spaces for cars, and who pays for them? Everybody does every time they write a check for the rent or mortgage, shop at a grocery store, or buy tickets for a movie. Free parking is not really free because its cost is bundled into higher prices for everything else. Off-street parking requirements ensure that everybody pays for parking even if they walk, bicycle, or ride the bus. Because motorists pay for parking indirectly, the cost of parking rarely deters anyone from owning or driving a car, and the result is increased automobile dominance, traffic congestion, air pollution, and urban sprawl. Parking requirements thus help explain why America's attempt to be urbanized and fully motorized at the same time is destroying both the benefits of cities and the advantages of the private car.[99]

Parking requirements are not the only source of bias toward automobile travel, of course. UCLA planning professor Brian Taylor explains how the funding mechanism for the U.S. Interstate Highway System shifted transportation planning decisions from cities to state highway departments dominated by civil engineers.[100] The federal government matched state construction expenditures for Interstate Highways in urban areas on a nine-to-one ratio, but with the requirement for uniform design standards, regardless of location. This extraordinarily generous matching arrangement skewed urban transportation investment toward more freeways with more lanes, bigger interchanges, and higher speeds. States paid only 10¢ for every $1 they spent on the new highways, and cities paid nothing. The more the freeways cost, the more cities wanted them, in part because of all the jobs created by the massive construction projects.

Parking requirements operate in a symbiotic relationship with freeway construction: more freeways increase the demand for free parking at the destinations made more accessible by car, and the parking supply automatically keeps pace with the increased demand. The freeway system is here to stay, but if cities remove off-street parking requirements, the price of parking will begin to cover some of its costs.

Suppose cities had always charged market prices for curb parking and had let private decisions determine the quantity of off-street parking. Parking would not be free, but few people would complain about a shortage of it. Gold is scarce and expensive, for example, and is essential for many purposes, but there is no shortage of it: shortages result from underpricing. Parking requirements and free parking have helped to create the illusion that, all things considered, almost everyone prefers to drive everywhere alone, but everyone actually prefers the best value, and parking requirements keep the cost of driving so low that solo driving is the cheapest form of travel. If all drivers had to pay for their own parking, fewer people would "prefer" to drive everywhere.

PRECEDENT COAGULATES INTO TRADITION

Off-street parking requirements exemplify MIT planning professor Lloyd Rodwin's lament that planners often pursue short-term goals:

> Empirical studies of planning activities…showed most planning to be more ad hoc than comprehensive, and that most decisions involved the short term rather than the long term.[101]

In the politics of parking requirements, planners and politicians weigh the interests of voters (who want free parking and no spillover) against the interests of developers (who must pay for the required spaces).[102] Both of these are short-term concerns. No one takes into account how the required parking increases traffic congestion and air pollution, which are problems that can be shunted onto tomorrow. Even planners ignore how parking requirements degrade urban design and corrupt urban form. Parking requirements are never used as strategic instruments to achieve long-term goals. Instead, they are tactical responses to solve immediate and purely local spillover problems.

Another MIT planning professor, Dennis Frenchman, recommends that planners should instead emphasize longer-term solutions:

> Right now, the [planning] profession is focused primarily on resolving problems of the present, and developing solutions to current problems— inching forward into the future. I would argue that we need to extend our time horizon by studying where trends are leading and what kind of city may emerge.[103]

Frenchman's criticism of the planning profession in general applies to parking requirements in particular. Few urban planners can seriously contend that minimum parking requirements and ubiquitous free parking are long-term strategies to make great places and create sustainable cities. Urban planning is supposed to coordinate many individual actions toward a desired collective outcome, but planners do not consider the cumulative consequences of all the parking spaces they require for each land use.[104] Because free parking encourages driving, off-street parking requirements help explain why the U.S. had 1.2 motor vehicles per licensed driver in 2002 and slightly more than one vehicle per person of driving age.[105] Whatever future we are inching toward, planners ensure that we will park free when we get there. Parking requirements are often nothing more than precedent coagulated into tradition, and planning for parking is typically planning for *free* parking, which then biases travel choices toward driving. As University of Washington professor of architecture and urban planning Anne Vernez Moudon says, "The car is not the enemy, nor is the elimination of cars the solution. It is our *societal bias* toward cars that must be questioned."[106] Similarly, in his book on American downtowns, San Diego State University urban geography professor Larry Ford says:

> The problem is not the automobile. There are plenty of cars and traffic jams in European cities, but the urban planning and design there does not simply revolve around making space for the car. In American downtowns, however, that has too often been the case. For years, downtowns have been decimated as buildings have been cleared and streets widened in an effort to get more cars into the city. Since most cars are driven only a few hours per week, stor-

age is a big problem. Parking lots often take up more space than any other land use.[107]

Cars are here to stay, but the question remains: who should pay for parking them? To show the bias inherent in American parking requirements, consider an alternative approach. In Tokyo, residents must present proof that they own or have leased an off-street parking space before they can register an automobile. The parking requirement is thus linked to car ownership, not to housing ownership. Cars obviously need somewhere to park, but we should place the cost where it logically belongs—on car owners.

AN ANALOGY: BLOODLETTING

I previously used lead poisoning as an example to show how long-established medical practices have harmed patients. To conclude this chapter on how parking requirements harm cities, I will turn to another medical analogy. Jane Jacobs made it first in *The Death and Life of Great American Cities*, when she compared urban renewal programs to bloodletting:

> With bloodletting, it took years of learning to know precisely which veins, by what rituals, were to be opened for what symptoms. A superstructure of technical complication was erected in such deadpan detail that the literature still sounds almost plausible.... Medical analogies, applied to social organisms, are apt to be farfetched, and there is no point in mistaking mammalian chemistry for what goes on in a city. But analogies as to what goes on in the brains of earnest and learned men, dealing with complex phenomena they do not understand, do have a point. As in the pseudoscience of bloodletting, just so in the pseudoscience of city rebuilding and planning, years of learning and a plethora of subtle and complicated dogma have arisen on a foundation of nonsense.[108]

Until it was abandoned in the early twentieth century, bloodletting was the longest established of all medical treatments. Physicians had many pseudoscientific terms for what they were doing—"phlebotomy" and "venesection" meant opening a vein to remove blood as a therapeutic treatment. There were elaborate diagrams that showed precisely how much blood to take, from which part of the body, and when, to treat every conceivable ailment. Naturally, physicians collected a fee for each venesection performed.

Although bloodletting was a standard way to treat many ailments for more than 2,000 years, some physicians doubted the practice. Perhaps the most famous reservations were expressed after the death of George Washington. The youngest of the three physicians in attendance recom-

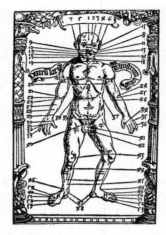

Figure 5-7. Venesection manikin, sixteenth century. Numbers indicate locations where in certain diseases venesection should be undertaken. (From Stoeffler, 1518, as illustrated in Heinrich Stern, *Theory and Practice of Bloodletting*, New York, 1915. Photo courtesy of NLM.)

mended against bleeding, but his senior colleagues bled Washington four times during the last day of his life, taking between five and six pints of blood. A month later, one of the senior physicians wrote to the other and admitted that their young colleague was probably right:

> You must remember that he was averse to bleeding the General, and I have often thought that if we had acted accordingly to his suggestion, when he said, "he needs all his strength—bleeding will diminish it," and taken no more blood from him, our good friend might have been alive now. But we were governed by the best light we had; we thought we were right, and so we were justified.[109]

Planners are in much the same position today. They are governed by the best light they have; after all, the American Planning Association and the Institute of Transportation Engineers are the two main sources of data used to set off-street parking requirements. All zoning ordinances contain elaborate tables stating precisely how many parking spaces are required, just as medical texts once contained elaborate tables stating precisely how much blood to let (see Figure 5-7).[110] Planners think they are right, and so they feel justified. Few practicing planners are rebellious or rash enough to say that parking requirements are nonsense on stilts.

Parking requirements also resemble bloodletting in the public's uncritical approval. George Washington himself insisted on being bled even before his doctors arrived, and most patients assumed that bleeding must be beneficial. One eighteenth-century physician observed:

> People are so familiarized to bleeding that they cannot easily conceive any hurt or danger to ensue, and therefore readily submit, when constitutional fear is out of the question, to the opening of a vein, however unskillfully advised.[111]

Similarly, most people today assume that planners know how many parking spaces every land use needs, and few doubt the need for parking requirements, "however unskillfully advised." On a more positive note, there is another parallel between parking requirements and bloodletting: just as putting an end to bloodletting produced huge benefits, so too will removing off-street parking requirements.

CONCLUSION: FIRST, DO NO HARM

A great planning disaster, as Peter Hall defined it, is a planning process that costs a lot of money and has gone seriously wrong. The word "disaster" usually refers to something that goes suddenly wrong, like a shipwreck, but parking requirements are not a disaster in this sense. Instead, parking requirements slowly and mysteriously sap a city's strength, just as lead poisoning slowly and mysteriously debilitates a human being. Cities do not die, of course, but parking requirements weaken cities in subtle ways. They distort transportation choices toward cars, and thus increase traffic congestion, air pollution, and energy consumption. They reduce land values and tax revenues. They damage the economy and degrade the environment. They debase architecture and urban design. They burden enterprise and prevent the reuse of older buildings. And they increase the prices for everything except parking. Perhaps words such as blight, distress, and torment best describe how parking requirements afflict cities. Planners and politicians mean well when they establish parking requirements, but as Graham Greene wrote about Alden Pyle, the protagonist of *The Quiet American*, "I never knew a man who had better motives for all the trouble he caused." Could things be any worse if there were no planning for parking at all?

Daniel Boorstin, the University of Chicago historian who later became the Librarian of Congress, said, "To know our disease, to discover what we suffer from, may itself be the only possible cure."[112] Planners have disastrously misdiagnosed the parking problem as not enough parking spaces, and cities have imposed off-street parking requirements as the cure. Instead, parking requirements are a disease masquerading as a cure.

CHAPTER 5 NOTES

1. Hall (1982) conducted case studies of several great planning disasters, such as the Anglo-French Concorde supersonic airliner, of which only 16 were eventually built at immense cost. Bunnell (2002, 16-18) points out that none of the seven cases that Hall studied were of conventional urban planning practices. Two cases (of San Francisco's Bay Area Rapid Transit System and Sydney's Opera House) had technology problems and major cost overruns, but are not disasters in most peoples' eyes. Off-street parking requirements are, however, a conventional planning practice that costs a lot of money and has gone seriously wrong.

2. The *2001 National Household Travel Survey* found that 87 percent of trips less than 50 miles, and 90 percent of trips greater than 50 miles, were made by personal vehicle (United States Department of Transportation 2003a, 21 and 25).

3. Whyte (1988, 314).

4. Duany, Plater-Zyberk, and Speck (2000, 162-63).

5. Plans of other towns also show that parking occupies more land than all other uses combined. In their book on visualizing change in small towns and rural areas, Julie Campoli, Elizabeth Humstone, and Alex Maclean (2002, 32) present an aerial view of Manchester, Vermont, showing that parking occupies far more land than buildings. Their aerial views of many small towns show the disruptive gaps that parking lots insert between buildings.

6. "Plenty of Space to Park," *The Buffalo News*, July 10, 2003.

7. Halperin (1963, 191). Oakland is not unusual among Bay Area cities. A letter the Fremont Chamber of Commerce sends to all new residents brags, "With 173,000 residents Fremont is the 4th largest city in the Bay Area. We are an exceptionally well planned city, which is proven by the fact that we have no paid parking lots or parking meters."

8. See Karban (1982) for an explanation of predator satiation. In this analogy, cars (or drivers) are the predators, and parking spaces are the prey.

9. Williams and Taylor (1986, 4).

10. Fulton (1999, 130-31). Similarly, Harvard professor of real estate development Richard Peiser (2003, 173) explains that a three-story apartment building with 900-square-foot apartments will have a footprint of 300 square feet per apartment (900 square feet divided by three stories). If each apartment has two parking spaces, and if each parking space occupies 300 to 350 square feet of land, two parking spaces per apartment will occupy 600 to 700 square feet of land. The footprint for each apartment's parking is thus at least twice the footprint for each apartment.

11. The floor-area ratio (FAR) is the total floor area in a building divided by the land area of its site. If the zoning allows a FAR of 1.0, the maximum floor area cannot exceed the area of the building's site.

12. The Planning Advisory Service (1991) surveyed the parking requirements in 127 cities. The median parking requirement for the cities that base their requirements for fast-food restaurants on gross floor area is 10 spaces per 1,000 square feet

13. Fulton (1999, 131) makes a similar point: "A restaurant will usually be required to have far more parking available than a retail shop. The ability of the landowner to open a restaurant will depend not on the zoning, but on the ability to build or secure enough parking. If the parking can't be worked into the project, the landowner may be forced to open a retail shop instead of a restaurant."

14. Garreau (1991, 120).

15. Washington State Department of Ecology and City of Olympia (1995).

16. Litman (1998, 10). Litman (2003) describes the *Online TDM Encyclopedia*, which presents many promising mobility management strategies. It is available online at www.vtpi.org.

17. Section 5.3.3 of the SmartCode states "The Functions specified in Section 6.4 [residential, lodging, office, and retail] shall be as limited in intensity by the Required Parking." The SmartCode is available online at www.dpz.com/index.htm.

18. Section 6.4 of the SmartCode. The SmartCode does require less parking than most zoning ordinances, and it has relatively few categories of land use. It also allows on-street parking to count toward the required parking, and reductions for shared parking are allowed. A city can also reduce or eliminate the parking requirements in any particular location. Duany says these limited reforms are "achieved without freaking out the conventional bean-counters for whom the essence of planning is parking and traffic numbers" (message to The Practice of New Urbanism listserve on May 25, 2002).

19. Jacobs (1993, 305-6).

20. "Rethinking San Francisco's Parking Requirements," San Francisco Planning Department, 2002, available online at http://sfgov.org/planning/neighborhoodplans/index.htm.

21. "Wallflowers in a Hot Market," *Los Angeles Times*, March 20, 2001. The building has 380,000 gross square feet (320,000 rentable square feet) of office space, and 697 parking stalls. The rectangular parking structure is clad in imported Indian ruby red granite, and the triangular office tower is clad in sapphire blue reflective glass. The building's design complied with the principles of feng shui, a traditional Chinese system of divination that seeks to bring structures into harmony with natural forces. Doors, elevator shafts, and stairwells were placed to ensure that luck would not pour out of the building ("Empty Downtown L.A. Office Tower May Be Getting Its Fill," *Los Angeles Times*, May 24, 2003). The building was sold in 2003 to a developer who intends to convert it into residential condominiums.

22. Dunphy (2000, 79).

23. Parking requirements can also prevent a church from occupying a site. *The San Diego Union-Tribune* reported on a typical dispute about church parking. The Community of Praise Baptist Church rented an aging storefront for their services in a part of National City, California, that is zoned for churches. Six months after occupying the vacated furniture store with no off-street parking, the church found it had neglected to check the city's parking requirements. In defense of the church, a member of the city council who drove past the church on Sundays and saw available parking argued that the church offered more customers to local businesses and placed more people in the high-crime area during times when the area was a ghost town. "The Lord placed us here," Pastor E. M. Williams said. Nevertheless, the planning commission voted 4-3 to deny an occupancy permit because there weren't enough parking spaces ("Churchgoers Face Eviction over Parking," *San Diego Union-Tribune*, September 13, 2003).

24. Dunphy (2003).

25. "A Little Landscaping Can Change a Lot," *Milwaukee Journal Sentinel*, August 8, 2004.

26. Southworth and Owens (1993, 282-3). Liebs (1985) explores the history of how cars affected roadside commerce and architecture.

27. Because the earliest cars were expensive, the earliest garages were former stables and coach houses on large estates, often with quarters for a chauffeur. As automobile owner-ship spread to the middle class, garages became practical sheds facing onto alleys. By the late 1930s, garages became more substantial, and the house and the garage were often designed as a matched set. During the late 1940s, garages moved forward and were attached to the house, and they now poke forward toward the street, occupying much of the frontage of many houses. John Brinckerhoff Jackson (1980), Drummond Buckley (1992), David Gebhard (1992), Larry Ford (1994 and 2000), and Kira Obolensky (2001) relate the history of domestic garages. Jackson says that Radburn, New Jersey, was the first development that was designed with the awareness of the garage as an essential adjunct to the dwelling.

28. U.S. Census Bureau's *1995 Property Owners and Managers Survey*.

29. Dorsett (1998).

30. Brinkman (1948, 27).

31. Mark Frauenfelder, "How I Came to Love the Dingbat," *Los Angeles Weekly*, October 1, 1999, available online at http://boingboing.net/dingbats.html. "Tuck-under" parking is the term sometimes used to describe a building where some or all of the ground floor is used for parking instead of living space. One distinguishing feature of a dingbat is that its tuck-under parking occupies the full front of the building, without garage doors.

32. That is, the cost of the required parking per apartment exceeds the land cost per apartment.

33. Bertha (1964). Before 1961, Oakland's zoning ordinance did not even mention off-street parking in residential districts.

34. Because the cost per dwelling unit increased by 18 percent and the density per acre fell by 30 percent, the total investment in housing construction per acre fell by 18 percent (1.18 x .7 = .82).

35. Bertha (1964, 108-20).

36. Bertha (1964, 118).

37. Landowners pay for parking requirements through lower land values, and this can distort our understanding of the requirements' cost. Land values fell by 33 percent after Oakland began to require one parking space per dwelling unit, so we cannot use this new, lower land value to estimate the cost of the required parking spaces. Because imposing the parking requirement itself reduces density and land values, we must use the *pre*-require-ment land value to estimate the cost of required parking spaces.

38. Jia and Wachs (1998) used the statistical technique of hedonic regression analysis to estimate how off-street parking spaces affect the sale prices of housing units, while hold-ing constant the effects of other variables. They estimated how much a parking space increases the market value of a single-family house, not how much it increases the cost of constructing one. The estimated value of $47,000 per space does, however, suggest the value of a curb space—and how much cities could earn by renting curb parking spaces to residents, rather than giving the curb cuts to homeowners free (see Chapters 17 and 19). It also suggests that the housing market gives developers an incentive to build off-street parking and planners do not need to require it.

39. Adler (1985, 376).

40. Hermosa Beach, California, for example, allows a homeowner or tenant to buy a permit to park on the street in the width of their own driveway for a one-time fee of $35. All other restrictions on parking (such as no parking during certain hours for street cleaning) still apply. The permit, which includes the address of the owner or lessee of the property, must be displayed on the dashboard on the vehicle when it is parked on the street in front of the driveway. These permits are especially convenient for guests.

41. Willson (1995).

42. We can use Willson's model to calculate that increasing the parking requirement for offices from 2.5 to 3.8 spaces per 1,000 square feet would reduce land values by 32 percent and density by 30 percent. In comparison, when Oakland introduced its off-street parking for apartments, Brian Bertha estimated that land values fell by 33 percent and density fell by 30 percent. Willson did not rely on any information in Bertha's case study, and Willson's methodology was different. Nevertheless, the two independent studies came to a similar conclusion.

43. This total cost includes the costs of site clearance, site development, architect and other professional design services, project management, inspection, surveys, tests, construction, and contingencies.

44. The data are taken from a memorandum from the Office of the President of the University of California to the Regents' Committee on Grounds and Buildings, January 18, 2001. The two-bedroom apartments are 770 square feet, and the efficiencies are 385 square feet. In the budget submitted to the Regents, $4,520,000 in cost is shifted from parking to housing because the project displaces a surface parking lot, and the Housing Administration will pay the Parking Services to replace the surface spaces lost. Table 5-4 shifts this $4,520,000 back to parking cost to separate the two costs accurately; this shift does not change the total project cost of $144,770,000. The project is also described in the Final Environmental Impact Report for the UCLA Southwest Campus Housing and Parking project, State Clearinghouse No. 2000051014, January 2001.

45. Why does the project provide one parking space per bedroom? The UCLA Housing Services surveyed graduate students, and asked, If you were to choose to move into the proposed new housing for single graduate students, how many automobiles or motor-bikes/cycles would you be likely to bring to your apartment? Nothing was said about the price of parking, and parking is free in all other graduate student apartments that UCLA provides. Ninety-four percent of students answered they were likely to bring one car, and UCLA planners interpreted this as a demand for one parking space per bedroom, but few students will bring cars worth as much as the parking spaces ($21,000 per space).

46. North Westwood Village Specific Plan, Ordinance 163.202, effective March 5, 1988. If there are more than four habitable rooms, Los Angeles requires 3.5 parking spaces per apartment.

47. This assumes that the additional parking spaces would cost $20,972 per space, which is the average cost per space in UCLA's project. Providing 26 percent more parking spaces would probably increase the marginal cost per space, given the number of apartments. Therefore, this estimate for the cost of meeting the city's parking requirement is conservative.

48. Palo Alto Planning Commission (1995). Alma Place was awarded the first-ever Prometheus Prize for Architectural Excellence in Affordable Housing Design from the Housing Trust of Santa Clara County in 2002.

49. Part of the first level includes the lobby and offices, while all of the second level is parking.

50. The building contains 371 square feet per apartment, including the common areas for a lobby, laundry, meeting room, and vending machines (Palo Alto Planning Commission 1995, 16). The apartments alone average just 260 square feet, and they include a bathroom and a kitchen area with a microwave and mini-refrigerator.

51. Nelson\Nygaard Consulting Associates (2003, 20). Because the proposal was to reduce housing rents by $50 a month and charge $100 a month for parking, a resident without a car would have paid $50 a month less, and a resident with a car would have paid $50 a month more. None of the parking spaces could be rented to nonresidents because tax credit subsidies, which were a funding source for the project, may not be used for any portion of the development that does not directly benefit the residents.

52. Palo Alto Planning Commission (1995, 5).

53. Palo Alto Planning Commission (1995, 5 and 8).

54. Palo Alto Planning Commission (1995, 8).

55. Transportation and Land Use Coalition (2002, 12-3). As mentioned above, in an area along Wilshire Boulevard that has the best bus service in the city, Los Angeles requires 2.5 parking spaces for each dwelling unit regardless of the number of habitable rooms.

56. Section 23D.40.080 of the Berkeley Zoning Code.

57. Southern California Association of Non-Profit Housing (2004, 10). The requirement was for a hypothetical 100-unit development consisting of 10 studios, 40 one-bedroom units, 40 two-bedroom units, and 10 three-bedroom units. A similar study of 44 cities in the San Francisco Bay Area found that the parking requirements for apartment buildings ranged from 1 space per unit (in two cities) up to 3.5 spaces per unit, with an average of 1.9 spaces per unit (Cook et al. 1997, 19).

58. The *2001 National Household Travel Survey* reported 235 billion household vehicle trips and 2.28 trillion household VMT for the nation's 107 million households (Polzin, Chu, and Toole-Holt, 2003, 6 and 16).

59. Glaeser and Gyourko (2003) argue that zoning and other land-use controls help explain why the price of housing is far above its cost of construction in some areas of the United States.

60. In its survey of parking requirements in American cities, the Planning Advisory Service (1991) reported that the parking requirements in Hillsborough County, Florida, were 1 space per 1,000 square feet for a furniture store and 3 spaces per 1,000 square feet for a bicycle repair shop. Parking lots usually accommodate about 3 spaces per 1,000 square feet of surface area, including the area needed for access aisles. Therefore, a requirement of 3 spaces per 1,000 square feet of floor area implies adding a parking lot equal in area to the total floor area of the building it serves.

61. Duany, Plater-Zyberk, and Speck (2000, 163).

62. DeWitt et al. (2003, 14-15) describe these exemptions from parking requirements. Cincinnati exempts businesses with fewer than 2,000 square feet from parking requirements.

63. Communication from William Spikowski of Spikowski Planning Associates in Fort Myers, Florida, on August 5, 1999.

64. Many older buildings were constructed before parking was required or when parking requirements were lower. If these buildings are substantially remodeled or rebuilt, they must meet the higher parking requirements now in place. Parking requirements are not the only problem that has delayed redevelopment, but they retard redevelopment by making it more difficult and more expensive. The adjacent neighborhoods lack retail services, even food stores, and this discourages residential redevelopment.

65. DeWitt et al. (2003, 11). The Saint Paul Housing and Redevelopment Authority later purchased a nearby lot to meet the parking requirements for the building.

66. "Holy Land," *New York Times*, February 3, 2002. The desecration of historic sites to provide free parking has a long history. For example, here is a description of the federal government's parking policies in the 1950s, as related by a planning consultant to the District of Columbia: "The federal government has tried a variety of methods...to satisfy current parking requirements. The first and most obvious method is to use every inch of paved space for parking, regardless of the purpose for which it was designed. Typical examples of this expedient may be seen throughout the Federal Triangle, particularly in the Commerce Department Building. The usual pattern is to fill interior courtyards and their access roadways with cars in the manner of an overfilled parking garage, with aisles full. Another method is...to convert pleasantly landscaped front, side, and rear yards into paved parking areas with only a narrow stip of lawn retained to try to preserve the traditional appearance of a landscaped setting for federal buildings. A fine example of this is the Pension or old General Accounting Office Building.... Parking spaces are generally free...but they are usually allocated to the highest paid employees and become in effect a [tax-exempt] salary bonus" (Sutermeister 1959, 249-250).

67. Section 12.95.2 of the Los Angeles Municipal Code.

68. It is particularly inappropriate to require off-street parking for sidewalk cafés, which can add vitality to downtown streets and encourage both residential and office development. After Stamford, Connecticut, changed its parking regulations in 1992 to encourage sidewalk cafés, 40 new sidewalk cafés opened in its downtown. John Ruotolo of the Stamford Downtown Special Services District credits these cafés with encouraging both residential and commercial development in the downtown: "You walk down the streets and there are people there. There is a vitality there. There is a different kind of excitement everywhere you pass" (*Stamford Advocate*, July 28, 2004). Nearby Norwalk, Connecticut, requires 1 parking space for every 45 square feet of restaurant space, and no restaurant owners have been willing to provide year-round parking spaces for seasonal sidewalk dining space.

69. Section 9(E) of the Westwood Village Specific Plan. This specific plan was established by Los Angeles City Ordinance 164.305 (effective January 30, 1989). Available online at www.cityofla.org/PLN/complan/specplan/pdf/wwdvil.pdf. Other than a parking structure built by the city, no building has replaced a parking lot since Westwood Village's replacement parking requirement was enacted in 1989. The 50 percent replacement ratio is obviously pulled out of thin air.

70. Voith (1998a, 4-5). Also see Voith (1998b) for an analysis of relationships among agglomeration, access, and congestion.

71. Northwestern University urban economist Edwin Mills (1972, 53) explained, "Other things being equal, goods and services are produced downtown if their production functions permit substitution of capital and labor for land.... Therefore, understanding how the urban economy ticks is mainly a matter of understanding how markets combine land with other inputs in varying proportions at different places to produce goods and services." Off-street parking requirements increase the cost of combining land with other inputs and interfere with how the urban economy ticks.

72. Dueker, Strathman, and Bianco (1998, 28).

73. Fulton (2001, 254). The cost of the Disney Hall parking garage ($110 million) was 40 percent of the cost of Disney Hall ($274 million). Disney Hall is across First Street from the Los Angeles Music Center, which was built in 1964. Parking was also expensive for that project: the underground parking structure cost $13 million, and the Music Center cost $18 million (Fulton 2001, 237). Because Disney Hall has 293,000 square feet and 2,188 parking spaces, it has "only" 7.5 parking spaces per 1,000 square feet, rather than the 10 spaces per 1,000 square feet required by the zoning ordinance.

74. First Amendment to Walt Disney Concert Hall Philharmonic Sublease, Section 8.1:

"During each Winter Season throughout the Term, Philharmonic shall schedule and cause performances of orchestra concerts in the Concert Hall before a paying audience of at least one hundred twenty-eight (128) scheduled performances (not including open rehearsals with an invited audience)."

75. The construction start for Disney Hall was delayed until 2000 because the sponsors needed more time to raise the $274 million needed to pay for it. The $110 million spent on the parking garage was more than the funding gap that delayed the construction of the concert hall for several years. The cheaper stainless steel surface also has a practical disadvantage. The blinding glare of reflected sunlight from the stainless steel heats up nearby apartments, and parts of Disney Hall have been shrouded with a mesh blanket to kill the glare until a permanent solution is found.

76. Jacobs (1962, 19).

77. Wormser (1997, 14).

78. Kay (1997, 63). Similarly, in his book on American downtowns, Ford (2003, 262) says, "Strolling along a street is no fun when cars are barreling in and out of cavelike garages. The blank walls that dominate most parking structures also dilute the urban experience."

79. Kenworthy and Laube (1999, Chapter 3). The data are available only for CBDs because this is the only place where cities regularly survey the parking supply. Kenworthy and Laube provided transportation data for 46 cities, but parking space counts were available for only 44 cities.

80. A typical parking lot has about 325 cars per hectare (130 cars per acre), including the necessary space for access aisles. This density is equivalent to about 30 square meters (330 square feet) of land per parked car. Because each hectare of land accommodates 325 parking spaces, dividing the total number of CBD parking spaces by 325 spaces per hectare gives the total land area occupied by this theoretical parking lot.

81. The 2000 Census found that the entire Los Angeles urbanized area has the highest population density in the United States: 7,068 people per square mile (see Appendix F). The Texas Transportation Institute (TTI) annually surveys traffic data in 70 American cities and calculates the Roadway Congestion Index to rank them by the severity of their traffic congestion. Los Angeles has ranked highest on the TTI Roadway Congestion Index in every year since 1983 (Texas Transportation Institute 2003, Exhibit A-18).

82. Pucher (2003, Table 6).

83. Tables QT-H11 and DP-4 in Census 2000 show the relationship between housing tenure and car ownership. Available at www.census.gov.

84. The National Multi Housing Council (2000) used data from the U.S. Census Bureau's *1997 American Housing Survey* to calculate the vehicle ownership rates for occupied apartments in structures with at least five rental units. The vehicle counts include passenger cars, vans, SUVs, and light trucks owned or regularly used by a household member and ordinarily kept at home.

85. See United States Department of Transportation (2003a, 20) for automobile ownership rates.

86. See *United States v. City of Parma, Ohio*, 494 F. Supp.1049, 1052 (United States District Court for the Northern District of Ohio 1980).

87. *United States v. City of Parma, Ohio*, 494 F. Supp.1049, 1089 (C. N. D. Ohio 1980).

88. Tables HCT33B, HCT33D, HCT33H, and HCT33I in Census 2000.

89. *Hobson v. Hansen*, 269 F. Supp. 401, 497 (D. D. C. 1967).

90. "Housing Project a Costly Lesson for Taxpayers Policy: L.A.'s Casa Gloria was built for $233,000 a unit. Questionable decisions, inefficiencies of financing faulted." *Los Angeles Times*, May 16, 1994.

91. Millard-Ball (2002, 19).

92. In other words, drivers have a more elastic demand for shopping at any single store than do nondrivers. Segelhorst (1971, 28) points out that the CBD retailers validate for parking but not for transit. "The rationale is that transit shoppers are captive to the central business district, and that the extension of validation to include transit would be an unprofitable subsidy of transit customers by retailers." Or as Homer Simpson explained, "If we buy a new car, we get our parking validated for free!"

93. Lan and Kanafani (1993).

94. Bacon (1993).

95. If two goods are complementary—like cars and parking—an increase in the price of one will reduce the demand for the other.

96. Dunn (1998, 16). This is Dunn's sole reference to parking in *Driving Forces: the Automobile, Its Enemies, and the Politics of Mobility.*

97. For example, James Flink is the nation's foremost historian of the automobile, but the word parking does not appear in the index of any of his three volumes on the history of the automobile (Flink 1970, 1976, and 1988). Similarly, in his essay on "Cars and Their Enemies," James Q. Wilson (1997) mentions parking only once, to say that the critics of cars recommend heavy restrictions on parking. But the main—almost the only—parking policy in the U.S. is just the opposite—to require parking, not restrict it.

98. Warner (1992, 9).

99. Owen (1959, 3). Although he wasn't referring specifically to parking requirements, Brookings Institution economist Wilfred Owen pointed out the conflicts between motorization and urbanization in his book, *Cities in the Motor Age.*

100. Taylor (2000).

101. Rodwin (2000, 18).

102. Existing businesses with no off-street parking must rely on the nearby curb parking supply to serve their customers. These existing businesses may thus insist that all new businesses meet the city's parking requirements, so that the customers of new businesses will not occupy the scarce curb parking. Existing businesses may also support off-street parking requirements for new businesses in order to hobble competition from the new businesses.

103. Frenchman (2000, 29).

104. In his survey of 70 regional transportation plans in the U.S., John Shaw (1997b) found that parking is typically not considered a key component of regional transportation systems and is often dealt with only as a minor element that "should be considered."

105. The U.S. Department of Transportation (2002, Tables MV-1 and DL-1C) reported that in 2002 there were 230 million registered motor vehicles, 223 million persons of driving age (above 16 years old), and 194 million licensed drivers. There were thus 1.03 vehicles per person of driving age, and 0.87 licensed drivers per person of driving age.

106. Moudon (1987, 16). Italics in the original.

107. Ford (2003, 265-266).

108. Jacobs (1961, 12-13).

109. Letter from Dr. Gustavus Brown to Dr. James Craik, January 21, 1800. The doctors agreed that Washington suffered from "inflamatory quinsy," and the problem is now diagnosed as a streptococcus infection. Bleeding was not the only treatment the doctors inflicted on Washington. They wrapped his throat with flannel that had been dipped in a solution of ammonia and a toxic preparation of the crushed, dried bodies of the cantharis beetle (Spanish fly). By mouth they administered a mixture of molasses, butter, and vinegar, a gargle of vinegar and sage tea, and an emetic of calomel and tartar. Other treatments were a poultice of wheat bran paste applied to the skin, and an enema. Ferling (1988, 506) and Lossing (1859, 319) describe the medical procedures.

110. Davis and Appel (1979) present a fascinating account of the history of bloodletting. Medical journals continued to publish articles advocating bloodletting until the 1920s. The profession of medicine existed for thousands of years before doctors were able to do much more good than harm (think of all the bloodletting with unsterilized instruments). The profession of urban planning is much younger, and planners undoubtedly do some harm along with all the good they do (think of all the required parking spaces that disfigure cities).

111. Dickson (1765, 1). Many patients died after bloodletting, of course, and physicians naturally thought that bloodletting did not work because the patient was already too sick. Similarly, merchants often blame downtown business problems on a lack of parking, and when a new public parking lot does not improve business, they can always say that even more parking is needed.

112. Boorstin (1962, 259).

6

The Cost of Required Parking Spaces

Discovery commences with the awareness of anomaly.

—*THOMAS KUHN*

The cost of meeting a parking requirement depends on the cost of the required parking spaces. Because most parking is free in the U.S., it may seem reasonable to assume that most parking spaces don't cost much, but in this chapter I will show that each space in a parking structure costs at least $125 a month. The estimate requires extended calculations, however, so readers like Kingsley Amis's *Lucky Jim*, "whose policy it was to read as little as possible of any given book," may wish to skim or skip the chapter if they accept that parking spaces cost this much.[1] In the next chapter I will use this estimate to show that the cost of all parking spaces in the U.S. exceeds the value of all cars and may even exceed the value of all roads. These findings point to an anomaly that requires an explanation: *if parking costs so much, why is it usually free?*

HOW MUCH DOES A PARKING SPACE COST?

There is no way to estimate the cost of surface parking without knowing the price of land, which varies by location. Depending on the price of land, a surface parking space can cost almost nothing or more than $100,000.[2] For structured parking, however, we can estimate a lower bound on the cost per space *without* knowing the price of land. Because a parking structure occupies land that could be used for surface parking, we can estimate the cost of the parking spaces *added* by the structure, and the relevant question thus becomes: *What is the cost per parking space added?*

Consider a 750-space parking structure built at UCLA on a site that had provided 200 surface spaces.[3] Although it contains 750 spaces, it adds only 550 spaces to the parking supply. The construction cost was $12.8 million, or $23,200 *per space added* ($12,777,000 ÷ 550 spaces).

We cannot credit the structure with providing the 200 parking spaces that would have been on the site if the structure had not been built, and calculating the cost for the 550 spaces *added* by the structure thus takes into account the opportunity cost of the land used for its footprint. We can therefore calculate the cost per parking space added by a parking structure without the need to estimate land values. Note, however, that by valuing the opportunity cost of land as a surface parking lot, this method neglects other alternative uses that might be more valuable. Because a parking structure is usually built only when land is too valuable to use for surface parking, the cost per space added by a structure is therefore a lower-bound estimate of the total cost (including land cost) of structured parking spaces.

Cost per Space Added by 15 Parking Structures

Using this method, I have estimated the cost of the parking spaces added by 15 parking structures built on the UCLA campus between 1961 and 2002. Table 6-1 shows the results.[4]

Column 1 shows when each structure was built, column 2 its name, and column 3 the number of spaces in it. Column 4 shows the number of potential surface spaces lost as a result of building the structure (no surface spaces are lost for the four that are underground).[5] Subtracting the lost surface spaces from the spaces in the structure gives the net number of spaces added (column 5). In total, the 15 structures contain 19,686 spaces and occupy sites that would have provided 3,110 surface spaces. They therefore added 16,576 spaces.

Column 6 shows the original cost of each structure in the year of construction, and column 7 converts this cost into 2002 dollars by adjusting for construction cost inflation. Column 7 thus shows how much each structure would have cost if it had been built in 2002.[6] Column 8 shows the original cost per space added, and column 9 converts this to 2002 dollars. For the structures built between 1961 and 2002, the average cost in 2002 dollars was $22,500 per parking space added.

The cost per space in a parking structure depends on two factors: the structure's cost per square foot and the number of square feet per parking space. First, the structure's cost per square foot depends on the quality of the design and materials and whether it is aboveground or underground.

Table 6-1. Cost per Parking Space Added by 15 Parking Structures

Year built	Structure name	Spaces in structure	Surface spaces lost	Spaces added by structure	Structure cost		Cost per space added	
					Year built	2002	Year built	2002
(1)	(2)	(3)	(4)	(5)=(3)-(4)	(6)	(7)	(8)=(6)/(5)	(9)=(7)/(5)
1961	5	765	219	546	$1,091,000	$8,421,000	$2,000	$15,400
1963	14	1,428	355	1,073	$1,745,000	$12,662,000	$1,600	$11,600
1964	3	1,168	213	955	$1,859,000	$12,985,000	$1,900	$13,300
1966	9	1,800	298	1,502	$3,490,000	$22,392,000	$2,300	$14,800
1967	8	2,839	666	2,173	$6,061,000	$36,896,000	$2,800	$17,000
1969	2	2,253	323	1,930	$5,610,000	$28,903,000	$2,900	$14,900
1977	CHS	921	319	602	$7,084,000	$17,980,000	$11,800	$29,900
1980	6	750	200	550	$6,326,000	$12,777,000	$11,500	$23,200
1983	4	448	0	448	$8,849,000	$14,229,000	$19,800	$31,800
1990	1	2,851	346	2,505	$52,243,000	$72,182,000	$20,900	$28,900
1990	RC	144	53	91	$2,040,000	$2,819,000	$22,300	$30,800
1991	SV	716	0	716	$14,945,000	$20,209,000	$20,900	$28,300
1995	3 Addition	840	118	722	$9,900,000	$11,831,000	$13,700	$16,400
1998	4 Addition	1,263	0	1,263	$33,217,000	$36,685,000	$26,300	$29,000
2002	7	1,500	0	1,500	$47,300,000	$47,300,000	$31,500	$31,500
Total		19,686	3,110	16,576	$201,760,000	$358,271,000	—	—
Average 1961-1969		1,709	346	1,363	$3,300,000	$20,400,000	$2,300	$14,500
Average 1977-2002		1,048	115	933	$20,200,000	$26,200,000	$19,900	$27,800
Average 1961-2002		1,312	207	1,105	$13,500,000	$23,900,000	$12,800	$22,500

Note: The *ENR* Construction Cost Index is used to convert the original construction cost to 2002 dollars.

A structure with superior architectural design or built underground will cost more per square foot. Second, the number of square feet per parking space refers to the efficiency of the structure's layout: more square feet per parking space means lower efficiency and a higher cost per space. For example, if the construction cost is $50 per square foot, an efficient structure with 300 square feet per space will cost $15,000 per space (300 x $50), while a less efficient structure with 400 square feet per space will cost $20,000 per space (400 x $50).[7]

Urban Density Influences the Type of Structure

Figure 6-1 shows the cost per space added by each structure (from column 9 in Table 6-1), and it reveals a striking pattern: the average cost is $14,500 per space added by the structures built in the 1960s and $27,800 per space added by the ones built since 1977. After adjusting for inflation, the spaces added since 1977 have cost 92 percent more than the spaces added in the 1960s. Although the newer spaces are more expensive, the type of parking structure rather than the year of its construction explains most of the variation in cost.

Figure 6-1. Cost Per Parking Space Added (2002$)

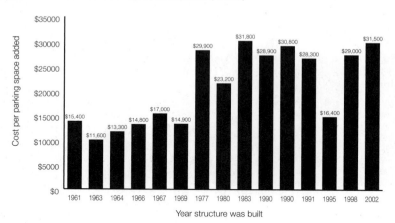

Year structure was built

The newer spaces are more expensive for two reasons. First, seven of the nine structures built since 1977 have some or all spaces underground, while no underground spaces were built in the 1960s. Underground parking requires expensive excavation, shoring, waterproofing, fireproofing, ventilation, and lighting. Second, the structures built since 1977 are smaller, averaging 39 percent fewer spaces than the ones built in the 1960s. Small structures are less efficient because the fixed costs of ramps, elevators, and stairwells are spread among fewer spaces. The above-ground Recreation Center (RC) structure is unusually small (only 144 spaces) and expensive ($30,800 per space added).[8]

The price of land does not enter these calculations, so it does not *directly* explain the high cost of parking spaces added since 1977. Nevertheless, it *indirectly* explains the high cost of new structures because the increasing scarcity of vacant land on campus has led to more expensive methods of construction that conserve land, such as building underground or on small sites.[9]

The UCLA parking structures built in the 1960s resemble those typically built in suburban areas where land is inexpensive and large undeveloped sites are available. In his study of suburban office developments in Southern California, Richard Willson found that the average land-and-construction cost for structured parking was $12,300 per space in 1995 ($14,700 per space when adjusted for construction cost inflation to 2002), which is almost identical to the average inflation-adjusted cost of $14,500 per space added by the suburban-style aboveground structures built at UCLA in the 1960s.[10] The lower cost of parking structures built at UCLA in the 1960s thus reflects the lower cost of building parking structures in suburban areas.

Structure Type Determines the Cost per Space

We can examine two parking structures built as additions to existing structures to explore why the cost per space increased after 1977. The two new additions are similar to the older original structures. The aboveground Structure 3 addition built in 1995 resembles the original aboveground Structure 3 built in 1964, and the underground Structure 4 addition built in 1998 resembles the original underground Structure 4 built in 1983 (Table 6-2). When we look at the cost per space in 1998 dollars, each addition cost almost the same as the original structure.[11] This close match shows that the cost per space added depends not on the year it was built but rather on the structure type—aboveground or underground.[12]

Table 6-2 also shows the cost of an underground garage constructed beneath Pershing Square in downtown Los Angeles in 1952.[13] The original cost of $2,500 per space is equivalent to $25,800 in 1998—close to the cost per space for the two underground garages built at UCLA in 1983 and 1998. In real terms, the cost of building underground parking changed little in half a century.

We can also compare the average cost of UCLA's aboveground parking structures with the national average. In *Building Construction Cost Data*, R. S. Means publishes cost estimates for various types of construction in

Table 6-2. Cost of Aboveground and Underground Parking Structures
(Cost per space added by five parking structures in Los Angeles)

	Aboveground (Structure 3)		Underground (Structure 4)		Underground (Pershing Square)
	1964 Original	1995 Addition	1983 Original	1998 Addition	1952 Structure
Current $	$1,900	$13,700	$19,800	$26,300	$2,500
1998 $	$12,200	$14,700	$28,600	$26,300	$25,800

The original portion of UCLA's Structure 3 (built in 1964) contains 1,168 spaces in five aboveground levels; the addition built in 1995 contains 840 spaces in seven aboveground levels.

The original portion of UCLA's Structure 4 (built in 1983) contains 448 spaces in two underground levels; the addition built in 1998 contains 1,263 spaces in two underground levels.

The Pershing Square Garage (built in downtown Los Angeles in 1952) contains 2,150 spaces in three underground levels.

The ENR Construction Cost Index is used to convert original construction costs to 1998 values.

the U.S., and parking garages are one category. In 2001, the median construction cost for aboveground parking garages was $12,000 per space, and the 75th percentile cost was $15,600 per space (25 percent of garages cost more than $15,600 per space).[14] Because construction costs in Los Angeles were 8.5 percent above the national average, the median cost for Los Angeles was $13,000 per space, and the 75th percentile cost was $16,900.[15] UCLA's cost of $14,500 *per space added* by aboveground structures was thus between the median and 75th percentile *cost per space* for Los Angeles. When the lost surface spaces are not subtracted from the number of spaces in each structure, the inflation-adjusted construction cost per space in UCLA's aboveground structures built in the 1960s was only $11,900 per space, which is below the national average cost for aboveground parking structures.

Cost of Other Parking Structures

The estimate of $22,500 a space added refers to all parking structures at UCLA, but comparable garages elsewhere cost as much or more. One good comparison is a 380-space municipal parking garage built in 1998 in Westwood Village, one block from UCLA. Its footprint previously provided 101 surface spaces, so the structure added 279 parking spaces. The construction cost was $8,622,000, or $30,000 per parking space added—37 percent higher than at UCLA.[16]

Parking spaces are also expensive in other cities. As Chapter 9 explains, some cities allow developers to pay a fee in lieu of providing the required parking spaces; the cities then use the revenue to provide public parking. To justify their in-lieu fees, some cities have carefully documented the cost of constructing public parking spaces. These costs are $18,000 per space in Lake Forest, Illinois; $32,400 per space in Walnut Creek, California; $37,000 per space in Beverly Hills, California; and $51,000 per space in Palo Alto, California.[17] Newspaper articles occasionally report the cost of public parking structures, such as a 750-space aboveground public parking garage in San Jose, California, built in 2002 at a cost $57,000 a space (including land cost).[18] The City of Seattle paid $61,000 per space for a 1,200-space garage beneath the Pacific Place shopping center.[19] The International Parking Institute makes annual awards for excellence in parking structure design, and the construction cost was $40,117 a space (excluding land cost) for a 511-space structure that was given the highest award in 2003.[20] Parking spaces can also cost much more. The Multilevel Parking Industry Association of Japan reported that underground garages built in Kawasaki, Nagasaki, Tokyo, and Yokohama have cost between $280,000 and $414,000 per space![21]

The average cost of $22,500 per space added by parking structures built at UCLA is thus not unusually high. If parking spaces cost this much, parking requirements intended to satisfy the peak demand for free parking grossly inflate the cost of urban development and greatly reduce the drivers' cost of using cars.

MONTHLY COST OF A PARKING SPACE

How much do parking spaces have to earn to repay their cost? To answer this question, we need to know the *monthly* cost of a parking space. We can convert the construction cost per parking space added into a monthly cost by assuming an interest rate and an amortization period. The original capital cost of each structure has already been converted into 2002 dollars (see Table 6-1). If future costs and revenues are also measured in 2002 dollars, we can convert the capital cost into a monthly cost by using the real interest rate (the interest rate after accounting for inflation), which is commonly assumed to be around 4 percent a year. A longer amortization period produces a lower monthly cost, so to be conservative we can assume 40 years.[22] At 4 percent interest, a $22,500 capital cost amortized over 40 years will require payments of $94 a month.[23] Therefore, the capital cost of a new parking space is equivalent to paying $94 a month for 40 years.

In addition to the initial capital cost, parking spaces have operation and maintenance costs. Parking structures take a beating from heavy vehicles driving through them every day, and they are prone to weather damage. The UCLA Parking Service spends $33 a month per space for administration, cleaning, insurance, lighting, maintenance, revenue collection, and security (see Table 6-3). The total cost per space added by the 15 parking structures built since 1961 therefore amounts to $127 a month ($94 + $33).

Table 6-3. Monthly Cost of a Parking Space (2002$)

Assumptions	
Capital cost per space	$22,500
Amortization period	40 years
Interest rate	4 percent
Cost per space per month	
Capital cost	$94
Operating and maintenance cost	$33
Cost per space per month	**$127**

This estimate of $127 a month per space is low because it is based on the following conservative assumptions.

1. Land is valued at its opportunity cost for surface parking, but a parking structure is built only when land is too valuable to use for surface parking, so the land value may be much higher.
2. The opportunity cost of land is measured only for the structure's footprint, but a parking structure requires additional land for access roads and landscaped setback.
3. No land cost is calculated for underground parking structures, although they occupy space that could be used for other purposes, such as storage and mechanical equipment.
4. The operation and maintenance cost per space for parking structures is calculated for the entire parking system (including surface lots). But structures have higher costs for elevators, lighting, ventilation, security, and maintenance than do surface lots.
5. Property taxes are excluded because UCLA is a tax-exempt institution.
6. Structures are optimistically assumed to have a useful life of 40 years.
7. The interest rate is only 4 percent a year.[24]

Given these conservative assumptions, the 15 parking structures built at UCLA since 1961 cost *at least* $22,500 per space or *at least* $127 a month per space.

This figure of $127 a month per space is also low compared with the debt service for UCLA's newest parking structure, built in 2002 at a cost of $31,500 per space. At an annual interest rate of 6.125 percent for 27 years, the debt service is $201 a month per space (see Table 6-4). This may seem expensive, but consider the financial situation of anyone who borrows the money necessary to buy land and build a parking garage. Revenue of more than $127 a month per space would probably be necessary to cover the debt service, operating costs, property taxes, and insurance for the structure. The cost estimate of $127 a month per space is also low when compared to the price of parking in many commercial spaces. A survey of 59,000 parking spaces in downtown Seattle in 2002, for example, found the average price of commercial parking was $200 a month.[25] A similar survey of 32,000 parking spaces in downtown Bellevue, Washington, in 2002 found the average price of commercial parking was $138 a month.[26] And a nationwide survey of the prices charged for structured parking in 43 Central Business Districts (CBDs) in the U.S. in 2003 found the average price for unreserved parking was $141 a month.[27] (Despite these high prices, employer-paid and validated parking reduces the cost of parking for most drivers to zero. Therefore, the posted prices for parking in down-

Table 6-4. Debt Service for Parking Structure 7

1. Total cost of structure	$47,282,000	
2. Number of parking spaces in structure	1,500	
3. Cost per parking space	$31,500	per space
4. Interest rate	6.125%	per year
5. Term	27	years
6. Annual debt service per debt-financed space	$2,414	per year
7. Monthly debt service per debt-financed space	$201	per month

Source: Memo from the UC Office of the President to the UC Regents, November 7, 2001.

town spaces are evidence more of the high cost of providing parking than of what drivers pay for it.) Finally, University of Michigan economics professor Richard Porter estimated that the cost of the 4,500 public parking spaces in structures and lots in Ann Arbor was $160 a month per space.[28] Therefore, the estimated cost of $127 a month per space for parking structures at UCLA is low when compared to the cost of both private and public parking elsewhere in the U.S.

The cost of $127 a month per space for structured parking is low by national standards. In her book *Parking Structures*, Mary Smith shows that both surface parking and aboveground structured parking cost about $12,000 per space if the price of land is $30 per square foot. Structured parking is cheaper than surface parking only at land prices above $30 per square foot ($330 per square meter or $1.3 million per acre).[29] At a land price of $30 per square foot, the capital-plus-operating cost for an unattended aboveground garage is about $150 a month per space.[30] Because structured parking costs even more than $150 a month per space at higher land prices, a parking structure must earn at least $150 a month per space to pay its way.

We should also distinguish between the cost per space of a parking structure and the cost per *occupied* space. In his case studies of office developments in Southern California, Richard Willson explains that the cost per space in the structure usually underestimates the cost per occupied space because some spaces always remain empty. He argues that the cost of these empty spaces must be allocated among the occupied spaces if parking fees are to cover the total cost:

> The costs of providing unused spaces would have to be spread over those who use the facility. Since many of the parking facilities are half empty, this fee is much higher than the fee for a single occupied space. For the surface-lot case studies, the utilization-adjusted break-even fee averages $92 per month. Each all-day parker would have to be charged that amount if the total parking

revenue were to equal the cost of providing the parking facility. For the parking-structure studies, the utilization-adjusted break-even fee averages $161 per month.[31]

These calculations suggest that $127 a month per space is a *conservative estimate* of the cost for a structured parking space. There are also, however, the external costs to consider.

EXTERNAL COSTS OF A PARKING SPACE

Beyond the capital and operating costs of providing parking spaces, we can estimate how additional parking spaces increase other costs in the transportation system. After all, planners require developers to provide parking spaces because they expect drivers to use them. We should therefore ask: do the required parking spaces increase vehicle travel? If so, how will this added vehicle travel increase the external costs of traffic congestion and air pollution?

Induced Travel

Parking spaces do not *create* travel demand, of course, but a larger supply of parking reduces its market price and therefore reduces the price of vehicle travel. In the short run, the lower prices induce those who were already driving to drive even more. Some who would have stayed home begin driving. And some who would otherwise walk, cycle, or ride public transit shift to driving. In the long run, the lower price of parking leads to increased vehicle ownership and thus further increases vehicle travel.[32] Parking spaces do not create vehicle travel, but they do enable it.

The phenomenon of vehicle travel induced by new parking spaces (added vehicle-*storing* capacity) is similar to the phenomenon of vehicle travel induced by new roads (added vehicle-*carrying* capacity). As Don Pickrell explains, road construction increases vehicle travel by increasing its speed and reducing its time price.[33] Similarly, parking requirements increase the supply and reduce the money price of parking. Because cars spend most of their time parked, the price of parking (if motorists pay for it) can be a large part of the cost of vehicle travel. But many transportation analysts neglect the price of parking in estimating the demand for vehicle travel, probably because parking is usually free to drivers almost everywhere. But where drivers do pay for parking, it strongly influences travel behavior: the higher the price of parking, the more travelers ride public transit, carpool, bike, or walk to their destinations.

Using information from the environmental impact report (EIR) for UCLA's newest parking structure, I will provide an example of how new parking spaces increase vehicle travel and how the increased vehicle travel increases traffic congestion and air pollution. These estimates are specific to one case, but they show that new parking spaces can create substantial external costs.

Environmental Impacts

The EIR was conducted for UCLA's 1,500-space Parking Structure 7, which was built in 2001–2003.[34] The EIR provides full documentation for nearly every aspect of the structure, including the predicted number of vehicle trips and vehicle miles travelled (VMT) it will generate, and the

Table 6-5. External Costs of a Parking Space ($/Month)

Panel 1. VMT per parking space

Trips per space (trips/month)	Trip length (VMT/trip)	VMT per space (VMT/month)
(1)	(2)	(3)=(1)x(2)
82.6	8.8	**727**

Panel 2. Congestion cost per parking space

VMT per space (VMT/month)	Congestion price ($/VMT)	Congestion cost ($/month)
(4)=(3)	(5)	(6)=(4)x(5)
727	$0.10	**$72.70**

Panel 3. Emissions cost per parking space

	Emissions per space (lbs/month)	Emissions price ($/lb)	Emissions cost ($/month)
	(7)	(8)	(9)=(7)x(8)
ROG	1.32	$3.84	$5.07
CO	13.79	$2.22	$30.61
NO_x	1.37	$5.88	$8.06
PM_{10}	0.03	$4.87	$0.15
SO_x	0.07	$3.96	$0.28
			$44.16

Panel 4. Total external costs per parking space

Congestion ($/month)	Emissions ($/month)	Total ($/month)
(10)=(6)	(11)=(9)	(12)=(10)+(11)
$72.70	$44.16	**$116.86**

Source: Intramural Field Parking Structure Environmental Impact Report, State Clearinghouse Number 1999091001, University of California, Los Angeles, May 2001.

vehicle emissions from the cars traveling to and from it. Table 6-5 shows the data on vehicle trips and vehicle emissions estimated in the EIR.

Congestion cost: $73 a month per space. The full cost of an automobile trip includes not only the cost borne by the driver but also the external costs of congestion the driver imposes on other travelers. When a car enters a road that is already near its carrying capacity, it slows down all the other vehicles already on the road. Slowing these other vehicles increases everyone else's travel time and fuel consumption. Nothing alerts individuals to these external costs of their driving, and most drivers are unaware of or indifferent to the external costs their own driving creates.[35]

Using trip generation rates estimated specifically for UCLA parking structures, the EIR reports that 1,500 new parking spaces will generate 5,630 one-way vehicle trips per weekday, or 3.8 trips a day per space, implying a parking turnover rate in the structure of 1.9 vehicles a day per space.[36] If we assume that the structure is used only 22 weekdays a month (i.e., no trips are calculated for the weekends), each space will generate 82.6 vehicle trips a month.[37] The EIR reports that the average distance for vehicle trips to campus is 8.8 miles, so each space will generate 727 VMT a month per space (82.6 x 8.8). We can use this estimate to calculate how adding a parking space increases the cost of traffic congestion in Los Angeles.

Several transportation analysts have estimated the cost of traffic congestion in Los Angeles, and their results suggest the value of reducing peak-hour vehicle travel is at least 10¢ per VMT. In 1991, Michael Cameron estimated that the external cost of vehicle travel in Los Angeles ranged from 10¢ to 37¢ per VMT.[38] He also estimated that a peak-period congestion toll of 15¢ per VMT would be needed to reduce congestion enough to raise average freeway speeds to 35-40 miles an hour. At this speed, the external cost of congestion produced by drivers would be 15¢ per VMT. After an extensive literature survey in 1992, Kenneth Small also concluded that a peak-period charge of 15¢ per VMT (in 1990 dollars) would be appropriate on congested freeways in Los Angeles.[39] Using a large-scale transportation model with data for 1991, Elizabeth Deakin and Greig Harvey estimated that if the appropriate congestion charges were imposed on Southern California's highway network, they would average 10¢ a mile.[40] Finally, in 1991 Patrick DeCorla-Souza and Anthony Kane estimated that the cost of reducing congestion by adding new highway capacity to serve peak users in Los Angeles would be 20¢ per peak-hour VMT.[41]

If we value the congestion cost of 727 VMT a month at the low end of these values for Los Angeles—10¢ per VMT—the external cost of congestion amounts to $73 a month per new parking space.

Emissions cost: $44 a month per space. Vehicle emissions are another major external cost of driving. Los Angeles has the worst air pollution in the nation, and motor vehicles produce most of it.[42] As Kenneth Small and Camilla Kazimi report, transportation accounts for 75 percent of total reactive organic gas (ROG) emissions in Los Angeles, 98 percent of carbon monoxide (CO), 83 percent of oxides of nitrogen (NO_x), and 68 percent of oxides of sulfur (SO_x).[43]

Using the vehicle emission factors estimated by the South Coast Air Quality Management District (SCAQMD), the EIR calculated the total emissions per weekday for vehicles traveling to and from the new structure. Column 7 of Panel 3 of Table 6-5 shows the vehicle emissions per space per month created by these vehicles.

Putting a dollar value on the cost of pollution is not easy, but one reasonable method is to use the SCAQMD's threshold values for the cost-effectiveness of emissions-reduction measures (see column 8).[44] I have used these official values as an estimate of the cost of the pollution emissions created by additional vehicle travel. The external cost of vehicle emissions induced by a new parking structure thus amounts to $44 a month per space. This estimated cost of $44 for 727 VMT implies an emissions cost of 6¢ a mile.

With an emissions cost of 6¢ a mile and a congestion cost of 10¢ a mile, the total external cost of vehicle travel is 16¢ a mile. For the average trip length of 8.8 miles, the total external cost per trip to or from Parking Structure 7 is thus $1.41. In another attempt to calculate the external costs of vehicle travel, in 2001 Kaan Ozbay, Bekir Bartin, and Joseph Berechman estimated that the marginal external cost for a 10- to 15-mile highway trip in New Jersey was $1.25, or 8¢ to 13¢ a mile.[45] The estimate for Los Angeles may be slightly higher because Los Angeles has worse traffic congestion and air pollution.[46]

Total external costs: $117 a month per space. The fourth panel shows that the total induced external costs of a new parking space amount to $117 a month: $73 for added congestion and $44 for added pollution. Although this may sound high, the estimate is based on uniformly conservative assumptions.

1. The VMT and the vehicle emissions are estimated only for weekday trips.
2. The congestion cost per VMT is taken from the bottom of the range of estimates for Los Angeles.
3. The average one-way trip distance is only 8.8 miles, while the average one-way automobile commute to work in Southern California is 15 miles.[47]

4. Greenhouse gas (CO_2) emissions from 1.1 million VMT per month are ignored.
5. The congestion and pollution costs associated with building the structure are ignored. In addition to the estimated impacts of *using* the parking structure, *constructing* it required excavating the 10-acre site to a depth of 31 feet. Removing 222,000 cubic yards of earth required 26,000 truck trips (with a peak of 63 truck trips an hour) through campus and Westwood Village, along Wilshire Boulevard to the San Diego Freeway, and eventual disposal.

Despite these conservative assumptions, the external cost of $117 a month for a new parking space still seems surprisingly high, but this may be only because no one has bothered to estimate it before.

These external costs are calculated for Los Angeles, and they would be lower in cities that have less traffic and cleaner air. (But that raises an important point: new parking spaces create even higher external costs in cities that are already polluted and congested.) In any case, one can easily vary the four assumptions in the calculation—the trip generation rate, the average trip distance, the vehicle emission rates, and the costs of pollution and congestion—to see how they affect the external costs of increased driving induced by new parking spaces in other places. The pollution costs of new parking spaces may be especially high in developing countries where the vehicle emissions and population densities are higher. For example, Mutasem El-Fadel and Hayassam Sbayti at the American University of Beirut studied the environmental impacts of a proposed 2,000-space parking garage in the center of Beirut. They estimated that it would increase the ambient levels of CO by 29 percent and of NO_2 by 38 percent in the already polluted air. These increases in pollution would occur because most Lebanese cars are old and poorly maintained; the average age of the fleet was 14 years.[48] With dirtier cars and higher population densities, the external cost of new parking spaces in developing countries may be far higher than in the U.S.

New parking spaces also induce increases in other external costs associated with vehicle travel: noise, greenhouse gas emissions, and accident costs not paid for by the drivers who cause the accidents. Consider also the ecology of parking lots. They increase the impervious surface area in a city, reduce the area for water to percolate into the soil, and increase stormwater runoff. Parking lots also accumulate oil drippings that contain toxic metals, such as chromium, and the runoff then pollutes water supplies. After heavy rain, the runoff enters storm sewers at an accelerated rate, contributing to the risk of flooding. The faster runoff also erodes the banks of streams and rivers, and adds more sediment to the water.[49] Finally, poorly designed parking lots and structures often degrade the townscape. When these other costs above and beyond traffic congestion and air pollution are considered, the estimate of $117 a month for the external cost of a new parking space becomes even more conservative.

This brings us to the great imbalance between what parking costs and what drivers pay for it. UCLA spends $201 a month per debt-financed space in the parking structure we have been using in this example (see Table 6-4). When the external cost of $117 a month is added, the total social (internal plus external) cost associated with a new parking space is $318 a month. In 2002, the price for a permit to park on campus was $54 a month—only 16 percent of the total social cost per parking space. Drivers pay far less than the marginal social cost of driving to UCLA, but this is merely one example of the much larger problem: almost all parking is grossly underpriced.

Drivers who pay $54 a month for a permit to park in Structure 7 surely do not realize that their parking spaces cost more than $200 a month or that the congestion and pollution added by their vehicle trips cost more than $100 a month. Drivers base their travel decisions only on the prices they personally face. On the day Structure 7 opened, UCLA's *Daily Bruin* interviewed drivers who park there. Consider this response from a third-year psychology student: "I didn't have a permit before so I had to van-pool. For me, having a permit is awesome."[50] Awesome indeed. Paying only $54 a month to park in a space that cost $31,500 to build *is* awesome. That's quite a subsidy, and there is probably no better bargain on campus. The large subsidy for parking drew this student from a vanpool to solo driving, and thus increased traffic congestion and air pollution. Each individual driver enjoys a parking subsidy, but the whole society suffers.

Economists and planners often propose parking policies as possible ways to *reduce* the external costs of traffic congestion and air pollution. For example, Dutch transportation economist Erik Verhoef says, "Since virtually every car has to be parked at the end of the trip, parking policies may offer a potentially strong instrument for influencing traffic flows."[51] But by increasing the supply and reducing the price of parking spaces, off-street parking requirements make parking itself yet another external cost of vehicle travel and thus *increase* traffic congestion and air pollution. Although parking spaces themselves do not directly increase traffic, the lower price of parking does. We own more cars and drive them more often than we would if we paid market-rate prices for parking. The costs of congestion and pollution are hard to measure and to attribute to individual drivers, which is why they remain external costs. In contrast, charging for parking is easy, so there is no reason why it should be an external cost. By increasing vehicle travel, off-street parking requirements increase the total external costs of driving and make an already bad situation far worse.

CONCLUSION: THE HIGH COST OF REQUIRED PARKING SPACES

Cities require a precise number of parking spaces for every land use, and one would therefore expect to find many studies of how much these spaces cost. Where are they? Perhaps planners have not studied the cost of parking simply because they rarely think about it when they set parking requirements. This neglect sounds unwise, and it is. Two unstated assumptions—that parking is free, and that its cost is irrelevant—lie behind parking requirements in zoning ordinances. Cities therefore require developers to supply enough parking spaces to meet the peak demand for free parking, regardless of the cost.

Parking structures at UCLA have cost *at least* $22,500 per space added, or $127 a month per space. These estimates were made with conservative assumptions, including a low interest rate, a long amortization period, a low opportunity cost of land, and no taxes. In addition, the external cost of congestion and pollution associated with driving to and from a parking space amounts to *at least* $117 a month. When both the internal and external costs are calculated, the total social cost of a new parking space comes to *at least* $244 a month. But the cost of parking at UCLA is not the important point. The important point is that parking is expensive for everyone except drivers.

CHAPTER 6 NOTES

1. Amis (1958, 18). Jim Dixon, a university lecturer, is the protagonist of *Lucky Jim*.

2. Because a typical parking lot has about 330 square feet per space (for both the parking spaces and for circulation of cars to access the spaces), a parking space will have a land cost of $100,000 where land is worth $300 a square foot.

3. The example is UCLA's Parking Structure 6, which was built in 1980 and is described in Table 6-1.

4. The UCLA Parking Service is one of the largest single-site parking systems in the nation, with 21,000 parking spaces in structures and surface lots. One atypical structure is excluded from the list of structures. This "demountable" structure was prefabricated and was intended for removal (and reassembly elsewhere) at a later date. It was placed on a portion of Lot 32, remote from the main campus, and its appearance would be unacceptable on the main campus. In regard to its location, Bob Hope said, "It takes four years to get through UCLA, or five if you park in Lot 32." The construction contracts for all the structures were competitively bid, so the cost records are accurate and detailed, and they include the costs of planning and design.

5. Surface parking lots at UCLA occupy 851,725 square feet of land and contain 2,591 parking spaces, for an average of 329 square feet per surface space (including access lanes). Therefore, each structure's footprint was divided by 329 square feet to estimate the number of surface spaces lost. No surface parking spaces are assumed to be lost for underground parking structures.

6. To estimate the increase in the cost of construction since each parking structure was built, the 20-city average of the *ENR* Construction Cost Index for 2002 was divided by the *ENR* Construction Cost Index for the year in which the parking structure was built. This ratio was multiplied by the original construction cost to show the construction cost expressed in dollars of 2002 purchasing power. The *ENR* Construction Cost Index, a widely accepted measure of cost inflation in the construction industry, is published in the magazine *ENR* (formerly *Engineering News Record*) and is available online at www.enr.com. The index rose from 847 in 1961 to 6,538 in 2002.

7. Mary Smith (1999, 532) explains how cost per square foot of floor area and efficiency together determine the cost per space. Retail customer parking with high turnover requires larger spaces than office employee parking and is thus less inefficient (more square feet per space), and angle parking is less efficient than perpendicular parking.

8. The high cost is due to the small footprint and the resulting inefficient layout of the structure (more square feet of structure per parking space). The structure has parking spaces only on one side of the aisles (it is "single loaded") while larger structures are "double loaded" with parking spaces on both sides of the aisles.

9. The high cost of construction in Los Angeles can explain only a small part of the high cost of adding recent parking spaces at UCLA because the *ENR* Construction Cost Index for Los Angeles in 1998 was only 14 percent above the median Construction Cost Index for all the 20 cities that *ENR* monitors.

10. Willson (1995, 39). The construction cost is adjusted by the *ENR* Construction Cost Index.

11. The *ENR* Construction Cost Index is used to convert the original construction costs to 1998 dollars. The original aboveground structure contains 39 percent more parking spaces than the aboveground addition, and its footprint is twice as large as that of the addition. Economies of scale help explain the original structure's slightly lower cost per space. The underground addition is almost three times the size of the original underground structure, and economies of scale may help explain the newer structure's slightly lower cost per space.

12. The cost per parking space added by a parking structure should vary less among different locations and over time than does the cost of most other real estate. For example, measuring a standard unit of housing is difficult because houses vary greatly in size and quality. Housing values also vary greatly among locations and over time because of differences in land values. A parking space may be the most uniform unit of real estate on earth.

13. Klose (1965, 190) gives the original cost of constructing the Pershing Square garage. Because the *ENR* Construction Cost Index rose faster than the Consumer Price Index between 1952 and 1998, the cost of constructing parking spaces rose relative to other prices.

14. R. S. Means (2001, 483).

15. R. S. Means (2001, 618). In another publication, *Square Foot Costs*, R. S. Means (2002, 130) reports that the construction costs for a five-level aboveground garages ranged from $20.25 to $84.05 per square foot. With an average area of 330 square feet per parking space, the construction cost ranges from $6,700 to $27,700 per parking space.

16. Letter from Vitaly Troyan of the Los Angeles Bureau of Engineering, October 12, 1999. The parking structure—on Broxton Avenue in Westwood Village—has two levels underground and four levels aboveground. Like the RC structure on the UCLA campus, the Broxton Avenue Structure has a small footprint and an inefficient layout, with single-loaded aisles.

17. In Lake Forest the cost of $18,000 per space is the land-and-construction cost of surface parking lots. In Walnut Creek the cost is $32,400 per space added by a municipal parking structure (as calculated by the method shown in Table 6-1). In Beverly Hills the cost of $37,000 per space refers to the average estimated land-and-construction cost of municipal parking spaces for projects that applied to pay the in-lieu fees between 1978 and 1992; the highest cost was $53,000 per parking space. In Palo Alto, the cost of $50,994 is the cost per space added by two municipal parking structures (calculated by the method shown in Table 6-1).

18. Kate Folmar, "Bold Downtown Project Cost $58 Million, to Include Restaurants, Shops, Banquet Hall," *San Jose Mercury News*, January 5, 2003.

19. Washington State Department of Transportation (1999, 6).

20. *The Parking Professional*, August 2003, p. 18 and 35. The six-level structure (two underground and four aboveground) was built at the Texas Medical Center in Houston, Texas. Giant 90-foot-long x 60-foot-tall water walls were used to mask the structure, and a computer program creates a series of animated sequences of falling water at various rates and densities to create a continuous show. Jackson & Ryan were the architects.

21. Land cost does not explain the high cost per space because all spaces are underground. The 120-space Heiwa Kouen garage in Nagasaki cost $280,000 per space; the 500-space Yokohama-eki Higashi-guchi garage in Yokohama cost $304,000 per space; and the 380-space Kawasaki-eki Higashi-guchi Chika garage in Kawasaki cost $414,000 per space. These values are calculated with an exchange rate of $1=110 Yen. Several factors contribute to these high costs. Underground parking garages are often built in front of an existing railway station, and they must be built in stages without closing off surface traffic. The Shinkawa garage in Tokyo was built under a river. Regulations for earthquake-resistant construction are also more strict in Japan than in the U.S. Even if these garages were fully occupied all day every day, they wouldn't pay for themselves. See Multilevel Parking Industry Association of Japan (1997).

22. UCLA's first parking structure, built in 1961, required extensive reconstruction 30 years later. The structure built in 1963 was demolished 36 years later to redevelop the site. The structure built in 1964 required extensive repairs 35 years later. The other structures built in the 1960s do not meet current design or earthquake safety standards. The structure built in 1977 needs extensive repairs and may be demolished. Forty years is thus a long period over which to amortize the capital cost of a parking structure. One would normally not want to amortize a loan over a period longer than the expected economic life of the structure financed by the loan. Since the payment of $94 a month is calculated in dollars on 2002 purchasing power, it would have to increase over time at the rate of inflation to maintain its real value.

23. Varying the assumptions about a parking structure's lifespan and the interest rate will affect the equivalent monthly capital cost per parking space. For example, with a 4 percent interest rate, a 30-year life raises the monthly cost per space to $113, while a 100-year life reduces it to $80. With a 50-year life, a 3 percent interest rate reduces the monthly cost per space to $76, while a 5 percent interest rate increases it to $107.

24. The revenue bonds issued to finance parking structures at UCLA bear interest rates of 6.1 percent, 8.25 percent, and 7.74 percent, and one revenue bond has a variable rate that can float between 4 percent and 9 percent. These are all tax-exempt interest rates, and taxable bonds issued to finance commercial parking structures will bear higher interest rates. The revenue bonds include a risk premium to compensate for the risk involved in the lender's investment, but the bonds are secured by the revenues of the entire parking system (including surface spaces), not by the revenues of the particular parking structure financed by a bond. The revenue bonds can be a safe investment for the lender even if the investment in a new parking structure is risky for UCLA. The appropriate risk premium for investment in a single structure is therefore higher than implied by the interest rates on existing UCLA Parking Service bonds.

25. Puget Sound Regional Council (2003, 10).

26. Puget Sound Regional Council (2003, 27).

27. Colliers International (2003, 28).

28. Porter (1999, 162-63) estimated that the cost of Ann Arbor's 4,500 public parking spaces was $8.8 million a year.

29. Similarly, University of Pennsylvania professor of urban design Jonathan Barnett (2003, 52) says, "Land costs need to be well over $1 million an acre before land-cost, by itself, makes it advisable to build a garage instead of at-grade parking."

30. Smith (2001, 24 and 27). Smith says a common rule of thumb is that the first level of an underground parking structure costs 1.5 times the above-grade costs, with the multiplier doubling for each additional underground level.

31. Willson (1995, 35). After seeing Willson's estimate, the Chicago Regional Transportation Authority (1998) commissioned similar case studies at office developments in 10 Chicago suburbs. These studies found that the peak parking demand was only 68 percent of capacity. The utilization-adjusted break-even fee for these parking spaces ranged from $96 to $103 per month.

32. In the long run, the reduced price of parking will increase both the total person-miles of travel by all modes and vehicle travel's share of this total. The number of person-miles of travel by walking, cycling, and public transit will decline.

33. Pickrell (2001).

34. Intramural Field Parking Structure Final Environmental Impact Report, State Clearinghouse Number 1999091001, University of California, Los Angeles, May 2001. Because UCLA commissioned the EIR, the structure's environmental impacts are unlikely to be overestimated.

35. External effects are not deliberate creations but are the unintended or incidental by-products of an activity. Even if drivers are aware of these external effects, they are unlikely to feel guilty about them because, after all, everyone else is doing the same thing.

36. 5,630 trips ÷ 1,500 spaces = 3.753 one-way trips or 1.9 round-trips a day per space.

37. 3.753 × 22 = 82.6 one-way trips a month. This calculation assumes that the parking spaces are used on 22 weekdays a month and not on weekends. This neglect of weekend traffic produces a conservative estimate of vehicle trips and VMT per month.

38. Cameron (1991). Because traffic congestion is even worse without a toll, the congestion-related external costs of vehicle use are presumably higher than 15¢ per VMT where there are no tolls.

39. Small (1992).

40. Deakin and Harvey (1996, 7-8). Deakin and Harvey's estimate included tolls on the arterials and collector streets as necessary.

41. DeCorla-Souza and Kane (1992).

42. U.S. Environmental Protection Agency (1995). Los Angeles is the only region in the EPA's most-polluted category of "extreme nonattainment" of national air quality standards. The four other categories of nonattainment are, in decreasing seriousness: severe, serious, moderate, and marginal.

43. Small and Kazimi (1995).

44. South Coast Air Quality Management District (2000, 29). If the cost per ton of emissions reduced by a proposed control measure is less than the SCAQMD's threshold value, the measure is considered cost effective and is required. Because the SCAQMD presumably does not require emission controls that cost more than the value of the emissions reduced, we can interpret these threshold cost-effectiveness measures as the SCAQMD's estimate of the value to society of reducing emissions. These values refer to the cost of emissions in 2000.

45. Ozbay, Bartin, and Berechman (2001, 100). They defined the marginal external costs as "the costs auto users are not held accountable for, including those every user imposes on the rest of traffic, such as the costs of congestion, accidents, air pollution, and noise" (Ozbay, Bartin, and Berechman 2001, 82).

46. The Texas Transportation Institute (TTI) annually surveys traffic data in 75 American cities and calculates the Roadway Congestion Index to rank them by the severity of their traffic congestion. Los Angeles has ranked highest on the TTI Roadway Congestion Index in every year since 1983 (Texas Transportation Institute 2003, Exhibit A-18). The TTI estimated that Los Angeles drivers experienced 739 million person-hours of delay in congested traffic in 1997 and that the time wasted and excess fuel consumed in this congested traffic was worth $12.4 billion a year. To put this estimated cost in perspective, the construction cost of the magnificent Getty Center that opened in Los Angeles in 1997 was approximately $1 billion. Therefore, the TTI's estimated cost of traffic congestion in Los Angeles equals the cost of constructing a dozen Getty Centers every year.

47. Annual surveys conducted between 1989 and 1996 found that average one-way vehicle commute distances ranged from 14.8 to 16.9 miles (Southern California Association of Governments 1996). In calculating the VMT reductions associated with reducing a vehicle trip to work, the SCAQMD assumes an average one-way distance for each avoided vehicle commute trip of 15 miles.

48. El-Fadel and Sbayti (2001, 19).

49. Albanese and Matlack (1998) found that the parking lots at eight shopping centers in Hattiesburg, Mississippi, were occupied well below capacity even at the periods of peak demand. The runoff from these parking lots increased the sediment in nearby streams and reduced the number and diversity of fish in the streams.

50. *UCLA Daily Bruin*, April 9, 2003.

51. Verhoef (1996, 96). He shows that under certain circumstances (each car driver uses an equal amount of road space per trip, congestion is equally spread over the road network, and all drivers have the same parking duration), the optimal parking fee can substitute for the optimal road toll. Downs (1992) also discusses parking policies to reduce traffic.

Putting the Cost of Free Parking in Perspective

Instead of buildings set in a park, we now have buildings set in a parking lot.

— *LEWIS MUMFORD*

We can now put the cost of parking in perspective by comparing it with other costs of the transportation system. These comparisons show that "free" parking greatly reduces the driver's cost of vehicle travel and therefore seriously distorts individual travel choices toward cars.

TOTAL SUBSIDY FOR PARKING

For many land uses, the area devoted to parking exceeds the floor area of the building it serves. We have no trouble understanding that office buildings cost a lot of money, so it should not surprise anyone that the parking lots or structures (often bigger than the buildings they serve) also cost a lot. Furthermore, curb parking spaces usually line both sides of the adjacent streets. When we consider both curb spaces and off-street spaces in cities, the land and capital devoted to parking probably exceed that devoted to travel.

Mark Delucchi of the University of California, Davis, conducted what is by far the most comprehensive evaluation of the total cost of motor vehicle use in the U.S. He estimated both monetary costs (such as for vehicles, fuel, roads, and parking) and nonmonetary costs (such as for air and

Table 7-1. Annual Capital and Operating Cost of Off-Street Parking Spaces ($billions per year in 1990–1991)

	Low	High
Bundled residential parking	$15	$41
Bundled nonresidential parking	$49	$162
Municipal and institutional parking	$12	$20
Priced parking	$3	$3
Total cost of parking	**$79**	**$226**
Total parking subsidy	**$76**	**$223**
Priced parking as % of total parking	**4%**	**1%**

Source: Delucchi (1997, Tables 1-5, 1-6, and 1-7).

water pollution). Because inputs and assumptions for the estimates are uncertain, he presented both low and high estimates for each value. For the years 1990–1991, he estimated the annualized capital and operating cost of off-street parking at between $79 billion and $226 billion a year (see Table 7-1).[1]

Delucchi points out that most parking is not priced separately but is instead bundled with other goods and priced as a package. He estimated that drivers paid only $3 billion a year for parking, while the rest of the cost was bundled into the prices for goods, services, and housing. As a result, drivers paid somewhere between 4 percent ($3 billion ÷ $79 billion) and 1 percent ($3 billion ÷ $226 billion) of the total cost of parking. The other 96 to 99 percent of the cost of parking was hidden in higher prices for everything else.

Delucchi also estimated the annualized capital and operating cost of public roads (including the curb parking spaces) at between $98 billion and $177 billion, close to the estimated cost of parking spaces. If drivers paid only 4 percent of the cost of roads, most people would condemn this as outrageously unfair, but drivers pay at most 4 percent of the cost of off-street parking, and they complain loudly whenever its price increases.

Because Delucchi included the cost of curb parking in the cost of roads, the total cost of the parking supply (both off-street *and* on-street) is underestimated. Consider a 36-foot-wide residential street, with two 10-foot-wide travel lanes and two 8-foot-wide parking lanes: curb parking takes up 44 percent of the road space. Clearly, curb parking spaces account for a significant share of the total cost of roads, and an accurate estimate of the total subsidy for parking would take curb parking into account.[2] The U.S. Department of Commerce estimates that the total value of roads is 36 percent of the value of all state and local public infrastructure (which also includes schools, sewers, water supply, residential buildings, equipment, hospitals, and parks). Because curb parking occupies a substantial share of road space, it must be a substantial share of all state and local public infrastructure as well.[3] Since drivers do pay gasoline taxes while they are driving, but do not pay gasoline taxes while their cars are parked, curb spaces are subsidized far more than the travel lanes. Free curb parking may be the most costly subsidy American cities provide for most of their citizens.

Since drivers paid only $3 billion a year for parking in 1990–1991, the subsidy for off-street parking was between $76 billion and $223 billion a year. Because the U.S. gross domestic product was $6 trillion in 1991, the subsidy for off-street parking amounted to between 1.2 percent and 3.7 percent of the nation's economic output.[4] American cars and light trucks logged 2 trillion miles in 1990, so the off-street parking subsidy amounted to between 4¢ a mile (if the subsidy was $76 billion) and 11¢ a mile (if it was $223 billion).[5] In comparison, the average variable cost for gasoline, oil, maintenance, and tires for cars in 1990 was 8.4¢ a mile.[6] The subsidy for off-street parking was therefore somewhere between 48 percent and 131 percent of the drivers' cost for gasoline, oil, maintenance, and tires.

Delucchi's estimate refers to 1990–1991. Adjusted for inflation and the increase in the number of vehicles and off-street parking spaces since then, the total subsidy for off-street parking in 2002 was between $127 billion and $374 billion.[7] Because the U.S. gross domestic product had grown to $10.5 trillion in 2002, the subsidy for off-street parking as a share of the economy amounted to between 1.2 percent and 3.6 percent, almost exactly the same as in 1991. This subsidy is huge by any comparison. In 2002, the federal government spent $231 billion for Medicare and $349 billion for national defense.[8] National defense!! Can the subsidy for off-street parking be that big??? Well, why not? Since the 1950s, most American cities have required every new building to provide ample off-street parking. American households now have more cars than drivers, and their cars are parked 95 percent of the time. Because motorists rarely pay anything for parking, their cars live almost rent free. American cars and light trucks logged 2.6 trillion vehicle miles of travel in 2002, so the subsidy for *off-street* parking ranged between 5¢ a mile (if the subsidy was $127 billion) and 14¢ a mile (if it was $374 billion).[9] If we use the rule of thumb that increasing the gasoline tax by 1¢ a gallon increases gasoline tax revenues by about $1 billion a year, it would take an increase in the gasoline tax of between $1.27 and $3.74 a gallon to offset the subsidy for off-street parking.[10] Removing the subsidies for off-street parking would thus produce the same effect on travel as increasing the gasoline tax by between $1.27 and $3.74 a gallon. Because parking costs so much and motorists pay so little for it, the hidden subsidy is truly gigantic.

CAPITAL COST OF THE PARKING SUPPLY

The previous estimate referred to the *annual* cost of the parking supply. We can also estimate the *capital* cost of the parking supply, and the surprising result is that the cost of all parking spaces in the U.S. exceeds the value of all cars and may even exceed the value of all roads.

Value of Vehicles and Roads

The Department of Commerce has estimated the capital value of all fixed reproducible tangible wealth (i.e., excluding land value) in the U.S. for the years 1929 to 1997. Two categories of this estimate are the capital value of vehicles (all cars and trucks) and of roads (all streets and highways).[11] Table 7-2 shows the number of registered vehicles and the capital value of vehicles and roads for the years 1990 to 1997. The last row of the table shows that there were 208 million registered vehicles in 1997, and the Department of Commerce valued this vehicle stock at $1,144 billion. The average value per vehicle was therefore $5,507 ($1,114 billion ÷ 208 million). Although this value may seem low, the average age of all vehicles in 1995 was 8.3 years, and 62 percent of all vehicles were more than five

Table 7.2 Capital Value of Vehicles and Roads in the United States, 1990–1997

Year	Registered vehicles (million)	Capital value of vehicles		Capital value of roads		Capital value of vehicles and roads	
		Total ($billion)	Per vehicle ($/vehicle)	Total ($billion)	Per vehicle ($/vehicle)	Total ($billion)	Per vehicle ($/vehicle)
(1)	(2)	(3)	(4)=(3)/(2)	(5)	(6)=(5)/(2)	(7)=(3)+(5)	(8)=(7)/(2)
1990	189	$844	$4,473	$971	$5,144	$1,816	$9,616
1991	188	$856	$4,550	$994	$5,285	$1,850	$9,835
1992	190	$884	$4,645	$1,018	$5,349	$1,903	$9,994
1993	194	$927	$4,774	$1,059	$5,457	$1,986	$10,231
1994	198	$994	$5,018	$1,134	$5,724	$2,127	$10,742
1995	202	$1,055	$5,234	$1,218	$6,043	$2,273	$11,277
1996	206	$1,110	$5,380	$1,285	$6,224	$2,395	$11,605
1997	208	$1,144	$5,507	$1,359	$6,542	$2,503	$12,049

Sources: U.S. Department of Commerce (1998, Tables 3, 11, & 13), and Appendix H for number of vehicles.

years old.[12] The depreciation of the older vehicles explains the low average value of $5,507 per vehicle.

Are Parking Spaces Worth More Than Vehicles?

There are more parking spaces than vehicles because drivers must be able to park wherever they go, and many parking spaces are vacant much of the time. Cities typically require enough parking spaces to satisfy the *peak* demand for parking at every land use—at home, work, school, restaurants, shopping centers, movie theaters, and hundreds of other places—so that drivers can have convenient access to all addresses at all times. To see the result, think of what happens during the middle of the night when almost all vehicles are parked at home: almost all the spaces necessary to meet the peak demand for free parking at all other land uses are empty.

Cities require a specific number of parking spaces for every land use, but no city collects data on its total parking supply. As a result, no one knows the total number of parking spaces in the U.S. The eminent land-use planner Victor Gruen estimated that every car has at least one parking space at home and three or four waiting elsewhere to serve the same car.[13] To be conservative, suppose there is one parking space per car at home and only two elsewhere (at work, school, supermarkets, and so on), or only three parking spaces per vehicle.[14] Suppose we also make the conservative assumption that the average land and capital cost per parking space is only $4,000, an extremely low value given the evidence cited and calculated in Chapter 6. Given these two conservative assumptions, the value of the parking available per car is $12,000 (3 spaces per car x $4,000 per space), or more than twice the average value of a car ($5,507). If so, the total parking supply is worth more than twice the value of the total vehicle stock.

Are Parking Spaces Worth More Than Roads?

We can use similar reasoning to compare the cost of parking spaces with the value of roads. The Department of Commerce estimated that the depreciated construction value of all roads (excluding land value) was $1,359 billion in 1997. With 208 million vehicles owned in 1997, roads were therefore worth $6,542 per vehicle. This value may seem low, but many rural roads are old and in poor condition, so their depreciated value can be quite low. If there are 3 parking spaces per vehicle and the average value of parking is $4,000 per space, the parking spaces would again be worth $12,000 per vehicle. If so, the parking supply is worth almost twice the value of all roads ($6,542 per vehicle).[15]

Finally, the total capital value of all vehicles *and* roads was $2.5 trillion in 1997, or $12,049 per vehicle (the last row of columns 7 and 8), about equal to the value of parking per vehicle. Because parking lanes occupy both sides of most urban streets, we should also attribute part of the cost of roads to parking rather than to vehicle movement. When both off-street *and* on-street parking spaces are taken into account, more infrastructure may be devoted to idle cars than to moving ones.

Another rough approximation suggests a huge disparity in what motorists pay for parking and what they pay for roads. Total receipts for public and private parking facilities in the U.S. were only $6.6 billion in 1997.[16] In comparison, motorists paid $90 billion for fuel taxes, vehicle taxes, and tolls in the same year.[17] Parking spaces may be worth more than all roads, but motorists paid only 7 percent as much for parking as they did for road-use taxes and tolls.[18]

Most analysts agree that construction of the interstate highway system greatly spurred the dominance of the automobile in urban transportation. Gasoline taxes financed the construction of these highways, so motorists did at least pay for them. Most analysts fail to notice, however, that parking takes up far more land than the interstate system does, costs far more, and is far more essential to automobile use, but motorists rarely pay anything for parking. Off-street parking requirements, far more than interstate highways, have spurred the dominance of the automobile in urban transportation.

NEW PARKING SPACES COMPARED WITH NEW CARS

Another way to put the cost of free parking in perspective is to compare it with the price of new cars. Column 2 of Table 7-3 shows the original (non-inflation-adjusted) cost per space added by the parking structures built at UCLA since 1961 (from column 8 of Table 6-1). Column 3 shows the average price of a new car purchased in the U.S. in the year the structure was built. Finally, column 4 shows the ratio between the average cost of a new parking space and the average price of a new car.[19] On average, a new parking space has cost 17 percent more than a new car. Drivers may not realize it, but many parking spaces cost more than the cars parked in them, especially because cars depreciate in value much faster than parking spaces do.[20] When we consider that many cars cost less than the parking spaces they occupy, and that many parking spaces are vacant much of

Table 7-3. Cost of New Parking Spaces at UCLA Compared with the Price of New Cars

Year built	Cost per parking space	Average price of new car	Space cost as % of car price
(1)	(2)	(3)	(4)=(2)/(3)
1961	$2,000	$2,841	70%
1963	$1,626	$2,968	55%
1964	$1,946	$2,954	66%
1966	$2,323	$3,070	76%
1967	$2,789	$3,216	87%
1969	$2,907	$3,557	82%
1977	$11,762	$5,814	202%
1980	$11,499	$7,574	152%
1983	$19,752	$10,606	186%
1990	$20,859	$15,042	139%
1990	$22,350	$15,042	149%
1991	$20,873	$15,475	135%
1995	$13,712	$17,959	76%
1998	$26,300	$20,364	129%
2002	$31,500	$21,440	147%
Average 1961–2002			117%
Average 1961–1969			73%
Average 1977–2002			146%

Sources: Column 2 is from Table 6-1, column 8. Column 3 is from *Ward's Automotive Yearbook 2003* (page 270), and earlier editions.

the time, it is not surprising the parking supply is worth more than the vehicle stock.

The previous estimates have referred to the annual and capital costs of the total parking supply. We can also investigate the parking subsidies for individual trips. The next comparison shows that free parking at work subsidizes more than half of the average driver's variable cost of driving to work alone.

FREE PARKING COMPARED WITH THE COST OF DRIVING TO WORK

Nationwide, 95 percent of automobile commuters park free at work.[21] As a result, cities that base their parking requirements on the peak parking occupancy observed at existing worksites tend to require at least enough spaces to meet the *peak* demand for *free* parking. The resulting parking subsidies can be put in perspective by comparing the cost of providing free parking *at* work with the price that commuters pay for driving *to* work. For this comparison I will use an example based on the average distance for the journey to work in the U.S.

Free Parking Reduces the Cost of Automobile Commuting by 71 Percent

Consider an urban area where the cost of providing a structured parking space is $127 a month, as estimated in Chapter 6 (see row 1 of Table 7-4). If a commuter drives to work 22 days a month, it costs $5.77 per work day to provide a parking space at work ($127 ÷ 22 = $5.77). Because parking spaces provided for commuters usually serve only one car a day, a solo driver who parks free at work therefore receives a parking subsidy of $5.77 a day, which is greater than the round-trip transit fare for almost any commute trip (row 3).[22] As University of Pennsylvania professor of transportation Vukan Vuchic points out:

> With parking charges, car travel is more expensive than transit. Providing "free parking," however, creates a situation in which many commuters who select a mode on the basis of direct costs believe that they "save money" only by driving. This confirms the experience of many cities that "free parking" is a major—often the most important—factor in the encouragement of car commuting. It may represent the dominant obstacle to diversion of trips from cars to transit or to any other mode.[23]

Now let's take this parking subsidy, express it in cents per mile traveled, and compare it with the other costs of commuting. The *2001 National Household Travel Survey* found that the average round-trip commute distance in the U.S. was 26.2 miles, so if the parking subsidy is $5.77 a day, it is 22¢ per mile driven to and from work (row 5).[24] In comparison, the average operating cost of an automobile (for gasoline, oil, maintenance, and tires) was 13.6¢ per mile in 2001 (row 6).[25] The subsidy for free parking at work is thus 62 percent greater than the cost of driving to and from work (22¢ ÷ 13.6¢).

The average solo commuter paid $3.20 a day for vehicle operating costs (row 7). The driver's total variable cost of automobile commuting (operating cost plus parking cost) was therefore $3.20 a day if the employer paid for parking or $8.97 a day if the driver paid for it (row 8). Free parking at work thus subsidized 64 percent of the total variable cost of automobile commuting. In an earlier study of commuters in Toronto, Canadian transportation economist David Gillen estimated that free parking at work subsidized 85 percent of the total variable cost of driving to work.[26]

Table 7-4. Parking Subsidies Compared with Commuting Costs

Variable	Measure	Source
1. Parking subsidy per month	$127 per month	Table 6-3
2. Working days per month	22 days	
3. Parking subsidy per day	$5.77 per day	$127/22 days
4. Average round-trip distance to work	26.2 miles	*NHTS*
5. Parking subsidy per mile driven	22¢ per mile	$5.77/26.2 miles
6. Average automobile operating cost per mile	13.6¢ per mile	*Ward's*
7. Automobile operating cost per day	$3.20 per day	26.2 miles x 13.6¢ per mile
8. Total variable trip cost per day	$8.97 per day	$5.77 + $3.20
9. Parking subsidy as share of variable trip cost	64 percent	$5.77/$8.97
10. Average fuel efficiency	20 miles per gallon	*Ward's*
11. Gasoline consumed per work trip	1.3 gallons	26.2 miles/20mpg
12. Gasoline tax equivalent of parking subsidy	$4.44 per gallon	$5.77/1.3 gallons
13. Average federal and state gasoline tax per gallon	37¢ per gallon	USDOT
14. Federal and state gasoline tax per mile	1.9¢ per mile	37¢/20 miles
15. Parking subsidy/gasoline tax	12 (ratio)	22¢/1.9¢

Sources: Average trip distance is from the *2001 National Household Travel Survey (NHTS)*. Average variable operating cost (for gasoline, oil maintenance, tires) and fuel efficiency in 2001 are from *Ward's Motor Vehicle Facts & Figures 2002*.

Average gasoline tax rate in 2001 is from U.S. Department of Transportation (2001, Table MF-121T).

If the variable cost of driving to work is $3.20 a day and the cost of parking is $5.77 a day, charging for parking at work increases the out-of-pocket cost of driving to work by 180 percent. This large increase occurs because the cost of parking is such a large share of the cost of commuting. The percentage increase is smaller in countries where gasoline taxes are higher, but is still substantial. Belgian transportation economists Stef Proost and Kurt Van Dender estimated that charging for parking in central Brussels (where 70 percent of automobile commuters park free) would increase the commuters' costs of driving to work by 60 percent.[27]

Free Parking Is Worth More Than $4 per Gallon of Gasoline

One way to understand how charging for parking could change commuter choices is to imagine another cost increase of equivalent value, such as a gasoline tax. In 2001 the average fuel efficiency of cars and light trucks was 20 miles per gallon (row 10), while the average round-trip commute distance by private vehicle was 26.2 miles, so the average commute consumed 1.3 gallons of gasoline a day (row 11).[28] If a commuter parks free in a space that costs $5.77 a day and burns 1.3 gallons of gasoline on the way to and from work, the parking subsidy is equivalent to $4.44 per gallon of gasoline (row 12). Removing the subsidy for workplace parking would thus have the same effect on commuting as increasing the gasoline tax by $4.44 a gallon! The existing gasoline tax rate of 37¢ a gallon (row 13) would have to increase by 1,100 percent merely to offset the subsidy provided by free parking.[29]

In the long run, charging for parking would increase the cost of driving to work by even more than a $4.44-per-gallon gasoline tax. In response to the gasoline tax, motorists would buy more fuel-efficient cars or work closer to home, and the fuel consumed per work trip would decrease, but improved fuel efficiency will not cut the cost of parking.[30] So long as a car needs to be parked, the driver will pay for it, and the disincentive to solo driving is unavoidable.

Free Parking Is Worth 22¢ per Mile Driven to Work

For the average trip to work, free parking subsidizes the cost of a typical commute by 22¢ a mile (row 5). We can compare this subsidy with the cost paid per mile for the existing gas tax. The average combined federal-and-state gasoline tax in 2001 was 37¢ a gallon.[31] If fuel efficiency is 20 miles a gallon, the gas tax increases the cost of driving by 1.9¢ a mile (row 14). The subsidy per mile for parking *at* work is thus 12 times the gasoline tax per mile for driving *to* work (row 15). For shorter trips, of course, this ratio is even higher.

Other research also suggests that the cost of parking is higher than the cost of driving. In a study conducted for the Conservation Law Foundation, Apogee Research estimated that the cost of parking ranged from 25¢ per vehicle mile of travel (for all travel, not just commuting) in Boston and Cambridge to 11¢ per vehicle mile in the suburbs; because drivers usually parked free, they paid almost none of this cost.[32] The average cost of gasoline and oil was about 5¢ per vehicle mile, so the subsidy for parking was at least twice the fuel cost of driving.

To recapitulate, three comparisons show that free parking at work subsidizes a major cost of commuting by car. First, it reduces the out-of-pocket cost of driving by 64 percent. Second, it is equivalent to a subsidy of $4.44 per gallon of gasoline. And third, it subsidizes the cost of driving by 22¢ per mile, which is 12 times the gasoline tax per mile. Free parking is an offer that few commuters will refuse.

PARKING SUBSIDIES COMPARED WITH CONGESTION TOLLS

We can also compare how much parking subsidies reduce the cost of driving with how much congestion tolls would increase it. Most transportation economists agree that traffic congestion cannot be removed, or even significantly reduced, without charging a toll—such as the one that London introduced in 2003—for driving during peak hours. Economists argue that congestion stems from the government's failure to charge a higher price for driving during peak hours—an error of *omission*. But local governments impose minimum parking requirements to increase the supply and reduce the price of parking—an error of *commission*.

Michael Cameron and Kenneth Small independently estimated that a toll of 15¢ a mile (in 1990 dollars) would be necessary to achieve free flow during peak hours on Los Angeles highways.[33] Elizabeth Deakin and Greig Harvey estimated that the appropriate tolls on all congested roads in Los Angeles in 1991 would average 10¢ a mile.[34] Table 7-4 shows that free parking at work can *reduce* the cost of commuting by 22¢ a mile. Therefore, employer-paid parking reduces the cost of driving to work by more than the recommended congestion tolls would increase it.[35]

The average car is parked 95 percent of the time, so if most parking remains free, most drivers would pay congestion tolls only during the brief time they are traveling between two free parking spaces.[36] Parking charges complement congestion tolls, and Edward Calthrop, Stef Proost, and Kurt Van Dender showed that parking fees and congestion tolls combined would make transportation much more efficient than would either one alone. They used a simulation model of transportation in Brussels to analyze the effects of (1) charging fees for all parking in the Central Business District (CBD), (2) charging a congestion toll for all cars entering the CBD, and (3) charging both parking fees and a congestion toll.[37] They found that when parking fees and congestion tolls are introduced together, both the optimal parking fee and the optimal congestion toll are lower than when either one is introduced alone. But they also found that parking fees alone produced 96 percent of the benefit that parking fees and congestion tolls together would produce, while congestion tolls alone produced only 72 percent of this benefit. If a city had to choose either parking fees *or* congestion tolls, parking fees would produce higher benefits.

Two earlier comparisons of parking fees and congestion tolls yielded similar conclusions. In 1980, José Gómez-Ibáñez and Gary Fauth estimated that either a $1-a-day parking surcharge or a $1-a-day congestion fee on local streets in central Boston would about double the average traffic speed and would produce almost the same net transportation benefits.[38] In 1967, J. Michael Thomson estimated that parking fees in central London could produce about half the benefits of a peak-period congestion toll for all cars entering central London.[39] Thomson also estimated that half the total benefits of reduced congestion during the peak hours would accrue to bus passengers and operators because the reduced automobile congestion would increase bus speeds. At the time of the study, two-thirds of all the on-street parking spaces in central London were free.

Thomson estimated that the optimal congestion toll in 1967 would be £0.30 a day (£3.44 or $5.51 in 2003 prices) and would have increased the average peak-hour speed of traffic by 25 percent. In 2003 (35 years after Thomson's research), Transport for London introduced a congestion toll of £5 ($8) a day for entry into central London; during the first six months of the toll system, traffic into the zone declined by 16 percent, and the time spent either stationary or traveling less than 10 kilometers (6 miles) per hour declined by about 25 percent.[40] The £5-a-day toll is modest compared to the price of curb parking in the congestion-charge zone (which ranged up to £4 an hour in 2004) and even more modest in comparison with the price of all-day commuter parking in London. Because 81 percent of automobile commuters to central London park free at work, market-priced parking should therefore produce even greater reductions in traffic congestion.[41]

Parking fees are sometimes recommended to reduce congestion. Although the basic problem is seen to be the absence of congestion tolls, parking fees are proposed as a way to compensate for the political reluctance to impose the tolls.[42] But this proposal neglects the political reluctance to charge parking fees that are high enough to pay even for the cost of the parking spaces themselves. Cities do not use parking fees to compensate for the lack of congestion tolls, but instead do just the opposite. Cities underprice parking and thereby make traffic congestion even worse. Many proposed transportation pricing policies—congestion tolls or higher fuel taxes—are intended to make driving more expensive, but actual parking policies make it cheaper.

Most transportation analysts seem to think about parking only as it relates to something else they are interested in, such as traffic congestion or air pollution. Few seem to worry that the parking itself is being managed so inefficiently.[43] Nevertheless, charging prices to allocate parking spaces efficiently will also reduce congestion, air pollution, and energy consumption. Charging for parking is simple, and it often means no more than ending an inappropriate subsidy. Because both congestion tolls and parking fees promote transportation efficiency, and because the technology needed to charge for parking is so much simpler than that needed to charge for driving in congested traffic, it makes sense to end parking subsidies *in* the CBD before charging tolls for trips *to* the CBD.

Traffic congestion discourages vehicle travel (including bus travel), while parking fees specifically discourage solo driving. Congestion increases the time it takes to get from place to place, but people can respond by adjusting their places of employment or residence. They may reduce the distance to work, perhaps, or choose to live and work in a less congested area, but they continue to drive to work alone, and the time it takes to get to work remains stable even as the average travel speed decreases.[44] By slowing bus travel, congestion may even shift some transit passengers to solo driving. In contrast, parking fees encourage carpooling, walking, biking, or riding transit to work. These adjustments do reduce solo driving, which congestion does not.

SIMPLE ARITHMETIC

Another way to put free parking in perspective is to compare the cost of parking a car with the cost of driving it. In 2001, the average cost of operating a car (for gasoline, oil, maintenance, and tires) was 13.6¢ a mile, and the average car was driven 11,766 miles a year, so the total operating cost was $1,600 a year, or $4.38 a day.[45] If there were only three parking spaces per car, and if the average cost per space were only $1.46 a day, the average cost of parking a car would also be $4.38 a day. But because the average capital and operating cost of providing a parking space is surely more than $1.46 a day ($44 a month), the cost of parking exceeds the driver's cost of gasoline, oil, maintenance, and tires. Nevertheless, drivers pay for parking on only 1 percent of their trips. Total parking subsidies are thus probably higher than the total cost of operating all cars.

A final way to visualize the cost of free parking is to consider the total space needed to park all our cars. Suppose cars are packed closely together in a lot so each parking space is only 200 square feet, with no room to maneuver. If there are three parking spaces per vehicle, the area needed for parking is 600 square feet per vehicle. Because the U.S. had 230 million motor vehicles in 2002, the total parking area would be 4,950 square miles, about the size of Connecticut or larger than Delaware and Rhode Island combined.[46]

CONCLUSION: A GREAT PLANNING DISASTER

For any planning regulation, we should ask not only who will benefit from it, but also who will pay for it. With free parking, everyone seems to benefit, and no one seems to pay, so the cost of parking requirements has not been an issue for planners. But when we compare the cost of parking with other costs in the transportation system, we can see that the parking supply is probably worth more than all the motor vehicles in the U.S. Because drivers pay almost nothing to park, the subsidy is staggering, about the size of the Medicare or national defense budgets. In attempting to understand how these parking subsidies affect transportation and land use, we should follow the good advice of Deep Throat, who in an underground parking garage in 1972 reportedly told *Washington Post* writer Bob Woodward during his Watergate investigation, "Follow the money."

A cost of somewhere between $127 billion and $374 billion a year for off-street parking has been shifted into higher prices for everything else. This cost disappears from sight when drivers park free, but it does not cease to exist. Instead, free parking increases the demand for driving, which in turn increases the subsidy necessary to meet the peak parking demand. Minimum parking requirements are truly a great planning disaster—perhaps the greatest of all time.

CHAPTER 7 NOTES

1. Delucchi (1997, Tables 1-5, 1-6, and 1-7). Delucchi makes several conservative assumptions that tend to underestimate the cost of off-street parking. The lower bound of $79 billion a year is based on an estimate of 125 million nonresidential off-street parking spaces, and the upper bound of $226 billion a year is based on an estimate of 200 million spaces (Delucchi and Murphy 1998, Table 6-1). Because the U.S. had 189 million motor vehicles in 1990, this implies at most 1.06 nonresidential off-street parking spaces per vehicle. But using data based on off-street parking requirements for a variety of land uses, Murphy and Delucchi (1997, Table 6-1) estimate an upper bound of 895 million nonresidential off-street parking spaces in 1990, or 4.5 times more than the number of spaces used to calculate the upper bound of $226 billion a year for the subsidy for off-street parking. The huge uncertainty in calculating the cost of parking is perhaps explained by the ambiguity of how to count parking spaces. For example, many residents park in their driveways, so perhaps the driveways should be counted as parking spaces. On the other hand, residential garages not used for parking should not be counted as parking spaces. Many businesses were started in garages (the most famous being Reader's Digest, Walt Disney, Hewlett-Packard, Apple Computers, and Amazon.com). Buddy Holly and countless other musicians started out in garages, and some garage bands never leave their garages. Considering all the alternatives to parking cars in them, we should not count the cost of all residential garages as a cost of parking, but we should also not underestimate the number of nonresidential parking spaces.

2. Because on-street parking spaces are so difficult to count, Delucchi included their cost in the cost of roads. Some researchers do not consider the cost of parking to be a part of the cost of automobile transportation at all. In his book on *Financing Transportation Networks*, for example, University of Minnesota transportation economist David Levinson (2002) estimates the cost of automobile transportation but excludes the costs of parking because "they are outside the strictly defined transportation sector," similar to U.S. defense costs that some people attribute to the defense of the Middle East oil-producing regions (Levinson 2002, 42–43). Excluding the cost of parking gives an incomplete account of the transportation system's total cost, to say the least.

3. U.S. Department of Commerce (1998, Table 11). In 1997, the value of state and local roads and highways ($1.3 trillion) was 36 percent of the value of all state and local infrastructure ($3.7 trillion). Other infrastructure categories are a much smaller share of total infrastructure: educational buildings (18 percent), sewer systems (8 percent), water supply (5 percent), residential buildings (4 percent), equipment (4 percent), hospitals (3 percent), conservation and development (2 percent), and other (20 percent). These estimates exclude land value; because land value is a larger share of the total cost of roads than of the cost of other public infrastructure, including land value in the estimate would increase the share of total public infrastructure devoted to roads.

4. For the estimate of the U.S. gross domestic product, see Table B-1 in the *Economic Report of the President, 2004*, available online at www.gpoaccess.gov/eop/.

5. See *Ward's Automotive Yearbook 2003* (p. 269) for the total vehicle miles of travel in 1990.

6. See *Ward's Motor Vehicle Facts and Figures 2001* (p. 64) for the average variable cost of passenger cars in 1990.

7. Because there were 189 million motor vehicles in the U.S. in 1990, the parking subsidy was between $402 and $1,180 a year per vehicle. Adjusted for inflation to 2002, it was between $554 and $1,628 a year per vehicle. If there were only 3 parking spaces per vehicle, the parking subsidy per vehicle would thus be between $15 and $45 per parking space per month; these values are very low for the cost of a parking space in most cities, so even Delucchi's high estimate for the parking subsidy may be too low. Because parking requirements are intended to satisfy the peak demand for parking at every land use, it seems rea-sonable to assume that the off-street parking supply (and the total parking subsidy) increases in line with the number of cars. Some older cities were built before parking requirements were imposed, so the parking subsidy for new development probably exceeds the average parking subsidy for all development, and the total parking subsidy may therefore increase faster than the number of cars. Because the U.S. had 229,619,979 motor vehicles in 2002 (United States Department of Transportation 2002b, Table MV-1), Delucchi's estimates imply that the total parking subsidy was between $127 billion (if the subsidy was $554 per vehicle) and $374 billion (if the subsidy was $1,628 per vehicle).

    8. See Tables B-70 and B-80 in the *Economic Report of the President, 2003*, available online at www.gpoaccess.gov/usbudget/fy04/pdf/2003_erp.pdf.

    9. See *Ward's Automotive Yearbook 2003* (p. 269) for the total vehicle miles of travel in 2002.

    10. See Table 7-4. The average combined federal-and-state gasoline tax in 2001 was 37¢ a gallon. Because the average fuel efficiency was 20 miles a gallon, the gasoline tax increased the cost of driving by 1.9¢ a mile (37¢ ÷ 20). The subsidy for off-street parking is at least 2.6 times greater than the tax on gasoline (if the subsidy was 5¢ a mile) and may be 7.9 times greater (if the subsidy was 15¢ a mile).

    11. The capital value of an asset is measured as the cumulated value of past gross invest-ment in that asset minus the cumulated value of past depreciation. See Katz and Herman (1997) for the methodology for estimating the capital value of cars and roads. The values are expressed in current dollars for each year (i.e., they are not indexed for inflation).

    12. Hu and Young (1999, Table 20).

    13. Gruen (1973, 89). When Peter Newman and Jeffrey Kenworthy assembled their sourcebook of transportation statistics for cities, most cities were able to estimate the total number of parking spaces only in the Central Business District (CBD), and in some cases not even there. Newman and Kenworthy (1989, 31-32) report that the cities' parking data were almost always collected on an irregular basis by consultants in response to specific needs in specific areas.

    14. Erik Verhoef (1996, 97) reports that in the Netherlands there are three parking spaces available for every car.

    15. This estimated value in roads excludes the value of land. Therefore, the value of park-ing spaces must also exclude the value of land to make a valid comparison with the value of roads. The U.S. had 230 million motor vehicles and 4 million miles of roads in 2002, or about 58 cars per mile of road (U.S. Department of Transportation 2002b, Tables MV-1 and HM-20). If there are only three parking spaces per car, there are 174 parking spaces per mile of road or one parking space for every 30 feet of road.

    16. The *1997 Economic Census* found that private parking lots and garages in the U.S. had total receipts of only $5.2 billion in 1997 (U.S. Census Bureau 1997). Parking lots and garages are code 81293 in the North American Industry Classification System. The U.S. Department of Transportation (2002a, Table 3-A) reported that the total receipts of all pub-lic parking facilities were $1.4 billion in 1997. The receipts of parking lots and garages overstate what drivers pay for parking because parking operators receive revenue that drivers don't pay if someone else pays it for them—as with validated and employer-paid parking.

    17. Motorist payments for motor-fuel and motor-vehicle taxes and tolls were $90 billion in 1997. See U.S. Department of Transportation, Federal Highway Administration, Office of Highway Policy Information, *Highway Statistics 1998*, Table HDF, Disposition of Highway-User Revenues. Available online at www.fhwa.dot.gov/ohim/hs98/hs98page.htm.

18. Another comparison shows the size of parking subsidies. KPMG Peat Marwick (1990) estimated that in 1989 the annual capital plus operating cost of parking spaces provided free to automobile commuters in the U.S. amounted to $52.1 billion. The American Public Transit Association (1997) reported that in 1989 the federal, state, and local governments provided $8.7 billion in total operating subsidies for all public transportation in the U.S. Therefore, the parking subsidy for automobile work trips was six times the operating subsidy for all public transportation trips for all purposes.

19. Data for the average price of a new car are taken from the *Ward's Automotive Yearbook 2000* (page 284) and from earlier editions of the same publication.

20. In the 1960s, the cost of a new parking space averaged 73 percent of the price of a new car. Parking spaces have remained the same (or become smaller) since the 1960s, while the quality of new cars has improved significantly, but a new parking space more than doubled in cost when compared with the price of a new car.

21. The *1995 Nationwide Personal Transportation Survey* found that 95 percent of all automobile commuters park free at work (U.S. Department of Transportation 1995a). The *2001 National Household Travel Survey* did not ask commuters whether they paid for parking at work (U.S. Department of Transportation 2003a).

22. Some commuters will be absent from work, so more commuters can be offered parking than there are spaces. On the other hand, a parking system operates most efficiently with a vacancy rate of between 5 and 15 percent, so that drivers do not need to search the entire system for the last few available spaces. The absentee rate found in parking studies is usually between 5 and 15 percent, so these two factors are assumed to cancel each other.

23. Vuchic (1999, 77).

24. *2001 National Household Travel Survey* (United States Department of Transportation 2003a).

25. *Ward's Motor Vehicle Facts & Figures 2002.*

26. In a study of commuters to the Toronto CBD, David Gillen (1977a) found that the average cost of parking at work was $1.56 a day and the average automobile variable cost (fuel, oil, tires) for driving to work was $0.28 a day. The total variable cost of a vehicle trip to work was thus $1.84 a day ($1.56 + $0.28), and free parking at work subsidized 85 percent of the total variable cost of driving to work ($1.56 ÷ $1.84).

27. Proost and Van Dender (2001, 401). Because vehicle operating costs are proportional to trip length, while the parking fee is independent of it, charging for parking produces even greater increases in the cost of driving for shorter trips. Charging for parking substantially increases the cost of driving to work because each commuter's car takes up a lot of space at work. A typical employment density in office buildings is four persons per 1,000 square feet, or 250 square feet of office space per employee. In comparison, parking lots and parking structures typically have about 330 square feet per space (half for the parked car, and half for the access aisles). Because a car parked at work typically occupies about a third more space than its driver does, charging for parking can substantially increase the cost of driving to work.

28. *Ward's Motor Vehicle Facts & Figures 2002.* The average fuel efficiency was calculated by dividing the total Vehicle Miles Travelled (VMT) for cars and light trucks by the total fuel consumption of cars and light trucks.

29. We are lucky our cars are not fueled by other common liquids such as Diet Snapple ($10 a gallon) or Evian water ($21 a gallon).

30. Richard Muth (1983) examined how the rapid rise in gasoline prices during the 1970s affected the cost of commuting. After correcting for general price inflation, the price of gasoline almost doubled between 1973 and 1980, but Muth estimated that the cost per mile for driving to work increased by only 5 percent. Two reasons explain this small increase in commuting cost. First, petroleum costs were only about one-fifth of the cost of the 10-year average cost of operating an automobile (including gasoline, oil, depreciation, repair and maintenance, replacement tires, accessories, sales tax, and taxes on gasoline and tires). Second, average car size declined and automobile fuel efficiency increased as a result of the gasoline price rise.

31. United States Department of Transportation (2001b, Table MF-121T). The federal tax was 18.4¢ per gallon, and weighted average of the state tax rates was 19.08¢ per gallon. The state tax rates ranged from 7.5¢ per gallon in Georgia to 29¢ per gallon in Rhode Island.

32. Apogee Research (1994, 99 and 109). Apogee estimated the sum of the costs for both residential and nonresidential parking spaces, not including the cost of on-street parking spaces. Apogee assumed that the capital cost of a residential garage was only $2,400 and that it would be depreciated over 80 years, so the estimate of residential parking cost seems conservative (Apogee Research 1994, 110).

33. PAS Report 532, *Parking Cash Out,* describes these congestion toll estimates by Michael Cameron (1991) and Kenneth Small (1992).

34. Deakin and Harvey (1996).

35. In response to a congestion toll, drivers would travel at off-peak hours, shift to untolled roads, or move closer to work, so the congestion toll per work trip would decrease. Therefore, charging for parking would in the long run increase the cost of driving to work by even more than would a congestion toll of 22¢ a mile.

36. See Appendix B for the evidence that drivers park free for 99 percent of their trips and that the average car is parked for 95 percent of the time.

37. "Pricing of parking and road use need to be simultaneously determined. As the level of parking fee becomes more efficient, or as the number of free parkers is reduced, so the level of optimally determined cordon charge falls. Additionally, by introducing a cordon charge, the level of the optimally determined parking fee falls" (Calthrop, Proost, and van Dender 2000, 64). Without parking fees, the optimal congestion toll was $3.70 per trip. With parking fees of $1.90 per trip (the estimated cost of providing parking spaces), the optimal congestion toll fell to $3.10 per trip. In the base case, they assumed that drivers park free for 70 percent of their trips. The cordon charges vary by time of day but parking fees do not. European Currency Units (ECU) are converted at an exchange rate of $1 = 1ECU.

38. Gómez-Ibáñez and Fauth (1980)

39. Thomson (1967). The optimal increase in the price of parking was £0.0375 an hour (£0.43 or $0.69 in 2003 prices), and it increased the average peak-hour speed of traffic by 14 percent. The optimal congestion toll was £0.30 a day (£3.44 or $5.51 in 2003 prices), and it increased the average peak-hour speed of traffic by 25 percent. Thomson did not model the effects of parking fees and a congestion toll. The 1967 prices are converted to their 2003 equivalents by the UK Retail Price Index and are converted at an exchange rate of £1 = $1.60. In 2003, Transport for London introduced a charge of £5 a day for entry into central London.

40. Transport for London (2003).

41. Baker (1987, 535) reports the results of a survey showing that 81 percent of commuters to central London park free at work.

42. For example, Glazer and Niskanen (1992, 124) say, "We thus do not address the role of parking fees in allocating more and less desirable parking spaces to users." They examine "the second-best solution: the optimal parking fees if the road-usage fee is too low." They do not examine what happens if the parking fee itself is too low to allocate spaces efficiently.

43. An exception is Eric Verhoef (1996, 112) who presents a sophisticated analysis of parking policies with two goals: "(1) optimizing the level of congestion on an urban road network and (2) optimizing the activity of parking itself." He concludes that parking fees are a first-best way to allocate scarce parking space but a second-best way to regulate other road transport externalities.

44. Gordon and Richardson (2001) explain how stable regional travel times can coexist with substantial increases in route congestion, and they present evidence showing that the average commuting time in the U.S. has not changed significantly since 1969 and perhaps has not changed since 1934.

45. *Ward's Automotive Yearbook 2003*, pp. 268-269. The total operating cost of driving a car is $1,600 a year (11,766 miles per year x 13.6¢ per mile), which is equivalent to $4.38 a day ($1,600 ÷ 365).

46. The area of 200 square feet per parking space is conservative because it does not include the area needed for access aisles in parking lots and garages. The total area needed for parking is 4,950 square miles (230 million vehicles x 600 square feet per vehicle ÷ 27,878,400 square feet per square mile). The land areas of Connecticut, Delaware, and Rhode Island are 4,845 square miles, 1,954 square miles, and 1,045 square miles, respectively.

8

An Allegory: Minimum Telephone Requirements

The right to have access to every building in the city by private motorcar, in an age when everyone possesses such a vehicle, is actually the right to destroy the city.

—*LEWIS MUMFORD*

We are so accustomed to plentiful free parking that we may not see—or may not *want* to see—its costs and consequences clearly. To gain a new perspective, imagine what would happen if urban planners arranged to have the charges reversed for all telephone calls, so the called parties, not the callers, pay for telephone calls.[1] Let's further imagine that the cost of all the reversed charges are bundled into every property's mortgage or rent payment, without separate itemization, so that nobody seems to pay for using the phone.

Because all calls are free to the callers, the demand for telephone use soars. To avoid chronic busy signals, cities set minimum telephone requirements so that each new building provides at least enough telephone lines to handle the peak number of calls. Soon everyone expects every building to have at least one telephone line for each occupant plus additional lines for fax machines, computer modems, and burglar alarms. Developers pass the cost of providing this telephone capacity on to the occupants, raising the price of all goods and services, including housing.

To help urban planners predict telephone demand, telephone engineers survey the maximum number of telephone lines engaged during the peak calling hour at a handful of properties, and the Institute of Telephone Engineers (ITE) publishes the results in a manual of "telephone generation rates" for every land use. Urban planners then consult the ITE manual to set minimum telephone requirements that will satisfy the maximum telephone demand at hundreds of different land uses. Minimum telephone requirements differ wildly among cities, with no explanations asked or given. Urban planners set individual telephone requirements without considering the price of telephone calls or the cost of providing telephone capacity. In setting the individual requirement for each land use, planners ignore the cumulative effects of the whole system of requirements.

The federal government inadvertently spurs peak-hour calling by exempting employer-paid telecommuting subsidies from income taxes and then heavily subsidizes local mail service to reduce solo telecommuting at peak calling hours. The government spends more and more on mail service to carry a shrinking share of all communication.

Attempting to reduce peak-hour calls, some cities exempt the Central Business District (CBD) from minimum telephone requirements, but developers continue to provide ample telephone capacity anyway, because it is available everywhere else and everyone has become accustomed to having it. In desperation, a few cities cap the number of telephones allowed in the CBD, but with every call free to the caller the problems of telephone congestion become insoluble. A telephone demand management (TDM) industry springs up.

Finally, imagine that telephone calls have the same environmental effects as vehicle trips. Excessive telephone use pollutes the air, depletes natural resources, and risks global warming. Planners search frantically for solutions to all these problems without even noticing the effects of minimum telephone requirements.

Minimum telephone requirements are a joke, but minimum parking requirements are real. Cities *do* require at least enough parking spaces to satisfy the peak demand for free parking, which *does* increase vehicle travel. Excessive vehicle travel *does* pollute the air, deplete natural resources, and risk global warming. Minimum parking requirements have short-circuited the price system in the markets for both transportation and land, and have created many unintended but not unforeseeable consequences. Cities would look and work much better if prices rather than planners governed most decisions about the quantity of parking. Like the automobile itself, parking is a good servant, but a bad master.

CHAPTER 8 NOTE

1. With free parking, the locations visited pay the cost of providing the parking. With collect telephone calls, the locations called pay the cost of telephone calls. Providing free parking for 99 percent of all automobile trips is like providing 800 numbers for 99 percent of all telephone calls.

9

Public Parking in Lieu of Private Parking

A mass of metal is laboriously transported from one place to another. Then it is abandoned for the day, obstructing pedestrians who are attempting a less selfish method of locomotion.

— A. J. P. TAYLOR

Off-street parking requirements have a flimsy theoretical and empirical basis, cost an enormous amount of money, and create immense harm. Unfortunately, they are also legislated in zoning ordinances and firmly entrenched in planning practice, so major reforms are difficult. In Part III of this book, I will propose a way to eliminate parking requirements altogether, but I realize that this will not happen soon. In the meantime, we can make significant reforms within the existing system. Some cities have already embarked in two promising directions:

1. *Provide Public Parking in Lieu of Private Parking.* Some cities give developers the option to pay a fee in lieu of providing the required parking spaces. The cities then use the revenue to provide public parking spaces to replace the private parking spaces the developers would otherwise have provided.
2. *Reduce Parking Demand Rather Than Increase the Parking Supply.* Some cities give developers the option to reduce parking demand instead of increasing the parking supply. To reduce parking demand, developers typically provide incentives—such as transit passes

for commuters—that encourage travel by the alternatives to solo driving.

These two reforms can reduce costs for developers, improve urban design, increase public transit ridership, reduce traffic congestion, and save commuters money. This chapter examines the first reform (in-lieu fees), while Chapter 10 examines the second (reduce parking demand).

In-lieu fees give developers an alternative to providing the required parking spaces on-site. To learn about in-lieu programs, I surveyed planning officials in 47 cities that offer them: 25 in the United States, 7 in Canada, 6 in the United Kingdom, 6 in Germany, 2 in South Africa, and 1 in Iceland (see Table 9-1).[1] I consulted the officials who administer the in-lieu fees and examined the fee ordinances and supporting documents. The survey results are summarized in four sections: (1) the benefits of in-lieu fees, (2) problems with the fees, (3) how cities set the fees, and (4) who decides whether to provide the parking or pay the fee.

Table 9-1. Surveyed Cities with In-lieu Fees

United States	Canada	United Kingdom
Berkeley, California	Burnaby, British Columbia	Brent
Beverly Hills, California	Calgary, Alberta	Harrow
Carmel, California	Hamilton, Ontario	Kingston upon Thames
Chapel Hill, North Carolina	Kitchener, Ontario	Redbridge
Claremont, California	Ottawa, Ontario	Sutton
Concord, California	Toronto, Ontario	Waltham Forest
Culver City, California	Vancouver, British Columbia	
Davis, California		
Hermosa Beach, California	**Germany**	
Kirkland, Washington	Dresden	
Lafayette, California	Frankfurt	
Lake Forest, Illinois	Hamburg	
Manhattan Beach, California	Munich	
Montgomery County, Maryland	Nuremberg	
Mountain View, California	Würzburg	
Mill Valley, California		
Orlando, Florida	**South Africa**	
Palm Springs, California	Johannesburg	
Palo Alto, California	Port Elizabeth	
Pasadena, California		
San Francisco, California	**Iceland**	
San Rafael, California	Reykjavik	
Santa Monica, California		
State College, Pennsylvania		
Walnut Creek, California		

BENEFITS OF IN-LIEU FEES

Planning officials reported that in-lieu fees provide several benefits for both cities and developers. These benefits fall into seven categories.

1. *Flexibility.* Developers gain a new option. If providing all the required parking spaces on-site would be difficult or too expensive, developers can instead pay the in-lieu fee.

2. *Shared Parking.* Public parking spaces built with the in-lieu revenue allow shared use among different sites whose peak parking demands occur at different times (a bank and a bar, for example), and fewer spaces are needed to meet the combined peak parking demands.

3. *Park Once.* When all businesses have individual parking lots, they want only their own customers to park there. Once customers have left the store, the owners want them out of the lot as soon as possible, requiring the customers to drive to another private lot in order to make a second stop in a nearby business. Shared public parking allows drivers to park once and visit multiple sites on foot, thereby reducing vehicle traffic and increasing foot traffic.

4. *Historic Preservation.* Parking requirements can discourage adaptive reuse of historic buildings if the additional parking spaces required for a new use are difficult to provide on-site. By removing the requirement for on-site parking spaces, in-lieu fees make it easier to restore historic buildings and to rehabilitate historic areas. The owner of an old brownstone, for instance, may want to rehabilitate it and turn it into a restaurant but cannot because it lacks the required parking. Without the in-lieu option, the building may stay unused, or—worse yet—be torn down and replaced by a parking lot. With the in-lieu option, however, the building is restored, more people find work, the neighborhood gets a new place to eat, and the city earns higher tax revenues.

5. *Consolidation.* Some cities also allow developers and property owners to pay in-lieu fees to remove the existing required parking spaces. This option consolidates scattered parking spaces, assists infill development, improves urban design, and encourages conversion of parking lots to higher-and-better uses that provide more services, yield more revenue, and employ more people.[2] All property owners, not just developers, can use more of their land for buildings and less for parking.

6. *Fewer Variances.* Where providing the required parking is difficult, developers often request variances to reduce the parking requirements for their sites. These variances weaken the general plan, require administration, and create unearned economic windfalls for

some developers but not others. By making fewer variances necessary, in-lieu fees allow cities to create a level playing field for all developers.

7. ***Better Urban Design.*** Parking requirements typically result in surface parking lots for smaller buildings that cannot support their own parking garages. Because in-lieu fees allow stores to meet their parking requirements without on-site parking, they allow continuous storefronts without "dead" gaps created by parking lots. Developers can undertake infill projects without assembling large parcels for on-site parking, and architects have greater design freedom. The public parking structures consume less land than would be required if each site provided an on-site parking lot, and cities can place the structures where they interfere least with vehicle and pedestrian circulation. To improve the streetscape, some cities dedicate the first floor of public parking structures to retail uses. The in-lieu policy thus contributes to a better-looking, safer, and more walkable city.

CONCERNS ABOUT IN-LIEU FEES

Officials in all the surveyed cities recommended the in-lieu policy, but some reported that developers were initially skeptical. The following four points summarize the developers' concerns, as well as potential solutions.

1. ***Lack of On-Site Parking.*** Parking is a valuable asset for any development, and a lack of on-site, owner-controlled parking can reduce a development's ability to attract tenants and customers. This may be a valid objection, but its solution is simple: developers can provide the required parking rather than pay the fee.

2. ***High Fees.*** Cities may not build and operate parking facilities as cheaply as the private sector. Cities may pay extra to improve the architectural design of parking structures, for example, and these higher costs may increase the in-lieu fees. Although this might happen, most cities set their in-lieu fees lower than the cost of providing a public parking space. Economies of scale in public parking can further reduce the fees because the structures spread the fixed cost of ramps, elevators, stairwells, and curb cuts among more parking spaces.[3] Cities also have access to lower-cost, tax-exempt financing. Again, developers who feel the in-lieu fee is too high can always provide the required parking themselves.

3. ***No Guarantees.*** Cities use the in-lieu fee revenue to finance public parking, but they don't guarantee when or where the spaces will be provided.[4] To address this concern, some cities build the public parking first and accept in-lieu fees only for the number of public spaces already provided. The cities then use the in-lieu fees to retire the debt

incurred to finance the spaces. Other cities refund the in-lieu fees if they haven't built the public parking within a certain time. Cities can also allow developers to defer payment of the in-lieu fees until the public parking spaces are built.

4.   *Fewer Parking Spaces.* Cities use in-lieu fees to finance public parking spaces, but they don't commit to provide one public space for every private space not provided. Oftentimes they provide fewer. Pasadena, for example, provides two public parking spaces for each three in-lieu fees paid. When this happens, the in-lieu programs reduce the total number of parking spaces. A smaller parking supply may lead to fewer customers and put businesses at a competitive disadvantage. Cities provided two responses to this last concern. First, the more efficient use of shared public parking enables a smaller parking supply to meet the combined peak parking demand. Instead of many individual parking lots underused much of the time, the city has fewer but larger parking facilities used throughout the day. Second, if the city collects in-lieu fees to finance public parking spaces instead of granting variances to reduce parking requirements, the in-lieu policy actually *increases* the parking supply.

While these concerns should not be ignored, planning officials in most of the surveyed cities said in-lieu fees have become a form of administrative relief for developers who find it difficult to provide the required parking on site. In practice, the in-lieu fees give developers an alternative to providing expensive on-site parking spaces, and the shared public parking gives downtown the park-once advantages of shopping malls.

HOW DO CITIES SET THE IN-LIEU FEES?

There are two basic approaches to setting in-lieu fees. The first is to calculate the appropriate fee per space on a case-by-case basis for each project. The second is to charge a uniform fee per space for all projects. One city, Beverly Hills, has employed both methods, and we can review its experience to learn why most of the surveyed cities have opted for uniform fees.

Case-by-Case Fees

Until 1994, Beverly Hills calculated an in-lieu fee for each project based on the estimated cost per space (for both land and construction) to build a public parking structure nearby. The per-space fee set for each project was the sum of (1) the average construction cost per space and (2) the value of 60 square feet of land (the average land area per space for a municipal parking structure) within a 300-foot radius of the site. The average in-lieu fee turned out to be $37,000 per space, and the highest was $53,000; that is, one developer was willing to pay the city $53,000 for permission *not* to provide a parking space that the zoning required.[5]

The case-by-case approach was complicated, time consuming, and expensive to administer, requiring a land-value appraisal to estimate the cost of public parking near each project. After waiting four to six months for the city to calculate the fee, applicants usually appealed to the city council to reduce it. Developers also complained that not knowing the fee in advance created uncertainty in project planning and financing.

Uniform Fees

To address these problems, in 1994 Beverly Hills adopted uniform in-lieu fees, which have proved to be easier for the city to administer and for developers to use.[6] With the fees set ahead of time, developers can easily incorporate them into financial analyses and can decide early in the development process whether to provide the parking or pay the fee. These two benefits of simplicity and certainty help explain why most cities set uniform fees.[7]

Most cities have no explicit policy regarding how often to revise their fees, and some fees haven't changed for many years. A few cities, however, automatically link their fees to an index of construction costs. Beverly Hills and Palo Alto, for example, adjust their fees annually by the *ENR* Construction Cost Index, which measures cost inflation in the construction industry.[8]

Kirkland has two unusual in-lieu options. First, the developer can pay an initial fee of $6,000 per parking space not provided, and the property owner must then purchase one parking permit in a public lot for every three spaces not provided. This one-for-three ratio is based on the estimate that employees typically use one-third of the required parking spaces. The second option is to pay no initial fee, but in every subsequent year the property owner must buy one parking permit in a public lot for each space not provided. The agreement to purchase annual public parking permits is an obligation that runs with the land and is binding on subsequent property owners for as long as the required on-site parking is not provided. These two options reduce the capital cost of development, and they encourage the use of public parking. Property owners may cancel the annual in-lieu agreement anytime if they provide the required on-site parking.

Santa Monica has a novel in-lieu arrangement for its popular Third Street Promenade commercial district. Instead of providing the required parking, developers can pay an in-lieu fee of $1.50 a year per square foot of floor area (regardless of the use), and the money finances public garages built behind the stores.[9] Basing the fee on floor area rather than on parking spaces gives a break to land uses with high parking requirements. Santa Monica requires one space for every 80 square feet for theaters, for example, so a theater's in-lieu fee is only $120 a year per parking space not provided (80 x $1.50); this modest fee helps explain why many movie theaters—and other uses with high parking requirements, such as restaurants—have opened on the Promenade.[10] The parking is hidden behind the Promenade, resulting is a dense, pedestrian-friendly streetscape with superior urban design and continuous storefronts.

Some German cities have a graduated schedule of in-lieu fees (known as *Ablösebeträge*) that are highest in the city center and decline toward the periphery. Hamburg's fee, for example, is $20,705 per space in the city center and $11,300 per space in the surrounding area.

Vancouver has the most sophisticated method for calculating its in-lieu fee. The fee ($9,708 per space) is the expected cost per space in a public parking structure, minus the expected revenue from the charges for parking in the structure.[11] The in-lieu fee is thus the share of the total cost of a public parking space that parkers do not pay. Developers who pay the in-lieu fees do not subsidize the city, and the city does not subsidize developers. Instead, developers subsidize parking.

Many cities set their in-lieu fees below the cost of a public parking space. Hamilton, Lake Forest, and Toronto, for example, set their fees at half the estimated land-and-construction cost of providing parking spaces.[12] Mountain View, Orlando, and Walnut Creek set their fees equal to the construction cost per space for municipal parking structures, excluding the cost of the land.[13]

When asked *why* cities set the in-lieu fees below the cost of providing a parking space, planners typically answered that the fee would be "too high" if the city charged the full cost. But that, sadly, is the point. When in-lieu fees reveal the full cost of providing the required parking, everyone can see that it is *too high*. Parking requirements hide the cost of parking in the cost of development. Only if the full cost of parking is out in the open, where everyone can see it, can we think about it properly. And yet, when in-lieu fees threaten to reveal this cost, cities respond by setting below-cost fees. There seems an almost pathological need to hide the cost of parking, as though it ceases to exist if it is hidden.

Who Decides?

Most cities allow developers to choose whether to provide the parking or pay the fee, but a few cities *require* developers to pay the fee. Calgary, for example, requires developers to pay fees for half the spaces and to provide the other half. Orlando requires developers to pay fees in lieu of the first required space per 1,000 square feet and allows them to choose whether to pay fees for the rest. Carmel and Lake Forest require developers to pay fees in lieu of all the parking. Officials cited several reasons why they require developers to pay the fees rather than to provide the parking. Requiring the fees:

- encourages shared parking;
- discourages the proliferation of surface parking lots;
- emphasizes continuous shopfronts along the street;
- improves pedestrian and bicycle circulation;
- reduces traffic congestion; and
- improves urban design.[14]

WHY PAY THE FEE RATHER THAN PROVIDE THE PARKING?

When given the option, how does a developer decide whether to pay the in-lieu fee or to provide the required parking? The issue is not simply whether the in-lieu fee is less than the cost of an on-site parking space. Developers who pay in-lieu fees receive permission to build without providing the required parking spaces, while developers who provide the required parking spaces receive permission to build *and* own the on-site spaces, which are a valuable asset. Therefore, some developers will provide parking spaces that cost even more than the in-lieu fees because on-site parking spaces add value to a development, while payment of an in-lieu fee does not.

The developer's decision to provide the required parking or pay the in-lieu fee depends on the costs and benefits in each case (see box). Suppose the capital cost of an additional on-site parking space is $15,000.[15] Suppose also that an additional on-site parking space will add $6,000 to a project's capital value.[16] In this case the net loss per additional parking space is $9,000 (the $15,000 cost minus the $6,000 benefit). If the in-lieu fee is less than $9,000 per space, the developer should pay the fee rather than provide the parking.

Pay the fee or provide the parking?

Capital cost of an additional parking space:	$15,000
Capital value added by an additional parking space:	- $ 6,000
Net loss per additional parking space:	$ 9,000

Conclusion: Pay the fee if it is less than $9,000 per space.

A decision to pay the in-lieu fee rather than provide on-site parking implies that each additional parking space costs much more than it adds to a development's value. Developers in Beverly Hills, for example, paid average in-lieu fees of $37,000 per space between 1978 and 1992. The developers' willingness to pay these high fees for permission *not* to provide the required parking indicates the high cost parking requirements can impose on urban development.

The cost of meeting a parking requirement is not always an exaction from the developer. We can distinguish three cases in which none, some, or all of the requirement is an exaction:
1. If the developer voluntarily provides all the required parking, the requirement does not impose any exaction.[17]
2. If the developer provides all the required parking but would prefer to provide fewer spaces, the developer's loss on the involuntarily supplied parking is an exaction.
3. If the developer pays the in-lieu fee for all the required parking, then all of the requirement is an exaction.

Even where the parking requirement is not an exaction, the in-lieu fee can show the developer's cost to comply with the requirement because it provides an estimate of the cost of providing a new parking space.

THE IMPACT FEES IMPLICIT IN PARKING REQUIREMENTS

Off-street parking requirements resemble impact fees used to finance the public infrastructure—such as roads and schools—that development makes necessary. Alan Altshuler and Jose Gómez-Ibáñez define impact fees as "mandated expenditures by private land developers, required as a price for their obtaining regulatory permits, in support of infrastructure and other public services."[18] Most cities levy these impact fees in proportion to a building's floor area. San Francisco, for example, charges a one-time impact fee of $5 per square foot of new office space and uses the revenue to finance public transit. Off-street parking requirements resemble impact fees because cities require developers to provide infrastructure—parking spaces—as a price for obtaining regulatory permits. When cities *require* developers to pay in-lieu fees rather than provide parking spaces, the in-lieu fees *are* impact fees.

By putting an official dollar value on the cost of parking spaces, the in-lieu fees produce an unintended side effect: they reveal the cost of satisfying the off-street parking requirements. The cost of providing the required parking is usually bundled into the total cost of development with no separate accounting, but the in-lieu fees bring the cost of required parking spaces out in the open. We can therefore use the in-lieu fees as a way to estimate the cost of satisfying a city's parking requirement. This estimate can be thought of as a "parking impact fee" that is implicit in the off-street parking requirement. The simplest way to explain a parking impact fee is to calculate it for one land use—office buildings.

Parking Impact Fees for Office Buildings

The *parking impact fee* imposed by a parking requirement depends on (1) the number of parking spaces required and (2) the in-lieu fee per space. Table 9-2 shows the parking requirements and the in-lieu fees for office buildings in the Central Business Districts (CBDs) of 29 cities in 1996 (the year the survey was conducted).[19] The last column of the table shows how the off-street parking requirements and the in-lieu fees combine to produce parking impact fees.

To see how a parking requirement and an in-lieu fee translate to an impact fee, consider the first row of the table. Palo Alto requires 4 spaces per 1,000 square feet of floor area, and its in-lieu fee is $17,848 per space.[20] A developer who provides no parking must pay the city an in-lieu fee of $71,392 per 1,000 square feet of office space ($17,848 x 4), or $71 per square foot ($71,392 ÷ 1,000). The parking requirement and the in-lieu fee, combined, are therefore equivalent to an impact fee of $71 per square foot of office space. According to *Building Construction Cost Data* (an annual publication that reports the cost for many types of construction), in 2001 the median construction cost for one- to four-story office buildings was $74 per square foot and was $78 per square foot for five- to 10-story office buildings.[21] Palo Alto's parking impact fee for a new office building is thus about the same as the cost of constructing the building itself.

If the in-lieu fees are equal to the cost of providing new parking spaces in the CBD, the parking impact fees show the cost of meeting the city's

Table 9-2. Parking Impact Fees for Office Buildings in 1996

City (U.S. cities in regular text; *Non-U.S. cities in italic text*)	In-lieu parking fee ($/space)	Parking requirement (spaces per 1,000 square feet)	Parking impact fee ($/square foot)
(1)	(2)	(3)	(4)=(2)x(3)/1,000
Palo Alto, California	$17,848	4.0	$71
Beverly Hills, California	$20,180	2.9	$59
Walnut Creek, California	$16,373	3.3	$55
Kingston upon Thames, *United Kingdom*	$20,800	2.3	$48
Carmel, California	$27,520	1.7	$46
Mountain View, California	$13,000	3.0	$39
Sutton, United Kingdom	$13,360	2.7	$36
Harrow, United Kingdom	$14,352	2.3	$33
Hamburg, Germany	$20,705	1.5	$32
Lake Forest, Illinois	$9,000	3.5	$32
Mill Valley, California	$6,751	4.4	$30
Palm Springs, California	$9,250	3.1	$28
Reykjavik, Iceland	$13,000	2.2	$28
Claremont, California	$9,000	2.9	$26
Concord, California	$8,500	2.9	$24
Davis, California	$8,000	2.5	$20
Orlando, Florida	$9,883	2.0	$20
Kitchener, Ontario	$14,599	1.3	$19
Chapel Hill, North Carolina	$7,200	2.5	$18
Kirkland, Washington	$6,000	2.9	$17
Hermosa Beach, California	$6,000	2.6	$16
Berkeley, California	$10,000	1.5	$15
Burnaby, British Columbia	$7,299	2.0	$15
Vancouver, British Columbia	$9,708	1.0	$10
State College, Pennsylvania	$5,850	1.3	$8
Ottawa, Ontario	$10,043	0.7	$7
Calgary, Alberta	$9,781	0.7	$7
Port Elizabeth, South Africa	$1,846	2.3	$4
Waltham Forest, *United Kingdom*	$2,000	0.9	$2
AVERAGE			
U.S. cities	**$11,197**	**2.8**	**$31**
Other cities	**$11,458**	**1.7**	**$20**

In-lieu fees and parking requirements are for the city center in 1996. In-lieu fees and impact fees are expressed in U.S. dollars. Multiply the required spaces in column 3 by 1.076 to find the parking requirement in spaces per 100 square meters. Multiply the impact fee in column 4 by 10.76 to find the parking impact fee in dollars per square meter.

off-street parking requirement. Several cities explicitly set their in-lieu fees below the land-and-construction cost per parking space, so in these cases the parking impact fees may underestimate the developer's cost to supply the required parking. The estimated impact fees range from $2 per square foot in Waltham Forest to $71 per square foot in Palo Alto. The final two rows of the table show that the average parking impact fee in the U.S. ($31 per square foot) is 55 percent higher than in the other countries ($20 per square foot). The U.S. cities have slightly lower in-lieu fees, but their impact fees are higher because they require much more parking (2.8 spaces per 1,000 square feet in the U.S., versus only 1.7 per 1,000 square feet in the other cities).[22]

The results in Table 9-2 show that parking requirements significantly increase the capital cost of office buildings. If the average parking impact fee is $31 per square foot, and the average cost of constructing a five- to 10-story office building is $78 per square foot, the required parking adds 40 percent to the cost of the office building. Developers who provide the required parking must also pay for the operating costs of the spaces—cleaning, lighting, repairs, security, insurance, and property taxes. Because the in-lieu fees are based only on capital costs, the parking impact fees underestimate the total cost that parking requirements impose on development.

Although some in-lieu fees are high, they do not impose a burden on urban development; instead, they merely give developers a new option that can reduce the burden of meeting a parking requirement. The parking requirements impose the burden on development, while the in-lieu fees merely quantify the cost. Normally, the cost of parking is hidden in the overall cost of development, but the in-lieu fees expose the extraordinarily high cost of providing all the required parking spaces.

What Explains High Impact Fees?

Figure 9-1 shows the pattern of parking requirements and impact fees for office buildings in the 29 cities. The horizontal axis shows the parking requirement in spaces per 1,000 square feet of gross floor area, and the vertical axis shows the fee per parking space not provided. Each equal-impact-fee curve shows combinations of parking requirements and in-lieu fees that produce the same impact fee. The lowest curve, for example, shows that a requirement of one space per 1,000 square feet and an in-lieu fee of $10,000 per space create an impact fee of $10 per square foot of floor

**Figure 9-1. Parking Requirements, In-lieu Fees, and Parking Impact Fees
(for office buildings)**

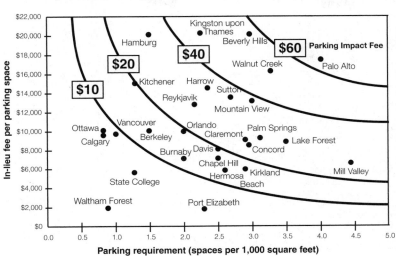

area, as do all other combinations of parking requirements and in-lieu fees along the curve.[23]

A horizontal band of cities with similar in-lieu fees ranging from $6,000 to $10,000 per space have very different parking impact fees because their parking requirements differ greatly. For example, Lake Forest on the right and Calgary on the left have similar in-lieu fees ($9,000 and $9,781), but Lake Forest's parking impact fee ($32 per square foot) is almost five times Calgary's ($7 per square foot) because Lake Forest's parking requirement (3.5 spaces per 1,000 square feet) is five times higher than Calgary's (0.7 spaces per 1,000 square feet).[24]

Do urban planners consider the cost of parking spaces when they decide how many to require? If they did, cities with higher in-lieu fees (which imply a higher cost of parking spaces) should have lower parking requirements. Figure 9-1 would show a downward sloping pattern of cities with high fees and low requirements in the upper-left corner, and cities with low fees and high requirements in the lower right corner. But Figure 9-1 shows scant relationship between in-lieu fees and parking requirements. The coefficient of correlation between the in-lieu fees and parking requirements is only 0.06, which implies almost no relationship between the cost

Table 9-3. Parking Impact Fees for Land Uses with Highest Parking Requirements in 1996

City (U.S. cities in regular text; Non-U.S. cities in italic text)	In-lieu parking fees ($/space)	Land use	Parking requirement (spaces per 1,000 square feet)	Parking impact fee ($/square foot)
(1)	(2)	(3)	(4)	(5)=(2)x(4)/1,000
Beverly Hills, California	$20,180	Restaurant	22.2	$448
Palm Springs, California	$9,250	Cabaret	28.6	$264
Mountain View, California	$13,000	Assembly hall	18.0	$234
Kingston upon Thames, United Kingdom	$20,800	Food superstore	7.7	$160
Davis, California	$8,000	Funeral home	20.0	$160
Sutton, United Kingdom	$13,360	Food superstore	8.5	$114
Kitchener, Ontario	$14,599	Manufacturing	7.7	$112
Calgary, Alberta	$9,781	Billiard parlor	10.3	$101
Ottawa, Ontario	$10,043	Church	9.8	$98
Claremont, California	$9,000	Theater	10.0	$90
Hermosa Beach, California	$6,000	Theater	13.0	$78
Burnaby, British Columbia	$7,299	Art gallery	10.3	$75
Palo Alto, California	$17,848	All uses	4.0	$71
Mill Valley, California	$6,751	Assembly hall	10.0	$68
Harrow, United Kingdom	$14,352	Garden center	4.6	$67
Hamburg, Germany	$20,705	Garden center	3.1	$64
Walnut Creek, California	$16,373	Nonresidential	3.3	$55
Kirkland, Washington	$6,000	Restaurant	8.0	$48
Carmel, California	$27,520	Commercial	1.7	$47
Concord, California	$8,500	Restaurant	4.0	$34
Port Elizabeth, South Africa	$1,846	Recreation hall	18.6	$34
Reykjavik, Iceland	$13,000	Nonresidential	2.2	$28
Lake Forest, Illinois	$9,000	Restaurant	2.5	$23
Orlando, Florida	$9,883	Nonresidential	2.0	$20
Chapel Hill, North Carolina	$7,200	Offices	2.5	$18
Berkeley, California	$10,000	Nonresidential	1.5	$15
Vancouver, British Columbia	$9,708	Nonresidential	1.0	$10
Waltham Forest, United Kingdom	$2,000	Shops	4.5	$9
State College, Pennsylvania	$5,850	All uses	1.3	$8
AVERAGE				
U.S. cities	**$11,197**		**9.0**	**$99**
Other cities	**$11,458**		**7.4**	**$73**

In-lieu fees and parking requirements are for the city center in 1996. In-lieu fees and impact fees are expressed in U.S. dollars. Multiply the required spaces in column 4 by 1.076 to find the parking requirement in spaces per 100 square meters. Multiply the impact fee in column 5 by 10.76 to find the parking impact fee in dollars per square meter. The land uses are those with the highest minimum parking requirement in each city.

per space and the number required. When planners set parking requirements, cost does not seem to matter.

Parking Impact Fees for Other Land Uses

Higher parking requirements produce higher parking impact fees. Table
9-3 shows each city's parking impact fee for the land use with the city's
highest parking requirement. The first row shows that Beverly Hills
charges $20,180 per required space not provided and that it requires 22.2
parking spaces per 1,000 square feet of restaurant space (one space per 45
square feet). The parking requirement and the in-lieu fee together impose
a parking impact fee of $448 per square foot of restaurant space (22.2 x
$20,180 ÷ 1,000).[25] In comparison, the median construction cost of a restau-
rant in Beverly Hills is $122 per square foot.[26] In other words, the parking
impact fee is 3.7 times the cost of building the restaurant itself.

The highest parking impact fees range from $8 per square foot for all
land uses in State College up to $448 per square foot of restaurant space
in Beverly Hills. The variation in parking requirements explains most of
the variation in the impact fees.[27] Palm Springs and Vancouver, for example, have similar in-lieu fees ($9,250 and $9,750), but Palm Springs' parking impact fee ($264 per square foot) is 26 times Vancouver's ($10 per
square foot) because Palm Springs highest parking requirement (28.6
spaces per 1,000 square feet) is 29 times higher than Vancouver's (1 space
per 1,000 square feet).

Figure 9-2 arrays cities according to their parking impact fees for the
land uses with the highest parking requirements, similar to Figure 9-1 for
office buildings. The cities' relative positions shift substantially between
the two figures because their highest parking requirements differ greatly
from their office parking requirements.[28] In more ways than one, parking
impact fees are all over the map.

A Follow-Up Survey

The initial survey of in-lieu fees was conducted in 1996, and I repeated it
in 2002 for the American cities in the sample (see Table 9-4).[29] The first row
shows that Palo Alto had raised its in-lieu fee to $50,994 per space, equal
to the cost per space added by the city's two newest municipal parking
structures. The two structures contain a total of 902 spaces, and they were
built on the sites of two surface parking lots that had provided 189 spaces,
so the net gain was 713 spaces. Because the total cost of the two structures
was $36.36 million, the cost per space added was $50,994 ($36.36 million

Figure 9-2. Parking Requirements, In-lieu Fees, and Parking Impact Fees (for land uses with the highest parking requirements)

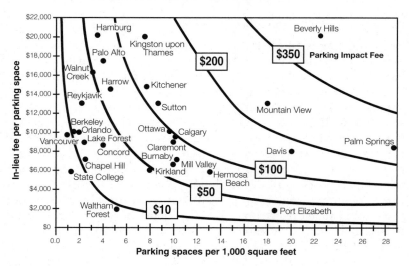

Table 9-4. Parking Impact Fees for Office Buildings in U.S. Cities in 2002

City	In-lieu parking fees	Parking requirement (spaces per 1,000 sq. ft.)	Parking impact fee	All other impact fees	Ratio
	($/space)	(1,000 sq. ft.)	($/sq. ft.)	($/sq. ft.)	(percent)
(1)	(2)	(3)	(4)=(2)x(3)/1,000	(5)	(6)=(5)/(4)
Palo Alto, California	$50,994	4.0	$204	$3.75	2%
Carmel, California	$49,980	1.7	$83	$0.00	0%
Mountain View, California	$26,000	3.0	$78	$0.00	0%
Beverly Hills, California	$22,678	2.9	$66	$5.88	9%
Hermosa Beach, California	$12,500	2.6	$36	$0.00	0%
Claremont, California	$9,000	4.0	$36	$2.75	8%
Mill Valley, California	$7,543	4.4	$33	$0.00	0%
Lake Forest, Illinois	$9,000	3.5	$32	$0.00	0%
Chapel Hill, North Carolina	$12,000	2.5	$30	$0.00	0%
Davis, California	$8,000	4.4	$20	$4.08	20%
Berkeley, California	$12,000	1.5	$18	$0.00	0%
Kirkland, Washington	$6,000	2.9	$17	$4.71	27%
State College, Pennsylvania	$10,000	1.3	$13	$0.00	0%
Palm Springs, California	$4,000	3.1	$12	$2.31	19%
Concord, California	$2,500	2.5	$7	$4.45	62%
AVERAGE	**$16,146**	**3.0**	**$46**	**$1.86**	**4%**

Note: In-lieu fees, parking requirements, and impact fees are for the city center in 2002.

÷ 713).[30] The parking requirement and in-lieu fee combined are equivalent to an impact fee of $204 per square foot of office space ($50,994 x 4 ÷ 1,000). The average parking impact fee for the sample is $46 per square foot of office space, a 48 percent increase from 1996. Most of this increase was caused by higher in-lieu fees, not by higher parking requirements; nine cities increased their fees, while only two reduced them.

One city, Palm Springs, reduced its in-lieu fee from $9,000 per space in 1996 to $4,000 per space for new buildings, and only $2,000 per space for existing buildings when a change of use would trigger a higher parking requirement. The goal was to revitalize the downtown, where parking requirements hindered the reuse of older buildings. The lower in-lieu fees have stimulated economic activity and have led to the opening of many new restaurants on Palm Canyon Drive, the city's main drag. When the new uses increased parking demand, the city then persuaded the property owners on one block to pool all their individual surface parking lots behind their buildings, and the city constructed a public parking structure on the combined site.

Column 5 in Table 9-4 shows the total impact fee that each city levies on office development to pay for all other public purposes—such as arts, fire protection, parks, roads, sanitation, and schools. The average combined impact fee for all these other purposes is $1.86 per square foot of office space.[31] The average parking impact fee of $46 per square foot of office space is therefore 25 times higher than the development impact fees these cities levy to pay for all other public purposes combined.[32] As another benchmark, the impact fees to finance schools in California are limited to a maximum of 41¢ per square foot of commercial space.[33] The average parking impact fee is therefore 112 times higher than California's highest school impact fee. Cars park free, but the public schools are shortchanged.

Parking Impact Fees Compared with Traffic Impact Fees

Some cities are beginning to charge traffic impact fees for new development. A survey in California found that 59 percent of counties and 56 percent of cities impose traffic impact fees to finance road improvements.[34] Of these jurisdictions, 42 percent base their fees on a proposed project's number of vehicle trips per day, 34 percent on the project's size (square feet, number of dwelling units), and 23 percent on the estimated number of peak-hour vehicle trips. In Salinas, for example, the one-time fee is $140 per daily vehicle trip, and the number of trips is calculated by multiplying the size of the project times its trip generation rate.[35] Since the daily trip generation rate for a downtown office building is 10 trips per 1,000 square feet, the traffic impact fee is $1,400 per 1,000 square feet ($140 x 10), or $1.40 per square foot of office space. Although this traffic impact fee is only 3 percent of the average parking impact fee of $46 per square foot of office space, it is yet another way to force nonmotorists to pay for driving and parking. The subsidy for driving increases the demand for parking, and the subsidy for parking increases the demand for driving.

CONCLUSION: THE HIGH COST OF PARKING REQUIREMENTS

In-lieu parking fees give developers a new option—pay a fee rather than provide the parking required by zoning. The city then uses the fee revenue to provide public parking spaces. In-lieu fees are a modest reform, but they have several important benefits. They encourage shared parking, reduce the demand for variances, improve urban design, and support historic preservation. The in-lieu fees also serve another important purpose: they reveal the high cost of the parking requirements themselves. When expressed as an impact fee, the cost of providing the required parking dwarfs the impact fees that cities impose for all other public purposes combined. If impact fees reveal a city's priorities among public services, most cities' highest priority is free parking.

As with most impact fees, it is not clear exactly who pays for the required parking, but someone has to—landowners, investors, workers, developers, and users of real estate. It *is* clear that drivers don't pay, but it would be a mistake to assume that because drivers don't pay, nobody pays. The cost of parking doesn't cease to exist just because drivers park free. Given the high cost of required parking spaces and their harmful consequences, planners should not uncritically assume that the demand for parking automatically justifies off-street parking requirements. Demand depends on price, but planners rarely think about the price drivers pay for parking or what the required spaces cost. Because drivers park free for 99 percent of their trips, parking requirements that satisfy the existing demand for parking will satisfy the demand for free parking, no matter how much it costs. In-lieu fees unveil the high cost of free parking.

CHAPTER 9 NOTES

1. These 47 cities were all I found with in-lieu fees when I conducted the study in 1996. To find the cities, I searched the literature on parking requirements, requested leads from professional parking associations, and sent requests for information to parking e-mail lists. I also asked the representatives of each city with in-lieu fees if they knew of any other cities with in-lieu fees (a "snowball" sample). Planners in several cities were unaware that any other cities had in-lieu fees, and I found only five published references to in-lieu fees: Public Technology (1982), Higgins (1985), Weant and Levinson (1990), and Topp (1991 and 1993). Additional cities in Germany have in-lieu fees (*Ablösebeträge*), but as explained later, most of these cities' fees are calculated on a case-by-case basis and therefore cannot be used to calculate the parking impact fees shown in Tables 9-2 and 9-3.

2. Mary McShane and Michael Meyer (1982, 136) explain the benefits of consolidating parking spaces in fewer locations: "When parking is scattered in many small lots, average walk time for users from parking lot to final destination is shortened, but the average walk time for non-users from origin to destination tends to be lengthened because of the decreased density of non-parking activities. When parking is consolidated, non-drivers benefit because higher densities of non-parking activities are encouraged."

3. It is cheaper, for example, to build one structure with 1,000 parking spaces than 10 structures that each have 100 spaces.

4. The "nexus" between an in-lieu fee and the cost of providing a public parking space legally justifies the fee in American cities. The nexus requirement does not, however, imply that cities must use the in-lieu revenue only to provide public parking. Cities can also use the revenue to finance a variety of transportation improvements that reduce parking demand. For example, British and German cities use the in-lieu revenue to improve public transportation.

5. Staff Report for the City of Beverly Hills Planning Commission, April 22, 1992.

6. The new in-lieu fees were $25,000 per space on Rodeo Drive, $20,000 per space on Beverly Drive, and $15,000 per space elsewhere in the city, and the fees are indexed by the *ENR* Construction Cost Index (Sec. 10-3.3310 of the Beverly Hills Municipal Code).

7. Thirty-eight of the 47 surveyed cities set uniform fees. Among the nine cities that set variable fees on a case-by-case approach, Culver City's fee is the assessed value of 300 square feet of land under the development. Hamilton's and Toronto's fees are half the land-and-construction cost of providing a new parking space near the development site. Johannesburg's fee is the land value of a surface parking space at the development site. Frankfurt's fee depends on the land-and-construction cost of a parking space, with a maximum fee of $16,025. San Rafael's fee is the fair-market value of the land that would otherwise have been devoted to the required parking, plus the cost of paving and other improvements. Montgomery County allows developers to pay a property tax surcharge instead of providing the required parking.

8. The *ENR* Construction Cost Index is published in the magazine *ENR*, and is available online at www.enr.com.

9. City of Santa Monica, "Mall Assessment District and Parking Developer Fee. " Available online at http://santa-monica.org/economic-development/mall.htm. Any property that includes residential uses receives a 50 percent credit against the in-lieu fee.

10. The annual in-lieu fee for a theater is $120 per space not provided because it is 80 square feet of theater per parking space x $1.50 per square foot. The parking requirement for retail is one space per 300 square feet, so the annual in-lieu for that use is $450 per space not provided. Drivers pay to park in the public garages for the Promenade, so the many new restaurants and theaters have not created a parking shortage; instead the parking prices are adjusted to keep demand from overwhelming the supply.

11. This net present cost of a public parking space is the net present value of all capital and operating costs minus the net present value of all revenues paid by those who park in the space over its usable life. The net present cost is measured by: (1) the land-and-construction cost of the structure minus (2) the present discounted value of the net operating income during the expected 30-year life of the structure minus (3) the present discounted value of the residual value of the structure after 30 years. The in-lieu fee therefore equals the expected value of the parking subsidy implicit in constructing a new public parking space.

12. "Since the payment of the $9,000 per space 'in lieu of' fee only allows for a property owner to establish a business, the fee has never been intended to cover the full cost of providing a parking space.... Historically, the 'in lieu of' fee has been placed at a level that is roughly equivalent to fifty percent of the cost of providing a parking space" (Memo to Lake Forest Plan Commission, February 1, 1993, page 2). Planners in several cities said that the council members wanted to set their in-lieu fees high enough to pay for public parking spaces, yet low enough to attract development. But when the council members were confronted with staff reports showing the actual cost of constructing a parking space, they couldn't cope with it and set fees well below the cost.

13. Hartmut Topp (1991, 14) reports that the in-lieu fee in German cities is limited to 60 to 80 percent of the cost to build a parking space in the area concerned.

14. Berkeley requires developers of lots under 30,000 square feet to pay fees instead of providing the parking. Waltham Forest requires developers to provide the first 0.2 required parking spaces per 1,000 square feet and to pay fees for the rest. German cities allow developers in the Central Business District (CBD) to provide only part of the required parking and require them to pay fees for the rest. For example, developers may provide at most 25 percent of the parking required for land uses in the center of Hamburg and must pay fees in lieu of providing the rest of the parking.

15. The capital cost of a parking space is not just the land cost for surface parking or the land-and-construction cost for structured parking. Providing the required parking may also preclude a far more valuable use of the land for another on-site purpose.

16. An additional parking space adds to the development's capital value by the net present value of additional revenues minus operating costs associated with having the additional parking space. If the additional parking space precludes a more valuable use of the property, the additional parking space can even reduce rather than increase the value of the property. In other words, cities may require developers to pay for parking spaces that reduce rather than increase the value of their property.

17. Chapter 5 showed that an individual developer may voluntarily supply all the parking required at a site, but this voluntary provision is in part due to the free parking everywhere else. Therefore, the whole system of requirements increases the total parking supply beyond what the market would provide, even if some individual developers voluntarily supply all the parking spaces required at their individual sites. The exaction component of a parking requirement at each site is thus higher when we consider the effects of the whole system of requirements.

18. Altshuler and Gómez-Ibáñez (1993, vii).

19. Office buildings were chosen for Table 9-2 because they are the most uniformly defined land use among cities. All the cities in Tables 9-2 and 9-3 require parking spaces in proportion to gross floor area. Eighteen of the 47 surveyed cities don't appear in Tables 9-2 and 9-3 because either their in-lieu fees or their parking requirements aren't comparable with the other cities. Brent, Culver City, Dresden, Frankfurt, Hamilton, Johannesburg, Nuremberg, San Rafael, and Toronto don't have fixed fees; instead these cities establish the fee for each specific case, usually taking into account the appraised land value at the site. Montgomery County's fee is based on the property tax. Manhattan Beach ($25,169 per space) requires parking only for the building area that exceeds a floor area ratio of 1:1. Lafayette ($8,500 per space), Munich ($16,025 per space), Redbridge ($8,624 per space), and Würzburg ($12,820 per space) require parking on the basis of net rather than gross floor area. San Francisco ($17,135 per space) doesn't require parking spaces in the CBD. Pasadena allows developers to pay an annual fee ($100 a year per parking space in 1992 and subsequently indexed to the Consumer Price Index) per parking space not provided. Santa Monica's fee is $1.50 a year per square foot of floor space. Fees are converted into U.S. dollars at the 1996 rates of U.S. $1 = 1.37 Canadian dollars; 1.56 German marks; 66.57 Icelandic kronur; 3.84 South African rands; and 0.60 British pounds.

20. In 2002 Palo Alto increased its in-lieu fee to $50,994 per space, which was the cost per space added by the most recent municipal parking structure.

21. R. S. Means (2001, 484).

22. The parking impact fees range widely outside North America. Three British cities (Harrow, Sutton, and Kingston upon Thames) have high impact fees ($33 to $48 per square foot) because their in-lieu fees are high. Another British city (Waltham Forest) has the lowest impact fee in the table ($2 per square foot) because both its in-lieu fee and its parking requirement are low. The British term for an in-lieu fee is "commuted payment." All the British cities in the survey are boroughs of outer London. The inner London boroughs no longer use commuted payments because they have replaced their minimum parking requirements with restrictions on the maximum number of parking spaces allowed.

23. Minimum parking requirements impose no burden if developers would voluntarily provide the required number of parking spaces. Developers will therefore prefer a low parking requirement with a high in-lieu fee to a high parking requirement with a low in-lieu fee, even if the parking impact fee is the same in both cases.

24. Cities with very different in-lieu fees can have similar parking impact fees. For example, Hamburg and Mill Valley have similar impact fees ($32 and $30 per square foot) but for different reasons. Mill Valley has a high parking requirement with a low in-lieu fee while Hamburg has a low parking requirement and a high impact fee. Mill Valley's in-lieu fee is less than a third of Hamburg's, but Mill Valley requires almost three times more parking spaces. The figure shows the relative contributions of parking requirements and the cost of parking spaces in creating the impact fees. If we draw a diagonal line between the lower-left and upper-right corners of the diagram, the cities above the line have high in-lieu fees in relation to their impact fees, while cities below the line tend to have high parking requirements. Seventy-five percent of the cities outside of the U.S. lie above the diagonal, while 52 percent of the cities in the U.S. lie below the diagonal. When compared with cities in other countries, American cities require more parking but have lower in-lieu fees.

25. The in-lieu fee of $20,180 per space is the median of Beverly Hills' three in-lieu fees. To encourage the expansion of restaurants that have been in business for at least two years, Beverly Hills offers a reduced in-lieu fee of $6,265 per space, which is 35 percent of the construction cost per space for municipal parking structures, excluding land cost. Beverly Hills requires one parking space per 45 square feet of restaurant area, so this reduced in-lieu fee is equivalent to an impact fee of $139 per square foot of restaurant area ($6,265 ÷ 45). The in-lieu fee is far below the cost of providing a parking space, but the parking impact fee is still extremely high—comparable to the construction cost of a new restaurant.

26. R. S. Means (2001) reports that the median construction cost for a restaurant in the U.S. was $112 per square foot in 2001, and that construction costs in the Los Angeles region are 8.5 percent above the national average.

27. The r^2 for the correlation between minimum parking requirements and impact fees is 0.60, and the r^2 for the correlation between in-lieu fees and impact fees is 0.12.

28. The coefficient of correlation between the parking impact fees for offices (column 4 in Table 9-2) and the parking impact fees for land uses with the highest parking requirements (column 5 in Table 9-3) is only 0.43. Therefore, cities with the highest impact fees in Figure 9-1 don't necessarily have the highest impact fees in Figure 9-2.

29. Orlando, Florida, is not in the table because it no longer offers the in-lieu fee option. Instead, Orlando requires developers who want to provide more than the required number of spaces to pay a fee for each additional space. Walnut Creek, California, is also not in the table because its fee is now based on the cost of constructing a municipal parking structure at the time the fee is paid.

30. Memo CMR:346.02 from the Palo Alto City Manager to the City Council, July 22, 2002.

31. Altshuler and Gómez-Ibáñez (1993, 40) report that a 1991 survey of 100 U.S. cities found that the combined impact fees for all purposes (roads, schools, parks, water, sewers, flood control, and the like) averaged $6.97 per square foot of office space.

32. We can also compare parking impact fees with the impact fees to support public transit. For example, San Francisco levies the highest transit impact fee in the U.S.—$5 per square foot of new office space—to subsidize the San Francisco Municipal Railway. The *average* parking impact fee in the cities with in-lieu fees is more than eight times the *highest* transit impact fee in the country.

33. The limit of 25¢ per square foot was established in 1986 and is indexed to inflation (California Governor's Office of Planning and Research 1997, Chapter 5). The value was 41¢ per square foot in 2002.

34. Lawler and Powers (1997).

35. Salinas's Traffic Impact Fee is available online at www.ci.salinas.ca.us. The city uses its own table of trip generation rates to calculate the traffic impact fees. The table (based on the ITE *Trip Generation* manual and other data) was adopted in 1988 and has not been changed since.

10

Reduce Demand Rather than Increase Supply

The more parking spaces you provide, the more cars will come to fill them. It is like feeding pigeons.

—*HUGH CASSON*

The logic behind off-street parking requirements is simple: development increases the demand for parking, so cities require enough off-street spaces to satisfy this new demand. Off-street parking requirements thus ensure that cars will not spill over onto the neighborhood streets. This logic suggests another potential reform within the existing system of off-street parking requirements: if developers reduce parking demand, cities should allow them to provide fewer parking spaces; that is, cities can give developers the option to reduce parking demand rather than increase the parking supply. I will illustrate this "pay or pave" option with three strategies to reduce parking demand: (1) employer-paid transit passes, (2) parking cash out, and (3) car sharing.

TRANSIT PASSES IN LIEU OF PARKING SPACES

Offering transit passes to commuters can significantly reduce parking demand. One survey of commuters whose employers began to offer free transit passes found that their drive-alone share fell considerably—from 76 percent before they offered transit passes to 60 percent afterward—and that their transit share more than doubled. These mode shifts reduced commuter parking demand by approximately 19 percent.[1]

Because free transit reduces parking demand, a city can reduce the parking requirements at sites providing transit passes to all commuters. Suppose, for example, that free transit passes reduce parking demand by 1 space per 1,000 square feet of floor area; providing free transit passes can in this case substitute for providing 1 required parking space per 1,000 square feet.[2]

Eco Passes

Several transit agencies—in Dallas, Denver, Salt Lake, and San Jose, for example—offer employers the option to buy "Eco Passes," which give all their employees the right to ride free on all local transit lines. This arrangement reduces to zero the employees' marginal cost of riding public transit and therefore makes transit (in terms of perceived monetary cost) similar to driving and parking free. Because many commuters won't ride transit even when it is free, the transit agencies' cost per Eco Pass holder is low, and the agencies can therefore sell the Eco Passes at a surprisingly low price. In California's Silicon Valley, the Santa Clara Valley Transportation Authority (SCVTA) charges between $5 and $80 a year per employee for Eco Passes, depending on the employer's location and number of employees (see Table 10-1).[3] The passes allow unlimited free rides on any SCVTA bus or rail line, seven days a week.

The price of an Eco Pass is much lower than that of a conventional pass. Because frequent riders often buy the conventional passes, transit agencies must price them on the assumption that buyers will use them frequently. The price of an Eco Pass is much lower because employers buy the Eco Passes for all commuters regardless of whether they ride transit. The SCVTA's price for its Eco Pass ranges from 1 to 19 percent of the price for its conventional pass ($420 a year).

Table 10-1. Eco Pass Price Schedule, Santa Clara Valley Transportation Authority (annual price per employee)

Employer's location	Number of employees			
	1–99	100–2,999	3,000–14,999	15,000+
Downtown San Jose	$80	$60	$40	$20
Areas served by bus and light rail	$60	$40	$20	$10
Areas served by bus only	$40	$20	$10	$5

Source: Santa Clara Valley Transportation Authority, 2002.

A numerical example can help explain Eco Pass pricing. Suppose a firm with 100 employees offers conventional transit passes for all commuters who do not take a free parking space. The price of a conventional transit pass is $400 a year, and 20 commuters choose to ride public transit. In this case, the firm pays $8,000 a year for 20 conventional passes ($400 per employee x 20 employees), which amounts to $80 a year per employee ($8,000 a year ÷ 100 employees). If, however, the transit agency charges $80 a year per employee for Eco Passes for all 100 commuters, it receives the same $8,000 a year for the Eco Passes ($80 per employee x 100 employees) that it would receive from the sale of 20 conventional passes at $400 a year.

Firms pay the same total amount for 100 Eco Passes or 20 conventional passes, but Eco Passes offer a key advantage. With conventional passes, a firm offers commuters free parking *or* free transit. With Eco Passes, the firm can offer everyone free parking *and* free transit; therefore, even commuters who normally drive to work may ride transit occasionally. The firm's cost of offering Eco Passes to all commuters is no higher than the cost of offering conventional passes to commuters who don't take a free parking space.[4] Offering Eco Passes to all commuters is also simpler than determining who qualifies for a conventional pass each month.

If an employer offers Eco Passes to everyone rather than conventional passes only to nondrivers, transit ridership should increase, and this may increase the transit agency's cost of providing service.[5] But if the transit system has excess capacity on its buses and trains—and most American transit systems do—its costs will not increase, and the system will become more efficient, with a lower cost per rider. Only 27 percent of the seats on American public transit are regularly occupied.[6] If Eco Passes induce more commuters to ride public transit, they may be filling otherwise empty seats.

Cost-Effectiveness of Eco Passes

We can estimate the cost-effectiveness of Eco Passes by comparing their cost with what they save on parking. Two of the cities served by the SCVTA—Mountain View and Palo Alto—have in-lieu parking fees that allow us to estimate the savings on required parking (see Chapter 9). For the cost-effectiveness comparison I will make two sets of assumptions: one conservative and the other optimistic. In the conservative case, all the assumptions are chosen to show high costs and low savings from the Eco

Passes. In the optimistic case, all the assumptions are chosen to show low costs and high savings. Table 10-2 shows the two estimates.

In 2002, Mountain View charged $26,000 per required parking space not provided, and Palo Alto charged $50,994 (row 1 of Table 10-2).[7] Because Mountain View requires 3 parking spaces per 1,000 square feet of office space, and Palo Alto requires 4 spaces per 1,000 square feet, developers must pay an in-lieu fee of $78 per square foot of office space in Mountain View if they do not provide the required parking and $204 per square foot in Palo Alto (row 3).

A survey of Silicon Valley commuters before and after their employers offered Eco Passes found that commuter parking demand declined by approximately 19 percent.[8] In this case a city could reduce the parking

Table 10-2. Cost-effectiveness of Eco Passes (Silicon Valley)

	Assumptions	
	Conservative	Optimistic
1. In-lieu parking fee ($/parking space)	$ 26,000 (Mountain View)	$ 50,994 (Palo Alto)
2. Parking requirement (spaces/1,000 square feet of floor area)	3 (Mountain View)	4 (Palo Alto)
3. Capital cost of required parking ($/square foot of floor area)	$ 78 (3x$26,000/1,000)	$ 204 (4x$50,994/1,000)
4. Reduction in parking demand (%)	19%	19%
5. Capital savings on required parking ($/square foot of floor area)	$ 15 ($78x19%)	$ 39 ($204x19%)
6. Annual cost per employee for Eco Passes ($/employee/year)	$ 80	$ 5
7. Employees per 1,000 square feet (employees/1,000 square feet of floor area)	4	4
8. Annual cost per square foot for Eco Passes ($/square foot of floor area/year)	$ 0.32 ($80x4/1,000)	$ 0.02 ($5x4/1,000)
9. Capital savings per $1 of annual cost for Eco Passes ($/year)	$ 46 ($15/$0.32)	$ 1,938 ($39/$0.02)
10. Annual cost of Eco Passes as % of capital savings (%/year)	2.2% ($0.32/$15)	0.1% ($0.02/$39)

Conservative assumptions: Low in-lieu fee, low parking requirement, high Eco Pass cost.

Optimistic assumptions: High in-lieu fee, high parking requirement, low Eco Pass cost.

requirement by 19 percent for office developments that offer Eco Passes for all commuters (row 4). If the Eco Passes reduce parking requirements by 19 percent, they reduce the capital cost of parking by $15 per square foot of office space in Mountain View and by $39 per square foot in Palo Alto (row 5).

Firms in Silicon Valley pay between $5 and $80 a year per employee for Eco Passes (row 6). If there are 4 employees per 1,000 square feet of office space (row 7), Eco Passes therefore cost from 2¢ to 32¢ a year per square foot of office space (row 8).[9] The advantage is obvious: for every square foot of office space, spending between 2¢ and 32¢ a year on Eco Passes will reduce the one-time capital cost of required parking by between $15 and $39.

We can convert these per-square-foot figures into the potential capital savings per annual dollar spent for Eco Passes. With the conservative assumptions, the Eco Passes cost 32¢ a year (the high annual cost) and save $15 for required parking (the low capital savings). In this case, spending $1 a year for Eco Passes will save $46 on the initial capital cost of providing the required parking (row 9). With the optimistic assumptions, Eco Passes cost only 2¢ a year and save $39. In this case, spending $1 a year for Eco Passes will save $1,938 on the cost of required parking.

These two cases suggest that a developer who spends $1 a year for in-lieu Eco Passes (after the building is constructed and is earning money) saves between $46 and $1,938 on the initial capital cost of required parking—an incredible bargain even under conservative assumptions. Although the building will supply 19 percent fewer parking spaces, the Eco Passes reduce parking demand by 19 percent, and the smaller parking supply will satisfy demand. Beyond reducing parking demand, the Eco Passes also provide a new fringe benefit to every employee in the building.

Row 10 shows the annual cost of Eco Passes as a percent of the capital cost saved for the required parking. With conservative assumptions, the annual cost for Eco Passes is 2.2 percent of the capital savings for required parking. With optimistic assumptions, the annual cost is only 0.1 percent of the capital savings. If the developer's cost of capital is above 2.2 percent a year, the Eco Passes will therefore save more on annual interest payments for parking than they cost in annual payments for transit. In-lieu Eco Passes are a good investment.

These estimates refer only to Mountain View and Palo Alto, but the low cost of reducing parking demand compared with the high cost of increasing the parking supply shows that Eco Passes can greatly reduce the cost of meeting a parking requirement. Both estimates also understate the cost-effectiveness of Eco Passes because they refer only to capital costs. Since there will be fewer parking spaces to operate and maintain, Eco Passes will also reduce operating and maintenance costs for the required parking, which average about $500 a year per space for structured parking.[10] Finally, developers who provide the in-lieu Eco Passes can still offer free parking to all commuters who want to drive because the reduced parking supply will meet the reduced parking demand.[11] All else being equal, most employees would prefer to work for a firm that offers free parking *and* free public transit than for a firm that offers only free parking, and the free transit passes are therefore a tax-exempt fringe benefit that helps attract and retain workers.

Benefits of Eco Passes in Lieu of Parking Spaces

Providing Eco Passes in lieu of required parking converts an upfront capital cost for parking spaces into an annual subsidy for transit, and many developers may want to make this trade. The Eco Passes can yield benefits for developers, property owners, employers, commuters, transit agencies, and cities. A brief description of the benefits to each party shows that everyone can win from the in-lieu Eco Pass arrangement.

Developers and property owners. Some developers may hesitate to provide fewer parking spaces than the city requires because they fear that it will make a project less desirable to tenants. Eco Passes can skirt this obstacle: by luring some commuters from cars to transit, Eco Passes should reduce parking demand, and free transit for all tenants should increase the project's marketability. Eco Passes can also help a developer to meet traffic mitigation requirements, reduce a project's environmental impact, and perhaps lead to a speedier approval process.

Conventional in-lieu fees give developers no site-specific benefit beyond permission to build without providing the required parking. The public parking spaces financed by in-lieu fees benefit all developers in the surrounding area, not just the developers who pay for them.[12] In contrast, Eco Passes provide a site-specific benefit (free transit for all employees in the development) to the developers who buy them, and nothing to other developers. For this reason, developers may be more willing to buy in-lieu Eco Passes than to pay conventional in-lieu fees that finance public parking structures everyone can use.

Fewer parking spaces also translate into savings after a building is constructed. The capital cost of parking is a heavy fixed burden for a new building that has yet to be leased. The annual cost of Eco Passes, in contrast, varies with the number of workers in the building, so the cost is low if the building is half-empty. Paying a variable cost for Eco Passes instead of a fixed cost for parking spaces can therefore reduce the developer's risk and improve the feasibility of project finance.

Developers and building owners can offer the Eco Passes to all commuters in a building, and this added amenity should allow higher rents. Alternatively, they can transfer the cost of the Eco Passes to employers by requiring all tenants to offer Eco Passes to their employees. Either way, Eco Passes can be more profitable than free parking.

Employers. By shifting some commuters from cars to transit, Eco Passes can save employers some of the money they now spend to subsidize parking. The added fringe benefit of free transit for all commuters will also help recruit workers. Eco Passes are a tax-deductible expense for employers and a tax-free benefit for commuters. Employers will earn higher profits if they save more on reduced parking subsidies than they spend for Eco Passes.[13]

Commuters. Eco Passes clearly benefit commuters who ride transit to work, and commuters who usually drive to work can consider the passes a form of insurance for days when their cars aren't available. Eco Passes offer commuters day-to-day flexibility in commuting; public transit is always an option, not a long-term commitment. Commuters can also use their Eco Passes for nonwork trips. In the Silicon Valley survey, 60 percent of commuters reported using their Eco Passes for purposes other than commuting, with an average of four nonwork trips a month.

Public transit agencies. Eco Passes are a demand-side transit subsidy paid for by the private sector. If developers can provide Eco Passes instead of required parking spaces, Eco Pass sales will increase. The reduction in parking subsidies will finance the Eco Passes and will provide a reliable revenue source for transit agencies. Transit planners can also increase service to sites where developers make long-term commitments to purchase Eco Passes because the demand for transit will be higher where all commuters can ride free. These service improvements will benefit all riders, not just Eco Pass holders, and they may attract additional riders who pay the full fare.

Cities. Parking requirements increase the supply of parking whereas Eco Passes increase the demand for public transportation. Providing Eco Passes in lieu of required parking will therefore convert a supply-side subsidy for cars into a demand-side subsidy for transit. The appropriate reduction in required parking depends on how much Eco Passes reduce parking demand, and cities should specify the reduction they will grant for offering Eco Passes rather than oblige developers and landowners to seek a variance in the parking requirement. Like other zoning variances, parking variances are not granted routinely and must be supported by evidence; the burden of proof is shifted to the developer, who must prove that some parking spaces will not be needed. A special study to provide data supporting the application for a parking variance may cost several thousand dollars, with no guarantee that the variance will be granted. If cities specify the by-right reduction in parking requirements for developers who offer Eco Passes, parking demand management will become more feasible and profitable. Seattle, for example, reduces the parking requirement for a development by up to 10 percent if transit passes are provided to all employees and if transit service is within 800 feet of the development.

Cities can offer bigger reductions in required parking in transit-oriented developments (TODs) because Eco Passes will reduce parking demand more at sites with better transit service. In these areas, substituting Eco Passes for parking spaces will allow higher density without more vehicle traffic. A survey of TODs in California, however, found that cities did *not* reduce the parking requirements at seven of the 11 sites studied.[14] Many cities appear to assume that more transit will not reduce parking demand and, conversely, that more parking will not reduce transit demand.

Eco Passes in lieu of parking spaces can significantly reduce the cost of TODs because parking spaces are more expensive in denser areas. A study by the California Department of Transportation points out the higher burden of parking requirements in TODs:

> Increased densities in TODs, coupled with the goal of improving accessibility for pedestrians to transit stations, often means building structured parking garages. Parking spaces in structures can cost from $10,000 to $30,000 each, compared to about $5,000 per space for surface parking.... These increased costs can negatively affect the financial feasibility of projects, even if they are otherwise profitable. Hence, if the design and location of TODs enable a reduction in the number of parking spaces needed, the cost savings can be significant.[15]

If cities do not reduce the number of spaces required in a TOD commensurate with the increased cost per space in structures, the cost of the required parking will be higher in a TOD than in a conventional development. Suppose, for example, a city requires 4 spaces per 1,000 square feet of floor area in a conventional development, and the developer's cost of surface parking is $5,000 per space; the cost of the required parking is thus $20 per square foot of floor area (4 x $5,000 ÷ 1,000). Suppose also the city requires only 2 spaces per 1,000 square feet in a TOD, and the developer's cost of structured parking is $20,000 per space; the cost of the parking required for a TOD is thus $40 per square foot of floor area (2 x $20,000 ÷ 1,000), or twice the cost in a conventional development. Allowing a TOD developer to offer low-cost Eco Passes in lieu of high-cost parking spaces can thus improve the TOD's financial feasibility.

A study of travel patterns in California found that, in practice, TOD employers are far more likely to offer commuters free parking than a transit subsidy. In Los Angeles, for example, 89 percent of all commuters who worked in a TOD in Hollywood were offered free parking, while only 19 percent were offered a transit subsidy. In Orange County, 87 percent of commuters in a TOD in Anaheim were offered free parking, while only 8 percent were offered a transit subsidy. In San Diego, 83 percent of commuters in a TOD in Mission Valley were offered free parking, while only 17 percent were offered a transit subsidy.[16] The TODs were also embedded in regions where free parking was the norm, and this free parking elsewhere had a major influence on the TOD residents' travel behavior. Among TOD residents, only 5 percent of those whose employers offered free parking rode transit to work, while 45 percent of those whose employers did not offer free parking rode transit.[17] TODs will have little effect on travel behavior if parking remains free everywhere, even in the TODs themselves, and transit remains expensive.

Providing Eco Passes instead of parking spaces will increase transit ridership, reduce the cost of transit-oriented development, improve urban design, reduce the need for variances, and reduce traffic congestion, air pollution, and energy consumption. These benefits will come at low cost if the transit system has excess capacity, as most do. Furthermore, cities that offer the in-lieu option will encourage job growth because development costs will be lower than in neighboring cities that require parking spaces with no in-lieu alternative. Reducing the demand for parking will also shift land from parking spaces to other uses that employ more workers and generate more tax revenue.

In-lieu Eco Passes are simpler than conventional in-lieu parking fees because they eliminate the need to construct, operate, and maintain parking structures. Cities can enforce property owners' obligations to purchase the in-lieu Eco Passes by imposing covenants or conditional use permits on land for which the required parking is not provided. The transit agencies will have a strong financial incentive to ensure that property owners buy the required Eco Passes, and they can help in the enforcement process, since their contracts at each site will automatically show whether property owners are fulfilling their obligations.[18]

Transit Passes Instead of Parking Spaces for Various Land Uses

The preceding calculations refer to providing transit passes at employment sites. But cities can also allow transit passes instead of parking spaces at other land uses, such as universities, theaters, stadiums, hotels, and apartments.

Some universities contract with their local transit agencies to accept their student (and in some cases faculty and staff) identification (ID) cards as transit passes. The ID cards function as Eco Passes and reduce the demand for parking on campus. These programs are generically known as Unlimited Access, and they have spread rapidly during the past decade.[19] Unlimited Access programs do not provide free transit; instead, they are a new way to pay for transit. The university pays the transit agency, and all eligible members of the university community ride free. When UCLA began its Unlimited Access program in 2000, for example, the faculty/staff bus mode share for commuting to campus rose from 8.6 percent before the program began to 20.1 percent afterward. The number of faculty/staff bus riders increased by 134 percent, and the number of solo drivers fell by 9 percent.[20] If universities offer these Unlimited Access programs, cities can waive some of the required parking the universities would otherwise have to build.

A similar arrangement can be offered for stadiums that offer free transit passes to all ticket holders. The University of Washington has a contract with Seattle Metro that allows stadium tickets to serve as transit passes on the game day. Between 1984 (the year before the program began) and 1997, the share of ticket holders arriving at Husky Stadium by transit increased almost five times (from 4.2 percent to 20.6 percent).[21] Including a transit pass in the ticket price is particularly appropriate for any land use where the peak parking demand occurs infrequently, perhaps only a few days each year. Building enough parking to meet this peak demand is extremely wasteful because additional public transit service can be provided on event days to serve the peak at a far lower cost. Although not related to the issue of parking requirements, public transportation was free to all passengers with tickets for the games during the 2004 Athens

Olympics, and attendees used public transportation for almost all their trips. Tickets to concerts and athletic events also serve as transit passes on the event day in many German cities. If season ticket holders have a free transit pass for every event, they have a stronger incentive to consider public transport as an alternative, and their savings on paying for parking can be considerable.

The transit-in-lieu-of-parking arrangement can be extended to all manner of land uses. Hotels that offer transit passes to every guest, for example, may attract more visitors who don't bring cars. Guests can avoid the hassle and expense of renting a car, reinforcing tourists' willingness to try public transit in a new city where they don't have a car. Even without any regulatory incentive, some hotels already offer free shuttles to popular destinations or offer guests free tokens on public transit. More hotels will begin to offer free transit passes if cities reciprocate by reducing their parking requirements. Coronado, California, for example, reduces the parking requirements for hotels and motels that offer free transit tickets to guests.[22]

A city can also reduce parking requirements for apartment developers who offer free transit passes for residents. The Centre Area Transportation Authority in State College, Pennsylvania, charges about $100 a year per apartment (depending on location) to give all residents transit passes for the lines serving their apartment buildings. Participating developers are encouraged to include transit amenities in their site designs (bus shelters and bus pull-off lanes). Apartment owners advertise these transit passes as one of the amenities they offer. The apartment transit passes attract tenants who own fewer than the average number of cars and are appropriate in areas with good transit service and a smaller parking supply.

In-lieu Eco Passes are not just for new development—cities can also allow property owners to remove some of the parking spaces required for existing land uses if they offer transit passes. The in-lieu option will allow parking lots to be converted to infill development, raising density and improving urban design without increasing traffic. The new development will also provide more jobs and yield more taxes than the former parking lots, which are perhaps the least fiscally productive of all land uses. Portland, Oregon, for example, is turning a park-and-ride lot at a rail station into a TOD.[23] Converting free parking lots at rail stations into TODs with Eco Passes can increase rather than reduce transit ridership.

Finally, a city can require developers to reduce parking demand if they want to provide more parking spaces than the zoning requires. If the minimum parking requirement for an office building is 4 spaces per 1,000 square feet, for example, and a developer wants to provide 5 per 1,000, a city could require the developer to offer Eco Passes at the site in exchange for permission to build the extra spaces. This would not restrict the maximum number of parking spaces, but developers would have to try to reduce parking demand before they received permission to increase the parking supply. Offering transit passes could reduce parking demand enough that a developer would no longer want to provide more than the required number of spaces.

In summary, a small annual outlay for transit passes can substantially reduce the large capital cost of required parking at many land uses. This new in-lieu option will save money for developers and employers, give commuters a new choice, fill empty seats on public transit, and reduce traffic congestion and air pollution.

PARKING CASH OUT IN LIEU OF PARKING SPACES

Another way to reduce parking requirements is to offer commuters the option to "cash out" their employer-paid parking subsidies. Giving commuters the choice between free parking or its equivalent cash value shows that even free parking has a cost—the forgone cash. The option to cash out raises the effective price of commuter parking *without* charging for it. Commuters can continue to park free at work, but the cash option also rewards those who carpool, ride public transit, walk, or bike to work.

California law requires many employers who offer free parking to offer commuters the cash-out option as well. Case studies of employers in California show that the cash-out option reduced driving to work by 11 percent.[24] Because cash out reduces parking demand, it can also reduce the parking requirements for new development. The law addresses this issue by mandating that cities reduce parking requirements for the developments that offer parking cash out:

> The city or county in which a commercial development will implement a parking cash-out program...shall grant to that development an appropriate reduction in the parking requirements otherwise in effect for new commercial development.[25]

The legislation also gives developers the option to substitute parking cash out for some of the required parking spaces at *existing* developments:

> At the request of an existing commercial development that has implemented a parking cash-out program, the city or county shall grant an appropriate reduction in the parking requirements otherwise applicable based on the

demonstrated reduced need for parking, and the space no longer needed for parking purposes may be used for other appropriate purposes.[26]

In other words, employers can offer parking cash out if they want to expand their operations onto land previously used for required parking. This option will provide growing companies the opportunity to expand in place rather than seek larger quarters elsewhere.

Does Parking Cash Out Reduce Parking Demand?

Cities should reduce the parking requirements for developers who offer parking cash out, but the California legislation does not specify by how much; it says only that the reduction should be "based on the demonstrated reduced need for parking." This is a rather ambiguous standard, but the reduction in the number of cars driven to work after offering cash out suggests the appropriate reduction in requirements. Table 10-3 shows the results found in case studies of employers in Southern California who offer parking cash out.[27]

The upper panel of the table (commuter demand) shows how parking cash out reduces the number of cars driven to work per commuter. Cities usually require parking spaces in proportion to floor area, so the cars per commuter have been converted into cars per 1,000 square feet.[28] To estimate the total number of spaces required for all purposes (not just commuters), we must also consider visitor parking, the percentage of commuters who are parked at the time of peak parking demand, and the share of spaces that must be left vacant to ensure that arriving cars can find a place to park. The lower panel of Table 10-3 (non-commuter demand) shows these other components of parking demand.

Commuter parking. When employers offered free parking *without* the cash option, commuters parked 3.2 cars per 1,000 square feet of building area. *With* the cash option, commuters parked 2.8 cars per 1,000 square feet. Parking cash out therefore reduced commuter parking demand by 0.4 spaces per 1,000 square feet, or 13 percent.

Visitor parking. Visitors also occupy parking spaces. Using the results of a survey of office buildings in San Diego, Thomas Higgins estimated that visitor parking demand is 0.1 spaces per employee.[29] With 4 employees per 1,000 square feet, visitor parking demand is thus 0.4 spaces per 1,000 square feet.

Vacancy factor. A parking system operates most efficiently at an occupancy rate between 85 and 95 percent of capacity, so entering cars don't

Table 10-3. Parking Cash Out Reduces Parking Demand

Commuter demand (location/case number)	Cars parked per 1,000 square feet when employers pay for parking			
	Without cash out	*With* cash out	Reduction	
			#	%
(1)	(2)	(3)	(4)=(3)-(2)	(5)=(4)÷(2)
Downtown L.A. (5)	2.9	2.2	-0.7	-24%
Downtown L.A. (8)	2.9	2.4	-0.5	-16%
Century City (1)	3.0	2.7	-0.3	-9%
Century City (4)	3.7	3.3	-0.3	-9%
Century City (3)	3.4	3.1	-0.3	-9%
Santa Monica (6)	3.6	3.3	-0.3	-9%
Santa Monica (7)	3.5	3.3	-0.2	-5%
West Hollywood (2)	2.3	2.2	-0.1	-5%
Case study average	3.2	2.8	-0.4	-13%
Non-commuter demand				
Visitor parking	+0.4	+0.4	0	0
Vacancy factor	+0.3	+0.3	0	0
Peak parking factor	-0.2	-0.2	0	0
Total parking demand	**3.7**	**3.3**	**-0.4**	**-11%**

Source: Shoup (1997b, Table 1). The eight case studies are ranked in descending order of the reduction in parking demand (Column 4).

have to search throughout the entire system to find a vacant space. The Parking Consultants Council recommends that the number of spaces should be between 5 and 10 percent greater than the estimated demand.[30] Adding 10 percent to the estimated commuter and visitor demand increases the required number of parking spaces by 0.3 spaces per 1,000 square feet.

Peak parking factor. The "peak parking factor" is the percent of drivers parked at the time of peak demand. Peak parking demand is less than the total number of cars driven to work because not all drivers park during the peak parking accumulation. A survey in downtown Los Angeles found that 94 percent of commuters parked at the time of peak demand.[31] In other words, the peak parking demand is 6 percent lower than the number of cars driven to work. The peak parking demand is therefore 0.2 spaces per 1,000 square feet less than the number of cars driven to work.[32]

Total parking demand. The resulting estimate of parking demand is 3.7 spaces per 1,000 square feet if the employer pays for parking without the cash option, and 3.3 spaces per 1,000 square feet with it (see total parking demand at the bottom of Table 10-3).[33] This result indicates that parking cash out reduces parking demand by about 11 percent, suggesting that cities can reduce parking requirements by 11 percent for developments that offer the cash option. Although this figure depends on the circumstances in each location, we can use it to estimate the cost-effectiveness of using cash to reduce the demand for required parking spaces.

Cost-Effectiveness of Parking Cash Out

Parking cash out converts a parking subsidy into a cash grant commuters can use for any mode of travel. We can estimate the cost-effectiveness of parking cash out by comparing its cost with the resulting savings on providing the required parking (see Table 10-4).

Suppose the required parking costs $10,000 a space (row 1).[34] The previous case studies show that parking cash out reduces peak parking occupancy by 0.4 spaces per 1,000 square feet of office space (row 2), so it reduces the cost of required parking by $4 per square foot of office space (row 3). Employers spent only $24 a year per employee to offer parking cash out to all employees (row 4).[35] The cost is low (only $2 a month per employee) because employers saved almost as much on parking as they paid in cash to commuters. If there are 4 employees per 1,000 square feet (row 5), parking cash out costs 10¢ a year per square foot of office space (row 6).

We can convert these figures into the capital savings on parking per annual dollar spent for cash out. If the ongoing cost to offer parking cash out is 10¢ a year per square foot of office space, and the up-front savings on constructing the required parking is $4 per square foot, every $1 a year spent for parking cash out saves $40 on the initial capital cost of required parking (row 7). The annual cost of parking cash out is only 2.5 percent of the capital savings on required parking (row 8). If the cost of capital is above 2.5 percent a year, parking cash out thus saves more than it costs.

Table 10-4. Cost-effectiveness of Parking Cash Out

1. Capital cost per parking space	$ 10,000 per space
2. Reduction in parking demand	0.4 spaces per 1,000 square feet
3. Capital savings on parking	$ 4 per square foot ($10,000 x 0.4/1,000)
4. Annual cost per employee for cash out	$ 24.23 per employee per year
5. Employees per 1,000 square feet	4 employees per 1,000 square feet
6. Annual cost per square foot for cash out	$ 0.10 per square foot per year ($24.23 x 4/1,000)
7. Capital savings per $1 of annual cost for parking cash out	$ 40 per year ($4.00/$0.10)
8. Annual cost of parking cash out as % of capital savings (%/year)	2.5% per year ($0.10/$4.00)

Cash out also reduces operating and maintenance costs (including property taxes) for parking because fewer spaces are required. In addition, offering commuters the option to cash out their parking subsidies is a valuable fringe benefit that helps to recruit and retain workers. All things considered, parking cash out is a good investment.

CAR SHARING

Another possible in-lieu policy is to provide shared-car parking spaces instead of private parking spaces. A convenient shared-car option may convince some residents to skip buying a second (or even first) car, and thus reduce the demand for parking. In a study of San Francisco's City CarShare program, Robert Cervero and Yu-Hsin Tsai found that nearly 90 percent of the members were from 0-1 vehicle households, well above the 71 percent share of such households in the city. At the end of City CarShare's second year, 29 percent of the members had disposed of one or more cars, while only 8 percent had increased their vehicle ownership; as a result, 21 percent of the members reduced the number of vehicles they owned. They made 6.5 percent of their trips and drove 10 percent of their vehicle miles travelled (VMT) in shared cars.[36]

Consider how the in-lieu car-sharing arrangement might work for a 100-unit apartment house in a city that requires one parking space per apartment. Suppose that making one shared car available for the residents leads ten households in the building to choose not to buy a personal car. In this case, the city can allow one shared-car parking space to substitute for ten private parking spaces, and the number of required spaces would drop from 100 to 91. The developer would contractually commit to providing the shared-car arrangement for the residents as long as the private parking spaces are not provided. The reduction in required parking spaces could also be much greater. In San Francisco, for example, the Planning Department granted a variance to construct the 141-unit Symphony Towers apartments with only 51 parking spaces (rather than the required 141 spaces), in part because the developer committed to provide two parking spaces for the car-sharing operator City CarShare. Charges for the parking spaces in the building were unbundled from the apartment rents.[37]

A shared car in the garage of an apartment building would be like something between a taxicab and a private car available for every resident, and it would make the apartments more desirable for the tenants. The arrangement would save money for both the developer (who provides fewer parking spaces) and residents (who own fewer cars) without eliminating anyone's ability to use a car when needed. The car-sharing organization would also gain members and would be able to locate its cars in more locations, making membership in the club even more beneficial.

The shared-car option can be extended to many land uses. Cities can allow hotels, office buildings, and universities, for example, to provide some shared-car parking spaces in exchange for a reduced parking requirement. By making most parking free to drivers, off-street parking requirements have reduced the demand for car sharing. In contrast, offering developers the option to provide shared-car parking spaces in lieu of private parking spaces can increase the demand for car sharing, reduce development costs, and reduce the demand for driving.

POLICIES APPROPRIATE TO THEIR LOCATIONS

These three policies—Eco Passes, parking cash out, and car sharing in lieu of required parking spaces—are appropriate where most employers and developers offer free parking, most commuters drive to work alone, and public transit has excess capacity. All three of these conditions are met in most U.S. cities. Ninety-one percent of all commuters drive to work in the U.S., 95 percent of automobile commuters park free at work, and only 27 percent of the seats on public transit are occupied.[38] Most cities require ample on-site parking, and they can reduce parking requirements for developers who agree to offer Eco Passes or parking cash out for all commuters.

Eco Passes and parking cash out are not useful in cities where few employers offer free parking, few commuters drive to work alone, and public transit is already packed—but these places almost certainly do *not* require excessive off-street parking. In the many cities that do require excessive off-street parking, however, offering developers the option to reduce the cost of required parking by Eco Passes, parking cash out, and car sharing makes sense for everyone.

CONCLUSION: OFFER THE OPTION TO REDUCE PARKING DEMAND

Conventional in-lieu fees give developers the option to finance public parking spaces rather than provide the required private parking spaces. Cities can also give developers the option to reduce the demand for parking rather than increase the supply, and this modest reform will create substantial benefits for all parties:

1. The reduced demand for parking can shift land from parking spaces to activities that employ more workers and yield higher tax revenue.
2. By reducing the number and size of parking lots, reducing the demand for parking improves urban design.
3. Employers use their savings from providing less parking to offer new fringe benefits—Eco Passes or parking cash out—for commuters. This new fringe benefit resembles a wage increase that helps recruit and retain workers.
4. Commuters gain new fringe benefits—free public transit or cash payments—beyond the usual offer of free parking at work.
5. Developers and property owners save money. They can replace a high capital cost for parking with a low annual cost for public transit, parking cash out, or car sharing. Fewer vehicle trips reduce a project's environmental impact and can help developers satisfy traffic mitigation requirements.
6. Supply-side capital subsidies for required parking are converted into demand-side subsidies for public transit, and the increased transit ridership enables transit agencies to improve service.
7. Fewer vehicle trips reduce traffic congestion, air pollution, and energy consumption.

Eco Passes and parking cash out are cost effective because paying for a transit ride to and from work is much cheaper than paying for a free parking space at work. Case studies suggest that developers can save at least $46 on the capital cost of required parking for each $1 a year they spend on Eco Passes. They can also save $40 on the capital cost of parking for each $1 a year they spend to offer parking cash out. The low cost of reducing the demand for parking compared with the high cost of increasing the supply shows that Eco Passes and parking cash out are cost-effective strategies. These cost-effectiveness comparisons were made in places famous for their addiction to cars: Silicon Valley (for Eco Passes) and Southern California (for parking cash out). If Eco Passes and parking cash out can reduce parking demand in these two places, they can probably achieve good results in other cities.

CHAPTER 10 NOTES

1. Santa Clara Valley Transportation Authority (1997). The number of cars driven to work by solo drivers fell by 21 percent. Because some commuters switched from carpools to transit and because carpoolers drive fewer than one vehicle per person, the total number of cars driven to work fell by only 19 percent. The transit share increased from 11 percent before the free transit passes, to 27 percent afterward.

2. As an administrative precedent for purchasing transit passes in lieu of providing the required parking, some cities allow property owners to purchase parking permits in public garages in lieu of providing the required on-site parking. For example, Kirkland, Washington, allows a property owner to pay an annual in-lieu fee of $1,020 per required parking space not provided, and the owner receives a parking pass to a public garage for each fee paid. This obligation runs with the land and commits future property owners either to pay the annual fee or to provide the required parking.

3. See the SCVTA's Web site www.vta.org/eco_pass.html for details of the Eco Passes. The Eco Pass's price includes a guaranteed ride home. On any day they ride transit to work, commuters are entitled to a free taxi ride home in the event of illness, emergency, or unscheduled overtime. The public transit systems in Boulder and Denver, Colorado, and Salt Lake City, Utah, offer similar Eco Pass programs.

4. Eco Passes avoid the problem of "adverse selection." The concept of adverse selection was developed in the context of insurance coverage. Adverse selection describes the tendency for people with a greater potential of loss to purchase more insurance. This tendency leads to higher loss payments, and then to higher insurance premiums for everyone who is insured. Similarly, adverse selection increases the cost of conventional transit passes sold to the public. Because frequent transit riders often buy monthly passes, transit agencies must price these passes on the assumption that passholders are frequent riders. There can also be adverse selection among employers. Firms with many commuters who ride transit will have an incentive to buy the Eco Passes, and this will tend to increase the transit operators' cost.

5. In the example, 20 percent of commuters opt for the conventional transit passes. Because all commuters get Eco Passes, and not just those who ride transit every day, the daily transit ridership may increase. Although some commuters who had opted for the conventional transit passes rather than parking spaces may begin to drive to work on some days, those who previously drove to work every day may begin to ride transit occasionally.

6. See U.S. Federal Transit Administration (1998) for data on annual passenger miles and annual vehicle revenue miles for public transit systems in the U.S. Dividing the 17.5 billion passenger miles traveled on bus transit in 1997 by the 1.6 billion vehicle revenue miles of service on bus transit gives an average occupancy of 10.9 passenger miles per bus mile ($17.5 \div 1.6 = 10.9$ passengers per bus). Dividing the average bus occupancy of 10.6 passengers by the average bus capacity of 40 seats gives an average seat occupancy of 27 percent ($10.9 \div 40 = 27$ percent); that is, if all passengers are seated during their trips, only 27 percent of bus seats are occupied. This calculation overestimates the number of bus seats that are occupied because some passengers stand rather than sit. An average bus occupancy of 10.9 passengers may seem low, but Davis and Diegel (2002, Table 2.11) estimated that the average bus occupancy was only 9.2 passengers in 2000. Naturally, some transit vehicles are packed at rush hours, but this must be a small percentage of all transit vehicle-miles for the average occupancy to be only 27 percent. If Eco Passes increase ridership during the hours when capacity must be increased to carry more riders, the marginal cost of the additional riders can be high.

7. See Table 9-4 for the cities's in-lieu fees in 2002.

8. Santa Clara Valley Transportation Authority (1997).

9. Suppose the Eco Pass costs $80 a year per employee. If there are 4 employees per 1,000 square feet of office space, the Eco Passes cost $320 a year per 1,000 square feet of office space (4 x $80), or 32¢ a year per square foot of office space ($320 ÷ 1,000). The SCVTA charges the highest price of $80 a year per employee only in downtown San Jose, and the highest price elsewhere is only $60. The table thus overstates the highest cost of Eco Passes in Mountain View and Palo Alto by 33 percent, and the calculations in Table 10-2 are even more conservative.

10. Mary Smith (1999, 535). This estimate excludes property taxes.

11. If the off-street parking requirements satisfy the commuter demand for free parking, employers have enough spaces to offer everyone free parking. If cities offer a reduction in parking requirements equal to the reduction in parking demand caused by the in-lieu Eco Passes, the required parking supply still meets the demand for free parking, but everyone also can ride transit for free.

12. The developers who pay the conventional in-lieu fees to finance public parking structures thus inadvertently subsidize their competition, who also benefit from the public parking spaces.

13. For example, if the Eco Passes cost $40 a year per employee and they reduce the demand for commuter parking by 19 percent (as found in Silicon Valley), Eco Passes save more than $40 a year per employee on parking subsidies if the firm had been spending more than $211 a year per employee to subsidize parking (because reducing a parking subsidy of $211 a year by 19 percent saves $40 a year). Many firms spend far more than this break-even value of $211 a year ($17.60 a month) per employee to subsidize parking.

14. California Department of Transportation (2002, Appendix B).

15. California Department of Transportation (2002, 1).

16. Lund, Cervero, and Willson (2004, 88).

17. *Ibid.* (64).

18. Employees will also know whether their employer continues to offer the Eco Passes, and they might report an employer who failed to comply with a covenant to provide Eco Passes.

19. Universities have given their programs a variety of names—such as BruinGO, ClassPass, SuperTicket, and UPass. See Brown, Hess, and Shoup (2001) for a survey of 35 Unlimited Access programs. There were more than 60 programs by 2002.

20. Brown, Hess, and Shoup (2003).

21. University of Washington Transportation Office (1997).

22. "The parking requirement for a hotel or motel facility may be reduced by the City during parking plan review by up to twenty percent if…complimentary transit tickets are provided to customers and employees, free use of bicycles is similarly provided, and telephones, faxes, computers with modems, and other business machines are readily available on site" (Section 86.58.230E of the Coronado Municipal Code). Many hotels in German cities have also arranged for their hotel guest identification to serve as a transit pass.

23. Portland TriMet (2002, 3-11).

24. Shoup (1997b, Table 1). This research will also be available in PAS Report 531, *Parking Cash Out* (forthcoming).

25. California Health and Safety Code Section 65089.

26. *Ibid.*

27. These case studies are evaluated in Shoup (1997b).

28. Shoup (1997b, Table 1) shows the numbers of cars driven to work per commuter before and after giving commuters the option to cash out their parking subsidies. A downtown Los Angeles employee survey found an average office occupancy density of 4.2

employees per 1,000 square feet (Barton Aschman Associates 1986). The absentee rates (for sickness, vacations, telecommuting, and travel) at the eight case study firms ranged from 5 percent to 27 percent, with an average of 10 percent of employees absent on each day. Given an occupancy density of 4.2 employees per 1,000 square feet and average employee absentee rate of 10 percent, Table 10-3 shows the number of cars driven to work per 1,000 square feet before and after employers offered commuters the option to cash out their parking subsidies.

29. Higgins (1993) assumed a daily average of 0.5 visitors per employee, a visitor parking turnover rate of four per day, and a visitor drive-alone share of 85 percent. If there are 0.5 visitors per employee per day, if 85 percent of these visitors arrive by car, and if visitor parking spaces turn over four times per day, the visitor parking demand is (0.5 x 0.85)/4 = 0.1 parking spaces per employee.

30. Parking Consultants Council (1992, 5).

31. Wilbur Smith and Associates (1981). Hartmut Topp (1991, 7) reports that the peak parking factor for commuter parking in Frankfurt, Germany, is about 85 percent.

32. Commuters drive 3.2 cars per 1,000 square feet when employers offer free parking without the cash option. The peak parking demand is 0.2 spaces per 1,000 square feet less than this because 6 percent of these cars aren't parked at work at the time of peak demand.

33. The estimates in Table 10-3 do *not* show that parking demand is *exactly* 3.7 or 3.3 spaces per 1,000 square feet of office space. The wide variation among the case-study sites shows that there is not one "right" number of parking spaces for all office buildings. Nevertheless, the evidence does show that the cash option reduces parking demand and that cities can allow developers, property owners, and employers to offer parking cash out instead of providing some of the required spaces.

34. The assumed cost of $10,000 per space is lower than the cost per space (in 2002 dollars) for any of the 15 parking structures built at UCLA since 1961 (see Table 6-1).

35. Shoup (1997b, 207).

36. Cervero and Tsai (2003, 5, 24-25). The typical shared-car trip was 5.5 miles and cost $32. The typical shared car was leased out for seven hours per day.

37. U.S. Environmental Protection Agency (2004, 25). Symphony Towers is located at 724 Van Ness Avenue, and is described on the San Francisco Housing Action Coalition's web site at www.sfhac.org/images/HAC_Board_1.pdf. As an added incentive to participate in carsharing, developers might even offer to pay every resident's small annual membership fee in the carshare organization. In Los Angeles, for example, one shared-car plan has a $25 annual fee plus a charge of $10 per hour. See the Flexcar web site at www.flexcar.com.

38. See Shoup (1997b, 201) for data on free parking at work and the share of commuters who drive to work, and Brown, Hess, and Shoup (2001) for the share of occupied seats on public transit.

Part

II

Cruising for Parking

As he turned from Oberlin Avenue round the corner into Third Street, N.E., he peered ahead for a space in the line of parked cars. He angrily just missed a space as a rival driver slid into it. Ahead another car was leaving the curb, and Babbitt slowed up, holding out his hand to the cars pressing on him from behind, agitatedly motioning an old woman to go ahead, avoiding a truck which bore down on him from one side. With front wheels nicking the wrought-steel bumper of the car in front, he stopped, feverishly cramped his steering-wheel, slid back into the vacant space and, with eighteen inches of room, maneuvered to bring the car level with the curb. It was a virile adventure masterfully executed.

—SINCLAIR LEWIS, Babbitt

CHAPTER

11

Cruising

My father didn't pay for parking, my mother, my brother, nobody. It's like going to a prostitute. Why should I pay when, if I apply myself, maybe I can get it for free?

—GEORGE COSTANZA

When a resource is communally owned, the right of "first possession" means that anyone has a right to the resource once they capture it. With fish in the ocean, for example, anyone who catches a fish can keep it, so no one has any incentive to leave fish to breed because anyone else can catch them. Communal ownership of ocean fisheries has led to widespread overfishing, the depletion of many species, and an increase in the effort needed to catch them.[1] In 2003, a study published in *Nature* found that since the 1950s industrial fishing fleets have stripped the ocean of 90 percent of large fish, such as giant tuna, swordfish, and marlin.[2] "Fishermen used to go out and catch these phenomenally big fish," said Ransom Myers, a Canadian fisheries biologist and one of the study authors, "but cannot find them anymore. They're not there. We ate them."[3]

Free curb parking is another example of communal ownership because it is available to all drivers on a "first-come, first-served" basis.[4] The curb spaces are like fish in the ocean: a parking space belongs to anyone who occupies it, but if you leave it, you lose it. Where all the curb spaces are occupied, turnover leads to a few vacancies over time, but drivers must cruise to find a space vacated by a departing motorist. Drivers have been cruising for free curb parking since shortly after the automobile was invented, congesting traffic, creating air pollution, and wasting energy.

CRUISING THROUGH THE TWENTIETH CENTURY

Cruising wasn't a problem when only a few rich people owned cars, but as the number of drivers increased, the search for open curb spaces became more and more difficult. In a travel book from the 1920s, *Touring New England on the Trail of the Yankee*, Clara Whiteside described the problems she encountered while on an automobile tour in Connecticut:

> We started out to view the town.... Round and round the blocks we drove trying to find a place to park.... Every curb was black with backed-in cars... "There's a place!" Alas! it was the wrong side of the street. So on we would go to the next corner hoping to be able to turn but invariably the traffic officer would firmly signal us, till time after time, we would find ourselves...in the very center of things, entangled in the traffic.[5]

Apart from the disappearance of traffic officers at every corner, cruising for parking has changed little since the 1920s. Where curb parking is free and off-street parking is expensive, some drivers doggedly search for a free curb space rather than pay to park off-street. Parking surveys in Seattle in 2000, for example, found "spaces were often readily open in off-street *pay* lots, although *free* on-street parking was full to overflowing."[6]

Everyone intuitively understands the choice between cruising and paying, but we know almost nothing about the collective consequences of cruising. For example, how many of the cars on congested streets are simply hunting for curb parking rather than going somewhere? How much fuel does this cruising waste, and how much air pollution does it create? Cruising is individually rational because it saves the driver some money for parking but is collectively irrational because it takes time, congests traffic, wastes fuel, and pollutes the air.

Cruising presents a paradox; it is an aspect of transportation that analysts know little about, while everyone else knows a lot about it. All drivers, at one point or another, have cruised, and depending on where they live, cruising may be a large part of their everyday life. Consider New York, America's capital of cruising. To allow for street cleaning, New York prohibits parking for a 90-minute period on one side of the street on Mondays, Wednesdays, and Fridays, and on the other side on Tuesdays, Thursdays, and Saturdays.[7] During the 90 minutes each day when parking is prohibited on the side of the street being cleaned, residents cruise for new parking spaces or double park on the other side where parking is permitted. The city suspends the alternate-side regulations on 32 legal and religious holidays each year, but New Yorkers must move their cars on other days.[8]

New Yorkers have been cruising for alternate-side parking for many years. Frank McCourt (author of *Angela's Ashes*) describes one person's obsession with parking during the 1950s:

> Harry Ball...drives Virgil crazy with his parking problems.... He's got this big car...and he goes nowhere with it.... He moves it from one side of the street to the other, back and forth, back and forth. Sometimes he brings the little aluminum beach chair and sits near his car looking for a parking spot to open for next day. Or he walks around the neighborhood looking for a spot and if he finds one he gets excited and gives himself a heart attack rushing to his car to drive it to the new spot which is now gone and so is the one he was in and there he is driving around with no spot, cursing the government. I was with him once and he nearly ran down a rabbi and two old women.... He could park that car in a garage for eighty-five bucks a month but that's more than Harry pays for rent and that'll be the day Harry Ball ever wasted a penny.[9]

Harry Ball was concerned only about his own pennies, of course, and not about the costs that his search for free parking imposed on everyone else.

Journalists often discuss cruising, and the *New York Times* sometimes gives tips on how to do it properly. A 1987 article, for example, recommended:

> keeping the eyes open for a hand clenched into a fist...because it means they're holding car keys and if you trail them you can get their parking space [or] keeping eyes open for the exhaust that means someone is starting up a parked car [or] to look for red lights on cars, an indication that they might be about to move.[10]

The obsession with parking in New York carries over onto TV sitcoms. In a *Seinfeld* episode, George explains his strategy to Elaine: "Look, I have my system. First I look for the dream spot right in front of the door, and then I slowly expand out in concentric circles." He refuses to pay for off-street parking because, he says, "It's like going to a prostitute. Why should I pay when, if I apply myself, maybe I can get it for free?"[11]

In some places cruising becomes a matter of legal dispute. In a 1975 ruling on the constitutional validity of off-street parking requirements, the Colorado Supreme Court stated:

> Studies of traffic problems uniformly find air pollution to be related to autoists moving slowly around block after block seeking a place to park. In these days of environmental concern, we cannot believe that it is unconstitutional to require those who invite large numbers of people to their establishments—who in turn clog the streets, air and ears of our citizens—to provide parking facilities so that automobiles may be placed in a stall and stilled.[12]

"The Alternate-Side-of-the-Street Jitterbug"

By William E. Geist

New York Times, January 16, 1985

Johnny has a job that is believed to exist only in New York. Johnny is a car shepherd. One of those distinctly New York vocations that grows out of some distinctly New York problem.

"When you can't pay the exorbitant garage prices," one of Johnny's clients said, "and you can't drive around and around and around one more block looking for parking spaces—which are like gold around here—or you'll crack up, then you go to Johnny."

Johnny tends to a flock of about 20 cars, keeping them on the move from one side of the street to the other and out of trouble for fees ranging from $25 a month for old customers to $60 for new customers.

"I don't want any more customers," said the gray-haired tender of cars who is also a building superintendent, "but they pay whatever I ask. The garages around here cost more than $200 a month, and some people are also too lazy to get up and move their cars."

A car shepherd on West 78th Street claims to be making as much as $150 a month for some of his cars.

"There are times," said the client, "when I don't see my car for six weeks and have no idea where it is." Johnny knows. On some of Johnny's streets, alternate-side-of-the-street parking regulations specify that cars must be off the street between 8 A.M. and 11 A.M.; on other streets, the hours are 11 A.M. to 2 P.M.

"I pay any parking tickets," Johnny said. "If they tow, I drop dead. It costs me over $100."

On this cold and blustery morning, Johnny had to jump start some of the cars and unfreeze door locks. He has been doing this for 20 years, but said the job had become far more difficult, with fewer and fewer parking places to be found.

[I]llegal double parking has become a practice accepted by authorities in Manhattan, and where the police have decided to ticket the double-parkers, vehement protests have been mounted by New Yorkers over their right to double-park illegally.

Veterans of double-parking streets tell of strange tactics to keep from being blocked in. Notes on windshields such as "Don't Block—Woman in Labor" seem to have no effect whatsoever, they say. "Try to get a choice end spot so you can just drive out or back out," one veteran said, "and don't park next to a tree, because that way you can't drive down the sidewalk."

Gerald Mayer was something of a folk hero to suffering motorists in his neighborhood on West 79th Street. Mr. Mayer prided himself on always finding a parking space on the street.

"I tried to make it a game," he said, "otherwise you go out of your skull."

"You have to have the eyes of a hawk and quickness at the wheel," Mr. Mayer said. "You have to watch people's hands for keys and listen for the jingle. You have to get to know what the doctors and dentists and shopkeepers in the neighborhood look like, what kinds of cars they drive and what time they leave every day.

At one time, he said, there was a funeral parlor in the neighborhood where you could park illegally and the police would think you were one of the bereaved.

Mr. Mayer recently retired and did not need his car anymore. Out of the goodness of his heart he gave it to his son, who also lives in Manhattan. His son quickly recognized the ploy and gave it back.

Transportation researchers occasionally mention cruising. In a World Bank study of transportation problems in Central American cities, for example, Anthony Churchill says, "The low price of parking gives rise to queuing and even worse forms of congestion as vehicles circulate vainly seeking a place and as the motorist, in desperation, parks illegally."[13]

These anecdotes confirm what everybody knows: drivers cruise for curb parking. Cruising creates a mobile queue of cars that are waiting for curb vacancies, but drivers cannot see how many cars are in the queue because the cruisers are mixed with other cars that are going somewhere. Nevertheless, a few researchers have estimated how many cars are cruising, and how long it takes to find a curb space. They have watched videotapes of traffic flows, interviewed drivers who park at the curb, and have themselves cruised. The following 16 studies of cruising, conducted between 1927 and 2001, are listed in chronological order. The resulting estimates depend on the locations studied, but between 8 and 74 percent of the cars in traffic were cruising for parking, and the average time to find a curb space ranged from 3.5 to 13.9 minutes.

DETROIT

The first research on cruising was, appropriately, conducted in Detroit. In 1927, Hawley Simpson (who later became president of the Institute of Traffic Engineers) measured cruising for parking by counting cars as they repeatedly passed observation points at two locations in Detroit's Central Business District (CBD) between 2 p.m. and 6 p.m. (Table 11-1). At one location, 76 cars went by a total of 360 times, for an average of 4.7 passes per car (with one car passing the same point 24 times). At a second location, 188 cars passed the same point a total of 689 times, for an average of 3.7 passes per car (with one car passing the same point 17 times). Simpson estimated that 19 percent of the cars passing the first observation point, and 34 percent of the cars passing the second, were cruising.

Curb spaces at both locations were fully occupied for most of the day. At the peak hour, Simpson counted 28 percent more parked cars than legal parking spaces and found that 40 percent of the parked cars violated some parking regulation. Only 22 percent of the cars parked at the curb stayed more than one hour, but they occupied 60 percent of the available parking-space-hours in the downtown district. In making this calculation, Simpson pointed out that the correct measure of parking space consumption is not simply the number of parked cars at any one time but is instead the number of parked cars multiplied by the length of time they stay: *parked-car-hours*. During a day, a large number of cars that stay for a short time typically contribute very little to the total accumulation of cars parked at any one time, while a few cars that park all day account for

Table 11-1. Cruising in Detroit

Location	Number of cars cruising	Number of trips passing same point	Average trips per car	Maximum trips per car	Cruising as % of traffic
One	76	360	4.7	24	19%
Two	188	689	3.7	17	34%

Source: Simpson (1927, 85).

most of the cars parked at any one time. A few cars staying a long time can thus occupy most of the available parking capacity, while many cars staying a short time occupy a relatively small share. Reducing the average parking duration therefore increases the number of cars that can park at the curb during a day.

Simpson also predicted many of the problems that later arose from free off-street parking. "Rather than assisting in solving the street traffic problem" he said, "it may very probably have the opposite effect by inducing a large amount of unnecessary vehicle usage. Free storage is an economic fallacy."[14]

WASHINGTON, D.C.

In 1933, the U.S. Bureau of Public Roads tested how long it took to drive six-mile trips along three different routes to the Department of Commerce building at 15th and E Streets, NW, during the morning rush hour.[15] Researchers used stop watches and odometers to measure the time and distance for each segment of the trip—driving to 15th and E, searching for a curb space, and then walking to the Commerce building. Table 11-2 shows the results. The average driving time was 25 minutes, the average search time to find a curb space was eight minutes, the average walking time to the Commerce building was nine minutes, and total trip time was 42 minutes. Driving accounted for 60 percent of the total trip time, cruising for 19 percent, and walking for 21 percent. The total trip time was 68 percent longer than it would have been if the drivers had been able to park at the destination without cruising. The driving speed for the six miles to the Commerce building was 14.2 miles per hour, but when the subsequent search and walking times were added, the total trip speed fell to 8.5 miles per hour. This slow speed must have been especially annoying because the researchers made their time trials in a vehicle that was "the last word in motor car design, so accurately streamlined that hardly a particle of dust will accumulate on its fenders and body surfaces."[16]

Table 11-2. Driving, Cruising, and Walking Times for Six-Mile Trips
in Washington, D.C. (minutes)

	Driving	Cruising	Walking
Trip segment time	25.4	8.0	9.0
Share of total trip time	60%	19%	21%

Source: Hogentogler, Willis, and Kelley (1934).

NEW HAVEN AND WATERBURY

The next research on cruising was undertaken 27 years later, in 1960. Matthew Huber, then at the Yale Bureau of Highway Traffic and later a professor of civil engineering at the University of Minnesota, surveyed 3,200 curb parkers and 2,700 off-street parkers in the CBDs of New Haven and Waterbury, Connecticut, to learn how far they had cruised before finding a parking space. Drivers were interviewed as soon as they parked, and each was asked to retrace the route followed between the trip origin and the parking space (a map of the CBD was provided with each interview to help drivers trace their routes). Drivers could begin searching for parking *before* they reached their destinations, Huber said, and drivers were asked to identify where their searches began. The interviews were equally distributed between a relatively quiet summer period in July, an average fall period in November, and the pre-Christmas rush in December.

The average distance cruised before parking at a curb space was 1,041 feet in New Haven, and 930 feet in Waterbury (Table 11-3).[17] Eighteen percent of the off-street parkers reported that they had searched for a curb space before parking off the street, and they cruised an average of 2,377 feet in New Haven, and 1,613 feet in Waterbury. Huber's data also showed that cruising for parking amounted to at least 17 percent of total vehicle miles travelled (VMT) in the New Haven CBD.[18]

LONDON

In a PBS *Mystery* episode, Cordelia Gray returned late to her London detective agency and explained, "I spent half an hour trying to find a meter."[19] Work done by Britain's Road Research Laboratory shows that Ms. Gray was not alone in her cruising and that she inconvenienced more people than the clients waiting in her office. In 1965, researchers conducted park-and-visit tests mimicking the search for curb parking in London. They drove to an address and then recorded the time taken to find a curb space. The search times required to find a space in three different areas of London averaged 3.5, 3.6, and 6.1 minutes.[20]

Table 11-3. Cruising in New Haven and Waterbury, Connecticut

	Distance (in feet) cruised before parking					
	New Haven		Waterbury		Total	
	Curb	Off-street	Curb	Off-street	Curb	Off-street
Men	1,011	2,034	908	1,615	952	1,793
Women	1,129	2,683	993	1,610	1,049	2,137
All	1,041	2,377	930	1,613	977	1,963

Source: Huber (1962).

Cruising for parking congests traffic and increases travel time for every-one, including bus riders. Buses and cruising cars generally use the same traffic lane closest to the curb, and because travel time accounts for most of the capital and operating cost of buses, cruising for underpriced curb parking increases both the time and money cost of bus travel. When the Road Research Laboratory conducted its park-and-visit tests, the number of people traveling on buses in central London during peak hours was almost twice the number traveling in cars. Cruising for curb parking therefore created more delay for bus riders than for car drivers.[21]

In addition to slowing buses, traffic congestion also prevents them from keeping to their schedules, and the resulting irregular service further reduces the transit system's ability to carry passengers. F. J. Lloyd says that both these effects were shown when closure of the Suez Canal in 1957 caused severe fuel rationing and sharply reduced traffic congestion in central London:

> Not only did the buses run regularly and freely, but the experience was that they were able to carry the large number of additional passengers who pre-sented themselves, with no increase at all in the volume of scheduled services. To run buses faster... is not the entire aim and object. Buses must be run reg-ularly and to schedule, and it is then possible to carry a given volume of pas-sengers with a smaller number of buses. During Suez the buses were better utilized and the service efficiency was greatly improved.[22]

Where fuel is plentiful and cheap, however, more people want to drive their own cars. More driving increases the demand for parking, and com-petition for the same curb parking supply creates even more cruising. By congesting traffic, cruising slows buses, puts them off their schedules, and increases their cost. The slower, less reliable, and more expensive transit service then discourages passengers and diverts them from buses to cars, which further increases congestion and accelerates transit's downward spiral.

PARIS

Using a transportation simulation model of Paris in 1977, Hubert Levy-Lambert found:

> Moderate pricing of private automobile parking in the streets (50 cents per hour in the center, 25 in the outskirts) [$1.68 and 84 cents in 2002 dollars] would reduce private traffic by 24 percent, increase peak-hour speed from six to nine miles per hour, and create a surplus of about $163 million in 1975 [$545 million in 2002 dollars], most of it being the money value of 600,000 hours of transportation time saved per day.[23]

Levy-Lambert estimated that 68 percent of the total time savings would accrue to drivers and 32 percent to public transport riders.

FREIBURG

In 1977 the German Automobile Club set up video cameras at each intersection in central Freiburg and used them to follow randomly selected cars as they traveled from one intersection to another. The researchers estimated that an astonishing 74 percent of the 800 cars tracked on camera were cruising for parking and would have parked immediately had they found a space. On average, these cars hunted six minutes before finding a place to park. The cameras revealed another notable finding: cruising, the researchers reported, produced psychological changes among drivers as they crept along in search of a parking space:

> This fixation on a parking space turns many drivers into unscrupulous maniacs. When all else fails, they will pull into any available space in a no-stopping zone, on the sidewalk, or even in an intersection.[24]

Where cruising for curb parking constitutes three-fourths of the total traffic, it can substantially degrade the transportation system, the environment, and even mental health.

JERUSALEM AND HAIFA

In 1984, Ilan Salomon conducted a study of commuters to the CBD of Jerusalem to examine car owners' decisions about whether to drive to work and where to park. Despite the general perception of a severe parking problem in the CBD, he found that 90 percent of car owners drove to work. In the sample of 849 drivers who responded to a mail-back questionnaire about their work trips, the median search time for a parking space between 8 a.m. and early afternoon was nine minutes. The questionnaire also asked respondents for their comments on parking in the center of Jerusalem, and Salomon summarized their views:

> Parking is viewed as a 'free public good' which drivers believe should be supplied by the authorities. Hence, the solution suggested by the respondents most frequently relates to the construction of more facilities and the reduction of rates.[25]

When faced with a parking shortage, most drivers' natural response is to recommend more parking spaces and bigger subsidies, not higher parking prices.

Yoram Shiftan conducted a study of 200 people arriving at the Carmel Center Business District in Haifa in 2002, asking drivers how long they had searched to find a parking space. Two-thirds of them had cruised for more than five minutes before parking, and one-third for more than 10 minutes.[26]

CAMBRIDGE

In 1985, Marianne O'Malley examined cruising in the Harvard Square business district of Cambridge, Massachusetts. Drivers saved money by cruising because the meter price of curb parking was 50¢ an hour while the commercial price of off-street parking was $3 an hour. To measure the resulting search time, she conducted a series of park-and-visit tests:

> To determine the mean length of cruise, I cruised to three randomly selected locations. Each of my thirteen cruises was done between 10 a.m. and 3:30 p.m. My strategy was to drive to the location and then try to find a space within a quarter mile radius.[27]

She found that it took, on average, 11.5 minutes to find a parking space in Harvard Square, with a range from two to 25 minutes, and that the average distance cruised was 1.27 miles. The average walking distance from the parking space to the intended destination was 0.25 miles, which took about 7.5 minutes. She also estimated that 30 percent of the cars in Harvard Square traffic were searching for curb parking.[28]

CAPE TOWN

In 1993, Peter Clark conducted a survey of curb parkers in Cape Town, South Africa, and found that the average search time in the central city area was 12.2 minutes.[29] The median search time was 10 minutes; 22 percent of drivers searched for less than five minutes, and 4 percent for more than 25 minutes. Sixty percent of parkers reported that they had difficulty in finding a curb space, and short-term parkers appeared to care far more about the time they spent searching for parking than about its price. Using a stated-preference analysis, Clark estimated that the price elasticity of demand for curb parking was -0.22, while the search-time elasticity was -0.61; that is, drivers were three times more sensitive to the time it takes to find a curb space than to the price of parking in it. The -0.22 price elasticity of demand suggests that a 10 percent increase in the price of parking would reduce the number of cars parked on the street by only 2 percent. The survey also indicated that most of this 2 percent would continue to come to the central city area, but would park off-street.[30]

NEW YORK

New York earned a new place in the pantheon of parking tales in 2002, when Calvin Trillin published *Tepper Isn't Going Out*, the first parking novel. Murray Tepper, the protagonist, obsesses about parking so much that once he has a good spot, he sits in his car and reads the newspaper, reluctant to abandon the prized real estate he has captured. Cruising plays an important role in the novel—not just the frustration of the hunt but the exhilaration of victory. Witness this exchange between Tepper and his daughter:

> "Daddy...I remember when you used to keep the car on the street and switch it from one side of the street to the other every night, because of the alternate-side parking rules. I remember when I was a little girl sometimes Mom and I would have to wait dinner for you while you looked for a place to park that would be legal for the next day. And then you'd come in and you'd say, 'Guess what? A beautiful spot!' That was nice. You managed to keep the car on the street, and every night you had a little victory. Or maybe I just remember the victories. Maybe there were nights when you looked and looked and had to give up."
>
> "That's one of the odd things about alternate-side parking," Tepper said. "There isn't exactly any way to give up."
>
> Even so, he sometimes missed those evenings circling the blocks of the Upper West Side. Most of the neighborhood was governed by the alternate-side parking regulations, for street-cleaning purposes, and he knew from long experience which sides of the streets said, NO PARKING 8AM-11AM MON-WED-FRI, and which said, TUES-THURS-SAT, and which said, improbably, MON-THURS or TUE-FRI, and which, just to keep you on your toes, said, 11AM-2PM instead of 8AM-11AM. What he often had trouble keeping in his mind was which day of the week the next day—the relevant day—would be, and he was in the habit of repeating it, half under his breath, as he searched for a spot regulated by a sign that did not mention it.

As he moved down the street, looking for a spot that alternate-side parkers call "good for tomorrow," he'd say "Tuesday, Tuesday, Tuesday" over and over, almost as if he were chanting some sort of mantra. He'd listen intently for the sound of an ignition being turned. He'd glance quickly from side to side, hoping to spot the flicker of a dashboard light that would indicate someone had just opened a car door and might be about to pull out. There were nights when he was totally confident of finding a spot. There were nights when he could almost imagine himself with a large tattoo on his arm that said, BORN TO PARK. There were nights when he knew that it was only a matter of time before he'd slip into a NO PARKING MON-WED-FRI spot, emitting, as the car came to rest against the curb, a final "Tuesday!" loud enough to startle passersby.[31]

Trillin hesitates to call his book the ultimate New York novel, but he does say that it is the ultimate New York parking novel. In an interview with the *New York Times*, Trillin described his own skill in finding what he calls a Beautiful Spot:

It has to be in a place where there aren't many other spots. The difficulty enhances the beauty of the spot.... You go around a corner and people are double parked and suddenly you spot a space that a lesser parker—if I may use that phrase—a lesser parker would not have spotted. You just hear the click of an ignition. The driver gets in his car and pulls out, and you pull in backwards in one seamless movement.[32]

Trillin isn't the only New Yorker who has evolved special skill in finding alternate-side parking spots, of course. Consider the scientific approach of Columbia University professor Horst Störmer, who won the Nobel Prize in physics in 1998 for the "discovery of a new form of quantum fluid with fractionally charged excitations." In an interview published in 2000, Störmer described his strategies for finding curb parking in Manhattan:

I'm driving an old, banged up car—because I'm parking in the street. I figure that I'm never going to pay more for parking than the lease for a car. And in New York, you have to pay more for parking than to lease a decent car. So every night I try to find a parking space. It's a real challenge, and usually I succeed. Almost all the time I've been living in New York, about five years full-time now, I've been able to find a space. When they have a parade or something I have to go into a garage, but otherwise I find a space. And then of course there's alternate side parking. Till eight o'clock you're fine, but then you have to move your car. Which is actually not bad; it gets you out of bed, and going. You do develop strategies. For example, you know how to drive fast down a road, and not mistake hydrants for parking spots. I know where the hydrants are. And also, parking spots are very rare. So the probability of finding two parking spots next to each other is very rare. It goes like n squared. And typically in front of a hydrant you have about two openings—it's about two parking spots long. So you can go relatively fast. You don't have to look at those where there's two behind each other. So you only go for spots where there's one. That's great, because a lot of people who don't realize that drive slow, and you can overtake them, and then you're in front of them, and you can see the whole street. That really gives you a big advantage, because all these parking spots are waiting for you, rather than for the person who you just overtook.[33]

Cruising for parking is not the best use of a Nobel-Prize-winning physicist's time, or anyone else's. Because alternate-side-of-the-street parking takes so much time, however, many street-parkers have learned how to make use of it. During the time when there is no parking on one side of the street that is being cleaned, some drivers sit in their double-parked cars on the opposite side of the street, awaiting the chance to reclaim a spot once the street sweepers brush by. In an article on what these double-parkers do while waiting for a parking space, the *New York Times* reported:

> For Hillary Morehouse, moving her white Chrysler PT Cruiser to either side of West 22nd Street is a trip to the movies. She cranks up the air conditioning, plugs her Apple iBook in the car's lighter, and watches DVDs.[34]

New York presents abundant opportunities for serious research on cruising, but it is surprisingly understudied. John Falcocchio, Jose Darsin, and Elena Prassas are the only academics who have attempted to estimate the time it takes to find a curb space in New York and the share of traffic that is cruising.[35] In 1995 they estimated the time spent searching for curb parking in the Manhattan CBD by interviewing drivers who parked at the curb on weekdays (Table 11-4). The average time to find a curb space was 7.3 minutes between 8 and 10 a.m., and 10.6 minutes between 11 a.m. and 2 p.m. They also measured the curb space occupancy rate on the blocks where the parkers were interviewed, and found that it was the single most important factor affecting search time. They also estimated that the search for curb parking created about 8 percent of the total vehicle-miles traveled in the Midtown, West Side area.

Table 11-4. Cruising Manhattan

Location	Average search time (minutes) 8 a.m.–10 a.m.	11 a.m.–2 p.m.	Cruising as % of traffic
Midtown, West Side	6.3	7.9	8%
Midtown, East Side	7.7	10.2	n.a.
Downtown, Fulton Street	12.4	13.9	n.a.
Average	**7.3**	**10.6**	**n.a.**

Source: Falcocchio, Darsin, and Prassas (1995).

SAN FRANCISCO

San Francisco is another city where the hunt for curb parking devours time that should be spent on more important things. "You spend half your life," one resident told the *San Francisco Chronicle*, "driving around looking for parking in this town, which is bad for your marriage."[36]

To explore the causes and consequences of cruising, Robert Saltzman of San Francisco State University developed a simulation model of cruising for parking. The Four-Block Short-Term On-Street Parking (FSTOP) model simulates the behavior of drivers who circle the block until they find a parking space, or leave if they haven't found a space after a certain number of circuits. Saltzman tested the model with data gathered on West Portal Avenue, where the meter price was 50¢ an hour:

> As with many urban commercial districts, San Francisco's West Portal Avenue is a wonderful place to shop, dine, and accomplish many kinds of essential errands. Along West Portal's six-block commercial area there are over 200 one-hour metered parking spaces for driving customers who wish to patronize nearby businesses. The difficulty, however, is that the occupancy rate of these parking spaces usually exceeds 95% for most of every day. For those who drive to the area, finding a convenient parking space can be a frustrating, time-consuming, and even dangerous experience.[37]

When the parameters were adjusted so that FSTOP's output matched the observed or estimated data, the average search time to find a space was 3.2 minutes. Because only 49 percent of the drivers who cruised for a curb space on West Portal Avenue eventually found one, the total search time per driver who did find a curb space was 6.5 minutes (3.2 ÷ 0.49).[38]

Saltzman observed that 25 percent of all parkers were guilty of a meter violation (overstaying the paid time or not paying at all). Another 9 percent fed their meters to gain additional time above the one-hour limit. Summarizing his findings, Saltzman concluded:

On-street metered parking systems in San Francisco and in many other U.S. cities have seen very little change in the way they have been managed for decades. Though heavily utilized in many places, they are not proactively managed by city officials. As a result, neither the parking public nor the businesses they patronize are served as well as they could be.[39]

SYDNEY

Finally, on the far side of the world—in Sydney, Australia—cruising is about the same as everywhere else. In 2001, transportation economist David Hensher found that the average search time before finding a curb parking space in downtown Sydney was 6.5 minutes.[40] He also estimated that drivers were willing to pay 3.5 times their wage rate to reduce search time; that is, someone who earns 10¢ a minute at work is willing to pay 35¢ to reduce search time by one minute. Drivers thus appear to view cruising for parking as especially hard work.

CRUISING WITHOUT PARKING

Like all social behavior, cruising is a complex phenomenon, and it can be done even without parking. The Eno Foundation reports a variant of cruising termed "mobile parking," which is an alternative to stationary parking:

> Most parking studies have considered only standing vehicles. Some few have taken into consideration the "mobile parked vehicle." By "mobile parking" is meant those vehicles in which a driver rides around, for lack of a parking space, while someone else shops or attends to other business.[41]

Mobile parking can be cheaper than stationary parking. The average operating cost for a new vehicle was 12¢ a mile in 2002.[42] At 10 miles an hour, the operating cost of driving a car is therefore $1.20 an hour. Where parking costs more than $1.20 an hour, cruising is cheaper than parking.

In another publication from the Eno Foundation, Wilbur Smith and Charles LeCraw identified yet another kind of cruising, termed "live" parking:

> In many cases, short term parking is accomplished through "live" parking in which the driver remains in the vehicle, usually with the motor idling while a passenger leaves, transacts business or makes a delivery. Many cities permit this type of parking on streets where "no parking" prohibitions prevail, in unoccupied loading zones, and at other places where vehicles could not be left without the driver. Some cases are known in which live parking is permitted as "double parking," but such practice is not recommended.[43]

Mobile parking and live parking can be costly, especially for employers. In the college town of Provo, Utah, for example, the Provo *Daily Herald* reports, "Provo zoning inspectors sometimes travel in pairs when they make trips to the area south of Brigham Young University—one to make the inspection and the other to drive the car so they don't have to search for a parking spot."[44] That is, the city underprices curb parking and then deals with the resulting parking shortage by sending two planners to do the work of one. While one planner conducts a zoning inspection, the other either waits in the car or drives around congesting traffic, polluting the air, and wasting energy.

CONCLUSION: A CENTURY OF CRUISING

Table 11-5 summarizes the results of 16 studies of cruising in 11 cities. Between 8 and 74 percent of traffic was searching for parking, and it took between 3.5 and 13.9 minutes to find a curb space. But these studies dating back to 1927 are mainly of historical interest. The data were probably not very accurate when they were collected, and the results depended on the time of day, the specific place, and the season when the observations were made. Still, cruising today is similar to what drivers have done since

Table 11-5. Twentieth-Century Cruising

Year	City	Share of traffic cruising (percent)	Average search time (minutes)
1927	Detroit (1)	19%	
1927	Detroit (2)	34%	
1933	Washington		8.0
1960	New Haven	17%	
1965	London (1)		6.1
1965	London (2)		3.5
1965	London (3)		3.6
1977	Freiburg	74%	6.0
1984	Jerusalem		9.0
1985	Cambridge	30%	11.5
1993	Cape Town		12.2
1993	New York (1)	8%	7.9
1993	New York (2)		10.2
1993	New York (3)		13.9
1997	San Francisco		6.5
2001	Sydney		6.5
Average		**30%**	**8.1**

The numbers after Detroit, London, and New York refer to different locations within the same city.

Sources: Simpson (1927), Hogentogler, Willis, and Kelley (1934), Huber (1962), Inwood (1966), *Bus + Bahn* (1977), Salomon (1984), O'Malley (1985), Clark (1993), Falcocchio, Darsin, and Prassas (1995), Saltzman (1997), and Hensher (2001).

the 1920s, and the studies at least show that searching for underpriced curb parking has wasted an enormous amount of time and fuel for many decades. The studies are selective because researchers study cruising where they expect to find it—on streets where curb parking is underpriced and overcrowded. But because curb parking is underpriced and overcrowded in the busiest parts of most of the world's big cities, the sun never sets on cruising.

Even a small search time per car can create a surprising amount of traffic. Consider a congested downtown area where it takes three minutes to find a curb space. If the parking turnover is 10 cars per space per day, each curb space generates 30 minutes of cruising time per day, and if the average cruising speed is 10 miles an hour, each curb space generates five VMT per day. As estimated in Chapter 19, the average block is surrounded with 33 curb parking spaces, so cruising for parking creates 165 VMT a day per block. Over a year, this amounts to 60,000 VMT per block (equivalent to more than two trips around the earth). Because this cruising adds to already congested traffic, it makes a bad situation even worse.

If on-street parking is cheaper than off-street parking, cruising may be individually rational. Collectively, however, it congests traffic, wastes fuel, causes accidents, and pollutes the air. Cities create all these problems when they underprice curb parking. Underpricing of anything creates a shortage, and curb parking is no exception. The shortage of curb parking in turn creates the demand for off-street parking requirements that increase the cost of all urban development. Underpriced curb parking amounts to gross mismanagement of scarce urban land, with widespread ramifications for transportation, cities, the economy, and the environment.

CHAPTER 11 NOTES

1. Gordon (1954) explains the economics of common-property fisheries.

2. Myers and Worm (2003).

3. "Seas Being Stripped of Big Fish, Study Finds," *Los Angeles Times*, May 15, 2003.

4. Scarce but free curb parking resembles what Berkeley economist Siegfried Ciriacy-Wantrup (1952, 141) termed a *fugitive* resource: "Resources are called 'fugitive' because they must be 'captured' through use." In a congested area where many cars are cruising, curb parking is fugitive because, if you aren't the first person to see a space being vacated, someone else will get it. UCLA economist Harold Demsetz (1967) defined three forms of property ownership: communal, private, and state. Communal ownership means that everyone in a community has a right to use the property, private ownership means that individual owners can exclude others from using the property, and state ownership means that the state can exclude anyone from using the property. In this framework, free curb parking represents communal ownership. Drivers spend time and fuel searching for the free curb spaces, just as fishing fleets spend time and money searching for the free fish. The time needed to find a parking space increases as more drivers want to park, just as the effort needed to catch fish increases as more fishing boats put to sea. The time limits on curb parking are similar to the limits on the time of year when fishing is allowed or to the limits on allowable catches for each species.

5. Whiteside (1926, 124).

6. Seattle Strategic Planning Office (2000, 15), italics in the original. The surveys were conducted in 35 study areas in 26 neighborhoods.

7. O'Donnell (1995, 16). The alternate-side parking prohibitions were reduced from three hours to 90 minutes on many residential streets in 2000 after the Department of Sanitation determined that 90 minutes was enough time for the street-cleaning machines to do their job.

8. For example, New York suspends the alternate-side regulations on Idul-Adha, Immaculate Conception, and Shavuot. The New York City Department of Transportation gives additional information on these regulations at www.ci.nyc.ny.us/html/dot/home.html. Residents who are already parked on side of the street where parking is permitted throughout the day expect to be blocked in during the time when parking is prohibited on the other side of the street, and some of them also double park if they expect to use their cars during the street-cleaning hours.

9. McCourt (1999, 324-5).

10. Enid Nemy, "The Magic Gift of Finding Parking Spaces and Taxis," *New York Times* (January 11, 1987).

11. *Seinfeld*, "The Parking Space." Several other *Seinfeld* episodes deal with parking: "The Alternate Side," "The Handicap Spot," and "The Parking Garage."

12. Williams and Taylor (1986, 8) say that this 60-page legal decision on the constitutionality validity of off-street parking requirements is the longest in American planning law. The 1959 decision of the Colorado Supreme Court (*City & County of Denver v. Denver Buick, Inc.*, 141 Colo 121, 347 P2d 919 (1959)) found that off-street parking requirements were unconstitutional because they violated private property rights, but it was later overruled by a 1975 Colorado Supreme Court decision (*Stroud v. City of Aspen*, 532 P2d 720 (Colo 1975)).

13. Churchill (1972, 111). There is also recreational cruising, which is ritual of American youth. The Beach Boys sang, "Well she got her daddy's car, And with the radio blasting, Goes cruising just as fast as she can now, And she'll have fun, fun, fun, 'Til her daddy takes the T-Bird away." Teens aside, most cruising is not an end in itself.

14. Simpson (1927, 88). Simpson served as president of the Institute of Traffic Engineers (which later became the Institute of Transportation Engineers) from 1939 to 1941.

15. Hogentogler, Willis, and Kelley (1934). They made two trips on each of the three routes: from 16th Street and Alaska Avenue, from 37th Street and Tunlaw Road, and from Chevy Chase Circle.

16. Hogentogler, Willis, and Kelley (1934, 197).

17. Huber (1962, Table 7). The reported cruising distance for drivers who parked off-street was for those drivers who first cruised for curb parking and then parked off-street; they had a higher average cruising distance than did those who found a curb space, perhaps because the unsuccessful cruisers parked off-street after being unusually unlucky in the search for curb parking. Men were more likely than women to park at the curb: women comprised 26 percent of curb parkers but 57 percent of off-street parkers (Huber 1962, Table 3). Because cars possessed poor maneuvering capabilities in tight places at that time, parallel parking was a difficult chore for drivers who didn't have power steering and automatic transmissions, and this may help explain the gender difference.

18. Huber found that the average distance cruised for curb parking was 823 feet more in December than in November, and for off-street parking was 655 feet more. He estimated that, when compared with November, cruising in December created an additional 3,379 VMT per day, which was the equivalent of increasing total vehicle travel in the CBD by 20 percent. Because cruising increased VMT by 20 percent in December when compared with November, cruising VMT was at least 17 percent of total VMT in December (20% ÷ 120% = 17%).

19. The 1997 television episode, *An Unsuitable Job for a Woman*, based on the novel of the same name by P.D. James (1972) was presented by WGBH Boston.

20. Inwood (1966).

21. Thomson (1967, 367). Smeed and Wardrop (1964, 309) reported that "of the total bus and car passengers on central London streets the proportion travelling by bus is 70 percent between 9:30 a.m. and 5 p.m., and 77 percent in the peak travel period between 5 and 6 p.m."

22. Lloyd (1967, 371).

23. Levy-Lambert (1977, 303). The 1975 values are converted to their 2002 equivalents by the U.S. Consumer Price Index-All Urban Consumers. See also Levy-Lambert (1974).

24. *Bus + Bahn*, "Kommentar überflüssig," (August 1977, p. 2). Topp (1993, 85) reports that illegal parking is widespread in German cities, amounting to 40 to 50 percent of total parking. He also reports that, "Search traffic is repeatedly quoted as reaching peaks of 50 to 70 percent of the total car traffic in a city center," but says that accurate measurements are difficult (Topp 1993, 91). Another study of parking in the center of Aachen, Germany, reported that during normal traffic periods up to 40 percent of the drivers in the city center were searching for parking (Organisation for Economic Cooperation and Development 1980, 57).

25. Salomon (1984, 208).

26. Shiftan (2002, 41). Yehuda Gur and Edward Beimborn (1984) developed a model of parking choice that included "looking time," which they defined as the time a driver must spend waiting to find a parking space. They tested the model in Haifa, and although they didn't report the looking times, their model shows that "the amount of time spent looking or waiting for a parking space is an increasing function of the utilization level of the parking area" (Gur and Beimborn 1984, 55).

27. O'Malley (1985, 8).

28. O'Malley (1985) estimated the share of traffic that was cruising by observing the share of newly vacated parking spaces occupied by the first driver who saw the space. See

Chapter 14 for a discussion of this method. The walking speed of two miles an hour takes into account waiting at stop lights to cross intersections.

29. Clark (1993a, 5).

30. Clark (1993b, 5).

31. Trillin (2001, 15-16). Consider also the parking regulations imposed by the Saint Paul, Minnesota, Department of Snow Emergency, as related on Garrison Keillor's *Prairie Home Companion* radio show of November 1, 2003. "In the event of snowfall we will plow the north side of residential streets between 8:45 and 11:35 this evening, followed by the south side, unless the snowfall is more than three inches, in which case one of the following will apply: cars with even-numbered license plates can park on odd-numbered sides of the street on Mondays, Tuesdays, or Thursdays, or on the east side, whichever is closest." After one resident got tired of moving his car back and forth, his wife recommended, "I have an idea. This time, just close the garage door and maybe they won't see our car."

32. Mel Gussow, "For Trillin, Parking Is an End, Not a Means," *New York Times* (February 2, 2002). Despite his expertise, Trillin now rents a garage and no longer parks on the street.

33. Abrahams (2000).

34. David Wallis, "Private Places in Public Spaces: The Zen of Alternate-Side Parking," *New York Times* (October 26, 2003).

35. Falcocchio, Darsin, and Prassas (1995). The Midtown, West Side research area is bounded by 6th and 10th Avenues between 54th and 57th Streets. The Midtown, East Side research area is bounded by Lexington and Madison Avenues between 25th and 33rd Streets. The Downtown, Fulton Street research area is bounded by Fulton Street, Park Row, the Brooklyn Bridge, and Gold Street. Cruising VMT are the product of the number of cars that park at the curb, the average search time per parking, and the average traffic speed in the area. (Parkings per hour) x (vehicle hours of cruising per parking) x (miles per hour) = VMT of cruising per hour.

36. Steve Rubenstein, "Car-sharing Program Can Free S. F. Drivers from Parking Hassles," *San Francisco Chronicle*, March 9, 2001.

37. Saltzman (1997, 79).

38. The calculation of 6.5 minutes of search time per driver who parked at the curb includes the search time of the other drivers who searched for but were unable to find curb parking. The observations of search time in other cities did not include the additional search time of drivers who were unable to find parking, so the average search times in these other cities may understate the total search time in those cities.

39. Saltzman (1997, 89).

40. Hensher (2001, 118).

41. Eno Foundation (1942, 16).

42. *Ward's Motor Vehicle Facts & Figures 2002.*

43. Smith and LeCraw (1946, 15).

44. "Solutions to South Provo Parking Issues Elude Officials," *Provo Daily Herald*, March 2004.

12

The Right Price for Curb Parking

It is no doubt ironic that the motorcar, superstar of the capitalist system, expects to live rent-free.

— *WOLFGANG ZUCKERMAN*

Free *curb* parking initiates the process of planning for free *off-street* parking. If curb parking is free, and developers do not supply enough off-street spaces to satisfy the demand for free parking, neighbors will complain about parking spillover (real, anticipated, or only imagined). These complaints lead urban planners and elected officials to increase the off-street parking requirements until the spillover problems are resolved. Rather than charge the right price for on-street parking, cities attempt to require the right quantity of off-street parking.

Planners usually do not have cruising on their minds when they set parking requirements. Instead, planners require off-street parking spaces to mitigate the effects of development, with free curb parking generally assumed as given. They try to estimate the traffic volume a project will add, as well as the number of parking spaces needed to accommodate the added traffic. Relying on the price of parking to match demand with supply is not an option in the present system.

Off-street parking requirements have become so entrenched in urban planning that complaining about them may seem futile, almost like complaining about gravity. Most drivers consider free curb parking an entitlement, and almost everyone takes off-street parking requirements for granted, as though they were absolutely essential. But free curb parking is *not* an entitlement, and more off-street parking is *not* the only way to keep curb spaces available. A better strategy is to charge the fair-market price for curb parking.

IS CURB PARKING A PUBLIC GOOD?

Some people think cities should not charge for curb parking because it is a public good, but curb parking is exactly the opposite of what economists define as a public good. Public goods have two economic characteristics. First, they are nonrival in consumption: one person's use does not reduce the amount left for everyone else. My listening to a radio broadcast, for example, doesn't prevent anyone else from listening. Second, public goods are nonexclusive: once the good has been produced, charging for it is difficult because no one can be excluded from receiving its benefits.[1] Again, once a radio program has been broadcast, charging the listeners for tuning in is difficult. Radio programs are therefore public goods, even if they are privately provided. Curb parking has *neither* characteristic of a public good, even if it is publicly provided. First, it is rival in consumption because only one car can occupy a parking space at a time. Second, charging for parking is easy. Curb parking spaces are much closer to *private* goods than to *public* goods. Moreover, the social costs of *not* charging for curb parking—traffic congestion, air pollution, accidents, wasted time, and wasted fuel—are enormous.

TIME LIMITS

Most cities deal with a shortage of curb parking by limiting the time allowed in curb spaces; that is, cities undercharge for curb parking and rely on time limits to create turnover. Columbia University economist and Nobel Laureate William Vickrey published several articles on parking, and in 1954 he explained why time limits are an inefficient way to manage parking spaces:

> Such regulations are, almost necessarily, highly inefficient in the rationing of parking space. If no one would want to park more than the allotted time, the regulation has no effect, while if there is someone who has an urgent need to park for two hours, say, in a one-hour space, he will be barred and have to go elsewhere to a less convenient space even if his need is greater and he would have been willing to pay much more for the privilege than would the two one-hour parkers he might displace.[2]

Time limits are not only inefficient but also difficult to enforce. Surveys often show that more than half of all cars parked in zones with time-limited free parking either violate the time limit or are in an illegal space. In Seattle, for example, a study of on-street parking in 35 areas found that the *average* parking duration in spaces with a one-hour time limit was 2.1 hours.[3] Even if they don't violate the time limits, drivers can evade them by moving their cars regularly. In describing the daily game of "parking bingo" played by downtown workers in Fresno, California, the *Fresno Bee* reported, "Employees even leave in pairs during the day to trade prime stalls...workers fend off rogue cars by standing in the space."[4] A study in Alexandria, Virginia, found that school custodians regularly moved teachers' cars to a new curb space every three hours to evade the time limits.[5] The school district thus spent the public's money to defeat the city's regulations. Time limits invite this sort of cumbersome and illegal evasion. Enforcement is expensive, and the city earns income only from fines—a politically unpopular revenue source with high collection costs.

THE RIGHT PRICE

Rather than limit the duration of curb parking, cities can charge the right price for it. What is this right price? The right price will balance the demand for parking—which varies over time—with the fixed supply of curb spaces. The right price may be high or low, but there will be no shortage, and drivers will not have to search for a parking space.

If the goal of right pricing is to achieve a curb-space vacancy rate that allows drivers to park without cruising, what would this rate be? Traffic engineers usually recommend that about 15 percent of curb spaces—one space in every seven—should remain vacant to ensure easy ingress and egress.[6] This cushion of vacant spaces eliminates the need to cruise, and a few spaces will generally be vacant within a block or two from any point. If we accept this recommendation, the right price for curb parking will vary throughout the day. At noon in the Central Business District (CBD), for example, when everyone is going to lunch or running errands, and couriers are jockeying to get close to their destinations, the price of curb parking will be high. At 7 p.m. in the same place, when most people have headed home, the demand will plunge, and the price will go down with it. Figure 12-1 illustrates this market-clearing price for curb parking (the price at which the quantity demanded equals supply). The supply of curb spaces on a street is fixed, so a vertical line positioned at the 85 percent occupancy rate represents the supply of curb spaces available with a 15 percent vacancy rate. The demand curve for curb parking slopes downward, and the point where it intersects the vertical supply curve shows the price that will "clear the market" for curb spaces. (The market-clearing price equates the quantity demanded and quantity supplied, and achieves market equilibrium. The market is "cleared" of shortages and

Figure 12-1. The Market Price of Curb Parking

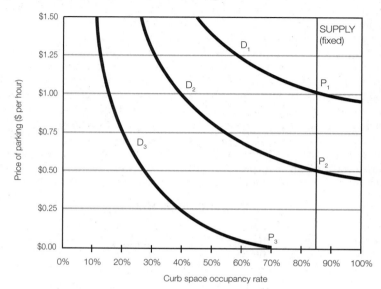

surpluses.) If the price is too low, overcrowding and cruising result. If it is too high, many spaces remain vacant and a valuable resource is underused. In this hypothetical example, when parking demand is high (curve D_1), $1 an hour is the right price. When demand is moderate (curve D_2), 50¢ an hour is the right price. And when demand is low (curve D_3), the occupancy rate is only 70 percent even with free parking, so the right price is zero. Even a low price is too high if many spaces are empty, and a high price is too low if all spaces are full.

William Vickrey recommended this variable-price policy in 1954. He proposed that parking meters should be interconnected and that curb parking prices should be set

> at a level so determined as to keep the amount of parking down sufficiently so that there will almost always be space available for those willing to pay the fee.... The meters could be arranged so that whenever more than say 3 out of 20 spaces [15 percent] are vacant, there would be no charge; whenever only 3 spaces are unoccupied, a slight charge would be made; the charge would become higher as more spaces are occupied, and would be quite high if all of the spaces become occupied.[7]

Parking should be free when occupancy is less than 85 percent at a zero price because it is then a public good in the sense that the marginal cost of adding another user is zero. But as demand increases, the public good becomes crowded, and it takes time to find a vacant space, so the marginal cost of adding another user increases. Because curb parking is in fixed supply, the price must increase to keep spaces available. Curb parking is a congestible public good with charges needed only when the occupancy would exceed 85 percent at a zero price.[8] The price that achieves an 85 percent occupancy rate is not a "free market" price; rather, it is a public price for a public service and should be set to achieve the public goals of improving transportation, land use, and the environment. With this pricing policy, Vickrey noted that "there would be an incentive for each parker to park as far as possible in locations where the demand is light, and there will be a natural tendency for the long-term parkers to park somewhat further away from the areas of heaviest demand."[9] The goal of pricing is to manage parking efficiently, and the city receives the revenue resulting from efficient management.

Regarding prices as a way to manage traffic, British transportation economist Phillip Goodwin distinguishes between two policies.[10] The first is "get the prices right: where travel is currently undercharged, getting the price right will reduce traffic." The second is "let's decide how much traffic we want, and then use prices to achieve it." Setting an 85 percent target occupancy rate for curb parking represents the second policy; for a typical block, this means one vacant space on each side of the street. Administrators do not choose the right price for curb parking; instead, the right price emerges as a result of choosing the right occupancy rate.[11] Once the target occupancy rate is selected, the meters can be dynamic, networked, self-organizing, and always "on."

If cities charge the right price for curb parking, they can do away with time limits as a way to create parking turnover. Cities can rely on prices alone to maintain a few curb vacancies and to create turnover. Prices cannot constantly fluctuate to maintain an occupancy rate of *exactly* 85 percent, of course, but they can vary frequently enough to avoid chronic overcrowding or underuse. If about 15 percent of spaces are vacant, the price is right.[12]

How would cities charge variable prices for curb parking throughout the day? The basic idea is simple, and Chapter 15 describes a variety of electronic parking meters that can charge variable prices. Suppose experience shows the right price to achieve a few vacancies is zero from midnight to 6 a.m.; 25¢ an hour from 6 a.m. to 8 a.m.; $1 an hour from 8 a.m. to 6 p.m.; and 50¢ an hour from 6 p.m. until midnight. Suppose also that you arrive at 7 a.m. and want to stay three hours. How much money should you put in the meter? The first quarter you insert will give you one hour (until 8 a.m.). Each additional quarter after that will give you another 15 minutes. So you will have to pay $2.25 for the three hours (25¢ for the first hour, and $1 an hour for the next two). The meter shows the price of parking during each hour, and you simply get less time for your money during the peak hours. If you wanted to park for 24 hours, you would pay $13.50 (nothing for midnight to 6 a.m., 50¢ for 6 to 8 a.m., $10 for 8 a.m. to 6 p.m., and $3 for 6 p.m. to midnight). (See Table 12-1.)

Prices can be reviewed periodically to examine whether they are producing the target occupancy rate. If a parking shortage occurs regularly at any time—at lunchtime, for example—the city can reduce the number of minutes given for each quarter inserted. If a parking surplus occurs at any time, the city can increase the number of minutes for each quarter. With newer multispace electronic meters, the parking authority can monitor occupancy rates, remotely reconfigure the price schedules, and send the new rates wirelessly to all the meters in a neighborhood (see Chapter 15). These balancing adjustments will preserve vacancies during the peak hours and fill spaces that would otherwise be vacant during the off-peak hours. This arrangement differs only slightly from existing meters that have a uniform rate during the daytime and are free at night.

The familiar image of pushing quarters into a parking meter is used only to illustrate getting less time for your money at peak hours; with electronic meters that accept payment by credit cards, debit cards, and cell phones, the transactions are cashless and drivers don't have to carry a pocketful of change to pay for parking. Multispace meters can also display information on an interactive graphic screen, including variations in the price schedule. The information can be multilingual, include graphics, and guide the user through transactions. New York City, for example, uses multispace meters in central Manhattan to charge variable prices of $2 for the first hour, $3 for the second hour, and $4 for the third hour during the daytime, and $2 an hour during the evenings and on weekends.

Because cities now post the price of curb parking only on the meters themselves, drivers already have to park at the curb and go to the meter before they see how much they will pay. Different prices at different times of the day therefore will not increase drivers' uncertainty about the price of parking for any trip. Prices are also much easier to understand than

Table 12-1. Hypothetical Fee Rates for Parking Meters

Time of day	Price per hour	Minutes per 25¢
Midnight–6 a.m.	Free	
6 a.m.–8 a.m.	$0.25	60
8 a.m.–6 p.m.	$1.00	15
6 p.m.–midnight	$0.50	30

many of the existing signs for curb parking. If the prices are posted on the meters, there will be no uncertainty about how much drivers should pay for the time they want, and because these prices will produce vacancies everywhere, anyone who parks at the curb and then decides to leave because the price is too high will at least not have wasted any time in finding a curb space. Drivers usually learn from experience the price of curb parking in areas they frequently visit, and they can also learn to expect that the price will vary in predictable ways. As an aid in trip planning, cities can post the price schedules for curb parking on their web sites so that drivers can decide where to park before they make their journey. Eventually, in-vehicle navigation systems can include the pattern of both curb and off-street parking prices at the drivers' destinations.

A variable price for curb parking may seem impractical at first, but the price of metered curb parking already changes between daytime (when the meters operate) and nighttime (when parking is free).[13] Congestion tolls in Asia, Europe, and the U.S. vary to match the changing demand for travel with a fixed supply of road space. The price of gasoline also fluctuates in response to the balance between supply and demand, and it is hard to imagine gasoline being sold any other way. Indeed, when gasoline prices were controlled for a brief period in the 1970s, the results were disastrous. The long lines of cars at filling stations dramatically showed the disadvantages of not letting prices fluctuate according to supply and demand. Cruising for underpriced curb parking creates a similar phenomenon. Cruisers are mixed in traffic with those actually going somewhere, but they are comparable to cars waiting in line for underpriced gasoline, and they do more harm. Waiting in line for gas visibly wastes drivers' time, but cruising also invisibly congests traffic, pollutes the air, and squanders fuel.

The price of most commercial parking varies by time of day and day of the week. Parking lot operators instinctively raise prices whenever their occupancy rates regularly approach 100 percent, and some operators claim they do not own a "full" sign because they never need one. To set the prices for on-street parking, cities can use the traditional four-step process that commercial operators use to set prices for off-street parking:

1. Look to see if your lot is full or empty.
2. Check your competition.
3. If you are full and they are empty, raise your price.
4. If you are empty and they are full, lower your price.

Curb parking should not be priced *exactly* like privately owned off-street parking, however. Commercial operators aim to maximize private profits, not social benefits, and they can maximize profits with substantial vacancy rates because they face downward-sloping demand curves.[14] If the capital and operating costs of a parking lot are fixed regardless of the occupancy rate, the owner will achieve maximum revenue and profits at the occupancy rate where reducing the price to attract additional customers produces no additional revenue, even if the lower price attracts more customers. In other words, the number of new customers gained by lowering the price is not enough to offset the loss of revenue from existing customers who also pay the lower price. Figure 12-2 illustrates a case where the maximum revenue for a 100-space parking lot occurs with only a 50 percent occupancy rate. Price is on the X-axis, and the demand curve is a downward-sloping straight line, with 100 percent occupancy when the price is zero, and zero occupancy when the price is $1 an hour. The 85 percent occupancy rate occurs at a price of 15¢ an hour, and the total revenue is $12.75 an hour (15¢ x 85 occupied spaces = $12.75). The maximum revenue of $25 an hour occurs at a price of 50¢ an hour (50¢ x 50 occupied spaces = $25). If the goal is 85 percent occupancy to ensure the efficient use of the available parking supply, the total revenue is only about half the maximum possible revenue.[15]

Although profit-maximizing parking lot owners often operate with high vacancy rates, their pricing strategy shows how parking prices can be var-

Figure 12-2. Parking Prices, Occupancy, and Revenue

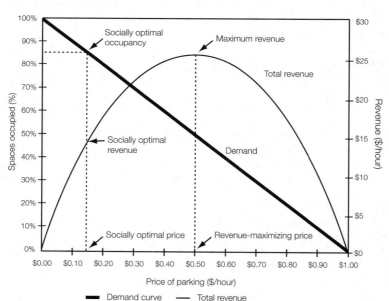

ied to manage a variable demand for curb parking spaces and to prevent the overcrowding that can seriously disrupt the transportation system.

Cruising and double parking are direct results of underpriced curb parking, and they greatly shrink the capacity of downtown streets. One double-parked car on a congested street can block an entire lane and back up traffic as far as the eye can see because all drivers must merge into the narrowed road space. Double parking and cruising do not stem from the private market's failure to supply the right amount of off-street parking. Instead, they stem from the government's failure to charge the right price for curb parking. If cities price curb parking to ensure a few vacancies, any increase in demand for the fixed supply of curb spaces will trigger an increase in their price, and shortages will not occur. Developers and merchants will be able to choose how many on-site spaces they want to supply for their customers, and cities will reap the value of any spillover parking as public revenue. The purpose of right-priced curb parking is not to gouge drivers or to maximize revenue. Instead, the right price for curb parking is *the lowest price that will avoid shortages*.

EXTERNAL COSTS OF CURB PARKING

Market prices for curb parking will eliminate cruising and allocate the available spaces efficiently among parkers. Curb parking also has external costs, however, and these costs may justify even higher prices for curb parking. Using the results of a Road Research Laboratory survey in England, in 1961 Alan Walters estimated the speed of urban traffic as a function of the traffic flow, the number of vehicles parked on both sides of the road, and the number of pedestrians crossing the road. The elasticity of speed with respect to the number of cars parked at the curb was -0.1, which suggests that a 10 percent increase in the number of parked cars reduces the speed of traffic by 1 percent.[16] Walters then estimated the external cost per vehicle-hour of curb parking by considering two factors: (1) the decrease in traffic speed for a small increase in the number of vehicles parked at the curb and (2) the total cost of the existing traffic flow. He estimated that the marginal external cost of curb parking was £0.11 per vehicle-hour in 1961 prices (£1.52 or $2.44 per vehicle-hour in 2002 prices).[17]

More recently, Taraknath Mazumder at the Indian Institute of Technology has analyzed how entering and exiting a curb parking space affects the traffic flow. He explains that a driver who intends to park at the curb starts decelerating before reaching the vacant space, and this starts a chain reaction. The vehicles following the decelerating vehicle also decelerate to maintain a safe headway distance from the preceding vehicle. Slight changes in the flow are propagated through the traffic flow as "shock waves" that quickly reduce speeds. Similar disturbances occur when a parked vehicle leaves the curb and enters the traffic flow. After a vehicle has parked or unparked, the following vehicles then accelerate to resume the normal speed, creating another shock wave similar to the deceleration phase, but in the reverse direction.[18] These traffic disturbances occur even if curb parking is priced to ensure vacancies and eliminate cruising. They are related to the number of parking events (entering or exiting a curb space) rather than to the number of cars parked at the curb. Each vehicle that parks at the curb creates two traffic disturbances, one while entering the curb space and one while leaving it. For a given parking duration and turnover rate, however, the number of parking events, and thus the external cost of curb parking, is proportional to the number of cars parked at the curb.

Mazumder videotaped traffic flows on three streets in Calcutta and used the results to estimate how the traffic disturbances created by curb parking reduced travel speeds. The average speeds on the three streets fell by 8 percent, 16 percent, and 18 percent. He also estimated that the external cost of curb parking exceeded the benefits to the curb parkers on the two streets where parking was free, while the benefits of curb parking exceeded the external costs on the one street where parking was priced.[19]

The external cost of curb parking clearly depends on a street's traffic flow. If traffic is light and turnover is low, the external cost will be low because few or no cars in traffic will be slowed by the cars entering and exiting the curb spaces. But if traffic is heavy, each parking entry and exit can significantly delay a large number of travelers. For this reason, the external cost of curb parking can exceed the market price needed to produce an 85 percent occupancy rate. If curb parkers impose external costs on other motorists, the price they pay for parking should at least cover this cost, even if the market-clearing price is lower. The price that produces 85 percent occupancy is thus the minimum that should be charged, and the question remains as to how high the price should be or whether curb parking should even be allowed. At hours and in places where the external cost is high enough, cities commonly prohibit curb parking to eliminate the traffic disturbances created by cars entering and exiting the curb spaces, and also to create an extra lane of travel on the roadway.

DEMAND-RESPONSIVE PRICES

Why are market-rate prices for curb parking so rare? Typically, a city council must pass a resolution to change parking meter rates anywhere in the city. Meter rates are therefore a political rather than an economic issue, and councilmembers naturally hesitate to raise the price that voters pay for parking. As a result, meter rates change infrequently, and the price of parking does not vary to match demand and supply. The fixed prices for curb parking lead to shortages when demand is high and to overcharges when demand is low. Given this inflexibility, how can cities charge market-rate prices for curb spaces?

Target Occupancy Rate

Market-clearing prices for curb parking present a classic conflict between economic efficiency and political popularity: the prices are necessary for efficient allocation, but they seem to be politically impossible. One way to skirt this conflict is to redefine the goal of parking policy. Instead of voting directly on the price of curb parking, a city council can establish a target occupancy rate—such as 85 percent—and instruct the parking authority to set the right prices to achieve this average rate. The parking authority can then monitor occupancy and charge the *lowest* price consistent with achieving the target rate. The political debate will no longer be about prices, but about occupancy rates, and the city council can dodge the responsibility for individual meter rates. Impersonal market forces, rather than individual councilmembers' votes, will determine the right price of curb parking. The target occupancy rate is the goal, and the price of curb parking is the means to achieve this goal.

If a city prices curb parking to achieve a target occupancy rate, drivers will be no more surprised to find that a vacant curb parking space is available at the peak hour than grocery shoppers are surprised to find blueberries on supermarket shelves in December or that prices fluctuate. The target occupancy rate is a clear goal to aim for, and everyone can see whether it is being achieved. Because many drivers are willing to pay for convenient curb parking and most cities need money to pay for public services, market-priced curb parking can make spaces available everywhere, improve transportation efficiency, and raise public revenue.

A Precedent: HOT Lanes

Market prices for crowded curb parking resemble congestion tolls for crowded freeways. Letting drivers' demand set congestion tolls is unusual but not unprecedented. On the I-15 freeway north of San Diego, single-occupant vehicles (SOVs) can pay a variable toll to use the high-occupancy vehicle (HOV) lanes, and the toll revenue is used to pay for additional public transit service in the corridor. Previously, the HOV lanes had excess capacity while the adjacent mixed-flow lanes suffered severe congestion. Irate solo drivers complained that the HOV lanes were an underused failure and argued that the lanes should be opened for use by all drivers. To take advantage of the unused capacity, the San Diego Association of Governments (SANDAG) instead offered solo drivers the option to buy permits to use the excess capacity on what are now known as high-occupancy/toll (HOT) lanes. As the demand for permits increased, however, higher tolls were needed to prevent congestion on the HOT lanes. Unwilling to pay more, solo drivers again protested. SANDAG's Board of Directors, which set the SOV tolls, did not want to raise them in the face of strong public opposition. Instead, the board chose a computerized system of SOV tolls that float up and down to ensure that the average speed stays above the target minimum of 54 miles an hour in the HOT lanes.[20] Demand automatically determines the tolls necessary to prevent congestion. High demand leads to high tolls, and low demand leads to low tolls. In a report to the California Legislature, SANDAG described the system:

> The per-trip fee varies dynamically in response to traffic conditions on the HOV lanes. The intent of variable fees is to keep the lanes free-flowing while maximizing their use…. Traffic volume data are used to determine when fees should be changed and to what level. The per-trip fee to use the HOV lanes at a fixed time (e.g., 7:15 a.m.) may not be the same from day to day or from month to month, because the fees are based on real-time conditions in the HOV lanes. System operations are based on a simple look-up table with maximum rates for various time periods. Every six minutes, data from the loop detectors at the tolling zone are read…and compared to a table to determine the price, which is then displayed on the electronic toll display signs. The price generally changes at $0.25 intervals and the system is structured such that the normal maximum price increase in any six-minute interval is $0.50.[21]

The toll for a solo driver typically ranges between 50¢ and $4 according to the amount of traffic, but it can rise as high as $8 in extraordinary circumstances, such as an accident in the free lanes. This dynamic pricing resembles a continuous auction for the available space in the HOT lanes, with tolls automatically adjusted every six minutes to clear the market: solo drivers participate in this auction by their decision whether to pay the tolls. Tollees thus pay the lowest price that will guarantee a fast trip in the carpool lane. If prices increase, public officials can simply wash their hands and say they didn't do it—the solo drivers did!

The I-15 pricing experiment is a great success.[22] The demand-determined tolls guarantee free-flowing traffic, and they provide a practical precedent for demand-determined parking prices. Parking prices need not change every six minutes, but they can change in response to changes in demand for the fixed supply of curb spaces. The solution to chronic overuse or underuse is obvious: *adjust the price*.[23] Putting the price of parking on automatic pilot to achieve a target occupancy rate—such as 85 percent—provides cover for public officials who fear voter opposition to price increases. In effect, demand—not the city council—sets the price necessary to prevent parking shortages. The city thus charges parkers the lowest price that will guarantee them a space.

Just as congestion tolls are adjusted up and down to achieve a target speed, parking prices can be adjusted up and down to achieve a target occupancy. The idea of charging dynamic, demand-determined parking prices is not new, and William Vickrey recommended them in 1954.[24] The primitive metering technology in the 1950s made Vickrey's idea appear outlandish, and his proposal became one of what he called his "innovative failures in economics."[25] Vickrey said that the proposal "was published with a gratuitous note by the editor to the effect that of course I agreed that the real solution was off-street parking, which was hardly true and certainly not warranted by anything I had written."[26]

CAN PRICES MANAGE CURB PARKING DEMAND?

If curb parking prices automatically adjust to achieve a target vacancy rate, drivers themselves will set parking prices through their own travel behavior. Curb parking can operate like a normal market—*after* elected officials have decided on the appropriate vacancy rate needed to make curb parking available without cruising.

Prices are a simple way to deliver a message about scarcity, but can they really manage curb parking efficiently? One well-designed and well-evaluated experiment showed that properly priced curb parking not only ensures vacancies but also improves the operation of the entire transportation system. This experiment is by far the most extensive research on the effects of parking prices ever undertaken. Conducted in central London in 1965, it showed the effects of curb parking price increases. The price of curb parking quadrupled in one area, doubled in the second, and remained unchanged in the third (see Figure 12-3).

To study how the price increases affected travel times, Britain's Road Research Laboratory conducted 620 park-and-visit tests before and after the price increases. Researchers drove to a chosen address and then recorded the time taken to find a vacant curb space. The driver also recorded the time taken to park the car at the curb, the time taken to walk to and from the address visited, and finally the time taken to unpark the car. The total park-and-visit time therefore measured the added travel time compared with the travel time experienced when drivers can park at the curb near the address they are visiting, without cruising.[27] If at least one parking space remains vacant on every block, drivers do not need to cruise, and they can park close to their destinations. Not spending time cruising and walking a long way to the destination decreases the time

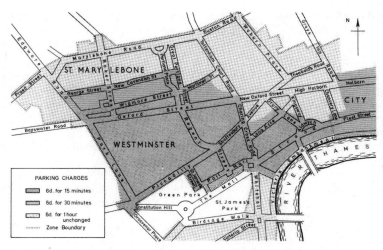

Figure 12-3. Distribution of New Parking Meter Charges in London Parking Zones, May 1965

price that drivers pay for a trip. The time price of travel fell when the money price of curb parking increased.

The Road Research Laboratory's drivers visited each of 31 addresses, 10 times before and 10 times after parking prices increased. The addresses were not randomly chosen but were instead important business and tourist destinations, such as the National Gallery. Fifteen addresses were in an area where the price of curb parking quadrupled to £0.10 an hour (£1.56 or $2.50 an hour in 2002 prices).[28] Eleven were in the area where the price doubled to £0.05 an hour (£0.78 or $1.25 an hour in 2002), and five were in an area where the price remained unchanged at £0.025 an hour (£0.39 or $0.62 an hour in 2002).

Table 12-2 shows the average park-and-visit times in the three areas before and after the parking price increases. Where prices quadrupled, the average park-and-visit time declined by 66 percent. Where prices doubled, the average park-and-visit time declined by 38 percent. And where prices did not change, the average park-and-visit time remained almost the same. The reductions in park-and-visit time saved drivers 8.35 minutes of travel time per trip where prices quadrupled and 3.08 minutes where prices doubled.

Where parking prices increased, the park-and-visit time fell because all three of its components—cruising, parking, and walking—declined. The reduced search time accounts for most of the reduction in the park-and-

Table 12-2. Park-and-Visit Times Before and After Parking Prices Increased in London (minutes per trip)

Parking price change	Search time			Parking time			Walking time			Total park-and-visit time			
	Before	After	Change	Before	After	Change	Before	After	Change	Before	After	Change	% Change
Quadruple	6.10	1.04	-5.06 **	0.56	0.37	-0.19 **	6.04	2.94	-3.10 **	12.70	4.35	-8.35 **	-66% **
Double	3.46	1.40	-2.06 *	0.50	0.42	-0.08	4.19	3.24	-0.95	8.14	5.06	-3.08 *	-38% *
No change	3.55	3.32	-0.23	0.47	0.52	0.05	5.75	5.53	-0.22	9.77	9.37	-0.40	-4%

** statistically significant at 1% level.
* statistically significant at 5% level.
Source: Inwood (1966, Table 2)

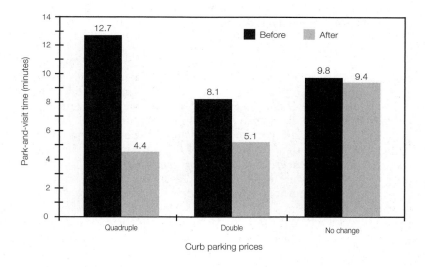

visit time. The average search time declined by 83 percent where parking prices quadrupled and by 60 percent where parking prices doubled. The elasticity of search time with respect to the price of curb parking was -1.26 where prices quadrupled and -1.18 where prices doubled.[29] These results suggest that where all curb spaces were occupied, a 10 percent increase in the price of curb parking reduced the average search time necessary to find a parking space by about 12 percent.[30]

Table 12-3 shows the park-and-visit times at each of the 15 destinations in the area where parking prices quadrupled. The park-and-visit times declined at 14 of the 15 destinations, with the declines ranging up to 95 percent.

Predictability of travel time is an important goal for a transportation system, but the time needed to find underpriced curb parking is highly unpredictable. When all curb spaces are occupied, the major determinant of search time is luck. Finding a space may take less than a minute if you pull up just as someone else is pulling out, or it may take half an hour. Drivers who want to avoid arriving late must therefore begin their trips early in case it takes a long time to find a parking space. The last row in Table 12-3 shows that the standard deviation (a measure of expected variability) of the total park-and-visit time decreased by 59 percent after parking prices increased.[31] Since raising the price of curb parking reduced the variability in the time required to find a curb space, it also reduced the *uncertainty* of travel time, which is yet another benefit of right-priced parking.

The three photographs of Grosvenor Square in Figure 12-4 show how the increase in meter rates led to an increase in curb vacancies, which in turn reduced the park-and-visit times. Photograph (a), taken just before parking meters (the first in Britain) were installed in 1958, shows that all curb spaces were occupied and many cars were double parked.[32] Photograph (b), taken just before the meter rates increased in May 1965, shows that all spaces were still occupied, but double parking had disappeared. Photograph (c), taken in August 1965 after parking prices quadrupled, shows that vacant spaces appeared and drivers could park near the addresses visited without cruising. After the price increase, the average time that drivers spent cruising fell from 6.1 minutes per trip to 1.04 minutes, or by 83 percent (Tables 12-2 and 12-3). The reduced search time accounted for 61 percent of the park-and-visit time saved after the price increase.[33]

The addresses where the price of curb parking quadrupled are in one of the wealthiest residential precincts on earth. The photographs in Figure 12-4 were taken on Grosvenor Square in Mayfair—names almost synonymous with wealth—where one might doubt that raising parking prices to £0.10 an hour in 1965 could dramatically reduce demand. But the Road Research Laboratory's evidence showed that even here parking demand was sensitive to price. Note especially the decline in the number of Rolls Royces parked (and double parked) at the curb as the price of curb parking increased.

Market-rate prices for curb parking in a place like Grosvenor Square are not unfair. Writing in the middle of the last century (when many motorists still assumed curb parking should be free as a matter of right), the economists Alan Day and Ralph Turvey argued that cities should charge for on-street parking because motorists do not have "the right to leave motor cars in the road any more than the right to leave pianos there." To be fair, they said, on-street parking in London should cost as much as parking in adjacent off-street garages:

Table 12-3. Park-and-Visit Times Before and After Parking Prices Quadrupled in London (minutes per trip)

Destination	Search time Before	Search time After	Parking time Before	Parking time After	Walking time Before	Walking time After	Total park-and-visit time Before	Total park-and-visit time After	Change	% Change
Cumberland Hotel	2.91	2.45	0.73	0.41	6.20	4.47	9.84	7.33	-2.51	-26%
British Standards Institution	1.56	0.09	0.51	0.23	3.61	0.56	5.68	0.88	-4.80	-85%
Selfridge's Store	2.90	2.10	0.49	0.55	4.01	5.20	7.40	7.85	0.45	6%
Fenwick's Store	10.88	2.37	0.50	0.64	6.83	5.71	18.21	8.72	-9.49	-52%
Canada Office	1.59	0.20	0.69	0.22	4.73	1.42	7.01	1.84	-5.17	-74%
Claridge's Hotel	5.53	1.38	0.77	0.80	5.71	2.29	12.01	4.47	-7.54	-63%
Berkeley Square House	4.90	0.44	0.85	0.51	7.23	1.58	12.98	2.53	-10.45	-81%
Queen's Theatre	13.18	0.46	0.45	0.46	6.57	2.92	20.20	3.84	-16.36	-81%
Peter Robinson's Store	10.97	1.05	0.58	0.22	7.37	3.96	18.92	5.23	-13.69	-72%
John Lewis Store	9.48	1.48	0.50	0.47	8.10	2.93	18.08	4.88	-13.20	-73%
Stuart House	8.06	0.11	0.55	0.22	6.36	0.37	14.97	0.70	-14.27	-95%
Ritz Hotel	11.49	1.00	0.54	0.20	8.63	5.60	20.66	6.80	-13.86	-67%
Charles House	2.82	1.08	0.35	0.15	4.46	2.07	7.63	3.30	-4.33	-57%
National Gallery	2.50	0.75	0.29	0.21	6.49	2.83	9.28	3.79	-5.49	-59%
Bush House	2.68	0.67	0.56	0.19	4.30	2.24	7.54	3.10	-4.44	-59%
Average	**6.10**	**1.04**	**0.56**	**0.37**	**6.04**	**2.94**	**12.70**	**4.35**	**-8.35**	**-66%**
Standard deviation	4.14	0.78	0.15	0.20	1.53	1.72	5.38	2.47	-4.44	-59%

Source: Inwood (1966, Table 2)

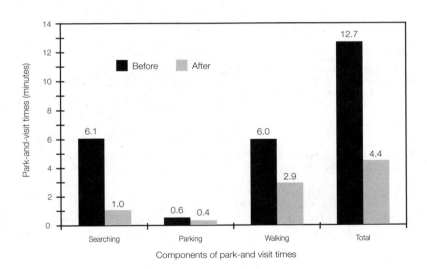

(a) Before the first West End parking meters, Feb. – March 1958 (note double banking on right)

(b) With parking meters at 6 pence per hour. April, 1959 (all available meter space occupied—typical of conditions until May, 1965.)

(c) With parking meters at 2 shillings per hour August, 1965 (plenty of vacant meter space)

British Road Research Laboratory

Figure 12-4. Grosvenor Square; effects of parking meter price increases on availability of curb parking.

The reason why a charge [for on-street parking] should be made is basically one of fairness. It can be assumed that visitors parking in garages would do so because they could not find a vacant space in any permitted [on-street] parking place. If parking in the garage costs, say 2s. 6d. [two shillings and six pence, or £0.125], this means that they would be prepared to pay about the same for space in the street. Why should those visitors lucky enough to arrive when a [street] space was vacant obtain free what someone else would be willing to pay 2s. 6d. for?... As a general rule, then, the parking meter should charge at approximately the same rate as neighbouring garages. This rate would not be the same in different parts of town nor should it be, since space is not equally scarce in different parts. Where space is most scarce it must be most expensive so that the incentive to economise in its use is strongest.[34]

Underpricing curb parking is no fairer than giving discounts on other public services merely on the basis of chance. Everyone would be outraged, for example, if cities allocated public housing on a first-come, first-served basis to anyone who wanted it, even to a rich miser. Allocating curb parking by cruising is not only unfair (in the sense that it randomly rewards a few lucky drivers), but it also wastes drivers' time and increases traffic congestion. Curb parking is a valuable public asset, and underpricing it is fiscally, socially, and environmentally irresponsible.

Pricing curb parking to ensure a few vacancies and reduce cruising does not mean that travel will become unaffordable. As drivers adapt to the higher monetary cost of parking and lower time cost of driving, they can employ several strategies to economize on parking:

1. They can reduce their parking durations.
2. They can carpool and split the cost of parking.
3. They can park off-street.
4. They can divert some trips to off-peak hours when parking is cheaper.
5. They can make more trips by public transit, cycling, and walking.

Each strategy reduces peak-hour parking use. Note especially that diverting trips to walking, cycling, high-occupancy vehicles, and public transit reduces *vehicle* travel without reducing *human* travel. The many ways to economize on parking show public transit is not the only alternative to solo driving and the availability of public transit is not a prerequisite to charging market prices for curb parking.

The phenomenon of latent demand makes it difficult to predict the price that will maintain a 15 percent curb vacancy rate. For example, suppose that raising the price of curb parking reduces the average parking duration by 15 percent. This might seem sufficient to create vacancies and eliminate cruising. But some of the vacant spaces may be quickly filled by drivers who had been cruising or who had opted instead to park off-street, and the appearance of even a few vacancies may attract new drivers who had previously been deterred by the shortage of parking. The price necessary to maintain a few curb vacancies will therefore be higher than what would be necessary to reduce the parking duration by 15 percent. Still, the evidence suggests that market prices for curb parking can create enough vacancies to guarantee easy parking access and eliminate cruising.

TWO LATER OBSERVATIONS

The Road Research Laboratory discontinued its park-and-visit studies after 1965, but while on a visit to London in 1983, I repeated the measurements for the 15 addresses in the area where meter prices had quadrupled in 1965. Although the price of meter parking had increased from £0.10 an hour in 1965 to £0.60 an hour by 1983, the general price level had increased even faster, so the real price of meter parking (after accounting for inflation) had fallen 19 percent since 1965.

A vacant meter space on Grosvenor Square—or anywhere else—was a rare sight. I visited each address once. The average search time was 7.9 minutes, not very different from the 6.1 minutes the Road Research Laboratory found in 1965 before meter prices increased, and well above the 1.04 minutes after meter prices increased. The longest search time was 27 minutes at the National Gallery, where I was caught in (and contributed to) a huge traffic jam. Excluding the observation for the National Gallery, the average search time was 6.6 minutes, almost the same found 18 years earlier before meter prices increased in 1965.[35] This result shows that if meter prices do not keep up with parking demand, all the old problems return (see Table 12-4).

Parking meter rates in London have increased rapidly in recent years. In July 2001, I again visited Grosvenor Square. The meter rate was by then £4

Table 12-4. Park-and-Visit Times in London in 1983 (minutes per trip)

Destination	Cruising	Parking	Walking	Total
Cumberland Hotel	14.05	0.10	15.42	29.57
British Standards Institution	1.33	0.67	3.07	5.07
Selfridge's Store	11.83	0.82	9.17	21.82
Fenwick's Store	15.23	0.62	3.38	19.23
Canada Office	3.70	0.60	6.45	10.75
Claridge's Hotel	4.48	1.02	3.77	9.27
Berkeley Square House	2.87	1.42	3.87	8.16
Queen's Theatre	5.00	0.30	15.00	20.30
Peter Robinson's Store	2.68	0.77	6.67	10.12
John Lewis Store	8.28	0.00	9.00	17.28
Stuart House	1.85	0.98	1.00	3.83
Ritz Hotel	8.32	2.07	7.67	18.06
Charles House	1.08	0.58	3.53	5.19
National Gallery	26.67	0.58	13.00	40.25
Bush House	11.25	1.25	12.70	25.20
Average (1983)	**7.91**	**0.79**	**7.58**	**16.27**
Average (1965) **before price increase**	**6.10**	**0.56**	**6.04**	**12.70**
Average (1965) **after price increase**	**1.04**	**0.37**	**2.94**	**4.35**
Standard deviation (1983)	6.77	0.51	4.51	9.93

(about $6) an hour, and there were a few vacancies, with cars frequently either entering or leaving a parking space, suggesting high turnover. These observations indicate that market-rate parking prices can create curb vacancies and turnover even in a wealthy area with high parking demand.

CONCLUSION: CHARGE THE RIGHT PRICE FOR CURB PARKING

Cruising is not the only form of queuing, of course. When going to a movie you may search for a parking space, wait in line to buy a ticket, wait in another line to gain admission, and then in yet another line to buy popcorn before the movie begins. But these other forms of queuing are different from cruising because they only waste your time. Cruising also congests traffic, wastes fuel, and pollutes the air. Cities thus create serious problems when they underprice curb parking. If cities charge the right price for curb parking, drivers will always be able to find a convenient place to park at their destination, without cruising. "Get the prices right" is an axiom in public economics, and the right price for curb parking is the lowest price that will keep a few spaces vacant everywhere. But if cities charge the wrong price for curb parking, drivers waste an astonishing amount of time and fuel in cruising and create a catastrophic amount of traffic congestion and air pollution.

CHAPTER 12 NOTES

1. See Friedman (2002, 596) or Stiglitz (1988, 75) for the definition of public goods.

2. Vickrey (1954, 62).

3. Seattle Strategic Planning Office (2000, 16). Drivers have been violating time limits for a long time. Miller McClintock (1924, 360) wrote, "Theoretically, these provisions [time limits] do away with the 'street hog' and make it possible for the drivers of vehicles to use the street in rotation. In actual practice, however, they have but little effect, for they cannot be enforced. It is estimated in most cities that if the entire police force had no other duty than the enforcement of parking restrictions, they would not be able to accomplish the task well. Evasion is made easy by the fact that owners can move their cars a short distance and thus gain the use of the street for another interval." In 1937, the Chairman of the Traffic Committee of the Rochester Engineering Society reported "In the eleven annual surveys we made in Rochester, where there were no meters, over 50 percent of all cars have overstayed their time limits, and I believe this same ratio obtains in every city in the state, because time-limit parking without meters cannot be enforced 100 percent"(Brown 1937, 54). In a survey of nonmetered parking, Buxton Williams and Jon Ross (2003) found that 45 percent of the parking spaces were illegally occupied. Even in normally law-abiding Germany, Hartmut Topp (1991, 4) reports that 40 to 50 percent of total parking is illegal.

4. These periodic parking maneuvers waste time and occasionally lead to confrontations. "Patrick Ortiz, 42, acknowledges he can do it [fend off another car] only so long, based on a driver's determination and 'depending on the size of the car'" (*Fresno Bee*, July 16, 2000). University of Chicago law professor Richard Epstein (2001, 13) says, "confrontations do happen when would-be parkers ask a family member or friend to stand guard by occupying the parking place until they are able to arrive—sometimes only for a minute but often for longer periods of time.... The practice therefore necessarily reduces the carrying capacity of the road and often leads to ugly confrontations when frustrated drivers seek to edge their way into parking places defiantly occupied by their redoubtable holders."

5. Olsson and Miller (1979).

6. Brierly (1972), May (1975), and Witheford and Kanaan (1972).

7. Vickrey (1954, 64). Vickrey may be the first to recommend what are now known as pay-by-space meters, with several conventional meters mounted on a single post, and with numbers painted on the pavement to identify which space corresponds to which meter. He speculated that "Possibly five to seven spaces is about as many as can conveniently be controlled together on this basis" (Vickrey 1954, 67), and this turns out to be the number of spaces typically controlled by a modern pay-by-space meter. He even noted that snow on the ground will cover the numbers painted on the sidewalk and will create a difficulty with this arrangement.

8. Bryan Ellickson (1973) analyzes congestion of public goods, which he calls crowding. "When the addition of another consumer increases the resources required to maintain the level of public good consumed by all, we will refer to the public good as 'crowded'" (Ellickson 1973, 417).

9. Vickrey (1954, 64). Quite aside from eliminating shortages, market prices allocate parking spaces to the drivers who value them the most, which is a great advantage. Edward Glaeser and Erzo Luttmer (2003) explain how rent control in New York allocates valuable apartments to some residents who place a low value on them, such as those who use them for only a few weeks a year. Similarly, with underpriced curb parking, some drivers occupy spaces on which they place a low value, while other drivers who place a high value on parking must circle the block searching for an opening.

10. Goodwin (2001, 29). These two approaches have been called price-type and quantity-type policies to dealing with externalities.

11. Vickrey (1955, 618) wrote, "Metering of curb parking on marginal cost principles would thus require rather substantial fluctuations in the rate per hour as the degree of occupancy fluctuates in the neighborhood of 100 percent." He thus envisioned a very steep supply curve, not a vertical one implied by a target occupancy rate, such as 85 percent. To derive this supply curve, he recommended estimating the marginal social cost of cruising and using this cost to set the price of curb parking. Because this estimate of social cost requires so much information, a target occupancy rate is much simpler to aim for and would produce much the same result.

12. Most cities cite turnover as the goal of installing meters, but market prices will create high turnover even without time limits. If the goal is to create even faster turnover, Robert Saltzman (1994) recommends that price per hour should increase for longer parking durations. For example, the price of parking for three hours would be more than three times the price of parking for one hour. Time limits on curb parking, however, shift the demand curves downward, reduce the market-clearing price of parking, and reduce the revenue from curb parking. Cities can, of course, choose a target occupancy rate lower than 85 percent if they want fewer cars parked on the street. To create more road space for traffic, a city can ban parking on one side of a street, for example. Or to take into account the random variability of parking demand, a city can aim for an average occupancy of 75 percent so that the actual occupancy rate will reach 100 percent less often.

13. Conventional meters are free at night even though the curb spaces may be crowded. Free parking at night probably stems from the idea that parking meters are intended to create turnover. It does not make sense to have one-hour parking meters enforced at 3 a.m., but it does make sense to charge for parking if it is scarce. When spaces are allocated by prices rather than time limits, the price may be lower at night but need not be zero.

14. Richard Epstein (2001, 25) states that "Presumably, the ideal system [of charging for curb parking] is one in which the City maximized its revenue from use." But this confuses the goals of a city with the goals of commercial parking operators, who aim to maximize profits, not social benefits. If the goal of pricing curb parking is to achieve a 15 percent vacancy rate, higher prices and a lower occupancy rate can increase revenues but leave too many spaces empty.

15. In a study of parking in downtown Los Angeles, for example, a survey in 2003 found that the occupancy rates of off-street parking lots and garages was only 38 percent on Saturday afternoon, and only 10 percent on weekday evenings (Kimley-Horn and Associates 2003). A parking survey in Tempe, Arizona, found that only 52 percent of all spaces were occupied on a Friday evening when parking was hard to find (Minett 1994). Commercial parking operators face downward-sloping demand curves because they are in "monopolistic competition." If all costs are fixed regardless of the occupancy rate, the owner will maximize revenue and profits at the price where the elasticity of demand is unity. If demand is inelastic (less than unity), raising prices will increase revenue and profits. If demand is elastic (greater than unity), reducing prices will increase revenue and profits. If costs are fixed, maximum profits will accrue only at the price where the elasticity of demand is unity. Commercial parking operators charge higher prices for short-term than for long-term parking because at the same price per hour the demand for long-term parking is more elastic than the demand for short-term parking. Operators divide the supply between long- and short-term parking to take advantage of the differing elasticities of the two demands. Similarly, early-bird rates discriminate in favor of commuters who do not have monthly permits, presumably because they arrive early and are more sensitive to the geographic pattern of prices than are the occasional all-day parkers who usually arrive later. Where operating costs increase with higher occupancy rates, a profit-maximizing owner will raise prices above the unit-elastic price because a reduced operating cost will compensate for the reduced total revenue. At times when the maximum revenue is less than the cost of remaining open, the parking lot will close.

16. Walters (1961). This elasticity was estimated for conditions of average traffic flow and speed, number of cars parked at the curb, and number of pedestrians. The elasticity was -0.17 when the number of cars parked at the curb was one standard deviation above the average. The parking turnover rate would also presumably affect the traffic flow.

17. This external cost was estimated for conditions of average traffic flow and speed, number of cars parked at the curb, and number of pedestrians. The marginal external cost would be lower if the price of parking reduced the number of parked cars. The 1961 value was converted to 2002 prices by the British Retail Price Index and then converted to U.S. dollars at an exchange rate of £1 = $1.60. Walters (1961, 162) acknowledged the slender empirical basis for his estimate, but he concluded that "efficient prices should be charged for roadside parking."

18. Mazumder (2004, 8-10). Yousif and Purnawan (1999) studied drivers' parking maneuvers when entering and leaving curb spaces in Manchester, England. They found that entering a parking space creates more delay for the moving traffic because the parkers force the moving traffic to either reduce speed, swerve, or sometimes stop. When leaving, drivers usually wait and choose an acceptable safe gap in the moving traffic, and therefore have a smaller effect on the traffic flow.

19. Mazumder (2004, Chapter 5). The reductions in speed were caused by the cars entering and exiting the curb spaces, rather than by the cars that remained at the curb. The traffic flows on the three streets were reduced by 4 percent, 9 percent, and 5 percent.

20. The goal is to maintain at least Level of Service C in the HOT lanes. The *Highway Capacity Manual* defines Level of Service on a road in six letter-grade categories, with A referring to the highest quality and F to the lowest. Level of Service C on a freeway refers to an average speed of greater than 54 miles an hour and a maximum density of 30 passenger cars per lane-mile (Transportation Research Board 1985, 3-8).

21. San Diego Association of Governments (1999, 8). Phase I, with monthly passes, ran from December 1996 through March 1998. Phase II, with electronic toll collection and per-trip charges using variable pricing, began in April 1998. Information about the project is available online at http://argo.sandag.org/fastrak/info.html.

22. See Hultgren and Kawada (1999, 24) for a discussion of how dynamic pricing shifts the toll-setting responsibility from politicians to drivers. SANDAG refers to the I-15 HOV lanes open to SOVs as Express Lanes, and they refer to the program as the FasTrak program. Information on the project is available online at www.sandag.cog.ca.us/. Because otherwise-unused capacity on HOV lane is being sold to solo drivers, some people are better off and no one is worse off—the program is Pareto-optimal.

23. In his debate with Friedrich Hayek over the efficiency of socialist economies, Oskar Lange (1936) proposed that socialist managers should employ the trial-and-error method to set prices: move prices up when shortages appear and down when excess supply appears. Market-clearing prices for curb parking thus have a good capitalist *and* socialist pedigree. Lange's advice turned out to be wildly unrealistic for managing socialist economies, but it works well for a parking lot.

24. Vickrey (1994, 1-2) proposed varying the rates charged by groups of parking meters according to the number of occupied spaces in the area, "the idea being to make parking free or nearly so whenever there are plenty of vacancies, and to vary the charge at other times to correspond to the cost to others of having to look further for a space." The original proposal was published in Vickrey (1954) and was reprinted in Vickrey (1994).

25. The title of Vickrey's 1992 Presidential Address to the Atlantic Economic Society was "My Innovative Failures in Economics" (Vickrey 1993). He noted that demand-determined parking prices were his first venture into marginal-cost pricing.

26. Vickrey (1993, 2). Vickrey's original 1954 proposal for market-priced curb parking was republished in Vickrey (1994, 56-65). In a preface to the 1954 article, the editor wrote about Vickrey's proposal that "unfortunately, the complexity of the system proposed is such that there is much room for doubt as to its practicability.... Of course, Mr. Vickery [*sic*] agrees that no substantial part of the parking problem can ever be solved with on-street parking no matter how efficiently such space is utilized" (Vickrey 1954, 62).

27. Inwood (1966, 2) states: "A car is driven to a chosen address, and a timed street search for a vacant parking meter space (within approximately one-quarter of a mile of the address visited) then takes place. When a vacant meter space has been found, the time taken to park the car at the curb is recorded, as are the times taken to walk to and from the door of the address 'visited.' Finally, the time taken to extract the car from the meter bay is recorded. In central London the strategy used in searching for vacant meters is determined very largely by the restriction of movement to available one-way streets leading to the nearest known meter parking places, examined in the order of their nearness to the address visited."

28. The pound sterling is adjusted to 2002 values by the British Retail Prices Index and converted to dollars at an exchange rate of $1.60 = £1.

29. Elasticity is calculated using the midpoint formula for elasticity of demand. See Mansfield (1983, 533) or Samuelson and Nordhaus (1989, 425) for an explanation of the midpoint formula.

30. The 12 percent reduction in search time results from the 10 percent increase in parking price multiplied by the -1.2 elasticity of search time with respect to the price of parking.

31. The standard deviations in the last row of Table 12-2 refer to the average values at the 15 sites, and the standard deviations of the 150 individual observations (ten at each site) would be higher. Table 12-2 thus understates how market-priced curb parking will reduce the uncertainty of travel time.

32. In his research on parking in Haarlem (the Netherlands), D. van der Goot (1982) found curb space occupancy rates (number of parked cars as a percentage of parking spaces legally available) of up to 400 percent. In his attempt to predict parking locations, he estimated that drivers were dissuaded from parking only when the legal curb space occupancy rates exceeded 120 percent.

33. Tables 12-2 and 12-3 show that the 5.06-minute decline in search time accounted for 61 percent of the 8.35-minute decline in the total park-and-visit time where parking prices quadrupled.

34. Day and Turvey (1954, 411).

35. Discussing the effects of the increased meter charges in 1965, Inwood (1966, 4) predicted, "Past experience of London street parking suggests that the reduced meter congestion following the introduction of the 2 shillings [£0.10] an hour charge may not continue undiminished for very long, and it would be unwise to infer that the charge is too high and ought to be reduced." He was right.

13

Choosing to Cruise

One has only to observe a flustered driver, desperately trying to park his car when there is no parking to be found, in order to see that we do not always act in accordance with the rationality principle.

— *KARL POPPER*

How do you choose whether to cruise or to pay? This chapter presents a simple model to help answer this question. Developing a model of rational cruising may seem pointless because some drivers resist paying for parking under any circumstances and do not seem to behave rationally when they cruise. But even though an economic model cannot predict how *everyone* chooses to cruise, we should not assume most drivers are irrational. In any case, the model shows how to be rational when you cruise, and its predictions are testable.

TO CRUISE OR TO PAY

To set the scene for the model, suppose curb parking is free but so crowded you have to spend time hunting for a space.[1] You can park off-street without waiting, but you have to pay for it. Given the trade-off between spending time to find curb parking or spending money to pay for off-street parking, should you cruise or pay? The answer depends on how long it takes to find a curb space, and how much money you save by parking at the curb.

Drivers do not explicitly calculate whether to cruise or to pay, but several factors influence the choice. To model the choice, consider the following variables (and their dimensions).

> p price of curb parking ($/hour)
> m price of off-street parking ($/hour)
> t parking duration (hours)
> c time spent searching for parking at the curb (hours)
> f fuel cost of cruising ($/hour)
> n number of people in the car (persons)
> v value of time spent cruising ($/hour/person)

First, consider how much you save on parking if you can find a curb space. The price of parking at the curb is p dollars per hour, and the price of parking off-street is m dollars per hour, so parking at the curb rather than off-street saves $m - p$ dollars per hour. The amount you save by parking at the curb is the duration (t) multiplied by the difference between the prices of off-street and curb parking, or $t(m - p)$. For example, if curb parking is free, off-street parking costs $1 an hour, and you park for two hours, you save $2 by parking at the curb.[2]

Second, cruising has a fuel cost. If your car consumes fuel at a rate of f dollars per hour of cruising, and you cruise for c hours, the total cost of fuel spent for cruising is fc. For example, if the fuel cost is $1 per hour of driving and you cruise for 6 minutes (0.1 hour), the fuel cost is 10¢.[3]

Third, cruising has a time cost. The value you place on saving time depends on your income as well as many factors unique to each trip: whether you are in a hurry, the weather, the scenery, safety, and so on. The value of time will vary from person to person, but even the same person will place a higher or lower value on time depending on the circumstances. Each person's time cost of cruising is the value of time (v) multiplied by the time spent cruising (c), or vc. Because every person in the car must spend the same time cruising, the total time cost for everyone in the car is the number of people in the car (n) multiplied by each person's time cost (vc), or nvc. So if you are alone in the car, you value time savings at $9 an hour, and you cruise for six minutes before parking, your cost of time spent cruising is 90¢ ($9 x 1 x 0.1). Adding a passenger in the car doubles the time cost to $1.80, a second passenger makes it $2.70, and so on.[4]

The money saved by parking at the curb and the cost of cruising for a curb space are:

$t(m - p)$	(1)	money saved by parking at the curb
fc	(2)	monetary cost of cruising for curb parking
nvc	(3)	monetized cost of time spent cruising for curb parking
$fc + nvc = c(f + nv)$	(4)	monetary and (monetized) time cost of cruising for curb parking

What is the maximum time you would spend cruising (denoted as c^*) before it would be cheaper to park off-street? There is no cost difference between cruising and paying if you expect to spend exactly c^* minutes to find a curb space, so you are indifferent between the two choices.[5] This equilibrium occurs when the money saved from parking at the curb, $t(m - p)$, equals the money and time cost of cruising, $c^*(f + nv)$. So if you expect it will take longer than c^* to find a curb space, you should pay to park off-street. But if you expect it will take less than c^*, you should cruise.

The break-even point occurs where the cost of cruising equals the savings from parking at the curb:

$$c^*(f + nv) = t(m - p) \qquad (5)$$

Solving for c^*, we find the search time at which you are indifferent between cruising and paying is:

$$c^* = \frac{t(m - p)}{f + nv} \qquad (6)$$

At time c^*, you realize no *net* savings by parking at the curb instead of off-street. The money the city loses from underpriced curb parking does not accrue to you or to anyone else but is instead dissipated in time and fuel spent cruising. And because each driver in congested traffic imposes time delays on all other drivers, cruising makes all drivers, even those who are not trying to park, worse off. Cruising for parking is one of those cases where, as British transportation expert Philip Goodwin put it, "Adam Smith's individuals pursuing their own best interests do not add up to Jeremy Bentham's greatest good for the greatest number."[6]

EQUILIBRIUM SEARCH TIME: AN EXAMPLE

We can use an example to illustrate the equilibrium search time. Suppose you want to park for one hour ($t = 1$), off-street parking costs $1 an hour ($m = 1$), and curb parking is free ($p = 0$). You thus save $1 by parking at the curb rather than off-street. If you drive 10 miles an hour, and if your car gets 20 miles per gallon of gasoline, cruising consumes $1/2$ gallon of gasoline an hour. If gasoline costs $2 a gallon, the fuel cost is thus $1 an hour ($f = 1$). You are alone in the car ($n = 1$) and your time is worth $9 per hour saved ($v = 9$). The equilibrium search time, c^*, is

$$c^* = \frac{t(m - p)}{f + nv} = \frac{1(1-0)}{1+(1\times9)} = 0.1 \text{ hour} = 6 \text{ minutes}$$

In this case it is worth spending up to six minutes to find a curb space. If fuel costs $1 an hour, and you cruise for six minutes (0.1 hour), you spend 10¢ for fuel. You save $1 on parking for an hour, so your net saving from parking at the curb is 90¢ ($1 saved on parking minus 10¢ spent for fuel). In a sense, you "earn" $9 an hour (90¢ saved for 0.1 hour of cruising). If you value time savings at $9 an hour, six minutes is the search time that leaves you indifferent between searching for curb parking and paying to park off-street immediately. You are no better off parking free at the curb after searching for six minutes than if you had paid $1 to park off-street immediately.

This example suggests three results. First, "free" curb parking is not really free. Although its costs are not out of pocket (like money put in a parking meter), they are incurred all the same—as the time and fuel used to find a curb space. Free curb parking leaves the driver no better off, and everyone else is worse off because cruising congests traffic and pollutes the air. The city also loses the money it would have received had it charged the market price for curb parking.

Second, since the time drivers spend in cruising is the price they pay for curb parking, this price depends on each person's opportunity cost of time.[7] In this example, solo drivers who value time savings at more than $9 an hour (or carpools who collectively value their time at more than $9 an hour) should pay to park right away, and those with a lower value of time should cruise. Free curb parking thus attracts solo drivers who place a low value on saving time. Areas where curb parking is free, and where solo drivers place a low value on saving time, should therefore have long search times.

Third, because the equilibrium search time for cruising declines when the monetary price of curb parking increases, raising the price of curb parking reduces the time-and-fuel cost of cruising by an equivalent amount. The curb parking revenue is thus not like a tax that transfers revenue from motorists to the government, but is instead a fee that reduces the motorists' time-and-fuel cost of cruising by as much as it increases their monetary cost of curb parking. The *net* burden on curb parkers is therefore zero because motorists save on cruising what they pay for parking, and the reduction in private waste is converted into new public revenue.

THE WAGES OF CRUISING

Cities create the incentive to cruise when they charge less for curb parking than the price of adjacent off-street parking. To suggest how strong this incentive can be, Table 13-1 shows the prices of curb and off-street parking at noon on a weekday at 20 sites in Southern California. Column 3 shows the price for curb parking nearest each site, and column 4 shows the price for the first hour of off-street parking. Curb parking is cheaper than off-street parking at every site. On average, the price of parking at the curb is only 14 percent of the price of parking off-street ($0.78 ÷ $5.67).

Column 5 shows the money that a driver who parks for one hour will save by parking at the curb rather than off-street. Suppose, for example, you want to visit the Los Angeles City Hall for an hour to visit the department of city planning. Curb parking costs $1.50 and off-street parking costs $3.30, so parking at the curb will save $1.80. The savings range from 50¢ (at the Long Beach City Hall) to $9 (at the House of Blues in West Hollywood), and the average saving for parking at the curb is $4.89. These savings create the economic incentive to cruise.

Now suppose it takes six minutes to find a curb vacancy at each of these sites. How much money does a driver "earn" per hour of time spent to find a curb space? Column 6 answers this question (if we neglect the driver's relatively minor cost of fuel, as most drivers probably do). At Los Angeles City Hall, a driver who cruises for six minutes and saves $1.80 earns $18 an hour ($1.80 ÷ 0.1 hour). The wages of cruising range from $5 an hour at Long Beach City Hall to $90 an hour at the House of Blues, and the average for all sites is $49 an hour. If it takes only six minutes to find a curb space, the time is well spent.

The average cruising time is not six minutes everywhere, of course, and the wages of cruising do not really range as high as $90 an hour. The higher price for off-street parking at some sites should increase the average search time or lead drivers to park farther away in cheaper spaces and walk a longer distance to their destinations. Nevertheless, curb parking saves money at most sites, and this saving is what encourages drivers to cruise rather than pay for an off-street space. Although drivers who take longer to find a curb space "earn" less money per minute of cruising, they also create more traffic congestion and air pollution, and this cost is borne by everyone collectively, not by the cruisers individually. Drivers who cruise do not pay all the costs of their choice.

The structure of prices for off-street parking complicates the decision to cruise. The prices in the table for one hour of off-street parking do not mean, for example, that it costs $10 *per hour* to park at the House of Blues, because the price of the first hour at some off-street parking facilities is more than half the all-day price. Many off-street facilities charge a flat fee for the first two or three hours, which explains the high cost for only one hour of parking. And the price of curb parking at the House of Blues needn't be $10 an hour to eliminate the incentive to cruise. To end cruising, the price of curb parking needs to be only high enough to create a few vacancies because at that level cruising becomes pointless. At most sites, however, the price is too low, leading to a shortage of curb parking as well

Table 13-1. The Wages of Cruising in Southern California (for parking one hour at the curb after cruising for six minutes)

Site	Location	Price of parking for 1 hour		Reward for cruising 6 minutes and parking at the curb for 1 hour	
		Curb	Off-street	Savings from curb parking	Savings per hour of cruising time
(1)	(2)	(3) $/hour	(4) $/hour	(5)=(4)-(3) $	(6)=10x(5) $/hour
Biltmore Hotel	Downtown LA	$2.00	$7.00	$5.00	$50
Chinese Theatre	Hollywood	$1.00	$8.00	$7.00	$70
Coliseum	Downtown LA	$0.25	$6.00	$5.75	$58
House of Blues	West Hollywood	$1.00	$10.00	$9.00	$90
LA City Hall	Downtown LA	$1.50	$3.30	$1.80	$18
LA County Museum	MidWilshire	$0.50	$5.00	$4.50	$45
LA MTA	Downtown LA	$0.00	$6.00	$6.00	$60
LA Music Center	Downtown LA	$1.50	$8.00	$6.50	$65
Long Beach City Hall	Long Beach	$2.00	$2.50	$0.50	$5
MGM Plaza	Santa Monica	$0.35	$6.30	$5.95	$60
Pasadena City Hall	Pasadena	$1.00	$6.00	$5.00	$50
Pasadena Playhouse	Pasadena	$0.00	$1.00	$1.00	$10
Reagan Office Building	Downtown LA	$1.50	$6.75	$3.70	$37
Santa Monica City Hall	Santa Monica	$0.50	$4.20	$3.70	$37
Santa Monica Pier	Santa Monica	$0.50	$7.00	$6.50	$65
So. Cal. Assn. Gov.	Downtown LA	$2.00	$8.00	$6.00	$60
Union Station	Downtown LA	$0.00	$6.00	$6.00	$60
UCLA	Westwood	$0.50	$7.00	$6.50	$65
USC	Downtown LA	$0.25	$6.00	$5.75	$58
Venice Beach	Venice	$0.00	$5.00	$5.00	$50
Average		**$0.78**	**$5.67**	**$4.89**	**$49**

Assumption: A solo driver parks for one hour at noon on a weekday and cruises six minutes to find a curb space.

The prices refer to the first hour of parking nearest each site.

The data were collected in 2001–2002

as countless complaints about the "parking problem." For example, here is the grievance of one disgruntled student who couldn't find a curb space near UCLA (where curb parking cost 50¢ an hour and off-street parking costs $7 a day). It appeared in the campus newspaper, the *Daily Bruin*:

> When I looked for parking about an hour before my 9:30 discussion in which we were reviewing for a midterm the following day, parking was nowhere to be found.... After 45 minutes of circling the block, I decided I'd have to buy parking or risk being late for class.[8]

Underpriced curb parking created this frantic (and ultimately unsuccessful) cruising.

Figure 13-1. The Price of Parking in Southern California (for parking one hour at noon on a weekday)

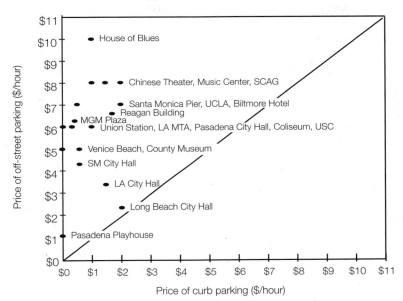

To see whether curb parking is underpriced in other parts of the country, I collected similar data on the price of curb and off-street parking for an hour at noon at the same location—City Hall—in 20 cities throughout the U.S.[9] Table 13-2 shows the results. The average price is $1.17 an hour at the curb and $5.88 an hour off-street. Cruising saves drivers the most money in New York, where the off-street parking is $14.38 for the first hour, but curb parking is only $1.50. Cruising saves money in all cities except Palo Alto (where both curb and off-street parking are free) and San Francisco (where both cost $2 an hour). In the 20 cities, the average price of curb parking is only 20 percent of the price of off-street parking, and the highest price of curb parking is only $2 an hour.

One explanation for Boston's high price for off-street parking ($11) is the cap the city has placed on the number of off-street parking spaces available downtown. The parking inventory is frozen at its 1975 level—35,500 spaces. Developers who want to build new parking spaces must buy licenses owned by existing parking facilities that have closed.[10] This cap on the parking supply drives up the market price of off-street parking, but it has also produced an ironic outcome: combined with the low price of curb parking, the higher price of off-street parking increases the incentive

Table 13-2. The Wages of Cruising at City Hall (for parking one hour at the curb)

City	State	Price of parking for one hour ($ per hour)		Savings for finding a curb space ($ per hour)
		Curb	Off-street	
(1)	(2)	(3)	(4)	(5)=(4)-(3)
Baltimore	MD	$2.00	$6.00	$4.00
Berkeley	CA	$0.75	$1.00	$0.25
Boston	MA	$1.00	$11.00	$10.00
Buffalo	NY	$1.00	$3.00	$2.00
Cambridge	MA	$0.50	$4.00	$3.50
Chicago	IL	$1.00	$13.25	$12.25
Houston	TX	$0.25	$1.50	$1.25
Long Beach	CA	$2.00	$2.50	$0.50
Los Angeles	CA	$1.50	$3.30	$1.80
New Orleans	LA	$1.25	$3.00	$1.75
New York City	NY	$1.50	$14.38	$12.88
Palo Alto	CA	$0.00	$0.00	$0.00
Pasadena	CA	$1.00	$6.00	$5.00
Philadelphia	PA	$1.00	$3.00	$2.00
Portland	OR	$1.00	$1.50	$0.50
San Diego	CA	$1.00	$6.00	$5.00
San Francisco	CA	$2.00	$2.00	$0.00
Santa Barbara	CA	$0.00	$5.00	$5.00
Santa Monica	CA	$0.50	$4.20	$3.70
Seattle	WA	$1.00	$8.00	$7.00
Average		**$1.17**	**$5.88**	**$4.71**

Assumptions: A solo driver parks for one hour at noon on a weekday. The prices refer to the first hour of parking in the spaces nearest the City Hall. The data were collected in 2001–2003.

to cruise. Boston limits the private off-street parking supply but fails to price its own public curb parking properly. A survey of parking prices in 53 North American cities in 2003 found that the average price for off-street parking in the Boston Central Business District (CBD) was $390 a month, and $30 a day.[11] In contrast, Boston charges the same price ($1 an hour) for all meters in the city. Far from using prices to manage the demand for curb parking, Boston encourages drivers to cruise for it.

Boston's off-street parking cap makes sense as a way to reduce congestion on routes *to* the city, but its failure to follow through with market prices for curb parking increases congestion *in* the city. Everyone would criticize off-street parking operators if long lines of cars regularly spilled into the streets and congested traffic because the lots and garages were always full. Nevertheless, cities create the same result with curb parking by underpricing it, and nobody notices because the cars hunting for curb parking are hidden in the general traffic flow. Even worse, the cruising wastes fuel, pollutes the air, causes accidents, and degrades the pedes-

Figure 13-2. The Price of Parking at City Hall (for parking one hour at noon on a weekday)

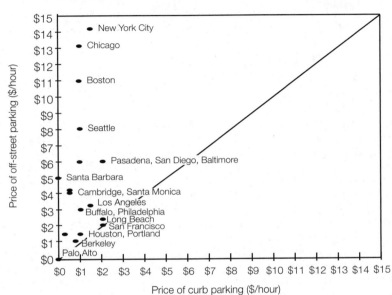

trian environment. Cities create this cruising by underpricing their curb parking.

Underpriced curb parking is not only an American phenomenon, of course. In his book on *Great Cities and Their Traffic*, J. Michael Thomson observed:

> For historical reasons all cities have inherited a tradition of free parking, and as space on the streets became scarcer many cities thought it right to provide off-street car parks free of charge. Only when driven by a desperate need to control the emerging parking chaos did most cities introduce parking charges, first off-street and then on the streets themselves. Today the level of charges is usually well below the economic cost.[12]

As a result, drivers circle for underpriced curb parking all over the globe.

RENT SEEKING

Payments for curb parking are rent for the temporary use of public land, and in that sense cruising may be viewed a form of "rent seeking" behavior in response to the potential savings from parking at the curb. When curb parking is underpriced (i.e., when the rent is too low), drivers spend time and fuel in their competition for cheap curb parking. In her analysis of competitive rent-seeking behavior, Stanford University economics professor Anne Krueger explains how scarce resources are squandered in rent-seeking situations:

> Rent seeking results in a divergence between the private and social costs of certain activities.... Rent seeking activities are often competitive and resources are devoted to competing for rents.[13]

The waste of time and fuel devoted to cruising dissipates the land rent cities would earn if they charged market-rate prices for curb parking spaces.[14] Curb parkers spend their time and fuel in cruising, the city loses potential rent from curb parking spaces, and everyone shoulders the added costs of traffic congestion and air pollution. Searching for underpriced curb parking is a negative-sum game.

Underpriced curb parking is the crux of the cruising problem. Cities create the incentive to cruise by setting the price of curb parking below the price of adjacent off-street parking.[15] The 45-degree lines from the origins in Figures 13-1 and 13-2 show where curb and off-street parking prices are equal. All combinations of curb and off-street parking prices in the upper left triangle represent places where curb parking is cheaper than off-street parking, and all but two of the observations fall in this triangle. By underpricing curb parking, cities encourage citizens to cruise. In contrast, market-priced curb parking will cut the waste of time and fuel spent in the competition to find a cheap curb space. It will also produce public revenue, divert long-term parkers to off-street spaces, open up more curb spaces for short-term parkers, and reduce traffic congestion and air pollution.

TWO PRICING STRATEGIES

Cities can use two pricing strategies to discourage cruising. The first is to charge the market price for curb parking. As indicated by equation 6, when the prices of curb and off-street parking are equal ($p = m$), the equilibrium cruising time (c^*) is zero. If curb parking costs the same as off-street parking, why drive around hunting for a curb space? Since curb parking (after you spend time and fuel to find it) costs the same as off-street parking, you don't save any money by cruising. If all curb spaces are occupied and there is no economic incentive to cruise, you should park off-street without wasting time and fuel.[16]

If curb parking remains free, however, a second strategy to discourage cruising is to reduce the price of off-street parking to zero. The logic is the same: if off-street parking is free, why search for a curb space? Since the prices of curb and off-street parking are again equal ($m = p = 0$), the equilibrium time is again zero. Cities can therefore reduce cruising either by charging market prices for curb parking or by requiring enough off-street spaces to reduce the price of off-street parking to zero. Although the price of curb parking is one of the few policy variables that cities directly control, almost all American cities have chosen to require ample off-street parking rather than to charge market prices for curb parking.

ELASTICITIES

Table 13-3 shows how each of the variables in the model affects the decision whether to cruise or to pay. The second column shows the partial derivatives of c^* (the maximum time a driver is willing to cruise) with respect to the variables in the first column. Six factors affect the decision to cruise: (1) the price of curb parking, (2) the price of off-street parking, (3) parking duration, (4) the price of fuel, (5) the number of persons in the car, and (6) the value of time.

The third column shows the elasticity of c^* with respect to each variable. The coefficient of elasticity is denoted by η (the Greek letter *eta*). These elasticities show how a small change in each variable increases or decreases the time a driver is willing to cruise. Five results stand out.

First, the elasticity of search time with respect to the price of curb parking depends only on the prices of curb and off-street parking. Figure 13-3 shows this elasticity, given the values of other variables assumed above.[17] The elasticity is low when curb parking is cheap, which means that raising the price—say, doubling it from 10¢ to 20¢ an hour—will have little effect on curb vacancies. This result may lead some to conclude that the demand for curb parking is inelastic and that raising its price won't produce vacancies. But as the price of curb parking approaches the price of off-street parking, even a small increase can create curb vacancies and reduce congestion. The demand for curb parking may be completely inelastic until its price approaches that of off-street parking, at which point it suddenly becomes very elastic.[18] Because the variables that affect the elasticity vary from place to place and according to the time of day, we cannot estimate a single price elasticity of demand for curb parking at even one location, let alone all locations. If demand is elastic, a small price increase can reduce curb congestion without producing much revenue. If demand is inelastic, however, the price increase needed to reduce curb congestion will yield substantial revenue.

Second, when curb parking is free, the elasticity of search time with respect to the price of off-street parking is +1. Therefore, reducing the

Table 13-3. Equilibrium Search Time (c^*)

Variable	Partial derivative of c^*	Elasticity of c^*
p (curb parking price)	$\dfrac{\partial c^*}{\partial p} = +\ \dfrac{t}{f+nv} < 0$	$\eta_p = +\ \dfrac{p}{m-p} < 0$
m (off-street parking price)	$\dfrac{\partial c^*}{\partial m} = +\ \dfrac{t}{f+nv} > 0$	$\eta_m = +\ \dfrac{m}{m-p} > 0$
t (parking duration)	$\dfrac{\partial c^*}{\partial t} = -\ \dfrac{m-p}{f+nv} > 0$	$\eta_t = +\ 1$
f (fuel cost of cruising)	$\dfrac{\partial c^*}{\partial f} = -\ \dfrac{t(m-p)}{(f+nv)^2} < 0$	$\eta_f = -\ \dfrac{f}{f+nv} < 0$
n (number of persons)	$\dfrac{\partial c^*}{\partial n} = -\ \dfrac{tv(m-p)}{(f+nv)^2} < 0$	$\eta_n = -\ \dfrac{nv}{f+nv} < 0$
v (value of time)	$\dfrac{\partial c^*}{\partial v} = -\ \dfrac{nt(m-p)}{(f+nv)^2} < 0$	$\eta_v = -\ \dfrac{nv}{f+nv} < 0$

Notes:
The length of time (c^*) a motorist is willing to search for curb parking is:

$$c^* = \frac{t(m-p)}{f+nv}$$

The elasticity (η_i) of c^* with respect to variable i is:

$$\eta_i = \frac{\dfrac{\partial c^*}{\partial i}}{\dfrac{c^*}{i}}$$

price of off-street parking by 10 percent reduces the time you are willing to cruise by 10 percent.

Third, the elasticity of search time with respect to parking duration is +1. A longer parking duration justifies a proportionally longer cruise. For example, a driver who wants to park twice as long as another is willing to hunt twice as long to find a curb space, all else being equal. Curb parking is best suited for quick trips and high turnover, but drivers who want to park for a long time have a stronger incentive to search for the curb spaces.

Fourth, the elasticity of search time with respect to fuel cost depends on the cost of fuel, the number of people in the car, and the value of their time. If the fuel cost is much lower than the time value, an increase in fuel

Figure 13-3. Curb Price Elasticity of Search Time

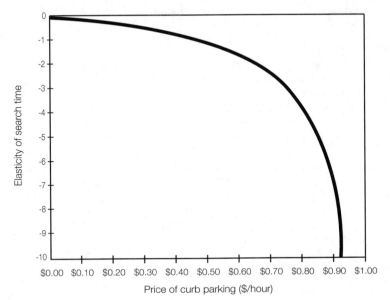

cost has little effect on willingness to cruise. If cruising costs $1 an hour for fuel, and time is worth $9 an hour, a solo driver's elasticity of cruising with respect to the price of fuel is only -0.1. Raising the price of gasoline by 10 percent therefore reduces the time drivers are willing to cruise by only 1 percent. If you are willing to hunt for six minutes to find curb parking when gasoline costs $1 a gallon, for example, raising the price of gasoline to $1.10 a gallon reduces the time you are willing to search by only four seconds.

Finally, the elasticity of search time is the same with respect to the number of people in a car and the value of their time. More people in a car and a higher value of their time thus have the same effect on willingness to cruise. The lone motorist who values time at $8 an hour and a carpool of four persons who each value time at $2 an hour are both willing to cruise for the same length of time, all else being equal, so underpriced curb parking chiefly attracts solo drivers.

A NUMERICAL EXAMPLE

If we make some simplifying assumptions, we can use a numerical example to illustrate how the price of curb parking affects the transportation system. Consider a steady-state equilibrium where the number of drivers who want to park at the curb and the length of time they want to park depend on the price of curb parking. Demand and supply are perfectly balanced at a price of $1 an hour: all spaces are occupied, and a new car arrives to park at the curb at exactly the time that a parked car is leaving. At prices below $1 an hour there is a shortage of curb parking, and at higher prices there are vacant spaces.[19]

To keep the arithmetic simple, consider an area that has 100 curb spaces. Columns 1 and 2 of Table 13-4 show how the price of curb parking affects the quantity of curb space demanded; at a price of $1 an hour, 100 drivers want to park at the curb, so demand exactly equals supply, and the occupancy rate is 100 percent (column 4).[20] At a price of $1 an hour, then, all the curb spaces are occupied, but someone is always leaving when someone else is arriving, so cruising isn't necessary. If the price is lower than $1 an hour, however, the excess demand leads to cruising. At a price of 70¢ an hour, for example, 111 drivers want to park at the curb; because there are only 100 spaces, 11 cars must cruise while waiting for a curb vacancy to appear (column 5).[21]

The price of parking affects not only the number of drivers who want to park at the curb, but also how long they will park after they find a space. Column 6 shows the average parking duration as a function of price; for example, it is 60 minutes when the price is $1 an hour but rises to 67 minutes when the price is 70¢ an hour.[22] Cheaper curb parking thus increases the number of curb spaces demanded and reduces the turnover rate (which is the inverse of the average parking duration); at a price of $1 an hour, the turnover rate is one car per space per hour, but at 70¢ an hour it falls to 0.9 cars per hour (column 7). Turnover creates openings for new cars to park at the curb, so underpriced curb parking has two undesirable effects: it increases the number of drivers who want to park at the curb and reduces the number of vacancies that occur during an hour.

By increasing the number of cars cruising and reducing the turnover rate, a lower price for curb parking increases the average search time per space. At a rate of 70¢ per hour, the turnover rate per space is 0.9 cars per hour; when we multiply this turnover rate by the 100 curb spaces, the aggregate parking turnover is 90 spaces per hour (column 8), or 1.5 spaces per minute. At the same price of 70¢ an hour, 111 drivers want to park in the 100 curb spaces, so 11 drivers must cruise. If we divide the 1.5 spaces available per minute by the 11 cars cruising for parking, the probability for an individual cruiser of finding a curb space within the next minute is 13 percent (column 9). The average time spent cruising, in turn, is simply the 11 cruisers divided by 1.5 spaces that become available each minute, or eight minutes (column 10). Reducing the price of curb parking thus increases the number of cars cruising, reduces the number of new vacancies each hour, and increases the average time needed to find a vacant space.

Reducing the price of parking below $1 an hour also reduces the revenue from the 100 curb spaces. At a meter price of $1 an hour the revenue is $100 an hour. Reducing the price cannot increase the number of parked cars, however, so the revenue declines proportionally (column 11). Increasing the price to more than $1 an hour, in contrast, does not increase the revenue proportionally because some spaces become vacant and yield no revenue at all. Increasing the price by 50 percent from $1 to $1.50 an hour, for example, increases revenue by only 33 percent. Maximum revenue is not necessarily the right goal for pricing curb parking, however, because it can lead to underuse of a valuable public resource—curb parking spaces that serve visitors to the area.

Columns 12, 13, and 14 show the effect of curb parking prices on the share of traffic that is cruising.[23] If the meter price is 70¢ an hour and if we assume that 100 cars an hour are traveling along the street rather than cruising for parking, 67 percent of the total traffic on the street is cruising. Finally, column 15 shows the Vehicle Miles Travelled (VMT) per hour caused by the cruising cars.[24] At a meter price of 70¢ an hour, cruising for the 100 curb spaces creates 113 VMT per hour or a little more than 1 VMT per space per hour.

Figure 13-4 presents the results from Table 13-4. The price of curb parking—the independent variable—is shown on the X-axis, and the dependent variables are shown on the Y-axis. When the price is below $1 an hour, all the curb spaces are occupied, and some cars are cruising. Raising the price toward $1 an hour still leaves all curb spaces occupied, but the number of cruising cars and their average cruising time decline. When the price is above $1 an hour, some spaces are vacant, drivers can park as soon as they arrive, and no cars are cruising. Although this simple numerical example assumes a perfect steady-state match between arrivals and departures, and neglects random variations in curb parking demand, it shows how the price of curb parking affects many important transportation variables. Underpriced curb parking reduces turnover, increases the time it takes to find a curb vacancy, reduces public revenue, and increases vehicle travel for cruising. Market-priced curb parking, in contrast, increases total public revenue and eliminates cruising.

COMPLICATIONS

The decision to cruise is far more complex than a simple model can portray, of course, and I will suggest five potential complications. First, the value of saving time is not constant. Different people place different val-

Table 13-4. Cruising as a Function of the Price of Curb Parking

Price	Curb parking demand and supply		Occupancy rate	Number of cruisers	Parking duration	Turnover rate	Vacancies per hour	Chance of parking in next minute	Average cruising time	Parking revenue	Cruising flow	Through flow	Cruising as % of traffic	Cruising VMT
	Demand	Supply												
$/hour	Parked-car-hours/hour		%	cars	minutes	cars/hour	spaces/hour	%	minutes	$/hour	cars/hour	cars/hour	%	VMT/hour
(1)	(2)	(3)	(4)=(2)/(3)	(5)=(2)-(3)	(6)	(7)=60/(6)	(8)=100x(7)	(9)=(8)/60/(5)	(10)=60x(5)/(8)	(11)=(1)x(3)x(4)	(12)=(8)x(5)	(13)	(14)	(15)=10x(5)
$0.50	123	100	100%	23	74	0.81	81	6%	17	$50	407	100	80%	231
$0.60	117	100	100%	17	70	0.86	86	9%	12	$60	291	100	74%	166
$0.70	**111**	**100**	**100%**	**11**	**67**	**0.90**	**90**	**13%**	**8**	**$70**	**199**	**100**	**67%**	**113**
$0.80	107	100	100%	7	64	0.94	94	23%	4	$80	122	100	55%	69
$0.90	103	100	100%	3	62	0.97	97	50%	2	$90	57	100	36%	32
$1.00	**100**	**100**	**100%**	**0**	**60**	**1.00**	**100**	**100%**	**0**	**$100**	**0**	**100**	**0%**	**0**
$1.10	97	100	97%	0	58	1.03	103	100%	0	$107	0	100	0%	0
$1.20	95	100	95%	0	57	1.06	106	100%	0	$114	0	100	0%	0
$1.30	92	100	92%	0	55	1.08	108	100%	0	$120	0	100	0%	0
$1.40	90	100	90%	0	54	1.11	111	100%	0	$127	0	100	0%	0
$1.50	89	100	89%	0	53	1.13	113	100%	0	$133	0	100	0%	0

Figure 13-4. Results of Changing the Price of Curb Parking

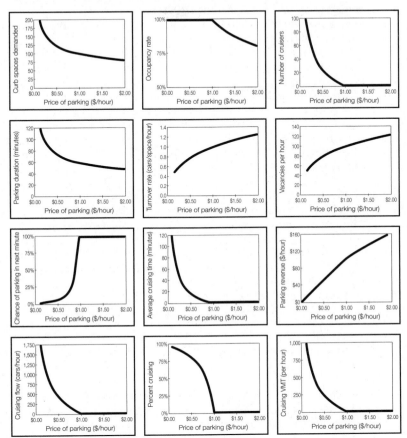

ues on time savings, and the same person may place different values on saving time on different days, at different hours, and for different trips. Even for a specific trip, the value of saving time may increase as you cruise because the likelihood that you will arrive late at your destination increases the longer you hunt for curb parking. You may therefore drive around for a while and then, getting desperate, pay to park off-street.

Second, you don't know in advance how long it will take to find a curb space. In a normal queue you can see how many people are ahead of you and how fast the queue is moving, so you can roughly estimate how long it will take to be served. But to cruise is to wait in a queue of unknown length, where the next person called to the window is determined by lottery. You may find a curb space in the next minute, or it may take half an hour. How long it will take to find a curb space is therefore a random variable with a distribution and an expected value that are both unknown. Previous experience with cruising in the area may give you an idea of what to expect, but you still don't know how many other drivers are cruising or how frequently curb spaces turn over. Nevertheless, clues gathered while driving around may alter your guess about how long it will take to find a curb space. You may see that other cars ahead of you also appear to be cruising, and this information lowers the likelihood of finding a curb space soon. You may therefore drive around for a while to size up the probability of finding a curb space within a reasonable time.[25] Compared with normal queuing, cruising is risky behavior, and drivers who are risk averse may choose to pay for off-street parking immediately rather than take a chance on finding a curb space. On the other hand, drivers who are risk takers and who enjoy the thrill of the hunt will increase both the average search time and the external costs of cruising.

Although the information gained while cruising will help to make a decision on whether it is worthwhile to continue cruising, the spent time is a sunk cost that should not affect the decision. The problem is similar to the example of putting coins into a broken parking meter, as suggested by Yale psychology professor Robert Sternberg:

> Many of us have had the unpleasant experience of putting money into a parking meter, turning the knob, and finding that our money has not registered. Do we put in more coins, move to another space, or hope we will not get a fine? The problem of "sunken costs" is one we all face in one form or another. We invest in something; the investment turns out to be less than successful, but we have already invested, so we might keep investing in the hope that eventually the investment will pay off. But how long is long enough to decide that it might be time to look for another investment—or parking space.[26]

If some drivers consider their sunk cost in time spent cruising as a reason to continue cruising, their behavior will increase the average search time to find a curb space.

Third, curb and off-street parking are not perfect substitutes for one another, and drivers do not choose between them only on the basis of price. If you lack change for the meter or want to stay longer than the time limit, you may park off-street even if it is more expensive. On the other hand, curb parking may be more convenient, especially for a very short stop, or it may seem safer than an underground garage. William Vickrey explained that because curb parking is in most cases more convenient than off-street parking, it must be priced higher than adjacent off-street parking to create curb vacancies and discourage cruising.[27] Beverly Hills, for example, charges $1 an hour for curb parking in its CBD and offers two hours of free parking in its municipal parking garages; nevertheless, the curb spaces are often fully occupied, which suggests that drivers strongly value the convenience of curb parking. In a survey of 1,040 drivers who parked in off-street facilities in Ann Arbor, Michigan, Stephen Deering et al. found that 42 percent of the respondents would have preferred to park on the street.[28] And in a survey of 1,560 shoppers in Cardiff, Wales, Amanda Nelson found that 51 percent of women said they were anxious when using parking structures after dark, while another 32 percent said they never parked in structures after dark. The price of curb parking may therefore have to be much higher than the price of adjacent off-street parking to create an acceptable curb vacancy rate. The market price for curb parking is not simply equal to the price of adjacent off-street parking but is instead the level that leads to about an 85 percent occupancy rate. If women prefer curb parking more strongly than men do, market prices for curb parking may increase the share of curb parking spaces occupied by women drivers.

Fourth, you may not know the cost of parking in all locations or how far you will have to walk to the final destination. You may thus drive to your destination and then begin looking around, or simply park at your destination without making any comparisons if the monetary cost of parking is not very high.

Finally, there are options beyond the simple choice between cruising and paying. You can also park in an illegal curb space and risk getting a ticket. Or you can drive to a nearby area where curb parking is readily available or where off-street parking prices are lower, and then walk farther to your destination. But despite these and other complications, the basic lesson is the same: if cities charge too little for curb parking, drivers will cruise.

IS CRUISING RATIONAL?

These calculations assume that drivers act rationally when they park their cars. Do they? Economists do, of course. Consider this anecdote from Gary Becker's Nobel Prize lecture:

> [I was] driving to Columbia University for an oral examination of a student in economic theory. I was late and had to decide quickly whether to put the car in a parking lot or risk getting a ticket for parking illegally on the street. I calculated the likelihood of getting a ticket, the size of the penalty, and the cost of putting the car in a lot. I decided it paid to take the risk and park on the street. (I did not get a ticket).[29]

Becker won his Nobel Prize "for having extended the domain of micro-economic analysis to a wide range of human behavior and interaction, including nonmarket behavior," so his own rational behavior should not surprise us.[30]

Rational behavior is at the core of economic analysis, and the philosopher Sir Karl Popper argued that it is also at the core of all social science.[31] But Popper added that rationality is not a universal law, and he used the search for parking to illustrate irrational behavior:

> One has only to observe a flustered driver, desperately trying to park his car when there is no parking to be found, in order to see that we do not always act in accordance with the rationality principle.[32]

Some drivers may consider situations where "there is no parking" and where "there is no *free* parking" to be identical. Nevertheless, if a driver wants to choose rationally between cruising for parking and paying for it, a simple model can explain the rudiments of the decision. Citing the flustered driver searching for parking as evidence that we do not always act rationally, Popper concluded, "Any model, whether in physics or in the social sciences, must be an oversimplification. It must omit much, and it must overemphasize much."[33] Or as Albert Einstein put it, "Make everything as simple as possible, but not simpler."

Drivers don't use a mathematical model when deciding whether to cruise, but all the model's assumptions are reasonable, and all its predictions are testable hypotheses. A model cannot predict how everyone will behave, but it does suggest how to behave if you want to be rational in your own cruising. You can even test the model's predictions by referring to your own experience. Suppose you want to park at a site where curb parking is free, but all the curb spaces are occupied. Off-street parking costs $1 for every 15 minutes but is immediately available. Would you be less likely to search for a curb parking space if you were in a hurry to reach your destination? If you had passengers in your car? If you intended to park for only a short time? If your answers to these questions are yes, the model correctly predicts your choices.

THE ROLE OF INFORMATION

Aside from underpriced curb parking, poor information about off-street parking availability also leads to cruising. If prices don't respond to demand to keep a few spaces vacant, motorists must drive around looking for a place to park. To reduce searches for off-street spaces, cities are experimenting with parking guidance systems that alert drivers to off-street parking availability.[34] One of the most sophisticated is the

STADTINFOLKÖLN (CityInfoCologne) in Cologne, Germany, which sends travel information to personal computers, in-car displays, and variable message signs at strategic places on approaches to the city. Here is how it works:

> Individual parking garages are equipped with "add-and-subtract" loop detectors which record the exact number of spaces left vacant in each facility. This data is transmitted to a central computer, which displays the information on variable message signs. The software analyzing the data takes into account the rate at which a given parking facility fills up (based on historical data), and displays the predicted occupancy status at the time the motorist is expected to reach the facility. When available space at a facility falls below a certain minimum, the message sign changes to flashing, thus warning motorists that they run the risk of being turned away at the garage of their choice for lack of space.
>
> STADTINFOLKÖLN also plans to provide forecasts of available metered on-street parking. These forecasts of available metered on-street parking will be based on algorithms derived from historical occupancy data of metered parking spaces on any given day of the week and at any given time. The forecasts of available on-street parking will be combined with data from the instrumented parking garages to provide a comprehensive status of parking availability in Cologne's city center at any given time.[35]

If a city can predict curb space occupancy from historical data, it can also raise meter rates when overoccupancy is expected and reduce them when underoccupancy is expected. Adjusting prices to keep curb spaces available is far simpler than broadcasting warnings about recurring shortages.

Better information is always valuable, but the need for information about parking availability stems in part from distorted prices. If mispriced parking creates shortages in some places and surpluses in others, cities can provide better information on these shortages and surpluses to help motorists find vacant spaces, but research on the effects of parking guidance systems rarely mentions the price of parking.[36] An alternative approach is to charge the right price for parking at each site so that parking lots never need to put out the "full" sign, and everyone can park anywhere they want if they are willing to pay the fair-market price.

To deal with chronic parking shortages, the European Union is sponsoring a test of an internet-based system (called e-PARKING) that enables drivers to make advance parking reservations. When reserving a space, the driver is given an access code that allows the parking garage to recognize the driver's identity on arrival, and the driver is then given access to the garage "at the touch of a mobile phone button."[37] The European Union's e-PARKING initiative shows the absurd (and expensive) lengths to which governments will go to solve a problem that would disappear if cities simply charged market prices for parking spaces.

Charging the right prices for parking and providing information on the resulting geography of prices will help motorists find the combination of price and location that suits them best. In-vehicle navigation systems that now provide digital maps and audio directions for drivers may eventually provide real-time information on the pattern of curb and off-street parking prices at the drivers' destinations. If you plug in how long you want to park and the value you place on reducing the walking time to your destination, the navigation system may ultimately be able to tell you exactly where to park.

If I had to choose between better prices and better information as the way to solve the parking problem, I would choose better prices. The two together are better than either alone, but it is a mistake to neglect price reform and instead deploy advanced technology to disseminate information about the shortages and surpluses caused by distorted prices. Should the Soviet Union have dealt with price-induced shortages for everything by developing elaborate and expensive technology to broadcast real-time information about the length of all queues for all products? Market prices contain an immense amount of information about fluctuations in supply and demand, and these prices are a simple way to convey information to motorists. Demand-responsive parking prices can make vacant parking spaces available everywhere, and the parking guidance systems can advise motorists about the different prices at different locations.

CONCLUSION: AN INVITATION TO CRUISE

Where curb parking is underpriced and overcrowded, some drivers will search for a curb space rather than pay to park off-street. This chapter has presented a model of how drivers decide whether to cruise or to pay. The model predicts that charging the market price for curb parking—a price at least equal to the price of adjacent off-street parking—removes the economic incentive to cruise. In setting the prices for curb parking, the government therefore plays a large part in determining whether drivers cruise. Cruising is simply a driver's individual response to the government's pricing policy. Underpriced curb parking is a perverse public subsidy because it encourages drivers to do something that harms other people and may not even benefit the drivers themselves. Governments must then throw good money after bad by spending more to fix the congestion and pollution problems they have created. Getting the price of curb parking right will benefit almost everyone.

CHAPTER 13 NOTES

1. For the model, I assume you are indifferent between curb and off-street parking if the price and the time required to find a space are the same in both cases. I also assume that you pay only for each minute parked in both cases. In reality, curb parking is often more convenient if a space is available right where you want to park. Curb parking is also often available in smaller increments (such as 6 or 10 minutes) while off-street parking is available only in larger increments (such as 20 or 30 minutes).

2. I assume you know in advance how long you want to park and you pay only for the exact time that you park. The parking charge is a linear function of the number of minutes you park, with no advance commitment to how long you park. Chapter 15 describes parking meters that allow you to pay for the exact time that you park, determined *ex post*.

3. If gasoline costs $1 per gallon, and your car gets 20 miles per gallon, cruising costs 5¢ per mile. If you cruise at 20 miles per hour, the fuel cost of cruising is $1 per hour.

4. The cost of time spent cruising, v, may differ among persons in the car. If everyone's value of time is weighted equally, we can interpret v as their average value of time.

5. The time spent walking from the parking space to the final destination is neglected here, but Chapter 18 presents a model of both parking and walking.

6. Goodwin (1997, 2). Goodwin was speaking of traffic congestion in general, rather than cruising for parking in particular.

7. Smolensky, Tideman, and Nichols (1972, 95) say, "Queues can be viewed as prices assessed in time, and time prices, like money prices, ration according to the tastes, income and opportunity costs of buyers." Arnott, Rave, and Schöb (forthcoming) explain that the full price of curb parking is the cost of time spent cruising plus the parking fee, and say that raising the parking fee does not alter the equilibrium full price of parking because the reduction in time cost equals the increase in parking fee.

8. Letter to the *Daily Bruin*, August 20, 2001. Cruising for parking is also a problem at rural universities. Consider this newspaper account of the parking problems caused by a growing student population at the University of Texas of the Permian Basin in Odessa, Texas: "The growth has left students such as Windy Quilodran, a senior English major, avoiding the peak class times and having to park further from classrooms and lecture halls. Quilodran said she dropped a class that would have fulfilled one of the last requirements for her degree after she spent more than 40 minutes driving around the campus one day. 'You spend your whole morning driving around in circles,' Quilodran said " (UTPB Hires Shuttle Bus to Ease Crowded Parking, *Odessa American*, September 9, 2003).

9. The cities are an opportunistic sample of places where my research assistants and I visited and were able to gather the data. Nevertheless, the sample shows that curb parking is probably much cheaper than off-street parking in many big and small cities. City Hall was chosen because it is a standard reference point that everyone can recognize.

10. Boston Transportation Department (2001). The Boston Air Pollution Control Commission administers the "parking freeze" in Boston Proper (the downtown). The number of spaces available to the general public is frozen at the 1975 level, but the Boston Air Pollution Control Commission may grant exemptions to private off-street parking available exclusively to employees, guests, or customers in a building. Residential parking is not capped. The total off-street parking supply increased by only 9 percent between 1977 and 1997, and in 1997 the 35,500 public parking spaces represented 60 percent of the total 59,100 off-street spaces in Boston Proper. Additional freezes apply in East Boston, South Boston, and at Logan Airport. Portland, Oregon, had a similar limit on the number of parking spaces—known as the parking lid—in the CBD. It was replaced in 1995 by limit on 0.7 spaces per 1,000 square feet of net leasable area, in part because historic buildings without any parking were losing nearby surface parking lots and were increasingly difficult to lease (Portland TriMet 2002, 3-9).

11. Colliers International (2003, 28-29). The highest price for unreserved parking in Boston's CBD was $600 a month, and the lowest was $285 a month.

12. Thomson (1977, 63-64).

13. Krueger (1974, 291). Krueger also explains that most people do not perceive themselves as rent seekers in their competition for rent. Similarly, H. Scott Gordon (1954, 135) says, "Common-property natural resources are free goods for the individual but scarce goods for society. Under unregulated private exploitation, they can yield no rent; that can be accomplished only by methods which make them private property or public (government) property, in either case subject to a unified directing power."

14. Frech and Lee (1987, 98) state, "A queue will be in equilibrium when the implicit cost of a commodity (computed as the value of time spent in the queue plus the explicit money price being charged) equals the price necessary to reduce the quantity demanded to the quantity supplied." Similarly, Gordon (1954, 132) says, "the rent which [fisheries] are capable of yielding is dissipated through misallocation of fishing effort. This is why fishermen aren't wealthy, despite the fact that the fishery resources of the sea are the richest and most indestructible available to man. By and large, the only fisherman who becomes rich is one who makes a lucky catch or one who participates in a fishery that is put under a form of social control that turns the open resource into property rights." Tollison (1982, 76) says, "resources spent in the pursuit of a transfer are *wasted* from society's point of view. These expenditures add nothing to social product (they are zero-sum at best), and their opportunity cost constitutes lost production to society." In their article on free entry and rent seeking, Higgins, Shughart, and Tollison (1988, 128) conclude that, "in a market where the award is based on 'effort,' entry fees are nonrefundable, and contestants are risk neutral…rents are completely dissipated."

15. As transportation consultant Herbert Levinson (1982, 217) says, "It is essential that curb parking be more expensive than parking in adjacent off-street lots."

16. If drivers prefer curb to off-street parking, the price of curb parking must rise above the price of off-street parking to create curb vacancies and discourage cruising.

17. The price of off-street parking is $1 an hour ($m = 1$). You want to park for one hour ($t = 1$). The cost of fuel for cruising is $1 an hour ($f = 1$). You are alone in your car ($n = 1$). And you value your time at $9 an hour ($v = 9$).

18. For example, when the price of curb parking is 25¢ an hour and the price of off-street parking is $1 an hour, $\eta_p = -(.25)/(1 - .25) = -0.33$; therefore, raising the price by 10 percent reduces the time drivers are willing to cruise by only 3.3 percent. But when the price of curb parking is 75¢ an hour, $\eta_p = -(.75)/(1 - .75) = -3$; therefore, raising the price by 10 percent reduces the time drivers are willing to cruise by 30 percent. Even this large reduction in search time may not produce many curb vacancies, however. If curb parking is cheaper than off-street parking, the main effect of raising the price of curb parking is to reduce cruising, not to produce curb vacancies, because drivers continue to take any available curb spaces.

19. The random nature of curb parking arrivals and departures means that a cushion of vacant spaces is needed so that drivers can usually find a place to park near their destinations. The vacancy rate will fall as more curb parkers arrive than leave and will increase as more leave than arrive, but a few vacancies will allow most drivers to park as soon as they arrive. In a perfect knife-edge balance, a new car arrives to park at the curb exactly at the time a parked car is leaving.

20. The assumed relationship between price of curb parking and the quantity demanded is $q = 100p^{-0.3}$, and the price elasticity of demand for curb parking is -0.3.

21. At meter prices below $1 an hour, the time cost of cruising is a surcharge on the money price of curb parking, and this time cost will limit the demand for curb parking. For simplicity, I have ignored this time cost in calculating the number of drivers who want to park at the curb. In reality, the time cost of cruising will limit the number of cruisers when the meter price is below $1 an hour, and column 5 overstates the number of cruisers.

22. The assumed relationship between price of curb parking and parking duration is $d = 60p^{-0.3}$, and the elasticity of parking duration with respect to price is -0.3.

23. If there are three curb spaces per 100 linear feet of curb, the length of curb with 100 spaces is 3,000 feet (0.57 miles), and a car that is cruising at 10 miles an hour makes 18 circuits of the curb per hour. The total number of cars that travel around the block in an hour is thus 18 times the number of cruisers in column 5.

24. The total cruising VMT in a hour is the number of cruisers (in column 5) multiplied by their average speed of 10 miles an hour.

25. Thompson and Richardson (1998) develop a model of parking search behavior that explains how drivers choose among off-street parking facilities. They consider parking choice as a search process in which drivers make a number of linked decisions based on updated knowledge gained from experience. Surprisingly, their model suggests that long-term experience doesn't necessarily lead to better parking choices.

26. Sternberg (2001, 190).

27. Vickrey (1954, 64). Similarly, Topp (1993, 85) says, "The most convenient parking spaces are the on-street spaces where parking fees are also usually less than in parking garages. Those spaces—and even the illegal ones—generate more search traffic and waiting cars than spaces in parking garages."

28. Deering et al. (1998, 15).

29. Becker (1993, 389).

30. See the Nobel e-Museum online at www.nobel.se/economics/laureates/index.html.

31. Popper (1985, 359) maintains that to model a social situation we need "no more than the assumption that the various persons or agents involved act *adequately*, or *appropriately*; that is to say, in accordance with the situation" (emphasis in the original).

32. Popper (1985, 361).

33. Popper (1985, 361). In my oversimplification, I neglect that the decision to cruise is part of a larger decision of whether to make the trip. Richard Arnott and John Rowse (1999, 98-99) developed a parking model that does incorporate cruising into the trip-making decision: "Our basic model is as follows. The city is located on the outside of a circle and is spatially symmetric. There is a fixed number of parking spaces per unit of distance. The demand for parking is derived from the demand for trips. Trip opportunities are generated according to an exogenous, stochastic, time-invariant process. A trip opportunity provides a benefit to a specific individual if she travels to a specific location and visits there for a specified period. She sits at home waiting for a trip opportunity. When she receives an opportunity, she decides whether to accept it, and if she does so, what mode of transport to take. If she drives, she decides how far from her destination to start cruising for parking, then takes the first available parking spot and walks to her destination." While Arnott and Rowse do embed cruising in the larger decision of whether to travel, they don't consider the difference in the prices of curb and off-street parking as an incentive to cruise, which is at the center of my analysis.

34. Khattak and Polak (1993) explain how parking information influences drivers' behavior.

35. "Cologne's Intelligent Parking Management System," *Innovation Briefs*, Vol. 13, No. 3, May/June 2002. Available online at www.innobriefs.com/.

36. For example, see Hester, Fisher, and Collura (2002) for off-street parking, and Basu and Little (2002) for curb parking.

37. See "Cutting the Search Time" in *ITS International*, January/February 2002, Vol. 8, No. 1, p. 65. The European Road Federation's description of the E-PARKING project is available online at www.erf.be/projects/pr_eparking.htm. In Singapore, the city's system of electronic road pricing has now been extended to garages. A driver's entry and exit from the garage is recorded electronically, and the charge is deducted from the car's credit balance, just as it would for paying a toll on the road, and the driver doesn't need to stop on the way in or out of the garage (Fabian 2003, 10).

14

California Cruising

Everything is interesting if you look at it deeply enough.
— RICHARD FEYNMAN

Cruising for parking plays an important role in Los Angeles life, and journalists often comment on it. The *Los Angeles Times*, for example, describes cruising on Melrose Avenue—a popular shopping district built before the city required off-street parking:

> Most shoppers who come in cars must vie for limited one-hour metered spaces along the avenue or for free spaces on the crowded side streets. The result is a frustrating search up and down and around the surrounding streets.[1]

And in a *Los Angeles Times* interview, a Hollywood screenwriter mentions that he continued cruising even after his fortunes suddenly improved:

> We were going to a meeting with a director and spent 20 minutes looking for a street parking space instead of leaving the car with the valet.... Then I realized, I think we can afford to valet now. We're meeting with the director of a $30-million film, and we're looking to put money in the meter.[2]

Many stores and professional offices validate off-street parking so their customers won't have to search for curb parking. Consider this story of a writer on her way to plastic surgery in Beverly Hills, where the validated parking appeared to be divine intervention:

Driving down Wilshire Boulevard I realized I had no business going to a cosmetic surgeon…. I'm Irish Catholic—we're supposed to grit our teeth and offer our suffering up to the poor souls in Purgatory, not high-tail it to some medical Sodom and Gomorrah where faces are peeled, breasts inflated and botulism is considered a panacea. By the time I had decided to turn around, I was there already, and when I found out the doctor validated parking, well, I took it as a sign from God.[3]

If you won't pay for off-street parking and you aren't validated, you're condemned to the purgatory of cruising for curb parking.

The model in Chapter 13 shows that underpriced curb parking creates the incentive to cruise. To test this prediction, my research assistants and I searched for parking in Los Angeles, using the park-and-visit method that Britain's Road Research Laboratory developed to measure search times in London (see Chapter 12). We made 240 observations at four locations in Westwood Village, a 15-block commercial district near the UCLA campus, and the average time to find a curb space was 3.3 minutes. While this is not much time for each driver to spend cruising, it adds up because many drivers park in Westwood Village every day. Over a year, cruising for parking in Westwood creates enough vehicle travel to make 38 trips around the earth.

PARK-AND-VISIT TESTS IN WESTWOOD VILLAGE

Westwood Village is a neighborhood commercial district bordered by the UCLA campus on the north and west, and by residential neighborhoods with parking permit districts on the south and east. (See Figure 14-1.) The village was developed in the 1920s and 1930s, and although it has lost some of its original Mediterranean charm and coherency over the years, it also gained many movie theaters, offices, shops, and restaurants. Most buildings are two or three stories, but high-rise office buildings line Wilshire Boulevard along its southern border. When the park-and-visit tests were conducted in 1984, the village contained 470 metered curb spaces and approximately 3,400 off-street spaces in 20 surface lots and parking garages. Curb spaces thus amounted to about 14 percent of the total parking supply. Although curb parking was fully occupied during the peak hours, off-street parking was always available. A subsequent parking study commissioned by the Los Angeles Department of Transportation in 1994 found that 1,200 off-street spaces in Westwood Village (35 percent of the total) were vacant during the peak hour (2 p.m.).[4]

During the 1984 study period, the price of metered curb parking was 50¢ an hour from 8 a.m. to 6 p.m. on Monday through Saturday with a one-

Figure 14-1. Westwood Village

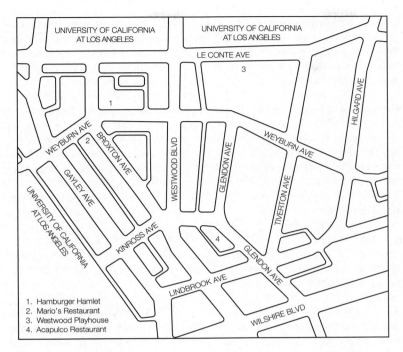

1. Hamburger Hamlet
2. Mario's Restaurant
3. Westwood Playhouse
4. Acapulco Restaurant

hour time limit, and parking was free after 6 p.m. with no time limit. In contrast, the price of most off-street parking was $1 an hour during the day, and $2 or $3 per entry in the evening. The incentive to cruise was therefore stronger in the evening: during the day, parking at the curb rather than off-street saved 50¢ for an hour, but at night saved $2 to $3 for any duration.[5]

The model of cruising in Chapter 13 suggests that search times should be longer after 6 p.m. when curb parking becomes free. To test this prediction, my research assistants and I cruised for curb parking between 4 p.m. and 8 p.m. on weekdays at four different addresses. We visited each address 10 times during each hour, for a total of 160 observations. For each visit we drove to the address and then circled the block until we found a curb space.[6] Because all curb spaces were occupied almost all the time, we rarely found a vacant space when we arrived. Instead, we usually searched until we found a parked car about to vacate a space and then waited for it to leave.

Most drivers who are hunting for parking try to avoid following directly behind other cars that appear to be cruising so as to maximize their chances of being the first to find a vacant spot. For this reason, the process of using cars to measure cruising times may influence the very behavior being studied.[7] To avoid this potential pitfall and get some exercise as well, we decided to make most of the observations by riding bicycles to simulate cars hunting for parking. Because cyclists do not influence cruisers' parking decisions, using bicycles probably improved the accuracy of the park-and-visit tests.[8] Furthermore, the average cruising speed by car in Westwood is only 8 to 10 miles an hour because every intersection has a stop sign or traffic light, so a cyclist can easily keep up with the vehicle traffic. For the tests, each bicycle was equipped with a cyclometer that measured elapsed travel time, distance traveled, and average speed. We were careful to behave like motorists in traffic that was moving or waiting to move so the search time by bike should have closely approximated the time by car.

CHEAPER CURB PARKING CREATES MORE CRUISING

Table 14-1 shows the results of the park-and-visit tests conducted between 4 p.m. and 8 p.m. on weekdays. The average search time before finding a space was 6.2 minutes between 4 p.m. and 5 p.m. It rose to 7.8 minutes between 5 p.m. and 6 p.m., 9.4 minutes between 6 p.m. and 7 p.m., and 9.7 minutes between 7 p.m. and 8 p.m. The times did not differ much among the four locations, but in all cases they did increase sharply after 6 p.m. when parking became free.[9] Furthermore, search times between 5 p.m. and 6 p.m. were higher than those between 4 p.m. and 5 p.m. This may be explained by the fact that drivers who parked at 5 p.m. could pay 50¢ for the first hour and stay free for as long as they liked after 6 p.m., which was much cheaper than evening rates for off-street parking.

Table 14-1. Search Time for Curb Parking in Westwood Village

Hour	Price of curb parking	Search time (minutes)				
		Acapulco Restaurant	Hamburger Hamlet	Mario's Restaurant	Westwood Playhouse	Average
4pm-5pm	$ 0.50	6.6	5.7	5.4	7.2	6.2
5pm-6pm	$ 0.50	7.6	6.8	7.6	9.0	7.8
6pm-7pm	$ 0.00	8.7	9.8	8.5	10.6	9.4
7pm-8pm	$ 0.00	8.3	9.2	10.0	11.1	9.7
Average		7.8	7.9	7.9	9.5	8.3

Note: Cruising times are the average of 10 observations at each site during each hour. The price of curb parking was 50 cents per hour before 6pm, and free after 6pm. The price of off-street parking was $1 per hour before 6pm, and $2 per entry after 6pm.

The average search time after 6 p.m. (when curb parking became free) was 36 percent longer than between 4 p.m. and 6 p.m. (when the price was 50¢ an hour). The increased search time during the evening does not reveal the effect of price alone because the time limit on curb parking also changed. The purpose and characteristics of the trips (including the parking duration) probably differ between daytime and evening as well.[10] Nevertheless, one conclusion is clear: because curb parking was free after 6 p.m., drivers found it worthwhile to cruise more than nine minutes to find a curb space.

As noted, the times were similar among the four locations, probably because they are close to one other. The times were almost identical at the Acapulco Restaurant, Hamburger Hamlet, and Mario's Restaurant, and only 17 percent higher at the Westwood Playhouse (see the last row of the table).[11] One hypothesis to explain this similarity is that drivers probably migrate to the blocks where search time is shorter, until the times become similar on adjacent blocks.[12] Although drivers don't know how long it will take to find a curb space on any block, the natural tendency to avoid following another driver who appears to be hunting for a curb space should spread cruisers evenly among adjacent blocks.

To estimate conditions throughout the rest of the day, we made additional observations between 8 a.m. and 4 p.m. Because the average search time between 4 p.m. and 8 p.m. varied so little among different blocks, we conducted the additional tests only at the Hamburger Hamlet, where the average search time between 4 p.m. and 8 p.m. was closest to the average for all four addresses. Again, we made 10 visits to this address in each hour, for a total of 80 observations (Table 14-2).[13]

The second column in the table shows the average search time during each hour from 8 a.m. to 8 p.m. Before 10 a.m., the time at which most shops opened for business, many of the curb spaces were vacant, and the search time was zero. Vacancies dwindled after 10 a.m., and the search times rose correspondingly, reaching their peak during the evening. Averaged across all hours, as shown in the last row, the time required to find a parking space was 3.3 minutes.[14] These results show that the average cruising time depends on more than simply the difference between the prices for curb and off-street parking. Because the time limit for curb parking was one hour, the varying demand for short-term parking during the day must also have affected cruising times, as did the end of time limits after 6 p.m.

CRUISING FOR A YEAR

If individual drivers spend an average of 3.3 minutes searching for parking, what is the total time spent cruising by *all* drivers during one day? To

Table 14-2. A Day of Cruising in Westwood Village

Hour	Average search time (minutes)	Parking turnover per meter (cars)	Search time per meter (minutes)	Total search time (hours)	Cruising distance per parking (VMT)	Cruising distance per meter (VMT)	Total cruising distance (VMT)
(1)	(2)[1]	(3)[2]	(4)[3]	(5)[4]	(6)[5]	(7)[6]	(8)[7]
8am-9am	0.0	1.9	0.0	0	0.0	0.0	0
9am-10am	0.0	2.3	0.0	0	0.0	0.0	0
10am-11am	0.9	1.2	1.1	8	0.2	0.2	113
11am-noon	2.0	2.1	4.2	33	0.3	0.6	296
noon-1pm	4.4	1.5	6.6	52	0.6	0.9	423
1pm-2pm	3.5	1.8	6.3	49	0.4	0.7	338
2pm-3pm	4.1	1.4	5.7	45	0.5	0.7	329
3pm-4pm	3.4	1.0	3.4	27	0.5	0.5	235
4pm-5pm	6.2	1.2	7.4	58	0.9	1.1	508
5pm-6pm	7.7	1.3	10.0	78	1.2	1.6	733
6pm-7pm	9.4	0.3	2.8	22	1.4	0.4	197
7pm-8pm	9.7	0.7	6.8	53	1.4	1.0	461
Average	**3.3**	**1.4**	**4.5**	**35**	**0.5**	**0.6**	**303**
Total	—	**17**	**54**	**426**	—	**7.7**	**3,633**

Notes:
1. In Column 2, search times from 8 a.m. to 4 p.m. are the average of 10 observations per hour; search times from 4 p.m. to 8 p.m. are the average of 40 observations per hour from Table 14-1.
2. Parking turnover in Column 3 was derived from continuous observations of all meters on Weyburn between Broxton and Westwood for a day.
3. Column 4 = (Column 2) x (Column 3).
4. Column 5 = (Column 4) x (470 parking meters)/(60 minutes).
5. Column 6 shows the average cruising distance taken from odometer readings.
6. Column 7 = (Column 3) x (Column 6).
7. Column 8 = (Column 7) x (470 parking meters).

answer this question, we began by measuring the turnover rate per space (the average number of cars that park at a meter during the day). To sample this rate, we continuously observed all the parking spaces on a block of Weyburn Avenue (the site of the Hamburger Hamlet) between 8 a.m. and 8 p.m. on a weekday, recording the arrival and departure time for each car that parked on the block (column 3). As shown in the last row of column 3, an average of 17 cars per space parked at the curb between 8 a.m. and 8 p.m. During a day, the total search time per space is the average time per search multiplied by the parking turnover rate (column 4 = column 2 x column 3). Based on this calculation, the last row of column 4 shows that each curb space generated about 54 vehicle-minutes of cruising between 8 a.m. and 8 p.m.

The total time spent cruising for *all* metered spaces is simply the average time per space multiplied by the 470 meters in the village.[15] Between noon and 1 p.m., for example, the search time per space was 6.6 minutes, so drivers spent a total of 52 *vehicle-hours* in cruising for parking between noon and 1 p.m. (6.6 minutes x 470 spaces ÷ 60 minutes). The last two rows of column 5 show that all drivers combined spent an average of 35 vehicle-hours cruising for parking per hour, with a total of 426 vehicle-hours per day.

Two Round Trips to the Moon

One way to visualize the average 35 vehicle-hours spent cruising during an hour is to imagine that all the cruisers are painted bright yellow. A view of Westwood from the air would then show 35 bright yellow cars mixed in the traffic flow. Some cars find curb spaces, but as they do, new cars arrive to take their place in the "reserve army of the unparked." Because the village encompasses only 15 city blocks, 35 cruisers amount to about two cars continuously circling each block. Another way to think of 35 cruisers is to compare them with the 470 curb spaces in the village: for every 100 curb spaces, seven cars are hunting for parking; that is, 107 cars want to park in 100 curb spaces, so seven cars must "wait" in the traffic flow.

This cruising produces an astonishing amount of excess vehicle travel. To estimate its magnitude, we used odometer readings to measure the average cruising distance, which ranged from zero between 8 a.m. and 10 a.m. to 1.4 miles between 6 p.m. and 8 p.m. (column 6). The average cruising distance during the day was half a mile.[16] We can use this distance to estimate the excess vehicle miles travelled (VMT) that each curb space generates. Between noon and 1 p.m., for example, individual drivers cruised 0.6 miles before parking (column 6), and the turnover rate was 1.5 cars per space (column 3), so drivers cruised a total of 0.9 miles per curb space during this hour (column 7). The cruising distance per space ranged from zero between 8 a.m. and 10 a.m. to 1.6 miles between 5 p.m. and 6 p.m., with each space generating 7.7 VMT of cruising per day. Because there are 470 metered spaces in Westwood Village, cruising for parking generated a total of 3,600 VMT per day. Cruising during the single hour between 5 p.m. and 6 p.m. generated 20 percent of the total cruising during the day (733 ÷ 3,633), perhaps because anyone who parked then could claim a space for the whole evening (the meters stopped operating at 6 p.m.).[17] Cruising was thus greatest during the rush hour, when traffic was already most congested.

With these data we can now put cruising in Westwood in perspective. Every day, cruisers within this 15-block district drove farther than the distance across the U.S.[18] Over a year, their cruising created 945,000 excess VMT—equivalent to 38 trips around the earth or two round trips to the moon.[19] The obvious waste of time and fuel is even more appalling when we consider the low speed and fuel efficiency of cars in the cruising mode. Drivers encounter a stop sign or traffic light at every intersection, usually have to wait for pedestrians to cross, and may have to wait in traffic while a curb space is being vacated; as a result, the average cruising speed is only 8 to 10 miles an hour. If we optimistically estimate that drivers average 20 miles a gallon, cruising 945,000 miles a year wastes about 100,000 hours (11 *years*) of drivers' time, consumes 47,000 gallons of gasoline, and produces 730 tons of CO_2 emissions.[20] Cruising for curb parking in Westwood Village thus consumes enough gasoline to fuel the cars of 44 average U.S. households for all their travel (including cruising) in an entire year.[21] No wonder everyone thinks Westwood has a parking problem!

Simple Arithmetic

Two round trips to the moon every year? In a small commercial district? Although it seems hard to believe, simple arithmetic shows that cruising for curb parking can easily create this much excess vehicle travel in a similar area in any city. The result depends on only four variables:
1.   The cruising time before parking in a curb space
2.   The turnover rate for curb spaces
3.   The average cruising speed
4.   The number of curb spaces

To keep the arithmetic easy, suppose drivers cruise three minutes before finding a curb space, the parking turnover rate is 10 cars per curb space per day, drivers cruise at 10 miles an hour, and the area has 500 curb spaces. We can estimate the total cruising VMT per year in four steps:
1.   Cruising three vehicle-minutes for parking at a curb space 10 times a day creates 30 vehicle-minutes of travel per curb space per day.
2.   Cruising for 30 minutes at 10 miles an hour creates five VMT per curb space per day.
3.   Cruising five VMT a day for 365 days a year creates 1,825 VMT per curb space per year.
4.   Cruising 1,825 VMT per space per year for 500 spaces creates 912,500 VMT per year.

Four realistic assumptions and four simple multiplications thus yield 912,500 VMT per year for cruising. The estimate of 945,000 VMT per year for cruising in Westwood is thus only common sense backed up by close observation and careful counting.[22] As Yogi Berra said, you can sometimes see a lot just by looking. But a precise estimate for Westwood is *not* the important point. The important point is that cruising for parking can inflate vehicle travel tremendously. If one curb space generates 1,825

VMT of cruising a year, the cruising for 14 curb spaces is equal to the distance around the earth.[23] Charging the right price for curb parking can eliminate all this cruising.

Cruising around the Average Block

These alarming numbers raise an obvious question—is Westwood typical? As it turns out, Westwood's curb parking supply appears to be average for commercial areas. A study of all nonresidential curb parking in Portland, Oregon, found that the average block is 253 feet long and has 3.3 parking spaces per 100 linear curb feet. At this rate, the average block has eight curb parking spaces on each side and 32 parking spaces on its perimeter.[24] This is close to the average of 31.3 curb spaces per block in Westwood Village (470 curb spaces ÷ 15 blocks).

Because the size and number of curb spaces of a block in Westwood appear close to the norm, we can use the data collected in Westwood to estimate the effect of cruising around an average commercial block that is 253 feet long and has eight curb spaces on each side. In the top panel of Figure 14-2, curb parking is underpriced, all spaces are occupied, and two cars are circling the block looking for a space (the average number of cruisers around each block during the day). The average driver cruises 0.5 miles before finding a curb space (see the next-to-last row of column 5 in Table 14-2).[25] Because the perimeter of a block that is 253 feet long on each side is 0.2 miles, the average driver circles the block 2.5 times before parking (0.5 ÷ 0.2). Each curb space generates 0.6 VMT of cruising per hour (column 7), so the 32 spaces surrounding the block generate an average of 20 VMT per hour, 240 VMT per day, and 62,000 VMT per year.[26] If cruising creates 20 VMT per hour around each block, and each circuit is 0.2 miles, cruising would, by itself, create a vehicle flow of 100 cars per hour around the block.[27]

The small distances cruised by each driver add up quickly because the turnover rate is 17 cars a day per space. With 470 meters in the village, 7,990 cars park at the curb each day (17 x 470), and 2 million park each year. Because so many cars park at the curb, a small cruising distance for each driver creates an amazing amount of traffic. Although the average driver circles the block only 2.5 times before parking, cruising in the aggregate creates 945,000 VMT a year.

In contrast, the bottom panel of Figure 14-2 illustrates what happens if the price of curb parking is set high enough to produce one vacancy for each eight spaces (a 12.5 percent vacancy rate). There is no incentive to cruise because drivers can find a vacant curb space anywhere they want to park, or they can park off-street for a comparable price, and the search time is therefore zero. Now imagine that the price of curb parking varies

Figure 14-2. Curb Parking Prices and Cruising

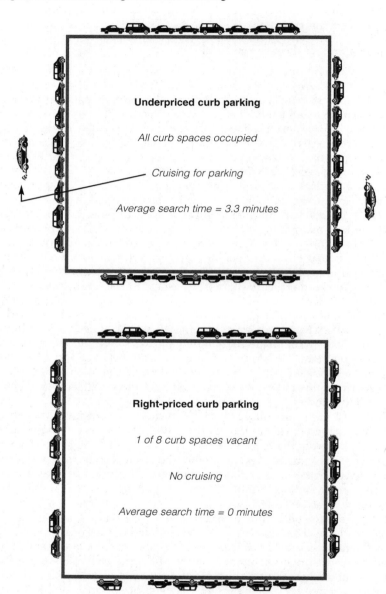

Underpriced curb parking

All curb spaces occupied

Cruising for parking

Average search time = 3.3 minutes

Right-priced curb parking

1 of 8 curb spaces vacant

No cruising

Average search time = 0 minutes

in response to parking demand to keep roughly one out of every eight spaces vacant in the village throughout the entire day. Demand-responsive pricing policy can eliminate 945,000 VMT of cruising for parking every year. Underpriced curb parking creates an astonishing amount of traffic, and market-priced curb parking can eliminate it.

Even More Cruising

The estimate of nearly 1 million VMT a year for cruising in Westwood Village may seem high, but it covers only 8 a.m. to 8 p.m. on weekdays. Considerable additional cruising occurs after 8 p.m. because all the curb spaces are fully occupied until well after 10 p.m., and whenever a car vacates a curb space during this period, the first driver to see it almost always parks in it. Curb parking is fully occupied on Saturday and Sunday as well, so additional cruising occurs then. Cruising for parking therefore creates more than 945,000 VMT a year in the village.

The estimate also excludes drivers who first hunt for a curb space and then park off-street. They fail to find a curb space, but they still congest traffic. Torn between the desire to save money and the desire to save time, cruisers sometimes slow as they pass off-street parking lots and look up to read the posted prices. To investigate whether off-street parkers had first searched for curb parking, we surveyed drivers who parked in the off-street lot on Broxton Avenue between 10 a.m. and 8 p.m. on a weekday in November 1984. Of the 150 respondents, 51 percent said their parking would be validated. Of those who paid for their parking, 35 percent said that they had first searched for curb parking before parking off-street. Seventeen percent of the drivers who parked in the off-street lot had therefore cruised for curb parking (49% x 35%). Because these drivers who failed to find parking at a meter eventually gave up and parked off-street, the distance they cruised is not included in the estimate of 945,000 VMT a year (which is the distance driven before actually finding a curb space). As mentioned in Chapter 11, a similar share (18 percent) of off-street parkers in New Haven and Waterbury Central Business Districts (CBDs) had searched for curb parking before parking off-street, and they had cruised twice as far as those who did find a curb space. Therefore, excluding the distance driven by those who first tried to park at the curb but then parked off-street leads to an underestimate of the total VMT cruised for curb parking in Westwood.

Finally, some drivers who are unsuccessful in finding a curb space leave without parking at all. I don't know how common this is, but people have told me of occasions when they drove around the village looking for curb parking and left in disgust when they failed to find it (paying to park off-street was apparently out of the question). For these three reasons, 945,000

VMT a year is a very conservative estimate of the total cruising for parking in Westwood Village.

Cruising is an odd form of vehicle travel because it adds VMT without adding either vehicles *or* travel—the number of vehicles that can park at the curb does not increase, nor does real travel, because cars simply circle the block going nowhere. Cruising may even reduce travel to congested areas if potential visitors think, as Yogi Berra put it, nobody goes there anymore because it's so crowded. All the excess VMT refers to searching for curb parking *after* drivers have reached the village. The *impression* of crowding created by cruising can deter visitors who would be willing to pay for curb parking if they could find a space without cruising and therefore limits patronage of the businesses that cheap curb parking is supposed to help. Underpriced curb parking creates the wrong kind of crowding—too many cars and not enough customers.

What Share of the Traffic Was Cruising?

We don't know which cars in traffic are cruising for curb parking because we don't know their drivers' motives. Nevertheless, a few researchers have attempted to estimate the share of the traffic flow caused by searching for parking. The earliest study (in 1927) estimated that between 19 percent and 34 percent of the cars traveling in downtown Detroit were cruising for curb parking. Subsequent studies in other cities have estimated that between 8 percent and 74 percent of the traffic flow was cruising for parking (Table 11-4).

So what share of the total traffic flow in Westwood Village was cruising? When all curb spaces are occupied and no one can find a curb space without searching, a car that parks in a newly vacated space was probably cruising, and one that passes a vacant space probably was not. In this way, a vacant curb space "samples" the flow of traffic to reveal whether the cars approaching the space are cruising. Suppose half the cars in traffic are cruising and the other half are not. One would expect that in half the cases where a meter space is vacated, the first car to approach it will park there. Similarly, if 30 percent of cars are cruising, 30 percent of the first cars to approach a vacant space will park. Given this reasoning, the percentage of cases where the first car to approach a newly vacated space parks in it shows the percentage of traffic that is cruising.

To estimate how much of the traffic flow on one street in Westwood was cruising, we observed the curb space occupancy rate and whether the first car that approached a newly vacated space parked in it.[28] Table 14-3 shows results for all the curb spaces on Weyburn Avenue between Broxton Avenue and Westwood Boulevard (the block on which search times in Table 14-2 were measured) between 8 a.m. and 8 p.m. on a weekday.

Table 14-3. Curb Space Occupancy Rates, Search Times, and Share of Traffic Cruising

Hour	Price of curb parking ($/hour)	Curb space occupancy rate (percent)	Search time per parking (minutes)	Share of traffic cruising (percent)
(1)	(2)	(3)	(4)	(5)
8am-9am	$ 0.00	68%	0.0	20%
9am-10am	$ 0.00	72%	0.0	13%
10am-11am	$ 0.50	91%	0.9	39%
11am-noon	$ 0.50	97%	2.0	66%
noon-1pm	$ 0.50	98%	4.4	90%
1pm-2pm	$ 0.50	99%	3.5	96%
2pm-3pm	$ 0.50	98%	4.1	56%
3pm-4pm	$ 0.50	99%	3.4	71%
4pm-5pm	$ 0.50	99%	6.2	87%
5pm-6pm	$ 0.50	100%	7.7	91%
6pm-7pm	$ 0.00	100%	9.4	92%
7pm-8pm	$ 0.00	100%	9.7	94%
Average		**93%**	**3.3**	**68%**

Column 4 is taken from Column 2 in Table 14-2.
Columns 3 and 5 are taken from observations on Weyburn Avenue.

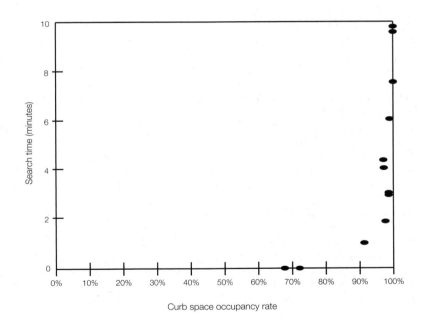

Weyburn Avenue is an east/west collector street, 55-feet wide and striped for two lanes of traffic in each direction, with a parking lane on each side. Parking was no problem before 10 a.m. when the occupancy rate was around 70 percent, and the search time was zero. But when the occupancy rate approached 100 percent after 11 a.m., the average search time increased rapidly (columns 3 and 4).

If most cars traveling along a street are cruising, most curb vacancies should be taken by the first cars that approach them, and this occurred after 11 a.m. on Weyburn Avenue. When a car left a curb space and created a vacancy, the first car that approached it usually parked in it. Between 7 p.m. and 8 p.m., for example, 94 percent of the first cars to approach a vacant curb space parked in it, which suggests that 94 percent of the traffic at that time was cruising for parking (column 5). Although it may seem hard to believe that most of the drivers in traffic were searching for parking, my own experience when collecting data confirms this. In the evening, when curb parking was free and there was no time limit, all it took to stop traffic was for someone to put a key in the door of a parked car because the first driver seeing this usually blocked a lane while waiting for the space.

The percentages in column 5 overestimate the share of traffic that was cruising when the occupancy rate was less than 85 percent because there is no reason to cruise when more than 15 percent of curb spaces are vacant. The first driver to see a vacant space may have just arrived at the destination.[29] But the curb space occupancy rate was more than 90 percent for most of the day, and the high share of newly vacated spaces taken by the first drivers to see them suggests that most cars were cruising for curb parking. On average, throughout the day, two-thirds of the cars on Weyburn Avenue were cruising for parking.[30]

The curb space occupancy rate also affects the time it takes to find a vacant curb space. The figure at the bottom of Table 14-3 shows the relationship between the curb space occupancy rate (from column 3) and the average search time (from column 4). When occupancy is below 90 percent, each new car that arrives to park simply increases the occupancy rate. But when the occupancy rate rises above 90 percent, each new car increases the time it takes to find a space. And when all curb spaces are occupied, an increase in parking demand increases the average search time but not the number of cars parked at the curb.

High occupancy rates and long search times are not uncommon. When Aaron Adiv and Wenzhi Wang (1987) studied curb parking in Ann Arbor, Michigan, for example, they found that the occupancy rate during the peak hours was 99.5 percent, and many cars were cruising:

Occupancy ratio, occupied space-hour/available space-hour, averaged 93.0 percent on Main Street throughout the day, and 99.5 percent around campus during the peak. Even off-peak averaged almost 80 percent. For all practical purposes, on-street meters are used all the time. It seems that demand exceeds supply. The surveyors observed…many vehicles that kept on cruising for on-street parking spaces.[31]

Similarly, in Westwood, when the curb occupancy approached 100 percent, both the search times and the share of traffic that was cruising increased sharply.

SIDE EFFECTS OF CRUISING

Underpriced curb parking is a hidden source of traffic congestion. The share of traffic that is cruising depends on both the number of cruisers and the number of travelers. Travelers and cruisers are mixed in the same traffic flow, but their goals are entirely different. Travelers want to drive fast, but cruisers creep along in the right lane, watching for any sign of a car about to leave a space. A parked car about to leave causes "parking foreplay" in which a cruiser stakes a claim to the space by waiting just behind it while it is being vacated. Cruisers also ask people who are approaching or entering parked cars whether they are leaving (both question and answer are often expressed in body language), and these negotiations further impede traffic.

Parking "side friction" (the traffic delay caused by cars entering and leaving curb spaces) can greatly reduce the capacity of the traffic lane next to the curb parking lane. This side friction becomes extreme when all curb spaces are occupied and a car in the traffic lane has stopped to claim a space being vacated; the stopped car not only blocks its own lane, but also slows traffic in the center lane as cars pull out of the blocked lane. Cruising thus increases the traffic flow, while parking foreplay and side friction reduce road capacity. While conducting the park-and-visit tests, I once watched a white Rolls Royce convertible block a lane of traffic on Westwood Boulevard while the driver patiently waited for a parking space being vacated by an identical Rolls. It would have been easier for the two drivers simply to swap keys than to unpark and park their cars.

In addition to delaying traffic, cruising also causes accidents. When a curb vacancy occurs on the opposite side of the street, for example, a cruiser will often make an illegal U-turn to claim the space, and I have seen this cause several accidents in Westwood. In a study of accident rates in 32 cities in 17 states, Thomas Seburn found that "an average of 18.3 percent of all accidents studied involved parking either directly or indirectly."[32] Similarly, Robert Weant and Herbert Levinson reported that approximately 15 percent of all traffic accidents involve parked cars, and that between 40 and 60 percent of all mid-block accidents involve parking.[33] Other estimates of the share of urban traffic accidents associated with curb parking range from 16 to 20 percent.[34] If some of these accidents are caused by cruising and aggressively pursuing *underpriced* curb parking, market-priced curb parking can reduce accident rates.

Finally, cruising degrades the environment for bicyclists and pedestrians. The added traffic and sudden stops associated with cruising impede bicyclists, and drivers who are waiting to claim curb spaces block the right lane, forcing bicyclists into the center of the street. Cruisers who are circling the block usually turn right at red lights to avoid waiting for the green, and this can intimidate pedestrians crossing at intersections. Cruising introduces unpredictability into the traffic flow, and the drivers who are focused on spotting a curb space may fail to notice bicyclists and pedestrians. This does not imply any sort of class conflict between drivers and pedestrians, however; many pedestrians are probably recent drivers who managed to find a parking space.

The side effects of cruising vary enormously according to the specific circumstances of each street and time of day—the width of the roadway, the traffic flow, and the turnover of cars parked at the curb. The external cost is especially high where curb parking is so crowded that drivers stop traffic in their lane while waiting for another car to leave. The high external cost of crowded curb parking suggests that the appropriate price for curb parking is *at least* the price that leads to a 15 percent vacancy rate.[35]

SOLO DRIVERS MORE LIKELY TO CRUISE

The model presented in Chapter 13 predicts that solo drivers are more likely to search for underpriced curb parking because they cannot split the cost of off-street parking with any passengers. A solo driver may be content to cruise as long as it takes to find a curb space, but the cumulative urgency of two or three passengers who are eager to eat dinner may persuade the driver to pay for off-street parking. To test this prediction, we observed the occupancy of all cars that parked at the curb and in an off-street parking lot on Weyburn Avenue between Westwood Boulevard and Broxton Avenue between 8 a.m. and 4 p.m. on a weekday (Table 14-4). Solo drivers occupied 69 percent of the cars parked at the curb, but only 53 percent of the cars parked off-street. Only 2 percent of the cars parked at the curb carried more than two passengers, compared with 13 percent of the cars parked off-street. As a result, the average vehicle occupancy rate of the cars parked at the curb was only 1.3 persons, compared with 1.7 persons for cars parked off-street. Underpriced curb parking thus allocates scarce curb spaces mainly to solo drivers and allows fewer people to visit local shops, restaurants, and theaters.

Table 14-4. Vehicle Occupancy Rates for Curb and Off-street Parkers

	Vehicle occupancy rate (persons/car)						Average vehicle occupancy rate	Number of cars observed
Place parked	1	2	3	4	5	6		
Curb	69%	29%	1%	1%	–	–	1.3	172
Off-street	53%	34%	5%	4%	2%	2%	1.7	225

MARKET PRICES CAN ATTRACT MORE PEOPLE

If curb parking is underpriced, drivers have an incentive to feed the meters and stay longer than the legal limit. Table 14-5 shows the distribution of curb parking durations on Weyburn Avenue between 8 a.m. and 4 p.m., calculated from the arrival and departure times of all cars that parked at the curb. Five cars that parked for more than two hours accounted for only 3 percent of all cars but 15 percent of the total occupied-space-hours. During the observations, one person dashed from a movie theater to feed his meter and rushed back in to see the rest of the film, while another asked my research assistant to feed the meter for him while he was in the theater. In contrast, cars that parked for 15 minutes or less accounted for 42 percent of all the cars parked at the curb during the day, but only 8 percent of the total occupied-space-hours (see columns 1, 3, and 8), and 60 percent of all curb parkers stayed for less than 30 minutes. These short-term curb parkers seem just the sort of customers the village wants—they park, hurry in to buy something, and leave quickly, vacating a curb space that another customer can use. When people want to stay in the village for longer times, they will find that off-street parking is a better bargain. The meter rates will therefore affect the kind of *trips* that curb parking serves, not the kind of *people* who park at the curb. Regardless of their income, gender, age, or ethnicity, for example, drivers will tend to park at the curb for a quick trip and off-street for a more extended stay.

Other studies have also found that long-term (and usually illegal) parking accounts for a large share of curb space usage, and this pattern of behavior is almost as old as the car. In his study of curb parking in the Detroit CBD in 1927, where the legal time limit was one hour, Hawley Simpson found that 22 percent of cars parked for more than an hour and occupied 60 percent of the space-hours used—exactly the same distribution found in Westwood, where the time limit was also one hour.[36] In a study of curb occupancy between 8 a.m. and 6 p.m in Paterson, New Jersey, Herbert Swan in 1922, found a similar distribution; 14 percent of cars parked for more than an hour and occupied 55 percent of the space-hours. "A large part of the downtown street congestion in Paterson,"

Swan wrote, "is due to machines cruising around in search of a place to park."[37] In 2001, the Boston Transportation Department found that the *average* parking duration at meters exceeded the legal two-hour time limit in four of the five corridors studied.

Table 14-5. Distribution of Curb Parking Durations

Parking duration (minutes)	Number of cars	Percent of cars	Accumulated cars		Total minutes parked			Accumulated parked-car-hours	
			Number	Percent	Average	Total	Percent	Number	Percent
(1)	(2)	(3)	(4)	(5)	(6)	(7)	(8)	(9)	(10)
0 - 15	72	42%	72	42%	6	436	8%	7	8%
16 - 30	31	18%	103	60%	20	612	11%	17	18%
31 - 45	21	12%	124	72%	37	779	13%	30	31%
46 - 60	10	6%	134	78%	50	496	9%	39	40%
61 - 75	17	10%	151	88%	68	1,152	20%	58	60%
76 - 90	9	5%	160	93%	83	745	13%	70	73%
91 - 105	4	2%	164	95%	99	397	7%	77	79%
106 - 120	3	2%	167	97%	116	348	6%	83	85%
120+	5	3%	172	100%	169	846	15%	97	100%
Total	172	100%	172	100%	34	5,811	100%	97	100%

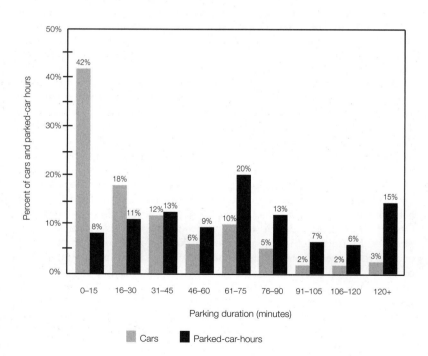

Underpriced curb parking increases parking duration, reduces turnover, and therefore reduces the number of trips curb spaces can serve. We can use the data on parking durations in Westwood to estimate how market-priced curb parking would increase the number of cars that park at the curb (Table 14-6). The results for underpriced curb parking are shown in column 1, and the estimates for market-priced curb parking in column 2. The average observed parking duration for all cars was 34 minutes, and the turnover rate (the number of spaces divided by the average parking duration) was 1.8 cars an hour per space (row 3). Because there are 470 meters in the village, this turnover rate means that during an average hour, 829 cars left a curb space and 829 new cars took their place (row 4). And because these cars had an average occupancy rate of 1.3 persons, 1,078 persons arrived every hour in the cars that park at the curb (row 6).[38] Clearly, reducing the average parking duration would increase the number of cars that can park at the curb during a day.

Now consider what would happen if the price of curb parking were set to produce an 85 percent occupancy rate (column 2). The average parking duration for the cars that did not exceed the time limit was only 17 minutes.[39] If the 38 cars that illegally stayed for more than an hour had parked off-street and their curb spaces were occupied by cars that parked the same average of 17 minutes, the turnover rate would be 3.5 cars per hour per space.[40] Although 15 percent of the curb spaces would be vacant, 1,410 new cars would park at the curb every hour (70 percent more than the 829 with underpriced curb parking). Market prices should also raise the number of persons in the cars that park at the curb. The cars that paid the market price to park off-street carried an average of 1.7 persons. If the vehicle occupancy rate of cars that pay the market price to park at the curb were also 1.7 persons per car, 2,397 persons an hour would arrive in the village in cars that park at the curb, more than twice the number who arrive when curb parking is underpriced.[41]

Halving the parking duration doubles the turnover rate, but the number of cars arriving increases by only 70 percent because 15 percent of all parking spaces stay vacant.[42] The number of *parked-car-hours* falls by 15 percent, but the *vehicle occupancy rate* increases by 31 percent, so the number of people in the village who are parked at the curb increases by 11 percent.[43] With market-priced parking, the number of persons *arriving* in the village during a day is 222 percent of the number arriving with underpriced parking, but they stay only half as long, so the number of curb-parked persons *in* the village during the day is 111 percent of that with underpriced parking.[44]

Underpricing creates the incentive for solo drivers to "squat" in scarce curb spaces, reduces turnover, and deters visitors by creating a shortage

Table 14-6. Curb Parking Prices, Occupancy, Turnover, and Arrival Rates

	Curb parking price			
	Low	Market	Ratio	Formula
	(1)	(2)	(3)=(2)/(1)	(4)
1. Curb space occupancy rate (%)	100%	85%	85%	
2. Parking duration (minutes)	34	17	50%	
3. Turnover rate (cars/hour/space)	1.8	3.5	200%	60/(2)
4. Cars parking at curb per hour	829	1,410	170%	470x(1)x(3)
5. Vehicle occupancy (persons/vehicle)	1.3	1.7	131%	
6. Persons arriving in Village per hour	1,078	2,397	222%	(4)x(5)

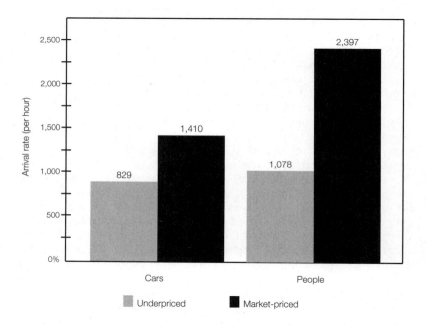

of convenient short-term parking. Market-priced curb parking will real-locate the curb spaces to visitors who place a higher value on their time. More spaces will also be available to short-term parkers who come for a quick purchase and leave immediately, so the curb parking spaces will generate more customers for local businesses. A low price for curb park-ing may sound good for business, but it is not. Careful study shows that raising the price of curb parking by just enough to create a few vacancies should improve business in Westwood Village and similar business districts.[45]

WAGES OF CRUISING IN WESTWOOD VILLAGE

To estimate the reward for cruising, consider a driver who arrived in Westwood between 6 p.m. and 7 p.m. (Table 14-7). After 6 p.m., most off-street lots charged $2 to park for the evening, while curb parking was free. Therefore, parking at the curb saved $2, minus the cost of the gasoline. The average distance cruised between 6 p.m. and 8 p.m. was 1.4 miles, which would use 0.14 gallons of gasoline (at 10 miles a gallon).[46] Since the price of gasoline was about $1 a gallon when the cruising was observed, the cost of gasoline for cruising was 14¢, and the net savings from curb parking was $1.86. The average search time between 6 p.m. and 7 p.m. was 9.4 minutes, so saving $1.86 for 9.4 minutes of cruising implies a savings of 20¢ per vehicle-minute ($12 per vehicle-hour) of cruising. Note that a solo driver saves the full $12 per hour by cruising while each member of a four-person carpool who split the cost of parking equally saves only $3 per hour. The higher reward for solo drivers helps explain both the higher share of solo drivers among curb parkers and the higher share of carpools among off-street parkers. At the average of 1.3 persons per car found for curb parkers, each person in the car saved 15¢ per minute ($9 per hour) of cruising. When these values are adjusted for inflation to the year 2002, the savings are 25¢ per minute or $15 per hour of cruising.

Table 14-7. The Economic Reward for Cruising

Savings on parking	$2.00	
Search time	9.4 minutes	
Cruising distance	1.4 miles	
Fuel efficiency	10 miles per gallon	
Fuel for cruising	0.14 gallons	(1.4 miles ÷ 10 mpg)
Price of gasoline	$1 per gallon	
Gasoline cost of cruising	$0.14	($1/gallon x 0.14 gallons)
Net savings from curb parking	$1.86	($2.00 – $0.14)
Net savings per vehicle-minute	$0.20 ($12 per hour)	($1.86 ÷ 9.4 minutes)
Persons per vehicle	1.3	
Net savings per person-minute	$0.15 ($9 per hour)	($0.20 ÷ 1.3 persons)

PERCEPTION VERSUS REALITY

Do drivers know how much they earn by searching for curb parking? To explore whether drivers accurately estimate their search times, we surveyed curb parkers. When we asked them how long they had cruised to find a space, their responses were, on average, 2.2 times what we had measured as the average search time (in column 2 of Table 14-2).[47] When we asked them how long they usually *expected* to search for parking, their responses were, on average, 3.7 times the observed time. This overestimation of search time means that drivers did not think they saved as much per minute of cruising as they actually did. For example, if drivers saved $1.86 by cruising for 9.4 minutes, they saved 20¢ per minute. But if they thought they cruised 2.2 times that long, they perceived a savings of only 9¢ per minute, less than half of what they actually saved. The over-estimation of cruising time also suggests that pricing curb parking to cre-ate a few vacancies will reduce *perceived* search time by more than twice the reduction in *actual* time.

Perhaps drivers overestimate how long they spend cruising because they think this time is wasted and boring. If so, drivers should place a high value on reducing the time spent cruising, and several studies have examined exactly this question. In 1991 Kay Axhausen and John Polak surveyed parkers in Birmingham, England, and Karlsruhe, Germany, to learn about the value of time associated with different components of travel by car—general in-vehicle time, search time, and walking time from the car to the final destination and back.[48] They estimated that com-muters were willing to spend $9.50 an hour to save search time in Birmingham and $21 an hour in Karlsruhe; shoppers were willing to spend $13 an hour to save search time in Birmingham and $59 an hour in Karlsruhe. They also estimated the drivers' cost of time spent cruising was 20 percent greater than the cost of general in-vehicle time in Birmingham and 51 percent greater in Karlsruhe; that is, drivers in Birmingham appeared to place the same value on reducing one minute of cruising *at* the destination as on reducing 1.2 minutes of driving *to* the destination, while drivers in Karlsruhe appeared to place the same value on reducing one minute of cruising as on 1.5 minutes of driving.

In 1997 Denvil Coombe et al. estimated the values that drivers who parked in the center of Bristol, England, placed on reducing search time and driving time.[49] They found that drivers valued search time at 7.6 pence a minute ($6.60 an hour) and valued driving time at 3.6 pence a minute ($3 an hour). Drivers thus appeared to be willing to spend about twice as much to reduce search time *at* the destination as to reduce driv-ing time *to* the destination.

The higher value that drivers place on reducing the time spent searching for parking helps explain why they think they spend longer cruising than they actually do—time appears to slow down when a driver is cruising. Drivers do not calculate precisely how much time they spend or money they save by cruising, but they do respond to the costs and benefits involved. The evidence suggests that drivers try to minimize the money-plus-time cost of parking. Charging market prices for curb parking will eliminate the time cost of cruising.

TURNING WASTED TIME INTO PUBLIC REVENUE

We can conduct a simple reality check on these cruising calculations. Suppose the price of curb parking in Westwood were raised just enough to eliminate cruising. How much time would drivers save, and how much revenue would the parking meters generate? There was no shortage of curb parking between 8 and 10 a.m., so the meter rate can stay at 50¢ an hour. But the curb spaces were fully occupied from 10 a.m. to 8 p.m., so the meter rates were too low. Suppose tripling the meter rate to $1.50 an hour would produce the desired 85 percent occupancy rate. How much additional revenue would this generate? The existing revenue at the current meter rate from 10 a.m. to 6 p.m. from Monday to Friday was about $500,000 a year (50¢ an hour x 8 hours a day x 5 days a week x 52 weeks a year x 470 meters). If meter rates were raised to $1.50 an hour from 10 a.m. to 8 p.m., and the occupancy rate were 85 percent, the new revenue would be about $1,250,000 a year ($1.50 x 10 x 5 x 52 x 470 x 85%). The added revenue would thus be about $750,000 a year ($1,250,000 − $500,000). Because eliminating cruising would also save about 100,000 hours of drivers' time wasted while cruising for underpriced curb parking, raising the price of curb parking would thus convert 100,000 hours of wasted time into $750,000 of public revenue, or about $7.50 of new public revenue per hour of drivers' time saved. This rough estimate of the value of saving drivers' time is similar to that found in the earlier studies and thus seems reasonable.[50] Because this calculation of potential meter revenue does not include the hours after 8 p.m. or all day on Saturday and Sunday, it underestimates both the number of cruising hours saved and the revenue that would be earned from right-priced curb parking. Right-priced curb parking is a fair and efficient way to raise public revenue, and Chapter 18 examines this issue in greater depth.

CONCLUSION: THE HIGH COST OF CRUISING

Underpriced curb parking creates a mobile queue whose members drive around rather than wait in line. The study of cruising for parking in Westwood Village found these results:

1. The average time to find a curb space was 3.3 minutes.
2. Search times increased when curb parking became free.
3. Solo drivers cruised more than did drivers of higher-occupancy vehicles.
4. In a day, cruising for parking created 3,600 excess VMT, which is greater than the distance across the U.S.
5. In a year, cruising created 945,000 VMT—equivalent to driving around the earth 38 times. It wasted 100,000 hours of drivers' time, consumed 47,000 gallons of gasoline, and produced 728 tons of CO_2.

Westwood Village has only 470 curb parking spaces, so raising the meter rates to produce a 15 percent vacancy rate would create only 71 vacancies. Because the village also has 3,400 off-street parking spaces, plus thousands more off-street spaces in the immediate surrounding area, these 71 curb vacancies would be a tiny share (less than 2 percent) of the total parking supply. Charging market prices to create this cushion of 71 curb vacancies would make parking convenient and eliminate cruising. It would also increase the efficiency of the 470 curb spaces, increase patronage of the businesses in Westwood, and increase public revenue from the parking meters.

Cities create the economic incentive to cruise by underpricing curb parking. Each driver may not think that three minutes is too long to spend cruising for a curb space, but the aggregate consequence is an astonishing amount of excess driving. Charging the right price for curb parking eliminates the incentive to cruise, and therefore reduces traffic congestion, energy consumption, accidents, and air pollution. If cities want to improve transportation, the economy, and the environment, charging the right price for curb parking is essential.

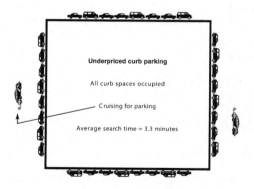

CHAPTER 14 NOTES

1. Sam Hall Kaplan, "Cars Versus Pedestrians on Melrose," *Los Angeles Times* (May 4, 1982, p. 6).

2. David Kronke, "Their Scripts Are the Victors," *Los Angeles Times* (July 9, 1995, p 26). Valet parking seems to be much more common in Los Angeles than elsewhere. Calvin Trillin says, "There's valet parking in Los Angeles. You drive up to the door of the restaurant and some kid from Honduras drives your car away for you. You don't even know where it is. You know, it's conceivable that there are people in Los Angeles who have never actually seen their car when its parked, except when it's inside their garage. That's very strange" (Trillin, 2001, 54).

3. "Tales from under the Knife," *Los Angeles Times*, January 14, 2002.

4. Kaku Associates (1994, 5, 12, and 14). The off-street vacancy rate was 56 percent at 10 a.m., 35 percent at 2 p.m., and 61 percent at 8 p.m. There were 3,408 marked spaces in 20 off-street facilities in the village. In addition to the off-street facilities within the village, several thousand off-street spaces are located in off-street facilities directly adjacent to the village. I am grateful to Francisco Contreras for designing Figure 14-1.

5. During the daytime the incentive to cruise is more complicated than just stated because many cars parked at the curb for less than an hour, and meter time could be bought in increments of five minutes, while most off-street lots charged for a minimum of one hour. Parking for half an hour would thus cost 25¢ at the curb, while parking off-street could cost up to $2.

6. I assume here that drivers do not begin searching for parking until they reach their destination, and then park in the first space they see, rather than keep cruising in search of a space nearer their destination. Cassady and Kobza (1998) examined strategies for choosing parking spaces in a mall's parking lot and found that passing up available spaces in search of a space nearer the mall's entrance increases the total time needed for the customer to reach the mall's front door after entering the parking lot.

7. The probability that a driver who is cruising will find a curb space during the next time period is equal to the number of parking spaces vacated per unit time divided by the number of cars cruising for parking. The more cars cruising and the lower the curb parking turnover, the lower the probability of finding a curb space. Drivers should thus avoid areas where other drivers appear to be cruising.

8. Cycling is also cheaper, produces no pollution, and makes cruising even enjoyable. I usually bike to UCLA, and the village is on my way to campus, so I made most of the cruising observations myself while on the way to or from work. Cruising also gave me a good excuse to visit my mother, who lived in the village.

9. The average search time was significantly higher after 6 p.m. at the 99 percent level of confidence for a *t* test of the difference between means.

10. The causal relationship between the price of curb parking and search time was clearer in London in 1965 because only parking prices changed, while in Westwood both parking prices and time restrictions changed in the evening.

11. The Hamburger Hamlet has since closed, Mario's Restaurant became a California Pizza Kitchen, and the Westwood Playhouse was renamed the Geffen Playhouse.

12. Another hypothesis is that blocks with similar commercial characteristics and a similar number of parking spaces will have the same number of cars searching for curb parking.

13. The search times between 8 a.m. and 4 p.m. refer to the Hamburger Hamlet only, while the search times between 4 p.m. and 8 p.m. refer to the average for all four addresses.

14. The average search time of 3.3 minutes per parking event between 8 a.m. and 8 p.m. is the total search time per metered space (54 minutes) divided by the number of parkings per space (17). The average search time is thus weighted by the parking turnover in each hour. The high search times per parking event in the evening are associated with low turnover, and the zero search times in the morning are associated with high turnover. The high turnover in the morning is explained by many short stops, such as to pick up doughnuts and coffee. The unweighted average search time is 4.3 minutes.

15. I assume that cruising for parking at the meters on the block containing the Hamburger Hamlet is similar to cruising for parking at other meters, as was found in the observations shown in Table 14-1.

16. The average cruising distance of 0.5 miles per parking event during the day is the total cruising distance per metered space (7.7 miles) divided by number of parking events per space (17). This average distance is thus weighted by the parking turnover in each hour. The high cruising distances in the evening are associated with low turnover, and the zero cruising distances in the morning are associated with high turnover. The unweighted average cruising distance is 0.6 miles.

17. Although the search time to find a curb space rose after 6 p.m., turnover declined because the time limits ended at 6 p.m. The total VMT for cruising during an hour is the product of the cruising distance per meter and the turnover rate; although neither the cruising distance nor the turnover rate was highest between 5 p.m. and 6 p.m., the combination of a high cruising distance *and* a high turnover rate produced the greatest amount of cruising for any hour. Ending the charge for curb parking and the time limits at 6 p.m. probably caused the greatest volume of cruising traffic in the peak hour between 5 p.m. and 6 p.m.

18. The driving distance from New York to Los Angeles is about 2,790 miles.

19. This cruising was for all the weekdays in a year: 5 x 52 x 3,633 = 944,580 VMT. The circumference of the earth at the equator is 25,000 miles, and 944,580 ÷ 25,000 = 38. This cruising took 110,760 vehicle-hours (= 5 x 52 x 426) because cruisers drove at only 8.5 miles per hour. The distance from earth to the moon is 239,000 miles. To put Westwood's annual cruising for parking in perspective, think about driving to the moon and back two times, crawling along at 8.5 miles an hour; it would take you 11.4 years. We can also make another comparison: the U.S. has 3.9 million miles of paved roads, so four years of cruising for curb parking in Westwood Village is equivalent to driving along every mile of roadway in the country (3,932,012 miles ÷ 945,000 miles per year = 4.16 years). See United States Department of Transportation (1999, Table HM-20) for the total miles of paved roads—highways, arterials, collectors, and local streets, both urban and rural—in the U.S.

20. Combustion of each gallon of gasoline produces 19.6 pounds of tailpipe CO_2 emissions. The full-fuel-cycle emissions (counting emissions from extraction, transport, and refining) are 57 percent higher than the tailpipe emissions alone, so a gallon of gasoline consumed for cruising produces 30.8 pounds of CO_2 (U.S. Department of Energy 1994a, 79).

21. The average American household consumed 1,067 gallons of gasoline for vehicle travel in 1994. See the United States Department of Energy (1994b, Table 5.2) Available online at www.eia.doe.gov/emeu/rtecs/toc.html.

22. The estimates for Westwood Village were 3.3 minutes of cruising before parking, a parking turnover rate of 17 cars per space per day, and a cruising speed of 8.5 miles per hour. Because the measurements were made only on weekdays, the total cruising was estimated for 260 days per year.

23. Because the average car in the U.S. is driven 11,766 miles year (*Ward's Automotive Yearbook 2003*, pp. 268-269), the cruising for seven curb spaces in Westwood Village is equal to the average annual VMT per car in the U.S.

24. Portland Metro Regional Transportation Planning (1995). The study found that two-thirds of the total curb length is available for parking, and the remaining third is committed to driveways, bus stops, fire hydrants, loading zones, and other no-parking uses. The 100 linear curb feet include both the parking and the no-parking zones. The average block with 253 feet of curb space thus has eight curb spaces (253 feet x 3.3 spaces per 100 feet = 8.3 spaces). See Chapter 18 for a discussion of the Portland study. Taylor, Young, and Bonsall (1996, Chapter 13) explain the methodology of conducting parking inventories. At the rate of 3.3 parking spaces per 100 feet, there are 172 curb spaces per mile.

25. The average cruising distance between 8 a.m. and 8 p.m. was 0.5 miles, and there are about 3.3 parking spaces per 100 linear feet of curb, so drivers passed 87 curb spaces before finding a vacancy (5,280 x 0.5 x 3.3/100 = 87). When the average cruising distance was 1.4 miles between 6 p.m. and 8 p.m., drivers passed 243 curb spaces before finding a vacancy. Gennaro Bifulco (1993) presents a model of cruising that includes the number of spaces passed before a vacant parking space is found. I am grateful to Jeremy Nelson for suggesting and creating Figure 14-2.

26. The cruising distance *per metered space* per hour is greater than the cruising distance *per car that parked at the curb* because the meters turn over more than once per hour. Column 8 of the next-to-last row of Table 14-2 shows that cruising around the 15 blocks creates 303 VMT of cruising per hour or 20 VMT per block per hour, which amounts to 240 VMT for the 12 hours between 8 a.m. and 8. p.m. If the block is 253 feet per side, its perimeter is 1,012 feet or 0.2 mile. Cruising creates 62,000 VMT around the block every year (240 x 5 x 52) or 1,900 VMT a year per curb space (62,000 ÷ 32). Drivers may not always circle the same block while cruising, but if the average search time is the same on all blocks, the path of cruising doesn't make any difference to the total amount of cruising.

27. If a block is 0.2 miles around, 20 VMT is equivalent to 100 circuits of the block (20 ÷ 0.2). If cruisers make 100 circuits of the block per hour, there is one circuit every 0.6 minutes (60 minutes ÷ 100 circuits), or one circuit every 36 seconds. If we again imagine that all cruising cars are painted bright yellow, someone standing on the sidewalk would see a bright yellow car pass in each direction every 36 seconds.

28. I am grateful to Jun Zhang for conducting the parking meter observations and analyzing the results. He was the first graduate student from mainland China to study urban planning in the U.S. After earning his M.A. at UCLA and his Ph.D at MIT, he became a senior economist at the World Bank.

29. The occupancy rate is the average over the hour, however, so all curb spaces could be occupied during some of the hour even when the average occupancy rate is only 90 percent, and this would cause cruising at some times during the hour even when the average occupancy rate is less than 90 percent. If there are vacancies all during the hour, no one would need to cruise, but some drivers who are the first to see a newly vacated space will take it; in this case, the share of spaces taken by the first car to pass them will overpredict the share of traffic that is cruising.

30. Table 14-3 shows that 68 percent of the total traffic flow on Weyburn Avenue was cruising. Earlier it was estimated that for every 100 cars parked at the curb, an average of seven cars were waiting in traffic to find a curb space. The difference between these two estimates is due to the different concepts they measure. For every 100 cars in motion, 68 of them were cruising, while for every 100 cars parked at the curb, seven more were cruising. Cruisers are a larger share of moving cars than of parked cars because more cars are parked than moving. A 22 percent reduction in the total number of curb spaces demanded may therefore be needed to create a 15 percent vacancy rate (15% + 7%).

31. Adiv and Wang (1987, 297). Italics in the original.

32. Seburn (1967, 42).

33. Weant and Levinson (1990, 242).

34. In an early study, Wilbur Smith (1947, 163) reported that 9.2 percent of accidents in urban areas involved parked cars, 5 percent involved cars leaving a parked position, and 2.6 percent involved cars stopped in traffic (some of them preparing to park); therefore, between 14 and 17 percent of urban traffic accidents were related to parking. Five percent of pedestrians killed and 9 percent of pedestrians injured in cities had entered the roadway from behind parked cars. In a report to the House Committee on Public Works, the U.S. Department of Commerce (U.S. Congress 1959, 61) reported, "In urban areas about 12 percent of all accidents involve parked vehicles and an additional 4 percent involve a vehicle leaving a parked position. Thus, 16 percent of all accidents in urban areas are directly related to curb parking." Paul Box (1970, 9) reported that "curb parking is directly or indirectly responsible for about *one-in-five* total urban accidents." In a study of bicycle fatalities in New York City from 1995 to 1998, Charles Komanoff and Michael Smith (2000, 2) found that three of the 72 fatal bicycle crashes involved "dooring" by drivers exiting their parked cars. Accidents related to curb parking should thus be considered in deciding whether to permit curb parking on any block.

35. Cruising for parking increases local traffic congestion, and this explains why most people expect ample off-street parking requirements to reduce traffic. But the resulting free parking increases the total amount of vehicle travel and thus increases regional traffic congestion. In contrast, market-rate prices for curb parking will reduce both local *and* regional traffic congestion.

36. See Simpson (1927, 84); this study was discussed in Chapter 12. Smith and LeCraw (1946, 36) reported that in a similar study of curb parking in Durham, North Carolina, in 1945, only 25 percent of curb parkers stayed for more than an hour, but they occupied 59 percent of the space-hours used.

37. Swan (1922, 498).

38. This calculation assumes that the turnover and vehicle occupancy for all cars that park in the Village are the same as observed those observed on Broxton Avenue.

39. Column 4 of Table 14-5 shows that 134 cars parked for 60 minutes or less, and column 8 shows they parked for a total of 39 hours (2,340 minutes); the average parking duration for these 134 cars was thus 17 minutes (2,340 ÷ 134).

40. Alternatively, we could assume that all the previous overtime parkers would instead stay the legal one hour.

41. Some of the new carpools that park at the curb may previously have parked off-street because they couldn't find curb parking, however, and some solo drivers who previously parked at the curb might park off-street.

42. Suppose, for example, there are 100 parking spaces, the occupancy rate is 100 percent, and the average parking duration is one hour, so that 100 cars arrive and depart every hour. Now suppose the price of parking increases, and the average duration declines to 30 minutes; if the average occupancy rate stayed 100 percent, 200 cars would arrive and depart per hour. If, however, the occupancy rate declines to 85 percent, 170 cars would arrive and depart every hour. Increasing the price of parking would thus double the turnover rate but increase the number of cars arriving and departing by 70 percent.

43. The vehicle occupancy rate increases from 1.3 to 1.7 persons per car (31 percent), and the curb space vacancy rate falls to 85 percent, but 131% x 85% = 111%, so the number of *parked-person-hours* increases by 11 percent.

44. This phenomenon is similar to what happens in an HOV lane compared with hyper-congested mixed-flow lanes. The density of vehicles in the HOV lane (cars per mile) is lower than in the mixed-flow lanes, but the flow (cars per hour) is higher, and because the number of persons per car is also higher, the number of persons per hour in the HOV lane is higher than in an adjacent mixed-flow lane.

45. Charging market prices for curb parking may increase meter revenue without significantly affecting retail sales, especially if metered spaces are a small part of the total parking supply. In her doctoral dissertation at the University of Illinois, Nancy Scannell (1992) used data on changes in the number of metered parking spaces over a period of eight years to examine the relationship between the number of metered parking spaces and retail sales in Chicago. The number of metered parking spaces fluctuates every year for a variety of reasons, such as street and sidewalk repairs, street widenings, changes from two-way to one-way streets or vice-versa, and decisions to ban on-street parking entirely. Scannell found no significant relationship between changes in the number of metered parking spaces and retail sales.

46. This fuel efficiency was measured for the 1966 Ford Mustang used to conduct the cruising experiments; it is 41 percent less than the 17 miles a gallon in average city driving for the same car. The fuel efficiency for cruising is low presumably because the average cruising speed in Westwood is so low; every intersection has a stop sign or traffic light, and cars usually have to wait for pedestrians to cross, so the average speed is only 8 to 10 miles an hour. The fuel efficiency of the average cruiser is difficult to estimate, but it has little effect on the calculations because the cost of fuel is a small part of the combined time-and-money cost of cruising.

47. Falcocchio, Darsin, and Prassas (1995) estimated search times in Manhattan by interviewing drivers who parked at the curb. If drivers overestimate the time they cruise, this method overestimates the average search time.

48. Axhausen and Polak (1991, 72-76). The original values in 1988 were £4.12 and DM 35.42 per hour for work trips, and £5.74 and DM100.86 per hour for shopping trips. These values were converted to U.S. dollars using purchasing power parities (£1 = $1.66 and $1 = DM2.49) and then adjusted to 2002 dollars by the U.S. Consumer Price Index.

49. Coombe et al. (1997, 67) used the Traffic Restraint Analysis Model (TRAM) to make these estimates, using a stated-preference approach.

50. Because a value of $7.50 an hour for time saved was calculated from the estimate that drivers spend 100,000 hours a year cruising for parking in the village, it suggests that the estimate of total cruising time is also reasonable.

Part

III

Cashing in on
Curb Parking

Plans are policies, and policies, in a democracy at any rate, spell politics. The question is not whether planning will reflect politics, but whose politics it will reflect.

—NORTON LONG

15

Buying Time
at the Curb

*I'll tell you how to solve Los Angeles' traffic problem. Just take all the cars
off the road that aren't paid for.*

— *WILL ROGERS*

Free curb parking is like rent control for cars. High demand for a limited
supply of free curb spaces predictably leads to shortages, and to deal with
this problem cities impose off-street parking requirements that increase
the cost of housing. Free parking for *cars* thus raises the cost of housing
for *people*. But suppose cities remove off-street parking requirements and
begin to charge market prices for curb parking. If cities charge prices to
keep about 15 percent of curb spaces vacant—flexible prices to balance
the variable demand for curb parking with the fixed supply of curb
spaces—drivers will always be able to find an available curb space at their
destinations. Market-priced curb parking will save time, reduce traffic,
conserve energy, improve air quality, reduce housing costs, and increase
public revenue. But two major problems—one practical, the other political—prevent cities from charging the right price for curb parking. The
practical problem is how to collect the revenue, and the political problem
is that everyone wants to park free. This chapter describes new technology that has removed the practical problem. The following two chapters
will propose a new strategy for distributing curb parking revenue to overcome the political problem.

FIRST PARKING METER

Because one of its residents, Carl Magee, invented the parking meter, Oklahoma City installed the world's first parking meters in 1935. *The Encyclopedia of Oklahoma History and Culture* tells the story:

> In Oklahoma in 1913 there had been an estimated three thousand cars; by 1930 there were five hundred thousand, most of which were registered in Oklahoma County and the capital city. The problem was that people who worked downtown occupied all of the parking spots every day, forcing retail customers to park far away from stores. The city had placed time limits on parking, with enforcement performed by traffic police who chalked tires, marked time, and gave tickets on hourly rounds. The parking situation came under scrutiny by the Oklahoma City Chamber of Commerce in 1932. Appointed chair of the Traffic Committee, Magee assumed the task of solving the problem.
>
> Magee decided that the situation required the invention of a small, windable, inexpensively made, mechanical device to "time" the use of each parking space. In 1932 he designed and built a crude model and on December 21, 1932, filed for a patent. In order to refine the concept and build a real working prototype, he joined forces with the Oklahoma State University Engineering Department.... On July 16, 1935, 175 meters were installed and tested on fourteen blocks in Oklahoma City, and when the system proved successful, the city placed meters all over downtown.
>
> The impact of the parking meter was threefold. First, it straightened out Oklahoma City's parking problem. Second, it brought revenue into the city coffers through meter money (a nickel an hour) and parking fines (a twenty-dollar fine for each violation). Third, it stimulated a huge growth in the assessed valuation of downtown commercial property. Carl C. Magee had started a trend, and parking meters sprang up in cities across the nation.[1]

The new parking meters were a great success. Oklahoma historian LeRoy Fischer says:

> On a hot July day in 1935, the world's first parking meters went into use. In the early morning, the meters were the subject of much interest by sidewalk crowds and motorists. There was not much use of the parking spaces at the early hours, as not much business was being done; normally, these spaces would have been full under the old conditions. As the morning hours passed, meter usage increased. Cars pulled into the metered spaces and moved out when their owners had finished their business, while in the unmetered zones the old congestion remained. Magee's idea of a coin-operated meter for the regulation of parking on city streets was proving itself, although at the time of

the initial installation most everyone had been skeptical of what the meters would accomplish. Within a few days other businesses were asking for meters on their streets, and within several months far more than the original 150 units had been installed. A new product had been born.... Newsreel cameramen came to take pictures of the installation.[2]

The meter sketched in Magee's patent application looks more streamlined than today's models, but one might easily mistake it for a parking meter now on any city street (Figure 15-1).

From the user's point of view, most American parking meters remain identical to the original 1935 model: you put coins in the meter to buy a specific amount of time, and you risk getting a ticket if you don't return before your time expires.[3] The main change in 70 years is that few meters now take nickels. In real terms, however, the price of most curb parking hasn't increased; adjusted for inflation, 5 cents in 1935 was worth 65 cents in 2004, less than the price of parking for an hour at many meters in 2004.

The original purpose of parking meters was to enforce time limits for curb parking and thus ensure turnover so that as many cars as possible could park in the limited number of curb spaces. The parking meter's main purpose is still the same: it limits the allowed time at the curb, and the prohibition against feeding the meter is intended to ensure turnover. The price of curb parking by itself, however, is usually too low to ensure vacancies or frequent turnover without time limits.

In the 1950s, optimists predicted that nuclear power plants would soon make electricity so abundant that it would be "too cheap to meter," but that prediction failed spectacularly.[4] By

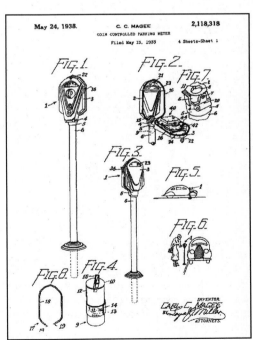

Figure 15-1. Patent for the Parking Meter

making parking spaces so abundant that there is no need to charge for them, however, urban planners have succeeded where nuclear physicists failed, and drivers now park free for most of their trips. Most parking *is* literally too cheap to meter, and one result has been the arrested development of American meter technology. Although the parking meter was invented in the U.S., most of the subsequent technological progress has been made in Europe, where the scarcity of parking creates a demand for more efficient and convenient metering. American cities now use parking meters almost exclusively in areas that were developed before zoning required off-street parking.

The technology of paying for most commercial goods and services evolved rapidly in the last century, with ceaseless innovation in cash registers, bar code readers, credit cards, debit cards, and smart cards. These innovations have made commerce more convenient for shoppers and more efficient for merchants. In contrast, the technology of paying for public utilities stagnated: electricity meters, gas meters, water meters, and parking meters have changed very little, or not at all. But if American cities remove off-street parking requirements and begin to charge market prices for curb parking, meter technology will advance rapidly.[5]

THE TECHNOLOGY OF CHARGING FOR CURB PARKING

Traditional curb parking meters require drivers to carry exact change and to decide in advance how long they want to park. Ensuing concern about the need to return before the meter expires can create "meter anxiety." Many drivers end up either paying for more time than they use or not paying enough and risking a ticket. New technology, however, allows drivers to pay for curb parking without carrying exact change and without deciding in advance how long they want to park. Buying time at the curb can now be as convenient as any other of life's daily transactions, like buying a loaf of bread or a quart of milk.[6]

New Parking Meters

Only a few American cities have installed advanced parking meters, but the resulting experience shows their effectiveness. I will use the case of Aspen, Colorado, to illustrate the advantages of the new meters. Aspen, a resort community, is hardly a typical American city, but until recently it suffered from the usual parking woes. With only 5,000 residents but 25,000 visitors a day during the winter and summer, curb parking is scarce. Until 1995 parking was free and restricted only by a 90-minute time limit. This created predictable problems, as described by Aspen's city manager:

Most of the downtown parking spaces in Aspen were being occupied by locals and commuters working in downtown and moving their cars every ninety minutes to avoid parking tickets in what we affectionately called the "90 Minute Shuffle." Few if any spaces were available for shoppers, restaurant patrons, and guests. The result was a commercial core full of employees' parked cars and streets congested with angry guests' and shoppers' cars endlessly trolling for a parking space.[7]

Aspen attempted to solve its parking problem by building a 340-space municipal garage in 1991. But the new garage did not solve the problem because curb parking remained free:

> Despite its convenient location and $1.50 a day rate, only during special occasions did it ever fill. On most days the garage remained over half empty, while tremendous congestion and competition raged for free on-street parking a block away.[8]

After several years of planning and preparation, Aspen began to charge for curb parking in 1995. The price is now highest in the commercial core—$1 an hour—and declines with distance outward. The city also established Residential Parking Permit (RPP) districts in neighborhoods surrounding the commercial area and allows nonresidents to park in these RPP districts for $5 a day. Aspen also introduced sophisticated new meters to make paying for parking more convenient for drivers. These meters have been widely adopted in Europe but remain unfamiliar in most American cities. In the remainder of this chapter, I will describe five of these new ways to pay for parking: (1) pay-and-display multispace meters, (2) pay-by-space multispace meters, (3) personal in-vehicle meters, (4) payment by mobile telephones, and (5) payment by satellite.

Pay-and-Display Meters

Aspen places one "pay-and-display" multispace parking meter in the middle of the block on each side of the street in the downtown district. After parking, drivers walk to the meter and pay for the length of time they wish to park. The meter delivers a receipt imprinted with the time and date for which parking has been purchased, and the driver displays the receipt inside the car's windshield. One inexpensive and unobtrusive pay-and-display meter can control 20 to 30 parking spaces. Aspen is one of only a few cities in the U.S. to use pay-and-display meters, but many European cities use them for both curb and off-street parking.

Aspen carried out an extensive public education program when it introduced the new technology. It gave one free $20 smart card to every Aspen resident to familiarize them with the new multispace meters, and it voided one parking ticket per license plate for violations of the new regulations. Parking control officers also carried smart cards and offered an hour of free parking to any drivers who were confused by the new system.[9] These consumer outreach efforts are often overlooked, but in Aspen they increased public acceptance of the new technology.

Multispace pay-and-display meters have several important advantages over traditional parking meters:

Duncan Parking Technologies

Figure 15-2. Pay-and-Display Meter

1. Ease of payment. Multispace meters accept payment by coins, bills, credit cards, smart cards, and cell phones.[10] Drivers thus don't need to carry exact change to feed the meters.

2. Flexible prices. Multispace meters have computer capabilities that allow charging different prices by time of day or day of the week, thus responding to variations in parking demand. Parking officials can remotely reconfigure the price schedule in any area and the new rates are sent wirelessly to all the meters in the neighborhood.

3. Better information. Multispace meters can show information on a large, interactive graphic screen, so they can convey complex information. They can be multilingual, display graphics, and guide the user through transactions with messages such as "Please insert your card other side up."

4. Better revenue control. Multispace meters automatically record how much money has been collected from credit cards, debit cards, bills, and coins. Each meter keeps a running tally of the day's receipts—sent wirelessly to a central site—allowing auditors to detect any discrepancies when the revenue is counted. Officials can monitor each unit's take in real time. These data are useful for audit purposes to ensure that all revenue is collected and deposited to the correct accounts.

5. Better data collection. The meters produce records of parking occupancy on each block by time of day and day of the week, and the resulting data can easily be displayed on a city's geographic information system. The information is useful to analyze usage patterns and set prices to manage the parking supply.

6. Proof of payment. The receipt is proof of payment for the parker's business and tax records. Parkers who receive an erroneous ticket can send in the receipt as proof of payment without going to court.
7. Economy. One multispace meter costs less to purchase and maintain than the 20 to 30 individual meters that it replaces. Payment by credit and debit cards reduces the cost of collecting, transferring, and counting bills and coins.
8. Less Out-of-Service Time. Cities can equip multispace meters with cellular communication devices that automatically report any mechanical failure to a central computer. Rapid service response can then make it likely that meters are up and running when motorists try to pay.
9. Preferential rates for residents. Where smart cards are used, cities can configure the system to allow residents to pay a preferential rate in their home neighborhood and pay normal rates elsewhere.
10. Better urban design. One multispace meter can replace up to 30 individual meters, and the pay-and-display procedure does not require marking individual curb spaces on the street. Multispace meters thus reduce street clutter by removing unnecessary hardware and signs. The meters can also be solar powered.
11. More spaces. Because conventional meters must be spaced to accommodate the longest cars, they are separated by more space than necessary for small cars. At unmarked curbs, smaller cars can fit into spaces too small for longer cars, and about 10 to 15 percent more cars can typically fit into the available curb space. Unmarked curbs also give a selective advantage to smaller cars.
12. Higher revenue per space. Because new pay-and-display parkers cannot use any unexpired time paid for by the departed parkers, each space yields higher revenue.

Pay-by-Space Meters

Pay-by-space meters are another multispace technology that makes curb parking more convenient. The city paints a number on the sidewalk beside each curb space and installs signs directing parkers to the nearby meter. Berkeley, California, installs one meter for every eight curb spaces, and they are simple for drivers to use. Parking consultant John Van Horn describes their operation:

> The driver parks his car, notes the space number and goes to the machine. He selects the space number and inserts the appropriate coins. The machine displays the amount of time purchased. Enforcement officers can easily see which spaces are in violation by observing small windows in the back of the machine. When a space is in violation, a red fluorescent dot appears [in the

window].… On the face of the machine, in addition to the space numbers, is an "information" button that when pressed gives the parker additional information about the unit and whatever else the city wishes to place on the display. The city has also placed its toll-free number on the machines, but so far has received no complaint calls.[11]

Pay-by-space meters resemble the pay-and-display meters, but have several additional advantages.

1. Convenience. Parkers who have entered the number of their space in the meter don't need to return to their vehicles because they are not required to display a receipt on the dash.
2. Grace time. The meters can offer a "grace period" before displaying a violation.
3. No meter anxiety. Parkers who pay by credit, debit, or smart cards, or by cell phones, can pay for more time than they expect to use, and can then obtain a refund for the unused time when they return. For those who have paid by cell phone, a text message can be sent to the phone when the meter time is almost expired, offering a chance to add time.
4. Networks. All multispace meters in an area can be networked, and drivers can extend the time on their space by paying at the nearest meter rather than returning to their vehicles.

After the meters were installed in Berkeley, the City Manager reported, "The feedback has been positive—as positive as you can get for a parking meter."[12]

Because of their computing capabilities, the multispace meters are well suited to varying the price of curb parking to achieve a desired vacancy rate for the curb spaces they control. Each meter knows the occupancy rate for all its spaces at each time of the day or week, so these data can be used to set the appropriate prices. Historical data can be analyzed to predict prices that will achieve the desired occupancy rate, or prices can be adjusted in real time to respond to the observed occupancy rates. Although at first glance it may appear difficult or impractical to vary curb parking prices in response to changing demand, one has only to look at off-street parking lots to see that many private operators continuously tweak their prices to manage the demand for their spaces.

Figure 15-3. Pay-by-Space Meter

Reino International

Personal In-Vehicle Meters

Aspen also uses personal in-vehicle parking meters to make paying for parking more convenient. These personal meters look like small pocket calculators, and motorists use them in combination with a stored-value smart card to pay for curb parking.[13]

The system works as follows. The city marks the zones where curb parking is priced, assigns a number to each zone, and posts on each block the zone number and meter rate. To pay for parking, the driver keys the zone number into the meter, inserts the smart card, switches the meter on, and hangs it inside the car's windshield with the liquid crystal display (LCD) visible. A timer in the meter deducts money from the smart card for the parking time elapsed until the driver returns and switches it off.[14] Enforcement personnel can easily determine whether a parked car's meter is running because they can see the zone code and elapsed time flashing in the LCD window. The meter shows the card's remaining prepaid value at both the beginning and the end of each use, and thus reminds motorists when they need to add value to their cards.

Europeans refer to the in-vehicle meter as an "electronic purse" because of its convenience. Paying for parking with an in-vehicle meter is like paying for a long-distance telephone call with a prepaid calling card. Callers pay for long-distance telephone calls according to where they call, when they call, and how long they talk. With in-vehicle meters, drivers pay for parking according to where they park, when they park, and how long they park.

In 1989, Arlington, Virginia, became the first local government to introduce in-vehicle parking meters in the U.S., and subsequent surveys have shown an overwhelmingly positive response from motorists.[15] Cities that use the in-vehicle meter system report the following advantages:

1. No need for cash. Drivers don't need coins, tokens, or exact change when parking because the in-vehicle meters operate like debit cards.

2. Accurate payments for parking. Drivers pay for the exact parking time they use—no more, no less. Drivers don't pay for any leftover time they don't use.

3. No meter anxiety. Drivers don't need to guess how long they will want to park and don't need to return to their cars by a specific time.

Figure 15-4. In-Vehicle Meter

Ganis Smart Park Systems

4. Safety. Where personal safety is an issue, drivers feel more secure because they pay for parking while still inside their cars. Drivers are also protected from bad weather while paying for parking.
5. Receipt for parking fees. The electronic memory of the in-vehicle meter can provide receipts for parking fees to use for expense accounts or tax purposes.
6. Mobility. The same in-vehicle meter can be used in several cities.
7. Faster turnover. In-vehicle meters encourage faster parking turnover because drivers pay for parking by the minute. Drivers don't use up excess time at the curb simply because they have already paid for it.
8. Low cost. The city doesn't need to buy, install, and maintain conventional post-mounted meters, and it doesn't need to collect, transfer, and count coins.
9. Revenue in advance. The city collects the parking revenue in advance and earns interest on the unused balances.
10. Adjustable prices. In-vehicle meters can charge different rates in different areas, at different times of the day and days of the week, and for different parking durations.
11. Grace periods. In-vehicle meters can automatically offer a preset "grace period" after the legal time limit at a space has expired.
12. Compatibility with conventional meters. Drivers can use their in-vehicle meters to pay for parking at conventional meters or multi-space meters. Cash customers who don't have in-vehicle meters can pay by putting coins in the conventional meters.
13. No theft or vandalism. Users insert the smart card in the meter when they key in the zone where they park and then activate the meter by removing the smart card. The debit for parking is deducted from the card when the driver inserts it in the meter for the next use. No one has any incentive to steal the meter because it has no monetary content and it cannot be activated without the smart card that stores the monetary value. In-vehicle meters also eliminate the risk of vandalism that is commonly directed at conventional meters.
14. Ease of enforcement. The parking-zone code flashes in the LCD window of a meter that is running, and enforcement personnel can easily see whether a car is paying for parking.
15. Fewer parking violations. Drivers with in-vehicle meters usually pay for parking rather than risk getting a ticket. If the expected cost of illegal parking (the fine multiplied by the probability of citation) exceeds the price of legal parking, people pay for parking to save money.
16. Statistical analysis. The times parked in each zone are stored in the smart card's memory and can be retrieved for statistical analysis

when value is added to the cards. Anyone who is concerned about keeping this information private can always pay cash or buy a new smart card rather than add value to an old one.

17. Better urban design. The in-vehicle technology saves valuable space on the sidewalk, removes unsightly meter clutter, and does not require painting stripes on the street to mark the curb spaces.

These advantages come at low cost to both drivers and the city. Aspen requires a one-time deposit of $40 per in-vehicle meter. Drivers can pre-pay for as much parking time as they want, and they can add value to their meters' remaining balance whenever they like. Drivers bought 300 meters in the first three days of the program, and by 1998 had bought more meters than the number of residents in the city.[16]

Compared with conventional parking meters, in-vehicle meters save time, space, and money. Murray Tepper, the parking connoisseur and hero of Calvin Trillin's novel *Tepper Isn't Going Out*, explains the problem with conventional meters:

"I've got a dollar and a half invested in this spot," Tepper said. "So there is good reason to be here at least until I get my money's worth. I read somewhere that the aggregate value of unexpired time left on meters people drive off from, just in New York alone, is the equivalent of the gross national product of something like thirty-eight different countries. I'll admit that it's hard to figure out what you're supposed to make of that statistic. I mean, it's not as if we could help the economy of those countries by staying longer at the meters. But there it is."[17]

With in-vehicle meters, drivers pay only for the time they park and so are rewarded for leaving early. This pay-as-you-park price structure makes better use of the scarce curb spaces because drivers don't spend excess time at the curb simply because they have already paid for it. Drivers save the money they would otherwise leave in unexpired meters, and because they don't park any longer than necessary, they make more spaces available for other drivers. Parking thrift saves space, time, and money. So there it is.

Payment by Mobile Telephone

In Europe, the cost of converting most parking meters to the Euro has spurred the development of even newer cashless payment systems for parking. For example, some cities in Holland and Sweden have introduced a system that allows drivers to use cellular telephones to pay for curb parking.[18] A driver parks, dials the city's number for parking payments, and keys in both the license plate number and the number of the district where the car is parked. After returning to the car, the driver dials the same number to end the payment. Drivers pay only for the exact time parked, and the city sends bills to motorists periodically. A transponder in the car's windshield shows enforcement officers that the car is registered for the payment system. Without stopping to inspect the car, the officers use a hand-held scanner to interrogate the car's transponder and check that it is paying. If it isn't, a parking ticket is issued electronically.

Apart from a simple transponder card necessary for each car, drivers don't need to purchase any special devices to participate in the program. In addition to the added convenience for drivers, the city benefits from reduced vandalism, lower collection costs, and lower maintenance costs. The system also provides real-time information on parking occupancy throughout the city, which helps planners evaluate and adjust their parking policies. Mobile telephone ownership by motorists is becoming ubiquitous in most countries, and phone-based payment systems (also called m-commerce or e-payments) are a convenient way to pay for curb parking.

Payment by Satellite

The European Union is evaluating the feasibility of using satellite technology to implement a pan-European road tolling system. Road tolls would be assessed electronically by the Global Positioning System (GPS), which would track information on the distance traveled, the time of travel, and the class of road used. If this plan is implemented, it could be extended to paying for curb parking as well. When a car is parked on-street, the system could charge its owner for the use of the road space, just as when cars are moving.[19] Combining charges for parking with tolls for driving would spread the cost of the satellite-based system over a much broader base of transactions and thereby reduce the cost of introducing the road tolls. The savings in the capital and operating cost of conventional parking meters, and the revenue from previously free curb parking, would also help finance the cost of the new GPS-based metering.

NOT TECHNOLOGY BUT POLITICS

Primitive technology once made it difficult to charge market prices for curb parking. Now, most parking seems too cheap to meter because off-street parking requirements increase the supply and reduce the price. The cost of parking is shifted from parkers into higher prices for everything else, and the plethora of free parking gives the false impression that charging for parking would cost a lot but bring in little revenue. The cost of parking is thus an external cost of driving. As Stanford economist and

Nobel laureate Kenneth Arrow observed, the existence of an externality is equivalent to the nonexistence of a market, which typically occurs either when property rights are not defined or the transaction costs are too high. But property rights for parking are (or can be) well defined, and new technology has greatly reduced the transaction costs of charging for it. The real barrier to charging the right price for curb parking is not technology but politics.

Almost every American adult owns a car and almost every car is parked most of the time. Free parking therefore seems to serve almost everyone's interest, and it may appear naive to recommend charging fair-market prices for curb parking, no matter how sophisticated the technology. Fortunately, Aspen's success with paid parking clearly shows that market prices for curb parking can be politically popular, even in the face of some initial protest. Opponents organized a "Honk if You Hate Paid Parking" campaign at the end of 1994, just before pay parking began. Aspen's city manager describes the scene:

> Precisely at noon on the Friday before the New Year, employees of the downtown shops and restaurants (and more than a few from City Hall) poured out of their workplaces, walked to their cars parked right in front a few steps away, and proceeded to honk their horns for half an hour in protest of the parking regulations that would soon go into effect.[20]

Some citizens, however, mounted a counter-demonstration to *support* paid parking:

> The local chapter of the Sierra Club added flavor with several of their members parading in gas masks, including one dressed as a clown riding a unicycle and carrying a sign that read, "Honk if You Love Dirty Air."[21]

Despite the initial protests, paid parking has worked well in Aspen. When parking was free, downtown curb occupancy during peak periods ranged from 95 to 100 percent and finding a space was difficult. Average occupancy declined to about 70 percent after paid parking began, and it became easy to park downtown. Aspen's citizens now overwhelmingly support the program:

> Much to the horn-honkers' chagrin, the paid-parking program was supported by a 3 to 1 margin by voters in the municipal election in May 1995.... Most downtown business people now agree that the attractiveness of available convenient parking for their shoppers and patrons has far offset any disadvantages of paid parking. Likewise, the Residential Permit program has helped residents of neighborhoods around the commercial core to find a place to park

in the block on which they live instead of several blocks away. The municipal parking structure now fills routinely during the winter and summer months and has begun to generate surplus revenues that can be reinvested in transportation improvements. The paid parking programs are generating about $600,000 a year in new revenues.[22]

On a typical day, Aspen has five times more visitors than residents. Seen from the residents' point of view, their town receives meter revenue paid mostly by tourists. Wouldn't *you* vote for that?

Beyond being politically popular, charging users in proportion to their use of curb parking is sound economic policy, as public finance economist Richard Bird explains:

> The appropriate initial position in formulating sound public policy is that any public service with an easily identifiable direct beneficiary should be paid for by that beneficiary, *unless* sound and convincing arguments in favour of a particular degree of explicit subsidy can be produced. This starting point is in complete opposition to that which many countries seem to have adopted, namely, that whatever subsidies now exist are right, so that the onus of proof with respect to any change lies with the proponents of change. This position may not be logical, but that is the one with which proponents of user charges almost certainly will have to deal.[23]

Charging tourists for curb parking is an unusual case where the proponents of a new user charge can easily deal with the standard argument that every existing subsidy is justified. Users pay for the benefits they receive, and most of these users are nonresidents who cannot vote.

CONCLUSION: HONK IF YOU SUPPORT PAID PARKING

Aspen's residents voted for paid parking because they found it has several important advantages. It makes vacant curb spaces available, reduces traffic congestion and air pollution, improves urban design, increases the use of off-street public parking, and generates substantial revenue from visitors.

Aspen's experience raises an important question: if paid parking works so well there, why don't more cities try it? The answer lies with what happens to the money fed into parking meters. The next two chapters argue that the residents of many cities will support fair-market prices for curb parking if each neighborhood gets to keep the curb parking revenue it generates. We already have the right technology to charge market prices for curb parking. Now we can also have the right politics.

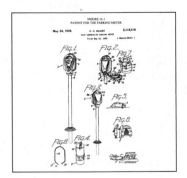

CHAPTER 15 NOTES

1. "Parking Meter," in *The Encyclopedia of Oklahoma History and Culture*, available online at www.ok-history.mus.ok.us/enc/parking.htm. Fischer and Smith (1969, 184) report that Oklahoma City paid $23 for each of the new meters, equivalent to $311 per meter in 2004.

2. Fischer (1970, 346). Carl Magee had pointed out that prior to the parking meter, "in spite of one-hour parking regulations, regular policing, and periodic crack-downs, something on the order of eighty percent of all automobiles remained parked on the streets in one location all or most of the day. These long-time parkers were primarily proprietors and employees of nearby downtown businesses" (Thuesen 1967, 115). In August 1935, the city conducted a survey of curb parking. In nonmetered zones, 60 percent of the parked cars were owned by merchants or people who worked downtown, with low turnover. In metered areas there was a rapid turnover of cars and an even flow of traffic (Fischer and Smith 1969, 201).

3. The Reverend C. H. North of Oklahoma City's Third Pentecostal Holiness Church was the first motorist cited for overstaying a parking meter's time limit. The Reverend "said that he was guilty, but maintained that he had gone to a store to get change and when he returned to deposit a nickel, he found a ticket on his windshield." This then-novel excuse persuaded the judge to dismiss the citation (Fischer and Smith 1969, 192).

4. In a talk to the National Association of Science Writers on September 16th, 1954, Admiral Lewis L. Strauss, Chairman of the U.S. Atomic Energy Commission, said, "It is not too much to expect that our children will enjoy electrical energy in their homes too cheap to meter." The modern, abundant, and clean energy from nuclear power plants would somehow be free, like curb parking.

5. What would cities do with all their old parking meters? They might follow Seattle's lead by converting them into "giving meters." Seattle has adapted unused parking meters to take change from passers-by, hoping that donors who are reluctant to give money to panhandlers will put coins in the meters; the money is used to pay homeless young people for taking part in community projects and for job training. "This is not a parking meter," say the signs on University Way. "This is a chance for new beginnings." Although city officials say the meters are a way to draw attention to the homeless and the services that help them, the mayor conceded that they are meant to discourage begging (*The Economist (U.S.)*, August 16, 2003, p. 26).

6. The technology of charging for curb parking will undoubtedly continue to improve rapidly in the future. Even the technology for parking a car at the curb has improved. Some cars in Japan have auto-pilot devices that park the car without any help from the driver. When the driver pulls up to a curb space, a screen shows a view of the adjacent parked cars. The driver touches the screen to indicate the location of the desired space, and the car takes it from there, using electronic sensors to judge its position and so allow it to avoid other parked cars and the curb. The driver does not have to touch the steering wheel or the accelerator while the car is parking itself. New technology may thus mark the end of the road for both the old-fashioned parking meter and the difficulty of parallel parking.

7. Ready (1998, 7).

8. Ready (1998, 10).

9. Ready (1998, 11). When Miami introduced pay-and-display meters in 2003, during the system's first days the city stationed one person per meter to answer questions, offer assistance, and troubleshoot. In addition, cars with expired receipts did not receive a citation, but a "warning card" that reminded customers about the benefits of the pay-and-display machines (*The Parking Professional*, August 2004, 28).

10. To pay by phone, the driver dials a toll-free number and enters how much time is wanted on the meter. A message is sent to the meter authorizing the transaction, and the driver's credit card is debited.

11. Van Horn (1999, 42-44). Van Horn reports an additional advantage of pay-by-space meters: "Berkeley has some areas where the parking rules change space by space. For example, in three of the spaces controlled by a unit, there is no parking from 7 a.m. to noon. In other spaces controlled by the unit, parking is available from 9 a.m. to 6 p.m. The machine displays which spaces are available during which times, and if a parker selects a space that is illegal during the that time, the unit will so note and not allow the parker to insert a coin."

12. "Parking Meters Going High-Tech in Berkeley," *San Francisco Chronicle*, August 30, 1999. Berkeley continues to suffer from vandalism against all its parking meters, however. Chapters 16 and 17 explain how returning meter revenue to pay for public investments in the neighborhoods where it is collected will increase the popular support for parking meters and discourage vandalism.

13. Several manufacturers's web sites demonstrate how the in-vehicle meters work. For example, see www.park-o-pin.de/start.htm and www.ganis-smartpark.com/. The in-vehicle meters are a hi-tech version of the simple voucher parking systems used in some cities, such as New Haven, Connecticut. Motorists buy a booklet of permits and use them by scratching off the appropriate panels indicating the date and the time they have parked and placing the vouchers on the inside of the car window.

14. If the driver overstays the time limit, the time display becomes negative and the excess time is shown; traffic enforcement officers can then issue a ticket just as they do when a conventional parking meter shows a violation. Alternatively, the city can set the in-vehicle meters to charge for parking at an accelerated rate for those who overstay the time limit.

15. *Public Technology*, November/December 1990, p. 4.

16. Ready (1998, 9). In 1996 Aspen received the International Parking Institute's Award of Excellence for its transportation and parking plan.

17. Trillin (2001, 14).

18. See "Dutch City Introducing Mobile Internet Cashless Parking," *Parking Today*, August 2001, pp. 24-26.

19. The European system would use the Galileo global navigation satellite system expected to deliver real-time positioning accuracy within one meter by 2008. Cars parked off-street in driveways or parking lots would, of course, not be charged for curb parking. Parking violations could also be detected by the system; because prices could replace time limits for curb parking, however, there would presumably be many fewer violations. Satellite technology may have to improve substantially to use it for charging for parking, but technology always improves over time.

20. Ready (1998, 7).

21. Ready (1998, 7).

22. Ready (1998, 8 and 12).

23. Bird (1997, 539).

16

Turning Small Change into Big Changes

If it is feasible to establish a market to implement a policy, no policy-maker can afford to do without one.

— J. H. DALES

The money you put into a parking meter seems to vanish into thin air. No one knows where the money goes, and everyone wants to park free, so politicians find it easier to require off-street parking than to charge market prices for curb parking.[1] But cities can change the politics of parking if they return curb parking revenue to pay for public services in the neighborhoods that generate it. If each neighborhood keeps all the parking revenue it generates, a powerful new constituency for market prices will emerge—the neighborhoods that receive the revenue. If *nonresidents* pay for curb parking, and the city spends the revenue to benefit the *residents*, charging for curb parking can become a popular policy rather than the political third rail it often is today. To explain this proposal, I will describe how it might work in two settings: business districts (in this chapter) and residential neighborhoods (in the following chapter).

PARKING BENEFIT DISTRICTS

Consider an older business district where most stores have no off-street parking and vacant curb spaces are hard to find. Cruising for free curb parking congests the streets, and everyone complains about the parking shortage. Charging market-rate prices for curb parking would increase turnover and reduce traffic congestion, and the convenience of a few vacancies would attract customers who are willing to pay for parking if they don't have to spend time hunting for it. Nevertheless, merchants fear that charging for parking would keep customers away. Suppose in this case the city creates a "parking benefit district" in which all the meter revenue is spent to clean the sidewalks, plant street trees, improve store facades, put overhead utility wires underground, and ensure public safety. The meter revenue will help make the business district a place where people want to be, rather than merely a place where everyone can park free. Returning the revenue generated *by* the district *to* the district *for* the district can convince merchants and property owners to support the idea of market-priced curb parking.[2]

Right Prices Will Attract More Customers

Keeping a few curb parking spaces vacant is like having inventory in a store, and everyone understands that stores adjust prices to balance supply and demand. Similarly, a city can reduce the price of curb parking if there are too many vacancies (too much inventory) and increase it if there are too few spaces (too little inventory). The *right* price for curb parking is the *lowest* price that keeps a few spaces available to allow convenient access. If no curb spaces are available, reducing their price certainly cannot attract more customers—just as reducing the price of anything else in short supply cannot increase sales. If a department store is sold out of the hottest toy at Christmas, for example, lowering the price of that toy cannot attract more buyers. So how can lowering the price of parking in an area where all spaces are occupied attract more customers? A below-market price for curb parking simply leads to cruising and traffic congestion. The goal of pricing is to produce about 85 percent occupancy so that drivers can quickly find places to park near their destinations.

Underpriced curb parking cannot increase the number of cars parked at the curb because it cannot increase the number of spaces available. What underpriced curb parking *does* do is create a parking shortage that keeps potential customers away. If it takes only five minutes to drive somewhere else, why spend 10 minutes cruising for parking in a business district where all the curb spaces are occupied? Because short-term parkers are less sensitive to the price of parking than to the time it takes to find a space, charging enough to create a few curb vacancies can attract customers who would rather pay for parking than not be able to find it.[3] Spending the meter revenue for public improvements that make the area more attractive can then draw even more customers.

Parking availability is a key point in attracting customers. Using a survey of 1,704 households in the Netherlands, Harmen Oppewal and Harry

Timmermans examined how parking fees, parking occupancy, and time limits affected the probability that customers will visit shopping centers.[4] Shoppers disliked higher parking fees, as expected, but they also disliked crowded parking and limits on parking durations. Using prices to eliminate crowding and time limits can therefore improve shoppers' evaluation of parking at destinations that now have underpriced but scarce curb parking. Market prices can create a few curb vacancies, increase turnover, reduce search time, and attract customers who are now kept away by parking shortages. Parking won't be free, but it will be more convenient.

The parking turnover rate depends on how users respond to prices. If the price of curb parking increases, curb parkers can stay a shorter time, and longer-term parkers can park off-street. Both responses will increase curb parking turnover, so more cars can park at the curb during a day. Shoppers who want to make a quick purchase will find convenient curb spaces available, while those who want to linger or stroll around will find it cheaper to park off-street. Drivers who are unwilling to put a few coins in a parking meter probably wouldn't spend much money in the adjacent shops, and their places at the curb can be taken by customers who do want to buy something.

The purpose of charging market prices for curb parking is *not* to maximize meter revenue, but to allocate curb spaces more efficiently—to drivers (and their passengers) who are willing to pay for parking if they don't have to waste time cruising for it. If meter prices are just high enough to ensure a few vacancies on each block, shoppers who stay for only a short time won't pay much to park on each trip, and those who arrive in higher-occupancy vehicles can split the parking cost, so they won't pay much per person. In short, the right price for curb parking: (1) ensures that everyone can park without cruising; (2) encourages short-term parking, thereby increasing turnover; and (3) favors shoppers who arrive in higher-occupancy vehicles. Right-priced curb parking can therefore attract more customers who collectively spend more money while shopping.

One Side of the Street at a Time

Right-priced curb parking can spread in the same way that parking meters spread after their debut in 1935. Cities did not simply plant the meters all over the city on one day and then start collecting revenue from them on the next. Instead, cities usually installed meters on only one side of the downtown streets to show people how the meters worked. Oklahoma City's city manager explained the process:

> The two sides provided comparisons which are obvious. On the unmetered side is confusion. On the metered side is order, sufficient room for every car to

be parked and driven out quickly and easily, and there are usually parking spaces open.[5]

By 1937, only two years after the first meters were installed in Oklahoma City, 20,000 meters had sprouted on the sidewalks of 35 cities, and they were well received. After surveying the use of parking meters in these cities, Leon Brown reported in *American City*:

> Merchants and shoppers both are in favor of them. When one side of the street has them, merchants on the other side demand them. When one town has them, the merchants of nearby towns demand them, showing that they draw out-of-town shoppers rather than driving them away.[6]

Parking benefit districts can be introduced in the same way. Suppose the city charges the market price for curb parking on one street in a commercial district, just high enough to ensure a few vacant spaces. Everyone who wants to shop on that street can easily find a curb space, and the meter revenue is earmarked to clean the sidewalk, trim the trees, or improve storefront facades along the street. Parking remains free on all the other streets, where all curb spaces remain occupied with sluggish turnover. Everyone complains about the parking shortage on the free streets, and cars cruising for free parking congest traffic. No meter revenue is available to clean the sidewalk, trim the trees, or improve the storefronts. On which street would *you* prefer to have a business?

Merchants may oppose charging for parking on the grounds that it will drive away customers, but this fear is often unfounded. Parking consultant Mary Smith explains that many customers are short-term parkers who care more about the convenience than the cost of parking:

> When Circle Centre, a public-private joint venture, retail and entertainment center in downtown Indianapolis was about to open, there was much speculation in the press regarding whether or not it could succeed with the relatively modest parking fee of $1 for the first three hours. The fee structure then jumps to $2 per hour.... However, in the end, the parking fee was not an issue to shoppers; and the project is among the top five percent of retail centers nationally, in terms of annual sales per square foot.... If there is any negative effect of parking in downtowns vis-a-vis the suburban shopping center, it is the lack of *convenient* parking, not lack of *free* parking.[7]

If merchants realize that convenient parking is more important to customers than free parking *and* are guaranteed that their business districts will receive all the meter revenue, they will soon support market-rate prices for curb spaces.[8]

A LOGICAL RECIPIENT: BUSINESS IMPROVEMENT DISTRICTS

Curb parking revenue is a benefit in search of a beneficiary: the funds need the right recipient to generate political support for market prices. In commercial areas, Business Improvement Districts (BIDs) are the logical recipients. In a BID, property owners assess themselves to pay for supplemental public services beyond the level provided by the city.[9] In essence, BIDs are a form of "cooperative capitalism," and they provide local public services that cities either do not provide (such as sidewalk cleaning) or do not provide at a satisfactory level (such as security). Property owners are willing to pay for these added "clean and safe" public services because they recognize their property's value depends on the quality of the surrounding environment. The assessments are roughly proportional to the benefits each property receives, and because all property owners pay their fair share, the cost to each can be small. The economic incentive for property owners to establish a BID is that their expected commercial return will exceed their individual assessments.

BIDs have multiplied rapidly since 1965 when the first one was established in downtown Toronto, and many cities now encourage local businesses and property owners to create them. These organizations have a good track record, their legality is well established, and their operating principles are familiar to public officials and business owners. BIDs are therefore ready-made, legitimate recipients for curb parking revenue. Suppose a city offers BIDs the parking meter revenue earned within their boundaries. This arrangement amounts to a matching grant from the city: if businesses tax themselves to pay for public improvements, the city will contribute the area's curb parking revenue to help finance the effort. The added parking revenue will either reduce the assessments businesses must pay or increase the public services the district can provide. Either way, the matching grant encourages local businesses to form BIDs, and the meter revenue can thus elicit self-help efforts from the benefitted businesses.

Earmarking curb parking revenue to fund BIDs and giving them a say in setting the parking prices for their area will encourage businesslike management of the parking supply. Each district can examine how other districts deal with curb parking, and they can weigh the benefits and costs of alternative policies. The BIDs will have every incentive to choose the best policy for curb parking in their area because they will be the first to benefit from good decisions and the first to suffer from bad ones. BIDs can increase their revenue by installing more parking meters, extending meter hours, or increasing meter rates. More important, charging market prices for curb parking will maintain a few vacancies and encourage turnover, making more curb spaces available to short-term parkers and thereby increasing the productivity of the parking supply.

If meter money disappears into the general fund, no one is disturbed to see a car parked at an expired meter. As a result, parking enforcement officers are perhaps society's least-esteemed public servants. In *The Delicate Art of Parking*, a 2003 Canadian mockumentary film about parking enforcement, a dedicated meter reader says, "The true meaning of parking enforcement is to provide an essential service to the people of this city and the overall better good of society. I'm an honest, hardworking person. I get up every morning knowing that I play a vital role in keeping the streets unobstructed and the traffic flowing." But a citizen interviewed on the street says, "The meter reader! I'd just like to line them all up and just shoot them."[10]

The meter readers for other public utilities arouse no similar hostility. Gas, electric, and water meters measure exactly how much service each household has consumed, and the meter readers simply record this past consumption. Conventional parking meters are far less convenient than these other meters because drivers must pay in advance for the time they expect to use. The parking meter reader's function is not to measure how much time a driver has used but is instead to give a ticket to anyone who overstays the time they paid for. The special resentment toward parking meter readers suggests that the method of payment, not the payment itself, is the main problem with parking meters. If parking meters charged, in arrears, only for the time a car has occupied a curb space (as with in-vehicle meters and payments by mobile phone), they would be less objectionable. Citations would still be needed for those who don't pay at all, but meters that charge only for the time used should reduce some of the resentment against parking enforcement officers.

Drivers will always oppose strict meter enforcement, but dedicating curb parking revenue to BIDs will create a new interest group who support effective enforcement. If a BID receives its own meter revenue, merchants who see cars parked at expired meters in front of their stores will see them as freeloaders occupying curb spaces that could be used by other drivers who would be willing to pay for parking if they could find a vacant space. BIDs that support better enforcement will receive more meter revenue, and the city will receive more citation revenue. In a survey of large cities' on-street parking policies, Allison de Cerreño found that, on average, the cities collected $5.10 in parking fines for every $1 of meter revenue. Business support for better parking enforcement can therefore provide substantial general revenue for cities.[11]

To the motorist, parking meters resemble a modern version of the rent collector for an avaricious feudal landlord. If the payments for parking do not fund a popular public service, it will be difficult to convince many people that cities should charge market prices for curb parking. Two cities in California—Pasadena and San Diego—have made progress toward reform by returning meter revenue to the business districts that generate it. Pasadena returns all the revenue, while San Diego returns 45 percent. An evaluation of these two cities' programs shows that they have helped revitalize older business districts by improving their parking, public services, and urban design.

PASADENA: YOUR METER MONEY MAKES A DIFFERENCE

Pasadena's downtown declined between the 1930s and the 1980s, but has since been revived as "Old Pasadena," one of Southern California's most popular shopping and entertainment destinations. Two policies—returning parking revenue to finance public improvements and reforming parking requirements—have played a major part in this revival.[12]

History

Old Pasadena was the original commercial core of the city and in the early twentieth century was an elegant shopping district. In 1929, Pasadena widened its main thoroughfare, Colorado Boulevard, by 28 feet, which required moving the building facades on each side of the street back 14 feet. Owners removed the front 14 feet of their buildings, and most constructed new facades in the popular Spanish Colonial Revival or Art Deco styles. A few owners, however, put back the original facades in an early example of historic preservation. The result is a handsome, circa-1929 streetscape that forms the center of Old Pasadena.

The area sank into decline during the Depression and, after the war, the narrow storefronts and lack of parking led many merchants to seek larger retail spaces in more modern surroundings. Old Pasadena became the city's Skid Row, with wonderful buildings in terrible condition. The area was known mainly for its pawn shops, porn theaters, and tattoo parlors, and by the 1970s much of it was a retail slum slated for redevelopment. Vacant stores lined the streets, and property owners let their buildings decay because the low rents did not justify repairs. Pasadena's Redevelopment Agency demolished three historic blocks on Colorado Boulevard to make way for Plaza Pasadena, an enclosed mall with ample free parking. New buildings clad in then-fashionable black glass replaced other historic properties (see Figure 16-1). The resulting "Corporate Pasadena" horrified many citizens and prompted the city to reconsider its plans for the area. In 1978 the city published the *Plan for Old Pasadena*, which stated, "if the area can be revitalized, building on its special char-

Demolition of Pasadena's Mather Building on the corner of
Colorado Boulevard and Marengo Avenue, July 7, 1971

The replacement building

Figure 16-1. Urban renewal in Old Pasadena

acter, it will be unique to the region."[13] But the *Plan* did not understate the problems, describing the area as unkempt, seedy, and unsafe:

> The area is commonly perceived as undesirable and unsafe. Comments heard about West Colorado include the following: "The area's been going downhill for years." "It's a bunch of dirty old buildings." "It's filthy." "It's Pasadena's sick child." "The area is unsafe."[14]

Although the city succeeded in having what was left of Old Pasadena listed in the National Register of Historic Places in 1983, commercial revival was slow to come, in part because most buildings had no off-street parking.

In the 1980s and 1990s, the city devised two creative parking policies that have contributed greatly to Old Pasadena's revival. First, it has returned parking meter revenue to finance public improvements. Second, it has allowed businesses in Old Pasadena to pay a modest fee to satisfy off-street parking requirements, making it possible for owners to rehabilitate an existing building or change its use without providing any new on-site parking spaces; two public garages in Old Pasadena provide the parking spaces individual properties would have had to provide.[15]

Parking Meters and Revenue Return

Old Pasadena had no parking meters until 1993. All curb parking was free and was restricted only by a two-hour time limit. Because employees parked in the most convenient curb spaces and moved their cars periodically to avoid citations, customers had difficulty finding places to park.[16] The city's staff proposed installing meters to regulate curb parking, but the merchants and property owners opposed the idea. They realized that employees occupied many of the most convenient curb spaces, but still they feared that meters, rather than freeing up space for customers, would discourage customers from coming at all. Customers and tenants, they assumed, would go to shopping centers with free parking. Meter proponents countered that anyone who left because they couldn't park free would make room for others who were willing to pay for parking if they could find a space, and that the want of convenient short-term parking kept many potential customers away. Proponents also argued that people who were willing to pay for parking would be likely to spend more money in the shops while they were in Old Pasadena.

Debates about the meters dragged on for two years before the city reached a compromise with the business and property owners: all the meter revenue would be used to pay for public investments in Old Pasadena. Parking meters came to be seen in a new light—as a source of revenue—and the desire for public improvements suddenly outweighed the fear of driving customers away. The business and property owners agreed to an unusually high rate of $1 an hour for curb parking and even to operating the meters in the evenings and on Sundays. The city also liked the arrangement because it wanted to improve Old Pasadena. The meters could provide the $5 million needed to finance the city's ambitious plan to improve Old Pasadena's streetscape and to convert its alleys into walkways with access to shops and restaurants.[17] In effect, Old Pasadena became a parking benefit district. Business and property owners bought into the proposal for parking meters because they were bought off with the resulting revenue.

Added public services and local control. The city worked with Old Pasadena's BID to establish the boundaries of the Old Pasadena Parking Meter Zone (PMZ) where the parking meters were installed. Only the metered blocks benefit directly from the meter revenue. The city also established the Old Pasadena PMZ Advisory Board, consisting of business and property owners who recommend parking policies and set spending priorities for the zone's meter revenue.[18] Local control and the added public services are largely responsible for the parking program's success. "The only reason meters went into Old Pasadena in the first place," said Marilyn Buchanan, chair of the Old Pasadena PMZ, "was because the city agreed all the money would stay in Old Pasadena."[19]

The city installed the parking meters in 1993 and then immediately borrowed $5 million to finance the "Old Pasadena Streetscape and Alleyways Project," with the meter revenue dedicated to repaying the debt. The bond proceeds paid for street furniture, trees, tree grates, and historic lighting fixtures throughout the area. Dilapidated alleys were turned into safe, functional walkways with access to shops and restaurants.

In 2001, Old Pasadena's 690 parking meters yielded $1.3 million, or $1,867 per meter (see Table 16-1). The PMZ earned additional revenue from valet parking services that use meter spaces, as well as from investment earnings on the meter fund balance, so the total revenue was $1.4 million ($2,096 per meter). The total capital and operating expenses for collecting the revenue amounted to $383 per meter (18 percent of total revenue).[20] Old Pasadena therefore received $1.2 million of net parking revenue ($1,712 per meter) to fund additional public services.

The first claim on this revenue is the annual debt service of $448,000 to repay the $5 million borrowed for the sidewalk and alley improvements. Of the remaining revenue, $694,000 was spent to increase public services in Old Pasadena. The city provides some of these services, such as additional police foot patrols, at a cost of $248,000. The city also allocated $426,000 of meter revenue to the area's BID (the Old Pasadena

Table 16-1. Old Pasadena Parking Meter Revenues and Expenditures for FY 2001

PARKING REVENUES

Meter charges	$1,288,012	$1,867	per meter for 690 meters
Valet at meters	$68,915		Valet use of meter spaces
Investment earnings	$89,067		Interest on fund balance
Total parking revenues	$1,445,994	$2,096	per meter

PARKING EXPENSES

Operating expenses

Personnel	$51,162		
Cash handling	$44,112		
City abatements	$34,425		
Materials and supplies	$10,335		
Vandalism replacement	$11,862		
Rent	$7,896		
Internal service charges	$2,335		
Total operating expense	$162,127	$235	per meter (11% of revenue)

Capital expenses

Parking meter lease payments	$66,338		
Parking meter replacement	$36,000		
Total capital expenses	$102,338	$148	per meter (7% of revenue)
Total parking expenses	$264,465	$383	per meter (18% of revenue)
NET PARKING REVENUE	$1,181,529	$1,712	per meter (82% of revenue)

EXPENDITURES IN OLD PASADENA

Operating expenditures in Old Pasadena

Security	$247,681	City of Pasadena	
Lighting services	$20,600	City of Pasadena	
Additional sidewalk and street maintenance	$410,796	Old Pasadena Management District	
Marketing	$15,000	Old Pasadena Management District	
Total operating expenditure	$694,077	59% of net parking revenue	

Capital expenditures in Old Pasadena

Debt service for streetscapes and alleyways	$448,393	38% of net parking revenue	
Total expenditures in Old Pasadena	**$1,142,470**	**97% of net parking revenue**	
Net income after all expenditures	$39,059	3% of net parking revenue	

Source: Memorandum from Pasadena City Manager to City Council Finance Committee, May 21, 2001.

Management District, which has the same boundaries as the PMZ) for added sidewalk and street maintenance, and for marketing (maps, brochures, and advertisements in local newspapers). The parking enforcement officers who monitor the meters until well into the night are official "eyes on the street," and their presence further increases security. Drivers who park in Old Pasadena finance all these public services, at no cost to the businesses, property owners, or taxpayers. The money seems to come out of thin air.

A virtuous cycle. As the area attracted more pedestrians, the sidewalks needed more maintenance. This would have posed a problem back in the days when Old Pasadena relied on the city for regular cleaning and maintenance, but now the BID has meter money to pay for the added services. The BID has arranged for daily sweeping of the streets and sidewalks, trash collection, removal of decals from street fixtures, and periodic steam cleaning of Colorado Boulevard's sidewalks.[21] Returning the meter revenue to Old Pasadena has thus created a "virtuous cycle" of continuing improvements. The meter revenue pays for public improvements, the public improvements make the area more attractive for visitors who pay for curb parking, and more meter revenue is then available to pay for public improvements. Giving the BID the responsibility for spending the meter money has reassured business and property owners that the city does not use it for any other purpose. To remind everyone where the money goes, the meters have stickers that say, "Your meter money will make the difference in Old Pasadena."

Figure 16-2. Pasadena parking meter

Public Parking Garages with Zoning Parking Credits

A second policy—public parking garages instead of private parking spaces—has also spurred Old Pasadena's revival. Under the city's "Parking Credit Program," businesses can pay the city a modest fee in lieu of providing the required off-street parking spaces, only $115 a year per space in 2001.[22] Because paying $115 a year is far cheaper than providing an off-street parking space, most businesses choose to pay the fee rather than provide the required parking. The low fees for the parking credits remove a barrier to the adaptive reuse of existing buildings, and the freedom from parking requirements is essentially the freedom to create new businesses.

Making adaptive reuse profitable. An example can show how the parking credits promote the prosperity of Old Pasadena. Few buildings have off-street parking because they were constructed before the city required it. Any existing business can continue to occupy its site without off-street parking if the use was established before the city required parking (see Chapter 3). Suppose a pawn shop (from the Skid Row days) occupies retail space with no off-street parking. Although Pasadena requires 2.5

spaces per 1,000 square feet for pawn shops, the pawn shop may operate without parking because it possesses a grandfathered right. But if the pawn shop closes and a restaurant wants to occupy the space, the change of use would trigger the city's parking requirement of 20 spaces per 1,000 square feet of seating area. If the proposed restaurant has 1,000 square feet of seating area, the city normally requires 20 off-street parking spaces, but the requirements in Old Pasadena are reduced 25 percent because of the area's mixed-use character, so only 15 spaces are required. Still, *without* the parking credit program, the restaurant cannot open unless it provides 15 off-street spaces. If by some engineering and financial miracle the restaurant could construct 15 parking spaces at a cost of $20,000 each, the cost would be $300,000, or $300 per square foot of seating area. *With* the program, the restaurant pays the city only $1,725 a year to buy 15 parking credits to satisfy the parking requirement (15 spaces x $115 per space), or only $1.73 a year per square foot of seating area. The option to pay a low annual fee for parking credits rather than a high up-front cost to provide the parking has allowed many new restaurants to open in Old Pasadena.

In most cities, parking requirements increase the cost of opening new businesses in old buildings and therefore reduce the returns to investment in historic preservation. Old Pasadena's parking credits reduce the cost of opening a business and thus make investment in adaptive reuse more profitable (see Figure 16-3). Off-street parking requirements are no longer a barrier to new businesses in Old Pasadena.

Figure 16-3. Building before adaptive reuse (left); New Saks Fifth Avenue (right): parking credits in historic Old Pasadena made investment in this adaptive reuse more profitable.

Financing shared parking. To accommodate the parking demand generated by new businesses, the city constructed two public parking structures and contributed to the construction of a private structure open to the public. Because the 1,567 public spaces are shared among different land uses that experience their peak parking demands at different times, fewer spaces can meet the total parking demand, and the city therefore issues 1.5 parking credits per space in the public garages. The parking credit program began in 1987, and by 2001 the city had allocated 2,350 credits. Businesses that buy credits to meet the city's parking requirements do not receive permits to park in the municipal structures; their customers and employees pay at the same rate other drivers pay. The parking credits do, however, link the public parking spaces with private development in Old Pasadena. This nexus allows businesses to satisfy the city's parking requirements without providing any additional on-site parking spaces.

Visitors to Old Pasadena receive 90 minutes of free parking in the public garages, after which they pay $2 an hour, up to a maximum of $6 a day. In 2001, the garages' total capital and operating expenses amounted to $4.84 million, while the parking fees brought in $3.25 million (see Table 16-2). Because drivers pay two-thirds of the garages' total annual capital and operating costs, the city can charge businesses a modest fee for the parking credits. The total parking credit payments were $229,000, only 5 percent of the total public parking expenses. The $1.59 million shortfall (annual expenses minus parking revenue) is made up by parking credits, investment earnings, tax increment revenue, and lease revenue for the ground-floor retail space. The parking credit system thus shifts most of the burden of paying for parking from businesses to drivers—where it belongs. Businesses pay so little for parking credits because drivers pay to use the public spaces. Marsha Rood, Pasadena's Development Administrator from 1983 to 2000, says, "Without the public parking structures, revitalization of Old Pasadena would not have happened— period."[23] Thousands of people can stroll among the shops, restaurants, and bars in part because the vehicles that brought all these pedestrians into the area are parked in the public garages.

Because the city reduces the off-street parking requirements in Old Pasadena by 25 percent and issues 1.5 parking credits per public space, Old Pasadena has fewer parking spaces than the rest of the city. Let's go back to the restaurant example where the city normally requires 20 parking spaces. The 25 percent parking reduction in Old Pasadena brings this down to 15 spaces. The restaurant can meet the requirement by buying 15 parking credits, and because the city issues 1.5 parking credits per space, 10 public spaces replace what would otherwise be 20 private spaces. Because the city effectively requires only 50 percent as many parking spaces in Old Pasadena as in the rest of the city, and parking credits pay for only 5 percent of the total expenses for the public parking structures, the restaurant's annual cost of meeting its parking requirement is only 2.5 percent of what it would be elsewhere in the city. The 25 percent reduction in parking requirements, the issuance of 1.5 parking credits per public parking space, and the low fees charged for the credits have effectively removed a barrier to opening new businesses, yet there are still enough parking spaces for everyone.

A dynamic pedestrian downtown. Drivers who don't want to pay $1 an hour for curb parking can always park free in the public garages for 90

Table 16-2. Old Pasadena Parking Structure Fund for FY 2001

PARKING REVENUES		
Monthly and hourly parking fees	$3,251,538	66%
Tax increment	$787,371	16%
Lease revenue	$313,089	6%
Investment earnings	$256,024	5%
Parking credits	$228,537	5%
Marriott revenue	$83,612	2%
Miscellaneous	$7,425	0%
Total parking revenues	$4,927,596	100%
PARKING EXPENSES		
Operating expenses		
Contract services	$1,010,576	21%
Utilities	$203,211	4%
Marriott expenses	$175,180	4%
Personnel	$109,320	2%
City abatements	$62,705	1%
Insurance	$49,665	1%
Internal service charges	$47,236	1%
OP Management District	$30,000	1%
Rent expense	$10,860	0%
Materials and supplies	$9,422	0%
Total operating expenses	$1,708,175	35%
Capital expenses		
Debt service for garage construction	$2,219,694	46%
Payback to General Fund	$350,000	7%
Debt service for Marriott construction	$209,000	4%
Seismic upgrade debt service	$133,958	3%
Bond amortization	$119,521	2%
Amortization cost of land	$96,333	2%
Total capital expenses	$3,128,506	65%
Total parking expenses	$4,836,681	100%
NET PARKING REVENUE	$90,915	

Source: Memorandum from Pasadena City Manager to City Council Finance Committee, May 21, 2001.

minutes, and the shared public parking encourages visitors to park once and walk throughout Old Pasadena.[24] The public garages are one block off Colorado Boulevard, with ground-floor retail and restaurants. The public parking avoids the usual haphazard distribution of small private parking lots attached to individual shops without regard to neighborhood design. If each separate business has its own parking lot for the exclusive use of its own customers, you cannot park once and walk from shop to shop, even where walking is convenient. Off-street parking requirements thus rule out a compact, walkable, park-once business district. If you are forced to drive between the nearby parking lots of different shops, your car is no longer transporting you; instead, you are transporting it. Shopping malls avoid this problem by having one parking lot for all stores, and their park-once advantage surely helps explain their popularity.

To ensure continuous shopfronts, Pasadena prohibits parking lots or parking structures that face Colorado Boulevard.[25] Pedestrians look at store windows rather than parking lots, and they don't have to look out for cars driving across the sidewalk to enter and exit off-street parking. Pasadena architect and urban designer Stefanos Polyzoides attributes much of the success of Old Pasadena to the "rules that allowed development to go forward with less than the traditional parking requirements. This has encouraged pedestrian activity in Old Pasadena, giving it a dynamic pedestrian environment."[26] Old Pasadena has a well-planned system of public parking rather than a random collection of private parking, and drivers pay most of the cost. Public parking does not mean free parking, and public parking structures largely financed by user fees have greatly contributed to Old Pasadena's striking success.

Unburdened from parking requirements, Old Pasadena has done well compared with the rest of the city. Its sales tax revenue increased rapidly after parking meters were installed in 1993 and is now higher than in other retail districts in the city (Figure 16-4). In 1994, Old Pasadena's sales tax revenue surpassed that of Plaza Pasadena, the nearby shopping mall—complete with free parking—that the city had assisted with a $41 million subsidy in the 1970s. With great fanfare, Plaza Pasadena was demolished in 2001 to make way for a new redevelopment with storefronts that resemble Old Pasadena.[27]

Parking subsidies have opportunity costs. Some cities restrict the use of curb parking revenue to fund off-street parking. The fallacy of this superficially appealing policy is clear when we recognize that alternative uses for the money may be far more valuable. Old Pasadena could have used its annual $1.2 million of meter revenue to subsidize the public garages, for example. The garages might then offer everyone three or four hours of free parking, rather than only 90 minutes. But parking subsidies have opportunity costs—the alternative possible uses of the money. Would Old Pasadena be better off today with more free parking but dirty sidewalks, dilapidated alleys, no street trees or historic street lights, and less security? It certainly doesn't appear so. Old Pasadena is now a place where everyone wants to be, rather than merely another place where everyone can park free.

A Tale of Two Business Districts

To examine how parking policies affect urban outcomes, we can compare Old Pasadena with Westwood Village, a business district in Los Angeles once as popular as Old Pasadena is now. In 1980, anyone who predicted Old Pasadena would soon outclass Westwood Village would have been considered crazy. Since the early 1980s, however, the village has declined as Old Pasadena thrived. What explains these different outcomes?

Except for their parking policies, Westwood Village and Old Pasadena are similar. Both are about the same size, both are historic areas, both have design review boards, and both have BIDs. Westwood Village also has a few advantages that Old Pasadena lacks. It is surrounded by extremely

Figure 16-4. Pasadena Retail Sales Tax Revenue

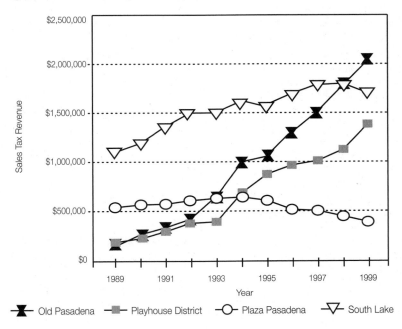

high-income neighborhoods (Bel Air, Holmby Hills, and Westwood) and is located between UCLA and the high-rise corridor of Wilshire Boulevard, both sources of many potential customers. Tellingly, although Westwood Village has about the same number of parking spaces as Old Pasadena, most merchants assume the village's decline must be the result of a parking shortage, a common lament among merchants everywhere whenever a business district has difficulty attracting customers. In Old Pasadena, however, parking is no longer a big issue. The *Los Angeles Times* has published many articles about the changing fortunes of Westwood Village and Old Pasadena, and a selection of headlines suggests the different outcomes that have resulted from their different parking policies (see sidebar).

Market-price curb parking helps businesses. First, consider the two cities' curb parking policies. A study in 2001 found the average curb-space occupancy rate in Old Pasadena was 83 percent, which is about the ideal rate to ensure available spaces for visitors.[28] The meters thus reduce the

---

Headlines from the *Los Angeles Times*, 1986-2004

OLD PASADENA

Old Pasadena Thanks Parking Meters for the Change (Mar 2, 2004)

An Upscale Urban Village Emerges in Genteel Pasadena (Nov 30, 2002)

Seedy Chic; Amid Old Pasadena's modern chain stores and restaurants are three beloved survivors of a less attractive past: porn, pawn and piercing shops (Feb 26, 2001)

Breathing New Life Into Old Main Streets; Small cities see a future in turning faded downtowns into pedestrian-friendly meccas (Jan 5, 1997)

Shopping's Change of Pace; Visitors to Old Town Pasadena find an eclectic, artsy world of diners, clothing shops, bookstores and theaters (Dec 2, 1994)

Pasadena Parking Meters in Old Town (Oct 3, 1993)

Pasadena Parking Meters Approved (Jul 15, 1993)

From Seedy to Trendy Redevelopment (Dec 22, 1992)

Pasadena Parking Plans Studied (Feb 28, 1991)

Saving Old Pasadena (Oct 1, 1989)

Pasadena Parking Problem Resolved (Nov 6, 1986)

Pasadena Parking Garage Gets OK (Jul 24, 1986)

WESTWOOD VILLAGE

Reviving the Village (Aug 20, 2002)

Westwood Rebirth, Stuck on Idle (Oct 22, 1999)

Revitalizing Westwood (Mar 1, 1998)

Westwood: the Village's Prospects for a Comeback (May 28, 1995)

Westwood Village Parking Meter Rates Cut in Bid to Attract Shoppers (Mar 4, 1994)

Westwood Yearns for a Return to its Glory Days (Aug 7, 1993)

Westwood Revitalization Effort (Oct 10, 1991)

Fix Westwood Village (May 26, 1991)

Westwood Looks to Recapture Old Aura (Oct 29,1989)

Glorious Past, Gloomy Future (Jun 12, 1988)

Parking Woes in Westwood Village (Sep 13, 1987)

congestion previously caused by drivers cruising for free parking. Because all the meter revenue stays in Old Pasadena, merchants and property owners understand that market-priced curb parking helps business. The meter revenue has financed substantial public investment in sidewalk and alley improvements that attract visitors to the stores, restaurants, and movie theaters.

In contrast, Westwood's curb parking is underpriced and overcrowded. A parking study in 1994 found that the curb-space occupancy rate was 96 percent during the peak hours, making it necessary for visitors to drive around searching for a vacant space. Nevertheless, the city reduced meter rates from $1 to 50¢ an hour in response to merchants' and property owners' plea that cheaper curb parking would stimulate business.[29] Because off-street parking in any of the 18 private lots or garages in Westwood costs at least $2 for the first hour, drivers have an incentive to hunt for cheap curb parking rather than park off-street. The result is a chronic shortage of curb spaces, underuse of the off-street spaces, and loud complaints about the parking shortage. The 1994 study found that only 68 percent of the village's 3,900 off-street parking spaces were occupied at the peak daytime hour (2 p.m.). Nevertheless, the shortage of curb spaces (the 518 curb spaces are only 14 percent of the total parking supply) creates the impression of an overall parking shortage.[30] Westwood's meter revenue disappears into the city's general fund, and its sidewalks and alleys are crumbling (see Figure 16-5).

Off-street parking requirements hinder investment. Next consider the two cities' off-street parking policies. Old Pasadena's parking credits make it easy to open a new business in an old building or to construct a new building on a vacant lot used for surface parking. In contrast, Westwood Village's parking requirements prevent many potential businesses from reusing old buildings. If a new use would require more parking spaces than the existing use, businesses must make up the difference, a difficult task. Furthermore, buildings vacant for more than a year must provide *all* the parking spaces required for any new use, making adaptive reuse prohibitively expensive.

Westwood Village also has a "replacement parking" requirement that freezes land used for surface parking. Anyone who wants to build anything on an existing parking lot must provide all the parking spaces required for the new use *and replace 50 percent of the surface parking spaces already on the land.*[31] With this replacement requirement, landowners "owe" the city half the parking spaces they have previously supplied voluntarily. The heavy burden of meeting the replacement requirement discourages development on surface lots.

Westwood Village   Old Pasadena

Westwood Village   Old Pasadena

Donald C. Shoup

Figure 16-5. Sidewalks and alleys of Westwood and Old Pasadena compared

Although the 1994 parking study found that 1,200 off-street spaces were vacant during the peak hour, the visible shortage of curb parking per-suaded Los Angeles to build a 380-space municipal parking garage in the village in 1998, at a cost of $30,900 a space (see Chapter 6). Because the curb spaces in front of the garage are free and thus always occupied, the perception of a parking shortage persists. New off-street spaces cannot solve a shortage of underpriced curb spaces because mispricing, not a raw shortage, is the real problem.

Twenty years ago, people from Pasadena would drive 20 miles to Westwood Village to shop, have dinner, go to a movie, and walk around. Now, people from Westwood drive 20 miles to Old Pasadena to shop, have dinner, go to a movie, and walk around. In an interview with the *Los Angeles Times* in 2004, longtime property owner and chair of the Old Pasadena PMZ, Marilyn Buchanan, explained how parking meters helped turn Old Pasadena around:

> We've come a long way. This might seem silly to some people, but if not for our parking meters, it's hard to imagine that we'd have the kind of success we're enjoying. They've made a huge difference. At first it was a struggle to get people to agree with the meters. But when we figured out that the money would stay here, that the money would be used to improve the amenities, it was an easy sell.[32]

In the same article, interviews with shoppers confirmed Buchanan's view. Consider this response:

> This place, it's perfect, really. They've kept the buildings and the streets well. That makes it so attractive. People are walking around because they like the way it looks and feels. It's something you just don't see in Los Angeles. As a driver, I don't mind paying more for what you have here. I tell you what: For this, I will pay.[33]

The Old Pasadena/Westwood Village comparison suggests that parking policies can help some areas thrive while leaving others trapped in a slump. Old Pasadena would still be struggling if it had not installed parking meters, had not built public parking structures, and had not established the parking credits program. Westwood Village would probably have retained its luster if it had always charged market prices for curb parking, had spent the revenue on public services, and had relaxed the off-street parking requirements. The clichés "Parking is Power" and "Parking is Destiny" have some validity, but they do *not* mean that curb parking should be free or that more parking is always better. Market-price curb parking that finances public investment helps an area to thrive, and well-designed public parking structures with ground-floor shops and restaurants are a great asset. Underpriced curb parking and ubiquitous off-street parking lots, on the other hand, can do great harm. The exactly opposite parking policies in Old Pasadena and Westwood Village have surely helped determine their different fates. As the signs on Old Pasadena's parking meters say, "Your meter money will make the difference in Old Pasadena." Old Pasadena has literally pulled itself up by its parking meters.

SAN DIEGO: TURNING SMALL CHANGE INTO BIG CHANGES

Returning the revenue to Old Pasadena was part of the bargain that created the necessary political support to install parking meters. The city's general fund lost no money from this arrangement because the city had no parking meters before it established the revenue-return policy. But what happens when a city already has more than 5,000 parking meters generating substantial revenue for the general fund? San Diego's successful experience shows how cities can return a share of parking meter revenue to business districts, even when this will reduce general fund revenue in the short run.

Until 1997, San Diego used all parking meter revenue to finance citywide public spending. BIDs in the older commercial areas argued that this policy was unfair. The newer parts of the city had ample parking and no meters, while the older parts had a parking shortage and their meter revenue did not come back to help solve the problem. Why should the city take meter revenue from areas with a parking shortage and spend it in areas with ample free parking? The BIDs had a good argument, and they convinced the city council that communities should be able to spend a part of their meter revenue to solve their own problems.

San Diego's City Manager was understandably reluctant to part with what had been general revenue. In a compromise, the city now returns 45 percent of parking meter revenue to the districts that generate it. When it adopted this policy in 1997, the city council explained the goal:

> The intent of this Policy is to retain a certain portion of the meter revenues collected for the benefit of the area in which the meter is located. These revenues will be used for a variety of neighborhood and business improvement projects. Parking Meter Districts (PMDs) will be established to provide an equitable mechanism for distribution of the funds.[34]

Each Parking Meter District's governing body must be either a BID, a nonprofit redevelopment corporation, or a community development corporation. The city council appoints each PMD's advisory board, and final approval of the spending rests with the council. PMDs may be established in areas with more than 100 parking meters, and each district includes both the metered area and the surrounding residential neighborhoods. The PMD's purpose is broader than merely improving parking and transportation, as suggested by the placement of its administration in the city's Community and Economic Development Department.[35]

The Revenue Split

San Diego returns 45 percent of the city's total meter revenue to the PMDs, and this revenue is divided among them in proportion to the number of parking meters they each contain. Three PMDs have been established— Downtown, Uptown, and Mid-City—and in Fiscal Year 2002 they received $2.2 million in meter revenue to spend for such purposes as parking, trans-

Table 16-3. Parking Meter District Revenues in San Diego

Area	Revenue
Downtown	$1,401,000
Uptown	$567,000
Mid-City	$195,000
Total	$2,163,000

portation, signage, maintenance, landscaping, and security. This meter revenue increases rather than replaces the existing municipal funding sources for each district.[36]

The metered neighborhoods clearly benefit from the revenue, but does the rest of the city lose out? Not necessarily. San Diego's general fund continues to receive 55 percent of the revenue. The incentive for PMDs to install additional parking meters, extend the hours of operation, and raise the rates to gain greater revenue for themselves can therefore increase the total meter revenue deposited in the general fund. If the PMD activities improve business conditions and taxable sales in the districts, additional sales tax revenue will also accrue to the city. Although diverting a share of the existing parking meter revenue to neighborhoods creates short-term loss to the general fund, it can eventually help the whole city. In recommending the revenue-return policy to the city council, San Diego's City Manager explained both the short-term loss and the long-term gains:

> Sharing the revenues and involving the business community in the development of parking solutions in the City's older commercial areas will create a short-term loss to the City's General Fund. However, it is possible that by doing so, other BIDs and redevelopment areas may decide to request the installation of meters, thus increasing revenues to make up for the portion directed to the area. A carefully administered, comprehensive parking meter management program will enhance sales tax revenues in the districts and contribute to the overall economic benefits of San Diego.[37]

San Diego's three PMDs pursue different goals to suit their different circumstances. The following sections explain the contexts of the three districts and the different priorities each has pursued. The results show there is no one-size-fits-all approach for parking benefit districts. Instead, revenue sharing is a flexible policy that can be adapted to each community.

Uptown District

The Uptown District consists of five communities—Bankers Hill, Hillcrest, Middletown, Mission Hills, and Park West—to the north and west of Balboa Park, with 38,000 residents. The Uptown Partnership, a nonprofit community development corporation, was established expressly to administer the PMD, and it has become a valuable addition to the "social capital" of its area. Community development corporations often have to spend much of their time scrambling to secure funds to stay alive, but the guaranteed meter revenue allows the Uptown Partnership to concentrate on the long-term goals for its community.[38] The partnership holds a monthly public meeting and publishes a newsletter covering its activities. The partnership has put its logo on every parking meter, explaining that its purpose is "Turning Small Change into Big Changes."

In the first year of the program, the Uptown District sought extensive community input and developed a five-year implementation plan with eight important community goals.[39]

1. Revitalize commercial districts.
2. Provide pedestrian-oriented commercial areas.
3. Encourage the design of building and circulation systems sensitive to pedestrians.
4. Improve traffic circulation.
5. Increase the availability of off-street parking.
6. Provide for safe and efficient movement of people and goods.
7. Establish a fully integrated system of vehicular, transit, bicycle, and pedestrian facilities.
8. Establish a focal point for transit services within the community.

The emphasis on pedestrians in this neighborhood plan is a refreshing departure from the typically narrow focus on cars in most transportation plans. The Uptown Partnership hosts "Feet First" walking tours and uses the events to discuss and assess the pedestrian environment. The partnership addresses parking, but also recommends, "Any approach to the parking problems in Uptown must be comprehensive. In addition to parking and auto circulation, the solution must address pedestrian circulation, and how the land is used."[40] The plan also proposed installing more parking meters, extending meter operation later in the evenings, and using multispace meters to improve the streetscape and increase revenue.

The Uptown Partnership does not attempt to solve parking problems in isolation from other aspects of the urban system. Rather, it uses its park-

Figure 16-6. The Uptown Partnership logo

ing revenue to address both parking and broader goals. The plan noted, for example, that the excessive width of some streets leads to speeding, and it proposed to reduce the number of traffic lanes on these streets, using the additional space for wider sidewalks or landscape improvements. One of the Uptown District's first completed projects was to plant trees in the median of Washington Street, greatly improving the appearance of a main commercial artery. Other streets were converted from parallel parking to diagonal parking,

Figure 16-7. Diagonal parking in the Uptown District

Figure 16-8. Uptown Information Kiosk

which creates more parking spaces and a wider buffer between the sidewalk and traffic.[41]

The Uptown Partnership sells debit cards that allow drivers to buy as much time on the meter as they want and to get a refund on unused time. The cards allow drivers to park without having the correct change, without having to guess beforehand exactly how long they will park, without having to worry about their meter running out if they are delayed, and without paying for more time than they use. The partnership also operates the Uptown Information Kiosk at the corner of Fifth and University Avenues, which sells parking meter cards, monthly bus passes, and transit tokens, and provides transit and tourist information (Figure 16-8).

Downtown District

The Downtown PMD is administered by the Centre City Develop-ment Corporation (CCDC), a public nonprofit corporation San Diego established in 1975 to plan and redevelop the 1,500-acre downtown area. Because the Downtown PMD has the same boundaries as the CCDC, it did not require a new institution to carry out its functions. The meter revenue augments the CCDC's other sources of revenue, enabling it to carry out projects not otherwise possible. The CCDC estimated that the downtown parking supply was adequate for the next few years but found that many drivers did not know where to find the available spaces. As a result, it decided to sponsor an extensive "Downtown Wayfinding Sign System." Consultants conducted interviews, focus groups, and public meetings to determine the best ways to direct visitors to major destinations and nearby parking. An environmental graphics firm planned and designed the signs using a historic tile motif and mapped the clearest and most logical routes in cooperation with the San Diego Traffic Engineering Division. The new signs lead drivers from freeway off-ramps to downtown landmarks such as the Gaslamp Quarter, the Convention Center, and the Embarcadero. Other signs direct drivers to public parking once they have reached their destination. The total cost of $550,000 for planning, designing, fabricating, and installing the wayfinding system was paid by the district's parking meter revenue.[42] (See Figure 16-9.)

Parking strategies in the Centre City Community Plan are not focused solely on increasing the parking supply. Rather, they also seek to achieve additional community goals, such as less land devoted to parking, fewer single-occupancy vehicle trips to the Central Business District (CBD), better public transit, and improved urban design. The following policies promote these specific goals:

1. The off-street parking requirement for multifamily housing is only 1/2 space per unit.

2. There are *no* parking requirements for nonresidential uses.
3. All parking for a project must be enclosed and architecturally integrated into the structure.
4. At least 50 percent of the street wall of structured parking must include street-level uses.
5. For office buildings, at least two levels of parking must be provided underground before the provision of any above-ground parking.[43]

Figure 16-9. Wayfinding Signs

These policies ensure that new parking is friendly to the urban environment, and new buildings developed under this code have replaced former surface parking lots. To replace the surface spaces lost, the CCDC built a 500-space, seven-story public garage with street-level retail stores in the historic Gaslamp Quarter in 2001 (Figure 16-10). The garage was financed by issuing $12 million of parking revenue bonds. The bonds' primary security is the net operating revenue from the garage and tax-increment revenues, but the CCDC also pledged its on-street meter revenue as added security for the bonds, which reduced the interest rate on the borrowing.[44] The CCDC is also building a second 1,230-space, $20-million public parking garage with street-level stores to serve the Gaslamp Quarter, the San Diego Convention Center, and the city's new ballpark for the San Diego Padres. Again, the pledge of meter revenue as security led to a lower interest rate on the revenue bonds.

Because the CCDC has built public parking garages and does not require off-street parking for nonresidential uses in the Gaslamp Quarter, many historic properties have been restored and converted to new uses—such as restaurants—that are often blocked by high off-street parking requirements. The market rather than the city's parking code now determines whether businesses open in the Gaslamp Quarter.[45] In addition to building public parking garages, the CCDC has installed more parking meters to increase turnover and make on-street parking more useful to businesses (the CCDC pays 45 percent of the installation cost and the city pays 55 percent, the same ratio in which they divide the meter revenue). As in Uptown, the CCDC has converted parallel parking spaces to diagonal

Donald C. Shoup

Figure 16-10. Public Parking Garage in the Gaslamp Quarter

ones on some of the wider streets, increasing the curb parking supply and calming traffic. It has also used meter revenue to improve sidewalks and plant street trees.

Mid-City District

Because the Mid-City District has fewer parking meters than the other two districts, it receives less money, but it has used this money well. It commissioned several creative parking studies, and one of the resulting conclusions surely applies to many older commercial districts: "The Mid-City area suffers not so much from the lack of parking, but from a host of challenges—including the perceived lack of parking—that have kept its commercial districts from realizing their full potential."[46] This simple statement is key to understanding the problems many older cities face, and it runs counter to the easy excuse that insufficient free parking is always to blame whenever a business district fails to thrive.

An inventory of all the on-street spaces in the Mid-City District found many abandoned driveways with unused curb cuts not available for on-street parking. The district sent letters to the owners of property adjacent to these unused curb cuts and offered to remove them at no cost to the property owners. As a result, the district has created 30 new curb parking spaces at a cost of only $2,000 each, a great bargain. Removing the non-functional driveways also improved the sidewalks for pedestrians.

The district's consultant also recommended converting wide streets to diagonal parking. Although the net gains in the number of on-street spaces were often small, the diagonal spaces are convenient and serve to calm traffic on streets that were unnecessarily wide. Among other projects the district has undertaken, it paid to reconstruct the curb, gutter, and sidewalk, and to plant street trees in front of a new off-street parking lot, while the property owner paid for all other improvements. The resulting project has increased the parking supply and improved the urban design of the street.

The district's consultant measured the occupancy rates of curb spaces and found a wide variation. The occupancy rate exceeded 100 percent on many blocks without meters and was below 50 percent on many metered blocks. The study showed that parking problems are extremely localized and meters can solve a shortage, but prices need fine tuning. Nevertheless, San Diego sets a single price ($1.25 an hour) for all parking meters in the city and has the same hours of operation everywhere, regardless of variations in the intensity of parking demand in different areas at different times. The underuse of parking meters in the Mid-City District shows why a citywide uniform price is not an appropriate way to manage curb parking demand.

Big Changes from Small Change

San Diego's PMDs show real achievements and even greater promise. Decentralizing control over curb parking revenue has allowed communities to make policy choices responsive to local priorities, such as landscaping, pedestrian convenience, better signage, and wayfinding. Making an area more pedestrian friendly is a particular benefit of local control. Planners who work for neighborhoods rather than for city transportation departments do not automatically assume pedestrians are merely drivers who have already found a parking space.

San Diego has established a Parking and Mobility Task Force, with representatives from city departments and the three PMDs. PMD staff effectively represent their communities' interests to the city and provide an alternative perspective to that of the city transportation engineers. The task force makes recommendations to the city manager on such issues as the installation of parking meters, parking enforcement, signal timing, and the violation of parking regulations by city vehicles. The task force also fosters cooperation among PMDs in experimenting with new parking and transportation policies. The Uptown District, for example, was the first to convert curb spaces from parallel to angled parking, and the other two districts followed the example after seeing the results.

The revenue from curb parking has financed many significant improvements in the three districts. Even more revenue would be available if the parking meter hours were extended to coincide with the hours of operation of adjoining businesses, but to date all meters in the city operate only from 8 a.m. to 6 p.m., Monday through Saturday. Parking demand is high in the evenings and on Sunday in both the Downtown and Uptown Districts, but the curb parking remains free and overcrowded.

San Diego's revenue-distribution formula reduces the incentive for PMDs to extend the meter hours in areas where parking demand is high. The Downtown District, for example, would receive only 29 percent of the additional revenue it generates. First, the city takes 55 percent and returns only 45 percent of the additional revenue to the PMDs. The city then distributes the meter revenue to the PMDs in proportion to the number of meters in each district; because the Downtown District has 65 percent of the city's meters, it receives 65 percent of the revenue returned to the PMDs, or only 29 percent of the revenue created by increasing its meter hours (45% x 65%). The incentive to earn more meter revenue is even lower in the other districts. The Uptown District receives only 12 percent of any additional revenue it generates (45% x 26%) and the Mid-City District receives only 4 percent (45% x 9%).

Why doesn't San Diego simply return 45 percent of each PMD's meter revenue? When the revenue return began, the city collected meter revenue on routes that included more than one district, and there was no way to link the revenue to the district in which it was collected. The city therefore audited the number of meters in each district and based each district's revenue on that number. With the subsequent installation of electronic parking meters, however, the city's Parking Management Division has established a tracking system, giving a unique number to each meter. The first digit of each meter number indicates which district it is in, and the revenue will in the future be returned on the basis of the actual meter revenue collected within each district. This new policy of returning to each district 45 percent of the revenue it generates will increase each district's reward for increasing the number of meters, their hours of operation, and their rates.

The neighborhoods' growing interest and expertise in parking management may soon lead to substantial changes in San Diego's parking policies. In 2003, the city manager appointed a task force with representatives from the PMDs, businesses, and other stakeholders to examine the city's parking management. They recommended shifting from a single meter rate throughout the city to rates that match supply and demand in each area:

The City's current approach of establishing time-limited areas with identical times and setting up all meters with identical fees does not effectively manage the varying demand for parking spaces.... [T]here is no one combination of rate and time that will meet the parking management needs throughout the City, and indeed there may be no one rate and time limit that meets the needs of even an individual community.... Parking meter rates should vary and meters should be operated during the days and hours that require management of the supply.... At some locations, metered parking provided at too low a rate may exacerbate parking and traffic impacts, while parking provided at too high a rate leaves metered spaces unused. Meters at different locations may have different rates (e.g., parking at a high demand meter location may cost $.25 for 5 minutes [$3 an hour] while a low demand meter might encourage longer term parking with $2 for 8 hours [$.25 an hour]). Permits may be provided to some users to park in otherwise restricted areas. Meters may be operated in evening hours in entertainment zones, and on Sundays and holidays in areas with high demand on those days.[47]

Giving neighborhoods more control over their curb parking helps everyone see the benefits of using flexible prices to match demand and supply.

The CCDC manages the Downtown PMD, but the other two PMDs include both the streets with parking meters and the surrounding neighborhoods, so they required new entities to administer the program. The need to organize and staff a new layer of government can be a barrier to creating a PMD and may help to explain why PMDs have been established only in areas that already had parking meters. To eliminate this barrier, the city could offer to share the parking meter revenue with any BID that installs meters. The guaranteed streams of meter revenue will strengthen existing BIDs and will also encourage merchants and property owners to organize new BIDs in areas without them. As merchants in areas without BIDs see how parking revenue can help revitalize business districts, they will want to form their own BIDs to bring the same kinds of improvements to their own areas. The increased number of metered spaces will improve transportation, provide revenue for neighborhood revitalization, and increase the revenue flowing to the city's general fund.

CONCLUSION: CASH REGISTERS AT THE CURB

Suppose American cities at the beginning of the twentieth century had chosen the parking policies Pasadena and San Diego adopted for their downtowns in the 1990s. The merchants and property owners who would have benefitted from the parking fees would have been less inclined to recommend free parking. Market prices would have made the scarce curb spaces available to customers rather than to commuters who parked all day in front of the stores where they worked. By creating a few vacancies, market prices would also have eliminated cruising for parking on downtown streets and thereby reduced traffic congestion. Public transit would have run faster, and the higher speeds would have reduced both the transit companies' costs and the riders' fares. With higher speeds and lower fares, public transit would have been more competitive with the automobile. Less congestion and better transit would have made the central-city shopping district more competitive with the suburbs. Instead, cities began to require off-street parking everywhere, and we now expect to park free at both ends of every automobile trip. We live with the resulting traffic congestion, urban sprawl, and air pollution.

The free-parking policies adopted in the early twentieth century are understandable, because neither parking meters nor BIDs had been invented. But both exist today, and the political challenge is now to get them working together.[48] If BIDs receive the revenue, every parking meter will resemble a cash register at the curb, and all businesses will see the advantages. Charging market prices for curb parking and dedicating the revenue to BIDs will help solve the transportation, land-use, and economic problems plaguing many central cities.

Older business districts are like shopping malls without free off-street parking. Merchants may fear that charging for curb parking in these business districts will drive customers away, but earmarking the revenue to pay for increased public services can mitigate these concerns and create the necessary political support for parking meters. A few curb vacancies will make the business district a convenient place to shop, not merely a place where drivers can park free after they cruise long enough. Spending the curb parking revenue to finance public amenities that draw customers will also give merchants an incentive to support paid parking. Charging the right price for curb parking will reduce the transportation problem, and using the revenue to pay for local public services will build better business districts, with no new taxes.

CHAPTER 16 NOTES

1. Who *does* receive the money that parking meters swallow, and how is it spent? In a survey of large cities in the U.S., de Cerreño (2002, 18) found that half the cities deposit the revenue in the general fund, while the others direct the funds to the city's department of transportation or to subsidize public transit. According to an earlier survey, 60 percent of all cities deposited their parking meter revenue into their general funds, and 40 percent deposited them into special funds that typically were used to provide public off-street parking (Robertson 1972). None of these revenue uses is so popular that voters want cities to charge higher prices for curb parking; politically, it is as if the money were incinerated. Most residents will place a higher value on the immediate, tangible benefit of free parking than on the possible long-run benefits of higher public services or lower taxes that would be made possible by charging higher prices for curb parking.

2. In Britain, earmarking is called "ring-fencing," as if a fence were put around the revenue to prevent its leaking out. This is a particularly appropriate description for a parking benefit district because the revenue is earmarked for any purpose in a specific neighborhood, not for a specific purpose in the whole city (such as public transit or a tax reduction). Harrington, Krupnick, and Alberini (1998) found in a survey in Southern California that residents were more willing to support congestion tolls if the revenue was returned to the public as a tax reduction than if the revenue use were unspecified.

3. Simon Haworth and Ian Hilton (1982) summarize studies of the elasticity of demand for parking. All the studies show that the demand for parking is less elastic for shorter parking durations.

4. Oppewal and Timmermans (2001).

5. *American City*, August 1936, p. 59. The meters were placed on one side of the street in one block and on the other side of the street in the next block, so each side of the street had alternating blocks of free and metered curb parking.

6. Brown (1937, 53). Fogelson (2001, 299-302) relates the early debates for and against parking meters.

7. Smith (1999, 538; 541).

8. If most consumers valued low prices more than convenience, thousands of products (such as pre-washed, pre-cut lettuce) would cease to exist, and everyone would cook their meals from scratch.

9. Lawrence Houstoun (1997, 9) explains the process of organizing and managing these self-governing public/private partnerships

10. The film's web site is www.thedelicateartofparking.com/. The city of Hialeah, Florida, has no parking meters, and a downtown businessman asked about them responded, "Absolutely not! We already have enough taxes." With meters, he said, "who do you think is going to get the money? The city. No, not another cent!" (*Parking Professional*, May 2004, p. 19).

11. De Cerreño (2002, B-4; B-14). Because stricter enforcement will increase the probability of citation for overtime parking, it will increase the incentive to pay for parking and the meter revenue will increase, but the fine revenue may either increase or decrease. If enforcement is so strict that everyone pays for parking, the fine revenue can decline to zero. If cities want to maintain fines as a source of revenue, they can increase the fines for violations rather than increase the effort to cite violators.

12. I am grateful to Douglas Kolozsvari for his partnership in our research on Old Pasadena. See Kolozsvari (2002) and Kolozsvari and Shoup (2003).

13. Arroyo Group (1978, 3). Information about the history of Old Pasadena is available on the web site of Pasadena Heritage at www.pasadenaheritage.org. This historic preservation organization was founded in 1977 in reaction to the Pasadena Redevelopment

Agency's plans for Old Pasadena. In the 1980s, Pasadena converted its redevelopment agency into a community development commission, which is organized according to the same laws and provisions as a redevelopment agency. The main difference is that the commission structure provides for more community participation and input.

14. Arroyo Group (1978, 25).

15. Section 17.68.025 of the Pasadena Municipal Code, available online at www.ci.pasadena.ca.us/cityclerk/municode.asp.

16. This problem is an old one. Smith and LeCraw (1946, 21) comment on "the practice which still exists today in some communities: one merchant parking his own car at the curb in front of his competitor's place of business. This attitude still prevails among long-time parkers, for studies have shown a large percentage of vehicles parked for a full day to belong to employers and employees of business establishments within the same block."

17. The city's general fund also did not *lose* anything in the process because there had been no parking meters anywhere in the city before the meters were installed in Old Pasadena. The general fund thus gained revenue from overtime fines at the new meters.

18. The Mayor appoints the seven members of the Advisory Board, subject to confirmation by the city council. See www.ci.pasadena.ca.us/commissions/parking_meter.asp.

19. Interview with Marilyn Buchanan, June 12, 2001.

20. Pasadena calculates the full costs of the parking meter program. For example, the charge of $51,162 for personnel includes not only staff who collect the meter revenue, but also office staff for customer service and management. The charge of $34,425 for city abatements includes overhead for the city manager, financial reports, and other general services provided by the city. The charge of $7,896 for rent is for a share of the office space occupied by the transportation department. The charge of $44,146 for cash handling includes the cost of counting the coins and armored car service. Finally, $39,000 (3 percent of the net parking revenue) remained after paying all capital and operating expenditures for additional public services in Old Pasadena and was carried forward to FY 2002.

21. Colorado Boulevard is steam-cleaned twice a month, and all the other streets in the district are steam-cleaned less frequently. The broken-windows theory suggests that frequent cleaning is an important step to discourage litter and graffiti.

22. The fee was initially set low to promote new businesses in Old Pasadena and was indexed annually by the Consumer Price Index. Because business is now booming, the city council increased the fee per credit to $240 in 2003, increasing to $720 per year in 2005. The parking credit policy is available online at www.ci.pasadena.ca.us/planning/deptorg/curplng/pkgcredit.asp.

23. Interview with Marsha Rood, June 6, 2001.

24. In contrast, a parking study in downtown Tempe, Arizona, found that 55 percent of the off-street parking spaces were restricted to use by employees, and 32 percent were reserved for customers who were made to move on after they finished their business; only 13 percent of the off-street spaces were available for public use. Because of these restrictions, the maximum occupancy of all spaces on a Friday evening—when parking was hard to find—was only 52 percent (Minett 1994).

25. Section 17.33.060 of the Pasadena Municipal Code.

26. Presentation at the Urban Planning Forum in the Pasadena City Hall on February 12, 2000, www.ci.pasadena.ca.us/mayor/PolyzoidesSummary.asp. Polyzoides was a cofounder of the Congress for the New Urbanism.

27. In 1998, Old Pasadena's sales-tax revenue also surpassed that of South Lake Avenue, formerly the city's premier shopping district, which has ample off-street parking but still has no parking meters. The Playhouse District followed Old Pasadena in establishing a Parking Meter Zone, and its sales tax revenue has been rising.

28. Meyer, Mohaddes Associates (2001, vi). Old Pasadena's parking meters operate until 8 p.m. Sunday through Thursday, and until midnight Friday and Saturday.

29. Kaku Associates (1994, 12). The meter rate increased from 50¢ to $1 an hour in the 1980s and was reduced to 50¢ an hour in 1994. Curb parking is free after 7 p.m. and on Sunday. In Chapter 14, I estimated that cruising for underpriced parking in Westwood Village creates about 70 percent of the traffic on some streets.

30. Kaku Associates (1994). The off-street occupancy rate was 44 percent at 10 a.m., 68 percent at 2 p.m., and 39 percent at 8 p.m. At the peak daytime hour (2 p.m.), 32 percent of the village's parking spaces were vacant.

31. Section 9(E) of the Westwood Village Specific Plan. This specific plan was established by Los Angeles City Ordinance 164.305 (effective January 30, 1989), available online at www.cityofla.org/PLN/complan/specplan/pdf/wwdvil.pdf. See also the discussion in Chapter 5. The only new construction in Westwood Village on a parking lot since the zoning began to require replacement parking has been a public parking structure that replaced a parking lot on Broxton Avenue. The village's 15 blocks have eight surface parking lots and 10 parking structures.

32. Kurt Streeter, "Old Pasadena Thanks Parking Meters for the Change," *Los Angeles Times*, March 2, 2004.

33. Ibid.

34. "Parking Meter Revenue Allocation & Expenditure Policy," City of San Diego Council Policy Number 100-18, effective on March 4, 1997.

35. Information about the Parking Meter District Program is available on the city's web site at www.sannet.gov/economic-development/business-assistance/small-business/pmd.shtml.

36. City of San Diego Manager's Report No. 02-247, October 23, 2002.

37. City of San Diego Manager's Report No. 96-221, October 24, 1996.

38. The Uptown Partnership's web site is www.uptownpartnership.org.

39. Uptown Strategic Mobility Plan, November 17, 1999, p.2.

40. Ibid., p. 4.

41. Uptown Parking District Strategic Plan and Implementation Guideline, Phase 1, May 6, 1999, p. 15. Some cities now require drivers to back into diagonal spaces when parking so they will drive forward when unparking. This is safer than backing into the traffic flow when unparking, and it is much safer for bicyclists who share the roadway with cars.

42. San Diego Centre City Development Corporation, "Wayfinding Sign System Unveiled Downtown," May 18, 2000.

43. These provisions for the Centre City Planned District are contained in Chapter 10, Article 3, Division 19 of the San Diego Municipal Code. The code is available online at http://clerkdoc.sannet.gov/Web site/mc/MunicodeChapter10.html.

44. Bonds that are backed by two or more revenue sources are called "double-barreled." Double-barreled bonds used to finance public parking garages can be backed by both the garage and the on-street meter revenues. The garage revenue is the first repayment source, and if it is insufficient, the meter revenue can be used. Double-barreled bonds are used when the projected revenue stream is uncertain, and the added security of the meter revenue increases the security of the bonds.

45. Most cities will not allow a new business to open unless it provides the parking required for the particular land use, and tracking land uses as tenants turn over is a problem for planners.

46. The parking studies were conducted by the Mission Group and are described on the Mid-City PMD's web site at www.theboulevard.org/Parking.htm.

47. "Managing Parking in San Diego: Report of the Parking Task Force," (Office of the City Manager, 2004, pp. 2, 5, and 7).

48. Many policy options are never considered because they are believed to be politically, legally, or administratively infeasible, or because they simply have not been proposed. Fulton and Weimer (1980) explain how they guided the proposal for parking permit districts through adoption and implementation in San Francisco.

17

Taxing Foreigners Living Abroad

The way to multiply big problems is to neglect small ones.
— HENRY SIMONS

Suppose you live near a business district that generates parking spillover into your neighborhood. Strangers park in front of your home all day, every day. You can't find a place to park on your own street, and neither can your guests. Urban planners have long had to deal with these complaints from citizens, as suggested by this passage from a textbook on zoning:

> Many people object to having the streets in front of their homes in constant use as parking lots, both from the purely esthetic standpoint, and for more practical reasons such as the inability of their own guests to find nearby parking, the difficulty of getting in and out of driveways, the narrowing of the roadway, the danger of children running out from between parked cars, and the hindrance to street cleaning and snow removal. The noise of car doors opening and closing and of engines starting up can also be an annoyance.... Usually, with little encouragement, any resident of the area involved in a zoning dispute can tell you about existing [parking] conditions.[1]

Many cities deal with spillover by establishing Residential Parking Permit Districts that reserve all curb spaces in a neighborhood for residents and their guests.[2] These permit districts prevent parking spillover from adjacent commercial areas but they also leave many unused curb spaces, indicating an overreaction to the spillover problem. As an alternative to curb parking that is first overused when free and then underused in a permit district, consider a profitable middleground: a market in curb parking.

A MARKET IN CURB PARKING

Suppose the city proposes to charge nonresidents for parking on your block and offers to give you all the revenue from the cars that park in front of your house. You and your guests can still park free in your curb spaces, but you can make these spaces available to others when you don't use them yourself. Suppose a price of 25¢ an hour leaves at least 15 percent of the spaces on your block vacant, so that anyone willing to pay that price can always find a place to park. You can therefore park in front of your house at no cost, or you can earn money for each space you make available to the public. The revenue can be substantial (remember, each parking meter in Pasadena yields about $1,700 a year; see Chapter 16). Your parking space might generate more than enough money to pay the property taxes on your house each year.

Many residents seem to think they own the parking spaces in front of their homes, or at least they act that way. So rather than fighting this thought, cities can accept it and take advantage of it by treating residents like the landlords they think they are. Cities cannot allow private citizens to charge for parking on public streets, of course, and most residents wouldn't want to see parking meters in front of their houses. But by slightly modifying the existing residential parking permit districts, cities can create political support for market-price curb parking without giving public revenue to private citizens and without installing parking meters.

My proposal is to create "parking benefit districts" in residential neighborhoods. Parking *benefit* districts resemble parking *permit* districts because residents can still park free on the streets in front of their homes. But the benefit districts differ from conventional permit districts in two important ways:

1. Nonresidents can park on the streets in a benefit district if they pay the fair-market price.
2. The city earmarks the resulting revenue to finance added public services in the district.

The price for nonresident parking in a benefit district can be set high enough to ensure sufficient vacancies for both residents (who park free) and nonresidents (who pay to park). The new revenue can finance additional public services in the neighborhood above and beyond those provided everywhere in the city. The city can clean the streets more often, fill potholes, repair sidewalks, plant trees, remove graffiti, preserve historic buildings, or put utility wires underground in neighborhoods where the benefit districts generate revenue. Seen from the residents' side of the bargain, charging nonresidents for curb parking resembles Monty Python's plan to solve Britain's economic problems by taxing foreigners living abroad.

RESIDENTIAL PARKING BENEFIT DISTRICTS

Parking benefit districts are a compromise between free curb parking that leads to overcrowding and permit districts that lead to underuse. The benefit districts are better for both residents and nonresidents: residents get public services paid for by nonresidents, and nonresidents get to park at a fair-market price rather than not at all.

Selective Public Goods

Political support for establishing a parking benefit district does not depend on a collective conviction that charging for curb parking will benefit the larger community—such as by reducing air pollution and traffic congestion. Support will come instead from the "selective individual benefits" that curb parking revenue provides for the district's residents. Harvard political scientist Arnold Howitt explains the crucial importance of providing selective benefits when proposing restrictions on cars:

> It is difficult to organise people to seek a "collective" or "public" good from which they would benefit regardless of their contribution to securing it. Citizens are more likely to take action for "selective" goods which are granted or withheld from specific individuals or small groups.... What prevents the emergence of more active support for auto restraint policies is the almost total absence of individuals or firms that might receive immediate, direct "selective" benefits.[3]

Most proposals for constraints on cars often suffer from their across-the-board nature. Because no one group benefits much more than another, the measures lack a natural constituency who will put time and money into advocating them. Parking benefit districts, in contrast, will finance selective benefits for the residents, and these benefits will generate the necessary political support to charge for curb parking. Residents who receive the benefits can vote for their member of the city council, while most nonresidents who pay for parking in the neighborhood cannot. Politicians think politically, and in supporting parking benefit districts they will not have to break free from parochial, place-based concerns to adopt a reform serving the wider public interest. By creating legitimate constituencies who enjoy selective public goods, parking benefit districts *rely* on parochial, place-based concerns to provide the incentive for reform. The political support for these benefit districts will come from self-interest, not ideological conviction, and no one needs to believe that charging market prices for curb parking is good transportation policy. In this case, residents who think locally will act globally whether they know it or not.

Parking benefit districts will not only increase residents' desire to charge for curb parking, but may also increase drivers' willingness to pay for it. If drivers see that the money they pay for parking goes to plant trees, clean and repair sidewalks, and increase security for themselves and their cars, they may feel this is a fair exchange. Parkers will get more for their money than simply time at the curb.

Once implemented, the benefit districts are likely to multiply and endure because they will create voting blocs who benefit from selective public goods paid for by someone else. The districts can also be put in place gradually, giving everyone time to adjust to them. Neighborhoods with the most parking spillover from nearby business districts will earn the most revenue. Nonresident parkers will become paying guests rather than freeloaders, and their numbers will be kept manageable by flexible prices designed to keep a few vacant spaces available.

Informal markets for off-street parking already operate in many older neighborhoods near sites that generate spillover parking. They often appear near the Los Angeles Coliseum, for example: residents park their cars on the street and charge nonresidents for the right to park in their driveways and yards. Figure 17-1 shows a scene photographed during the

Photo by Tom Zimmerman, collection of the Los Angeles Public Library

Figure 17-1. Residents charging for off-street parking at the 1984 Olympics

1984 Olympics. Just as residents can charge nonresidents for *off-street* parking, the city can charge nonresidents for *curb* parking. From the residents' viewpoint, charging for curb parking is simple because the city does the work. Neighborhoods with strong spillover demand might become more prosperous than their residents ever imagined they could be.[4]

Client Politics

Parking is political, and parking benefit districts fit into the category of "client politics" as defined by James Q. Wilson. Wilson explained that the incentive to engage in political action depends on whether the benefits and costs of a public policy are widely distributed or narrowly concentrated. Generally speaking, the policies that are easiest to implement tend to produce concentrated benefits and widely distributed costs:

> When the benefits of a prospective policy are concentrated but the costs widely distributed, *client politics* is likely to result. Some small easily organized group will benefit and thus has a powerful incentive to organize and lobby; the costs of the benefit are distributed at a low per capita rate over a large number of people, and hence they have little incentive to organize in opposition—if, indeed, they even hear of the policy.[5]

We can apply Wilson's model to parking benefit districts. Residents of a neighborhood have a strong incentive to organize because they receive additional public services paid for by the parking revenue. Nonresidents who park on the neighborhood's streets, in contrast, are transients who each pay a small share of the total cost and who therefore have little incentive or ability to organize in opposition. Indeed, it is the narrowly concentrated benefits and widely distributed costs that have motivated formation of the existing permit districts, which reserve curb parking exclusively for residents. Residents are stable, place-based groups who have the legitimate political power to form a parking benefit district, while nonresidents have no say in the matter. The residents' desire for local public goods at no cost to themselves will create the most effective way to overcome motorists' aversion to paying for parking they believe should be free. Conventional arguments against charging for curb parking, such as "The streets belong to everyone" (which really means the streets belong to motorists), will seem superficial and opportunistic when weighed against the neighborhood public benefits. Even drivers may be more willing to pay for parking if they don't have to spend time cruising for it and can see the revenue is used to provide public services they value. The principal justifications for parking benefit districts are pragmatic and political, not theoretical or ideological.

As cities shift toward market-price curb parking and away from off-street parking requirements, parking benefit districts will reduce traffic congestion, air pollution, accidents, and energy consumption. These wider social benefits will be above and beyond the "selective benefits" received only by the districts' residents, but no one will have to persuade residents of the value of these larger social goals; self-interest alone can justify the policy. Less traffic and cleaner air may therefore be seen as regional icing on the neighborhood cake.

Political and Administrative Feasibility

Policies that increase the cost of cars are never popular or easy to implement, but parking benefit districts are an exception. They appear to meet all seven of the criteria that Arnold Howitt deemed critical to the political and administrative feasibility of policies to restrain automobile use:

1. The smaller the geographical area affected, the fewer the persons likely to feel threatened economically or to have their travel habits interrupted. A small restraint area, therefore, is less likely to evoke political opposition.
2. Policies that extend existing restrictions seem less threatening than new types of restraints and therefore tend to generate less opposition.
3. New policies that can be adopted and implemented incrementally, rather than all at once, are less visible and less likely to evoke opposition. Successful implementation of the first step, moreover, helps to allay public concern about the potential impact of subsequent steps, which become easier to adopt and implement.
4. Schemes that do not require both local and state legislative approval are less vulnerable to opposition.
5. Policies are more likely to be successful if they do not depend on regular amendment.
6. Policies that generate revenue tend to be more attractive to elected executives and administrators.
7. Policies that require less interagency coordination and commitment of fewer organizational resources by key agencies are more likely to be implemented successfully.[6]

Parking benefit districts meet these feasibility criteria perfectly. Instead of bemoaning the fact that parking is political, planners can make the politics of parking work for public purposes.

Indiana University political scientist Elinor Ostrom argues the key to solving a commons problem is to "get the institutions right."[7] Parking benefit districts are institutions that will help secure consensus about curb parking among everyone whose agreement counts: voters, business own-ers, and politicians. If each neighborhood keeps its own parking revenue to finance public spending, all these interest groups will have an incentive to charge nonresidents the right price for curb parking. Note that *drivers* do not appear on this list of interest groups who can influence the politi-cal decisions about the price of curb parking in a benefit district. Almost all adults drive, but *nonresident* drivers will have little say on a neighbor-hood's choices, especially because the neighborhoods where these drivers live may also be charging nonresidents for curb parking. Because every-one can enjoy neighborhood public investments financed by everyone else's payments for curb parking, parking benefit districts will not merely create winners and losers but will instead create winners and big winners.

The Need for Earmarked Revenue

Residents will want to charge for curb parking only if their own neigh-borhoods receive the revenue; when a higher level of government takes the revenue, the opposite incentive is created. Explaining the general reluctance to raise curb parking prices in Munich, the Organisation for Economic Co-Operation and Development reported, "Little incentive exists in Munich for raising parking fees because the money thus col-lected does not go to the municipality but to the Free State of Bavaria."[8] If the state government receives the revenue, city officials are understand-ably reluctant to raise parking fees. Similarly, if the city government receives the revenue, neighborhood residents likewise oppose raising the fees. Residents have a legitimate interest in their own neighborhood's welfare, and cities can take advantage of this self-interest by earmarking curb parking revenue to pay for neighborhood public services. Market prices and earmarked revenue will show everyone that long-term storage for cars is not the best use of street space.

The explanation for free curb parking is not that planners and politicians have failed to see the light; instead, curb parking is free because drivers resist paying for it, and most voters drive. Public policies emerge from a balancing of political interests, and because drivers oppose paying for curb parking, we need a countervailing interest that benefits from the rev-enue. Earmarking the revenue to pay for neighborhood improvements will create this countervailing interest. Brookings Institution economists Clifford Winston and Chad Shirley say:

> Policy makers do not just happen to create inefficiencies. When economists estimate large welfare losses stemming from public policies as if the losses were simple oversights that officials could correct by paying closer attention to what they were doing, it is the economists, not the officials, who are not paying attention.[9]

Once we get the right economic interests, we will get the right parking policies.

One Block at a Time

The simplest way to convert an existing *permit* district into a new *benefit* district is to sell a few nonresident permits that allow employees of nearby businesses to park in the district during the day, when many residents have taken their own cars to work. District residents might be offered the option to accept two or three daytime permit holders on their block, with the revenue used to finance public improvements such as sidewalk repairs. Residents who benefit from parking fees paid by commuters will begin to see curb parking from the perspective of a parking lot owner—as a valuable income-earning property. If residents on one block agree to this arrangement, residents on other blocks will be able to see the effects and then decide if they too would like their block to have these benefits. In this way, permit districts can be converted to benefit districts one block at a time.

Parking benefit districts can be tested in a few neighborhoods as pilot programs, and residents can petition the city to establish the benefit districts just as they now petition for conventional permit districts. The benefit districts will be formed only if residents want them, but cities must first offer the option. Citizen demand rather than government mandate explains the rapid spread of parking permit districts throughout the U.S. If a few experimental parking benefit districts are successful and prove to generate significant revenue for their neighborhoods, they will spread rapidly in the same way permit districts have—by popular demand.

The choice of whether to form a parking benefit district and how much to charge for curb parking is inherently a local decision. If the residents of some blocks oppose selling the right to park on their street, they can always choose not to opt into a benefit district. The ability to form benefit districts will give neighborhoods more transportation, land-use, and public finance choices. Some neighborhoods may choose to retain free curb parking, off-street parking requirements, and no curb parking revenue, but this is the *only* choice that cities now give neighborhoods. Cities can offer the *option* of parking benefit districts and let each neighborhood make its own choice. The new public revenue will help put older neighborhoods and commercial districts back on their feet, and market prices for curb parking will benefit the whole city by reducing traffic congestion and air pollution.

Collecting the Revenue

Priced parking does not require a conventional meter at every space. New technology has overcome both the aesthetic and practical objections to charging for curb parking, and cities can use a variety of unobtrusive payment systems. Daytime permits, for example, are a cheap, simple, and inconspicuous way to allow nonresidents to park in existing permit districts. In Aspen, drivers buy a hang tag, scratch off the day and date, and display it in the windshield.[10] High-tech alternatives, such as in-vehicle meters, are also available (see Chapter 15).

The more sophisticated meter technologies require an up-front investment, which can be financed the same way the first parking meters were financed. Cities were initially unsure how the motoring public would react to the new meters, so manufacturers paid to install the first meters and recovered the cost from the resulting revenue. As reported in a 1935 issue of *American City*:

> The Dual Parking Meter Co., Oklahoma City, will install these meters without cost to the city, taking all receipts until these meters are paid for and become the property of the city free and clear.[11]

This arrangement is now commonly referred to as build-operate-transfer (BOT). Private enterprises build and operate public infrastructure, charge for its use until the cost is recovered, and then transfer ownership to the public sector. Parking meters were an early BOT project, and the same arrangement can pay the up-front costs of benefit districts. Private investors usually construct a BOT facility and then charge the users to repay the construction costs. In parking benefit districts, however, the facility—curb parking—is already there, and the only private investment needed is for the technology to collect the user fees. The private investment will involve almost no risk, and the benefit districts will require no public subsidy.

A Promising Precedent

Letting nonresidents pay to park in a residential permit district resembles letting solo drivers pay to drive in carpool or high-occupancy vehicle (HOV) lanes. On some freeways, California has begun to allow solo drivers to pay a toll to use carpool lanes with underused capacity, with the tolls set high enough to ensure that traffic continues to flow freely (see Chapter 11). These high occupancy/toll (HOT) lanes make better use of carpool lanes and give solo drivers a new option for occasions when they are willing to pay a higher price for faster travel.

Parking benefit districts are like HOT lanes because nonresidents pay to park in underused curb spaces, just as solo drivers pay to drive in underused carpool lanes. The biggest difference between the two arrangements is that charging nonresidents for curb parking is easier than charging solo drivers for using a HOT lane. HOT lanes therefore provide a good precedent for the simpler proposal to allow nonresidents to pay for curb parking in residential permit districts.

Dense Neighborhoods

Most citizens seem to think the right to park free in front of their house is written into the social contract, but in his book on *Twentieth-Century Sprawl*, Owen Gutfreund points out that if curb parking had been free in pre-automotive times, "urban residents would have been entitled to stable their horses and carriages on the public street in front of their homes."[12] Nevertheless, the right to park free in front of one's own home is now an ingrained social practice, and free parking for residents in a benefit district is probably necessary to generate political support.[13] In neighborhoods where most residents don't park on the street, however, a majority-rule solution may turn out to be market prices for all curb parking, even for residents. The densest neighborhoods don't have enough curb spaces for all the residents (let alone nonresidents) who want to park on the street, so the residents will have to pay for parking to avoid overcrowding the few curb spaces available, and more revenue will be available to pay for public services. San Francisco, for example, is considering a plan to restrict the number of resident permits to the number of curb spaces and to charge market rates for the permits. Existing permits would be grandfathered at the current below-market price, but new permits would be priced to equate demand with supply.[14]

Where a city returns parking revenue to the neighborhoods that generate it, expecting residents to pay for the curb parking they use is like expecting roommates who split their telephone bill to pay for the long-distance calls they make. A New Yorker who phones her boyfriend in Boston once a week, for instance, should pay less than her roommate who phones his boyfriend in Hawaii every day. If a group is small, if the common property is valuable, and if different members of the group make highly unequal use of this property, splitting the bill according to use seems much fairer than any other arrangement.

Curb parking revenue can be high in dense neighborhoods, and an anecdote from San Francisco will suggest how high. The doorman at a posh apartment house on Russian Hill uses the building's passenger loading zone to park cars for visitors, and he usually receives a $20 tip for this service. When a curb space opens up near the building, he quickly parks

From "The Ethicist," a weekly column in the *New York Times Magazine* (July 27, 2003)

Q: Two of my neighbors are in cahoots. When one pulls his car out of a spot, the other is always parked directly in front or behind and moves his car just enough to take up two spaces, so no other car can squeeze in. When the first car returns, the other moves back, restoring parking spots for both. Is it ethical for them to save spaces for each other, instead of leaving one for another parking-deprived New Yorker?

A: If either of them were ethical, they wouldn't use private cars in Manhattan, a city with excellent public transportation. Why should the non-car-owning majority allow the car-owning minority to store their private property, i.e. cars, on public property at no charge? Why should my every walk to the store be akin to a stroll through a parking lot? Why should that majority be subject to the many costs and risks to health and safety attendant on the private car?

the visitor's car in it. If a resident then comes home and can't find a curb space, the doorman creates a curb vacancy by moving the visitor's car back to the passenger loading zone, for which he receives another $20 tip.[15] Charging market prices for curb parking in this neighborhood will make life easier for both residents and visitors, and will divert revenue from tips for doormen to spending for public improvements.

Where land values are high and curb space is scarce, cities can allocate *all* curb parking purely by prices. Residents can be given "first refusal" rights, but they would have to pay the market price. Those who store several cars on the street would probably be the first to reduce their use of curb space, most likely by disposing of any rarely driven cars.[16] Charging residents will be less popular than charging nonresidents, but even those who do end up paying for curb parking in their own neighborhood may feel they get a good deal because they will be guaranteed a space close to their front door, without cruising. In addition, everything residents pay for parking will come right back to them as added spending for public improvements—sidewalk repair, street trees, and underground utilities—in their own neighborhood. Market prices will convert many curb spaces from long-term storage to short-term use that can serve more cars each day and bring in more revenue for the neighborhood.

In some crowded neighborhoods, residents who park at the curb hesitate to use their cars because they're afraid they won't be able to find a place to park when they return. For example, British journalist Ian Parker says:

London drivers fear the morning peak, and the evening peak, and the school run rush hour, and the West End theatre rush hour. They fear Saturday afternoon traffic and Sunday night traffic. And they fear the prospect of leaving a good London parking spot: when a car fills the space they have left, they feel troubled and adrift, regretting their recklessness. There are Londoners—they are real and many—who will take a taxi from home, rather than risk giving up a resident's parking space, a lovely space, right in front of the house.[17]

If curb parking is so overcrowded that residents are reluctant to leave their parking space for fear they won't find another one when they get back, this need to "hoard" a parking space reduces the value of owning a car, and increases the demand for parking even by those who would rather not be parked. In the very neighborhoods where parking is most valuable, drivers occupy spaces they don't need because they know these spaces will go to another parker under the "first possession" rule. People who would rather use their cars instead remain parked, and they reduce the number of spaces available to those who do want to park. And those who do find parking may have to walk a long distance to their ultimate destinations. Charging market prices for curb parking can thus increase the effective supply of convenient parking by releasing spaces that the users really do not want.

In any parking benefit district, residents will necessarily face a trade-off between parking spaces for themselves and public services for the neighborhood. The more permits they allocate to themselves, the less income they will receive from nonresidents. With conventional permit districts, cities simply give permits to all residents at a low price. One survey by the Institute of Transportation Engineers found that most cities place no restriction on the number of permits issued to each household and charge less than $10 a year for a permit.[18] Another survey by Gerard Mildner, James Strathman, and Martha Bianco found that most cities make resident permits available for any registered car owned by a resident.[19] Where parking is not sufficient to accommodate all the residents' cars, cities usually do not create permit districts, which suggests that where permits and pricing are needed most, officials simply throw up their hands and do nothing.[20] Even when cities do create permit districts in neighborhoods where parking is scarce, they can be quite freewheeling about the number of permits they issue, as shown by the outrage over romance novelist Danielle Steel's 26 residential parking permits in San Francisco's Pacific Heights neighborhood. Anyone who wants to park 26 cars on the street should certainly pay the market price. (See sidebar.)

In the densest neighborhoods, open access to free curb parking drives down its value to residents because they must spend so much time

Novelist Stirs Passion Over Parking

By John M. Glionna

Los Angeles Times, May 8, 2002

Romance novelist Danielle Steel is a woman of excess. She's dashed off dozens of bestsellers, married five times, produced nine children, and inhabits a sprawling compound that commands sweeping views of Alcatraz Island and the Golden Gate Bridge.

It turns out she has an appetite for parking places too.

The 54-year-old grande dame of fiction has amassed 26 residential permits in her tony Pacific Heights neighborhood—more than any other San Franciscan, city officials say.

In a traffic-clogged city where the number of cars dwarfs the number of parking spaces, where residents can circle for hours to find a spot, Steel's penchant for parking permits has unleashed passions not normally associated with her 50-odd romance novels.

Partially inspired by Steel's surplus, irked city officials Thursday will consider limiting the number of parking permits to three per household. Under present law, residents can buy an unlimited number of permits—at $27 per year each.

San Francisco has the nation's largest persquare-mile number of registered vehicles and one of the smallest numbers of per-capita parking spaces. About 500,000 vehicles compete each weekday for 320,000 street parking spaces, statistics show.

Crowded into 49 densely packed square miles, residents often wait two years for garage rental space. People wind up parking on sidewalks, often to find themselves later boxed in by other parking scofflaws.

Police issue 100,000 parking tickets annually specifically for sidewalk parking.

City officials said the uproar over Steel's parking permits signals a frustration felt by nearly every San Franciscan.

"Parking is at an extraordinary premium in this city, and the issue is definitely the biggest complaint we face as city officials," Supervisor Gavin Newsom said. "People hate to have to park on the sidewalk, and it moves them to organize so their voice is heard at City Hall."

The parking issue recently prompted "one of the most acrimonious public meetings" Newsom said he'd attended. "No one wanted to talk about homelessness or affordable housing," he said. "What they wanted to talk about were parking permits."

Not Steel. The prolific author whose books—including "Bittersweet," "The Gift" and "Fine Things"—have been translated into 28 languages in 47 countries, declined to discuss the permit controversy.

In 1988, the author and her then-husband, John Traina, a shipping consultant, paid $8 million for the home many consider the most elegant in San Francisco.

Perched on a hill surrounded by other multimillion-dollar mansions, the home features towering concrete walls, thick foliage and electronic surveillance. A sign outside the garage door warns: "No Parking." Steel's permits cover four Toyotas, three Mercedes, two Land Rovers, a Volvo, two antique 1940 Fords and a 2000 Jaguar, not to mention cars driven by her staff, records show.

When approached by a reporter, a man who said his name was Tony, Steel's parking director, refused to comment and hustled the visitor out a side service door.

"We never intended to provide cheap onstreet parking storage for people with too many vehicles," said Diana Hammons, a spokeswoman for the Department of Parking and Traffic. "You can't own a dozen cars and expect to park them on city streets."

searching for a space. If residents could always depend on finding a convenient space close to their front door, however, they would place a higher value on the right to park at the curb. Curb parking in a benefit district would be more valuable to residents because it would become much more dependable. The revenue could therefore be much higher than anyone expected and could finance a high level of public services. All the many residents of these dense neighborhoods would benefit from the public services, but only a relative handful would pay for parking because the limited number of curb spaces can serve only a small share of a large population. The denser the neighborhood, the more valuable the public services, and the smaller the share of residents who will pay for curb parking.[21]

In the densest areas like Manhattan, curb parkers could pay by the hour (as with in-vehicle meters) rather than by the month (as with permits). With hourly charges, residents would not pay for the curb time they do not use when they take their cars out of the neighborhood; the hourly charges are thus like a monthly permit with a rebate for every hour not used. In contrast, conventional flat-rate monthly permits encourage purchase by those who want to store their cars on the street most of the time because the permit holder's marginal cost of parking is zero for all hours of the month. Charging for curb parking by the hour rather than by the month will favor part-time over full-time users and produce more revenue. To save money, some residents who had previously stored their cars on the street when parking was free will shift to off-street parking, and more curb spaces will be available for visitors.

Residents object to paying for parking on the streets in their own neighborhoods, of course, but they also object to the problems caused by free parking. In a survey of 1,526 households in developments on the outskirts of Reading, England, John Noble and Mike Jenks at Oxford Brookes University found that residents owned 1.57 cars per dwelling, while their developments provided 3.37 parking spaces per dwelling (2.81 off-street and 0.56 on-street), or slightly more than two parking spaces per car.[22] Nevertheless, 41 percent of the residents were either dissatisfied or very dissatisfied with the provision of parking in their neighborhoods, in part because many residents parked their cars on the streets rather than in the garages: 38 percent of households with one-car garages never used them for parking, while 54 percent of the two-car garages were used for at most one car.[23] Many garages were instead used to store garden tools, household appliances, furniture, and other bulky items; others were used for workshops, playrooms, or business purposes. Where on-street parking is free, providing enough of it to satisfy all the residents can be very difficult and expensive. If cities return curb parking revenue to the neighborhoods that generate it, however, most people may eventually come to realize that charging fair-market prices for *all* curb parking, even for residents, is the best policy.

Transportation economist Douglas Lee at the Volpe Center points out that if cities begin to charge for curb parking, some landowners may want to convert their front yards into parking lots, and cities will therefore need to enforce their off-street parking regulations:

> A carefully designed and landscaped driveway with a well-tended garage at the end is seldom a detriment to the neighborhood, whereas a front yard that is left as dirt used only for parking is a blight to its neighbors. It is also a blight for its owner, but the cost to the neighborhood is much greater.... Regulations should be aimed at limiting the amount of off-street parking as well as its negative impact.... Restraints may include requirements for paving, screening, landscaping, setbacks, and drainage, with limitations on the share of the site covered by building and parking or by parking only.[24]

Most cities already regulate the design of off-street parking in residential neighborhoods, but charging for curb parking will make enforcing these regulations more important.

Optimum Size for a Parking Benefit District

By allowing local choices about public spending, parking benefit districts will foster neighborhood self-government. Because residents will collectively choose whether to charge for their curb parking and how to spend the revenue, this neighborhood responsibility will require grassroots decision making and new microlevel institutions of government.

A parking benefit district must be small enough to create the incentive to charge for curb parking but large enough to spend the revenue efficiently and fairly. Two precedents for parking benefit districts are business improvement districts and parking permit districts. Cities can manage curb parking, collect the revenue, and return it as additional public services, but businesses and neighborhood residents can set policy and monitor the outcome. Devolving to neighborhoods the authority for parking fits the principle of "subsidiarity" in a federal system of government—the principle that government action should be undertaken by the smallest jurisdiction able to perform it effectively.[25] The goal is to ensure that decisions are made as close to the citizens as possible. If we apply this principle to parking benefit districts, each neighborhood can decide its own policy about charging for curb parking and choose its own priorities for spending the revenue. Cities can collect the meter revenue and enforce parking regulations to take advantage of scale economies, although some cities already contract these tasks to private operators.[26]

What is the optimum size for a parking benefit district? It can be as small as a city block. Some local public goods—such as sidewalks, street trees, and underground utilities—serve mainly the blocks where they are located, and these blocks may be the most appropriate territory to form a parking benefit district. Yale law professor Robert Ellickson has argued that many neighborhoods can benefit from block-level institutions, which he calls "block improvement districts" (BLIDs, to distinguish them from the similar concept of business improvement districts, or BIDs). These microgovernments resemble the community associations developers now establish in most subdivisions.[27] The chief problem in establishing a BLID is finding the funds to finance it. Parking benefit districts can pay for local public goods and are thus a perfect revenue source for these microterritorial institutions. The appropriate spending authority must be microlevel before residents will agree to charge for their curb parking, and block-level institutions seem particularly appropriate to receive the revenue.[28]

Beyond the specific public goods they provide, Ellickson explains that block-level microgovernments also have important social and political advantages:

> A high level of solidarity is easier to maintain within a small group than within a large one.... Smallness also enhances the quality of internal gossip and the frequency of chance encounters.... [A]t the block level, social pressures to pull one's oar tend to be stronger than they are at the neighborhood level. Indeed, the act of creating a formal block-level organization such as a BLID might foster acquaintanceships that would then strengthen the informal social capital of the block's residents and property owners.... Block-level institutions are well scaled to strengthen members' involvement and skills in collective governance. Many commentators seek to revitalize civic life in the United States. They should welcome block organizations that might serve as incubators of local social capital. The proceedings of a block organization would provide easy opportunities for people to engage in meaningful debate, voting, office-seeking, and other forms of community participation. Candidates for office would be few. There would be little or no wait to speak at a meeting. Participants would be unlikely to be intimidated by the setting because the turf would be familiar and most faces known. On routine issues involving the block welfare, an ordinary owner or resident would have little reason to be cowed by the views of experts.[29]

Ellickson proposes a specific legal framework for these sublocal governments, and I won't speculate further on the administrative details because, as Niccolò Machiavelli warned, "There is nothing more difficult to plan or more uncertain of success or more dangerous to carry out than an attempt to introduce new institutions."[30] Parking benefit districts, however, do not require much in the way of new institutions, and they can be established as marginal improvements to existing institutions. As explained in Chapter 16, a simple first step is to allow BIDs to retain their curb parking revenue. The next step could be to sell daytime permits in existing residential permit districts and earmark the revenue to finance public services the residents choose. Microgovernments funded by curb parking revenue can evolve by small steps and, in the end, will help create communities of mutual interest as well as help residents take control of their neighborhoods.

Parking benefit districts can help to fill an important gap in the fiscal system. Where there is no funding mechanism, neighborhood collective action is difficult to organize. For example, you can't, individually, put your utility wires underground no matter how much you dislike the overhead wire blight in your neighborhood. Even if you would much prefer to have underground utilities, you may instead remodel your kitchen, which you can do without organizing neighborhood action. This problem contributes to what John Kenneth Galbraith termed "private affluence and public squalor."[31] In many older neighborhoods, for example, residents constantly remodel their kitchens and bathrooms while the sidewalks crack, street trees die, and overhead wires mar the view. Charging for curb parking and spending the revenue to finance neighborhood reinvestment—sidewalk repairs, new street trees, and underground utilities—will match public wants with private means.

If parking benefit districts improve older neighborhoods and families can enjoy better public services by staying where they are, fewer families whose incomes are rising will want to move out. Many residents would probably prefer to preserve or improve their established neighborhood rather than move to a new development where everything is well designed but uniform and unmistakably new. In Albert Hirschman's famous formulation of the alternatives for dealing with civic problems, parking benefit districts will give residents more opportunity to exercise "voice" and less need to choose "exit" as the way to improve their neighborhood.[32] By reducing the emigration of prosperous families, parking benefit districts can as a by-product bring about more social integration and social capital in older neighborhoods. They will, as then-Governor of Arkansas Bill Clinton recommended, "give the people a new choice, rooted in old values, a new choice that is simple, that offers opportunity, demands responsibility, gives citizens more say, provides them responsive government—all because we recognize that we are a community."[33]

Parking benefit districts can become a new institution of neighborhood government, and in describing the Supreme Court's landmark 1926 decision that legitimized zoning (*Village of Euclid* v. *Ambler Realty Co.*), Harvard law professor Charles Haar noted two ways to justify a new institution:

> At the center of the *Euclid* litigation rests a fascinating question of legal strategy—a recurring question faced by virtually all those who find themselves on the cutting edge of legal reform in the adversarial common law system. Should a new doctrine be acknowledged frankly as a novel approach designed to cope with changing circumstances, or should it be dressed in the reassuring garb of incrementalism, presented as the inevitable byproduct of the evolution of ancient legal principles?[34]

With parking benefit districts, planners and lawyers can have it both ways. They can argue that parking benefit districts are merely an incremental change to the established system of parking permit districts, but also a novel approach to financing neighborhood public services.

None of this suggests that governance in a parking benefit district will be easy. Condominium and homeowners' associations are microgovernments that assess monthly fees to maintain their common areas, and most of them manage their affairs amicably, but in others apathy punctuated by an occasional bitter dispute shows that neighborhood self-determination doesn't automatically produce communal solidarity. Nevertheless, an imperfect neighborhood government is probably much better than none at all. Because 16 percent of the U.S. population moves every year, and many people have few contacts with their neighbors, parking benefit districts can help to foster collective concern for a neighborhood's well being, not just individual concern for each family's well being.

Cap-and-Trade Approach

The simplest way to convert a parking permit district into a parking benefit district is to sell a limited number of daytime permits to nonresidents. This policy resembles the cap-and-trade approach to protecting the environment. In a cap-and-trade system, a government caps total pollution emissions and allows firms to trade permits for the right to emit the regulated pollutants. For example, electricity generation creates sulfur dioxide (SO_2) emissions, which are the chief source of acid rain. The 1990 Clean Air Act Amendments capped the total SO_2 emissions from electric utilities, allocated SO_2 emissions permits to utilities based on their emissions history, and then created a market letting utilities trade permits among themselves.[35]

A parking *benefit* district resembles the cap-and-trade approach because it limits the number of nonresident permits and sells them at the fair-market price.[36] The cap-and-trade approach works well to reduce air pollution from utilities, but can it really be applied to curb parking? Charging nonresident motorists for curb parking is much easier than charging factories for emissions, and selling nonresident parking permits is much easier than distributing emissions permits. Cities can sell parking permits within a neighborhood, while pollution rights must be sold by a higher level of government far removed from the problem. Pollution markets must, by their very nature, encompass a region, a nation, or (in the case of greenhouse gas emissions) the entire world, and they must therefore be adopted in giant policy leaps. Parking benefit districts can be adopted on an incremental basis—one block at a time.

Early Examples

Residential parking benefit districts sound good, but will they work? A few cities already charge nonresidents for parking in residential permit districts. As mentioned earlier, Aspen, Colorado, charges nonresidents $5 a day to park in permit districts. Businesses and nonprofit institutions located in a residential permit district receive one free permit and can buy additional permits for $600 a year.[37] Several other cities have also begun to charge commuters for parking in permit districts, and their experience shows residential curb parking can produce substantial public revenue.

Boulder, Colorado. In its Neighborhood Permit Parking zones, Boulder sells permits to residents for $12 a year and also sells Commuter Permits to nonresidents for $312 a year. Each permit is valid on a specific block face, and no more than four nonresident permits are sold on any block. The city periodically surveys the parking occupancy on all blocks in each permit zone and sells nonresident permits only on blocks that have a vacancy rate greater than 25 percent between 9 a.m. and 5 p.m. This approach ensures that each block has vacant parking spaces for both residents and commuters. Because many residents drive to work during the day and park on their own streets only in the evening, the commuters and residents effectively time-share the same curb spaces. Boulder's Parking Services department maintains a map showing all blocks on which permits have been sold and where permits are still available; the permits are sold on a first-come, first-served basis. Businesses can also buy nonresident permits and provide them to their employees. All revenue from nonresident permits is used to reduce the price of resident permits.[38]

Santa Cruz, California. The program in Santa Cruz is modeled after the one in Boulder. The city's goals were to make parking spaces available to commuters on underoccupied blocks and to return some benefit to residents for sharing their on-street parking with out-of-area commuters. Downtown employees pay $240 a year for commuter permits to park in nearby residential permit districts, while residents pay only $20 a year. The permits are valid Monday through Friday between 6 a.m. and 8 p.m. Each permit is valid on a specific block face, and only the blocks with occupancies less than 75 percent at peak hours are eligible for the permits. No more than four commuter permits are assigned per block.[39] The city intends to spend the revenue from the commuter permit program to benefit the permit districts but has not yet created a special fund to achieve this purpose.

Tucson, Arizona. In its ParkWise program, Tucson charges $2.50 a year for residential parking permits and from $200 to $400 a year for nonresidential permits, depending on location. The price of the nonresident permits is highest for the blocks nearest the University of Arizona and declines with distance from the university. The nonresident permits are valid between 8 a.m. and 5 p.m., and each permit is valid on a specific block face. The permits are also vehicle specific and must be attached to the car's rear window. Hanging tag permits are also available for an additional charge of $100 a year, and all vehicles using a hanging permit must be registered with the ParkWise program. The city may revoke a permit if the holder has three or more citations for parking in an unauthorized permit-program location during a year.[40] The program began in 1997, and Tucson currently has about 450 nonresident permits. All revenue from nonresident permits is used to reduce the price of resident permits.

West Hollywood, California. West Hollywood charges residents $9 a year for permits in its Preferential Parking Districts and charges nonresidents $360 a year for commercial permits that allow parking in the permit districts between 7 a.m. and 7 p.m. These "daytime" permits are available only to those who work or own a business in the area. The commercial permits are not block-specific, but the nonresidents are restricted to parking on one side of the street, with the other side reserved for residents. Because commuters want to park on the blocks as close as possible to their businesses, the most convenient blocks are crowded with commuters' cars while curb spaces on other blocks in the same permit district remain unused. For this reason, West Hollywood is considering a change to block-specific permits, with higher prices for the more convenient locations.

These four examples show the feasibility of charging nonresidents for parking in residential neighborhoods, although the cities do not guarantee to spend the revenue for public services on the blocks allowing nonresident parking; a lower price for resident permits is the neighborhoods' only special benefit. Where the permits are block-specific, there is an excess demand for the more convenient blocks, indicating that the price is below the market level. If cities guarantee to spend the resulting revenue on new public services that residents can see on their blocks, greater political support for market-price curb parking should emerge.[41]

BENEFITS OF PARKING BENEFIT DISTRICTS

In some neighborhoods, nonresidents' payments for market-price curb parking can yield more revenue than the existing property tax (see Chapter 19). Cities can use this new revenue to clean the streets, repair the sidewalks, plant trees, provide security, preserve historic buildings, or put utility wires underground. To suggest the potential of these neighborhood benefits, consider a specific case—using the revenue to repair broken sidewalks.

An Example: Repairing Broken Sidewalks

In Los Angeles, broken sidewalks are a common sight. About 4,600 miles of the city's 10,000 miles of sidewalks need repair or replacement, but the city can afford to make only temporary asphalt patches. In addition, the federal Americans with Disabilities Act (ADA) requires the city to make 123,000 sidewalk improvements (such as ramped curbs at intersections) to ensure access for people with disabilities, but the city can afford to make only about 900 of these improvements each year.[42]

Broken sidewalks are dangerous for pedestrians, and Los Angeles currently pays about $2 million a year to settle trip-and-fall lawsuits. Nevertheless, in 1998 voters turned down a proposed $770-million tax measure to repair the sidewalks.[43] Opponents argued that the proposed citywide tax did not guarantee the sidewalks in their own neighborhoods would ever get repaired, and they had a point. In a city with 4,600 miles of damaged sidewalks, many residents would have waited years before their taxes produced any improvements on their block.

Can the city repair the sidewalks without increasing taxes? It can—by creating parking benefit districts and using curb parking revenue to pay for the repairs. This approach can guarantee that all the sidewalks in many neighborhoods will get repaired quickly, without additional taxes. A city might require that the first claim on any curb parking revenue would be to bring the sidewalks up to ADA standards. After that goal has been achieved, the neighborhood could use the revenue for any other public purpose it chooses. Establishing sidewalk repairs as a funding priority might not conflict with a neighborhood's own preferences, because good sidewalks are an important element in neighborhood quality, and they can increase property values.

Figure 17-2. Broken sidewalks in a Los Angeles Parking Permit District

Figure 17-2 shows broken sidewalks in one Los Angeles parking permit district. The curb spaces are empty, the sidewalks are damaged, and the city has no money to make repairs. Converting the permit districts into *benefit* districts could generate enough revenue to repair the sidewalks at no cost to the residents. Permit districts shift the demand for parking somewhere else, but benefit districts can solve the parking problem and improve residential neighborhoods.

Until the residents of this neighborhood petitioned to establish a permit district, their curbs were jammed with parked cars—and additional cars were cruising for curb parking. The curb spaces in the permit district are now almost empty all day. But suppose the city sells a limited number of permits for commuters who work in nearby businesses to park in the district during the day. Each permit can be restricted to a specific block, and the number of permits can be limited so that each block has only a few nonresidents' cars parked at the curb.[44] Each block can choose whether to join the benefit district and use the revenue to have its sidewalks repaired, without federal or state grants or new taxes.

Could this scheme really work? Suppose the city charges $50 a month for each daytime parking permit in the benefit district (20 weekdays a month at $2.50 a day). The existing permit districts usually have at least two curb spaces in front of each house, and if a block has 10 houses on each side of the street, the 20 houses on the block have at least 40 curb spaces. If the city sells, say, one daytime permit for every five houses, the block will have four permits, or one nonresident's car for about every 10 curb spaces, and four permits priced at $50 a month apiece will yield $2,400 a year for the block (4 x $50 x 12). The cost of sidewalk replacement in Los Angeles ranges between $10 and $20 per square foot. Where sidewalks are five feet wide, the revenue would thus pay to repair or replace 24 linear feet (at $20 per square foot) to 48 linear feet (at $10 per square foot) of sidewalk a year, and the broken patches are usually only a few feet long. If only 24 feet of sidewalk are broken, the revenue would pay to repair the whole block in one year.[45]

Everyone can gain from a parking benefit district. First, the neighborhood gets its sidewalks repaired at no cost to the residents. Even residents with undamaged sidewalks in front of their houses gain when their neighbors' sidewalks are repaired because most residents walk within their immediate neighborhood. Second, commuters get parking spaces close to work. Third, employers save land and money by building fewer parking spaces. Fourth, the city faces fewer trip-and-fall lawsuits. Furthermore, the arrangement is voluntary because residents join the benefit district by petition, just as they join a permit district by petition. If a few blocks initially join the benefit district and have their sidewalks repaired, residents of the other blocks in the neighborhood will see the results and can decide to join later. Incremental block-by-block choices on whether to participate in a parking benefit district are a strong advantage of the proposal.

Parking benefit districts exemplify what Canadian economist J. H. Dales once recommended: "If it is feasible to establish a market to implement a policy, no policy-maker can afford to do without one."[46] Commuters are willing to pay for parking, while the nearby neighborhoods need money to repair their broken sidewalks. In this case, a market that matches the demand and supply for curb parking will work better—for everyone—than simply prohibiting curb parking for nonresidents.

Many neighborhoods can finance sidewalk repairs by charging nonresidents for curb parking. For example, the neighborhood around the Los Angeles Coliseum can probably earn significant revenue by charging nonresidents the market price for curb parking. Market-price parking in the neighborhoods around most colleges and high schools can probably yield significant revenue and also reduce conflicts occurring when stu-

Kids Learn Supply-and-Demand Lesson

By Eric Fidler, Winnetka, Ill.
Associated Press, November 30, 1997

Call it an early economics lesson. When rich kids have nowhere to park during high school, somebody is going to make some serious money.

Overwhelming demand and limited supply at New Trier High School—one of the state's wealthiest—is so bad that many pay hundreds, even thousands, of dollars a year to secure a space near school, either in a resident's driveway or a business's parking lot.

The 3,100-student school offers just 220 parking spaces to students, spots doled our by lottery, and only to seniors. Others must fend for themselves, with no street parking allowed.

Prime spots are so rare they become family legacies.

"I only got this because my sister had it, "said Chris Bartlett, a junior who parks his Toyota Celica convertible at nearby G&W Auto Clinic. "We handed it down."

Taking the bus to school isn't a desirable option for many image-conscious teens in this affluent, tree-lined suburb north of Chicago.

"I'd be leaving 20 minutes early," Bartlett said. "You have to wait outside. It's a pain."

Bob Woyner rents out four to six spaces at G&W. In the past, he's charged $500 a year, payable in advance. This year, it's $750.

The rent increase drew no protests.

"People just said fine," Woyner said. "Five hundred, 750, it's the same thing to these people."

Dylan Nagle got his spot at G&W through a sibling, too. Calling the school bus no fun, he feels lucky to have some-place to park his sleek Acura SLX there.

"It's kind of a hot thing around here," Woyner said. "I've had people say, 'How much is it? I'm willing to pay double.'"

The average income in the village of roughly 13,000 residents is about $150,000. While not everyone who attends the school is rich, the average house in town is valued at more than half a million dollars and it's common to see students driving Audis, BMWs, and Volvos.

"As a high school in the midst of a residential area, we're a different story," said Judy Brinton, New Trier's dean of students.

Even the school's highly coveted 220 student parking spaces come at a price: $270 a year.

With the school expected to grow by 1,000 students over the next seven years, the situation is only going to worsen, Brinton said.

"We don't have any place we can expand to," she said. "We don't have any empty fields we can pave."

A 1994 New Trier graduate, Kristen McGill, said the situation has been bad for years.

"Around here, kids are throwing two grand at the people for a semester," she said. McGill rented a spot in a driveway across the street from the school for $500, but that bargain ended after other students offered $2,000 for spaces.

"Finally, my senior year, they threatened to take it away," she said.

Asked why students didn't just take the school bus, McGill wrinkled her nose.

"You don't take the bus when you go to New Trier."

dents park in the surrounding neighborhoods. Many public schools have paved over student playgrounds to provide parking for teachers. Buying daytime permits for the teachers' cars in the surrounding neighborhoods can make valuable land available for classrooms and playgrounds at a modest cost. Writing in the *Los Angeles Times*, one parent described the school board meeting where conversion to a year-round schedule was being debated as a solution to overcrowded classes. "A teacher and union representative spoke passionately about how we couldn't build more classrooms on campus because, then, where would teachers park?"[47] Because of overcrowding and a shortage of recreational space, some Los Angeles schools offer their students only 15 minutes of physical education a week. In part, this problem stems from converting school grounds into parking lots for teachers' cars. Surely some neighborhoods would prefer to sell residential parking permits to their children's schools rather than have overcrowded classes, year-round schedules, and only 15 minutes of physical education a week.

Schools, commercial districts, medical centers, universities, and recreation sites are the leading sources of the parking spillover that leads nearby residents to establish conventional permit districts.[48] These districts sometimes allow nonresidents to park free for one or two hours, and they can easily begin to charge for parking. Enforcement will become much simpler because all vehicles will have to display some sort of permit or proof of payment, and enforcement officers will not have to chalk tires in a clumsy attempt to detect overtime parking by nonresidents. Where the sidewalks are seriously damaged and there is no money to make repairs, it does not make sense to offer time-limited free parking for nonresidents in permit districts. Nonresidents can park free for the allowed time, trip on the broken sidewalk, and then sue the city. Most cities appear to value free parking more than safe sidewalks, handicapped accessibility, and walkable neighborhoods. Parking benefit districts that pay for sidewalk repairs can reverse this unhealthy priority and provide many other public services. If the residents of a neighborhood want a particular public investment and have no other way to pay for it, why *not* charge nonresidents for curb parking?

Beyond providing revenue to invest in neighborhood public improvements, parking benefit districts will provide other important benefits. Consider these four: preserving historic districts, reducing locational conflicts, making neighborhoods safer, and increasing the housing supply

Preserving Historic Districts

Parking benefit districts are especially appropriate for neighborhoods built before the car arrived. Most older cities have neighborhoods of row houses without off-street parking spaces, and the residents must park on the streets. Many of these neighborhoods decayed during the twentieth century because they were inconvenient for families who owned cars. The natural response of car owners was to move to the suburbs where every house or apartment had its own off-street parking and on-street parking was plentiful. Even those who valued the architecture and the location of the old row houses found the neighborhoods inconvenient because there were never any vacant parking spaces. Residents who did own cars stored them on the street for free, but there were not enough spaces for everyone, and the curbs were overcrowded. As more affluent car-owning residents moved out, the row houses were left for families who were often too poor to own cars. Property values fell, and the land became less valuable in its existing use than for redevelopment in new uses. Many blocks of these row houses were then demolished to make way for offices and apartments with all the required off-street parking.[49] This pattern was common in Washington, D.C., and I vividly remember seeing the tragic decay and demolition of many blocks of fine row houses in the 1950s and 1960s. Even today, Washington has many streets of wonderful row houses in terrible condition, in part because curb parking is so difficult and because most people who own cars do not want to live without a parking space.

Suppose that in the twentieth century cities had always charged market prices for curb parking to guarantee a few vacant spaces and had spent the revenue to improve public services on the streets where the revenue was collected. Parking would not have been free, but anyone would have been able to find a vacant on-street space close to their front door. The absolutely key point is that prices must ensure vacant curb spaces on each block so that residents know they will always have a place to park when they come home, just as if they had their own garage in the suburbs. Almost as important, vacancies are necessary so that guests can always find a place to park. The guarantee of an available curb space at a fair-market price and added public services financed by the revenue would have kept the row-house neighborhoods desirable and prevented their decay. More relevant, parking benefit districts can now help revive and preserve many of the remaining row-house neighborhoods.

Parking benefit districts can also improve the design of individual buildings. Homeowners in older neighborhoods sometimes insert an incongruous garage into the front of a house because this is the only way they can guarantee themselves a parking space. For each off-street garage, however, the city must dedicate the adjacent curb space for a driveway, so adding a one-car garage removes one curb space (see Figure 17-3). As a result, the garage defaces a historic building, undermines the pedestrian environment, and does not increase the parking supply at all. Having a driveway is equivalent to having a dedicated curb parking space. If the property owner could pay for the exclusive use of a curb space without building an off-street space, the owner would save money and living space, the neighborhood would receive revenue for public improvements, and the historic fabric would be preserved. Some may object to this arrangement as the privatization of public streets, but curb cuts *already* dedicate the exclusive use of curb space to adjacent property owners. If cities instead offer to rent curb spaces to property owners (rather than give owners the curb cuts for free), residents could park in front of their houses. Building a garage would suddenly become a far more expensive way to park a car. The price charged for each curb space or curb cut should be its opportunity cost—what other drivers are willing to pay for it. In this case, instead of building a new garage *and* renting the curb space necessary for a curb cut to gain access to the garage, many property owners would want to rent the curb space itself, without building the garage.

Donald C. Shoup

Figure 17-3. Garage retrofitted into a historic house in St. Andrews, Scotland

If households can rent a curb space in front of their dwellings rather than install a curb cut, this arrangement will *increase* rather than decrease the amount of curb parking available to the general public. Curb cuts for driveways mean that no one can park in the affected on-street space, even if the residents are not using the off-street space. With dedicated curb spaces rather than curb cuts, however, residents can "sublet" their curb parking spaces to other motorists. You can park in your dedicated curb space when you need it, and when you don't need it you can make it available to others, at a price. This arrangement will increase the curb parking supply available to other residents of the neighborhood, as well as to nonresidents.[50]

Some British housing developments already assign curb parking spaces to specific houses. In their book on market-based urban order, Chris Webster and Lawrence Lai explain this parking arrangement:

> As a result of high housing densities on new estates and rising car ownership, many volume housing developers in the UK now contractually allocate on-street parking spaces in public access cul-de-sac developments to individual houses. The informal neighbour agreements that used to keep down the costs of organising parking arrangements are no longer adequate.[51]

Developers offer this contract because the residents are willing to pay more for a house in developments with dedicated curb spaces. The same logic suggests that the residents of older neighborhoods may be willing to lease curb parking spaces at market-rate rents, especially if all the revenue comes back to pay for neighborhood improvements.

Reducing Locational Conflicts

Neighborhoods differ, but their parking problems tend to be the same. If curb parking is free, most residents will say "Not in My Back Yard" to any nearby development with fewer off-street parking spaces than the zoning requires. For example, if the parking requirement for an office building is 4 spaces per 1,000 square feet, residents will oppose a nearby office building with only 1 space per 1,000 square feet because anticipated spillover parking from the new building would congest their streets and leave them no curb spaces to park their own cars.[52]

On the other hand, a parking benefit district can create a symbiotic relationship between commercial development and its nearby residential neighborhood because nonresidents who park in the neighborhood will pay for the privilege. Prices for curb parking can float in response to demand to produce any target curb vacancy rate the neighborhood desires. Commercial developments with few on-site parking spaces will increase the demand for the fixed supply of what the nearby neighborhoods sell to nonresidents—curb parking. If you owned a restaurant, wouldn't you appreciate a nearby office building with no employee cafeteria? If you owned a copy center, wouldn't you appreciate a nearby office building with no copy machines? Similarly, if you lived in a parking benefit district, wouldn't you appreciate a nearby office building with few parking spaces? The price of curb parking would limit the number of nonresidents' cars, and commuters who do pay to park on residential streets would pay to improve the neighborhood. In addition, the higher price for parking at an office building with fewer parking spaces will divert some commuters to carpools, public transit, cycling, or walking to work, and thereby reduce vehicle trips to the neighborhood. This combination of benefits—fewer vehicle trips and more public revenue—may lead residents to say "Do It in My Neighborhood" when a proposed development will attract business and create employment opportunities. Parking benefit districts can convert what planners call "locally unwanted land uses" (LULUs) into locally *wanted* land uses.

Parking benefit districts can also undercut the argument that employers must provide free employee parking to avoid creating parking problems on the nearby streets. For example, Verhoef, Nijkamp, and Rietveld examined the possibility of charging commuters for parking at the Free University in Amsterdam. Because curb parking was free in the surrounding neighborhood, they concluded that charging for parking at the university,

> will mainly result in a considerable shift of the 'parking burden' from the Free University onto the surrounding area, with an expectedly negative impact on the Free University's local image. Unless more stringent parking policies are implemented in the Free University's neighborhood, such a policy [charging commuters for parking] seems to provide no fruitful option.[53]

If the surrounding neighborhood were a parking benefit district, the Free University could improve its local image by charging commuters for on-campus parking because the increased demand for curb parking would increase the revenue available to pay for neighborhood public improvements.

Making Neighborhoods Safer

If curb parking spaces are common property that no one owns and everyone can use, no one cares for them. In *The Death and Life of Great American Cities*, Jane Jacobs says that the streets of a successful city neighborhood must have "eyes upon the street, eyes belonging to those we might call the natural proprietors of the street."[54] If neighborhoods keep the earnings from their curb parking, the residents will be more likely to keep a proprietary eye on the street to make certain their property is managed well. Parking benefit districts will also contribute to the goals of "defensible space" and "crime prevention through environmental design," concepts developed by architect Oscar Newman.[55] Like Jacobs, Newman emphasizes the importance of "territoriality" in making neighborhoods safer and recommends assigning portions of public spaces to individuals and small groups as their own private areas:

> In laying out the site of a housing development, buildings should be positioned so that the grounds can be subdivided and allocated to particular buildings. Residents should, as a result, be able to perceive particular areas of the project as being under their specific sphere of influence.... [P]arking areas should also be placed within these defined zones, as this will further assist residents in perceiving the grounds as their own and will aid them in exerting control over the grounds. Residents' supervision and control of the grounds surrounding their buildings is the most effective form of deterrent to crime and vandalism.[56]

Parking benefit districts will give residents a reason to supervise the streets. Because motorists are willing to pay more to park where they feel safer, residents will have a financial stake in the safety of visitors and their cars. Residents will want all the laws enforced in order to get all the money to which they are entitled, and they will strongly condemn any vandalism of cars or parking meters. Parking enforcement patrols who check to see whether nonresident motorists are paying will add yet another layer of supervision to make streets safer for drivers, pedestrians, bicyclists, and residents.

Market-price parking can make streets safer in yet another way. Although Rudyard Kipling wrote, "Transportation is civilization," fights over claims to a free parking space are common, and the ensuing rancor has even led to murder.[57] A few vacant curb spaces everywhere can calm our parking rage and make our cities more civilized; although parking won't be free, no one will have to fight (or die) for it. Fair-market prices will help to end the Hundred Years' War over curb parking.

Increasing the Housing Supply

Garages that have been converted into housing are termed granny flats, accessory apartments, and second units. They can substantially increase the supply of affordable rental units in good neighborhoods without any subsidy, but even in cities that allow them, parking requirements create a

steep barrier to garage conversions. Because cities require off-street parking for both the original house and the new flat, converting an existing
garage—no matter how roomy or how valuable as housing—into a
granny flat becomes almost impossible. Cities require enough off-street
parking spaces to prevent the cars formerly parked in the garages, plus
the cars of the new residents, from flooding the curb spaces and creating
more traffic.[58] But because most houses do not have enough land to
replace the parking spaces in the former garage *and* provide an additional
parking space for the new garage apartment, granny flats are out of the
question.

Parking requirements even prevent converting former coach houses into
apartments. Some Chicago neighborhoods built in the nineteenth century,
for example, have coach houses, and many of them were later converted
to granny flats. In 1957, however, Chicago banned living in buildings formerly occupied by horses; the previous conversions were grandfathered,
but new conversions were made illegal. (The real reason for banning
human habitation of buildings formerly occupied by horses was, of
course, parking, not public health.) Chicago's Metropolitan Planning
Council recently recommended a change in zoning to again allow converting coach houses to human habitation, with no off-street parking
required for the new housing. But cars, not horses, are the issue now.
Chicago Alderman Bernard Stone commented, "The real problem today
is that most existing coach houses are in areas where there already is a
lack of parking."[59]

Many residents strongly oppose granny flats in their neighborhoods
because of the parking problems they would create. As a planning commissioner in one Southern California city explained, she bought her house
in a neighborhood "where I wouldn't have to worry if I was going to be
able to park in front of my own house."[60] And who could blame her for
thinking that? Where curb parking is treated as common property free to
anyone, everyone will object to granny flats if the new residents park on
the street. Suppose, however, that a parking benefit district charges market prices for all curb parking in a neighborhood with granny flats.
Everyone will have an incentive to economize on curb parking. Some residents who formerly parked their cars at the curb will park off-street, and
others might sell an old car that isn't worth the price of a parking permit.
If some homeowners convert their garages into granny flats, the rising
price of curb parking will prevent the reduction in off-street spaces from
creating a curb parking shortage. The parking benefit district will also
provide added revenue for neighborhood public improvements.

When parking requirements prohibit converting garages into apartments, cities put free parking ahead of affordable housing. But in parking

benefit districts, planners can allow garage conversions to increase the housing supply and decrease the parking supply *without* creating a parking shortage, because everyone who is willing to pay the market price for parking will be able to find a convenient space. While parking requirements intervene in the housing market on the side of cars, parking benefit districts will allow people to bid space away from cars.[61]

The opportunity to produce second units without creating a parking problem can help to refute any argument that parking benefit districts will gentrify older neighborhoods in central cities. True, parking benefit districts will, by increasing neighborhood amenity, increase property values. But families who are willing to convert their garages into second units will find a new way to finance homeownership, and will at the same time provide a new supply of decent and affordable rental housing within walking distance of local stores and public transit. Higher urban land prices are not a bad thing if they lead to more housing, but off-street parking requirements prevent higher densities. Parking benefit districts will, in contrast, allow the market to supply less parking and more housing without generating more traffic.

CONCLUSION: CHANGING THE POLITICS OF CURB PARKING

The purpose of charging market prices for curb parking is to manage a scarce public resource, not to finance the cost of providing it. Governments often price public services to cover their cost, but curb parking doesn't seem to have any cost that justifies charging a price. Parking benefit districts will not finance curb parking but will instead create the necessary political support to charge market prices for it.[62]

Parking policy emerges from a political—not an analytic—process, and better analysis will not, by itself, affect this political process. But just as the technology of charging for curb parking has changed radically in recent years, so too can the politics. Voters will *want* their city to charge fair-market prices for curb parking if the revenue is returned to the right recipient—the neighborhoods that generate it. For transportation policy, the motive to charge market prices for curb parking is to manage demand; for neighborhoods, the motive is to finance public investment.

Parking benefit districts do not privatize curb parking, which remains publicly owned. Curb parking revenue pays for added public services, and the prospect of these services can persuade residents to rent space to nonresidents. The result is not to *privatize* curb parking but rather to *charge market prices* for it and to spend the revenue for public purposes. Private sector methods achieve public sector objectives. To borrow a Marxist term, the benefit districts will *commodify* parking—turn it into a commodity traded in markets. Commodity is an apt term here because it stems from the Latin *commodus*, meaning convenient. Benefit districts will make parking convenient, but the users will pay for it.

The twentieth century saw a great competition between two economic systems: central planning and market prices. Central planning is essential for some purposes, but it failed spectacularly where it governed too much of the economy. Parking is a perfect example of an economic activity where planners have usurped markets without justification. We have relied almost exclusively on the command-and-control approach to regulate parking, and we have failed spectacularly.

The only constraints on charging market prices for curb parking are now political. Aaron Wildavsky describes this situation perfectly: "Constraints are not mere obstacles, but are opportunities asking (daring, pleading) to be shown how they can be overcome."[63] Technology has overcome the practical constraints on charging for curb parking, and public concern has shifted to problems that free parking makes worse, such as traffic congestion, energy consumption, and air pollution. The political constraints on charging for curb parking are opportunities asking, daring, pleading to be overcome.

The *economic* rationale to charge market prices for curb parking is efficiency: the benefits far outweigh the costs. Drivers won't need to hunt for curb spaces, and cities won't need to require off-street parking. The *political* rationale for parking benefit districts is distribution: neighborhoods will be improved at no cost to their residents. Curb parking revenue needs the right recipient—its own neighborhood—before voters will support charging market prices for curb parking. Fair-market prices will solve the economic problem, and using the revenue to improve neighborhoods will solve the political problem.

CHAPTER 17 NOTES

1. Crawford (1969, 84).

2. Residential parking permit districts have spread rapidly throughout the U.S. since 1977 when the United States Supreme Court upheld the statute in Arlington, Virginia, that set up the first permit district in the country (see *County Board of Arlington County, Virginia, et al. v. Richards, et al.*; October 11, 1977). In 1974, Arlington enacted an ordinance that authorized residential parking permit districts, and the neighborhood of Aurora Highlands petitioned to became one. Commuters to nearby Crystal City, who had previously parked on the streets of Aurora Highlands, filed motions against the county, alleging that the permit districts denied them equal protection of the laws. The U.S. Supreme Court held that "the ordinance did not, on its face, violate the equal protection guarantee of the Fourteenth Amendment even though the ordinance discriminated between residents and nonresidents of the designated residential areas, since the Constitution neither outlawed the social and environmental objectives of the ordinance nor presumed that distinctions between residents and nonresidents of a local neighborhood were invidious, and since the equal protection clause required only that the distinction drawn by such an ordinance rationally promote the regulations's objectives."

3. Howitt (1980, 156-58). Mancur Olson (1965) analyzed how offering selective individual benefits as the reward for specific behavior can induce rational, self-interested individuals to act in their collective interests. Neighborhoods are not individuals, but individual residents can see that it is in their individual interest if their neighborhood becomes a parking benefit district. Olson also explained why there is a tendency for groups to underprovide public goods to their members; because parking benefit districts will finance neighborhood public goods from *nonresidents'* payments for parking, the only way to take advantage of the parking revenue is to spend it on public goods, which may therefore even become overprovided. See Olson (1965, 22-36) for a discussion of the optimal provision of public goods in small groups.

4. Each neighborhood will earn income from a valuable natural resource it owns, almost like silent screen star Norma Desmond (Gloria Swanson) in *Sunset Boulevard*, who explained to young screenwriter Joe Gillis (William Holden) the source of her wealth. "I own three blocks downtown. I've got oil in Bakersfield, pumping, pumping, pumping. What's it for but to buy us anything we want?" Each curb parking space will become a new source of neighborhood wealth, "pumping, pumping, pumping" revenue to buy any public services the residents want.

5. Wilson (1980, 369)

6. Howitt (1980, 163).

7. Ostrom (1990, 14).

8. Organisation for Economic Co-Operation and Development (1988, 119). The federal government also sets a maximum price that cities can charge for on-street parking. The long lead time to alter national legislation means that on-street parking prices lag behind the market rates for off-street parking.

9. Winston and Shirley (1998, 68).

10. Ready (1998, 10).

11. "Parking Meters in Oklahoma City," in the *American City*, August 1935, p. 61.

12. Gutfreund (2004, 81).

13. Free parking for residents in a benefit district is a political proposal, not an economic one. Moshe Adler (1985) points out that the existing permit districts may allocate curb spaces to residents who place a lower value on them than some nonresidents would. The allocation will be more efficient if everyone pays the market price for parking, just as *everyone* pays market prices for gasoline, tires, insurance, repairs, and the cars themselves. But concepts of equity often revolve around what has happened in the past; because residents are accustomed to parking free in front of their homes, everyone assumes that residents are entitled to free parking, no matter much circumstances have changed. Free parking for residents may therefore be a necessary political precondition for a parking benefit district.

14. Adam Millard-Ball (2002) describes San Francisco's proposal. One of the city's aims is to encourage residents who own garages to use them for cars rather than for storage and thus take some cars off the street.

15. San Francisco paints the curb white to designate passenger loading zones, and Howard Strassner of San Francisco explained this practice in white zones to me. Other cities also have informal curb parking brokers. For example, New York doormen move residents' cars from one side of the street to the other to deal with the alternate-side parking regulations.

16. Suppose, for example, 200 families live on a block that has only 20 curb parking spaces; charging the market price for curb parking can provide a net benefit for 180 families who do not park on the street, and a net cost to only 20 families who use the street as their garage. Hartmut Topp (1991, 10) reports that in Munich's inner-city districts, 30 percent of residents' cars are not moved during an average weekday. Douglas Lee (1987) discusses the policy of charging everyone the market price for curb parking.

17. Parker (2002, 306).

18. Institute of Transportation Engineers (2000). Even $10 a year is far too high a price for some citizens. Consider this letter to the editor that appeared in the *San Mateo Daily Journal* on July 14, 2004, in response to the city's proposal to charge $10 a year for resident permits in permit parking districts. An outraged citizen asked, "Why don't they measure how much air we breathe each day and start charging us for that?… I say 'Get rid of parking meters, parking permits and everything else you can think of other than paid parking garages that need to recoup their investment.' We are supposed to be living in a free country. Our First Amendment is supposed to guarantee life, liberty and the pursuit of happiness. My opinion is this: People should not have to constantly worry about feeding parking meters or be constantly worried about getting parking tickets."

19. Mildner, Strathman, and Bianco (1997).

20. Mildner, Strathman, and Bianco (1997, 114) say that "officials in cities that have areas with insufficient parking supply for all potential car owners have decided to avoid instituting permit zones for this very reason."

21. Curb parking spaces can serve a limited number of people, but public services are nonrival in consumption: one person's use does not reduce the amount left for everyone else. Therefore, the total benefits of public services, such as clean sidewalks, are higher in dense neighborhoods because more people enjoy them. The benefits of charging for curb parking and spending the money for neighborhood public services should thus be more popular in denser neighborhoods because the benefit/cost ratio will be higher. And because the number of curb spaces is fixed, the average per-person payments for curb parking will decline as density increases if the market price of curb parking increases less than in proportion to a neighborhood's population.

22. Noble and Jenks (1996, 18; 21).

23. Noble and Jenks (1996, 22; 26).

24. Lee (1987, 265).

25. See Schilling (1995).

26. Individual ownership and management of each curb parking space would probably suffer from marked *dis*economies of scale and high transactions costs.

27. See Gordon (2004) for an analysis of the microgovernments in common interest developments.

28. The smallest organizational level is the face-block (which refers to the properties that face each other across a length of street between two intersections), and a parking benefit district can consist of one or more face-blocks.

29. Ellickson (1998, 83-84). Robert Nelson (1999) also proposes legislation to retrofit community associations in older neighborhoods, and George Liebmann (2000) presents a comprehensive proposal for sublocal governments. Since parking benefit districts would generate revenue for sublocal governments, setting up the proposed block-level institutions should be greatly simplified. Parking benefit districts will, as Fred Foldvary (1994, 212) says about private communities, "unite governance with market competition in the provision of public goods." Earlier, Mancur Olson (1969, 483) proposed that "there is a need for a separate governmental institution for every collective good with a unique boundary, so that there can be a match between those who receive the benefits of a collective good and those who pay for it." He termed this alignment between revenue and responsibility "fiscal equivalence." Because many public investments (such as good sidewalks and underground utilities) benefit small areas, parking benefit districts can achieve fiscal equivalence between benefits and costs for many local public goods.

30. Similarly, referring to Nobel Laureate economist Friedrich Hayek's caution about social engineering, Bruce Caldwell (1997, 1885) wrote, "The conscious construction or imposition of social institutions is a tricky business. Many such institutions are the product of a long process of evolutionary development; they are themselves examples of complex self-organized adaptive orders. They have histories, and they perform functions that are not well-understood by outsiders."

31. In *The Affluent Society*, Galbraith (1958, 252-253, and 257) says in the years after World War II, "automobiles that could not be parked were being produced at an expanded rate.... The family which takes its mauve and cerise, air-conditioned, power-steered, and power-braked automobile out for a tour passes through cities that are badly paved, made hideous by litter, blighted buildings, billboards, and posts for wires that should long since have been put underground...in an atmosphere of private opulence and public squalor, the private goods have sway." Galbraith himself lives in a historic Cambridge neighborhood with free (permit) parking and overhead wires.

32. Hirschman (1970, 4, 30) said "exit" occurs when some members leave an organization if they are dissatisfied, while "voice" is any attempt to change, rather then to escape from, an objectionable state of affairs. He explained that exit belongs to the realm of economics, while voice belongs to the realm of politics.

33. Speech by Governor Bill Clinton on May 6, 1991.

34. Haar (1989, 334).

35. Ellerman et al. (2000) found that the cap-and-trade approach significantly reduced the cost of abating SO_2 emissions. Parked cars are not pollution, of course, but too many cars create severe parking problems.

36. In the traditional command-and-control approach to reducing air pollution, the government limits emissions for each pollution source but does not permit trading among regulated firms. A parking *permit* district resembles the command-and-control approach because it either prohibits parking by nonresidents or sets limits on how long they can park.

37. Carpools of three or more can also get a free daily permit. Aspen's regulations are available online at www.aspenpitkin.com/depts/61/residential.cfm.

38. Boulder's Commuter Permit program is authorized in Section 4-23 of the Boulder Municipal Code, and is described on the city's web site at www.ci.boulder.co.us/duhmd/Parkingservices/1resident.html.

39. Section 10.41.105 of the Santa Cruz Municipal Code states, "The local authority may, upon proof that sufficient street parking is available for residents in the area, sell permits to commuters who may pay to park on a specified street segment or block face." The Commuter Permits are described on the city's web site at www.ci.santa-cruz.ca.us/pw/index.html.

40. Tucson's "ParkWise" program is described on the city's web site at http://dot.ci.tuc-son.az.us/parkwise/parkwise.htm.

41. That is, the city agrees to a "maintenance of effort" for general public services provided in the new district. The parking revenue will provide *additional* public services in the district, above and beyond the services provided everywhere in the city.

42. City of Los Angeles, "Voter Information Pamphlet for the General Election on November 3, 1998." Available online at www.cityofla.org/CLK/election/elect98/vip/vip1198.htm.

43. A two-thirds (67 percent) Yes vote was required for passage, but only 43 percent voted Yes.

44. Visitor permits in existing permit districts are restricted to parking on the block of the resident who purchases the visitor permit. The proposed nonresident permits thus resemble the existing visitor permits, although the nonresidents would be paying guests.

45. If the number of curb spaces on a block is roughly proportional to the length of sidewalk, each block has about the same capacity to earn parking revenue to repair its sidewalks, regardless of the number of houses on the block.

46. Dales (1968, 100). Dales was, of course, talking about *legal* markets. Another advantage of a parking benefit district is that it can eliminate or at least reduce the illegal markets for resident permits in many permit districts where the nonresident parking demand is high. Black markets in curb parking often spring up where legal markets don't exist, and by creating a legal market in nonresident permits, a parking benefit district can convert illicit private gains into public revenue for the whole neighborhood.

47. Therese Lee, "The Good Overcomes the Bad and the Ugly," *Los Angeles Times*, September 7, 2003. All teachers in Los Angeles public schools are guaranteed free parking, but no other transportation benefit. Those who ride public transit, bike, or walk to school get nothing. The alarmingly high priority on parking is not limited to public schools. Consider this report of a planning commission meeting in San Mateo, California: "The controversial Junipero Serra High School expansion project returns to the Planning Commission tonight, when commissioners will review the first of three phases of construction anticipated at the all-boys Catholic school over the next decade… . Phase One of the plan calls for improvements to Serra's football and baseball fields and a new three-level parking garage…the school has scratched plans to build its new arts and music building during Phase One due to lack of funding" (*San Mateo County Times*, October 28, 2003).

48. Institute of Transportation Engineers (2000, 3). Writing in *Planning* magazine, James Andrews (2000, 22) says, "In Barrington, Illinois, neighbors recently complained about a multitude of cars parking at a house next to the high school. It turned out that one student's parents had bought the house not to live in, but to provide parking for him and his friends during school hours." And in Altoona, Pennsylvania, a survey of residents near a high school that generated spillover were surveyed about the possibility of setting up a resident parking permit district. The survey found, "many residents resisted paying for permission to park in the street when outsiders created the problem. Residents' first preference was that the high school move" (Andrews 2000, 23).

49. Shoup (1970) examines the time of land redevelopment.

50. Although he did not relate it to the issue of curb cuts, Gabriel Roth (1965a) proposed the idea of "householders' parking meters" that would allow residents to reserve the curb space in front of their homes for their own use or to make the space available to others. All the revenue would go to the city, and householders would be required to pay for the time they reserved the curb spaces for themselves.

51. Webster and Lai (2003, 63).

52. Spillover also provokes disputes over the scarce curb parking, but these disputes can have their bright side. Consider, for this example, this report from the *Los Angeles Times*: "About two years ago, a North Korean who worked in the state fisheries division was on a boat in the Yellow Sea when his transistor radio picked up a South Korean situation comedy. The radio program featured two young women who were fighting over a parking space in their apartment complex. A parking space? The North Korean was astonished by the idea that there was a place with so many cars that there would be a shortage of places to park them. Although he was in his late 30s and a director of his division, he had never met anyone who owned their own car. The North Korean never forgot that radio show and ended up defecting to South Korea last year. 'I realized that if there is a shortage of parking spaces, this is a different world than the one we know,' said the North Korean, who now lives in Seoul and asked that his identity not be revealed" (Barbara Demick, "For North Korean Regime, No News is Good News," *Los Angeles Times*, December 20, 2003). With market-price parking spaces, we can have the best of both worlds: cars and no shortage of places to park them.

53. Verhoef, Nijkamp, and Rietveld (1996, 399).

54. Jacobs (1961, 35).

55. Newman (1972, 1980, and 1996).

56. Newman (1980, 193).

57. Kipling (1909, 47). The *Los Angeles Times* (October 25, 1997) reported that "A New York City police officer who shot a man to death in an off-duty argument over a deli's parking space was convicted of murder Friday." The *Times* also reported a similar murder over a parking dispute on January 20, 2003. Parking also leads to murder in fiction; for example, see Simon Brett (1985). Richard Epstein (2001, 12) says, "The usual sociobiological logic behind a first possession rule is that all individuals have a strong, innate instinct to yield to others who have taken possession. Yet by the same token, they have an instinct to fight when they think that inchoate possession is theirs. Those conflicts arise when two people come at the same [parking] spot from different directions, and each thinks that he got there first."

58. Palo Alto, California, for example, requires each granny flat be detached from the main house and have two parking spaces of its own. Potential parking shortages aren't the only reason cities prohibit granny flats in single-family neighborhoods, of course, and some residents may simply oppose higher population density even if the new people come without cars.

59. "Coach House Plan May Reopen Door to Renters," *Chicago Tribune*, August 17, 2003.

60. "New Law on In-Laws," *Los Angeles Times*, October 12, 2003.

61. Parking is not the only reason why homeowners may object to allowing granny flats in their neighborhoods, of course, but it is a big reason. If parking benefit districts remove parking as an objection to granny flats, the other issues can be addressed more directly. And because granny flats will increase the revenue in a parking benefit district, the added public services paid for by curb parking may mitigate some of the other objections to allowing granny flats.

62. Consider the difference between toll roads and market-price curb parking. Highway tolls are usually justified on the grounds that they are needed to pay for road construction: the cost needs a financing mechanism. In contrast, parking benefit districts are needed to create the political will to charge for curb parking: the revenue needs a politically powerful group who wants to collect it.

63. Wildavsky (1979, 59).

18

Let Prices Do the Planning

There is nothing quite so practical as a good theory.

— ALBERT EINSTEIN

Cities have tried to manage parking almost entirely without prices. Rather than charge for curb parking, cities instead require off-street parking. The model of parking choice presented in this chapter suggests market prices are a much fairer and more efficient way to allocate parking spaces. It shows that carpoolers, short-term parkers, and those who place a high value on saving time will park close to their destinations, even though they have to pay more to do so. Solo drivers, long-term parkers, and those who place a low value on saving time will, in contrast, park in the peripheral spaces to save money. This pattern of individual parking choices will minimize society's collective cost of travel.

SPACE, TIME, MONEY, AND PARKING

Parking is all about space, time, and money, and it is perhaps the most spatial of all economic activities (as suggested by the name, parking space). Parking is thus ideally suited for analysis by traditional location theory. Suppose a city charges high enough prices for curb parking to keep one or two spaces vacant on every block. If drivers can pay to park anywhere without hunting for a space, a simple economic model explains how they will choose their parking locations.

To set the scene for the model, suppose the price of parking increases as you approach your destination. Parking closer to your destination will cost more money, but it will also save time spent walking from the car to the destination and back. Given the trade-off between spending money to park closer or spending time to walk farther, where should you park? Drivers do not use a theoretical model in deciding where to park, and some people may not even think about parking until it's too late not to. Others may look for a parking space that is merely satisfactory rather than optimal. Nevertheless, we can use a model to consider some factors drivers are likely to take into account, at least informally, if the price of parking increases as they approach their destination. To model the parking decision, consider the following variables:

d the distance from parking space to final destination (miles)

$p(d)$ the price of parking at distance d from the final destination ($/hour)

t parking duration (hours)

w walking speed between parking space and final destination (miles/hour)

n number of people in the car (persons)

v value of time spent walking ($/hour/person).

The *total cost* of parking at any location is the *money cost* of parking your car, plus the *time cost* of walking the rest of the way and back. The money cost of parking is the parking duration, t, multiplied by the price per hour, $p(d)$, or $tp(d)$.[1] For example, if the price of parking a half-mile from your destination is 50¢ an hour and you park four hours, you pay $2 for parking (4 x 50¢).

The time to walk from your parking space to the final destination equals the distance walked, d, divided by your walking speed, w, or d/w. Because you must also walk back to your car, the time to walk the round trip is $2d/w$. If you park a half-mile from your destination, you will walk one mile from your car to your destination and back. If you walk four miles an hour, you will spend a quarter of an hour walking (2 x 1/2 ÷ 4).

Your value of time, v, is the price you are willing to pay to save time spent walking to and from your final destination for this trip. The cost of time spent walking is therefore $2vd/w$, which is the value of time multiplied by the time spent walking. For example, if you walk 15 minutes and you value time at $8 an hour, the cost of time spent walking is $2. Your value of time varies, of course, depending on a number of factors: whether you are in a hurry, how tired you are, the weather, the scenery, safety, any packages you are carrying, whether you want the exercise, and many other circumstances unique to each trip.[2] The value of time can vary greatly from one person to another, one place to another, and one trip to another, but time is always money.

The total cost of walking also depends on the number of people in the car, n. Everyone in the car spends the same time walking from the car to the destination and back, so a group's total cost of time spent walking is

2*nvd*/*w*, which is each person's cost of time spent walking multiplied by the number of people in the car.[3] For example, if three people walk 15 minutes and each values time at $8 an hour, their collective cost of time spent walking is $6 (3 x 1/4 x 8).

In this example, the total cost for a three-person carpool to park one-half mile from their destination and walk the rest of the way is $8 ($2 for parking and $6 for walking). More generally, we can express (1) the money cost of parking the car and (2) the occupants' (monetized) time cost of walking if they park at distance *d* from the final destination as:

$tp(d)$ (1)   money cost of parking

$2nv \dfrac{d}{w}$ (2)   monetized time cost of walking to and from the destination

$tp(d) + 2nv \dfrac{d}{w}$ (3)   total cost of parking and walking.

The total cost associated with parking at any location is the sum of (1) the money cost of parking the car and (2) the monetized time cost of walking from the car to the destination and back. The *optimal parking location* is the distance from the final destination that minimizes (3) the total cost of parking and walking. (Appendix D presents a more complete version of this model, which takes additional variables into account.)

THE OPTIMAL PARKING SPACE

The money cost of parking is higher and the time cost of walking is lower for parking spaces closer to the destination. We can find the distance from the destination that minimizes the total cost of parking *and* walking by differentiating this cost (3) with respect to *d* and setting the result equal to zero.

$$\frac{\partial \left[tp(d) + 2nv \dfrac{d}{w} \right]}{\partial d} = t\frac{\partial p}{\partial d} + \frac{2nv}{w} = 0 \quad \text{and} \quad t\frac{\partial p}{\partial d} = -\frac{2nv}{w} \tag{4}$$

At the optimum parking spot, the changes in the money cost of parking ($t\partial p/\partial d$) and the time cost of walking ($2nv/w$) are equal in absolute value and opposite in sign for a small change in *d*. Parking closer to the destination increases the total cost because the money cost rises more rapidly than the time cost falls ($|t\partial p/\partial d| > 2nv/w$). Parking farther away also increases the total cost because the money cost falls less rapidly than the time cost rises ($|t\partial p/\partial d| < 2nv/w$). The optimal parking spot balances greed (the desire for money) and sloth (the desire to avoid walking).

GREED VERSUS SLOTH

We can use an example to show the tradeoff between greed and sloth in choosing a parking space that minimizes the total cost of parking and walking. Suppose the price of curb parking is $1 an hour at your destination and declines with distance from your destination according to a negative exponential formula.[4] More specifically:

$$p(d) = \$1e^{-2d} \qquad (5)$$

The price of parking is $1 an hour at the center and declines with distance from the center. Suppose you want to park 4 hours ($t = 4$), you are alone in your car ($n = 1$), you value time savings at $8 an hour ($v = \$8$), and you walk 4 miles an hour ($w = 4$). From equation (5), Figure 18-1 shows the cost of both parking and walking as a function of parking d miles from your destination.

At distance d from the destination the cost of parking one hour is $\$1e^{-2d}$, so the cost of parking 4 hours is $\$4e^{-2d}$. The exponential relationship implies that the price of parking increases faster as you get closer to your destination (the slope of the curve increases as d approaches 0). The time cost of walking from the parking space to the destination and back ($2nvd/w$) is $\$4d$, which *decreases* if you park closer to your destination.[5] You can spend money and save time by parking closer or spend time and save money by parking farther away.

So what distance from your destination balances greed and sloth? The total cost of parking *and* walking (the upper curve in Figure 18-1) reaches its minimum value ($3.40) at a distance somewhere between 0.3 and 0.4 miles from your destination. To minimize the cost of parking and walking in this example, you should park about a third of a mile from your destination and walk the rest of the way. Parking closer costs too much money, while walking from a more distant spot takes too much time.

We can find the optimal distance (denoted as d^*) that exactly minimizes the cost of parking and walking by substituting the formula for parking price as a function of distance (equation 5) into the formula for the minimum total cost (equation 4) and solving for d^*.

$$t\frac{\partial(\$1e^{-2d})}{\partial d} = -\frac{2nv}{w} \qquad \text{and} \qquad d^* = -{}^1\!/{}_2\log_e\left[\frac{nv}{tw}\right] \qquad (6)$$

Given the assumed values of $n = 1$ person, $v = \$8$ an hour, $t = 4$ hours, and $w = 4$ miles an hour, the value for d^* in equation (6) is 0.35 miles.[6] At the optimal distance of 0.35 miles from your destination the price of parking is 50¢ an hour and the cost of parking four hours is $2.[7] If you value time savings at $8 an hour for this trip and you walk four miles an hour, the time cost of walking is $2 a mile. Walking the round trip of 0.7 miles from your parking space to your final destination and back therefore costs $1.40.[8] The total cost of parking ($2) and walking ($1.40) is $3.40 for the trip if you park 0.35 miles from your destination.[9] If you are more than 0.35 miles from your destination, parking closer will increase the money cost less than it reduces the walking cost, so you should keep on driving.[10] If you are less than 0.35 miles from your destination, parking closer will increase the money cost more than it reduces the walking cost, and you have driven too far.[11]

PARKING DURATION AND VEHICLE OCCUPANCY

What determines the relationship between parking duration, vehicle occupancy, and optimal location? We can use equation (6)—which gives

Figure 18-1. The Cost of Parking and Walking (for a solo driver who parks four hours)

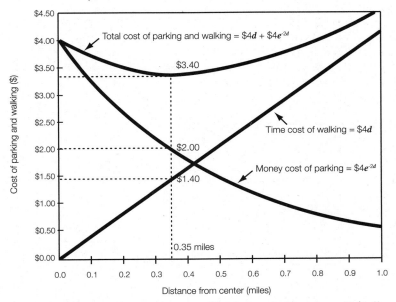

Assumptions: t=4 hours, n=1 person, v=$8 per hour, w=4 miles per hour, $p(d)$=1e^{-2d}$

d^*, the optimal walking distance from the destination—to show how different combinations of parking duration and vehicle occupancy influence where you should park. Higher values of n and v (number of passengers and their value of time) in the numerator pull the optimal parking spot closer to the destination, while higher values of t and w (parking duration and walking speed) in the denominator push it farther away.[12] For any combination of variables where $nv = tw$, the optimal parking spot is right at the destination because $nv/tw = 1$ and $\log_e (1) = 0$.

If we continue to assume that travelers value time savings at $8 an hour and walk four miles an hour, we can show how the optimal parking spot depends on parking duration and vehicle occupancy (see Figure 18-2).[13] For any parking duration less than two hours, all drivers, regardless of the number of passengers in the car, will find it cheapest (in money *and* time) to park right at the center. The optimal parking spot is at the center for solo drivers who park for up to two hours, two-person carpools who park for up to four hours, three-person carpools who park for up to six hours, and four-person carpool who park for up to eight hours.

Figure 18-2. Parking Duration and Vehicle Occupancy Affect Optimal Parking Location

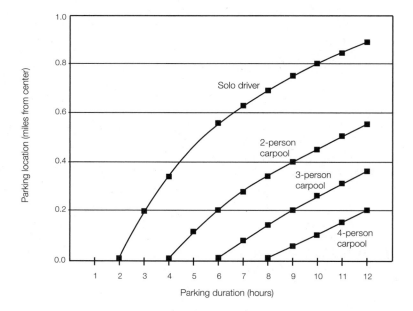

As parking duration increases on the horizontal axis, the optimal parking distance from the center increases on the vertical axis. The sensitivity to duration declines as carpool size increases, and solo drivers are more sensitive to parking duration than are carpools who split the money cost of parking. Market prices for parking therefore draw carpools and short-term parkers to the more convenient central spaces, while solo drivers and long-term parkers migrate to the cheaper peripheral spaces.[14] In the aggregate, people sort themselves in a sensible pattern that minimizes the total walking cost.

Consider the optimal parking spot for a two-person carpool who park four hours (see Figure 18-3). Their money cost of parking is $4e^{-2d}$, while their time cost of walking is $8d$.[15] To minimize the total cost of parking and walking, they should park right at their destination. The money cost of parking four hours is $4 ($2 a person), and the time cost of walking is zero. The only change from Figure 18-1 to Figure 18-3 is the addition of another person in the car; the optimal parking location shifts to the destination (walking distance = 0) and lowers the per-person cost for parking and walking from $3.40 for the solo driver (Figure 18-1) to $2 a person in

Figure 18-3. The Cost of Parking and Walking (for a two-person carpool that parks four hours)

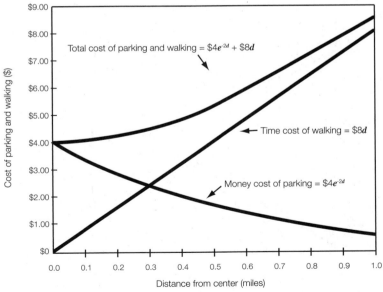

Total cost of parking and walking = $4e^{-2d} + 8d$

Time cost of walking = $8d$

Money cost of parking = $4e^{-2d}$

Cost of parking and walking ($)

Distance from center (miles)

Assumptions: t=4 hours, n=2 persons, v=$8 per hour, w=4 miles per hour, $p(d)$=$1e^{-2d}$

the two-person carpool (Figure 18-3). The money cost is $2 a person for both the carpoolers and the solo driver, but each person in the two-person carpool avoids the solo driver's time cost of $1.40 for the 10.5-minute walk.

As a final example, Figure 18-4 illustrates the case of a two-person carpool who park for eight hours. The money cost of parking eight hours is $8e^{-2d}$, while the time cost of walking is $8d$. To minimize the total cost of parking and walking, they should park 0.35 miles from their destination. The price of parking is 50¢ an hour, so the money cost of parking eight hours is $4 ($2 per person in the car). The time cost of walking is $2.80 ($1.40 per person in the car). The total cost of parking *and* walking is thus $6.80 ($3.40 per person in the car).

In each of these three examples, the optimal parking location is the best a driver can do under the circumstances (vehicle occupancy, value of time, parking duration, and walking speed). The results are intuitive. In the daily competition for the closest parking spots, carpools and short-term parkers can afford to park closer to their destinations than can solo drivers and long-term parkers.[16]

Figure 18-4. The Cost of Parking and Walking (for a two-person carpool that parks eight hours)

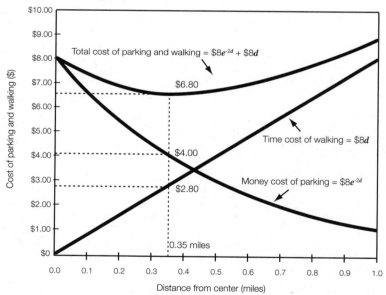

Assumptions: t=8 hours, n=2 persons, v=$8 per hour, w=4 miles per hour, $p(d)$=$1e^{-2d}$

THE INVISIBLE HAND

Each driver chooses the optimal parking spot for each trip—optimal for the individual driver, that is. We can show the aggregate effects of individual behavior by examining how four variables—n, v, t, and w—determine the optimal parking distance, d^*, from the destination. Recall equation (6) from the prior example:

$$d^* = -\tfrac{1}{2}\log_e \left[\frac{nv}{tw} \right] \qquad (6)$$

We can see that the ratio nv/tw determines each car's optimal parking location.[17] Because more persons (n) in the car and shorter parking durations (t) both lead drivers to park closer to their destination, market prices tend to allocate the best parking spaces to carpools and short-term parkers, a sensible outcome. In minimizing their own individual costs, drivers will tend to park in a pattern that also minimizes social costs.[18]

Three relationships among the four variables in the equation suggest that the value of time (v) is not the most important influence in determining where people will park. First, the factor nv in the numerator shows the number of people in a car is as important as the value of each person's time in determining parking location. For example, a carpool of four people who each value time at $5 an hour ($nv = 4$ x $5) will choose the same location as a solo driver who values time at $20 an hour ($nv = 1$ x $20), all else equal. Carpoolers are less concerned about the price of parking because they split the cost among more people. Carpools of people with a low value of time can thus bid the most convenient parking spaces away from solo drivers with a high value of time.

Second, the ratio of v/t in the equation shows parking duration is as important as the value of time in determining parking location. A solo driver who values time at $10 an hour and parks one hour ($v/t = \$10/1$) therefore chooses the same location as another solo driver who values time at $20 an hour and parks two hours ($v/t = \$20/2$), all else being equal. This helps to explain why short-term parkers are relatively insensitive to parking prices.[19] They are less concerned about the price per hour because they pay it for only a few minutes. Short-term parkers with a low value of time can thus bid the most convenient parking spaces away from long-term parkers with a high value of time.

Third, the ratio of n/t in the equation shows that the number of people in a car is as important as the parking duration in determining parking location. A solo driver who parks four hours ($n/t = 1/4$) chooses the same location as a two-person carpool who park eight hours ($n/t = 2/8$), all else being equal. (Figures 18-1 and 18-3 show that these two cases result in the same parking location.)

These results are not surprising and confirm what common sense would suggest. A high price per hour is no problem if you park only a short time or split the cost of parking among several people in the car. But a high price per hour *is* a problem if you drive by yourself and park a long time. These results also suggest that there is no single, sensible estimate of how far drivers are willing to walk from parking spaces to their final destinations. Willingness to walk depends on the parking duration, the number of people in the car, their walking speed, and their value of time. Someone who parks all day, for example, is probably willing to walk much farther than someone who parks only ten minutes.[20]

A higher value placed on time, all else being equal, leads to closer parking locations and shorter walks. Because higher-income drivers can place a higher value on their time, will they monopolize the best parking spaces? No, because the value of time is only one of the factors that determine the optimal parking location. Parking duration and the number of people in a car also affect location choice, so prices do not automatically allocate all the best parking spaces to drivers who place a high value on time. Many factors other than income also affect the value drivers place on saving time on any particular trip. Lower-income drivers may park at the center when they are in a hurry, while higher-income drivers may park at the periphery and walk when they have plenty of time.

Income does, of course, affect location choices when parking is priced, but if wealthier drivers do park closer to their destinations they will pay more for their parking, and market-priced parking will thus introduce a progressive charge on the wealthy. When cities require on-site parking everywhere, drivers pay nothing to park, and even the poor who cannot afford cars pay for off-street spaces they do not use. Directly charging drivers for their parking is much fairer than forcing everyone to pay for it indirectly.

CLASSIC MONOCENTRIC MODELS

The model of parking location resembles the classic monocentric model of housing location. Richard Muth explains how transport costs affect the optimum housing location:

> In the equilibrium location, the household's net savings on the purchase of a given quantity of housing and transport costs which would result from a very short move—either toward or away from the CBD [Central Business District]—would be equal to zero.... [T]he reduction in expenditure necessary

to purchase a given quantity of housing that results from moving a unit distance away from the market [equals] the increase in transport costs occasioned by such a move.[21]

If we substitute the words driver for household, parking for housing, walking for transport, and destination for CBD in this extract, Muth's statement describes the equilibrium parking location.[22] In addition, the assumptions in the parking model are almost identical to the assumptions in the Alonso-Mills-Muth housing model. As shown in Table 18-1, however, the two models differ in several important respects.

First, in the housing model, different households occupy different quantities of space, but they all occupy it for the same length of time—365 days a year. In the parking model, all cars occupy the same quantity of space—a parking space—but different cars occupy it for different lengths of time. In other words, in the housing model the quantity of space is variable but the length of time is fixed, while in the parking model the quantity of space is fixed but the length of time is variable.

Second, in the housing model travel refers to commuting between home and work, while in the parking model it refers to walking between a parking space and the final destination. In both models the price of travel affects choices the same way—a higher price of travel shifts the optimal location closer to the center.

Third, in the housing model the number of travelers refers to workers in the household, while in the parking model it refers to occupants of a car. In both models this number affects choices in the same way—more people in the house or car shift the optimal location toward the center.

Despite the monocentric model's theoretical elegance, a number of real-world factors reduce the accuracy of its predictions when it is applied to the study of housing choices. In contrast, a simple monocentric model should do much better in predicting parking choices, for several reasons.

Table 18-1. Comparing the Monocentric Models of Housing and Parking

Aspect of the Model	Housing Model	Parking Model
Location choice	Optimal housing location	Optimal parking location
Quantity of space occupied	Variable (house size)	Fixed (one parking space)
Length of time occupied	Fixed (365 days per year)	Variable (parking duration)
Travel	Commuting to work	Walking to destination
Travelers	Workers in household	Occupants of car
Destination	CBD	Trip-specific
Price information	Difficult to obtain	Readily available
Relocation frequency	Rare	Frequent
Quality of public schools	Important	Irrelevant

1. Drivers park frequently, and the relocation cost is low. If a driver sees a better deal, it is easy to park in a different spot for the next trip to the same destination. Over time, drivers can find the best parking location through a trial-and-error process. In contrast, families relocate infrequently because moving is difficult and expensive.
2. Drivers choose parking spaces for access to specific destinations because everyone in a car typically travels to the same place. Families, however, choose their housing locations for access to many destinations other than work. Furthermore, commuters travel to employment sites other than the CBD, and multiple commuters in the same household may travel to different work sites.
3. Parking spaces are a uniform commodity except for location, turnover is frequent, and prices are posted publicly. Housing, on the other hand, is a heterogeneous commodity, turnover is infrequent, and prices are negotiated.
4. Cadillacs park next to Chevrolets, and cars of many different colors and national origins park together in harmony. Families, in contrast, often pay close attention to their neighbors when they choose where to live.
5. Drivers ignore the quality of public schools when they choose where to park. Families, however, carefully consider not only schools but many other public services as well when they choose their housing locations.

Although this model cannot fully represent actual parking decisions and some of its assumptions may appear unrealistic, all its predictions are intuitively sensible and can be tested. Drivers obviously do not use a mathematical model when deciding where to park, nor do they have full information on the price of parking at every location. On the other hand, drivers usually do have good information on the parking prices for trips they make frequently, so their parking choices for these trips probably do reflect a balance between the benefits and costs of different locations.[23]

You can easily test the model's predictions yourself. Suppose the price of parking increases as you drive toward your destination. Do you park closer to your destination if you intend to park for a shorter time? Do you park closer to your destination if you have more passengers in your car? Do you park closer to your destination if you are in a hurry? Do you park closer to your destination if you have heavy packages to carry? If your answers to these questions are yes, the model correctly predicts your parking behavior. Some parking choices may be made for reasons we will never know, and no model can capture all the factors drivers take into account when choosing where to park. Even so, the standard monocentric model is a good place to begin research on the factors that affect parking locations.

EFFICIENCY

Market prices tend to allocate parking spaces quite efficiently. The most convenient parking spaces are occupied by carpoolers, short-term parkers, those who have difficulty walking, and those who place a high value on saving time. In contrast, the less convenient parking spaces are occupied by solo drivers, long-term parkers, those who enjoy walking, and those who place a low value on saving time. These individual choices in response to market prices minimize the travelers' total cost of walking from their parking spaces to their final destinations.

Demand-responsive prices for curb parking resemble spot prices for land (the spot price for a good or service is the price charged for immediate delivery). They reveal essential information about what drivers think parking spaces are really worth and the extent to which drivers are willing to trade money for time when parking. Drivers can choose parking locations according to how long they want to stay, how many people are in the car, how they value walking time (are they in a hurry, carrying heavy packages, tired, or short of money?), and many other circumstances of time and place that only individual drivers can know. As economic journalist John Cassidy says:

> By allowing millions of decision-makers to respond individually to freely determined prices, the market allocates resources—labor, capital, and human ingenuity—in a manner that can't be mimicked by a central plan, however brilliant the central planner.[24]

Letting market prices manage parking will also take a heavy burden off city councils, which now devote endless hours of uninformed debate to the micromanagement of parking for every land use. Even higher political bodies, all the way up to the President's Cabinet, will also save time, as suggested by this description of a cabinet meeting in which Daniel Patrick Moynihan participated: "a cabinet meeting which was mainly bitching about parking in federal buildings—all right, it was supposed to be about office space, but it was also about parking, it always is."[25] Bitching probably describes the discussion accurately, because what Joseph Schumpeter said about politics in general applies perfectly to the politics of parking in particular: "The typical citizen drops down to a lower level of mental performance as soon as he enters the political field. He argues and analyzes in a way which he would readily recognize as infantile within the sphere of his real interests. He becomes a primitive again."[26] If cities let prices take care of parking, politicians will be able to spend more time debating public issues that really matter.

With market-clearing prices for curb parking, drivers' individual choices will lead to a spontaneous, self-organized pattern of parking locations, with no help needed from planners (other than setting up the apparatus of market-priced curb parking to begin with, of course). If parking prices vary to create a vacancy rate of about 15 percent everywhere, the resulting price gradients will shift throughout the day as demand shifts. The outcome can be illustrated by a map that plots a set of contour lines, each one connecting points at which the price of parking is the same (like a weather map with isobars connecting points of equal atmospheric pressure). The isoprice (equal price) lines might be drawn in increments of 50¢ an hour, and the price gradient along any path toward the higher-priced parking would be determined by the frequency with which successive isoprice lines are crossed along that path. Where the isoprice lines are close together, the price of parking increases rapidly; where they are far apart, the price increases slowly. The decision to park some distance from a destination and walk the rest of the way is most likely to occur along the paths with the steepest price gradients because walking saves more money along these paths.

Wilbur Smith and Associates plotted a map of all-day parking prices in downtown Los Angeles in 1972, with isoprice lines showing three local peaks (see Figure 18-5).[27] Parking prices were far lower then, of course, and the hourly price at mid-day is now higher than the all-day price was then. Nevertheless, the map shows a clear pattern of prices, and it can be expected that similar patterns would emerge in comparable maps based on hourly parking rates in other cities. Furthermore, these patterns tend to shift throughout the day as activity patterns change. The peak parking prices might occur at employment centers during the day, at entertainment centers during the evening, and in high-density residential areas during the night. The individual gradients will form around many dispersed centers, much like anthills forming on a terrain that itself has larger peaks (the central business districts) and deeper valleys (low-density neighborhoods). Parking prices at any location will rise and fall during the day, and the local peaks will shift around like kittens fighting under a blanket.[28]

PRACTICALITY

"There is nothing quite so practical as a good theory," Einstein said, and right-priced curb parking is not only efficient in theory, but also workable in practice. Administrative costs were once a problem, but new technology has now made it possible to develop an efficient charging system. To illustrate the necessary characteristics of such a system, consider the criteria deemed essential to the success of a road-pricing system (another form of market charge for automobile use) laid out in the first government report on congestion tolls, the "Smeed Report," published in Britain in 1964. The Smeed Report proposed a system of road pricing almost identical to the congestion-charge system eventually established in

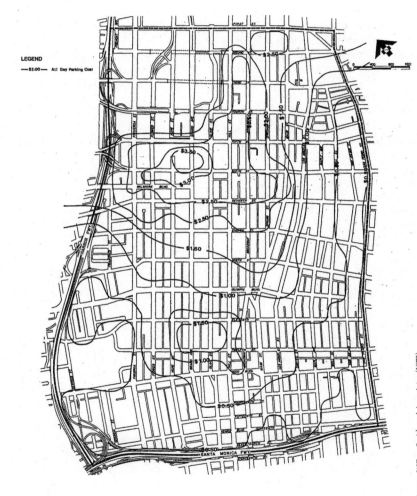

Source: Wilbur Smith and Associates (1972)

Figure 18-5. Parking prices in Los Angeles CBD

London in 2003, and it suggested nine criteria for a workable toll system. These criteria also seem appropriate for a market-priced parking system:

1. Charges should be closely related to the amount of use made of the roads.
2. It should be possible to vary prices for different roads (or areas) at different times of the day, week, or year, and for different classes of vehicle.
3. Prices should be stable and readily ascertainable by road users before they embark upon a journey.
4. Payment in advance and by credit should be possible.
5. The costs for individual road users should be accepted as fair.
6. The system should be simple for road users to understand.
7. The equipment for charging should possess a high degree of reliability.
8. The system should be reasonably free from the possibility of fraud and evasion, both deliberate and unintentional.
9. The system should be capable of being applied, if necessary, to the whole country.[29]

Because metering technology has greatly improved since the Smeed Report was published 40 years ago, a system for market-rate parking charges can easily meet these requirements.

The structure of parking prices at airports provides an example of what market-priced curb parking could look like. Everyone expects not only to pay for parking at airports, but also to pay higher prices for parking closer to the terminals. The expensive central spaces encourage short-term parking and carpooling, while the cheaper distant spaces attract long-term parkers and solo drivers. Many passengers use public transportation or shared-ride vehicles to get to and from the airports specifically to avoid paying for parking (which, incidentally, has become a major source of income for airports). In a similar vein, once people have become accustomed to market-priced curb parking, the idea of going back to free curb parking will start to seem as absurd as expecting free parking at airports (desired, perhaps, but understood to be neither realistic nor ultimately beneficial).

ENFORCEMENT

Parking regulations cannot be strictly enforced if legal parking options are unavailable, but regulation without effective enforcement merely creates confusion. To collect all the potential revenue from market-priced curb parking, cities must ensure that drivers do not park without paying—and enforcement is thus vital. Dedicating a share of parking revenue to the districts that generate it gives merchants, residents, and property owners a new incentive to support better enforcement because illegal parking would reduce the district's income. With effective enforcement, drivers will pay for curb parking as a matter of course, just as they expect to pay for everything else they consume.

To evaluate the likelihood that drivers will try to evade parking charges, we can calculate the expected value of the penalty for violation, which is the product of the fine for a violation and the probability of getting a ticket. Drivers can estimate this expected penalty when deciding whether to put money in a parking meter. Suppose the price of parking two hours at a meter is $2, a parking ticket is $25, and the probability of getting a ticket for an expired meter during two hours of nonpayment is 20 percent. The expected price of illegal parking for two hours is $5 ($25 x 20%), so it is rational to put $2 in the meter. Most models of parking choice assume drivers act in their rational self interest, rather than for moral reasons, in deciding whether to obey the law. For example, parking consultant Mary Smith says, "Cheating parking meters is a folk-crime: shaving the payment for the expected stay or not paying the meter is perfectly fine to the vast majority of Americans, if you get away without a ticket!"[30] In their model of the search for parking, Australian transportation researchers Russell Thompson and Anthony Richardson similarly "assume that parkers are rational and will behave dishonestly if the effect...[on the parkers] is positive."[31] British transportation researchers Ian Black, Kevin Cullinane, and Chris Wright explain that parking is well suited to the simple economic approach toward law enforcement because most parking violations do not involve the non-economic costs often associated with more serious law violations.

> The moral element of imposing costs on other people [by illegal parking] can be considered no different from that of costs during a journey in congested traffic. Of all "crimes," therefore, illegal parking probably falls firmly within the gambit of the economic approach with its emphasis on the monetary valuation of costs and benefits.[32]

The essence of parking enforcement is thus economic, and it is futile to rely on rules absent economic incentives. Quite simply, if the expected penalty for illegal parking (the fine multiplied by the probability of citation) is higher than the price at a meter, rational drivers will pay to park. Citations and fines, however, are politically unpopular. At best, they are like using a gun to rob a bank—you hope not to use it, but mere possession of the weapon induces cooperation. Booting a few repeat violators who have outstanding citations will help to collect the fines because drivers who see the booted vehicles will probably decide that paying for parking is the best policy.

Beyond booting, there are other promising proposals for parking enforcement. Cities can require drivers who park in loading zones to leave the key in the ignition, with the windows open. Drivers who park in zones with time limits can be required to leave their headlights on. To encourage parking between the marked lines, police can paint the part of a car outside the lines with flourescent Day-Glo colors. Steve Martin supports the death penalty for parking offenses.[33]

Drivers take the expected cost of getting a ticket into account when they decide whether to pay, and either a low fine or a low probability of citation will inevitably lead to an increased incidence of violations. A study in Boston in 2001, for example, found that the expected fine for illegal curb parking was often less than the charge for off-street parking for three or more hours, so the temptation to risk a ticket was strong.[34] J. R. Elliott and C. C. Wright, who studied the causes of the sharp increase in illegal parking in London in the early 1980s, explain how insufficient enforcement can lead to widespread noncompliance with parking regulations. They state that if enforcement falls below a certain level,

> drivers realise that the chances of being caught are reduced, more of them avoid paying the meter tariffs, and the traffic wardens find that they have more offenders to deal with. They issue more tickets, because each vehicle they come across is more likely to be illegally parked than before, but issuing the tickets takes a relatively long time and they will cover a reduced number of spaces per unit time. For any driver, the chances of being booked for non-payment fall even further, more drivers become offenders, and so on. The process is an accelerating spiral which ends in a collapse to a low-compliance state.[35]

This process creates a tipping-point or broken-windows phenomenon.[36] Once enforcement falls below a certain level, it collapses entirely.

Free-for-all parking creates antisocial behavior because drivers will often park illegally—by a fire hydrant, at a bus stop, or in a space reserved for the disabled—if no legal curb spaces are vacant. In Italy, for example, many cities have found it necessary to erect metal barriers along the curb to prevent drivers from parking on the sidewalks. In Manhattan, drivers sometimes wait impatiently to claim an illegal space if another car is vacating it, even if the other car is being towed away from beside a fire hydrant. The abuse of disabled parking placards is another deplorable and depressingly frequent violation. Scandals occur often, as in the case of 22 UCLA football players who were found to be using disabled placards for parking on campus.[37] The athletes got the placards by forging doctors' signatures for such conditions as asthma and palsy (see sidebar).

Where curbside parking is offered at market-rate prices vacancies will occur everywhere, and drivers will never "need" to park illegally. Furthermore, returning a share of parking revenue to neighborhoods will increase local support for enforcement.[38] Better enforcement and less illegal parking will, in turn, improve traffic flow for both cars and buses, and will improve the environment for bicyclists and pedestrians. Perhaps Calvin Trillin's fictional mayor of New York City, Frank Ducavelli (Il Duce), wasn't entirely wrong when he said, "Parking is the key to urban order…. A double-parked car is a call to lawlessness. It's like a sign inviting in the forces of disorder."[39]

BANNING CURB PARKING

Charging fair-market prices for curb parking is a better solution than either of the alternative policies cities tried in the early twentieth century—*free* curb parking or *no* curb parking. Before the parking meter was invented in 1935, all curb parking was free, and cars quickly filled the few curb spaces available in busy downtowns. Merchants parked in front of their stores but then complained they lost business because parking

Figure 18-6. Barriers in Milan, Italy, used to prevent cars from parking on sidewalks

---

Abuse of Disabled Parking Placards

Headlines from the *Los Angeles Times* about
UCLA Football Players' abuse of disabled parking placards

14 Bruins Charged with Getting Passes for Handicap Spots	July 9, 1999
There's No Spot for These Crimes; If Charges are True, Then UCLA Football Players Should Have the Wheelchair Thrown at Them	July 9, 1999
Bruin Tailgate Party Will Be Easy to Find	July 10, 1999
It's Fitting That These Guys Find Themselves in a Spot	July 10, 1999
UCLA Football Players' New Opponent: the Disabled	July 10, 1999
The Danger of Treating Athletes Like Gods	July 11, 1999
Severe Punishment Unlikely by UCLA; Dean of Students Says Students in Past Have Not Been Suspended or Expelled for 'Parking Violations'	July 13, 1999
Parking Scam Angers UCLA Athletic Director	July 14, 1999
This Isn't Good Sign for Bruins	July 24, 1999
14 to Please Guilty in Parking Scam	July 28, 1999
A Sorry Day for Bruins	July 29, 1999
UCLA is Sentenced in Court of Public Opinion	July 31, 1999
9 Enter Pleas in UCLA Parking Case	August 3, 1999
Parking Scandal Flares Anew	August 12, 1999
Handicapped Parking Scandal Will Return to the Spotlight this Week	August 23, 1999
Nothing Little about UCLA Predicament	September 11, 1999
Five More Charged in Parking Scandal	September 14, 1999
They're Parked in the UCLA Lineup	September 16, 1999
Fans Legally Park the Blame on Bruins	September 18, 1999

---

was inadequate. Furthermore, curb parking narrowed the roadway available for traffic, and cars cruising for curb parking increased the traffic flow. In combination, the reduced roadway capacity and the increased traffic drastically slowed not only cars but also the street railways that once carried most passengers to, from, and within downtown. Urban historian Robert Fogelson explains the problem:

> Inadequate parking was part of an even more serious problem, a problem that arose not so much because motorists had trouble finding a parking space as because most of them eventually found one. This was the problem of the

parked car, which was distinct from what was later referred to as the parking problem. What made this problem so serious was that it exacerbated the traffic problem.... [T]he parked car was an even greater obstacle to the flow of traffic than the moving car. The crux of the problem was that the streets were unable both to move motor vehicles and to store them. This was especially true in the central business district, which had the heaviest traffic and thus the greatest demand for parking space. Hence, downtown business interests were in a bind. If motorists could not park at their destination, the central business district would lose trade; but since parked cars increased traffic congestion, it would lose trade even if they could.[40]

In response to the traffic congestion caused by cars stored on the street, some cities attempted to ban curb parking completely. The least successful of these bans occurred in downtown Los Angeles in 1920. Free curb parking had been creating enormous traffic problems, but the ban on curb parking lasted less than a month. Los Angeles historian Bruce Henstell tells the story:

If there can be said to have been one instant, one point in time where the domination of the auto over all became complete, that moment came in April of 1920.... By 1920, there were more than 160,000 autos in Los Angeles.... Downtown autos challenged one another for the few precious inches of space available, traffic flowed like jelly.... A side effect of the traffic mess was that the streetcars couldn't get through and so were forty-five minutes to an hour late on every run through downtown.... [T]he city came up with a brilliant, innovative suggestion of banning [on-street] parking from downtown during peak hours.

Magically, the streetcars began making their schedules. The mayor pronounced himself happy. The traffic engineers were happy. "After the first day of the ordinance," editorialized a newspaper, "everybody seemed satisfied... except the motorists, the professional men, the business houses, and the police."... Earl C. Anthony, a prominent downtown businessman, was so infuriated that he planned a challenge to its constitutionality. After all, it clearly discriminated since it only regulated motorists, not pedestrians.... The city council caved in and repealed the ordinance. This despite the desperate pleas of the engineers that it had proved its workability.... The *Los Angeles Times* concurred. The experiment proved "Southern California throbs in unison with the purring motors of its automobiles."[41]

The ban was repealed after only 19 days. One reason was the fear the ban would drive business from the downtown to the suburbs, even though most of the cars parked on downtown streets were owned by commuters, not shoppers, and most people traveled downtown by street-car. The streetcars were already overcrowded, and many passengers with-out seats—"straphangers"—had to stand as the streetcars crept along in traffic. Critics suspected the parking ban was a plot by the street railways to increase their ridership and profits. After all, an industry maxim was, "The dividends are in the straps." Finally, automobile ownership was already widespread in Los Angeles, and by 1920 most people wanted to increase rather than restrict parking. Transportation historian Scott Bottles explains that the private car represented liberation from the slow pace and conformity of public transit, while the parking ban appeared to cast aside the future in favor of the past:

> The automobile, in short, stood as a symbol of urban and industrial progress. It answered an age-old need for rapid, personal transportation. To deny its use seemed absurd to its proponents. "The motor car means rapid transportation for the individual," insisted an automobile dealer. "It is conceded to be one of the greatest conveniences of modern life, and it is unthinkable to virtually bar it from the business district of the city." Why, the opponents of the ban asked, should the City Council ruin the value of such an important technological innovation. Gilbert Woodhill, manager of Western Motors, admitted that the streetcars had done "a great deal for Los Angeles" in past years, but they had not done as much as the automobile in recent years. To ban the automobile from parking on downtown streets was a backward step as far as he was con-cerned. A *Times* editorial agreed. "No other innovation has adapted itself so quickly and so universally to the needs of a generation.... And any city that endeavors to establish a blockade against the motor car by relegating it to the back streets and suburban lanes is making a serious mistake," the paper argued. The automobile, it pointed out, had won its place fairly in the eco-nomic and social life of the American people.... "As an agent of progress," the *Times* grandiloquently concluded, "it has outstripped the steam engine and telegraphy and stands second only to the printing press."[42]

Cars have become a prime ingredient of the American lifestyle, but this does not mean cities should devote two lanes of every downtown street to storing immobile automobiles. In 1925, Harvard transportation planner Miller McClintock explained that if curb parking were banned, the will-ingness to pay for off-street parking would provide a market test of the car's utility for each trip:

> What will become of all the cars that are now parked on city streets? The answer is twofold. Those owners who feel that under the changed conditions [a ban on curb parking], it is not worthwhile to use their automobiles in the city, will resort to some other means of transportation. This may seem to be an

undue hardship, but it should be noted that thousands of motorists in every large city have not been using their motors for personal transportation for a number of years, due to congestion which has resulted to no small extent because a relatively few individuals have demanded a right to store their cars upon public streets.

Those owners, for whom the automobile still possesses utility, even though they must pay for its storage, will continue to bring it into the prohibited parking area as before. After all, the ability of a transportation vehicle to bear the terminal charges at both ends of the run is not a very severe test of its utility. If a private passenger automobile is not worth enough to its owner to justify his paying 25 to 50 cents a day for its storage [$2.60 to $5.20 a day in 2003], it does not seem reasonable that the public should provide him with improved street space for the purpose. It is not impossible that prohibited [curb] parking may not only work for a desirable release of storage space for moving traffic, but that it may bring about a restriction of the amount of traffic on city streets by weeding out those vehicles which have no real business in the area.[43]

Although the Los Angeles parking ban lasted less than a month, CBD parking bans in other cities were more successful. Urban historian Paul Barrett, for example, explains how research by Miller McClintock helped persuade Chicago to ban curb parking in the Loop in 1927:

In 1926 McClintock reported that, of 68,621 department store patrons surveyed, just 6.7 percent had arrived by automobile and fewer than 1.5 percent had parked at the curb. Nearly 13 percent of the visitors to office buildings, 16 percent of restaurant patrons, and 18 percent of the book buyers had used automobiles to come to the Loop, but in each case less than 2 percent had parked at the curb. Motorists, it seemed, were more willing than anyone had thought to pay a small parking fee and walk from a garage to their destination.[44]

The Chicago ban on curb parking was a great success. In 1928, the number of cars entering the Loop increased by 14 percent, the speed of streetcars through the Loop increased, and the number of police required to enforce parking regulations fell.[45] Few people in Los Angeles, however, agreed with McClintock's argument that the willingness to pay for parking was a fair test of an automobile trip's utility. As a result, Los Angeles zigzagged between two extremes—from free curb parking to no curb parking and back to free curb parking—without ever exploring the middle ground of charging the market price for parking. Market-price curb spaces will provide convenient parking, buffer pedestrians on the sidewalk from traffic on the streets, and provide ample public revenue.

WHERE WOULD JESUS PARK?

In 2002 the Evangelical Environmental Network (EEN) created a stir when its What Would Jesus Drive? campaign argued that transportation choices are moral choices. The EEN explained on its Web site:

> The question, "What Would Jesus Drive?" is a more specific version of the well-known question, "What Would Jesus Do?" Christians ask themselves "What Would Jesus Do?" to help guide them in their daily decisions.... [T]he question actually becomes, "Lord, what would you have me do?" So our specific question then becomes, "Lord, what would you have me drive?"... Pollution from vehicles has a major impact on human health and the rest of God's creation. It contributes significantly to the threat of global warming. Our reliance on imported oil from unstable regions threatens peace and security. Obeying Jesus in our transportation choices is one of the great Christian obligations and opportunities of the twenty-first century.[46]

Regardless of your religion, your transportation choices do affect other people, and the world would surely be a better place if everyone were to drive cleaner and more fuel-efficient cars.

Thinking about their moral obligations to society may lead some motorists to choose a different car, but it won't lead many to choose a different parking space. Is there any sensible answer to the question, Where Would Jesus Park? Except for the obligation to obey handicapped parking rules, there seems to be no obvious moral dimension to the issue. Perhaps even more than in most other activities, people seem to think only of themselves in choosing where to park. After finding a good parking spot, few people would ask themselves, Does someone else need this space more than I do? Indeed, most parkers seem to act more like Homer Simpson than Ned Flanders.[47]

The opportunity cost of a parking space is what someone else is willing to pay for it, and the only way to let drivers know how much other people want to park in any space is to charge the market price for it. Choosing your parking spot on the basis of market prices will thus implicitly take into account the cost you impose on others when you choose to occupy any particular space. If you are a solo driver and want to park for a long time, for example, choosing a peripheral spot will save you money and also make the more central spaces available to people who arrive in carpools or want to park for a shorter time. In this way, using market prices to manage parking spaces will lead everyone, in pursuing their own self-interest, to consider the welfare of others. At least for parking, fair-market prices can resolve the moral dilemma that Daniel Defoe's rueful Moll Flanders described near the end of her tumultuous life in the eighteenth century: "We all want to do good, and we all want to do well. God grant that you don't have to choose."

In stark contrast to a system of market-priced curb parking, off-street parking requirements encourage narrow, self-interested behavior at the expense of others. Consider the dispute in 2002 over a 22-acre, $42 million megachurch proposed on the south side of Chicago. Naturally, anything that large raises land-use planning questions, and the opponents usually invoke parking requirements as a reason to reject a development or scale it back. Referring to the issue of whether 2,000 parking spaces would be enough for the new Salem Baptist church, the Reverend James Meeks said, "I don't care if Jesus is a member of your church, the City Council zoning board will not pass a project that doesn't have the proper amount of parking."[48]

Market-price curb parking, however, can reduce some of the conflicts created by proposed land uses. Consider the *New York Times* report of a Queens neighborhood "where Christians, Buddhists, Jews, Muslims and Hindus worship within blocks of one another without a hint of sectarian strife. When it comes to parking spaces, though, it is all-out war."[49] A flood of cars descends on the neighborhood every Sunday, and the residents complain bitterly about the ungodly noise, the crowds, and the cars that block their driveways. If this neighborhood becomes a parking benefit district, higher prices for nonresident parking on Sundays can manage demand and settle the strife. We need a new Golden Rule for the price of parking: *charge others what they would charge you.*

REMOVING OFF-STREET PARKING REQUIREMENTS

In contrast to the self-organizing efficiency of a market, most cities now require at least enough off-street spaces to satisfy the peak demand for free parking at every site, and the cost is shifted into higher prices for everything else. The result is both inefficient (prices do not reflect costs) and unfair (nondrivers subsidize drivers). If cities remove their parking requirements to eliminate this inefficiency, the ratio of parking spaces to people will decline (or rise more slowly), and parking prices will increase. Parking requirements cannot be eliminated all at once, of course. Instead, cities can dismantle their parking requirements gradually. Some cities have already removed parking requirements downtown, for example, and other business centers are obvious candidates. New subdivisions are another place to remove parking requirements because developers have every incentive to provide as much parking as residents are willing to pay for. Cities can then slowly remove parking requirements everywhere, hand in hand with creating parking benefit districts and charging market prices for curb parking.

Fewer parking spaces combined with higher prices for using them will affect demand and supply in many ways. On the demand side, higher parking prices will lead individuals to make a variety of transportation choices that reduce the number of parking spaces needed. For example, more people will drive in carpools (to split the cost of parking), more people will walk, cycle, or ride transit (to avoid parking charges altogether), more people will drive during off-peak hours (when parking prices will be lower), and many people will own fewer cars.

On the supply side, developers will begin to provide on-site parking spaces in response to market demand rather than zoning ordinances. Since prices will vary to maintain a few curb vacancies, spillover will no longer be a problem. Individual property owners and merchants can then choose how much on-site parking to provide based on business considerations, not zoning. Some may choose to provide their own off-street spaces, while others may offer to validate parking in nearby garages. Regardless of the strategy, all firms will be able to decide for themselves whether parking is worth its costs. Parking will increasingly become unbundled from other transactions, and professional operators will manage more of the parking supply. Over time, the prices for off-street parking will tend to cover the full cost of constructing and operating it, including the cost of land. Where the market price of parking does not meet these costs, more developers will choose not to build additional parking capacity. Where the market price of parking exceeds these costs, however, profit-making developers will step in to provide additional spaces. Everyone will understand there is no such thing as free parking, especially free underground parking.

The ITE data presented in Chapter 2 clearly show the demand for parking varies greatly among different sites, even for the same land use (such as a restaurant). If demand varies so much, how many parking spaces *should* each land use have? My suggestion is to treat parking spaces for a restaurant (or any other land use) in the same way we treat the restaurant itself. Planners don't say how many restaurants a city must have. We let the market provide as many restaurants as people are willing to pay for. Similarly, planners should let developers provide as many off-street parking spaces as drivers are willing to pay for. Charging drivers less than the cost-recovery price of a parking space provides a subsidy for driving. When cities require more parking than developers are willing to provide voluntarily, the result is to subsidize the car over other travel modes.

If cities do not require developers to provide off-street parking, how will the market finance all the parking spaces made necessary by development? I suggest the approach used to finance all other development: the prices drivers pay for parking can finance parking spaces because any other arrangement subsidizes parking and driving. Removing off-street parking requirements will merely shift the cost of parking out of the prices for everything else; the *net* effect will not increase inflation or the Consumer Price Index because increases in the price of parking will be offset by decreases in the prices of everything else.

Even if cities do not *require* off-street parking, many establishments will still offer it free. When people shop in a store, they often expect to park free while doing so. To meet these expectations, then, even without parking requirements, some businesses will continue to bundle the cost of parking with the prices charged for their goods and services. Other businesses, however, may decide *not* to provide free parking, which will enable them to offer lower prices for their wares. Individual consumers will thus have a choice: to park free in return for higher prices when they get out of their cars or to pay lower prices for everything except parking. While the average solo driver may prefer free parking, lower prices for everything else will appeal to those who carpool (and can thus split the parking cost), who use some alternative form of transportation (such as walking, biking, or riding mass transit), or who make larger-than-average purchases (and thus stand to reap a greater reward for what they buy).

The main point in this argument is *not* that it is always unwise for an establishment to subsidize the cost of parking by raising their prices for everything else. This decision, after all, ultimately depends on the preferences and expectations of the customers. Rather, the main problem lies in *requiring* all establishments to follow this practice. Market prices are a sensible bottom-up approach to planning for parking, while off-street parking requirements are a confused and costly top-down approach. Parking requirements in zoning ordinances are a disastrous substitute for millions of individual decisions—by developers, merchants, employers, and drivers—about how much a parking space is worth. We can rely on markets where they work well and reserve planning for the problems that arise when markets fail.

If cities de-require off-street parking, developers, property owners, and businesses can judge for themselves how much off-street parking they want to provide for their employees and customers. They will have every reason to make the right decision because they will pay for their own mistakes—and will prosper if they choose wisely. Urban planners who establish off-street parking requirements, in contrast, have no financial incentive to get things right. As a result, they often adopt dubious approximations (such as the golden rule of four spaces per 1,000 square feet) or copy the requirements of other cities. Urban planners simply do not know how many parking spaces each business, apartment house, or church in each different location needs, in part because they have no professional training to estimate parking demand.

Removing off-street parking requirements will not eliminate off-street parking but will instead stimulate an active commercial market for it. Both businesses and the city will have an incentive to make off-street parking available to the public where the market price covers the cost of providing it. If curb parking spaces are priced to clear the market and the revenue per space is not enough to cover the cost of constructing new off-street spaces, people apparently do not really want those new off-street spaces. People always want more parking spaces if someone else is paying for them, of course, but...

An active commercial market for public parking has two important benefits. First, it encourages shared use among sites where the peak parking demands occur at different times (e.g., banks and nightclubs) because paid parking is, almost by definition, shared. Shared public parking in one central location is inherently more efficient than private parking at every site because fewer spaces are needed to meet the combined peak demand, and each parking space is kept occupied for more of the time.[50] Shared parking also allows visitors to park once and visit multiple destinations on foot. For example, parking consultant Mary Smith says that Circle Centre, a successful retail/entertainment development in downtown Indianapolis, would have needed 6,000 parking spaces if it were built with unshared parking for every individual use, but 2,815 shared parking spaces were sufficient to meet the demand.[51]

Second, removing off-street parking requirements will favor commercial land uses that serve customers who can walk or bike from adjacent neighborhoods. Restaurants and stores that rely on walk-in trade, for example, will have lower costs if they don't have to provide parking spaces. Land and capital will shift from parking lots to new uses that employ more workers and generate more tax revenue. Emancipation from parking requirements will especially encourage adaptive reuse and infill development in older areas where providing more parking is difficult and will also favor development at locations with good public transit. In a sense, the absence of free parking, like its presence, is a self-perpetuating phenomenon. Market-priced curb parking and no off-street parking requirements will steer business investment toward activities whose customers and employees require less parking. The result will be more mixed-use and infill development near existing infrastructure and less greenfield development in outlying areas.

Planners set off-street parking requirements because the government fails to charge fair-market prices for curb parking, not because the market fails to provide enough off-street parking. Most cities now require every land use to satisfy the peak demand for free parking—regardless of the cost. If cities instead charge the right price for curb parking and deregulate off-street parking, developers and businesses can judge for themselves how many parking spaces to provide.

Edward Bassett, the New York lawyer and reformer who is considered the "father of zoning," made the connection between curb parking and off-street parking requirements. In 1926 he argued that if cities prohibit curb parking they will not need to require off-street parking because private owners will provide it in response to economic conditions:

> Some say that a way must be found to compel the private owner by law to set aside space for [off-street] parking. This cannot be done. The experience of cities is that the supply of downtown private parking space depends on the strictness of prevention of parking in the streets by the police. The city can undoubtedly prohibit parking in the public streets entirely. The degree to which private owners will furnish private parking space depends upon their willingness and the pressure of economic considerations.[52]

Bassett clearly saw that the mismanagement of curb space creates the parking problem. Perhaps because the parking meter had not been invented in 1926, Bassett recommended banning curb parking rather than charging for it. With today's metering technology, charging the right price for curb parking is far better than either banning curb parking or requiring off-street parking.

CONCLUSION: PRICES CAN DO THE PLANNING

Around the world, cars are multiplying, traffic is getting worse, the air is getting dirtier, oil is running out, greenhouse gases are accumulating, and cities need money. As one response, why not charge fair-market prices for curb parking and spend the revenue to improve neighborhoods? It works well where it has been tried.

One can debate the details of prices for parking but not the need for them. A simple model of parking choice shows that market prices produce reasonable results. Carpools, short-term parkers, those who have difficulty walking, and those who place a high value on saving time will occupy the best spaces. Solo drivers, long-term parkers, those who enjoy walking, and those who place a low value on saving time will occupy the peripheral spaces. The resulting pattern of parked cars will minimize the motorists' total cost of walking from their parking spaces to their final destinations.

Although market prices can allocate parking spaces fairly and efficiently, cities now require off-street parking everywhere—imposing enormous costs on the economy and the environment. Cities can and should regulate off-street parking to improve its *quality*, but they should deregulate its *quantity* and instead charge market prices for curb parking. If cities deregulate off-street parking and charge the right price for curb parking, market forces will improve transportation, land use, the environment, and urban life. You will not pay for my parking, and I will not pay for yours. Instead of planning without prices, we can let prices do the planning.

CHAPTER 18 NOTES

1. I assume that drivers know how parking prices vary with distance to their destination and how long they want to park. Alternatively, drivers may know only the expected value of how long they want to park. In either case, I assume that drivers pay only for the exact time that they park, determined *ex post*. The parking charge is a linear function of the number of minutes parked, with no advance commitment to how long one parks. Various in-vehicle and multispace parking meters allow drivers to pay only for the time parked, and they allow parking prices to vary according to the time of day and day of week.

2. Parking consultants Mary Smith and Thomas Butcher (1994, 31) explain that the path of travel strongly affects parkers' willingness to walk. "There are at least four variables related to path of travel: degree of weather protection, climate, line of sight (Can the parker see the destination form the parking space?), and 'friction' (interruptions and constraints on the path of travel, such as crossing streets with or without traffic signals, and natural and psychological barriers, such as railroad tracks or a change in neighborhood)…acceptable walking distances entirely within a parking facility are shorter than those for urban sidewalks… . Because the user of a facility walks down a parking aisle or follows a path between cars to reach the elevator, a high degree of 'friction' exists for this system. Also since parking structures are generally perceived as being less safe than open surface lots, the distinctions between walking within parking lots and structures should be recognized." Smith and Butcher present data implying that parkers are willing to walk between three and four times farther in the best pedestrian environments than in the worst ones. Although Smith and Butcher do not consider how the price of parking affects parkers' willingness to walk, their data suggest that curb parkers are willing to walk much farther to get to stores along a pleasant sidewalk than mall parkers are willing to walk through a parking lot or structure to reach the stores in a mall.

3. The cost of time spent walking (v) may differ among persons in the car. If everyone's value of time is weighted equally, we can interpret v as the average value of time.

4. Austin (1973) and Wilbur Smith and Associates (1972 and 1981) show that parking prices decline with increasing walking time from activity centers in Los Angeles according the negative exponential formula.

5. At distance d from the destination, the cost of walking to the destination and back for one person who values time at $8 an hour and walks four miles an hour is $(2 \times 1 \times \$8/4)d$, or $4d$. This linear relationship implies that the time cost of walking declines by $4 a mile as you approach your destination.

6. The calculation of the value for $-1/2\log_e(nv/tw)$ is as follows: $nv/tw = 1/2$; $\log_e(1/2) = -0.6933$; $-1/2(-0.6933) = 0.35$ miles. If pedestrians value time at $8 an hour and walk four miles an hour, the time cost of walking is $2 a mile.

7. At $d = 0.35$, $p(d) = \$1e^{0.7} = \$1(0.5) = 50¢$.

8. Another way to think about the time cost of walking is that walking 0.7 miles at four miles an hour (15 minutes a mile) takes 10.5 minutes. If time costs $8 an hour, 10.5 minutes cost $1.40.

9. If you want to spend four hours at your destination, the 10 minutes walking time must be added to the time at your destination, so the total parking duration is four hours and 10 minutes. The additional parking duration adds another 8.5¢ to the parking cost. This result shows you should park a bit closer to your destination when you consider the effect of walking time on the total parking cost. To simplify the discussion, this factor has been neglected. A negative value of d^* implies that you should park at your destination.

10. The time cost of walking from the parking space to the destination and back is $2nvd/w$. The derivative with respect to distance is $2nv/w$. Because $n = 1$, $v = 8$, and $w = 4$, the time cost of walking decreases by $4 per mile parked closer to the final destination $(2 \times 1 \times 8 \div 4 = 4)$. The money cost of parking is $t(\$1e^{2d})$. The derivative with respect to distance is $t(-2e^{2d})$. Because $t = 4$ and $d = 0.35$, the money cost of parking increases by $4 for each mile parked closer to the final destination $(4 \times 2e^{0.7} = 4 \times 2 \times 1/2 = 4)$.

11. The total money-and-time cost curve is almost flat between 0.25 and 0.5 miles from your destination because the slopes of the money-parking-cost and monetized-time-cost curves are about equal in absolute value but opposite in sign within this range. The total cost of parking and walking is about $3.40 anywhere between 0.25 and 0.5 miles from your destination. Parking less than 0.25 miles or more than 0.5 miles from your destination increases the total cost of parking and walking. The total cost of parking and walking is $4 *at* your destination and at 0.8 miles *from* your destination.

12. If $nv = tw$, then $-1/2 \log_e(nv/tw) = -1/2 \log_e(1) = 0$, so you should park at your destination. If $nv > tw$, then $-1/2 \log_e(nv/tw) < 0$; this result also implies that you should park at your destination, because you cannot park a negative distance from it.

13. The values in the figure are the solutions for d^* as a function of n and t when $v = \$8$ an hour and $w = 4$ miles an hour.

14. Consider the different parking durations necessary to make it worth walking 0.2 miles from the parking space to the center: three hours for a solo driver, six hours for a two-person carpool, nine hours for a three-person carpool, and 12 hours for a four-person carpool.

15. The walking cost of $\$8d$ in Figure 18-3 is double the walking cost $\$4d$ in Figure 18-1 because two people experience this cost. Carpoolers split the money cost of parking, but they don't split the time cost of walking.

16. The market allocation of closer-in parking spaces to carpools and short-term parking, and of farther-out spaces to solo drivers and long-term parking, resembles the pattern predicted by Johann Heinrich von Thünen in *The Isolated State* in 1826. In his commemorative essay on von Thünen's 200th birthday, Paul Samuelson (1983) describes this model and explains why hard-to-transport vegetables are grown in a ring immediately around a town, while easier-to-ship grain is grown in a ring farther outside the town.

17. This equation was derived from a specific negative exponential function for parking prices, but the argument nv/tw will always appear in the solution for the optimal parking location if parking prices increase monotonically as you approach your destination.

18. In linear-programming terms, the user-optimizing solution is the same as the system-optimizing solution.

19. If a driver parks only a short time at the destination, the cost of parking is a small part of the total cost of the automobile trips. Therefore, the elasticity of demand for automobile trips with respect to the price of parking is low for trips that involve a short parking time. In their research on the demand for parking at the San Francisco International Airport, Adib Kanafani and Lawrence Lan (1988) found that the price elasticity of demand for parking was -0.07 for durations of less than one hour, -0.95 for durations between six and seven hours, and -2.5 for durations of between three and four days.

20. Smith and LeCraw (1946, 18) present survey evidence showing that willingness to walk increases dramatically for longer parking durations.

21. Muth (1969, 22).

22. In the equilibrium location, the driver's net savings on the purchase of a given quantity of parking and walking costs that would result from a very short move—either toward or away from the destination—would be equal to zero.... [T]he reduction in expenditure necessary to purchase a given quantity of parking that results from moving a unit distance away from the market [equals] the increase in walking costs occasioned by such a move.

23. Parking guidance systems that display the price and availability of parking can give motorists the information they need to make rational parking choices. Research suggests drivers do pay attention to and act upon these guidance parking systems, although these systems usually focus more on the availability than on the price of parking (Haster, Fisher, and Collura 2002). Clearly, drivers must know about the spatial pattern of parking prices if these prices are to affect parking location. If cities begin to use prices to guarantee the availability of vacant parking spaces everywhere, availability will cease to be a dominant issue in parking choices, and prices will emerge as a stronger influence on drivers' parking location decisions.

24. Cassidy (2000, 44).

25. Takesuye (2001, 36).

26. Schumpeter (1942, 262).

27. The three peaks are at Sixth and Grand (the Biltmore Hotel), Twelfth and Olive (the Transamerica Building), and First and Spring (City Hall).

28. If parking prices are set to achieve a target vacancy rate, the isoprice lines will map the contour of prices that eliminate cruising. If curb parking is underpriced, another map could plot contour lines connecting points at which the search time is the same. Where parking is most underpriced, the search time would be greatest. Presumably, walking from parking spaces to final destinations would be most likely to occur along the paths with the steepest search-time gradients.

29. United Kingdom Ministry of Transport (1964, 7). Reuben Smeed chaired the panel that wrote the report. The panel included many of the famous names in British transportation economics, such as Michael Beesley, Christopher Foster, Gabriel Roth, J. M. Thomson, Alan Walters, and J. G. Wardrop.

30. Smith (1999, 543).

31. Thompson and Richardson (1998, 120).

32. Black, Cullinane, and Wright (1993, 267). When New Haven, Connecticut, introduced a voucher system of paying for curb parking, the *Yale Daily News* reported, "Yale students expressed differing opinions about the new parking voucher system. 'I've never in my life put anything in a meter,' Cameron Reeves '98 said. Other students said they will continue to ignore the parking laws in hopes of getting away with enough unpaid fees to cover the cost of tickets" (*Yale Daily News*, November 22, 1996).

33. These and other creative ideas about parking are available on the Halfbakery web site at www.halfbakery.com.

34. Boston Transportation Department (2001, 1).

35. Elliott and Wright (1982, 308).

36. James Wilson and George Kelling (1982) argue, "if a window in a building is broken and is left unrepaired, all the rest of the windows will soon be broken."

37. UCLA seems to be unusual only in the large number of football players who were caught misusing disabled parking placards because similar scandals have erupted on many campuses. In 2003, the quarterback at Florida State University earned national attention for parking in spaces reserved for the disabled. In a survey at a shopping center with 11 out of 314 parking spaces reserved for the disabled persons, City of New York University professor of management John Trinkaus found that the number of vehicles improperly parked in disabled spaces increased as the lot occupancy increased and in bad weather. Trinkaus (1984a, 114) concluded, "in the absence of police enforcement, general observance of parking for handicapped persons is normally practiced only when convenient." Trinkaus (1984b, 30) also found that the proportion of expensive to inexpensive cars improperly parked in handicapped spaces was about the same as that of all cars in the parking lot. He concluded that handicapped parking violations are more a function of prevailing cultural norms than of automobile purchase prices.

38. Cullinane (1993) presents a model that shows how the search times to find legal and illegal curb spaces affect the decision whether to park legally.

39. Trillin (2001, 89 and 205).

40. Fogelson (2001, 283). In his history of downtown business districts, Fogelson provides an excellent and extended analysis of how parking problems contributed to their decline.

41. Henstell (1984, 25-26). Henstell says that the first motorist charged with violating the new ordinance was James Wynne, 19, who refused to move his vehicle from in front of the store where he worked on First Street. See also Brilliant (1989, 71-72) and Fogelson (2001, 288-95).

42. Bottles (1987, 69-70).

43. McClintock (1925, 146). In 1924, McClintock also wrote, "It seems scarcely fair that cities should continue to provide space with a property value often as high as $25,000 for—and in 1931 the storage of cars which are not of sufficient utility to owners to warrant their paying from 25 to 50 cents for their housing" (McClintock 1924, 361). In 1931, Miller McClintock was one of the 30 founding members of the Institute of Traffic Engineers (which later became the Institute of Transportation Engineers) and served as its first vice-president.

44. Barrett (1983, 159). A subsequent survey of 864 Loop tenants found that 78 percent favored the parking ban. In a survey of 96,082 downtown patrons of 33 establishments (including stores, office buildings, banks, and restaurants) in 1926, only 19 percent had arrived by car, and only 1.6 percent had parked at the curb (Nau 1929, 85). Before Philadelphia instituted a parking ban on several downtown streets, a survey of department store customers found that only 2 percent of all shoppers had arrived by car and parked at the curb (Drake 1946, 112); 40 percent of all vehicles parked at the curb were in violation of the parking regulations.

45. Barrett (1983, 159).

46. See the organization's web site at www.whatwouldjesusdrive.org/. See also the related web site at www.highrock.com/personal/WWJD/.

47. As Miller McClintock asked "Why is it that men and women, normally courteous and considerate...should of a sudden revert to selfish, snarling savages the minute they get behind the wheel of an automobile?"

48. "Chicagoans Fight 'Megachurch' Plans," Morning Edition, National Public Radio, September 26, 2003.

49. "Religious Rites Welcomed; Parking Rights are Thornier," *New York Times*, March 29, 2004. Chapter 3 explains that the churches in New York are not required to provide ample off-street parking because of a loophole in the zoning code.

50. The Urban Land Institute (1983) explains the economics of shared parking. Lee Kjrohn, Planning Director in Manchester, Vermont, says, "We are looking at parking as a fundamental shared resource rather than a number of individual fiefdoms owned and controlled by individual parties" (*The Manchester Journal*, April 30, 2004).

51. Mary Smith (1996).

52. Bassett (1926, 60).

19

The Ideal Source of Local Public Revenue

The mode of taxation is, in fact, quite as important as the amount. As a small burden badly placed may distress a horse that could carry with ease a much larger one properly adjusted, so a people may be impoverished and their power of producing wealth destroyed by taxation, which, if levied in another way, could be borne with ease.

— HENRY GEORGE

Charging market prices for curb parking is not only sound transportation policy, but also sound fiscal policy. It can be related to the ideas of the nineteenth-century reformer Henry George, who argued that land rent is the most appropriate source of government revenue. We rarely consider curb parking spaces to be "rented," but they are, albeit on a small scale and for a short duration. A parking space is the smallest parcel of land commonly rented, but between 5 and 8 percent of urban land is devoted to curb parking, so charging the market price for it can yield substantial revenue.

HENRY GEORGE'S PROPOSAL

Born in Philadelphia in 1839, Henry George received no training in politics or economics, and his formal education ended with the seventh grade. He went to sea at 16, and halfway through his second voyage around the world he left his ship to become a journeyman printer in San

Francisco, which was beginning its transformation from a pioneer camp to a big city. The young George noticed that great wealth and extreme poverty were arising concurrently. Determined to explain—and remedy—this relationship, he began writing in his spare time. The result was *Progress and Poverty*, in which he contended that taxes on land are a "naturally ordained" source of government revenue for two reasons.

George's first point was that a tax on land is fair because communities rather than individuals create land values:

> The tax upon land values is, therefore, the most just and equal of all taxes. It falls only upon those who receive from society a peculiar and valuable bene-fit, and upon them in proportion to the benefit they receive. It is the taking by the community, for the use of the community, of that value which is the cre-ation of the community. It is the application of the common property to com-mon uses.[1]

George's second point was that taxes on land do not reduce the incen-tives to construct and maintain buildings. The need to raise cash to pay taxes may even prompt owners to put their land to its "highest and best" use (i.e., the one that yields the highest rent). Taxes on buildings, in con-trast, do reduce the returns from investment and thus reduce the incen-tives to construct and maintain buildings. Further, George argued, the added revenue from land taxes will allow cities to cut other taxes and stimulate economic growth:

> To abolish the taxation which now hampers every wheel of exchange and presses down upon every form of industry would be like removing an immense weight from a powerful spring. Imbued with fresh energy, produc-tion would start into new life, and trade would receive a stimulus which would be felt to the remotest arteries.[2]

In the most ambitious form of his proposal, George maintained that taxes on land can produce enough revenue to replace all other taxes in the economy. The land tax would consequently become the "single tax," replacing all taxes on labor and capital. The enterprise unleashed by this shift in taxation, he argued, would produce progress without poverty.[3]

These ideas were not entirely new. A century before Henry George began writing, Adam Smith also endorsed land value taxation in *The Wealth of Nations*:

> Ground-rents are a still more proper subject of taxation than the rent of houses. A tax upon ground-rents would not raise the rents of houses. It would fall alto-gether upon the owner of the ground-rent, who acts always as a monopolist, and exacts the greatest rent which can be got for the use of his ground.[4]

Henry George echoed Smith, but this did not give him credence in the economics profession. Most contemporary economists considered George a radical or even a crackpot, but his ideas attracted a huge popular following. Economic historian Mark Blaug says, "In the English-speaking world in the last quarter of the nineteenth century it wasn't Marx but Henry George who was the talking-point of all debates among fiery young intellectuals."[5] Running as a labor candidate, George narrowly lost the race for mayor of New York in 1886, but he drew more votes than the Republican candidate, Theodore Roosevelt, who dismissed George as "an utterly cheap reformer."[6]

Regarding the contemporary economists' harsh criticism of George, Joseph Schumpeter wrote in his *History of Economic Analysis*:

> Barring his panacea (the Single Tax) and the phraseology connected with it, [George] was a very orthodox economist.... Professional economists who focused attention on the single-tax proposal and condemned Henry George's teaching, root and branch, were hardly just to him. The proposal...is not *economically* unsound, except in that it involves an unwarranted optimism concerning the yield of such a tax.[7]

Many once-popular economic theories have disappeared without a trace since *Progress and Poverty* was published, but economists continue to discuss land value taxation. After first opposing George and then ignoring him, most economists now agree with his central proposition that property taxes are better placed on land than on buildings. For all his overblown rhetoric, Henry George was essentially right. Nine Nobel Laureates in economics, conservative and liberal alike, have endorsed land value taxation for the same reason that George gave: it raises public revenue without distorting private incentives.[8] "In my opinion," Milton Friedman said, "the least bad tax is the property tax on the unimproved value of land, the Henry George argument of many, many years ago."[9]

Richard Arnott and Joseph Stiglitz showed that, under certain assumptions, total land rent in a city will equal the total expenditure on municipal public goods, so perhaps land rent really can finance local government, a proposal economists had previously dismissed.[10] In homage to the

Figure 19-1. Illustration for Henry George's single tax

idea's originator, Arnott and Stiglitz dubbed their finding the "Henry George Theorem." Despite the efficiency and revenue potential of land value taxation, however, most cities continue to levy the same tax rate on land and buildings.

CURB PARKING REVENUE IS PUBLIC LAND RENT

George died in 1897, just as the car was born, so what do his ideas have to do with parking? There are two main connections. First, the revenue from curb parking is land rent that can be used to finance local governments. Second, underpricing creates a shortage of curb parking, which in turn leads cities to impose off-street parking requirements for every land use, and these parking requirements act like a tax on buildings. Free curb parking and off-street parking requirements are therefore the exact opposites of what Henry George recommended: cities fail to collect land rent from curb parking, and they impose a heavy tax on buildings. Consequently, cities can still obtain many of the benefits of land value taxation by adopting two related policies: *charge market prices for curb parking and remove off-street parking requirements.*

Curb parking spaces are in fixed supply, so the revenue derived from them is pure land rent.[11] Demand determines the rental value of curb spaces, which are publicly owned, and the city can use the revenue to pay for public services. Charging for curb parking fits well with Henry George's proposal and is actually far simpler than taxation as a way to collect land rent.

Table 19-1 compares market prices for curb parking and taxes on land values as ways to collect land rent for public purposes. The comparison suggests two important points, the first of which is the nature and source of the revenue. A price for curb parking is a user fee, not a tax, and it is paid by motorists, not landowners. Nevertheless, it has the advantages George ascribed to a land tax. Curb parking fees are paid only by motorists who occupy valuable public land and only in proportion to the time they occupy it. The revenue is a "taking by the community, for the use of the community, of that value which is the creation of the community."[12] Spending the revenue to pay for neighborhood public services is also the "application of the common property to common uses."

The second point is that charging for curb parking is easier than taxing land value. What George said about taxes on land better describes market prices for curb parking:

> There is no necessity of resorting to any arbitrary assessment. The tax on land values, which is the least arbitrary of taxes, possesses in the highest degree the element of certainty. It may be assessed and collected with a definiteness that partakes of the immovable and unconcealable character of the land itself.[13]

Table 19-1. Prices for Curb Parking Compared With Taxes on Land Values

Criterion	Market Prices for Curb Parking	Taxes on Land Values
Revenue source	Rent for the use of publicly owned land	Taxes on the value of privately owned land
Incidence	Drivers who park at the curb	Landowners when tax rates increase
Assessment	Cheap to measure and mark parking spaces Frequent turnover of curb parking spaces Easy to price accurately	Expensive to create cadastral records Rare sales of unimproved land Difficult to assess accurately
Efficiency	Eliminates cruising for free curb parking Reduces traffic congestion and air pollution Eliminates need for off-street parking requirements Reduces the disincentive to improve land	Reduces the disincentive to improve land
Equity	Drivers pay for public space they occupy	Landowners pay for public services

Despite George's optimism, assessing and taxing the value of land is not easy. Many books have been written on the difficulty of assessing land values (such as how to separate the values of land and buildings) and on the difficulty of taxing them (such as whether to tax annual rent or capital values).[14] But curb parking spaces are bare sites, identical except for location, and transacted constantly. They are like rental property with a high tenant turnover and a low transaction cost per new tenant. Curb parking thus resembles a spot market in rented land, which makes it well suited to market pricing. Rental prices can vary by hour of the day, day of the week, and time of the year. Mispricing is immediately obvious: if the price is too high, too many curb spaces will be vacant, while if it is too low, too many will be occupied. The solution is simple in either case: adjust the price. Curb parking can thus become the most efficient land market in any city.

PARKING REQUIREMENTS ACT LIKE A TAX ON BUILDINGS

The shortage of free curb parking fuels the political pressure for off-street parking requirements, which saddle all forms of development with increased costs and therefore increase the prices for everything except parking. Market-price curb parking thus produces another important fiscal benefit: it allows cities to remove off-street parking requirements, which act like a tax on buildings. Parking requirements differ from property taxes in that they are not related to the *value* of buildings, so they do not discourage investment in the quality and durability of buildings. But they do impose a burden in proportion to a building's *floor area*, and we can compare that burden with the ones imposed by impact fees and property taxes.[15]

Parking Requirements as Impact Fees

Many cities require developers to pay impact fees to finance public infrastructure—such as roads and schools—that development makes necessary. Parking requirements resemble these impact fees because cities require developers to provide the on-site parking spaces development supposedly makes necessary. A few cities also allow developers to pay a fee in lieu of providing the required parking; the cities then use the in-lieu revenue to provide public parking facilities. Chapter 9 explains how these in-lieu fees reveal the "parking impact fees" implicit in parking requirements. These impact fees depend on (1) the number of required parking spaces and (2) the cost per space. Table 9-4 in Chapter 9 shows the parking impact fees for one land use—office buildings in the central business district—for a sample of 15 cities in 2002. Palo Alto, with the highest impact fee, requires 4 spaces per 1,000 square feet of floor area, and its in-lieu fee is $50,994 per space. The resulting impact fee is $204 per square foot of office space: developers must pay $204 per square foot not to provide any parking ($50,994 x 4 ÷ 1,000 = $204). The average parking impact fee for all cities in the sample is $46 per square foot of office space. These impact fees may seem high, but they reflect only the cost of *constructing* parking spaces. Parking spaces also have operating costs for cleaning, lighting, repairs, security, insurance, and property taxes. Developers who provide their own spaces may thus pay even more than the impact fees calculated here.[16]

Parking Requirements Compared with Property Taxes

Most in-lieu fees are one-time payments not directly comparable to annual property taxes. The in-lieu parking fees in Montgomery County, Maryland, however, *are* property taxes. Montgomery County has established four "Parking Lot Districts" (Bethesda, Montgomery Hills, Silver Spring, and Wheaton), and in each district it levies a 0.28 percent surcharge on the annual property tax rate. The revenue is used to finance public parking facilities, and together the four districts provide a total of 22,000 public parking spaces. All taxable real property in a district is subject to the surtax, but owners can apply for an exemption by showing they meet the county's minimum parking requirements; that is, properties with the required parking are exempt from the surtax, but all other properties pay it. In effect, Montgomery County has discovered how to impose parking requirements retroactively: all older buildings not meeting current requirements must pay the tax surcharge that finances public parking.

Montgomery County's general property tax rate is 0.741 percent of assessed value. The total tax rate in Parking Lot Districts is 1.021 percent (0.741 + 0.28), so the parking surtax raises the tax rate by 38 percent (0.28 ÷ 0.741).[17] This provides a useful commentary on municipal priorities: the surtax for parking amounts to more than a third of the tax for education, health, libraries, police, social services, and transportation (property taxes are not, of course, the sole source of revenue for these public services). Still, developers pay this surtax for a simple reason: it is cheaper than providing the required parking spaces.[18]

Beyond providing public parking spaces, Montgomery County's in-lieu arrangement creates another benefit: it lets owners who pay the surtax convert their buildings to another use, regardless of the parking requirement for that use. As a result, parking requirements no longer freeze properties into their existing uses, and the new freedom to reuse older buildings has stimulated economic development. The county requires 25 parking spaces per 1,000 square feet of floor area for restaurants, for example, and exemption from this onerous requirement has been credited for the opening of hundreds of new restaurants in Bethesda, Silver Spring, and Wheaton.[19] Anyone who opens a 1,000-square-foot restaurant would obviously prefer to pay a 0.28 percent property tax surcharge than to provide 25 parking spaces in a commercial center with high land values. Willingness to pay the in-lieu fee suggests parking requirements impose a heavier burden on enterprise than does a substantial increase in the property tax rate.

The high tax rates implicit in parking requirements explain their large effects on development. Consider the results shown in the case studies in Chapter 5. Introducing a parking requirement of one space per dwelling unit in Oakland reduced housing density by 31 percent and reduced land values by 33 percent (see Table 5-2). Parking requirements impose major costs on development and distort the markets for both land and buildings. What Henry George said about abolishing taxes on buildings can also be said about abolishing parking requirements: it will remove a burden that "presses down upon every form of industry."[20]

Both property taxes and parking requirements place a burden on buildings, but property taxes at least provide public revenue. What do parking requirements provide? Free parking, which skews transportation choices toward cars, adds to congestion and pollution, and plays a part in many other problems. Henry George warned that property taxes discourage investment in buildings. In effect, parking requirements impose a tax on buildings to subsidize driving, so the harm is even greater.

WHAT WOULD ADAM SMITH SAY
ABOUT CHARGING FOR PARKING?

Although parking fees are user charges, not taxes, we can still evaluate them according to the traditional criteria for judging a tax. Economists from Adam Smith onward have recommended various ways to evaluate the tax structure, but none of their proposals differs greatly from Smith's four maxims:

I.   The subjects of every state ought to contribute towards the support of the government, as nearly as possible, in proportion to their respective abilities.

II. The tax each individual is bound to pay ought to be certain, and not arbitrary. The time of payment, the manner of payment, and the quantity to be paid, ought all to be clear and plain to the contributor, and to every other person.

III. Every tax ought to be levied at the time, or in the manner in which it is most likely to be convenient for the contributor to pay it.

IV. Every tax ought to be so contrived as both to take out and to keep out of the pockets of the people as little as possible, over and above what it brings into the public treasury.[21]

Curb parking revenue excels on all four criteria. Regarding the first criterion (ability to pay), car ownership is strongly correlated with income and those who cannot afford a car do not pay anything. As for the second criterion (certainty and transparency), market prices for parking are certain rather than arbitrary, and the amount, time, and manner of payment are clear to everyone. Regarding the third criterion (convenience), motorists pay small amounts for curb parking throughout the year as they use it, while landowners pay large lump sums once or twice a year. Curb parking revenue also performs well when judged by the last criterion (collection costs). In some cities, the cost of collecting curb parking revenue is only 5 percent of the gross revenue paid by motorists—the other 95 percent goes to the city.[22]

Except that it is a user charge rather than a tax, market-price curb parking is like Henry George on wheels. And because it eliminates cruising, market-price curb parking also saves time for motorists and reduces traffic congestion, air pollution, accidents, and fuel consumption. These nonrevenue benefits of charging for curb parking differ greatly from the nonrevenue costs of taxes that are a drag on the economy. (Several economists have estimated that each extra $1 raised by taxation *increases* other costs in the economy by about 30¢.[23]) User charges for curb parking can thus increase efficiency in two ways: first by reducing the cost of transportation, and second by raising enough revenue so that cities can reduce taxes that distort the incentives to work, save, and invest.[24]

REVENUE POTENTIAL OF CURB PARKING

We can estimate the revenue potential of curb parking in three ways: (1) per curb space; (2) as a share of total land rent; and (3) its ability to finance public improvements.

1. Revenue per Curb Space

The ground beneath our wheels is quite valuable. The average parking meter in Pasadena, for example, yields (after collection costs) $4.70 a day, which is $1,712 a year (see Table 16-1 in Chapter 16). In comparison, the median property tax for owner-occupied housing units in the U.S. was $1,188 in 2001.[25] Many houses have two curb spaces in front, so market-price parking spaces may yield more revenue than the current property tax in some neighborhoods.

The cost to construct off-street parking also suggests the potential revenue from curb spaces. To pay for itself, a parking structure must earn enough to cover the cost of constructing and maintaining the new spaces. In her book *Parking Structures*, Mary Smith estimates the capital-plus-operating cost per space for an unattended aboveground parking garage is at least $5 a day ($150 a month or $1,800 a year).[26] Before a parking structure is built, the nearby curb spaces should therefore be able to earn at least $5 a day.[27]

Because a typical curb space is 160 square feet, the rent per square foot would be $1.25 a year ($1,800 ÷ 160), a very high value for land rent. One curb space yielding $1,800 a year has a capital value of $36,000 if the interest rate is 5 percent ($1,800 ÷ 0.05); that is, if the parking space could be sold, it would be worth paying $36,000 for the right to collect its future revenue.[28] A typical curb space of 160 square feet would have a value of $225 per square foot ($36,000 ÷ 160). To put this value in perspective, a small 5,000-square-foot residential lot valued at $225 per square foot would sell for $1.1 million. An acre of curb parking (272 spaces) would be worth $9.8 million. But curb parking can be worth much more. For example, William Whyte, famous observer of city life, described the high opportunity cost of curb spaces on Lexington Avenue in Manhattan:

> By giving away land to parkers, or renting it for a pittance, cities are squandering some of the most valuable real estate that they have.... For a clue from

the marketplace, consider the case of the Korean wig seller. He used to pay a store owner on Lexington Avenue four hundred dollars a month for using 4 square feet of sidewalk for his wig stand. It wasn't the store owner's space to rent, of course; but as such charges go, it was reasonable, and the wig seller thought the business was worth it. In the curb lane adjacent, a diplomat used to park his Mercedes every weekday. And he parked it all day long. For using 180 square feet of space he paid nothing. If he had to pay at the same rate as the wig seller—one hundred dollars a month per square foot—he would have paid eighteen thousand dollars per month.[29]

A curb parking space may not earn the same rent per square foot as a wig stand, but who would have thought a wig stand could pay so much rent? In any case, Whyte's example shows that free curb parking in Manhattan has a high opportunity cost.

In 2002, a survey of the 28,737 curb spaces in Manhattan south of 59th Street found that only 6,904 (24 percent) were metered, so the untapped revenue potential must be immense.[30] At an average price of only $1 an hour, which is below the price of off-street parking in Manhattan, these parking spaces could earn $250 million a year.

Condominium parking spaces also show curb parking's revenue potential. In 2001, the *New York Times* wrote with amazement about the high price of these spaces in Manhattan and Brooklyn. (See sidebar.) Consider a building on Greenwich Street in TriBeCa, built in 1897 as a lantern fac-

Figure 19-2. The Wig Seller

William Whyte

For Sale: Minimalist Condos, No View

By Edwin McDowell

New York Times, July 29, 2001

It wasn't until Michael Friedman bought a car a year or two after moving from Manhattan back to his native Brooklyn in 1981that he remembered how his schoolteacher father, Louis, had circled the block again and again hoping to find a parking spot on the street. And after he finally found one, he hesitated to move the car from its space rather than repeat the ordeal.

Not so Michael, a lawyer. He parked his car in a garage in his Park Slope neighborhood so that he could come and go when he wanted. But in 1986, with the garage steadily raising its parking rates, he read about a free-standing six-story garage whose parking spaces were to be sold as condominiums. Since buying a parking space essentially meant having it as long as he wanted, Mr. Friedman took out a bank loan and bought one of the condo spaces for $29,000.

"I figured that if you plan to live in the area long enough, you'd come out ahead buying the space," said Mr. Friedman, who with his wife, Ruth Witztum, also a lawyer, has lived in Park Slope almost 20 years. Yet to this day incredulous acquaintances still sometimes ask, "What do you mean, you have a condo for your car?"

They might be more surprised if they knew that instead of driving to his law office in the Empire State Building, he commutes by subway. Or that his car is in the garage most of the time except on weekends. And still more surprised to know that numbers of condominium or co-op parking spaces in New York cost far more than the price Mr. Friedman paid for his.

For example, at 429-35 Greenwich Street in TriBeCa, where an 1897 lantern factory was converted into 28 condo apartments five years ago, the asking price for the 18 indoor condo parking spaces ranges from $45,000 to $80,000. One prospective buyer asked whether the $80,000 space included a new car.

The asking price for one of the 400 outdoor co-op parking spaces at Lincoln Towers on West End Avenue, ranges between $30,000 and $40,000, on the rare occasions that any become available.

In addition to the purchase price, owners of condo parking spaces pay a common charge, which at 429-35 Greenwich Street ranges from $75 to $130. And owners of parking spaces at co-ops pay a monthly maintenance, which at North Shore Towers in Queens ranges from $46 to $103.

But salespeople say that even tenants who are eligible to buy condo or co-op parking spaces are turned off by the cost, saying they would rather continue circling the block each day than pay what they consider a small fortune.

tory that was converted into condominium apartments and parking spaces in 1996. The market prices of the parking spaces range from $45,000 to $80,000, and on top of that the owners pay maintenance charges of $75 to $130 a month. Most people are staggered by these seem-

Figure 19-3. Cars parked free at the curb outside the Brimmer Street Garage in Boston

ingly outrageous prices because, after all, anyone can park free on the street. Small wonder, then, that Manhattan drivers cruise for curb parking: they have a chance to get, free, the most expensive space conceivable for storing a car.

The prices for condominium spaces have been increasing. In 1979, the Brimmer Street Garage on Beacon Hill in Boston became the first free-standing condominium garage in the U.S., with an initial price of $6,500 per space. In 2004, the *Boston Globe* reported that five of the 110 spaces in the garage had recently been sold for prices between $144,500 and $167,500 per space—plus a monthly condo fee of $163 and an annual property tax of $811. At an interest rate of 5 percent a year, these condominium parking spaces cost the owners about $30 a day.[31] In contrast, Boston charges residents nothing for permits to park on the street in "Resident Parking Only" districts. But the city has issued 3,933 resident permits for the 983 curb spaces in the Beacon Hill district, so although nonresidents are excluded, residents are not guaranteed a place to park.[32] The 4-to-1 ratio of permits to curb spaces helps explain why some residents are willing to pay a high price for an off-street space even when curb parking is free.

Market prices for off-street parking spaces are also high in other countries. In 1999, the London *Sunday Times* reported that a former hotel in Knightsbridge was being converted into apartments with prices ranging from £500,000 to £1.75 million. The marketing director said that one underground parking space was available for each apartment: "We're valuing them at £35,000 and selling them separately because not everyone wants one."[33] Small wonder, again, that not everyone wants a parking space when the price is £35,000 ($56,000). But these garage spaces turned out to be a bargain. Reuters news service reported than an underground parking space in Knightsbridge was sold for $177,000 in July 2003.[34]

All these prices pale in comparison to the $1.4 million that comedian Jerry Seinfeld spent to convert an old plumbing store into a garage around the corner from his duplex apartment in Manhattan. He bought the store in 1999, and four years of reconstruction work turned it into a 16-by 52-foot personal garage with room for four or five cars. "The truth about the garage is that I love the Upper West Side," Seinfeld said. "I circled the block every day for the four years it was being built looking for a space. If a spot had opened up anywhere during that time I would have immediately stopped construction."[35]

These examples of market prices for off-street parking in Boston, London, and New York suggest that the revenue from market-price curb parking in older cities can make a big contribution to local public finance. Many small payments, each for a short time, add up to a lot of money.

2. Revenue as a Share of Total Land Rent

A standard curb parking lane is eight feet wide. We can therefore compare the area of a parking lane with the area of the land it fronts. Where property lines extend 160 feet back from the street (a deep lot), curb parking occupies about 5 percent as much space as the property it fronts (8 ÷ 160). Where property lines extend only 100 feet back from the street (a shallow lot), a curb parking lane occupies about 8 percent as much space as the property it fronts. If market-price curb parking yields the same land rent per square foot as the property it fronts, the ribbons of public parking threaded throughout all cities can generate public revenue equivalent to between 5 and 8 percent of total land rent.[36] And because cities can charge for curb parking in front of land exempt from property taxes (such as schools, government buildings, and churches), curb parking can yield public revenue even where the property tax cannot. Curb parking spaces might therefore yield more than 5 to 8 percent of taxable land rent.

This 5 to 8 percent range depends on assumptions that can lead to either an overestimate or an underestimate: an overestimate because not all curb space is available for parking or an underestimate because curb spaces are also available along the sides as well as the front of a block. To obtain a more accurate estimate for one location, I measured the land area devoted to curb spaces surrounding 12 blocks in Westwood Village adjacent to UCLA (see Chapter 14) and compared it with the land area (excluding sidewalks and alleys) within these blocks. The curb parking space equaled 5.1 percent of the private land area.

What share of the curb length in a typical commercial district is available for parking? Studying a random sample of 129 commercial blocks, researchers in Portland, Oregon, recorded the total curb length, the curb length where on-street parking was allowed, and the remaining curb length where parking was prohibited (driveways, bus stops, fire hydrants, loading zones, and the like).[37] On average, only two-thirds of the curb length was available for parking. The researchers also counted the number of marked parking spaces available on each block and estimated the number of cars that could park in the unmarked curb length available for parking. On average, there were 3.3 parking spaces per 100 linear curb feet.

We can use the Portland data to make a rough estimate of the curb parking area surrounding the average city block.[38] The average curb length on one side of a block was 253 feet. If a block is square (253 feet on each side), the total area inside it is 64,000 square feet, and the perimeter available for curb parking is 1,012 linear feet. At 3.3 parking spaces per 100 curb feet, 33 spaces are available on the perimeter. If each curb space is 160 square feet (20 feet long and 8 feet wide), the total curb parking area around the perimeter is 5,280 square feet, which is 8.2 percent of the area inside the block.[39] For every 100 privately owned blocks, then, the city owns adjacent curb parking spaces equivalent to about eight more blocks. If market-price curb parking yields the same rent per square foot as the private property that it fronts, it will yield about 8 percent of total land rent.

The revenue potential of land devoted to curb parking should be at least double that of an adjacent off-street lot. A curb space occupies about 160 square feet while an off-street space often occupies about 320 square feet (160 for the parked car and another 160 for the access aisles). Curb parking thus requires about half the land per space that a parking lot does because it uses land more efficiently; at the same revenue per space, curb parking should therefore yield about twice the revenue per square foot of off-street surface parking. Access to off-street parking also requires curb cuts that remove curb spaces and thus reduces the net increase in the total parking supply. In the extreme, a one-car garage requires a curb cut removing one curb space and yielding no net increase in the parking supply.

Although the limited data suggest curb parking can yield substantial revenue, cities now collect almost nothing. In their survey of parking policies in 20 large metropolitan areas, Kenneth Dueker, James Strathman, and Martha Bianco found that 51 percent of parking meters are located in the Central Business District (CBD); two cities (Houston, Texas, and Portland, Oregon) did not have meters anywhere outside the CBD.[40] Cities therefore charge for only a tiny fraction of their curb spaces and collect only a tiny fraction of the potential land rent.

3. Revenue per Front Foot

Converting the revenue per *parking space* into the revenue per *front foot* shows the surprising ability of curb parking to finance public improvements. If a block has 33 parking spaces on its 1,012-foot perimeter and each space earns $1,800 a year, the block will earn $59,400 a year, or $59 a year per linear front foot.[41] This revenue can pay to clean and repair the sidewalks, plant and trim street trees, and provide other important public services. We can put the buying power of this revenue in perspective by comparing it to the cost of sidewalk replacement. In Los Angeles, the cost of replacing a sidewalk ranges between $10 and $20 per square foot. Only one or two years of parking revenue should therefore be enough to replace a six-foot-wide sidewalk in front of every property.[42] Because many curb spaces should be able to earn $5 a day ($1,800 a year), they can pay for substantial public improvements in their neighborhood.

Demand determines the rent of land, and parking spaces are no exception. Cities can collect whatever revenue the curb spaces produce at the prices needed to manage parking demand, and the added revenue can make the difference between poor and excellent public services in the adjacent neighborhoods. Front-foot finance is particularly appropriate to pay for "linear" public investments, such as sidewalks, streets, sewers, and underground utilities. Charging the right price for curb parking and spending the revenue to provide public services is much more sensible than offering free curb parking and requiring off-street parking spaces everywhere.

DIVISION OF CURB PARKING REVENUE

Although the curb spaces that fringe almost every block amount to between 5 and 8 percent of the land within the block, cities rarely charge for curb parking. Why not? In Chapters 16 and 17, I argued that money fed into a parking meter seems to vanish into thin air: no one knows where the money goes, and everyone wants to park free. Rather than charge for scarce curb parking, cities require off-street parking because hiding a cost is much easier than charging people for it and having the money disappear. But earmarking curb parking revenue to pay for neighborhood public goods will transform the politics that produce free parking. I do not mean earmarking the revenue to pay for a citywide public purpose such as public transit, but rather to pay for public purposes within a parking benefit district. There is a world of difference between feeding a meter and never seeing the money again and having someone else feed the meter to support your neighborhood. If *nonresidents* pay to park and cities spend the money to benefit *residents*, curb parking can become a popular source of public revenue. Residents who form a parking benefit district will be taking out a license to collect land rent.

One of the biggest potential advantages of paid parking is also its biggest weakness. Drivers don't want to pay for curb parking precisely *because* its revenue potential is so high: the more parking costs, the more drivers don't want to pay for it. Only by creating neighborhood interest groups that want the revenue will cities be able to charge the fair-market price for curb parking. Figure 19-4 shows, in a hypothetical case, how the division of curb parking revenue between a city and its neighborhoods can affect the total amount collected. The diagonal line from the lower left to the upper right shows that total parking revenue increases as the city gives a greater share of it to the neighborhoods: increasing the neighborhood's share of the revenue strengthens the political incentive to charge for curb parking. The two lower curves show the revenues that accrue to neighborhoods and the general fund, depending on the share of revenue returned to neighborhoods.

First, consider the lower left corner, which represents the current situation in almost every city: all curb parking revenue goes into the general fund, and nothing goes to the neighborhoods. Paying for parking seems

Figure 19-4. Distribution of Curb Parking Revenue

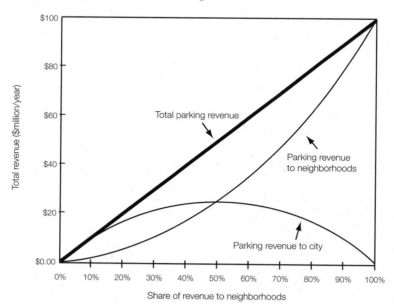

like paying rent to an absentee landlord. Because everyone objects to paying for parking, and no one sees a direct benefit from the revenue, no one supports the idea of charging for curb parking. Instead, everyone wants the city to require off-street parking for every land use so that spillover does not create parking shortages. In some areas the city sets limits on curb parking duration to create turnover, but strict enforcement is difficult and unpopular. If the city keeps all curb parking revenue for the general fund, it collects almost nothing because most people oppose parking meters. Cities in the U.S. collected only $1.43 per capita in net parking revenues in 1997—less than 1/2¢ per person per day—a small share of the enormous potential land rent from curb parking in a nation with 208 million motor vehicles.[43] Taking all curb parking revenue for the general fund is, from the neighborhood's point of view, a 100 percent tax rate that removes the incentive for residents to support charging for curb parking, so it yields almost no revenue. "High taxes, sometimes by diminishing the consumption of the taxed commodities," Adam Smith said, "frequently afford a smaller revenue to the government than what might be drawn from more moderate taxes."[44] So too with curb parking.

Now, consider the upper right corner, which represents the situation where cities return all curb parking revenue to the neighborhoods that generate it. No one wants to pay for parking—that will never change—but residents begin to think like landlords, not tenants, and they agree to form parking benefit districts that charge nonresidents for parking. Business owners also form Business Improvement Districts (BIDs) that use the curb parking revenue to finance public improvements in commercial areas. Because neighborhoods receive the revenue, citizens demand market prices for their curb parking, which in this example yields $100 million a year in new public revenue.[45]

Most curb parking is free because we are to the left side of the figure: all curb parking revenue goes into the general fund, and voters think like tenants, not landlords. Obviously, the curves are only an illustration, and cities do collect a small amount of curb parking revenue (mostly in the CBD), even if they deposit all of it in the general fund. Likewise, cities need not earmark *all* revenue for neighborhoods to generate the political support necessary for curb parking fees. How much cities can take for the general fund without significantly reducing the incentives to charge for curb parking is more a matter of politics than economics.[46] Nevertheless, the record in Pasadena (which returns all revenue to neighborhoods) shows that curb parking can yield substantial new revenue if the city returns it to the neighborhoods generating it.[47]

By itself, analysis that supports charging for curb parking will not go far. Everyone wants to park free, and rational arguments to the contrary are futile. The transportation benefits of market-price curb parking are simply not enough to justify the higher prices that drivers would have to pay. But another major benefit of market-price curb parking is government revenue. Unless the revenue benefits a group who can insist drivers should pay market prices for curb parking, the politics of parking will not change.[48] As Henry George said about the opposition to land value taxation, "It is not ignorance alone that offers opposition, but ignorance backed by interest, and made fierce by passion."[49] The same holds true for opposition to paying for parking. Nevertheless, returning revenue to the metered neighborhoods will create a countervailing interest and incite a passion to charge for parking.

SIMILARITY TO SPECIAL ASSESSMENTS

Many cities use special assessments to finance neighborhood public services. Residents typically petition the city to form assessment districts to pay for sidewalk repairs or street lights, for example, and property owners commonly pay in proportion to their street frontage. Similarly, residents can petition the city to form parking benefit districts to finance neighborhood public services, and curb parking will produce revenue in proportion to street frontage. One big difference between a parking benefit district and a special assessment district is who pays for it: property owners pay special assessments, while nonresident motorists will pay for curb parking.

Special assessment revenues in the U.S. totaled $3.5 billion ($13 per capita) in 1997.[50] One simple use for curb parking revenue is therefore to pay existing special assessments, relieving property owners of the tax burden while continuing to provide public services that have already passed the test of a neighborhood's willingness to pay. Cities have the accounting systems necessary to allocate special assessment revenue for neighborhood public services, so these districts are ready-made recipients for curb parking revenue and would require no changes in cities' standard operating procedures. In effect, a parking benefit district is a kinder, gentler special assessment district.

Special assessment districts are formed only after a community has decided it wants a public service enough to pay for it. The demand for a public service comes first, and the special assessment then finances it. Parking benefit districts lower the bar on a community's willingness to pay because everyone is eager to solve problems at someone else's expense. Even if a community has not yet identified a specific service it wants to finance, it may form a parking benefit district because once the money comes in, the residents can then decide how to spend it. Unlike special assessment districts that are organized around a common desire for a specific public expenditure, parking benefit districts are based on the common ownership of valuable land. The curb parking stays in public ownership, but the city establishes smaller communities to manage their common land. Because all the resulting revenue pays for local public services, these communities are more motivated to manage their land effectively. The city as a whole also benefits if curb parking pays for neighborhood public services because general revenue can instead pay for general public purposes.

PROPERTY VALUES

By solving the curb parking problem and financing public investment, parking benefit districts will improve neighborhoods and increase property values. Even for residents who don't have a parking problem and who don't place a high value on the added public services (such as street trees), the increased property values are an incentive to petition for a parking benefit district. In *The Homevoter Hypothesis*, Dartmouth College economics professor William Fischel says residents tend to "vote their homes" in the sense they consider the effect on the value of their homes when voting on municipal taxes and services. For most homeowners, the equity in their home is their largest asset, so even those who think curb parking should be free may vote to form a parking benefit district if they think the added public services will increase their property value.

Fischel points out that only about a third of American households have any children in public school, yet they vote to tax themselves to support the public schools, in part because good schools increase property values. Homeowners should be even more willing to vote for a parking benefit district because they won't have to pay anything.

AN ANALOGY: CONGESTION PRICING

Market prices for crowded curb parking resemble congestion tolls for crowded freeways because both are needed when demand would otherwise exceed the available capacity. But skeptics often view congestion tolls as a heavy-handed attempt to discourage people from driving during peak periods, and at first glance the tolls do seem unfair because many people have no choice but to drive in rush hours. After explaining the transportation advantages of congestion tolls, Berkeley planning professor Martin Wachs summed up their poor political prospects in a celebrated quote: "In addition to professors of transportation economics and planning—who hardly constitute a potent political force—I can think of few interest groups that would willingly and vigorously fight for the concept."[51] In their analysis of transportation pricing strategies for California,

Elizabeth Deakin and Greig Harvey explain the lack of political support for congestion tolls:

> The political acceptability of a transportation pricing measure will depend in large part on who supports it, who opposes it, and how strongly the respective groups feel about it…. The beneficiaries of pricing often will be harder to mobilize politically than the losers; for example, those who would share the benefits of toll revenues may be a large group but individual benefits may be fairly small. Travelers who place a high value on time may benefit greatly, but these benefits are, at least in advance of tolling, somewhat speculative. Many of the losers, by contrast, will see that they have an obvious and significant stake in opposing tolling, and their numbers may be large.[52]

Congestion tolls may be our single greatest opportunity to increase urban productivity, and their benefits can greatly exceed their costs, but motorists do not receive all the benefits. British transportation economist Philip Goodwin explains that if tolls raise the price of driving and reduce the traffic flow, drivers suffer a net loss:

> There are two groups of drivers—those who are paying more money, only partly offset by extra speed, and those who are now not enjoying a previously uncharged activity. So where is the benefit? The benefit only arises from the revenue which is collected. When it is spent sensibly, it can always generate greater benefit than that sacrificed by the drivers.[53]

Likewise, transportation economists Kenneth Small, Clifford Winston, and Carol Evans say that, aside from the collection costs, the tolls are "simply a transfer of purchasing power with negligible loss of resources."[54] In this transfer of purchasing power, drivers pay the tolls and get speedier travel, but if the government has not yet spent the toll revenue, the full consequences of the tolls *and* the resulting public benefits paid for by the tolls are not yet revealed.

The tolls are a transfer rather than a use of resources, but from the drivers' point of view they are a real cost. On the *receiving* end of this transfer, the toll revenue must provide real benefits to specific groups before anyone will actively support the tolls. If the potential beneficiaries from the toll revenue do not know who they are, they will not organize to support the tolls. To increase political support for congestion tolls, Goodwin proposes a "Rule of Three" for spending the resulting revenue: one-third for public transport improvements, one-third for road improvements, and one-third to increase general public spending or reduce taxes.[55] This proposed distribution of the revenue can create political support because, Goodwin argues, many of the benefits of congestion charges are "locked up" in the revenue collected and are realized only when the revenue is spent, just as many of the benefits of parking charges are realized only when the revenue is spent.[56]

Parking benefit districts suggest a politically promising use for congestion toll revenue. Parking benefit districts create *place-based* voting blocs of residents who want revenue to improve their neighborhoods. In a parking benefit district, the politically important people are the residents who *receive* the revenue, not the drivers who pay it. If neighborhoods retain the revenue they generate, *voters* will want to charge for curb parking. Parking benefit districts thus suggest a "Rule of One," because all parking revenue is spent in the neighborhood that generates it. Can a similar distribution of the revenue create political support for congestion tolls?

A Proposal: Place-Based Claimants for the Toll Revenue

Suppose a state charges tolls on all congested freeways and returns the revenues to the cities through which the freeways pass. With this pattern of revenue distribution, elected officials will want to charge nonresidents for driving through their cities, and the revenue recipients can become a political voice for more efficient transportation pricing.[57]

Consider how this proposal might work in Southern California. If cities receive the revenue, they will become powerful placebound political voices demanding congestion tolls. Cities already have strong lobbies in state legislatures, while many of the older, poorer cities bisected, trisected, and eviscerated by congested highways are in desperate fiscal plights. In Los Angeles County, the average per capita income in the 66 cities *with* freeways is $20,100 a year, and in the 22 cities *without* freeways is $35,100 a year, so congestion tolls will transfer money from richer cities to poorer ones (see Appendix G for a discussion of the distributional effects of congestion tolls). Consider the per-capita incomes in some cities *without* freeways: Beverly Hills ($65,500), Hidden Hills ($94,100), and Rolling Hills ($111,000). And consider the per-capita incomes in some cities *with* freeways: Compton ($10,400), Lynwood ($9,500), and Maywood ($8,900).[58] Congestion tolls can become an efficient, fair, and progressive source of public revenue for the benefitted cities.

Fiscalizing the Freeways

Freeways are an appropriate source of public revenue. Many cities already receive considerable revenue from land uses, such as auto dealerships and big-box retailers, that generate high sales taxes. Particularly since Proposition 13 was passed in California, fiscal considerations strongly influence land-use planning. Because property taxes are limited, cities strive to attract land uses that generate sales tax revenue. Dean

Misczynski, Director of the California State Library Research Bureau, coined the term "fiscalization of land use" to refer to the practice of making zoning decisions based on the resulting tax revenues and public service costs.[59] Cities rezone land to attract these tax generators—often at the expense of housing, manufacturing, and other land uses that do not generate significant tax revenues.

The toll revenue will not lead cities to compete for new freeways but will instead create political support to charge congestion tolls on the existing freeways. Although most transportation experts believe tolls are the only way to significantly reduce traffic congestion, little progress has been made toward adopting them. For example, University of California economist Charles Lave says, "It has been a commonplace event for transportation economists to put the conventional [congestion toll] diagram on the board, note the self-evident optimality of pricing solutions, and then sit down waiting for the world to adopt this obviously correct solution. Well, we have been waiting for 70 years now, and it's worth asking what are the facets of the problem that we have been missing? Why is the world reluctant to do the obvious?"[60] Likewise, Belgian transport economists Edward Calthrop and Stef Proost explain the advantages of pricing strategies in urban transportation but conclude, "Despite clear efficiency advantages, environmental taxes are rarely adopted in the transport sector. This seems strange: if the efficiency gains are waiting to be enjoyed, why do politicians so rarely seem to pursue them?"[61] The answer to this question, I would argue, is that the revenues need effective political claimants, and returning the toll revenue to cities with freeways can create these claimants.

As it turns out, most cities with freeways also have many low-income residents. This is no accident, in part because higher-income residents are successful at fending off noxious land uses. In 1965, for example, California approved the 9.5-mile Beverly Hills Freeway connecting the I-101 in Hollywood to the I-405 in Westwood and running straight through the heart of Beverly Hills. Construction was scheduled to begin in 1975 but never began at all, mainly because the City of Beverly Hills fought the project relentlessly. Prosperous cities that successfully push freeways into poorer cities will have a tenuous claim on the congestion toll revenue. Distributing the revenue to cities with freeways will compensate those who suffer from air and noise pollution, improve public finance in low-income cities, and create political support for congestion tolls. Instead of fiscalizing land use, we can fiscalize the freeways.

Congestion tolls cannot be implemented all at once, but they can be introduced in stages. High Occupancy/Toll (HOT) lanes already allow solo drivers to pay to use High-Occupancy Vehicle (HOV) lanes, and the two HOT facilities in Southern California show the policy is a great success (see Chapter 11). The European Union is planning to use satellite technology to charge congestion tolls on any kind of congested road. If the technology is successful, tolls can be introduced on freeways and surface streets one lane at a time.[62] Congestion tolls—the lowest price that will keep traffic flowing freely—can become a necessary pay-as-you-go fiscal resource for cities.

But let's get back to fiscalizing curb parking. The place-based nature of curb parking revenue helps explain why meter rates are unusually high in London (up to £4 an hour in 2004). The 33 boroughs of London, not the citywide Greater London Authority, receive all curb parking revenue, and these boroughs act like neighborhoods that collect money from outsiders. Residents can park free in their own permit districts, but outsiders must pay to park at the meters. The borough of Westminster in central London, for example, collects more revenue from parking than from property taxes.[63] Similar reasoning may also explain why London was the first large city in Europe to impose congestion tolls on motorists who drive into the center: commuters and visitors pay a toll of £5 a day, while those who live in the city center receive a 90 percent discount.[64] Many of the drivers who pay the toll do not live (or vote) in London, but the city keeps all the revenue, which is a powerful incentive for charging the tolls. If the toll revenue went to the national government rather than to the city, London would undoubtedly still have free, congested roads. Similarly, if curb parking revenue went to the Greater London Authority rather than to the 33 boroughs, London would still have cheaper but overcrowded curb parking.

APPROPRIATE PUBLIC CLAIMANTS

Roads and parking spaces are not the only public property that, through mismanagement, fails to produce significant revenue. Most people are aware of this problem, or at least of its symptoms, because newspapers occasionally report stories about how poor management of a public resource has made some special interests horribly rich. Radio and television stations pay nothing to use the broadcast waves; ranchers pay almost nothing to graze their cattle on federal land; and mining companies extract gold, silver, and other minerals from federal land without paying royalties to the government.[65] No one in particular has a strong incentive to devote time and effort to raising the prices charged for the radio spectrum, grazing lands, or mineral resources because the revenue simply disappears into the federal budget. But the special interests—broadcasters, ranchers, and miners—who directly benefit from underpricing have a strong incentive to lobby in Congress, so the public prices stay low.

Suppose, however, the federal government offered to share revenue from auctioning the radio spectrum with states in which broadcasters are located. Members of Congress would suddenly have a new incentive to charge broadcasters fair-market prices for using the spectrum. The revenue would create effective public claimants willing to fight for auctioning the spectrum because Senators and Representatives could take credit for bringing billions of dollars home to their states. Similarly, the federal government could share the public revenue from grazing and mining with the states and counties where the activities take place. Again, Senators and Representatives would have an incentive to support charging fair-market rents and royalties for using federal land because their own districts would receive a large benefit. This rent-sharing policy will lead state and local representatives to demand more money. In representing the interests of their constituents, members of Congress would see the advantages of market-rate prices, and the federal government's share of the new revenues would also increase.

The rents earned by public resources—from parking spaces to freeways to the radio spectrum—need the right recipients who will demand price reforms, and these right recipients are those for whom the benefits of efficient management are concentrated rather than dispersed. To use a much-maligned term, efficiency requires a special interest. Sharing federal public resource rents with states, counties, and neighborhoods will turn the residents into special interests, who will in turn become political advocates. They will champion public prices to serve the public interest rather than a private interest. As University of Chicago economist Henry Simons put it, "There is nothing seriously wrong with our institution of property or our institutional system save our proclivity to waste time in attacking or defending it and to neglect proper tasks of changing it continuously by wise collective experimentation."[66] If we experiment with sharing the rents from public resources among the right recipients, we can create the necessary political support for price reforms.

PARKING INCREMENT FINANCE

Rent sharing among levels of government may at first glance seem to take money away from the level that now receives it. To return to the case of parking, cities now receive all the meter revenue, and they are understandably reluctant to share it with anyone else. Where curb parking is now free, however, offering to return meter revenue to neighborhoods will not take any existing revenue from the general fund. This helps explain why Pasadena was willing to return all the revenue to Old Pasadena: the city previously had no parking meters anywhere, so it lost nothing. Where cities do charge for curb parking and keep the revenue for the general fund, however, returning any of it to neighborhoods can siphon away money the city is accustomed to receiving. This helps explain why San Diego returns only 45 percent of meter revenue to the neighborhoods: because it already had more than 5,000 meters in the city, sharing the revenue created a short-term loss for its general fund. San Diego's City Manager acknowledged this loss but argued the revenue sharing would encourage neighborhoods to install more parking meters to obtain more revenue for themselves and would eventually increase total revenue to the city (see Chapter 16).

Even a short-term loss to the general fund may deter some cash-strapped cities from returning any meter revenue to the neighborhoods that generate it. In this case, is there any way a city can create parking benefit districts without a cost to the general fund? Yes, if the city returns to neighborhoods only the *increment* in meter revenue—the amount above and beyond the existing meter revenue—that occurs after a parking benefit district is formed. We can call it "parking increment finance."

Parking increment finance closely resembles tax increment finance, which is a popular way to pay for public investment in redevelopment projects: cities allocate to local redevelopment agencies the increment in property tax revenue resulting from the increased property values in their project areas. Similarly, cities can allocate to BIDs the increment in parking meter revenue resulting from increased business activity in their districts.[67] If BIDs receive only the increments in their parking meter revenue, the city will keep all the meter revenue it already collects. BIDs will receive added public services without costing the city or themselves anything, while the guarantee of existing revenue to the general fund can reduce political concerns about assigning revenue to BIDs. Securing agreement to create a BID will be much easier if businesses know every additional dollar of curb parking revenue generated in their district will be reinvested in the area to finance its revitalization. If the parking revenue increment in a district is enough to finance the district's total expenditures, both businesses and the taxpayers will receive a free BID.

Parking increment finance will give BIDs a clear incentive to support installing meters, charging market rates, operating the meters for longer hours, creating more curb spaces with diagonal parking, and ticketing illegally parked cars. Better enforcement alone can substantially increase parking revenue. In a study of parking meter collections, management consultants Buxton Williams and Jon Ross found that, in a typical downtown case, cities collected only 41 percent of the charges that drivers should have paid for the time they spent at parking meters; 59 percent of the total potential revenue was not collected.[68] Broken meters accounted for the loss of 8 percent of potential revenue, while drivers simply failed to pay for 51 percent of the time they were parked at meters. In this case, stricter enforcement and better maintenance of the existing meters could more than double the curb parking revenue.

Parking increment finance differs from tax increment finance in one key aspect: critics argue that tax increment finance diverts to redevelopment districts money that should go to the general fund, or as economist Mason Gaffney put it, "Certain favored groups get the increment while everyone else gets the excrement."[69] Parking increment finance will clearly generate additional revenue, rather than divert existing revenue that would have accrued to the general fund, and because cities now charge nothing for curb parking in most neighborhoods, most parking benefit districts will automatically be parking increment finance districts.

EQUITY

Charging market-rate prices for curb parking is economically efficient, and it may become politically feasible, but is it fair? Many people will initially say no, but they may change their minds after they think about it. After all, the complaint that charging for curb parking is unfair can be made against charging for almost anything. Motorists pay for most other costs of owning and operating a car (gasoline, tires, repairs, insurance, and the vehicle itself), but few see this as unjust.[70] If people pay rent for housing, why shouldn't cars pay rent for parking?

Paying without Parking

To judge whether charging for curb parking is fair, we can compare it with the current alternative—off-street parking requirements that increase the prices of everything else. With off-street parking requirements, even households without cars pay for parking indirectly in the form of higher prices for everything they buy. In contrast, when curb spaces are priced at market rates, only parkers must absorb the cost. Charging for curb parking is thus fairer than imposing off-street parking requirements, especially for those who are too poor to own a car. The *2001 National Household Travel Survey* found that households with incomes less than $25,000 a year are nine times more likely not to own a car than households with incomes greater than $25,000 a year. Similarly, households living in a rented residence are six times more likely than homeowners not to own a car.[71] Because cars are unequally distributed in the population, charging drivers for the curb parking they use is fairer than forcing everyone to pay for off-street parking, even those who do not use it. Parking requirements take money from the poor to subsidize the better-off: drivers park without paying, while nondrivers pay without parking.

I am *not* saying we should pay more for parking. Off-street parking requirements already force everyone, including the carless, to pay too much for parking indirectly. I *am* saying we should pay for parking directly. Cities can *individualize*—decollectivize—the cost of parking, so that we pay less for parking if we use less. While we all want to park free, we should not elevate this wish into a social judgment that charging for curb parking is unfair, especially when we compare it with the alternative—off-street parking requirements that impose a heavy burden even on those with the least ability to pay. Almost everyone will be better off by paying only for the parking they use and *not* paying the high costs off-street parking requirements impose on everyone.

Paying for Parking

Skeptics may assume that paying for parking directly will ruthlessly segregate drivers by income and will harm the poor by reserving the best spaces for the rich. But the parking-location model in Chapter 18 shows several factors affect choices about where to park: parking duration, the number of people in the car, and the value drivers place on saving time for a specific trip. Drivers value time savings differently from one trip to another, and market-priced parking gives travelers a trip-specific, spur-of-the-moment ability to place a high value on their time. Poor people can be in a hurry, and drivers who cannot always afford to park in the best spaces can still choose to park in them on occasions when saving time is particularly important. Conversely, everyone can save on parking if they are willing to carpool, spend time walking, or ride public transit. Market prices will make curb parking spaces readily available for everyone, everywhere, all the time, so drivers can always choose where to park. Many people get upset when they can't find a place to park even if they are willing to pay for it, so they may feel that market-rate parking is better than free parking if it means they can always find a space. Market-priced curb parking will thus serve as a safety net drivers can use when they are in a hurry and an important trip is at stake.

In a similar vein, the cruising-for-parking model in Chapter 13 shows underpriced curb parking does not automatically benefit the poor. The same factors that influence the decision where to park also influence the decision whether to cruise. Someone who is in a hurry or has a car full of impatient people willing to split a parking fee is less likely to spend time circling the block. Again, income is only one of several factors that affect the value of saving time on a particular trip, and the same person can make different choices on different days. Because factors other than the value of time affect the willingness to cruise for parking, cruising does not automatically allocate free curb parking spaces to poor people. In other words, free curb parking is *not* an effective way to help the poor, especially because many of the poorest people cannot afford cars. Elderly, poor residents who travel very little pay for parking they don't use, while younger, richer, and more mobile residents use parking they don't pay for. Charging for curb parking may make a few of the poorest *drivers* worse off, even when the added public services financed by the revenues are taken into account, but it will make most of the poorest *people* better off.

Assuming the rich will monopolize market-priced parking spaces seems intuitive, but the fear is exaggerated. To examine how the price of curb parking affects the demography of curb parkers, Peter Clinch and Andrew Kelly at University College Dublin interviewed slightly more than 1,000 curb parkers before and after the price of curb parking was raised by 50 percent (to €1.90 per hour, which was still slightly lower than the cost of off-street parking) in the center of Dublin in 2001. One surprising change observed after the price rise was a 19 percent increase in the share of curb parkers who were women.[72] The average parking duration fell by 17 percent after the meter prices increased, durations longer than three hours fell by 39 percent, and durations of one-to-two hours increased by 32 percent. Perhaps because the turnover rate increased, the number of curb parkers who had cruised for 11 minutes or longer before finding a curb space also declined by 28 percent. The most surprising change was a 24 percent decline in the share of curb parkers who were in the highest social class. Who took their spaces? The upper middle class: their share increased by 24 percent.[73] The age profile of curb parkers did not change at all. In summary, raising the meter rate by 50 percent reduced the number of upper class males who parked at the curb, reduced the average parking duration, and reduced the cruising time needed to find a curb space. Who can object to these results on the grounds that charging for curb parking is unfair?

When High Occupancy/Toll (HOT) lanes were first proposed in California, critics contended they would become the exclusive province of the rich—"Lexus lanes," as California Senator Tom Hayden dubbed them. After the HOT lanes opened, however, Fords and Chevrolets were far more common than a Lexus. A variety of people use the lanes for a variety of reasons, and most people who travel in the HOT-lane corridors think the tolls are fair. In one survey, 84 percent of respondents said the HOT lanes are fair to the drivers who use them, and 80 percent said they are fair to those who do *not* use them.[74] Another survey showed the Lexus-lane concerns are not widely shared: 91 percent of those surveyed think the time-savings options provided by the HOT lanes are a "good idea," and 66 percent of drivers who do not use them support them. Eighty percent of the lowest-income motorists using the HOT lanes agreed with the statement, "People who drive alone should be able to use the I-15 Express Lanes for a fee."[75] The lowest-income users were more likely to support this statement than were the highest-income users, which suggests "Lexus liberals" are the ones who worry most about Lexus lanes. By extension, if neighborhoods can keep the curb parking revenue they generate, people of all incomes will probably agree that charging nonresidents the market price for curb parking is also fair.

Even egalitarians should recognize that equality does not mean parking should be free. Gasoline is a basic necessity for cars, but this does not mean gasoline should be free. Filling stations offer different grades of gasoline (with both self service and full service) at different prices, and this is not unfair. Parking spaces differ from one another chiefly in location, and different prices in different locations are likewise not unfair. Parking is a basic necessity for cars, but drivers who cannot find a free parking space do not deserve the same sympathy as the homeless. Hotel rooms are a basic necessity for tourists, but this does not mean cities should require free hotels everywhere. If cities established minimum hotel requirements to meet the demand for free hotel rooms, they would soon need the help of tourism demand management consultants. Camping or staying with relatives would come to be called "alternative accommodation," just as walking and cycling are now called "alternative transportation," without the need for anyone to ask "alternative to what?" Because solo driving is the norm, anything else is alternative—deviant?—transportation.

Minimum hotel requirements and free rooms are absurd, of course, because it is hard to imagine hotels could operate satisfactorily without charging guests. If cities priced parking spaces like hotel rooms, the parking industry would come to resemble the hospitality industry. Parking prices would vary by time and location, and the similarity doesn't end there. Many cities impose "transient occupancy taxes," a euphemism for taxes on hotel guests. These are politically popular taxes for good reason. Any tax paid by nonresidents is popular with voters, and nonresident curb parkers are the ultimate transient occupants. If transient occupancy taxes are fair for tourists, they should also be fair for motorists.

The economic, environmental, and equity implications of charging market prices for curb parking are even clearer in developing countries where the parking problems are more severe and most car owners are affluent. In Istanbul, for example, the *Chicago Tribune* reports:

> This city of 15 million has nearly doubled in population in the past decade and has an oversupply of honking horns and a shortage of parking spaces to go

with it. Drivers desperately seeking a place to park leave their cars in other people's yards, at bus stops and sometimes, when the search becomes too much, right in the middle of a busy street. People try gamely to protect parking spots with ramshackle chairs and removable steel posts. The problem has created a whole cottage industry, something residents call "the parking mafia." Affluent people hire guards to patrol the street in front of their villas and apartment buildings. Any business hoping to succeed—from a grocery store to a tanning salon to a tea garden—provides valet parking through the parking mafia. Such is the demand for slots in this overcrowded city that authorities say ad hoc parking barons have begun systematically burning buildings, claiming large numbers of the distinctive Ottoman-era wooden houses that provide character to residential areas.[76]

Market prices can certainly be used to manage curb parking demand and tame traffic in cities like Istanbul. Spending the revenue to provide basic public services, such as piped water, sewers, and sidewalks, will produce great benefits, largely at the expense of the car-owning elite. Because cities can borrow against the future stream of curb parking revenue, they can finance major public improvements in a short time.[77]

Regardless of a nation's income and culture, the politics of charging for curb parking are similar all over the world. Taraknath Mazumder of the Indian Institute of Technology says, "Most of the present decision-making regarding on-street parking in India relies on intuition and public opinion."[78] This situation may never change, but parking benefit districts will create new economic incentives that can change both intuition and public opinion because residents will see they personally benefit from market-priced curb parking. The changes in public opinion can then lead to better public policies for parking and transportation.

Lifeline Pricing

To ensure equity in curb parking, cities can offer "lifeline" credits for lower-income households, similar to the lifeline pricing arrangements for electricity and telephone service. For example, cities can give each low-income citizen a minimum parking credit without charge.[79] These credits will guarantee at least a minimum level of access, and those who don't own a car can use their credit to pay for parking when drivers offer them a ride. Because the city will charge for curb parking that was formerly free, the lifeline credits will not require a cash outlay. Instead, they will transfer income from those who own cars to those who don't. Charging market prices for curb parking and offering lifeline credits to the poor is fairer than requiring off-street parking everywhere.

Cities can also give lifeline credits to help disabled drivers who need to park close to their destinations. By creating a few vacancies everywhere, market-priced curb parking will improve access for the disabled because able-bodied drivers will never "need" to park in spaces reserved for the disabled. Because business owners and residents in a parking benefit district will lose revenue when a driver misuses a disabled placard to park free at the curb, they will actively support ticketing for this despicable behavior. As it is now, disabled placards are so widely misused, and detection of a violation is so difficult, the chance of actually getting a ticket is so low that even high fines for violations do not prevent misuse. In parts of Los Angeles, for example, so many disabled spaces are fraudulently occupied that legitimate users of disabled placards cannot find a parking space.[80] Reducing illegal parking in disabled spaces thus represents yet another advantage of charging the right price for curb parking and returning the revenue to neighborhoods.

Revenue Sharing

Charging for curb parking is fairer than requiring off-street parking, but will the resulting pattern of public spending also be fair? Suppose a rich neighborhood earns considerable curb parking revenue from nonresidents, while a poor neighborhood in the same city cannot earn anything because few nonresidents want to park there. The rich neighborhood will have plenty of money to spend on its public services, but the poor neighborhood will get nothing. This seems unfair, but it may also be uncommon, because the rich usually live far from land uses that create spillover parking. Still, many poor families also live in neighborhoods with no prospect of earning much curb revenue, and some rich people live at high densities on streets (such as Fifth Avenue or Wilshire Boulevard) that can earn substantial revenue. In these cases, a form of revenue sharing can counteract the potential for inequities in spending patterns. As described in Chapter 17, the city of San Diego shares parking meter revenue with its neighborhoods: 55 percent of the revenue goes to the city's general fund, and 45 percent goes to the neighborhoods that generate it. Revenue sharing can thus be used to redistribute income without breaking the link between curb parking and public services in a neighborhood. All neighborhoods will have an incentive to charge market prices for curb parking, but even the neighborhoods that cannot earn sufficient revenue will benefit.

Takings and Givings

Charging for curb parking that was formerly free may seem to be a "taking" by the community, but this is unfair only if motorists are assumed to have a private right to public property without payment. Motorists have not earned a right to park free, so it is more appropriate to think of free parking as a "giving" than of charging for parking as a taking. The giving, not the taking, needs justification. Why should the community give public land to motorists for their private use without any payment? Motorists pay gasoline taxes for the roads, but only when their cars are moving, not when they are parked, and motorists pay less in gasoline taxes the longer they park.

Charging for curb parking is less controversial than taxing land. The argument for taxing land rests on the idea that increments in land value are created by the community rather than by individuals, and therefore represent a less-than-legitimate source of private income. Charging for curb parking, in contrast, does not require an assertion of public rights in private land. On the contrary, it merely requires a reassertion of public rights (as opposed to private motorists' rights) to public land. Cities own curb parking and have the right to collect its full rental value, just as the owner of a private parking lot has the right to collect its full rental value. This is not to say Henry George was wrong in his views that the public should tax private land values, but rather that charging for curb parking is much easier to explain and defend. San Francisco State University political scientist Louis Wasserman says:

> The full single tax is not a serious fiscal proposal today, if only because there are no political prospects for its adoption anywhere on a national scale. But George's central principle—that the incidence of taxation should bear on the value of land rather than upon productive enterprise and improvements— remains a lively issue of fiscal reform.... What is typically sought by land taxers today is a modest advance along Georgist lines.[81]

A community can legitimately charge motorists who park their cars on scarce public land, and the result will be a modest advance along Georgist lines.

Biased Analysis

Most arguments in favor of market-price parking stress efficiency rather than equity. British transportation economist Gabriel Roth, for example, meticulously explained how market prices can efficiently allocate curb parking in his 1966 monograph, *Paying for Parking*. One would expect other economists to appreciate this point, but an unsigned review in the *Economic Journal* revealed a visceral prejudice against the idea:

> A solution to the parking problem, which is part of the wider urban road traffic congestion problem, is seen in terms of the free operation of the price mech-

anism without subsidy from local authorities or any other public body. No element of collective need is recognised; the doctor has to outbid all comers for a space to park outside his own surgery and, presumably, outside his patients' houses whenever the need arises. Consideration is not given to social costs and benefits, nor is it suggested that any should be given.[82]

This haughty, self-righteous dismissal of market-priced curb parking was written so long ago that doctors still made house calls "whenever the need arises," but is timeless in its easy assumptions that the "social costs and benefits" preclude using the "price mechanism" and the "collective need" for parking automatically justifies a "subsidy from local authorities." But free curb parking creates huge social costs in the form of traffic congestion, air pollution, and energy consumption. Free curb parking also creates the political demand for off-street parking requirements that increase prices, reduce density, and degrade urban design. Market-priced curb parking will reduce these social costs and will produce public revenue rather than require a public subsidy. Efficiency *and* equity are thus both good reasons to charge for curb parking.

Most arguments for free parking probably stem more from unenlightened self-interest than from a concern for social justice. In *Great Cities and Their Traffic*, J. Michael Thomson explained how unacknowledged self-interest can lead to a biased analysis of urban transportation problems:

> When approaching the subject of urban transport there is a danger of starting off with preconceived ideas and unconscious value judgments. Anyone concerned with the subject will have had years of personal experience as a *user* of urban transport; he will have acquired his own angle or viewpoint which, if not recognized, may lead to a biased analysis and assessment of the problem.

> Most of the people professionally responsible for urban transport are car owners and drive to their offices every day. The most powerful transport authorities are usually highway engineering departments occupying premises provided with free parking space to which most of the senior staff commute by car. The senior managers of public transport companies are more likely to arrive by car than by any one of their buses. And one of the first tasks of a team of consultants engaged to undertake an urban transport study is to acquire a fleet of private cars. It is beyond dispute that most important decisions affecting urban transport are made by people whose personal viewpoint of the problem is largely behind the wheel of a car.[83]

Drivers rarely think parking is too cheap or too plentiful, and if policy makers view the parking problem from behind the wheel of a car, what looks good for drivers probably looks good for society as well. Because motorists make most of society's decisions about transportation and land-use policy, "collective need" somehow justifies free parking. Policy makers have had years of personal experience as *users* of parking; they have acquired their own personal viewpoint that can lead to a biased analysis of the parking problem and to bad public policy.

A Precedent: Pay-as-You-Go Income Taxes

Charging for curb parking may seem like a radical way to pay for public services, but other fiscal reforms once considered radical now seem only commonsense. Consider the precedent of deducting income taxes from workers' paychecks. In *Washington Goes to War*, David Brinkley relates the strong liberal opposition to payroll withholding of income taxes. Before World War II, people paid taxes in quarterly installments on the income they had earned during the previous year. After the war began, income tax rates rose dramatically, but revenues lagged a year behind. The Chairman of the New York Federal Reserve Bank, Beardsley Ruml, conceived a solution: "pay as you go" he called it. Workers would pay taxes on income as they earned it, with the money deducted from their paychecks before they ever saw it. A problem with this scheme, however, disturbed liberals: "To begin a new year cleanly with a pay-as-you-go system," Ruml argued, "it would be necessary to forgive taxes for the previous year. Otherwise, people would have to pay two years of taxes in one year, an impossible burden for many."[84] But liberals believed that giving rich people a year's tax amnesty was unconscionable, especially in wartime. Brinkley explains the strong opposition:

> Liberals continued to balk. "The true content of the proposal," one opponent claimed, was simply to "make the rich richer and the poor poorer." And the president continued to promise to veto any bill that contained a tax-forgiveness clause.... Everyone agreed that the tax system was not working. Everyone (including the president) agreed that the pay-as-you-go system would work better. But bitter disagreements over a one-time (and largely imaginary) "windfall" for the wealthy had brought the whole process to a halt. Finally, Congress produced a bill that included a year's forgiveness for lower-income people, and only a partial forgiveness for the wealthy. The president did not mind that at all. He signed it. It took effect on July 1, 1943.
>
> The prolonged battle over the immediate effects of the plan had, apparently, prevented anyone from looking closely at the potential long-range results. For Beardsley Ruml...had produced a revolution in American public finance. When people became accustomed to paying taxes as they had always paid for automobiles—on the installment plan—Congress and the president learned, to their pleasure, what automobile salesmen had learned long before: that

installment buyers would be induced to pay more because they looked not at the total debt but only at the monthly payments. And in this case there was, for government, the added psychological advantage that people were paying their taxes with money they had never even seen. The term "take-home pay" now entered the language.[85]

Payroll withholding of income taxes is now so ingrained that the early opposition on the grounds it would harm the poor seems almost unbelievable. In the same way, once communities have begun to enjoy public services paid for by curb parking, opposition to charging for parking on the grounds it would harm the poor may in the future seem just as unbelievable. "Pay as you park" is fairer than our current system of paying without parking and parking without paying.

OPPORTUNITY COST OF CURB PARKING

Governments typically follow one of two approaches toward pricing public services: (1) price at cost, regardless of the market, or (2) price at market, regardless of the cost.[86] Free curb parking exemplifies the first approach because there is no obvious cost to cover. Market-price curb parking exemplifies the second approach: the price is determined by demand, not by cost. Curb parking can generate considerable revenue for a city because the market price of parking can greatly exceed the cost of collecting the revenue and maintaining the spaces. The cost of collecting the curb parking revenue does not increase the market price of curb parking but is instead subtracted from the gross revenue to yield the net revenue.

Aside from the cost of collecting the revenue and maintaining the road space, curb parking has an opportunity cost—the other possible uses of the space devoted to idle cars. Both sides of every road need not be used for parking, and many constituencies vie for the land. Pedestrians want wide sidewalks. Cyclists want bike lanes. Drivers want road space. Residents want street trees. Restaurants want sidewalk tables. Curb parking competes with all these other uses, so it can have a high opportunity cost. Cities take this into account when they prohibit curb parking on some streets during peak traffic hours because the roadway is too valuable to use as a parking lane.[87] Market prices for curb parking will reveal how much drivers think the curb spaces are really worth and will therefore help cities compare the value of a parking lane with the value of a wider sidewalk or an additional lane for cars or bicycles. As William Vickrey said, "The only objection to the use of a given space by a given individual is that he may thereby be depriving someone else of the privilege of using it."[88] The market-clearing price of parking reveals one oppor-

Figure 19-5. Sidewalks and street trees in Palo Alto

tunity cost of a parking space—the price other motorists are willing to pay for it. If cities charge market-clearing prices for their curb parking spaces—prices just high enough to create a few vacancies on every block at all times—these prices will show the value of a curb parking space. Knowing the value of the curb spaces can then help cities make informed judgments about the highest and best use of their valuable real estate. Cities may choose to eliminate a few parking spaces in popular pedestrian precincts, widen the sidewalks, and add room for sidewalk cafés or even wig stands. Palo Alto, California, for example, plants street trees in the parking lane rather than on the sidewalks, and widens the sidewalks at the intersections to make pleasant seating areas. A few curb parking spaces are lost, but the sidewalks are more inviting and pedestrian crossings at the intersections are easier.[89]

ECONOMIC DEVELOPMENT

Beyond their effects related to efficiency and equity in the transportation sector, parking benefit districts will also shift final demand from private consumption to local public investment, and this shift will alter the demand for different kinds of labor. Public spending for neighborhood public goods will create more jobs in the local economy than does private consumption because more of the goods and services that go into local public investment are produced locally rather than imported from outside the region.

To investigate this question, I have used a model of the Southern California economy to estimate how parking benefit districts will affect local employment and income. The Southern California Planning Model (developed by the Lusk Center Research Institute of the University of Southern California) is a 515-sector input-output model of the economy of Los Angeles, Orange, Riverside, San Bernardino, and Ventura Counties.[90] The model estimates not only the direct effects created by final demand, but also the indirect and induced effects created by intersectoral linkages. The model thus makes it possible to estimate the net effects of reducing private consumption and increasing public investment.

Spending money to repair sidewalks, for example, will divert resources from local private consumption to investment in local public infrastructure. Suppose parking benefit districts spend $1 million a year to repair their sidewalks, and motorists who pay for parking correspondingly reduce their other private consumption expenditures by $1 million a year. The effect of reducing private consumption is estimated by reducing the final demand for each consumption category in proportion to its share of consumption found in the *Consumer Expenditure Survey* conducted by the Bureau of Labor Statistics. The effect of increasing public investment in sidewalks is a bit more difficult to estimate because the input-output matrix, although highly disaggregated, does not have a specific category for spending on sidewalks. The closest analogy in the matrix is spending on roads, which seems similar in its labor and material demands to spending on sidewalks. The effect of increasing investment in sidewalks is therefore approximated by increasing the final demand for roads.

Table 19-2 shows the results of shifting $1 million a year from local private consumption to local public investment. The first row shows private consumption and public investment change by equal and opposite amounts, so there is no net change in final demand.

The second row shows raising public investment by $1 million a year will increase local wages by $840,000 a year. Lowering private consumption by $1 million a year, on the other hand, will reduce local wages by only $446,000 a year. Shifting final demand from private consumption to public investment will therefore increase total local wages by $394,000 a year ($840,000 – $460,000). Why is the net increase in local wages so dramatic? Local workers construct sidewalks, while many private consumption goods—such as cameras, cars, and clothes—are imported from outside the region, or even the country. Almost all the new jobs created for sidewalk construction will therefore be local, while many of the jobs lost from reduced private consumption will be offshore.[91]

The third row shows reducing private consumption by $1 million a year will eliminate 18 local jobs but increasing public investment by $1 million a year will create 22 local jobs. Therefore, the shift in final demand from private consumption to public investment will create four new local jobs. Why does the spending shift increase total wages by $349,000 a year but create only four new jobs? As the fourth row shows, the jobs eliminated as a result of reducing private consumption pay an average wage of $24,900 a year, while the jobs created by increasing public investment pay an average wage of $39,100 a year. In other words, not only does the shift from private consumption to public investment create 20 percent more jobs than it eliminates, but the created jobs also pay an average wage that is 57 percent higher than the eliminated jobs.[92]

The last row shows that local tax revenue will increase by $33,000 a year. This occurs because the shift in final demand toward local production stimulates taxable economic activity in the five-county region. Therefore, in this example, parking benefit districts will increase local tax revenue by 3 percent of the final demand they divert from private consumption to public investment.

These figures are rough approximations rather than precise estimates, and the results will vary depending on the specific public spending parking benefit districts choose to finance. Nevertheless, the logic is clear. By shifting demand from private consumption to public investment, parking benefit districts will make cities more prosperous.

In addition to improving the economies of cities, removing off-street parking requirements and increasing the price of parking can improve the national economy as well. We don't import parking spaces, but free parking increases the domestic demand for our two biggest imports: cars and fuel. In 2001 the U.S. imported $293 billion of motor vehicles and petroleum, accounting for 26 percent of total imports.[93] Because higher prices for parking will reduce the demand for cars and gasoline, they can sig-

Table 19-2. Local Effects of Shifting $1 Million from Private Consumption to Public Investment

	Private consumption	Public investment	Net increase
	(1)	(2)	(3)=(2)-(1)
Spending	-$1,000,000	+$1,000,000	$0
Wages	-$446,000	+$840,000	+$394,000
Jobs	-18	+22	+4
Wages/Job	$24,900	$39,100	+$14,200
Taxes	-$38,000	+$71,000	+$33,000

Source: Calculated by the Southern California Planning Model developed at the Lusk Center Research Institute of the University of Southern California. The local area consists of Los Angeles, Orange, Riverside, San Bernardino, and Ventura Counties.

nificantly reduce both imports and the trade deficit. Quite aside from this financial benefit, reduced gasoline consumption will reduce our national insecurity related to dependence on foreign oil.

MONOPOLY, FREE PARKING, AND HENRY GEORGE

Children first learn about free parking, city planning, and the economy when they play Monopoly. After throwing the dice, players move around the board and buy property, build hotels, go to jail, or park free. The players learn about being tenants when they land on another player's property and have to pay rent. They learn about being landlords when another player lands on their property and they collect rent. They learn about being owner-occupiers when they land on a property they have bought. They learn about investing when they take out mortgages to build houses. They learn about urban renewal when they remove houses to build hotels. And finally they learn about bankruptcy because the game ends when every player but one is bankrupt. But Monopoly misleads its players about two important features of the economy and city planning. The first is inflation because Monopoly's prices have remained the same since 1935. The second is off-street parking requirements because Monopoly doesn't have them.

Off-street parking requirements have a history similar to that of Monopoly, which ended up wholly different from how it started out. According to legend, Charles Darrow, an unemployed engineer in Philadelphia, invented Monopoly during the Great Depression. He sketched the game on his kitchen table, named the properties after streets in Atlantic City, made the houses and hotels from scrap lumber, used colored buttons for the tokens, and later sold the game to the Parker Brothers company for a fortune. But Monopoly has a much longer history, with links to Henry George. Elizabeth Magie, a single-tax advocate, patented a game similar to Monopoly in 1904. Called The Landlord's Game, it was meant to show the evil of land monopolies and was avidly played in the economics departments at Ivy League universities. In her patent renewal in 1924, Magie stated:

> The object of the game is not only to afford amusement to the players, but to illustrate to them how under the present or prevailing system of land tenure, the landlord has an advantage over other enterprises and also how the single tax would discourage land speculation.[94]

The Landlord's Game was more political and educational than fun, but players gradually changed its rules, abandoning the high-minded focus on land value taxes and instead emphasizing the thrill of land monopo-

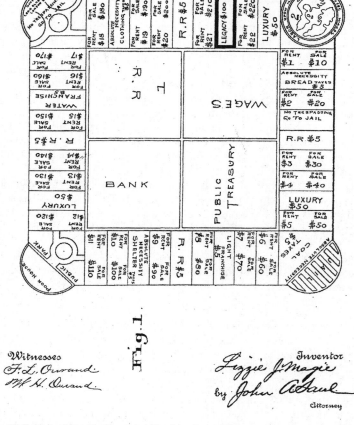

No. 748,626.

L. J. MAGIE.
GAME BOARD.
APPLICATION FILED MAR. 23, 1903.

NO MODEL.

PATENTED JAN. 5, 1904.

2 SHEETS—SHEET 1.

Figure 19-6. Patent applications for The Landlord's Game (this page) and Monopoly (opposite page)

Dec. 31, 1935.

C. B. DARROW

2,026,082

BOARD GAME APPARATUS

Filed Aug. 31, 1935

7 Sheets—Sheet 1

lies. By the time Darrow patented Monopoly in 1935, the game's purpose had shifted dramatically. Far from being an indictment of land monopolies, it now celebrated them; what had been condemned somehow became the goal. Along the way, the Georgist rhetoric in Magie's game was purged as well. The starting corner changed from "Labor upon Mother Earth Produces Wages" to "GO," while the corner opposite it changed from "Public Park" to "Free Parking." These changes from The Landlord's Game to Monopoly during the early twentieth century mirrored the decline of interest in land value taxation and the shift of interest from public parks to parking lots. People wanted free parking more than they wanted the single tax.

Monopoly looks nothing like what Elizabeth Magie intended, and in accepting what we have, we rarely stop to think about what we've lost. The same is true of free parking, which was originally intended to help cities but is now seen as an inalienable right around which we plan our cities at the expense of everything else. Because motorists don't pay for parking, society at large must pay for it in other ways—traffic congestion, air pollution, energy consumption, degraded design, urban sprawl, and the high opportunity costs for land. Every place we have to put a car is a place we could have put something else. When it comes to parking, we've forgotten land is not free.

Cities missed a great opportunity to collect land rent when cars created the demand for curb parking. The parking meter was invented in the same year Monopoly was patented (1935) so the means to charge for curb parking have long been available. But even reformers who demand confiscatory taxes on land do not want to pay for parking. At a Georgist conference, I once recommended market prices for curb parking as a way to collect land rent, and a prominent single-taxer wrote to me: "I hate to pay for parking." But Georgists don't need to advocate market prices for curb parking in order for the idea to succeed. If neighborhoods retain the curb parking revenue they generate, *voters* will advocate market prices for curb parking.

Charging for curb parking is a modest reform compared with taxing all land rent, and this is an advantage. Williams economics professor Roger Bolton argued land value taxation failed to gain acceptance because Henry George was too extreme:

> George's excessive enthusiasm in two respects—that all rent should be taxed and that governments should trust completely to a single tax on land—got in the way of his acceptance by professional economists. They also helped blind later generations to the possibilities of a modest increase in rent taxes as a substitute for other more objectionable taxes.[95]

Similarly, Robert Andelson and Mason Gaffney explained that much contemporary criticism of Henry George was "directed against the *single* tax, not against land-value taxation as merely one component of a public revenue system."[96] Charging for curb parking is a modest rather than a sweeping proposal, and if cities spend the resulting revenue to pay for neighborhood public goods, residents will see that charging market-rate prices for curb parking can improve transportation, land use, and public finance.

CONCLUSION: THE REVENUE IS UNDER OUR CARS

Free curb parking creates a classic commons problem, with many resulting pathologies. The "shortage" of curb parking causes cruising and creates the demand for off-street parking requirements, which then distort the markets for both transportation and land. In contrast, market-priced curb parking will reduce traffic congestion, air pollution, and energy consumption caused by cruising and also make curb parking more convenient. Eliminating the need for off-street parking requirements will, in turn, reduce development costs, make the land market more efficient, and improve urban design. Finally, the revenue from curb parking will either improve public services or reduce taxes that distort the economy, or both.[97]

With all these potential dividends, why is curb parking an insignificant source of public revenue? I offer two reasons. First, because off-street parking requirements hide the cost of parking in higher prices for everything else, most people have been fooled into thinking free parking really is free. Second, because no one seems to receive the money drivers put into parking meters, market-price curb parking lacks a political constituency. Planners and politicians therefore find it easier to require off-street parking than to charge for curb parking.

Cities can create the necessary political support for market-price curb parking if they return the resulting revenue to the neighborhoods—the parking benefit districts—that generate it. Every city has a few neighborhoods that are obvious candidates for parking benefit districts, and the idea can spread by example. When one neighborhood begins to finance public improvements from curb parking revenue paid by nonresidents, other neighborhoods will see the advantages and can petition for a similar arrangement. Cities can thus convert parking problems into public revenue. As Henry George predicted for land value taxation, market-priced curb parking can contribute to progress and help reduce poverty.

Parking benefit districts cannot, by themselves, completely solve the parking problem nor should we expect them to. No single proposal can solve a problem that creates so many conflicting interests and opinions.

Staunch conservatives often become ardent communists when it comes to parking, and rational people quickly turn emotional. Nevertheless, parking benefit districts offer a practical strategy to improve transportation and land use and to generate substantial public revenue. Curb parking will remain community property, but each community will be small enough to encourage efficient management. Market-price curb parking will also allow cities to remove the off-street parking requirements that place a heavy burden on all real estate development, a burden ultimately passed along to consumers in the form of higher prices for everything except parking.

If we continue to do what we've always done with curb parking, we will continue to get what we now have—the "parking problem," with all its ramifications. Fortunately, we can resolve this problem if we: (1) charge market prices for curb parking; (2) return the revenue to finance neighborhood public improvements; and (3) remove off-street parking requirements. No other source of public revenue can so easily bring in so much money and simultaneously improve transportation, land use, and the environment. All things considered, land rent from market-priced curb parking is an ideal source of local public revenue.

CHAPTER 19 NOTES

1. George (1879 [1938], 421).

2. George (1879 [1938], 434).

3. Most economists at first opposed George's ideas. Edwin Seligman of Columbia University declared, "Neither the American people nor the scientific student of finance will ever accept a scheme which is palpably unjust...and which seeks to put the burdens of the many on the shoulders of the few" (Cord 1965, 30). Seligman's argument assumes that only a few people own land, or at least that a large share of total land value is concentrated among the few. George considered the disdain he received from economists to be less an indictment of his ideas and more an illustration of their profession's failings. In his last book, *The Science of Political Economy*, he argued that economists opposed land value taxation because they were biased toward the interests of the rich and were increasingly influenced by schools of thought "admirably calculated to serve the purpose of those powerful interests dominant in the colleges...that must fear a simple and understandable political economy, and who vaguely wish to have the poor boys who are subjected to it by their professors rendered incapable of thought on economic subjects.... It is to this state that political economy in the teachings of the school, which profess to know all about it, has now come" (George 1898, 189).

4. Smith (1776 [1937], 795). John Stuart Mill (1965, 825) made a similar observation: "A tax on rent falls wholly on the landlord. There are no means by which he can shift the burthen upon anyone else.... A tax on rent, therefore, has no effect, other than its obvious one. It merely takes so much from the landlord, and transfers it to the state."

5. Blaug (1992, ix).

6. Cord (1965, 36) says, "Some well-known historians, such as John R. Commons, felt that the corrupt Tammany machine then in power used bribery and their control of the election machinery to deny him an election [George] actually won." See also Birnie (1939, Chapter XI).

7. Schumpeter (1954, 865), italics in the original. Schumpeter also noted that the French economist François Quesnay (1696-1774), who developed a system of analysis termed Physiocracy, proposed that taxes should be levied exclusively on the net rent of land—his proposed *impôt* [tax] *unique* was the original single tax. Adam Smith wrote that one of Quesnay's followers, the Marquis de Mirabeau, accounted the discovery of the Physiocratic system equal in importance to the invention of writing or the displacement of barter by money (Smith 1776 [1937], 643).

8. James Buchanan, Milton Friedman, Franco Modigliani, Paul Samuelson, Herbert Simon, Robert Solow, Joseph Stiglitz, James Tobin, and William Vickrey (see *Incentive Taxation*, November 1991, 1). Prest (1981) summarizes the history of economic thought on land value taxation. He says, "The first observation about urban land tax policy during the last century or so is...it survived. Whereas many other ideas in tax policy have come, gone, and been forgotten, we find the enormous interest taken in these matters in one form or another in the 1890s is in some ways parallelled in the 1970s" (Prest 1981, 105). Cord (1965) and Whitaker (1997) explain how and why contemporary economists criticized *Progress and Poverty*.

9. Blaug (1992, x).

10. Arnott and Stiglitz (1979). George argued the single tax could replace all other federal, state, and local taxes, while Arnott and Stiglitz found it might replace all other local taxes.

11. In economics, rent is a payment that is necessary to ensure efficient allocation of a resource among all potential users, but is not necessary to draw the resource into use. In the short run, market prices can ensure the efficient allocation of curb spaces, but no payment is necessary to draw the curb spaces into use. The long-run supply of curb parking is not perfectly inelastic, however, because cities can create more curb spaces by converting parallel parking to diagonal parking and thus converting more of the roadway from moving to parked cars. Nevertheless, the curb parking supply is fixed in the short run and the supply curve is a vertical line at the 85 percent occupancy rate (see Chapter 12).

12. C. Lowell Harriss (1972, 296) says about the incidence of taxes on land values, "In effect, the owner at the time of each jump in the tax rate will have suffered a loss of capital value—except as the spending of the funds adds offsetting benefits which enhance the demand for the property."

13. George (1879 [1938], 418) was unduly optimistic, but as Robert Andelson (1979, 387) pointed out, we should think of Henry George as a "perceptive guide rather than as an infallible oracle."

14. See, for example, Holland (1970). Pittsburgh, Pennsylvania, levied a higher tax rate on land than on improvements from 1913 until 2001, when a dispute over reassessments led the city to revert to a uniform tax rate on land and improvements.

15. Pollock and Shoup (1977) and Shoup (1978) present case studies to estimate how property taxes reduce investment in buildings. Fischel (2001b), Nechyba (2001), and Zodrow (2001) explain the uncertainty in estimating whether and how property taxes reduce investment in buildings. Parking requirements differ from property taxes in that they apply specifically to buildings, not to land, while property taxes apply to both land and buildings. Like the property tax on buildings, however, parking requirements can, by reducing the incentives to construct improvements, also reduce land values.

16. There is another way to calculate impact fees implicit in parking requirements. Chapter 7 explained that the construction cost of a parking space is about $13,000 if aboveground and about $25,000 if underground. Because the most common parking requirement for an office building is 4 spaces per 1,000 square feet of floor area, the required parking therefore costs $52 per square foot of office space if the parking is aboveground, and $100 per square foot of office space if the parking is underground. The average construction cost of an office building in Los Angeles, excluding the cost of parking, is about $150 per square foot. Providing the required 4 parking spaces per 1,000 square feet therefore increases the construction cost of the office space by 35 percent ($52 ÷ $150) if the parking is aboveground and 67 percent ($100 ÷ $150) if below ground.

17. The tax base for these tax rates is the "full cash value" of real property. These rates apply to Fiscal Year 2002. This information is available on Montgomery County's web site at www.co.mo.md.us/. This parking surtax understates the tax rate on buildings alone because the parking surtax applies to both buildings *and* land. Suppose the assessed value is 50 percent land value and 50 percent building value. If an owner chooses to pay the 0.28 percent surtax on total assessed value in lieu of providing the parking spaces required for the building, this amounts to a 0.56 percent surtax on the value of the building because no parking is required for the land alone. Any building (new or existing) that does not provide the required parking must pay the surtax.

18. When businesses provide on-site parking rather than pay the in-lieu fee, they do get the benefit of the parking spaces. They will pay the in-lieu fee only when it is less than the net loss (benefits minus costs) of the required parking spaces. Because parking spaces are worth something, the cost of the required spaces must be significantly greater than the in-lieu fee before a business would pay the fee (see Chapter 9).

19. Sec. 59-E-3.7 of the Montgomery County Zoning Ordinance: "Twenty-five parking spaces for each 1,000 square feet of floor area devoted to patron use within the establishment and 15 parking spaces for each 1,000 square feet of ground area devoted to patron use on the property outside the establishment."

20. David Segal (1977, 198-199) explains that in some cases property taxes alone can increase the parking supply. When developers have assembled the site for a new building, they must often wait several years before construction begins. Developers have a tax incentive to demolish existing buildings and convert the site to a parking lot while waiting to begin construction because the property taxes on a parking lot are lower than on a building. This phenomenon further increases the parking supply and creates more gaps in the urban fabric.

21. Smith (1776 [1937], 777-78).

22. A 1995 survey of parking meter costs (for collection, repairs, maintenance, and installation) and revenues in California found that the ratio of cost to revenue was 5 percent in both Santa Monica and West Hollywood, 9 percent in San Diego, 10 percent in San Luis Obispo, 11 percent in Beverly Hills, 19 percent in Sacramento, and 20 percent in San Jose (City of San Diego 1995). Since the highest meter rate was only $1 an hour, raising the meter rates to the market level would produce more revenue with no additional collection costs, and the ratio of cost to revenue would be even lower.

23. Drèze (1995, 114) explains the "marginal cost of public funds." Taxes that distort prices reduce efficiency and create a "deadweight" loss, which increases the cost of the tax revenue to the economy. The marginal cost of public funds is greater than an extra dollar of tax revenue because it includes the estimated deadweight loss associated with the higher tax rate. Different taxes, of course, have different deadweight losses. Hamond et al. (1997) describe the double dividend created by shifting the tax burden from "goods" like work and saving, and onto "bads" like pollution and waste.

24. This rationale for market-price curb parking is similar to the one that William Vickrey (1967, 136) offered for congestion tolls: "Given the serious financial plight of many urban governments, it would perhaps be desirable to use added charges on urban vehicular users to provide an appropriate source of additional funds. This would on the one hand be free of the baneful economic impact of most other revenue sources, such as taxes on property improvements or sales taxes, and on the other constitute a local resource more conducive to economical use of the proceeds than grants from larger jurisdictions, the spending of which is more often decided upon without adequate consideration of the tax consequences."

25. Property tax revenues are reported in the *American Housing Survey for the United States: 2001*, Table 1A-7, "Financial Characteristics—All Housing Units" (United States Census Bureau 2001a).

26. Smith (2001, 24; 27) shows structured parking is cheaper than surface parking only when the price of land is more than $30 per square foot.

27. If curb spaces earn much *more* than $5 a day, the revenue should justify constructing adjacent off-street spaces. The cost of constructing off-street parking should, in the long run, limit the price of curb parking. In turn, the availability of curb parking at market rates should limit the price of short-term off-street parking. In part because of the lack of curb vacancies, the price of the first hour of off-street parking is often 25 percent or more of the all-day rate, and this ratio should decline if curb parking is readily available. The current price of most curb parking understates its full revenue potential because minimum parking requirements have increased the off-street parking supply. The ability of curb parking to produce public revenue can therefore be seen only in cities that have never required off-street parking.

28. This is the net present value of a curb space. Because it is land value, there is no depreciation, and the time horizon is effectively infinite, so the capital value is the annual revenue divided by the interest rate. If parking prices increase at the inflation rate, the real interest rate should be used to discount future revenues. Five percent is a high estimate of the real interest rate and leads to a conservative estimate of the present value of a curb parking space.

29. Whyte (1988, 73-74).

30. City of New York Department of City Planning (2002, Table 10). The area includes all of Manhattan from 59th Street to the Battery, between the Hudson and East Rivers.

31. "Value Soars on Choice Hub Parking Spots," *Boston Globe*, April 14, 2004. At 5 percent, the annual interest on $167,500 is $8,375. When the condominium fee of $163 a month and the property tax of $811 a year are added, the total cost is $11,142 a year, or $30.53 a day. As recently as 1998 one space sold for only $27,000, so the price per space increased by 620 percent in six years. The Brimmer Street Garage does not allow vehicles like Chevrolet Tahoes, Ford Expeditions, and Hummers because they are too big. CNN reported that in 2004 the prices for condominium parking spaces ranged up to $250,000 in New York, $200,000 in San Francisco, and $80,000 in Chicago ("Boston Parking Spot Sold for $160,000," April 27, 2004).

32. Boston Transportation Department (2001, 63, 66). Despite the four-to-one overissuance of free resident parking permits, the Boston Transportation Department concluded, "Pricing strategies, such as higher fees for multiple stickers are not recommended as tolls to manage auto ownership because high fees would not affect auto ownership decisions in comparison to the high operating and insurance costs paid by Boston residents" (Boston Transportation Department 2001, 68). This argument for free parking is, of course, a flimsy pseudo-economic excuse probably intended to justify a political decision that had already been made. The high prices for off-street parking suggest that market prices for permits (to equate demand with supply) would reduce cruising, improve traffic, and produce substantial public revenue.

33. *Sunday Times*, December 12, 1999. The project is Harrods Mansions at No. 1 Hans Crescent in Knightsbridge.

34. Reuters, February 24, 2004. Another parking space in the same garage was bought by a mother for her three-year-old son for when he can drive.

35. "Park Avenue?" *Los Angeles Times*, June 7, 2004. The city gave Seinfeld—as to everyone else with off-street parking—a curb cut to access his new garage, thus eliminating an on-street parking space. The cost of Seinfeld's garage illustrates how the economics of car ownership in Manhattan resemble those in Hong Kong. In his study of how land use affects mode choices, Ming Zhang (2004, 357) says, "In Hong Kong, the after-purchase costs of owning and using private automobiles are among the highest in the world.... . Many in Hong Kong can afford to buy a car but cannot find or afford a place to park it."

36. Naturally, curb parking can earn either more or less rent per square foot than the adjacent land use does.

37. Portland Metro Regional Transportation Planning (1995).

38. Block length was defined by the property lines within the block, excluding the sidewalk.

39. Parking meters are typically 20 feet apart, but this varies. In Phoenix, for example, the standard length is 22 feet, with only 17 feet for the first and last spaces in rows of multiple meters (de Cerreño 2002, 16). Among rectangles of the same area, a square has the lowest ratio of perimeter to area. If blocks are not square, the ratio of parking area to area within the block will therefore be more than 8 percent. For example, if the block is 100 feet on the short side and 640 feet on the long side, it will still be 64,000 square feet, but its perimeter will be 1,480 feet, or 46 percent longer than the perimeter of the square block. The curb parking space would be 12 percent of the area of the block. Among square blocks, the ratio of perimeter to area declines as the area increases.

40. Dueker, Strathman, and Bianco (1998, 28).

41. $1,800 \times 33 = \$59,400$ and $\$59,400 \div 1,012 = \$58.70$.

42. If a sidewalk is six feet wide and the cost of sidewalk replacement is $10 per square foot, curb parking revenue of $59 per front foot would be enough to replace the sidewalk every year.

43. See U.S. Census Bureau (2000d, Table 45) for local government revenue and expenditure for parking in 1997. The U.S. Department of Transportation, Federal Highway Administration (1997b, Tables MV-1 and DL-1C) reported there were 207,753,660 registered motor vehicles and 182,709,204 licensed drivers in 1997.

44. Smith (1776 [1937], 835). The lower curve in Figure 19-4 is sometimes called a "Laffer Curve" after the economist Arthur Laffer, who is reputed to have sketched it on a cocktail napkin in 1974. See Monissen (1999) for a discussion of the Laffer Curve.

45. The $100 million of revenue is hypothetical. If, however, curb spaces yield $1,800 a year, a city with 56,000 curb parking spaces will earn a total revenue of $100 million per year. As the neighborhoods' share increases up to 50 percent, the revenue to the general fund also increases (revenues to the general fund are maximized at the 50 percent share if the total parking revenue curve is a straight line, which it need not be). If the city and its neighborhoods split the revenue equally, they each get $25 million a year. As the neighborhoods' share further increases to 100 percent, the revenue to the general fund declines to zero (the lower right corner) and the revenue to the neighborhoods increases to $100 million a year (the upper right corner).

46. As Richard Bird (1991, 268) says, "Tax reform is a political, not an economic, process. It results from the interplay of interests and actors characteristic of the political process rather than the application of the 'rational man' (or 'benevolent dictator') approach that underlies the conventional analysis of tax reform." The same is true of parking reforms.

47. See Chapter 16. If citizens believe cities will simply use the earmarked revenue to *substitute* for expenditures already made in neighborhoods rather than to *augment* these expenditures, parking benefit districts will have no appeal. Cities must therefore commit to a maintenance of effort for the services financed by benefit districts.

48. The land rent for curb parking is a transfer payment from drivers to the government. Drivers see this payment as a cost, and it should be counted as a benefit to the community. Although most drivers won't agree that charging market prices for curb parking is a good idea, the views of those who receive the revenue must be weighed in the balance.

49. Quoted in Cord (1965, 27). This was from an address in 1877 to the faculty and students at the University of California, where George was being considered as a candidate for a chair in political economy. He was not offered the post and was never invited to speak at Berkeley again.

50. U.S. Census Bureau (2000d, 4). Shoup (1990) explains how special assessments based on front-foot charges are used to finance neighborhood public investments. What neighborhood public purposes should be eligible for finance by a parking benefit district? One simple answer is any public purpose that can already be financed by a special assessment.

51. Wachs (1994, 16).

52. Deakin and Harvey (1996, 5-14, 5-15).

53. Goodwin (1989, 495).

54. Small, Winston, and Evans (1989, 86).

55. Goodwin (1995, 496) says "Of course, it is obvious that 'a third' is arbitrary.... But it is clear, easily understood, and, I think, capable of acting as a useful base for a consensus." Small (1992) proposes a similar tripartite division of the revenue.

56. The desire for revenue almost certainly hastened the advent of the parking meter. The first meters were installed in Oklahoma City during the Depression in 1935 when the city was close to bankruptcy. LeRoy Fischer and Robert Smith (1969) report the city's property tax base shrank by 29 percent between 1931 and 1934. The city manager estimated that the new parking meters would generate $75,000 a year in their first year, equivalent to $1 million a year in 2004. Were it not for this revenue, it seems unlikely Oklahoma City would have installed the parking meters.

57. Similarly, if VMT taxes were distributed to cities in proportion to the VMT they experience, a new constituency for VMT taxes would appear. If the congestion tolls or VMT taxes were assessed by means of satellite technology, geographic assignment of the revenue would not be difficult.

58. The per-capita incomes are from the 2000 census. When Southern Californians strike it rich, they apparently like to live on a hill far from the maddening freeways.

59. William Fulton (2001) discusses how the competition for sales tax revenue distorts land-use planning in California. Congestion tolls, of course, are user fees, *not* taxes. In many ways, congestions tolls are a better way to finance public services than property taxes are because the congestion tolls increase the economy's efficiency while property taxes reduce it. As Henry George might have argued, congestion tolls are rent for the use of scarce space. Toll sharing among cities with freeways will lead to "toll-seeking" behavior, which will generate the necessary political support for congestion pricing.

60. Lave (1995, 465). Similarly, Small, Winston, and Evans (1989, 86) say, "Seldom has applied economics produced an idea with such unanimous professional conviction in both its validity and its political unacceptability." They also explain why no other policies can reduce urban highway congestion, because none of these other policies accounts for the latent demand for peak-period highway travel.

61. Calthrop and Proost (2003, 544).

62. Fielding and Klein (1997).

63. City of Westminster, *Facts and Figures 2002/2003*.

64. See the web site of Transportation for London at www.transportforlondon.gov.uk/tfl.

65. The General Mining Law of 1872 allows mining companies to extract hardrock minerals from public lands without royalty. Enacted under President Ulysses S. Grant to encourage individual prospectors, the law also offers public land for sale at $5 an acre, perhaps the only price in the U.S. that has not increased since 1872.

66. Simons (1948, 33).

67. Casella (1985) and Johnson and Man (2001) explain Tax Increment Finance. For Parking Increment Finance, the revenue for the BID will presumably be the net increment in parking revenue after deducting the cost of collection.

68. Williams and Ross (2003).

69. Dardia (1998) explains that much of the total tax increment would in many cases occur without any redevelopment projects, and tax increment financing therefore diverts revenue from cities, counties, and school districts to subsidize redevelopment districts. Hormann and Segal (1998) argue that California's TIF-financed Community Redevelopment Agencies have played a strong role in business districts and have stifled the growth of BIDs that rely on self-help efforts.

70. Cities charge for admission to museums and many other public services one might argue should be free, but free curb parking is almost sacrosanct. Rather than being concerned about social equity or economic justice, most motorists probably want to keep their free lunch regardless of the social cost.

71. The *2001 Nationwide Household Travel Survey* found that 20.3 percent of households with incomes less than $25,000 a year don't own a car, while only 2.3 percent of households with incomes greater than $25,000 a year don't own a car; 17.6 percent of households whose residence is rented don't own a car, while only 3 percent of households whose residence is owned or otherwise nonrented don't own a car (United States Department of

Transportation 2003a, 20). Using data from the 1991-1993 Surveys of Income and Program Participation, Steven Raphael and Michael Stoll (2001, 109) calculated that African-American households own 0.67 cars per adult, Latino households own 0.73 cars per adult, and Caucasian households own 1.14 cars per adult.

72. The share of curb parkers who were women increased from 36 percent before the price increase to 43 percent afterward (Clinch and Kelly 2004a, Figure 3). Perhaps this change occurred because women are more averse than men to parking in off-street garages. Amanda Nelson (1997) found that 51 percent of women said they were anxious when using parking garages after dark, while another 32 percent said they never parked in garages after dark.

73. The share of curb parkers who were in the highest social class fell from 46 percent before the price rise to 35 percent afterward; the share who were upper-middle class rose from 38 percent before the price rise to 47 percent afterward. Clinch and Kelly (2004a, 3) conclude, "arguments that shifts in parking prices could have more serious equity concerns...are not substantiated by these data.... [T]he sole change was a transfer [of parking spaces] between the upper class and the upper-middle class." The categories of social class refer to the occupation of the head of the household and are standard in Irish market research surveys.

74. San Diego Association of Governments (2000, 36). In his survey of public opinion about road pricing, John Berg (2003, 7) reports that 94 percent of transit riders and 92 percent of carpoolers thought the I-15 toll program was fair.

75. United States Department of Transportation (2003b, 30).

76. "Parking Mafias Imperil Historic Homes in Istanbul," *Chicago Tribune*, April 11, 2004.

77. As soon as Pasadena installed parking meters in the Old Pasadena Parking Meter Zone, it borrowed $5 million against the future revenue and invested the proceeds in major streetscape and alley improvements (see Chapter 16).

78. Mazumder (2004, 2).

79. Cities can use the same lifeline-eligibility criteria for curb parking they use for other public utilities, such as telephone and electricity service.

80. That is, the share of disabled spaces that are illegally occupied approaches 100 percent!

81. Louis Wasserman (1979, 30)

82. *Economic Journal* 76, no. 301 (March 1966): 215. What Joseph Schumpeter (1942, 262) said about politics also applies to parking: "The typical citizen drops down to a lower level of mental performance as soon as he enters the political field. He argues and analyzes in a way which he would readily recognize as infantile within the sphere of his real interests. He becomes a primitive again."

83. Thomson (1977, 15).

84. Brinkley (1988, 218).

85. Brinkley (1988, 219).

86. Kenneth Button (1977, 43) says, "In practice, two quite distinct types of charging policy for parking spaces may be discerned: There is an administrative approach and an economic one. The former is concerned with cost recovery and is closely entwined with the highway engineer approach to urban traffic problems.... The economic way is to regulate charges in sympathy with the prevailing state of demand in the same way that other commodity prices vary. Charges are therefore based on the 'willingness to pay' principle." Button explains that when cities charge a low administrative cost for curb parking, the curb spaces are allocated according to drivers' willingness to pay the resulting search costs.

87. In 1929, the Committee on Parking Regulations of the National Highway Traffic

Association concisely concluded, "[Curb] parking…should be allowed at all times in business districts where it does not cost the traveling public more than it saves those who park…. The right to move a car is superior to the right to store a car on the public ways, and when or where parking causes a net economic loss to the public through hindrance to safe and convenient travel, there should be limitation of parking, both commercial and private" (Committee on Parking Regulations of the National Highway Traffic Association (1929, 139). In his analysis of the proper prices for curb parking, British transportation economist D. H. Glassborow (1961, 26 and 29) said, "Parking charges are…payments for the use of resources which could be used for other purposes. Quite simply, street parking is a problem where there is some other use for the space occupied by a parked vehicle…. Charges for street parking should not be regarded as payment to cover the cost of administration of a system of physical rationing…. The revenue from parking charges, after the cost of administration has been met, should be used to relieve the ratepayers as a whole and not be reserved to finance the construction of off-street parks. Certainly it should not be used to subsidize these car parks."

88. Vickrey (1954, 62).

89. University Avenue in Palo Alto has diagonal parking on one side of the street, and parallel parking on the other side. Roberta Gratz and Norman Mintz (1998, 95-96) describe how New Haven, Connecticut, eliminated parking spaces at the corner of Chapel and College Streets, across from Yale University, and created a pleasant public environment with trees, public seating, and a sidewalk café.

90. See Richardson et al. (1993) for a description of the Southern California Planning Model. I am grateful to Peter Gordon for using this model to estimate the effects of diverting final demand from private consumption to public investment.

91. Because more of the goods and services that supply local private consumption are imported, reducing local private consumption will reduce local wages by only 45 percent of the reduction in consumption. By contrast, more of the goods and services that supply local public investment are produced locally, so increasing local public investment will increase local wages by 84 percent of the increase in local public investment. Therefore, in this example, parking benefit districts will increase total local wages by 39 percent of the final demand they divert from private consumption to public investment.

92. The estimated wages of the created jobs in this example may be unusually high because roads are constructed for the public sector. In California, those who bid for work on state-financed construction projects must pay workers at the "most frequently occurring" wage rate in the region, and this is often the union scale. Private contractors who repair sidewalks may pay lower wages, but they will therefore have less incentive to substitute capital for labor. Shifting spending from private consumption to repairing sidewalks may thus create more jobs at lower wages than is estimated here for shifting the same spending to building roads. It is also worth noting, however, that most of the jobs created will be in the private sector and many of these jobs will be for workers with relatively few skills. The estimated the number of jobs lost is 17.9 and the number gained is 21.5, which are rounded in the table to 18 and 22.

93. United States Census Bureau (2002a, Exhibits 1, 6, and 9). The total ($104 billion for petroleum and $190 billion for motor vehicles) was equal to 82 percent of the trade deficit.

94. United States patent number 1,509,312 (September 23, 1924). After buying Darrow's patent, Parker Brothers subsequently bought Magie's earlier patent. Monopoly® is now the trademark of Hasbro, Inc. for its real estate trading game. See Orbanes (1988) for the history of Monopoly.

95. Bolton (1985, 11).

96. Andelson and Gaffney (1979, 284). Edwin Seligman (1931, 68) said, "a tax on land values is not necessarily a single tax. The essential feature of the single tax is the singleness of the tax." The essential feature of a tax on land value is not its singleness but its ability to raise revenue without distorting incentives. Similarly, curb parking revenue cannot replace all taxes, but cities can use it to reduce some taxes, such as property taxes. Free curb parking and onerous off-street parking requirements dramatically show that government ownership of land does not automatically capture land rent for the benefit of society.

97. Beyond these advantages of market-priced curb parking, the model of cruising in Chapter 13 suggests that if curb parking is underpriced, raising its price reduces the time-and-fuel cost of cruising by $1 for every $1 increase in motorists' payments for curb parking. The charge for curb parking is thus unlike a tax that transfers revenue from motorists to the government. The net burden on curb parkers is zero because the public revenue equals the reduced private waste of cruising. By reducing the traffic congestion caused by cruising, raising the price of curb parking in an area also reduces the time cost of travel for motorists who are driving through it rather than trying to park. Using a numerical example, Arnott, Rave, and Schöb (forthcoming) estimate that raising the price of curb parking can reduce the time cost of travel for in-transit motorists (those who are traveling rather than cruising) by $2 for every $1 increase in curb parking revenue. Every $1 increase in the curb parking revenue in an underpriced area thus reduces the motorists' cost of travel by $3: $1 in time-and-fuel savings for drivers who are searching for curb parking, and $2 in time savings for drivers who are traveling through. Their example depends, of course, on the amount of through traffic delayed by the cars cruising for parking.

20

Unbundled Parking

The point of cities is multiplicity of choice.

— JANE JACOBS

If cities required restaurants to offer a free dessert with each dinner, the price of every dinner would soon increase to include the cost of a dessert. To ensure that restaurants didn't skimp on the size of the required desserts, cities would have to set precise "minimum calorie requirements." Some diners would pay for desserts they didn't eat, and others would eat sugary desserts they wouldn't have ordered had they paid for them separately. The consequences would undoubtedly include an epidemic of obesity, diabetes, and heart disease. A few food-conscious cities like New York and San Francisco might prohibit free desserts, but most cities would continue to require them. Many people would get angry at even the thought of paying for the desserts they had eaten free for so long.

Cities don't require free desserts with every dinner, of course, but they do require off-street parking spaces for every building. As a result, the cost of parking is usually bundled into the prices for everything else, and most people drive wherever they go.[1] If cities remove these requirements, developers will be able to provide as few parking spaces as they choose. Some existing spaces will disappear as developers build infill projects on parking lots no longer required by law. Adaptive reuse of older buildings will also become less problematic because cities will no longer require property owners to provide additional parking spaces for new uses.

These responses to the liberation from parking requirements will reduce the supply and increase the price of parking. No one will be happy about paying for parking, but think of it this way: a dessert not included in the price of a dinner is still available, but not everyone will order it. Eliminating off-street parking requirements is like giving diners more control over what they eat, in that unbundled parking gives travelers more options. Unbundling will also lead to an increase in shared parking because everyone who is willing to pay for the parking can use it. In contrast, required parking is typically *not* shared since each specific site must provide its own spaces.[2] Moreover, businesses that have paid dearly to provide their own parking are not eager to let their competitors' customers use it. The growth of paid, shared parking will therefore allow a smaller parking supply to serve more trips, while the higher price of parking will increase travel by carpools, transit, biking, and walking. Removing off-street parking requirements will slowly but surely lead to shared parking, higher urban density, and a shift away from solo driving.

Unbundling will be simple where parking spaces are expensive and where the transaction costs of charging for them are low. Perhaps the simplest example is the case of apartment buildings that now typically offer two "free" parking spaces with every unit. Parking can be unbundled in this case by offering residents the option to lease the apartments and parking spaces separately. Residents can then choose how many parking spaces they are willing to pay for. I will use the example of separating the rent for parking spaces from the rent for apartments to show how unbundling can reduce the cost of housing.

PARKING COSTS UNBUNDLED FROM HOUSING COSTS

Landlords customarily bundle the prices for housing and parking in a single transaction. The bundled parking is not really free, of course. It just comes at no extra cost, so that residents think it is free and make their choices accordingly. Renting apartments and parking spaces separately will make the housing cheaper for those who think a second parking space (or even a first one) isn't worth the extra cost. If developers provide fewer parking spaces and pass the cost savings on to the residents, the housing itself will be cheaper.

An Example

Because cities require parking spaces as a condition for granting a building permit, developers usually don't separate the cost of parking from the other costs of an apartment building. As explained in Chapter 5, however, an apartment project on the UCLA campus unbundled these two costs because the housing and the parking were financed from separate budgets. Data from this project can thus illustrate the effects of charging

Table 20-1. Unbundling Reduces Apartment Rents and Increases Parking Rents

	Rent ($/month)						
Number of cars	Bundled parking			Unbundled parking			
	Apartment	Parking	Total	Apartment	Parking	Total	Saving
(1)	(2)	(3)	(4)=(2)+(3)	(5)	(6)	(7)=(5)+(6)	(8)=(4)-(7)
No car	$1,800	$0	$1,800	$1,400	$0	$1,400	$400
One car	$1,800	$0	$1,800	$1,400	$200	$1,600	$200
Two cars	$1,800	$0	$1,800	$1,400	$400	$1,800	$0

Assumptions:
Construction cost per apartment = $140,000.
Construction cost per parking space = $20,000.
Monthly rent = 1% of construction cost.
Bundled parking: two spaces for every apartment.
Unbundled parking: rent per space is $200 per month.

residents separately for apartments and parking spaces (see Chapter 5 and Table 5-4 for details of the project).

UCLA is exempt from zoning regulations, but if the project had been required to comply with the city's off-street parking requirements it would have needed 2.1 spaces per apartment. To keep the numbers simple, suppose each apartment costs $140,000, each parking space costs $20,000, and the city requires two parking spaces per apartment.[3] Further, suppose the monthly rent necessary to recover the cost of an apartment or a parking space is 1 percent of its construction cost.[4] Table 20-1 shows the results of bundling the parking cost into the apartment cost, as well as what happens when the two costs are unbundled.

If the cost of two parking spaces is included in the cost of each apartment, the apartments will cost $180,000 apiece ($140,000 + 2 x $20,000), and if the monthly rent is 1 percent of the construction cost, each apartment will rent for $1,800 a month regardless of how many cars the resident owns (see column 4). Suppose, however, the apartments and the parking spaces are rented separately. An apartment will then cost $1,400 a month, and each parking space will cost $200 a month. Residents without a car will pay $1,400 a month, those with one car will pay $1,600, and those with two cars will pay $1,800 (see column 7). Those who rent two parking spaces still pay the same total rent they would have paid if two "free" spaces had been bundled with their rent, but everyone else saves money. All unbundling has done is to release residents from the obligation to pay for parking spaces they think are not worth the cost.

The price of $200 a month is based on the construction cost of a parking space. From a marketing perspective, however, it may seem exorbitant, since everyone is accustomed to "free" parking. To avoid giving the impression of overcharging, a landlord can instead give residents a discount for not taking a parking space, just as restaurants and bars offer early-bird specials and happy hours for those who come early rather than add late fees for everyone else.[5] If the rent for an apartment is $1,800 with two free parking spaces (as in the case of bundled parking), a landlord can give a discount of $200 a month to a resident who has only one car, and $400 a month to a resident with no car.

Most people don't realize they already pay for parking in the rent for their housing. Unbundling does not increase the total cost for housing and parking, but rather splits it into two components and gives residents control over their parking costs. Residents can also be offered the choice of assigned or unassigned spaces, tandem or side-by-side spaces, or even valet parking, with all prices based on cost. Compact spaces can be priced less than full-size spaces since they are cheaper to construct, and this will encourage residents to buy smaller cars. Developers offer choices in the size and layout of apartments at different prices to suit different demands; offering choices in the number and type of parking spaces will also suit different demands, and the new choices will make the apartments themselves more affordable.[6]

Condominiums

Parking can also be unbundled in owner-occupied condominiums. Developers can offer the option to buy parking spaces separately from housing units or to lease parking spaces from the condominium association rather than buy them. Under the first option, the market would reveal how much residents value the parking spaces, and developers could cease building spaces residents do not think are worth the construction and maintenance costs.[7] Under the second option, the association could own the parking spaces as common property and lease them to the residents at a price that equates demand and supply. The rent from commonly owned parking spaces could then replace all or part of the association fees residents pay to maintain their association. Parking wouldn't be free, but those who own fewer cars would pay less. After unbundling, developers would find they could build condominiums with fewer parking spaces because residents would want fewer cars when they pay for parking separately.

Skeptics may doubt condominium owners will prefer to lease rather than to buy parking spaces, but it can easily become a mainstream practice. After all, people used to lease their apartments and buy their cars, but now the reverse is often true.[8] And if people choose to lease their cars, they may decide to lease their parking spaces as well. To begin with, the transaction costs for renting a parking space are much lower than for renting a car. Furthermore, the ability to vary the number of parking spaces you use is an advantage, especially because many bundled parking spaces cost more than the cars parked in them. Few people rent an expensive parking space they don't use. Unbundled parking simply gives people the option to decline a space they think is not worth the cost.

Like Cashing Out Employer-Paid Parking

Offering a discount for not taking a parking space in an apartment building resembles the option to cash out employer-paid parking at work. Employers who offer parking cash out praise its simplicity and fairness, and report that it helps recruit and retain workers. If commuters can cash out their employer-paid parking at work and also pay less for housing if they use less parking at home, they can double the savings from reduced car ownership. Cashing out free parking at both the work end and the home end of the commute trip will especially appeal to those who appreciate proximity rather than mobility as the way to gain access to activities.

What is the Right Number of Unbundled Parking Spaces?

If cities do not require off-street parking, how will developers know the right number of spaces to provide? This brings us back to the restaurant menu. How many desserts should the chef prepare if they aren't included free with the dinners? The truth, universally acknowledged, is that demand depends on price. The right number of desserts depends on how much the different kinds of desserts cost to prepare and how much the diners are willing to pay for them. So too with parking spaces. The right number depends on how much the spaces cost and how much residents think they are worth.

Constructing the second parking space per housing unit can be much more expensive than the first because of natural "break points" in the cost of parking spaces—points where the marginal cost per space jumps. One major break point occurs when surface lots cannot provide all the required spaces, and a parking structure is required. Another occurs when aboveground space is exhausted, and parking must be built underground. And with underground parking, additional break points occur with each successive level that must be excavated. The second parking space per apartment can thus be much more expensive than the first.

Returning to the UCLA example, the average cost of all the parking is $20,000 a space, but the first spaces may cost only $15,000 while the second ones cost $25,000. Yet while the second parking space costs more to construct, it is likely to be less valuable to residents than the first one since many households may get by with only one car. The high demand for the first space should thus not be confused with the lower demand for a second one, and unbundling can significantly reduce the cost of an apartment while only slightly reducing its value to residents. After all, you are much better off if you can save $200 a month by forgoing a second parking space you may think is worth only $50 a month.

A simple graph can illustrate how price affects the demand for parking, and how cost affects the supply. Figure 20-1 shows the demand for parking at two apartment houses as a function of the rent per space. Suppose the demand curve for parking is the same at both sites. Although different families will have different demands, the number of spaces demanded increases as the rent per space falls, with demand in both buildings for two spaces per unit when parking is free (point A). Now consider the marginal cost of parking spaces at the two sites. The lower curve shows how the marginal cost of providing an additional space at site 1 increases as the number of spaces increases. If the rent charged for a parking space covers the marginal cost of constructing it, residents will demand 1.5 spaces per apartment (perhaps half the residents will take one space, and the other half will take two) at a price of $50 a month (point B).[9] In this case, a developer will lose money by providing more than 1.5 spaces per apartment because the additional spaces will cost more than the residents are willing to pay for them. The upper curve shows the marginal cost per space at site 2 where parking costs more to construct, and in this case residents demand one space per apartment at a price of $100 a month (point C). Even if the demand for parking were the same everywhere (which it is not), the different construction costs at different sites imply that the number of parking spaces should not be the same everywhere.

Developers can compare the cost of parking spaces with the rates they believe the residents will be willing to pay for them. For example, at an interest rate of 10 percent a year and an amortization period of 30 years, each $1,000 in cost for a parking space requires $8 a month in debt payments. At this rate, a parking space that costs $20,000 must earn $160 a month in rent to cover its cost. If only a few residents are willing to pay more than $100 a month for a second parking space, developers will not voluntarily provide two spaces for every apartment. For the same amount of money, many residents might prefer bigger apartments with fewer parking spaces, so that is what the market will tend to provide.

If cities charge market-rate prices for curb parking, the price of off-street parking can guide the number of spaces developers provide, so that residents are not forced to pay for parking they don't think is worth the cost. But if curb parking remains free, cities that want to prevent spillover must require developers at both sites to provide two off-street spaces for every

Figure 20-1. Demand for Unbundled Parking

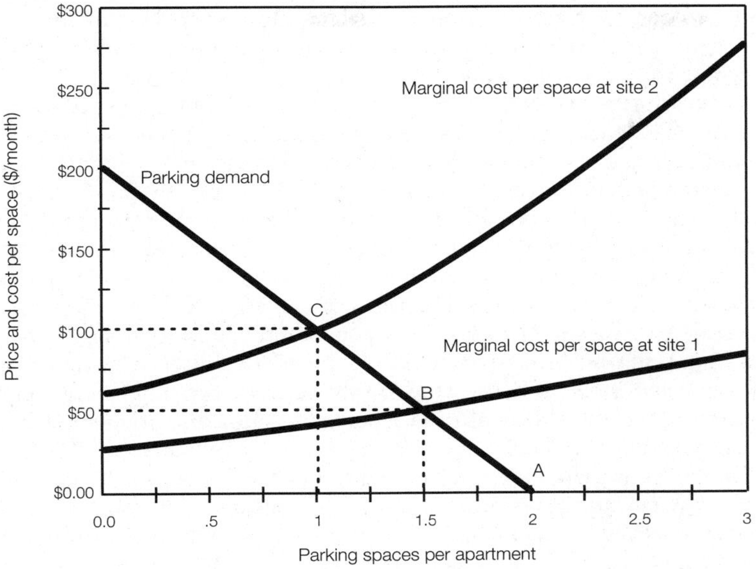

apartment, which is wasteful on several levels. To begin with, the economic waste associated with providing two parking spaces per apartment is measured by how much more the spaces cost than residents think they are worth.[10] In addition, the oversupply of bundled parking induces residents to spend more to buy and drive cars. The resulting traffic congestion and air pollution then compound the economic waste associated with too many parking spaces.

What Is the Right Size for Unbundled Parking Spaces?

Some cities allow developers to provide a share of the required parking as compact spaces so that more cars can fit within the same area. Many cities have abandoned this policy, however, and instead require "universal" spaces big enough to fit all cars. In their study of the parking requirements for Montgomery County, Maryland, for example, Steven Smith and Alexander Hekimian reported that the county adopted the dimensions of 8.5 feet x 18 feet for all parking spaces because the single size (1) simplifies parking regulations, (2) eliminates enforcement problems caused by large cars squeezing into compact spaces, (3) makes parking plan reviews easier, (4) avoids the need to change the maximum allowable percentage of compact spaces as the proportion of small cars in the fleet changes, (5) improves traffic circulation by eliminating the need to search for an appropriate size space in the facility, and (6) eliminates frustration and user complaints.[11] These reasons for the one-size-fits-all requirement suggest the problems created when planning replaces prices as the way to measure demand. If all parking is free, planners must devise clumsy, heavy-handed regulations that fail to discriminate among the different circumstances of many different people.

Off-street parking requirements eliminate any incentive to charge for parking in proportion to a car's size. When cars grow larger, cities typically respond by increasing the minimum width and length of the required parking spaces so that drivers can safely and comfortably open the doors of their bigger cars without marring the finish of adjacent vehicles in parking lots. Imagine the public health problems if people were always given, free, an entire new wardrobe of larger clothes whenever they gained weight. Because cities require wider and longer parking spaces when cars expand, the price of parking does not restrain the size of cars. In contrast, some garages in Europe include ceiling-mounted sensors at the entrance to measure each car's length. Smaller cars are automatically given a discount and are guided to smaller stalls.[12] If more garages give discounts for smaller cars, more drivers will buy small cars, and parking spaces can be smaller.

If cities stop specifying the minimum number and size of parking spaces, developers and property owners can respond to changes in the demand for different sized cars by re-striping and reconfiguring the parking spaces, and then by charging for the spaces according to their size. Suppose, for example, an apartment building is built with half compact spaces and half full-size spaces. If the demand for the cheaper compact spaces later increases, the building owner can re-stripe and convert some full-size spaces into a larger number of compact spaces. And if large Sports Utility Vehicles (SUVs) cannot fit into a full-size space easily, the owner can re-stripe to provide a few oversize spaces at a higher price, or perhaps an SUV owner can rent two compact spaces. If parking spaces are priced by their size, people will take these prices into account when choosing what size car to buy. A Chevrolet Aveo, for example, occupies only 57 percent of the space occupied by a Chevrolet Silverado.[13] If parking were priced in proportion to a car's size, Aveo owners would pay less than Silverado owners, and motorists would buy more Aveos. The size differences are also great in other countries. In Britain, a Mini Cooper takes only 54 percent of the space occupied by a Rolls Royce Phantom. In Japan, two Suzuki Cappuccinos can fit into the space occupied by one

Nissan Armada. And in Germany, three Daimler-Chrysler Smart Cars can fit into the space occupied by one Daimler-Chrysler Maybach 62. Because the size differences among cars are so large, charging for parking in proportion to a car's size is fairer than charging the same price for all cars regardless of their size.[14] After all, no one expects to pay the same rent for a 500-square-foot apartment as for a 1,500-square-foot apartment in the same building.

Two Markets for Unbundled Parking

Unbundled parking gives residents the option to save money on housing if they own fewer cars. Even where two free parking spaces are bundled into the rent for apartments, some families own only one car, and a few own no car. Because bundled parking forces these families to pay for parking spaces they don't use, they are an obvious niche market for apartments with unbundled parking. They can save on the cost of housing without giving up anything.

There is another niche market even among families who now own two cars. Unbundled parking increases the fixed cost of car ownership, and this higher fixed cost may lead some residents to decide not to buy a second car. Just as bundled parking increases spending on cars and driving, unbundled parking reduces it. Because the price of parking affects car ownership, the car ownership rates observed at sites where all parking is free give a distorted view of "the demand for parking." Residents who have to pay a high price for a second parking space may decide that a second car is not worth owning. They may, for example, choose to own one newer and higher-quality car in response to unbundling rather than two older, cheaper, and less reliable ones. Downsizing the number of cars but increasing their quality in response to unbundled parking can also increase the amount of money a household has available for nonautomobile expenditures.[15] The option to save money on both cars *and* parking will especially appeal to residents who enjoy walking or bicycling rather than driving for short trips.

Tiebout Sorting

Some apartment buildings were built before cities required off-street parking and provide few or no on-site parking spaces. Some residents are thus, in a sense, offered unbundled parking because they can select an apartment without a parking space if they choose to live in an old building. People therefore tend to sort themselves among apartments according to their demand for parking: those who want more parking can live in newer buildings, while those who want less parking can opt for older buildings. This residential sorting is similar to the idea that people "vote with their feet" by moving to the city that provides their preferred combination of public services and taxes, as public finance economist Charles Tiebout hypothesized.[16] Tiebout argued that households with similar tastes for public services and taxes tend to settle in the same jurisdictions. Similarly, households who own more cars will move to newer buildings with more parking spaces, and households who own fewer cars will move to older buildings. But this process is limited because older buildings are concentrated in older areas, and their supply is shrinking. In 2000, only 15 percent of owner-occupied units and 36 percent of renter-occupied units were built before 1960.[17] Because off-street parking requirements had become common by 1960, most housing now comes with ample parking, regardless of whether the residents want it. Tiebout sorting undoubtedly occurs, but it is a clumsy way to provide unbundled parking, and it becomes less effective as time passes.

PARKING CAPS OR PARKING PRICES?

In 1998 the British government established an Urban Task Force, chaired by the architect Lord Richard Rogers, to examine the causes of urban decline in England and to recommend practical solutions. In his introduction to the task force's report, *Towards an Urban Renaissance*, Lord Rogers wrote:

> We need a vision that will drive the urban renaissance. We believe that cities should be well designed, be more compact and connected, and support a range of diverse uses—allowing people to live, work and enjoy themselves at close quarters—within a sustainable urban environment.... An urban renaissance is desirable, necessary, achievable and long overdue.[18]

A controversial feature of the report was its proposal to set a maximum standard of one parking space per dwelling for all new urban residential development.[19] Local government authorities argued this recommendation is too prescriptive, ignores local circumstances, and conflicts with the projected growth of car ownership in Britain. House builders argued that new dwellings with only one parking space are difficult to sell because residents place a high value on residential parking even if they don't own a car. In a survey of London residents, Michael Stubbs of Oxford Brookes University found the paradoxical result that the more central the residence, the greater the desire for residential parking spaces. Respondents also mentioned it was difficult to resell a property with no parking. Typical responses in the survey included comments such as "In Central London parking is a must," and "London is impossible if you have a car and no space."[20] Although some planners recommend car-free housing as a way to increase density and improve design, developers are unlikely to build housing without parking if residents will not rent or buy it. Even those who do not own a car want flexibility because circumstances can change. If they do buy a car, they want a place to park it, and they want a place for guests to park.

In part, the demand for residential parking arises because it is bundled with housing, seemingly at no extra cost. You either have a parking space or you don't, and price is not mentioned. But with *unbundled* parking, residents can make separate housing and parking decisions. Those who don't own a car will be more willing to rent or buy an apartment without bundled parking if they know they can always rent or buy a convenient parking space whenever their circumstances change and they decide they want one. They won't have to move to a new apartment with bundled parking just because they buy a car. Bundling, in contrast, increases the demand for parking even by those who don't need it and who would rather live in a city less dominated by cars.

If parking is unbundled from housing and priced separately, prices can do the job of reducing the number of parking spaces. With parking priced to cover its cost, there is less need to cap the number of spaces in new development. If parking *is* capped, however, it should definitely be unbundled as well. Residents will be far more open to moving into housing with limited parking if they know they can always obtain a parking space if they are willing to pay the fair-market price for it. Market-price curb parking will complement the "cap and unbundle" approach to off-street parking. If curb parking is priced so that everyone can always find a place to park on their own street, residents will be even more willing to rent or buy an apartment without a bundled off-street space. People will not have to give up cars and change their lives in response to unbundled parking, but small changes made by enough people can make a big difference for cities and society.

EFFECTS OF UNBUNDLING ON VMT AND VEHICLE EMISSIONS

If you own a car, you'll also need a place to park it because the average car is parked 95 percent of the time. The demand for parking may therefore seem almost perfectly inelastic—an unquestioned necessity. But unbundling will shift parking from the cost of housing into the cost of car ownership, and the rent for a parking space will become part of the fixed cost of owning a car. Like insurance premiums and annual registration fees, parking will become another cost to consider in the decision to own and drive a car. Predicting the effects of car ownership costs on vehicle travel is complex, but Dutch transportation economist Gerald de Jong developed a model for this purpose.[21] He calibrated the model using data from the Netherlands and Norway, and then used it to estimate the long-run elasticity of annual Vehicle Miles Travelled (VMT) with respect to the annual fixed cost of owning a car. The estimates were -0.68 for the Netherlands and -0.48 for Norway; that is, a 10 percent increase in the fixed cost of car ownership reduced VMT by 6.8 percent in the Netherlands and 4.8 percent in Norway. If we assume the lower elasticity of -0.5, we can use the model to predict how the increase in the fixed cost of car ownership associated with unbundling will reduce annual VMT. Table 20-2 shows the results.

The American Automobile Association estimated the average fixed cost for a new car in 2002 was $5,800 a year and the median age of passenger cars in the U.S. was eight years.[22] Because 79 percent of the fixed cost of a new car is depreciation and finance charges, an eight-year-old car has much lower fixed costs (consisting mainly of insurance and registration fees). If we assume the fixed cost of the median-age car is $1,000 a year, we can estimate how unbundled parking will increase the fixed cost of owning both new cars and median-age cars, and how the increase in fixed cost will in turn reduce annual VMT.

Suppose the rent for a parking space is $50 a month, or $600 a year. For median-age cars, unbundling will increase the fixed cost by 60 percent, and if the elasticity of VMT with respect to fixed costs is -0.5, this cost increase will reduce annual VMT by 30 percent (-0.5 x 60%, see column 2). For new cars, unbundling will increase the fixed cost by only 10 percent and thus reduce VMT by only 5 percent, but the VMT reduction will be greater if the price of parking is higher. For example, if the rent for a parking space is $150 a month, or $1,800 a year, and the other fixed costs for a new car are $5,800 a year, unbundling will reduce VMT by 15 percent (column 4).[23]

Table 20-2. Unbundling Reduces Vehicle Travel (% reduction in annual VMT)

	Car's fixed cost ($/year)	Parking price ($/year)		
		$600	$1,200	$1,800
	(1)	(2)	(3)	(4)
New car	$5,800	-5%	-10%	-15%
Median car	$1,000	-30%	-60%	-90%

Columns 2, 3, and 4 show the percentage reduction in annual VMT.
Assumption:
Elasticity of VMT with respect to the fixed cost of automobile ownership = -0.5.
Sources: de Jong (1997) and *Ward's Automotive Facts and Figures 2002*, p. 64.

Unbundled parking will reduce car ownership rates. While no-car families may remain rare, one-car families will become more common. Unbundled parking will also make car-sharing programs more popular because people can save by splitting the cost of parking. Car sharing's greatest benefit is to divide the fixed cost of automobile ownership among a large group of potential users, and adding the cost of parking to the fixed ownership cost will increase this benefit. The car-sharing households face a higher marginal cost of driving because they pay per hour of use or per mile driven. In Los Angeles, for example, one car-sharing plan has a $25 annual fee plus a charge of $10 per hour; each hour includes 10 free miles, and additional miles are charged at 35¢ a mile.[24] If a family drives its second car only 10 hours a month, the cost of car sharing for the same time will be only $100 a month, which may be less than the cost of parking and insurance alone for the second car. Many families may therefore choose a shared car as a convenient substitute for a second car.[25] Because car sharing converts much of the fixed cost of car ownership into the marginal cost of driving, this higher marginal cost will further reduce VMT.

Housing is not the only land use where parking can be unbundled. Commuters who cash out their employer-paid parking subsidies, for example, will be able to save on parking at both the home and work ends of their commute trips. If stores and restaurants unbundle parking from the prices of merchandise and meals, everyone will be able to save on parking by using less of it. Unbundling will thus convert parking from a hidden, fixed cost of living into an explicit, marginal cost of owning and using cars.[26]

Unbundled parking will raise ownership costs proportionally more for the older and less reliable second (or third or fourth) cars in a household, which often consume more fuel and produce more pollution. When people consider the price of parking a rarely used car, it may come to be seen as an expendable luxury. As a result, unbundled parking will tend to cull from the fleet the cars that contribute least to mobility and most to fuel consumption and air pollution (the evaporative emissions from older cars while they are parked can be higher than the running emissions of new cars while they are being driven). Separating the costs of housing and parking will therefore selectively discourage ownership of the cars that impose the highest social costs. Using remote-sensing technology, University of Denver chemistry professor Donald Stedman estimated that the dirtiest 10 percent of all cars produce about 50 percent of all vehicle emissions.[27] Scrapping some of these gross polluters that are not worth the cost of parking can therefore greatly improve air quality. Unbundling will reduce both the number of cars and total VMT, and since the remaining cars will tend to be the cleaner ones, the reduction in emissions will exceed the reduction in VMT.

OBJECTIONS TO UNBUNDLING

If unbundling is such a good idea, why don't most landlords already do it? Parking often *is* unbundled in the older, denser parts of cities like New York and San Francisco, where parking is scarce. Parking condominiums have even been built for sale to residents who live in buildings that have no parking spaces (see Chapter 19). But most developers and landlords bundle parking with housing because the off-street parking requirements in zoning ordinances are so high. If cities require developers to provide two spaces per apartment, landlords cannot hope to rent the required spaces at a cost-recovery price. Many residents will think a second parking space, or even a first one, is not worth the high cost. Unbundled parking is rare because most cities require enough on-site parking spaces to satiate the demand for free parking.

Off-street parking requirements and bundled parking don't just happen, of course. Cities require off-street parking to solve problems that would occur if parking were not bundled into the prices for everything else. Consider the following potential problems that people might expect with unbundled parking: spillover, uncertainty, liability, transaction costs, and fairness. As we shall see, each can be successfully addressed *without* off-street parking requirements and bundled parking.

Spillover

Off-street parking requirements are intended to prevent parking spillover. If curb parking is free and new development doesn't provide enough off-street spaces, spillover will create a nuisance for everyone. Unbundling parking from housing will—if nothing else is done—create the spillover parking requirements are designed to solve.

To discourage spillover in residential neighborhoods, some cities prohibit overnight curb parking in order to prevent residents from using the streets as their garages. A more promising approach is to establish parking benefit districts that charge market prices for curb parking and spend the revenue to pay for public expenditures in the neighborhood (see chapters 16 and 17). If cities don't require off-street parking, curb parking can produce substantial revenue to pay for public services, which will then become another important benefit of unbundling.

Uncertainty

Another concern about unbundled parking is that without off-street parking requirements, some developers may provide too few spaces, and their projects will be unrentable. Consider the example of the two apartment houses presented earlier in Figure 20-1. Suppose the developer at the first site underestimates the demand for parking and provides only 1.25 spaces per apartment. One way to deal with this mistake is to raise the price of a parking space (or the discount for not taking one) until residents want only 1.25 spaces per apartment, which in this case is $75 a month per space. Parking prices can adjust to clear the market, just as the prices of apartments themselves adjust to clear the market, and these flexible prices will reveal how much residents really value the parking spaces. Another option is to offer all residents the option of one parking space at $50 a month, with the second space offered at a price that clears the market. Flexible prices can thus resolve any uncertainty in matching future parking demand with the available supply.

Another way to deal with uncertainty regarding future parking demand is to make some garage space convertible between parking and on-site storage, so the space can be used for whichever purpose is more valuable.[28] Demand for the on-site storage alternative in apartment buildings might be strong, as shown by the demand for space in commercial self-storage lockers. Homeowners often convert their garages to storage, and some apartment residents may want to do the same thing. Parking spaces will become more flexible, like other types of real estate.

The price of parking in a new apartment building can also adjust in a way that will benefit both landlords and residents. New office buildings often offer free parking during the initial leasing period when plenty of parking spaces are available, and the free parking is an incentive for early tenants. Parking charges are introduced only after the building is fully leased, and there is a need to limit demand. An apartment building can similarly offer free parking in the early stages of leasing when most spaces are vacant. Free parking will be an incentive for the first tenants, and parking charges can be introduced only after the building is nearly full (the leases must inform residents of this arrangement in advance, of course). In contrast, when parking is bundled into higher rent for the apartments, free parking is no incentive for the first tenants.

Urban planners have no training to estimate the demand for parking, and no financial stake in the success of a development. They do not know more than the developers do about how many parking spaces each project needs. They may, at best, know a little about the peak demand for free parking at a few land uses (see Chapter 2), but they know nothing about the marginal cost of parking spaces at any site or how to estimate the demand for parking as a function of its price. Markets will quickly reveal the demand for parking if cities cease requiring off-street spaces. Developers, landlords, and residents will all be able to make their own independent decisions about the right number of parking spaces. Market-priced parking will allow cities to evolve naturally in response to developers' costs and citizens' preferences, while parking requirements force evolution toward car dependency and sprawl. In planning for an uncertain future, flexible prices are far better than rigid requirements.

Liability

Legal liabilities help explain some cities' onerous transportation regulations. Excessive street widths, for example, are a defense against potential allegations that narrow streets contribute to automobile accidents. Legal rather than transportation concerns inhibit changing these regulations. But liability problems do not explain parking requirements. In their Central Business Districts (CBDs), Boston, New York, and San Francisco restrict rather than require off-street parking, while Cleveland, Milwaukee, and Philadelphia neither restrict nor require it. These examples show that, from a legal standpoint, cities can either restrict or ignore the number of off-street parking spaces. A failed Burger King, for example, is unlikely to prevail if it sues a city for negligently allowing fast-food restaurants to provide too little parking for their customers. Off-street parking requirements stem from cities' transportation and land-use planning policies, not from liability concerns.

Transaction Costs

Is parking too cheap to unbundle? If the cost of collecting the revenue outweighs the benefits of using prices to manage parking demand, free parking may be efficient; that is, parking may be too cheap to justify the transaction costs of charging for it. In the case of apartments, however, the transaction costs of charging for a parking space are minuscule compared with the cost of constructing it.[29]

The balance between the benefits of unbundling and the costs of transactions can differ greatly among different land uses, sites, and trips. If cities stop requiring off-street parking, the market will begin to sort out where unbundling is efficient. But it is wrong to assume that unbundling always involves higher transaction costs. Validated parking, for example, requires extra paperwork and accounting schemes to shield drivers from the parking charges that already exist. The parkers must also remember to have their parking tickets stamped, and forgetting to do this often leads to arguments at the exit kiosk, holding up everyone else waiting to leave. With validated parking, *bundling* increases transactions costs, and unbundling will reduce them.

Fairness

Will charging separately for parking harm the poor? To answer this question, we must remember that everybody pays for parking, but almost nobody pays for it directly. Everyone pays for bundled parking in the form of higher prices for everything else. If the cost of parking is bundled into the rent for housing, even those who can't afford a car must still pay for parking. Because the required parking spaces are a fixed cost, they represent a larger share of a lower income, and thus a greater burden for lower-income families. For example, if two required parking spaces add $100 a month to the rent for a family with an income of $24,000 a year, "free" parking consumes 5 percent of the family's income.

Unbundled parking will especially help those without cars because they will pay less for housing and nothing for parking. Unbundling will therefore benefit the poorest families more than anyone else. But will charging separately for parking harm poor families who give up a car—or decide not to buy one—to save the rent for an unbundled space? Again, we have to remember that bundled parking is not free; instead, it raises the cost of housing. How can the option to pay less for housing by taking less parking harm anyone, rich *or* poor? Those who rent the unbundled parking are no worse off, and those who don't rent it are better off because they have more money available for other things they value more.[30] The benefits to lower-income families are thus yet another advantage of unbundled parking.

CONCLUSION: THE HIGH COST OF BUNDLED PARKING

If the cost of parking is included in higher prices for everything else, we cannot pay less for parking by using less of it. Bundled parking hides the cost of owning and using cars, and it distorts choices toward cars and sprawl. The bloated parking supply required to satisfy the demand for free parking degrades urban design and drains life from city streets. By contrast, unbundled parking will reveal the cost of parking, reduce the prices of everything else, and give everyone the option to save money by conserving on cars and driving. Less driving will reduce traffic congestion, energy consumption, and air pollution. Fewer parking spaces will increase density and slow sprawl. As citizens cut back on driving in response to the rising price of parking, they will promote the public interest while pursuing their self-interest. Cities that remove off-street parking requirements will receive their just deserts.

TENANT | **BEAUTY SHOP**
NIGHT | **DAY**
PARKING | **PARKING**
8:30 A.M. *to* 5:30P.M.
NO VISITOR PARKING

CHAPTER 20 NOTES

1. Fang and Norman (2003, 1) say that bundling is "the practice of selling two or more products as a package deal, rather than selling each product separately.... The economics literature makes a distinction between *mixed bundling* and *pure bundling*. Mixed bundling refers to a pricing strategy where commodities included in a bundle can also be purchased separately, whereas pure bundling is used to describe a situation where the commodities in a bundle are not offered for sale separately." Validated parking is an example of mixed bundling; there is a price for parking, but the parking is free for those who buy something else from the firm that offers the validation. Residential parking is an example of pure bundling; a parking space is included in the price of a condominium, for example, but is not available otherwise.

2. Only at shopping malls, where many different uses are combined at one site, is it common for different uses to share free parking lots.

3. The actual construction cost of the project was $139,000 per apartment and $21,000 per parking space (see Chapter 5).

4. The monthly cost of 1 percent of the capital is a rough rule of thumb for rental housing and is used only for illustration. Obviously, the ratio depends on interest rates, taxes, operating costs, and other variables.

5. Similarly, some cities automatically reduce the fine for a parking citation if it is paid within a certain time rather than assess a late fee if the fine is not paid within the same time frame. An initial fine of $50 with a reduction to $35 if paid within a week, for example, is identical to one of $35 rising to $50 if not paid within a week. Although the lower fine with a late fee is the same as the higher one with a reduction for early payment, the issue is public relations: a late fee is a penalty, but a reduction for early payment is a reward.

6. The lower prices for smaller parking spaces should especially appeal to "green" residents who view oversized SUVs as "axles of evil" and "weapons of mass consumption."

7. The regulations could restrict ownership of parking spaces to residents to avoid any perception that "outsiders" are using their parking.

8. Similar reversals also occur. What use to be wired is now wireless (telephones), and what used to be wireless is now wired (cable television). Coffee drinkers are no longer surprised to see liquid sweeteners and powdered creamers. We should never underestimate consumers' adaptability to new circumstances. Owning rather than renting a parking space is a social convention that may easily change, just as other familiar conventions change.

9. I assume the real estate market is competitive and developers do consider the effect of their supply on the prices of apartments and parking spaces.

10. The magnitude of the waste is measured by the triangle above the demand curve, below the marginal cost curve, and to the left of a vertical line at two spaces per unit.

11. Smith and Hekimian (1985, 39). The ITE's recommended one-size-fits-all dimensions for parking spaces are 8.5 feet x 18 feet. In a survey of the parking requirements in the 27 cities in Dade County, Florida, John Bradley (1996) found that their required stall dimensions ranged from 8.5 feet x 18 feet (153 square feet) up to 10 feet x 25 feet (250 square feet). Many cities seem to take the ITE's recommendation as the minimum size and then require even larger spaces.

12. Several garages in Switzerland, and the National Car Park garage in Portman Square in London, have installed this technology.

13. An Aveo is 1.67 meters wide by 4.24 meters long, and occupies 7.07 square meters, while a Silverado is 1.99 meters wide by 6.27 meters long, and occupies 12.49 square meters.

14. Smaller cars reduce not only the demand for parking space, but also for road space. Because most of the road space used by cars in traffic is for the spacing between vehicles rather than for the vehicles themselves, however, reducing the average size of cars will reduce the demand for parking more than it reduces the demand for roads.

15. Downsizing the number of cars will reduce the fixed costs, such as insurance, of car ownership. The total insurance payments for one newer car can be significantly less than for two older cars. The repair costs for one newer car can also be less than for two older cars. The important point is that households will have more options with unbundled than with bundled parking. Some households with more than the usual number of drivers may even choose to rent *more* parking spaces than are commonly bundled free with the typical apartment.

16. Tiebout (1956). See Donahue (1997) and Fischel (2001b) for discussions of Tiebout sorting.

17. Table H-36 in Census 2000. These numbers are the averages for the nation, and most cities will have less variety. For example, Boston may have many more apartments with no or only one parking space, and Phoenix may have very few apartments with fewer than two parking spaces.

18. Urban Task Force (1999, 8).

19. Urban Task Force (1999, 105).

20. Stubbs (2002, 233).

21. De Jong (1997) explains that because of the fixed costs, car ownership is worthwhile only if you drive the car regularly. Households must therefore make a simultaneous decision on the ownership and use of a car.

22. *Ward's Motor Vehicle Facts & Figures 2002*, p. 64.

23. If residents pay for bundled parking in their rent, unbundling does not change the amount that car owners pay for parking. Unbundled parking does, however, increase the fixed cost of car ownership and decrease the rent for housing. For someone who gives up a second or third car after parking is unbundled, the lower rent will have an "income" effect on automobile use, so the elasticity of demand will slightly overstate the VMT reduction.

24. See the Flexcar web site at www.flexcar.com. Other plans with a higher fixed cost and a lower marginal cost are available for more frequent users.

25. In a study of one car-sharing plan in San Francisco, Cervero and Tsai (2003, 24-25) found that nearly nine out of 10 members were from households with no vehicle or only one.

26. We can think of how unbundling will reduce driving in another way. Andreas Schafer (2000) presents evidence showing that households' time and money budgets for travel are surprisingly stable over time. If unbundled parking raises the money cost of automobile travel, reducing the number of vehicles and VMT are two ways to make compensating reductions in the money cost of travel, to keep the travel budget stable.

27. Stedman (1994) used on-road testing technology to measure the emissions. He also found that found that the dirtiest 3 percent of vehicles emit 23 percent of the on-road CO emissions, and 27 percent of the hydrocarbon emissions (p. viii). The poorly maintained cars are driven fewer miles per year, but they emit far more pollution per mile; their evaporative emissions when parked are also far higher. Unbundling will reduce total VMT and disproportionately reduce the VMT by the dirtier cars, but will increase the VMT per car for the remaining cleaner cars.

28. Owners of office buildings sometimes convert parking spaces into storage space when the tenants are willing to pay more for storage more than for parking. This conversion is illegal if the parking spaces are required by zoning, but code enforcement is difficult if no one complains.

29. When UCLA economist Harold Demsetz (1964) examined the trade-offs between the costs of transactions and the benefits of accurate economic incentives, he used parking to illustrate the case where transactions costs were high enough to justify offering something free. "It is true that the setting and collecting of appropriate shares of construction and exchange costs [of parking] from each parker will reduce the number of parking spaces needed to allow ease of entry and exit. But while we have reduced the resources committed to constructing parking spaces, we have increased resources devoted to market exchange. We may end up by allocating more resources to the provision and control of parking than had we allowed free parking" (Demsetz 1964, 14). Demsetz was referring to parking in shopping centers. De Alessi (1983, 66) also used parking in shopping centers as an example to explain why some resources are not be priced because of the transactions costs, and he ignored the effect of free parking on travel demand. Richard Epstein (2001, 5) uses curb parking to examine the general trade-off between transaction costs and accurate price signals in allocating scarce resources: "It is only when the intensity of use increases that more complex legal regimes can pay their way."

30. Unbundling will also benefit families who turn down an expensive parking space in their apartment building and instead rent a cheaper space nearby so that they can save money on parking without giving up a car. As Thomas Sowell (1980, 128) says, "There is no reason to believe that people will generally make a better set of choices out of a smaller set of options, where the larger set includes all the options of the smaller set."

21

Time for a Paradigm Shift

How can a conceptual scheme that one generation admiringly describes as subtle, flexible, and complex become for a later generation merely obscure, ambiguous, and cumbersome?

— *THOMAS KUHN*

Princeton historian of science Thomas Kuhn said a paradigm is a conceptual scheme that has gained acceptance throughout a profession:

> [Scientists] whose research is based on shared paradigms are committed to the same rules and standards for scientific practice. That commitment and the apparent consensus it produces are prerequisites for normal science, *i.e.*, for the genesis and continuation of a particular research tradition.[1]

Kuhn argued that each profession's practices embody the current ruling paradigm and this paradigm frames the problems studied, the research methods used, and the criteria for evaluating the results. Furthermore, he said, the "normal" process of scientific inquiry focuses on the variables considered significant within the ruling paradigm. In other words, scientists fix on a train of thought and measure the relevant variables in extreme detail.

Because research in normal science is cumulative, Kuhn said, data that contradict the ruling paradigm are usually ignored or contested. Over time, however, if the body of contradictory evidence grows sufficiently large, a new paradigm that explains it may be adopted. When this type of paradigm shift occurs, scientists may discover a new set of relevant variables. Typically, these variables will not have been studied (or at least not studied with a high degree of attention or accuracy) in work from the former paradigm. In response, practitioners will improve the techniques for measuring the new variables and gather data consistent with and reinforcing the new paradigm. The process of normal science then begins anew, proceeding slowly along until contradictory evidence again builds up and triggers the next paradigm shift.

PARKING REQUIREMENTS AS A PARADIGM

Although urban planning is not a science, parking requirements resemble a paradigm, and the data collected to establish them are like the data collected in science. Urban planners knew almost nothing about parking demand when they began to require off-street parking. Planners and transportation engineers subsequently gathered data on the peak parking occupancy at various land uses. For example, each new edition of *Parking Generation* published by the Institute of Transportation Engineers includes new surveys at previously observed land uses, and surveys at new land uses (see Chapter 2).

The pseudo-empirical data collected to establish parking requirements are not only cumulative, as Kuhn described, but also circular. Planners use surveys of peak parking occupancy to set minimum parking requirements everywhere. In most cases, the large supply of required parking drives the market price of most parking to zero. As a result, most surveys of parking demand are conducted at sites that offer ample free parking, and the observed "demand" is correspondingly high. Following this circular logic, urban planners neglect both the price and the cost of parking when they set parking requirements, and the maximum observed parking demand becomes the minimum required parking supply.

Kuhn argued that our paradigms affect our theories and, in turn, our theories affect the way we experience the world. In planning for parking there is a further complication: like everyone else, planners don't want to pay for parking. Planners thus see the "need" for parking not only as a professional issue, but also as a personal one. Almost everyone's self-interest in the availability of free parking reinforces the paradigm of parking requirements. As Yale political scientist Edward Tufte explained, we suffer from "a bias toward policies with immediate, highly visible benefits and deferred, hidden costs—myopic policies for myopic voters."[2]

Parking requirements differ from a scientific paradigm in one key respect. Kuhn argued that education creates in students an intense commitment to the existing scientific paradigms. In contrast, planning education rarely, if ever, considers the single greatest arbiter of both transportation and land use—parking requirements. In practice, planning for parking is closer to sorcery than to science.

Discussing the difficulty of paradigm shifts in science, Kuhn asked, "How can a conceptual scheme that one generation admiringly describes as subtle, flexible, and complex become for a later generation merely obscure, ambiguous, and cumbersome?"[3] Without doubt, parking requirements are obscure, ambiguous, and cumbersome—an elaborate structure with no foundation. They also impose enormous costs and impede our progress toward important social, economic, and environmental goals. Planning for parking is ripe for a paradigm shift.[4]

The current debates about the transportation benefits of two recent movements in urban planning—New Urbanism and Smart Growth—provide an excellent opportunity to rethink off-street parking requirements in zoning ordinances. Many New Urbanist and Smart Growth planners argue that cities can reduce automobile dependency by altering land-use patterns and neighborhood designs. Skeptics, however, point to the lack of hard evidence that land use will affect vehicle travel. Consider, for example, *Travel by Design: The Influence of Urban Form on Travel*, by Marlon Boarnet and Randall Crane, by far the most rigorous study of how urban planning, through land-use controls, can influence travel behavior. Boarnet and Crane review previous research on the linkage between urban form and travel behavior, and conclude:

> There is little credible knowledge about how urban form influences travel patterns. Given the enormous support for using land use and urban design to address traffic problems, it was somewhat surprising…. [T]o find the empirical support for these transportation benefits to be inconclusive and their behavioral foundations obscure.[5]

Like almost everyone else, however, Boarnet and Crane do not examine how off-street parking requirements have debauched urban form and swelled vehicle travel. Parking is mentioned only once in *Travel by Design*, in a footnote, and no review of the book noted this neglect.[6] Off-street parking requirements have been a central element of both transportation and land-use policies for more than 50 years, and they profoundly distort travel patterns, but the invisibility of parking requirements in research on transportation and land use is almost total.

Parking requirements are especially difficult to reform because they are entrenched in zoning codes and embedded in an elaborate structure of permits, variances, covenants, court decisions, and entitlements. Their results have literally been cemented into the city. Not only will planners have to reject parking requirements, but so too will businesses, property owners, voters, and elected officials. To change enough minds, urban planners must offer society something better than off-street parking requirements, and planners *do* have something better to offer: parking benefit districts with market-priced curb parking. Specifically, cities should de-require off-street parking, charge market prices for curb parking, and spend the resulting revenue to pay for neighborhood public improvements. Removing off-street parking requirements does *not* mean off-street parking will disappear. Instead, where demand drives up the price of curb parking, developers will provide additional off-street parking of their own volition and charge for it accordingly

RETROFITTING AMERICA

Parking benefit districts can be retrofitted incrementally into existing neighborhoods. The new districts are not quite governments and not quite businesses, but they share some characteristics of each. They will manage their curb parking supply in a businesslike way, and the resulting revenue will support local public initiatives. Charging market prices for curb parking will improve transportation, and the public spending will improve neighborhoods. Removing off-street parking requirements will reduce the cost of development and will free up much urban land now legally dedicated to parking lots. In effect, cities have created an enormous land bank that can now be used for housing and other development if off-street parking requirements are removed.[7]

The results of removing parking requirements will be gradual rather than dramatic, but Jane Jacobs explains why we should favor small changes, and how they can add up to big improvements:

> Twenty years ago it was commonly believed that to benefit cities a plan must be sweeping and comprehensive. Small improvements and non-disruptive plans were sneered at as the band-aid approach. Slums were bulldozed to make way for monolithic public housing projects. Neighborhoods were bisected, trisected, and sometimes vivisected for links in city-wide expressway systems. Historic and humanely scaled landscapes were demolished to make way for highrise apartment or office buildings. Zoning was aimed at segregating the different components of city life from one another. Reality finally caught up with us: Not only was the destruction expensive, the results were disappointing socially, functionally and aesthetically.

> Even so, old ways of thinking die hard. Once people have taken it for granted that little worthwhile can be accomplished without the guidance of sweeping schemes—masterminding big change far into the future—they tend to be at a loss in finding constructive alternatives.

> Since we think with words even more than with diagrams, sometimes a simple change of phrase helps open our minds to possibilities and alternatives. Just so, nowadays a new term, retrofitting, has begun to enter the planning

vocabulary. Retrofitting means accepting what exists as a base, a given, and deliberately improving it with varied small changes. These little alterations, thought of and undertaken as opportunity offers, incrementally add up to a very significant improvement. By its very nature, this approach is economic, conserving, efficient, flexible, and responsive.[8]

Jacobs says that communities will choose the retrofitting approach if they share three values:

Belief that small improvements are worthwhile, faith that they add up, and recognition that they are all the more effective because they are not disruptive and all the more congenial because they can occur as opportunity offers and circumstance permits.[9]

In a similar vein, MIT professor of landscape architecture Ann Whiston Spirn says:

Incremental change through small projects is often more manageable, or feasible, less daunting, and more adaptable to local needs and values. When coordinated, incremental changes can have a far-reaching effect. Solutions need not be comprehensive, but the understanding of the problem *must* be.[10]

After cities emancipate themselves from off-street parking requirements, many small but significant reforms can follow from the basic understanding that "free" parking has a high cost. In Los Angeles, for example, the Getty Museum charges for parking but admits people free, while the Huntington Museum offers free parking but charges people for admission. Charging more for parking and less for people will improve city life.

AN ILLUSTRATION: ADVISING THE MAYOR

Some people seem to think that charging market prices for curb parking would require a massively difficult social change, like Prohibition or the Reformation. Nevertheless, it has worked smoothly where cities have established parking benefit districts. Although these districts represent only a marginal change to existing practices, they can produce major improvements. To put parking benefit districts in the broader context of transportation, land use, and public finance, suppose the mayor of a city in a developing nation asked your advice on how to deal with the parking problems caused by rapidly increasing car ownership. Consider two policies you might recommend: (1) keep curb parking free and require all development to provide off-street parking, or (2) charge market prices for curb parking and use the revenue to pay for local public services.

1. Off-street parking requirements will hide the cost of parking in the prices for everything else. They will collectivize the cost of parking, so everyone will pay for parking whether they use it or not. Free parking will encourage vehicle travel and discourage travel by foot, bicycle, and public transit. It will therefore increase energy consumption, traffic congestion, and air pollution. The city will be designed and built around free parking—at the expense of many other public goals. The nation will import more cars and fuel. The cost of required parking will be a hidden tax everyone must pay through higher prices for everything they buy, even if they do not own a car. The city will earn no curb parking revenue to pay for public investments.

2. Market prices for curb parking will "individualize" the cost of parking and give everyone an incentive to economize in using it. This policy will reveal the cost of parking and allow private choices to determine the off-street parking supply. Market prices will create a few curb vacancies so that drivers can always find a place to park near their destinations. The price of parking will restrain the demand for cars and will therefore reduce energy consumption, traffic congestion, and air pollution. More people will travel by foot, bicycle, carpool, and public transit. The nation will import fewer cars and less fuel. Because motorists will pay for parking directly, no one will be forced to pay for it indirectly. Curb parking revenue will pay for neighborhood public investments.

To help the mayor choose, you might suggest criteria for comparing the two policies, and Table 21-1 shows 12 that would be relevant. Parking benefit districts excel on 11 of these: air quality, climate change, energy consumption, housing prices, public revenue, public transportation, traffic congestion, urban design, urban sprawl, walking environment, and water quality.[11] Parking requirements excel on one criterion: free parking. Which policy would *you* recommend? In the aggregate, cities' choices between these two policies—or among other policies—will affect not just the individual cities, but the world. Consider, for example, what would happen if China and India were to adopt American-style parking requirements for all new development. Beyond the self-inflicted harm to the cities themselves, the consequences for global fuel consumption, air pollution, and climate change would be catastrophic.

A NEW STYLE OF PLANNING

Parking benefit districts will require a new style of urban planning. Planners now devote considerable effort to enforcing the parking requirements for new buildings or for changes in the use of existing buildings.

Table 21-1. Parking Requirements or Benefit Districts? Comparing Results

		Results	
	Criterion	Parking requirements	Benefit districts
1	Air quality	Worse	Better
2	Climate change	Faster	Slower
3	Energy consumption	Higher	Lower
4	Price of housing	Higher	Lower
5	Price of parking	Lower	Higher
6	Public revenue	Less	More
7	Public transportation	Worse	Better
8	Traffic congestion	Worse	Better
9	Urban design	Worse	Better
10	Urban sprawl	Faster	Slower
11	Walking environment	Worse	Better
12	Water quality	Worse	Better

As a result, they spend much of their time dealing with developers. With parking benefit districts, planners will more often work in partnership with neighborhoods, helping them decide how to manage curb parking and how to spend the public revenue it produces. In focusing on curb parking, city planners will also have to pay much more attention to streets, which they now largely neglect. As University of Washington professor of urban design Anne Vernez Moudon says,

> Streets have become a void in the mind of city planners. Transportation planning has been made separate from city planning and, accordingly, streets separate rather than link the different pieces of the city.[12]

The revenue from curb parking will refocus planners' attention on streets and neighborhoods. Because neighborhoods will have real money to spend and real choices to make, the residents' preferences will acquire new weight and real community participation will be necessary. Concentrating planners' attention on the task of improving older neighborhoods may well be one of the new parking paradigm's most important benefits.

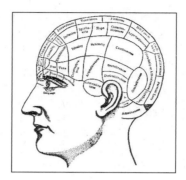

CHAPTER 21 NOTES

1. Kuhn (1996, 11). The *American Heritage Dictionary* defines a paradigm as "A set of assumptions, concepts, values, and practices that constitutes a way of viewing reality for the community that shares them, especially in an intellectual discipline."

2. Tufte (1978, 143).

3. Kuhn (1957, 76) was describing how latter-day astronomers looked back at the earth-centered concept of the universe.

4. Paradigm shifts are not easy, but planning paradigms have shifted before, as suggested by the names of various urban planning theories in the twentieth century: city beautiful, city practical, garden city, radiant city, rational planning, comprehensive planning, urban renewal, incrementalism, muddling through, advocacy planning, equity planning, participatory planning, progressive planning, radical planning, critical planning, strategic planning, communicative action, postmodernism, New Urbanism, and Smart Growth. No paradigm has ever been abandoned completely because each has some merit, but planning theory always moves on.

5. Boarnet and Crane (2001, 172).

6. Imagine a similar book that explored how air travel affects urban form but never mentioned airports. Would anyone fail to see the omission?

7. Some parking lots already serve as land banks for later development, and the interim use for parking is referred to as a "taxpayer" (Shoup 1969 and 1970).

8. Jacobs (1987, 27).

9. Jacobs (1987, 27).

10. Spirn (1984, 10). Italics in the original.

11. Water quality is included in this list for two reasons. First, paved parking lots increase the impervious surface area in a city, reduce the area for water to percolate into the soil, and increase stormwater runoff. Parking lots also accumulate oil drippings that contain toxic metals such as chromium, and the runoff then pollutes water supplies. Second, the revenue from curb parking can pay for piped water and sewers in parking benefit districts.

12. Moudon (1987, 16).

Part

IV

Conclusion

As our case is new, so must we think anew, and act anew.

—*ABRAHAM LINCOLN*

22

Changing the Future

> *I shall be telling this with a sigh*
> *Somewhere ages and ages hence:*
> *Two roads diverged in a wood, and I—*
> *I took the one less traveled by,*
> *And that has made all the difference.*
>
> —ROBERT FROST

In Monopoly, free parking is only one space out of 40 on the board. If Monopoly were played under our current zoning laws, however, free parking would be on every space. Parking lots might cover half of Marvin Gardens, and Park Place would have underground parking. Free parking would push buildings farther apart, increase the cost of houses and hotels, and permit fewer of them to be built at all. Smart players would soon leave Atlantic City behind and move to a larger board that allowed them to build on cheaper land in the suburbs. Connecticut Avenue would not be redeveloped with hotels, the railroads would disappear, and every piece on the board would move more slowly. Even the car would move slowly, but it would park free wherever it wanted.

If we played Monopoly according to our current zoning regulations, a large share of the money for every new building would disappear into the Community Chest, only to reappear as free parking. Every player would want the car as their token. Players who got the shoe as their token would cry foul, and they would be right—the system would not be fair because much of their money would be going to subsidize the car while everyone else gets left behind. We probably would not want our children to play by these unfair rules, and yet adult Americans play by these rules in real life every day. Mandatory free parking disfigures the landscape, distorts urban form, damages the environment, and wastes money that could be spent more productively elsewhere. Because we never see the money we spend on parking, it always seems someone else is paying for it. Everything *seems* all right, but I have tried to show in this book that a great deal is wrong with free parking and it is time to cry foul.

CURB PARKING AS A COMMONS PROBLEM

Parking will always be free where land is plentiful and cheap, but it is a grave mistake to think parking should be free everywhere. In Chapter 1, I argued most parking problems stem from treating curb parking as a commons. In England, the term "commons" originally referred to agricultural land everyone in a community could use, and "commoners" were citizens who enjoyed free use of the commons. Free curb parking is the modern urban counterpart of a medieval rural commons, and motorists are the new commoners: they can park free if they can find a space. But finding a vacant curb space often requires cruising, and cruising for parking is a natural outcome of a classic commons problem. Drivers waste their time circling the block while waiting for another car to leave, and in so doing they congest traffic, waste fuel, and pollute the air.

Although spending a few minutes searching for a free curb space is not a great burden for individual drivers, its aggregate consequences are astonishing. Chapter 14 showed that cruising for parking in a 15-block commercial district in Los Angeles created 945,000 vehicle miles travelled (VMT) a year—equivalent to driving around the earth 38 times! Because many cities have congested areas where drivers spend several minutes to find a curb space, cruising for parking in all the congested cities on earth generates a stupendous amount of excess vehicle travel, wastes an astronomical amount of fuel, and produces catastrophic levels of air pollution and CO_2 emissions.

Urban planners have not ignored the curb parking commons problem, of course, but they have chosen a costly solution: off-street parking requirements. In most U.S. cities, planners assume most people will travel everywhere by car and thus require each site to provide enough off-street parking spaces to satisfy the expected peak demand for parking. As a result, most new commercial buildings have parking lots or structures bigger than the buildings themselves, and almost everyone drives wherever they go: 87 percent of all trips in the U.S. are made by personal motor vehicles, and parking is free for 99 percent of these trips. Requiring all new buildings to provide ample off-street parking reduces cruising for free curb parking, but it also creates many new problems. It increases the cost and decreases the density of urban development, leading to faster sprawl; it fosters excessive reliance on the car, contributing to greater air pollution, traffic congestion, and energy consumption; and it degrades the transportation system for modes other than the car, including buses (which must crawl through the same congestion), cyclists (who must battle to share space with vehicles on the road and breathe their exhaust), and pedestrians (who must watch out for cars crossing the sidewalks to enter or exit off-street parking lots).

ENORMOUS PARKING SUBSIDIES

All this free parking is charity for cars. In 2002, the total subsidy for *off-street* parking was somewhere between $127 billion and $374 billion a year. If we also count the subsidy for free and underpriced *curb* parking, the total subsidy for parking would be far higher. In the same year, the federal government spent only $231 billion for Medicare and $349 billion for national defense. Do we really want to spend as much to subsidize parking as we spend for Medicare or national defense? Because parking costs so much and motorists pay so little for it, the hidden subsidy is truly gigantic. Spending so much to subsidize parking dramatically alters the transportation system, land-use patterns, the economy, and the environment—all in the wrong direction.[1]

A fundamental virtue of any public policy is transparency. Citizens should know not only what is being done, but also how much it costs and who will pay. The source of free parking is not transparent: the subsidy for it is not just high but also *hidden*. As drivers, we see only its benefits; as citizens, we bear its costs but do not recognize their source. The hidden nature of the subsidy leads us not to question the value of free parking. We have planned our cities since World War II as though parking really were free and thus not worth talking about. When we argue, for instance, about whether to rezone four acres of land for a Wal-Mart, three acres of which the city requires for a parking lot, we are missing something major in the discussion. Why can't the Wal-Mart and the parking lot each be considered on its own merits? Parking is now seen as a condition for development, rather than as a part of the development itself, to be scrutinized and evaluated on its own. Although parking is the single biggest land use in cities, it has managed to become always part of something else, and from that position it dominates cities.

A direct result of the failure to think critically about free parking is the tendency to take it for granted—to mistake it for a right rather than a privilege—so that most people do not see it as being any subsidy at all. Off-street parking requirements seem unquestionably necessary because without them development would create spillover and overcrowd all the free curb parking, which would be considered intolerable. Meanwhile, the other alternative, which is to charge market prices for curb parking, is also abhorrent because we are all accustomed to thinking of curb spaces as being "ours." Motorists have in effect taken the curb parking spaces by adverse possession. Cars have squatted free at the curb for so long it strikes most people as not just wrong but illegal—and un-American—to suggest drivers should pay market prices for parking.

Off-street parking requirements *might* be worth their enormous cost if their sole consequence were to force everyone to pay for parking indirectly through higher prices for everything else. After all, most trips in the U.S. are made by car, so it could be argued free parking simply shuffles money around among motorists and harms only the small minority who ride public transit, cycle, or walk where they want to go. Saddling the nonmotoring minority with a burden to subsidize the motoring majority raises a serious equity issue, but the number of people with a complaint is small, and their political power is even smaller. But parking requirements do far graver harm than simply penalizing a few nondrivers: they also have a host of other unintended consequences. They increase traffic congestion and air pollution, distort urban form, degrade urban design, increase housing costs, limit homeownership, damage the urban economy, harm the central business district, and penalize poor families. They also increase energy consumption, which helps explain why American motor vehicles now consume an eighth of the world's total oil production, more than half of it imported and paid for with borrowed money.[2]

Off-street parking requirements have produced consequences that the planners who invented them in the 1930s could never have imagined, and their costs are astounding. It is less excusable that planners today remain oblivious to the costs and consequences of the parking requirements they administer. Good intentions in urban planning have no value outside their consequences, and by that measure, off-street parking requirements are a catastrophe.

UNINTENDED CONSEQUENCES

Everyone is familiar with the problem of unintended consequences, but it was Harvard sociologist Robert Merton who in 1936 wrote the first analysis of the phenomenon. He identified five sources of unintended consequences: ignorance, error, immediacy of interest, basic values, and self-fulfilling prophecies. Each one of them contributes to the unintended consequences of parking requirements, which American cities were introducing when Merton wrote his classic article. We can consider each source in turn and relate it to the problems created by parking requirements.

Ignorance

"The exigencies of practical life frequently compel us to act with some confidence even though it is manifest the information on which we base our action is not complete," Merton said. Situations demanding immediate action of some sort "will usually involve ignorance of certain aspects of the situation and will bring about unexpected results."[3] Ignorance clearly applies to parking requirements. Planners must establish parking requirements for every land use, but they have almost no theory or data to help them estimate how many parking spaces are really "needed." They usually end up copying other cities' requirements or relying on unreliable surveys of the peak parking occupancy at suburban land uses with free parking and no public transit. As a result, cities typically require developers and property owners to provide too many parking spaces.

Error

"We may err in our appraisal of the present situation, in our inference from this to the future objective situation, in our selection of a course of action, or finally in the execution of the action chosen, " Merton said. Action, he explained, "tends to become automatic and undeliberative through continued repetition so that the actor fails to recognize that procedures which have been successful *in certain circumstances* need not be so *under any and all conditions*."[4] The demand for parking varies by location, time of day, day of the week, and week of the year. And yet, as Merton might have predicted, planners often make the mistake of applying the same parking requirements throughout the city. What was once the product of thought becomes instead routine, and what was once scrutinized and debated becomes uncritically accepted. Planners have no training in how to estimate parking demand, and most would be hard pressed to explain how their cities set the parking requirements for various land uses or to justify the differences between one use and the next. They do know, however, that parking requirements have been around since before they were born, and so they continue the tradition without asking how the parking requirements were established.

Immediacy of Interest

Unintended consequences will also occur "where the actor's paramount concern with the foreseen immediate consequences excludes the consideration of further or other consequences of the same act."[5] Planners are under tremendous pressure to resolve current land-use conflicts, and the future is typically left to take care of itself. Parking requirements serve to quiet disputes between neighbors and allow development to proceed, but who can seriously contend that minimum parking requirements and ubiquitous free parking are long-term strategies to make great places and create sustainable cities? Parking requirements help planners avoid immediate conflicts over current development, but they plant the seeds of many long-term woes.

Basic Values

Unintended outcomes are likely, Merton said, "where there is no consideration of further consequences because of the felt necessity of a certain action enjoined by certain fundamental values."[6] In a car-owning democracy, off-street parking requirements suit the basic values of most people, who do not see—or do not want to see—the long-term social, economic, and environmental costs of ubiquitous free parking.

Self-fulfilling Prophecies

Finally, Merton explained, "predictions of future social developments... become a new element in the concrete situation, thus tending to change the initial course of developments."[7] If planners assume everybody will go everywhere by car and cities require enough parking spaces to meet the peak demand for free parking at every land use, everything will be so dispersed that most people will have to drive wherever they want to go. Self-fulfilling prophecies about the need for parking help explain why we now make 87 percent of all our trips by car. City planners feel justified in requiring so many parking spaces because, after all, almost everyone drives everywhere. But if cities had *not* required any off-street parking spaces to begin with and had instead charged market prices for curb parking everywhere, we would now own fewer cars and use them more judiciously.

Off-street parking requirements produce many unintended and unwanted consequences, but cities impose them to deal with a very real problem: the overcrowding of curb parking caused by treating it as a commons. To solve the curb parking commons problem without imposing inept land-use regulations, cities can instead let the market do some work for the public good—the approach Brookings Institution economist Charles Schultze termed "the public use of private interest."[8]

ENCLOSING THE COMMONS

In a paradoxical description of problem solving, Berkeley professors of urban planning Horst Rittel and Melvin Webber wrote, "The information needed to *understand* the problem depends upon one's idea for *solving* it."[9] In the spirit of this statement, my understanding of the parking problem has been shaped by the idea of the traditional way to solve a commons problem: *enclosure*. In England, the communal rights to agricultural land were gradually converted into private rights through an enclosure movement that lasted several centuries.[10] "Enclosure" meant subdividing large areas of common land into smaller pieces of private property, and the procedure usually involved giving a small plot of land to each commoner as compensation for surrendering their former "commoning" rights. As the solution to a commons problem, enclosure now often refers to the establishment of legal rights to a previously unregulated resource.[11] In this modern sense of the term, the enclosure of curb parking does *not* imply private ownership of the curb space. Rather, I am using the term "enclosure" to mean charging market prices for curb parking and then spending the resulting revenue for local public improvements.

Agricultural enclosures in England greatly increased the productivity of farmland, but they also spelled the end of an established way of life, and scholars differ as to how painful the transition was. Oxford University historians Charles and Christabel Orwin, for example, speak of "the loss of the sense of personal responsibility in the members of the village community for its social institutions."[12] Others, however, think the social benefits of common-field agriculture have been exaggerated. London University geographer James Yelling says critics viewed the common-field system "not as an ennobling experience in 'pure democracy,' but as a morass of petty restrictions and a potent source of squabbles and individual friction."[13]

Like common-field agriculture, free curb parking also involves a morass of petty restrictions and is often a potent source of squabbles. Parking is one of the most heavily regulated aspects of urban land use, and the regulations are often bewildering—only residents can park on one street; nonresidents can park on the next street, but only for two hours; the third street may be free for everyone except on Friday mornings when all parking is prohibited; and the street after that may have meters or no parking at all. If cities begin to charge market prices for curb parking and spend the revenue to improve neighborhoods, future generations are unlikely to view this enclosure as diminishing anyone's personal responsibility for the community or unfairly dispossessing motorists of their ancient commoning rights. After all, drivers can still park; they just have to pay, and the results benefit everyone. Drivers will always be able to find a place to park if they are willing to pay for it, and the curb parking revenue will pay for valuable public services.[14]

PUBLIC PROPERTY, NOT PRIVATE PROPERTY

There is an important distinction between the separate issues of "public property" (a government owns it) and "open access" (anyone can use it free). With curb parking, public property is not the problem, and private ownership is not the solution. Instead, open access is the problem, and fair-market prices are the solution. Public ownership often leads to open access, of course, but it does not have to. Parking benefit districts with market-price curb parking will create public ownership *without* open access.[15]

Because curb parking spaces will remain public property, enclosure can help almost everyone. In contrast, agricultural enclosure converted communal farming and grazing rights into private property, and the process did harm some people, although the benefits and costs depended greatly on the circumstances. In his essay on the enclosure movement, the eighteenth-century agricultural expert Arthur Young wrote that where enclosure was done properly:

> [It] proves how much the poor are desirous of having property divided rather than in common.... They are converted by this property to as sober and regular a people as they were before licentious.... [N]othing tends so strongly to give the poor industrious and frugal habits as the prospect of acquiring, or the hope of preserving land.[16]

Despite the current political incorrectness of his phrasing, historians of the enclosure movement tend to agree with Young's evaluation. The Orwins, for instance, point out that open-field farming impeded progress because it distorted farmers' incentives and prevented new farming techniques from being adopted. If the yield from their investments had to be shared with others who did not contribute as much, individual farmers were reluctant to invest in new tools or study new agricultural methods. The commons, the Orwins conclude, "had served its day, and it had to go."[17]

Parking benefit districts can produce the economic benefits of agricultural enclosures without the social costs. "The magic of property turns sand into gold," Arthur Young observed, and the same alchemy can convert curb parking spaces into cash to pay for public improvements. Free curb parking is the product of good intentions, and most planners who implement off-street parking requirements are public-minded people trying to do what is best for their communities. But the costs of free parking are enormous, and the benefits, the more one examines them, are small in comparison. Free curb parking has served its day, and it has to go.

COMMONS, ANTICOMMONS, AND THE LIBERAL COMMONS

In 1968, Garrett Hardin published his famous article, "The Tragedy of the Commons." Thirty years later, in 1998, Columbia University law professor Michael Heller published "The Tragedy of the Anticommons," in which he analyzed the opposite problem. In an anticommons, Heller says, "multiple owners are each endowed with the right to exclude others from a scarce resource, and no one has an effective privilege of use. When too many owners hold such rights of exclusion, the resource is prone to underuse—a tragedy of the anticommons."[18] Free curb parking creates a classic commons problem: drivers waste time, congest traffic, and pollute the air while cruising for scarce curb spaces.[19] In contrast, residential permit districts that prohibit curb parking by nonresidents create an anticommons: residents don't own the curb spaces in their neighborhood, but they can keep nonresidents out. While free curb parking gives too much access to curb parking and overcrowds it, residential permit districts can give too little access, and a valuable resource is underused. As Heller says, "resources can become stuck in low-value uses at either end of the property rights spectrum. Whether this misallocation takes the form of overuse in a commons or underuse in an anticommons, the economic waste of resources results."[20] Free curb parking wastes resources in the form of cruising, while residential permit districts waste resources in the form of empty curb spaces.

Other authors have also reexamined the field of property rights, and their findings show commonly owned property need not lead to a tragedy. In a 1991 re-analysis of the commons problem in "The Tragedy of the *Unmanaged* Commons," Garrett Hardin says common ownership can be successful when it is combined with limited access.[21] Glenn Stevenson analyzes the economics of common property use and argues that open access, not common ownership, causes the tragedy.[22] Hanoch Dagan and Michael Heller also distinguish between common property and open access, saying open access implies free access to everyone, while common property can refer to resources owned or controlled by a finite number of people who manage the resource together and exclude outsiders.[23] Similarly, Yale law professor Carol Rose discusses cases where the difficulty of "individual propertization" leads to "limited common property" regimes that are "a commons on the inside, but property on the outside."[24] If residents of a neighborhood can park free on their own streets, while nonresidents have to pay, insiders will view their curb parking as a commons, but outsiders will see it as private property.

Dagan and Heller have further analyzed the spectrum of possibilities lying between private property at one end and a commons with open access at the other, and they propose a hybrid form of ownership termed a "liberal commons":

> For many resources, the most appealing ownership structure proves to be a participatory commons regime that also allows members the freedom to come and go. We call this structure a "liberal commons"—an ideal type of ownership

distinct from both private and commons property, but drawing elements from each. Any legal regime can qualify as a liberal commons when it enables a limited group of owners to capture the economic and social benefits from cooperative use of a scarce resource, while also ensuring autonomy to individual members.... Constructing a successful liberal commons is always challenging, but it is not an inherently contradictory or practically unattainable goal.[25]

Parking benefit districts fit the definition of a liberal commons perfectly. They provide an excellent example of how a neighborhood can capture the economic and social benefits from cooperative use of a scarce urban resource—land used for curb parking.

Urban planners have also been exploring how residents can pool property rights in pursuit of mutual gain. Cardiff University professor of urban planning Chris Webster explains, "Order emerges in cities as individuals seek to reduce the costs of cooperating with each other," and he uses curb parking as an example of a resource where inadequate property rights have hampered cooperation:

Access to on-street parking in front of a building is an attribute that many land users assume a right to, but have little control over in practice.... When residents possess no effective legal rights over the risk of neighborhood congestion, neighborhood quality and possibly viability are at the mercy of non-residents and non-conforming residents.[26]

In discussing solutions to urban problems, Webster points out that the property rights over a resource depend on both the value of the resource and the cost of assigning and enforcing the rights. As the value of a resource increases and the cost of assigning rights to it falls, societies will tend to reassign the property rights to it, and he again cites curb parking as an example:

On-road parking space in cities used to be a shared resource. Rising population numbers, density and car ownership increase demand and raise the wasteful cost of competition. Developers of new housing estates respond by assigning road spaces to individual houses or selling rights to shared car parks. Governments respond by redesigning roads, introducing resident-only parking and so on.[27]

Parking benefit districts are a logical next step in the assignment of property rights for curb parking. They will foster cooperation in managing valuable common land and will help to produce the type of urban order Webster describes:

Neighborhoods are a kind of urban order. They are shaped by organisational order as individuals pool rights over certain resources. They are governed by institutional order as spontaneous conventions and customs and organised rules and statutes seek to reduce the dissipation costs of conflict over shared resources. They are defined by the proprietary order secured by the institutions of private property. They are also defined by the institutions that attempt to allocate rights over shared resources. Indeed, it is the success of this type of institution that determines a neighborhood's fortunes.[28]

Parking benefit districts will improve the fortunes of neighborhoods by capturing the full economic and social value of urban land used for curb parking.

PUBLIC PROPERTY, BUT WITHOUT OPEN ACCESS

Parking benefit districts will convert communal rights into public revenue. Cities own all the curb parking spaces but tend to treat them as communal property with open access—parking is free for anyone who can find a space.[29] Even when cities do charge for curb parking, they usually charge less than the market price. In the case of curb parking, public ownership has not solved the commons problem, and this failure can be related to what John Stuart Mill termed the government's "inferior interest in the result."

> People understand their own business and their own interests better, and care for them more, than the government does, or can be expected to.... All the facilities which a government enjoys of access to information; all the means which it possesses of remunerating, and therefore of commanding, the best available talent in the market—are not an equivalent for the one great disadvantage of an inferior interest in the result.[30]

The higher the level of government, the less interest it has in local results. The federal and state governments, for example, have almost no interest in curb parking. Even for most local governments, the money from curb parking is just a drop in the bucket, not worthy of close attention. But for a neighborhood parking benefit district, the money received from curb parking will be the *entire* revenue stream, and when used to pay for public improvements, it can make a huge difference. For a city, free parking seems to have great benefits and few costs. For a parking benefit district, in contrast, the cost of free curb parking is much more obvious—it is everything the neighborhood could buy with the revenue from market-priced curb parking. Shifting the decisions about parking to the neighborhood level will thus create the great advantage of a superior interest in the result. In each neighborhood, the residents, businesses, and property owners will see the results every day.

Nothing in this argument says people will be happy about paying for parking or will think they are contributing to the greater good each time they pay. No one wants to pay for parking—that will never change—but who *wants* to pay for anything? We pay for things because we have to, not because we want to, and returning revenue to the metered neighborhoods will create a necessary constituency who want to charge for curb parking. If curb parking revenue pays for local public improvements, citizens will support a new enclosure movement that converts free curb parking into public revenue. Is that an intolerable burden on motorists? Parking is only one aspect of driving, and most other aspects aren't free. Nobody expects free gasoline, for example, which is just as well. The fact gasoline prices hit consumers where it counts—in their wallets—has spurred automotive technology toward greater fuel efficiency. But just as open-field agriculture slowed the improvement of farming methods, so too does free curb parking stall improvements in transportation and land use. And just as the enclosure of common fields reformed agriculture, so too can the enclosure of curb parking reform transportation, and the resulting improvements in urban land use may be even more far-reaching.

OTHER COMMONS PROBLEMS

Charging for curb parking can help solve several other difficult commons problems. Charging for parking will reduce traffic congestion, which is itself created by free access to scarce road space. Reducing vehicle emissions will reduce the air pollution created by our treatment of the atmosphere as a commons. Finally, charging for curb parking can contribute to solving another classic commons problem: global climate change.

Climate change is a complex issue, and addressing it will require complicated international treaties with targets, timetables, trading, monitoring, and sanctions. Signing an international treaty to deal with global climate change means all nations must agree to do things not individually beneficial in order to secure a collective benefit they each ultimately desire. The fear of a possible worldwide climate disaster may eventually compel concerted action, but it will be slow. In contrast, parking benefit districts require no complicated treaties and can be established quickly. And to the extent that higher parking prices can reduce consumption of fossil fuels, they can do some of the work we now look to international treaties to accomplish.

Although the connections may at first glance seem tenuous, charging for curb parking can indirectly help solve difficult regional, national, and even international problems. Pursuing local self-interest can thus help us reach much broader goals. Solving the smallest and simplest commons problem may thus make an impressive dent on much bigger and more complicated ones. Returning curb parking revenue to neighborhoods makes sense at the local, regional, national, and global levels. Getting the price of curb parking right will do a world of good.

TWO FUTURES

We cannot change the past, but we can change the future. Our unwise parking policies have damaged our cities, our economy, and our environment. These policies have produced a fiasco, but better policies can lead to great improvements. I will conclude by comparing the dramatically different outcomes of two alternative parking policies we can choose for the twenty-first century.

Free Parking

We can choose not to change anything. Cities can keep curb parking free and continue to require plentiful off-street parking for every land use. The cost of parking will remain hidden in higher prices for everything else. Free parking will skew our transportation choices toward cars, and we will continue to design our cities around this distortion. We will commit scarce land and capital to supply free parking, and as a result neglect many other goals. We will waste more time in traffic, consume more energy, import more oil, breathe dirtier air, and pay more for everything except parking. Everyone will pay for parking whether they use it or not. Cities will impose the high cost of free parking on everyone, even those too poor to own a car.

Parking Benefit Districts

We can, however, choose a better future. Cities can charge fair-market prices for curb parking, return the resulting revenue to pay for neighborhood public services, and remove the requirements for off-street parking. With this approach, the cost of parking will slowly become unbundled from the prices for everything else. Responding to this change, we will drive less. As a result, we will waste less time in traffic, consume less energy, import less oil, breathe cleaner air, and pay less for everything except parking. We will also have more revenue to pay for local public services.

A generation ago, many planners and politicians opposed market solutions to public problems almost as a matter of principle, but even skeptics who still doubt the merits of market prices for other public services can in good conscience recommend charging for parking. If cities underprice curb parking, they must require off-street parking everywhere—imposing enormous costs on the economy and the environment. Planners can and should regulate the quality of parking, but they should deregulate or limit its quantity. Instead of planning without prices, we can let prices do the planning.

THREE REFORMS

These three reforms—charge fair-market prices for curb parking, return the resulting revenue to neighborhoods to pay for public improvements, and remove the requirements for off-street parking—will align our individual incentives with our common interests, so that private choices will produce public benefits. We can achieve enormous social, economic, and environmental benefits at almost no cost simply by subsidizing people and places, not parking and cars.

CHAPTER 22 NOTES

1. Three criteria commonly used to evaluate the appropriateness of a subsidy are that it should be necessary, sufficient, and not excessive. We can evaluate the subsidies for parking by each of these criteria. "Necessary" means the outcome is both desirable and would not have happened otherwise. Free parking fails in this regard. Parking is necessary for most automobile trips, but it need not be free because most people would still get where they want to go even if they had to pay to park (just as they have to pay for gasoline). Many would continue to drive alone and to pay the full cost of parking, but some would begin to carpool, ride public transit, bike, or walk. "Sufficient" means the subsidy is large enough to provide the service demanded. Here again parking subsidies fail because there is never enough free parking or not enough of it exactly where everyone wants to park. Finally, "not excessive" means the public does not give away too much for what it gets back. Parking subsidies fail this test as well. We would get far better value for our money if we spent these subsidies for more important purposes.

2. In 2001, the U.S. produced 8.1 million barrels of petroleum a day and imported another 10.6 million barrels a day (Davis and Diegel 2002, Table 1.11). Petroleum imports totaled $104 billion, which accounted for 8 percent of total imports and equaled 29 percent of the balance of trade deficit (U.S. Census Bureau 2002a, Exhibits 1, 6, and 9).

3. Merton (1936, 900).

4. Ibid. (901), italics in the original.

5. Ibid. (901).

6. Ibid. (903).

7. Ibid. (903-4).

8. Schultze (1977). University of Southern California planning professors Peter Gordon and Harry Richardson (2001) refer to this approach as "market planning."

9. Rittel and Webber (1973, 161).

10. An Enclosure Act was an Act of Parliament authorizing the enclosure of common land in a particular locality. Turner (1980, 32) says there were 5,265 parliamentary enclosures in England from the first act in 1604 to the last in 1914. These enclosures accounted for 21 percent of the surface area of England but a much higher proportion of the area available for agricultural use.

11. Ross Eckert's *The Enclosure of Ocean Resources,* for example, refers not to fencing the ocean, but to extending national sovereignty and regulation into offshore territorial waters (Eckert 1979). This modern concept of enclosure stems from the long historical tradition of agricultural enclosures, but it does not imply private ownership of the "enclosed" resource.

12. Orwin and Orwin (1967, 171).

13. Yelling (1977, 215). In his history of the enclosure movement, William Curtler (1920, 65) wrote, "Contrary to the popular idea that enclosure was wholly a landlord's movement, modern investigation has clearly discovered that there was a distinct effort on the part of the peasantry, beginning as early as the fourteenth, and continuing in the fifteenth and sixteenth centuries, to abandon the open-field system and escape the compulsory co-operation with the lazy and shiftless."

14. Enclosure of the curb parking commons would certainly have occurred long ago if cities had not imposed off-street parking requirements as an alternative solution to the shortage of curb spaces. In his book on the economics of the open-field system in Britain, Carl Dahlman (1980) explains that collective ownership of grazing grounds persisted for centuries in part because of the economies of scale in livestock production. Similarly, open access to curb parking was once efficient when parking demand was low and curb space was plentiful. After car ownership became widespread, free curb parking would have been unworkable without ample off-street parking. Now that the cost of off-street parking is so high, charging market prices for curb parking is an appealing alternative to requiring off-street parking spaces.

15. A few cities contract with private operators to *manage* their curb parking spaces, but this is not the same as converting it to private ownership. Public ownership of curb parking with market prices to limit access will probably be much more efficient than private ownership of individual curb spaces. Converting the public parking spaces to individual ownership and operating a market in the privately owned curb spaces would have high transactions cost, and the politics would be acrimonious. Individually owned curb parking spaces might remain vacant much of the time because the transaction cost of renting them while the owners are not using them would be high. Publicly owned but market-priced curb parking spaces would have a higher occupancy rate, just as random-access spaces in a parking lot or garage have a higher occupancy rate than the named spaces do.

16. Young (1801, 500–501 and 521). Young also wrote that enclosure often did harm the poor, but this harm was not inevitable: "Instead of giving property to the poor, or preserving it, or enabling them to acquire it, the very contrary effect has taken place; and as this evil was by no means *necessarily* connected with the measure of enclosing, it was a mischief that might easily have been avoided, and ought most carefully to be avoided in the future" (Young 1801, 515, italics in the original). Young's description of enclosure eerily resembles modern discussions of welfare reform.

17. Orwin and Orwin (1967, 171). Joan Thirsk (1967, 200) wrote, "To those who observed or experienced some of the more ruthless enclosures of land in the Midland counties, all enclosers were agents of Satan and all enclosures inflicted grievous harm on the community. Such hardened opponents of change would hardly have recognized as part of the same movement the amicable enclosures taking place at the same time in some of the northern and west Midland counties." Similarly, James Yelling (1977, 214) says, "This error of transposing the effects of some enclosures on to others leads to the heart of the problem that the movement presents to the modern scholar. Almost all of the most easily demonstrated consequences of enclosure depended on circumstances. The necessary consequences, inevitably involved in any act of enclosure, were far less tangible, although perhaps of deep significance."

18. Heller (1998, 622). Carol Rose (1986, 723) has described another alternative to the tragedy of the commons where the commons is "not tragic, but comedic, in the classical sense of a story with a happy outcome." If the benefits to each participant in an activity increase when more people participate, the result is "the reverse of the 'tragedy of the commons': it is a 'comedy of the commons,' as is so felicitously expressed in the phrase, 'the more the merrier'" (Rose 1986, 768). Unfortunately, free curb parking is rarely a comedic commons.

19. Curb parking in a neighborhood can become so overcrowded that residents are reluctant to leave their parking space because they fear they won't find another space when they get back. Because people who would rather use their cars instead remain parked, they reduce the number of spaces available to those who do want to park. And those who do find parking may have to walk a long distance to their ultimate destinations. This inefficient allocation of curb parking space adds to the inefficiency caused by cruising.

20. Heller (1998, 626).

21. Hardin (1991).

22. Stevenson (1991).

23. Dagan and Heller (2001).

24. Rose (1998, 139); see also Rose (1999).

25. Dagan and Heller (2001, 553). Dagan and Heller propose legal regimes for this ownership structure and argue these regimes will directly address the tragedy of the commons, which is one of the core dilemmas of legal theory.

26. Webster (2003, 2596 and 2600).

27. Webster (2003, 2601). Demsetz (1964) makes a similar argument.

28. Webster (2003, 2610).

29. Alchian and Demsetz (1973, 19) say, "If the right to exclude is seldom exercised by the state, as in public parks or thoroughfares, then as a practical matter the users of the resource will treat it as communal.... The first driver to enter the public road has a right of use that continues for as long as he uses the road."

30. Mill (1965, 942).

The Practice of Parking Requirements

Striving to better, oft we mar what's well.

—-WILLIAM SHAKESPEARE

Cities have needed parking spaces ever since the two-wheeled chariot was invented in Sumeria about 5,000 years ago, but parking did not become a pandemic problem until the twentieth century, when cars appeared in great numbers. Columbus, Ohio, became the first U.S. city to establish a parking requirement for any type of land use when it began to require off-street parking for apartment houses in 1923. Fresno, California, in turn, became the first U.S. city to establish parking requirements for any land uses other than housing when it began to require off-street parking for hotels and hospitals in 1939.[1] Although off-street parking requirements are now 80 years old, no textbooks in urban planning or transportation planning explain them. The only articles on parking requirements published in the leading journals of the planning profession have severely criticized them, and no one has stepped up to defend them.[2] This appendix briefly describes how urban planners—with no theory, little training, and poor data—set and apply off-street parking requirements for hundreds of different land uses, and how this process has gone so far wrong.

THREE STEPS IN SETTING A PARKING REQUIREMENT

To set a parking requirement, an urban planner must (1) identify the land use, (2) choose the basis for the requirement, and (3) establish how many parking spaces to require per unit of the basis. Sometimes these three steps are simple and straightforward. For example, a typical parking requirement for an office building is 4 parking spaces per 1,000 square feet of the building's floor area. The land use is an office building, the basis for the requirement is floor area, and a developer must provide 4 parking spaces per 1,000 square feet of floor area.

For many land uses, however, the parking requirements are more complicated. Consider, for example, this parking requirement for automobile dealerships:

> 3.3 spaces for every 1,000 square feet of gross floor area of sales and showroom area; 3 spaces for every service bay in repair garage areas; 1 space for every vehicle customarily used in the operation of this use or stored on the premises.[3]

This parking requirement for automobile dealers has three bases—gross floor area, service bays, and vehicles—with a different number of parking spaces required per unit of each basis.

Planners must interpret some parking requirements on a case-by-case approach. Consider, for example, this requirement for a taxi stand:

> One space for each employee on the largest working shift, plus one space per taxi, plus sufficient spaces to accommodate the largest number of visitors that may be expected at any one time.[4]

This requirement also has three bases—employees, taxis, and visitors—but planners have considerable discretion in deciding how many spaces to require. They must estimate the largest working shift, the largest number of visitors expected at any one time, and how many cars they will park. If interpreted literally, this requirement appears to guarantee that the parking supply will accommodate the highest conceivable number of cars that could ever park at a taxi stand—and that most parking spaces will be vacant most of the time.

This parking requirement raises a raft of questions. First, requiring one parking space per employee and one space per taxi implies that all employees will drive to the taxi stand alone, park their own cars, and then take possession of a parked taxi. Is this a reasonable assumption? Might not, for example, some taxi drivers take their cabs home with them and then return with them the next day? Second, requiring one space per employee on the largest working shift implies planners know how many employees will work on this shift. Working shifts may vary seasonally with sharp but infrequent peaks. The use of taxis may rise during heavy downpours, for example, but fall at other times when the weather is pleasant enough for walking. So how many employees are we really talking about? Third, requiring sufficient spaces to accommodate the largest number of visitors that may be expected at any one time implies planners can know this number, which they cannot. Who, after all, are the visitors to a taxi stand, and why would they want to park there? Most people who visit a taxi stand probably don't bring their own cars, which is why they want a taxi. The largest number of visitors who may be expected at any one time is impossible to know in advance and will, in any event, occur only rarely. Finally, why should a city require any parking spaces at all for a taxi stand, other than those required to park the taxis?

Sadly, the complicated and puzzling taxi-stand parking requirement is not an anomaly, or at least not much of one. Throughout the U.S., parking requirements are laden with similarly baffling rules, which combine to make the provision of parking long on regulation and short on common sense. But we should not be too quick to blame planners for this situation—planners are being asked, after all, to perform a hard job for which they have not been trained. Setting the parking requirement for any single land use is a challenge, and planners must set parking requirements for hundreds of land uses. In its most recent survey of parking requirements in 2002, the Planning Advisory Service (PAS) found 662 land uses with distinct parking requirements as well as 216 different factors used as the bases for them.[5] A quick look at the 662 land uses in Planning Advisory Service Report 510/511 (2002) and 216 factors in Table A-1 helps to illustrate why parking requirements are not at all simple.

662 LAND USES

The first step in setting a parking requirement is to define the land use. This is not an easy task, since even the definition of "land use" is open to interpretation. In *Urban Traffic: A Function of Land Use*, Robert Mitchell and Chester Rapkin described various meanings of the term:

> The term "land use" (used so frequently in planning) has several specific meanings. It may refer to buildings or other improvements on the land, to the occupants or users of the land, to the major purposes of the occupancy of the land, or to the kind of activities on the land. Sometimes the term is employed without being defined specifically.[6]

Planners usually require parking spaces for land uses according to this last meaning: the major activities of the establishments based on the land.

The variety of uses and standards cited in the PAS Report is astonishing: batting cages and body-piercing studios, construction trailers and convents, dance halls and detoxification centers, jewelry stores and junkyards, libraries and liquor stores, monasteries and mortuaries, night clubs and nunneries, sauna baths and sawmills, taverns and truck-wash facilities. Because parking demand varies greatly among these land uses, and the parking demand varies greatly among different cities for the same land use, setting the parking requirements for every land use in every city is a daunting task.[7]

216 BASES

After the land use has been identified, the second step in setting a parking requirement is to decide how many parking spaces to require per... per what? To answer this question, planners seek to identify relevant factors that might help to predict parking demand. Table A-1 shows 216 factors planners have chosen as the bases for parking requirements.[8] Again, the variety is astonishing: barbers and bassinettes, chapels and children, fuel nozzles and funeral vehicles, gas pumps and golf holes, hearses and helistops, lodging rooms and lubricating racks, repair space and reposing rooms, taxis and teachers, waiting rooms and washing bays. With no help to be found in textbooks on land-use and transportation planning (but perhaps with some inspiration from Rube Goldberg or Heath Robinson), planners have identified these 216 factors that supposedly predict peak parking demand.[9]

Floor area is the most common basis for parking requirements, but this measure raises many questions about the definition of floor area: should it be gross area, leasable area, sales area, or some other measure? For example, some cities require parking for restaurants in proportion to the dining area only, excluding the kitchen, while others require parking in proportion to the gross floor area, including the kitchen. (Gross floor area is the building's total floor area, including cellars, basements, corridors, lobbies, stairways, elevators, and storage; it is measured from the building's outside walls.) If a city requires parking in proportion to *dining* area, a larger kitchen area does not require more parking spaces, so restaurants will tend to have larger kitchens. But if the city requires parking in proportion to the *gross* floor area, a larger kitchen does require more parking spaces, so the requirement constrains the kitchen size. The definition of floor area for a parking requirement can thus directly alter the use of the space inside buildings.

The factor used as the basis for a parking requirement can have serious unintended consequences. For example, cities can require parking for manufacturing sites in proportion to employees or floor area. Consider

Table A-1. 216 Factors Used as Bases for Minimum Parking Requirements

Active members
Administrative offices
Administrators
Air vehicles
Aircraft hangers
Aircraft tie downs
Alleys
Amusement devices
Archery targets
Assembly areas
Assembly halls
Assembly rooms
Athletic fields
Auditorium seats
Auditoriums
Automated Teller
   Machines
Bank windows
Barber chairs
Barbers
Bassinettes
Batting cages
Beauticians
Beauty chairs
Bedrooms
Beds
Bench length
Billiard tables
Boat berths
Campsites
Capacity in persons
Cashier floor area
Chairs
Chapel capacity
Chapels
Children
Classroom seats
Classrooms
Clergymen
Clients
Clubhouse area
Company vehicles
Courts
Customer circulation
   area
Customers
Dance floor area
Dental chairs
Dentist
Designed occupancy
Diamonds
Dining area
Dining/drinking space
Display area
Doctors
Dormitory units
Drive-in lanes
Drive-in windows
Driving tees

Dry boat storage area
Drying machines
Drying spaces
Dwelling units
Eating area
Efficiency units
Emergency room
   tables
Employees
Employees on largest
   shift
Enclosed floor space
Examination beds
Examining rooms
Facility vehicles
Faculty members
Feet of front wall
Fields
Fixed seats
Floor area for
   patron use
Flumes
Fuel nozzles
Funeral vehicles
Game tables
Garage area
Gas pumps
Golf holes
Grease racks
Greens
Gross floor area
Gross leasable area
Group home residents
Guestrooms
Guests
Hearses
Helistops
Holes
Homeless children
Inches of linear bench
Interments
Interments in one hour
Islands of gas pumps
Laboratories
Lanes
Largest chapel
Largest number of
   vehicles expected
Largest number of
   visitors
Leasable area
Leasable floor area
Licensed capacity
Loading area
Lodging residents
Lodging rooms
Lubricating racks
Managerial staff
Managers

Maximum anticipated
   membership
Maximum capacity
Maximum seating
   capacity
Mechanics
Members
Mobile home sites
Mobile homes
Motor vehicles
   serviced
Net floor area
Net leasable area
Offices
Operating vehicles
Operator stations
Outside display area
Par 3 holes
Parlor seats
Parlors
Passenger seating
Patient beds
Patient sleeping area
Patron seating
Patron serving area
Patrons
Pens
Persons
Persons lawfully
   permitted in pool
Persons of design
   capacity
Persons of licensed
   capacity
Persons of rated
   capacity
Playing fields
Pool surface area
Practitioners
Pupils rated capacity
Reception area
Rental display lot area
Rental floor area
Rental units
Repair space
Reposing rooms
Residents
Roomers
Rooming units
Rooms
Rooms designed for
   sleeping
Recreational vehicle
   sites
Sales floor area
Seating area
Seats
Seats for food service
Selling area

Service bays
Service capacity
Service stalls
Service windows
Shooting points
Showroom area
Skating rink area
Sleeping rooms
Sleeping units
Slips
Spectator seating
Square feet
Stables
Staff
Stalls
Storage area
Storage units
Stored vehicles
Students
Students of design
   capacity
Suites
Target area
Taxis
Teachers
Tee stalls
Tees
Tenants
Tie-downs
Total land area
Total membership
Total sales area
Trailer sites
Treatment rooms
Trucks
Units
Usable floor area
Users
Vehicles connected
   with such use
Vehicles customarily in
   operation
Vehicles maintained
Vehicles owned,
   operated by school
Vehicles stored on
   premises
Video game machines
Visiting doctors
Visitors
Waiting area
Waiting passengers
Waiting rooms
Washing bays
Washing machines
Washing modules
Washing spaces
Water area
Working area

Source: Planning Advisory Service (1964, 1971, 1991, 2002)

the effects of these two requirements: (1) one space per employee on the shift of maximum employment or (2) two parking spaces per 1,000 square feet of floor area.[10] If the city requires one space per employee, a firm cannot hire more staff without adding more parking spaces. Requiring parking in proportion to employees thus increases the cost of employing labor and may reduce the number of workers hired.[11] But if the city requires two parking spaces per 1,000 square feet, a firm cannot expand its plant without adding more parking spaces, even if the expansion adds no new employees. Requiring parking in proportion to floor area thus increases the cost of plant space and may reduce investment in plant size. The factor chosen as the basis for a parking requirement therefore affects firms' hiring and investment decisions. Given these effects, how should planners require parking for manufacturing sites and for hundreds of other land uses?

CONVERGENCE TO THE GOLDEN RULE

The third step in setting a parking requirement is to specify the number of parking spaces required. The problem is that planners do *not* know how many parking spaces a drive-in restaurant—or any other land use—needs. Most planners know little more about parking than the average citizen does. Copying another city's requirement is therefore an obvious strategy for anyone who needs to recommend a parking requirement for any land use. If cities do copy from one another, their parking requirements should converge over time. We can use two surveys of parking requirements for office buildings in 117 cities in Southern California to see whether this convergence occurs. Rex Link, a parking consultant, conducted the first survey in 1975. I repeated the survey in 1993 to analyze trends in these cities' requirements during the previous 18 years.[12]

The two surveys suggest cities do copy one another. In 1975 the most frequent requirement (the mode) was 4 spaces per 1,000 square feet. Of the cities requiring less than the mode in 1975, 65 percent had increased their requirement by 1993, and none had reduced it. Of the cities requiring more than the mode in 1975, 80 percent had reduced their requirement by 1993, and none had increased it. Only two of the 31 cities requiring 4 spaces per 1,000 square feet in 1975 had changed their requirement by 1993 (one up, one down). This convergence toward the mode doubled the percentage of cities requiring 4 spaces per 1,000 square feet from 27 percent in 1975 to 54 percent in 1993 (see Table A-2).

Practitioners sometimes refer to 4 spaces per 1,000 square feet as the "magic number" or "golden rule."[13] Because one off-street parking space (along with its share of ramps and aisles) occupies at least 300 square feet, 4 spaces occupy at least 1,200 square feet. Requiring 4 parking spaces per

Table A-2. Convergence Toward the Golden Rule: 1975–1993 (Parking Requirements for Office Buildings in 117 California Cities)

City	Parking spaces per 1,000 square feet			City	Parking spaces per 1,000 square feet		
	1975	1993	Change		1975	1993	Change
Placentia	8	4	-4	Brea	3.3	4	+0.7
Upland	6.7	6.7	0	Azusa	3.3	3.3	0
Los Alamitos	6.7	4	-2.7	Fontana	3.3	4	+0.7
Glendora	6.7	4	-2.7	Commerce	3.3	3.3	0
Duarte	6.7	4	-2.7	Hermosa Beach	3.3	4	+0.7
Lakewood	6.5	4	-2.5	Stanton	3.3	3.3	0
Buena Park	6	4	-2	San Marino	3.3	4	+0.7
San Jacinto	5.3	4	-1.3	Laguna Beach	3.3	4	+0.7
Hawaiian Gardens	5	3.3	-1.7	Tustin	3.3	4	+0.7
Bellflower	5	5	0	Santa Fe Springs	3.3	3.3	0
San Dimas	5	5	0	LaPalma	3.3	3.3	0
Inglewood	5	3.3	-1.7	Seal Beach	3.3	3.3	0
Walnut	5	5	0	Redondo Beach	3.3	3.3	0
Yorba Linda	5	5	0	South Gate	3.3	3.3	0
Paramount	5	3.3	-1.7	San Clemente	3.3	3.3	0
Pico Rivera	5	4	-1	West Covina	3.3	3.3	0
Arcadia	5	4	-1	Ojai	3.3	3.3	0
Pomona	5	4	-1	Gardena	3.3	3.3	0
La Verne	5	4	-1	Huntington Beach	3.3	4	+0.7
Signal Hill	5	4	-1	Bell Gardens	3.3	3.3	0
Monrovia	5	4	-1	Torrance	3.3	3.3	0
Ontario	5	3.3	-1.7	Westminister	3.1	3.1	0
Redlands	4.5	4.5	0	Culver City	2.9	3.8	+0.9
Fillmore	4.5	4	-0.5	Beverly Hills	2.9	2.9	0
Claremont	4.5	4	-0.5	Alhambra	2.9	4	+1.1
Costa Mesa	4.2	4	-0.2	Perris	2.9	4	+1.1
Anaheim	4	4	0	San Juan Capistrano	2.9	5	+2.1
Artesia	4	4	0	Riverside	2.6	2.6	0
Bell	4	4	0	Rialto	2.6	2.6	0
La Habra	4	5	+1	Ventura	2.5	4	+1.5
Cerritos	4	4	0	Carson	2.5	3.3	+0.8
Chino	4	4	0	Palos Verdes Estates	2.5	4	+1.5
Corona	4	4	0	Covina	2.5	3.3	+0.8
Cudahy	4	4	0	El Segundo	2.5	3.3	+0.8
El Monte	4	4	0	Oxnard	2.5	4	+1.5
Fullerton	4	4	0	Colton	2.5	4	+1.5
Hemet	4	4	0	Glendale	2.5	3	+0.5
Port Hueneme	4	4	0	Beaumont	2.5	5	+2.5
La Mirada	4	4	0	La Puente	2	3.3	+1.3
Lake Elsinore	4	4	0	Manhattan Beach	2	3.3	+1.3
Loma Linda	4	4	0	South El Monte	2	3.3	+1.3
Lomita	4	4	0	Santa Monica	2	3.3	+1.3
Maywood	4	4	0	Lawndale	2	3.3	+1.3
Montclair	4	4	0	San Fernando	2	3.3	+1.3
Monterey Park	4	4	0	Palmdale	2	3.2	+1.2
Newport Beach	4	4	0	Los Angeles	2	2	0
Norco	4	4	0	Burbank	2	3	+1
Norwalk	4	4	0	Pasadena	2	3	+1
Orange	4	4	0	Downey	2	2.9	+0.9
San Bernardino	4	3.3	-0.7	Industry	2	4	+2
Rosemead	4	4	0	Montebello	2	2.5	+0.5
Camarillo	4	4	0	Irwindale	2	4	+2
San Gabriel	4	4	0	Carpinteria	1.3	4	+2.7
Santa Barbara	4	4	0	Hawthorne	1.3	3.3	+2
Simi Valley	4	4	0	Long Beach	1	4	+3
South Pasadena	4	4	0	Vernon	1	2	+1
Thousand Oaks	4	4	0	**MEAN**	**3.6**	**3.8**	**+0.2**
Garden Grove	3.7	4	+0.3	**MEDIAN**	**3.5**	**4**	**+0.5**
Rolling Hills Estates	3.5	5	+1.5	**MODE**	**4**	**4**	**0**
Sierra Madre	3.3	3.3	0	**RANGE**	**7**	**5.7**	**-1.3**
Whittier	3.3	5	+1.7	**STANDARD DEVIATION**	**1.3**	**0.6**	**-0.6**

Note: The parking requirement is the number of spaces required per 1,000 square feet of gross building area for a three-story office building of 10,000 square feet.

1,000 square feet of floor area therefore commits at least 20 percent more space to parking than to buildings. After copying each others' parking requirements for many years, most cities now require more space for cars than for humans.

PARKING REQUIREMENTS AND REGIONAL CULTURE

When surveying the parking requirements for office buildings in Southern California, I noticed that many cities require parking spaces for more land uses than the PAS found in its national surveys of parking requirements. I counted 110 additional land uses with parking requirements in Southern California—above and beyond the 662 reported in the national survey reported in PAS Report No. 510/511. These additional land uses tell us something about Southern California's culture and economy, and they confirm some clichés about the region (see Table A-3).

Confirming our love of cars and everything about them, there are parking requirements for automobile display, drive-in dairies, drive-through establishments, lube-n-tune shops, tire recapping, truck storage, and used car sales. True to the stereotype about our love of finery are the parking requirements for cosmetic processing, custom dressmakers, millinery shops, shoe shops, and shoeshine kiosks. Finally, the parking requirements for self-defense studios and homes for the aged suggest that we look to the future with concern for our safety and hope for long life.

PARKING REQUIREMENTS AND PARKING TECHNOLOGY

In setting parking requirements, planners often confuse the number of parking spaces with the capacity to park cars in them because the capacity of a parking lot or garage to accommodate parked cars is an ambiguous concept. During the hours of peak demand, valet and stack parking can increase capacity by storing cars in tandem or in the access aisles, thus substituting labor for land and capital in parking cars. Automated garages, in turn, substitute capital investment and technology for parking spaces. Requirements for a minimum number of *parking spaces* eliminate the option to substitute labor for land and capital in providing *parked-car-hours*, which is the fundamental measure of what is ultimately consumed when drivers leave their cars. The capacity of a parking lot or structure is the number of parked-car-hours per hour it can provide. This capacity can be increased by devoting less space to each car, by reducing the time needed to park and unpark a car, and by decreasing the minimum vacancy rate necessary for efficient operation. Parking consumption also has quality dimensions, including the safety of the parked cars and their owners, the speed of parking and unparking, protection from weather, and the like. In focusing on the sheer number of parking spaces, off-street

Table A-3. 110 Additional Land Uses with Parking Requirements in Southern California

Aerobics studio
Amusement arcade
Animal care facility
Animal husbandry
Animal show
Apiculture
Architect
Art and antique shop
Art studio
Automobile display
Banquet caterer
Barber school
Biological laboratory
Blacksmith shop
Boat building or repair
Book bindery
Building contractor yards
Bulk food outlet
Cabinet or woodworking shop
Cannery
Card club
Caretaker's residence
Carpet and rug cleaning
Catering house
Catering services
Child care services
Childrens' home
Cold storage warehouse
Concrete products
Confectionary shop
Congregate care facility
Cosmetic processing
Cultural institution
Custom dressmaker
Dancing academy
Day nursery
Dead storage
Detached servants' quarters
Discotheque
Donut shop
Drapery shop
Drive-in cleaner
Drive-in dairy
Drive-through establishment
Electrical substation
Electronic game center
Employment agency
Engraving
Exercise room
Faxing center
Fish and meat processing
Frozen food locker
Game arcade
Gas storage plant
General appliance store

High technology manufacturing
Home for the aged
Horse show
Human service agency
Ice cream manufacturing
Large family day care center
Laundry services
Light sheet metal products
Lithographing or publishing
Live theater
Lube-n-tune
Manufacture of pottery
Manufacturing of neon signs
Methadone treatment facility
Millinery shop
Newspaper publishing
Non fast-food restaurant
Oculist
Open-air industrial use
Optometric clinic
Participating entertainment
Passive park
Performance theatre
Photofinishing drop-off/pickup
Picnic shelter
Printing and engraving shop
Professional studio
Ready-to-eat food restaurant
Recycling transfer
Religious group quarters
Scrap yards
Self-defense studio
Shelter for the homeless
Shoe shop
Shoe-shine kiosk
Spectator entertainment
Speculative industrial building
Stationery store
Stock brokerage
Studio
Swim club
Take-out restaurant
Ticket office
Tinsmith shop
Tire recapping or retreading
Tool and die works
Trailer park
Truck storage
Truck transportation yard
Unattended public facility
Used car sales
Vehicle sales
Video kiosk
Welding shop
Wholesale "open to the public" shop

parking requirements neglect many other important considerations in how the parking supply can most efficiently meet parking demand.

European and Asian cities have installed hundreds of automated garages that accommodate in the same volume twice as many cars as a conventional ramped garage. A driver pulls into the entryway of what looks like a single-car garage, steps from the car, and pulls a ticket. Sensors determine when all people have left the garage, so the drivers and passengers don't get parked along with their cars. After the occupants have left, the car is lifted on a pallet and transferred from the entry bay to a storage slot. When the driver returns and reinserts the ticket, the car is delivered, pointed outward, within one or two minutes. From the driver's point of view, the system works like valet parking, although the driver keeps the keys and no tip is expected. As an added advantage for urban design, the structure's facade can easily blend with the neighboring buildings (see Figure A-1).

Automated garages offer greater security for drivers, vehicles, and their contents, so the insurance costs are lower. Because the cars are parked mechanically and their doors stay closed at all times, the horizontal and vertical spacing between the parked cars is minimal. No space at all is needed for ramps, aisles, elevators, and stairs. These space-saving features are a particular advantage for underground parking. Conventional underground structures require expensive excavation, shoring, waterproofing, fireproofing, lighting, and ventilation, so reducing the volume of a structure greatly reduces its cost. Furthermore, automated garages do not require ventilation because the cars' engines are never running when

Figure A-1. Automated Parking Garage in Hoboken, New Jersey

the cars are inside and no exhaust emissions are generated. Compared with conventional garages, automated garages require only half the volume, and where land is scarce, they can reduce the capital and operating cost per parking space.[14]

Despite their advantages, automated garages are rare in the U.S., in part because most zoning codes require a certain number of physical parking spaces of a specific size, not a mechanical capacity to store the same number of cars. Furthermore, because the generous supply of required parking spaces has reduced the price of most parking to zero in the U.S., off-street parking requirements have reduced the potential profitability of automated garages and delayed their development.

Parking requirements have also retarded the adoption of technologies that allow conventional garages to satisfy demand with fewer spaces. Electronic signs, for example, can display how many spaces are vacant on each floor so that drivers can go directly to a level where spaces are available. In some garages, each stall has a ceiling-mounted detector that checks whether a vehicle is present or not. The detectors send their observations to a central computer, which updates signs on every level of the garage pointing the route to the nearest vacant space. The individual detectors are equipped with lights, visible along the whole aisle, showing whether a space is available—occupied stalls are red, and vacant ones are green—so drivers can easily see the nearest vacancies and avoid aisles with no vacancies.[15] The central computer can also display historical data on the occupancy and turnover rates of individual spaces and zones, and can provide the information necessary to analyze the operation of a garage and evaluate its performance. This technology is rare in the U.S., where the plentiful supply of parking makes efficient use less important.

WHAT WENT WRONG?

In attempting to assign a specific number of cars to almost every economic function in a city, parking requirements provide an interesting window onto the cities themselves and showcase their quirks and priorities. But cities are too complex to be ordered and catalogued, and no amount of rational planning, no amount of dogged, well-intentioned work, will ever measure everyone's "need" to park everywhere. Because this is what parking requirements are meant to do, it is little wonder they fail so spectacularly. Our current parking policies are aesthetically, economically, environmentally, and intellectually bankrupt.

Admittedly, requiring "enough" parking spaces in a new development does seem sensible. If some people drive to work, a new office building should have some parking spaces, shouldn't it? So what went wrong? Two things. The first problem is that planners require at least enough parking spaces to meet the peak demand for *free* parking, regardless of the cost. Second, and more fundamental, the parking requirements are unnecessary. After all, people also need food to live, but this does not mean planners should require every office building to provide a lunchroom big enough to supply a free lunch at noon for everyone who works in the building. But if all restaurants in the city were free, cities would soon need to impose lunchroom requirements for all office buildings, so that office workers would not overwhelm the nearby free restaurants. To satisfy the peak demand for free food, these lunchroom requirements would probably look exactly like off-street parking requirements. Developers could pay in-lieu fees for buildings that cannot provide their own lunchrooms, and cities would allow reductions in the requirements for buildings with shared lunchrooms. Everyone would soon find it even harder to lose weight, just as cities with off-street parking requirements now find it difficult to reduce traffic congestion, air pollution, and energy consumption. Fortunately, restaurants are not free, cities do not require lunchrooms, and many office workers eat light lunches or skip lunch entirely, in part because they must pay for what they eat. If cities begin to charge fair-market prices for curb parking and remove off-street parking requirements, they will likewise find it easier to reduce traffic and air pollution. And as people shift from driving to walking and cycling for short trips to save on paying for parking, some of us may even find it easier to lose weight.

APPENDIX A NOTES

1. Mogren and Smith (1952, 25). Hartmut Topp (1991, 12) says Germany began requiring building owners to provide off-street parking in 1939 when the *Reichsgaragenordnung* was enacted.

2. Shoup (1995, 1997, 1997a) and Willson (1995). Urban planners apparently feel no need to respond when articles in their profession's leading journals condemn a central practice of the profession. This silence suggests many planners don't read the journals, disagree with the criticism but don't have any response, or perhaps agree with the criticism but don't know what to do about it.

3. This is the parking requirement for an automobile sales establishment in Saint Louis County, Missouri (Planning Advisory Service 1991, 8).

4. This is the parking requirement for a taxi stand in Saint Clair Shores, Michigan (Planning Advisory Service 1991, 25).

5. Some of the 773 land uses in PAS Report 510/511 (2002) are duplicate names for what are essentially the same land uses. Abattoir, for example, is the same as slaughterhouse. When the 111 duplicate names are removed, there are 662 different land uses. The 15 surveyed cities are: Bellevue, Washington; Cambridge, Massachusetts; Davis, California; Grand Rapids, Michigan; Greensboro, North Carolina; Helena, Montana; Holland, Michigan; Iowa City, Iowa; Minneapolis, Minnesota; Pittsburgh, Pennsylvania; Portland, Oregon; Redmond, Washington; Richmond, Virginia; San Antonio, Texas; and Santa Cruz, California.

6. Mitchell and Rapkin (1954, 13).

7. The parking requirements for even the most frivolous-sounding land uses sometimes create serious debates. For example, Newport Beach, California, tripled its parking requirement for nail salons from one parking space for every 240 square feet of salon area to one space per 80 square feet in 1995. The planning commission had previously rejected the increase because the economic development committee had argued it would penalize new business. One member of the city council opposed the increase on the grounds that "I think this is targeting a successful industry…. I think it's antibusiness" (*Los Angeles Times,* April 1, 1995).

8. These 216 factors used as bases for parking requirements were reported in the surveys conducted by the Planning Advisory Service in 1964, 1971, 1991, and 2002. Additional factors are used by cities not included in the surveys.

9. Rube Goldberg (American) and Heath Robinson (British) sketched complex contraptions, often dilapidated from overuse, designed to perform simple tasks and usually run by overly serious attendants executing simple duties like cutting a string.

10. The Planning Advisory Service found these two requirements in its 1991 survey (PAS 1991, 18).

11. Requiring one parking space per employee increases the cost of employing labor but does not increase the cost of employing capital (computers, machines, etc.), and can thus encourage firms to substitute capital for labor in their production decisions.

12. Link (1975). The requirement was calculated for a 10,000-square-foot, three-story office building. A few cities included in Link's 1975 survey were not included in the comparison because the city's 1993 requirement was difficult to interpret. For example, in 1993 the City of Banning required "one parking space for each employee on the largest shift plus one space per 350 square feet of floor area." Therefore, building size alone is insufficient to calculate the required parking.

13. Willson (1995, 30).

14. Beebe (2000) describes the history and technology of automated parking garages. The garage operations have backup computer systems for each feature, and the high degree of redundancy greatly reduces the probability of mechanical error. Articles on automated parking garages are in *Parking Today* (January 1998 and March and May 2003), *Urban Land* (May 1998), *The Wall Street Journal* (February 13, 1999), *New York Times* (September 21, 2003), and *Slate* (April 1, 2004). The title of the *Slate* article by Josh Levin ("The Valet You Don't Have to Tip") suggests another advantage of robotic parking. See also the manufacturers' web sites at www.roboticparking.com/index.html and www.spacesaverparking.com/.

15. This guidance system is used in the Smart Park garage at the Baltimore-Washington International Airport. Information on the system is available at www.signalpark.com/functions.html.

B

Nationwide
Transportation Surveys

Were an alien visitor to hover a few hundred yards above the planet, it could be forgiven for thinking that cars were the dominant life-form, and that human beings were a kind of ambulatory fuel cell, injected when the car wished to move off, and ejected when they were spent.

—*HEATHCOTE WILLIAMS*

The U.S. Department of Transportation conducted the Nationwide Personal Transportation Survey (NPTS) in 1969, 1977, 1983, 1990, and 1995. In 2001, the name of the survey was changed to the National Household Travel Survey (NHTS).[1] I have used these surveys to estimate that (1) drivers park free for 99 percent of all automobile trips, and (2) the average car is parked 95 percent of the time.

DRIVERS PARK FREE FOR 99 PERCENT
OF ALL AUTOMOBILE TRIPS

For all automobile trips made on the previous day, the *1990 NPTS* asked drivers, Did you pay for parking during any part of this trip? (Unfortunately, this question was not asked in the previous or subsequent surveys.) Table B-1 shows the results.[2] Drivers parked free for 99 percent of their trips. The high percentage of trips ending with free parking is *not* a result of free parking at home—no one charges you, after all, when you pull into your own driveway—because the "did you pay for parking" question was asked about all vehicle trips *except* the trips ending at home.

Table B-1. Share of Vehicle Trips with Free Parking

Driver	Park Free	Metropolitan Area	Park Free
Sex		Atlanta	97%
Male	99%	Baltimore	97%
Female	99%	Boston	98%
All	99%	Buffalo	99%
		Chicago	98%
Age		Cincinnati	98%
16 - 30	98%	Cleveland	97%
30 - 50	99%	Dallas	99%
50 - 70	99%	Denver	99%
Over 70	99%	Detroit	99%
		Fort Worth	99%
Income		Houston	99%
Less than $20,000	99%	Los Angeles	97%
$20,000 - $40,000	99%	Miami	98%
$40,000 - $60,000	99%	Milwaukee	97%
$60,000 - $80,000	98%	Minneapolis-St. Paul	98%
$80,000 or more	98%	New Orleans	99%
		New York	96%
Education		Philadelphia	99%
Less than High School	99%	Phoenix	99%
High School	99%	Pittsburgh	99%
Bachelor's Degree	98%	Portland	99%
Graduate Degree	97%	San Diego	99%
		San Francisco	98%
		Seattle	98%
		St. Louis	98%
		Washington	98%

Source: Calculated from the *1990 Nationwide Personal Transportation Survey*.
Percentages refer to all drivers who responded Yes or No to the question:
Did you pay for parking during any part of this trip?
This question was asked for all vehicle trips except the trips that ended at home.

Regardless of their gender, age, income, education, or residence, drivers almost never pay for parking. The share of automobile trips with free parking declines slightly as income increases: drivers with an income less than $20,000 a year, for example, park free on 99 percent of all their trips, while drivers with an income more than $60,000 a year park free on only 98 percent of their trips. This does not mean lower-income drivers are more likely to be *offered* free parking. Instead, lower-income drivers *not* offered free parking are more likely to ride public transit, bike, walk, or not make the trip. A greater share of lower-income drivers park free because they are less likely to drive when they have to pay for parking.

The share of free parkers also declines slightly with increases in education. Drivers with less than a high school education park free on 99 percent of their trips, while drivers with a graduate education park free on only 97 percent of their trips. This does not mean higher education reduces the likelihood of being offered free parking. Instead, higher education probably increases the likelihood of paying to park mainly because education is correlated with income.

Most drivers probably feel they pay to park on more than 1 percent of *their* own automobile trips, and many do, especially those who live in older and more compact cities founded before the car arrived. But those who live in sprawling suburbs rarely, if ever, pay to park. The *2001 NHTS* found that American households make 235 billion vehicle trips a year.[3] If drivers pay to park for only 1 percent of their trips, they do pay 2.35 billion times a year, but they also park free 232.65 billion times a year.

The finding that Americans park free for 99 percent of their vehicle trips does *not* mean that 99 percent of all parking spaces are free to anyone who wants to park in them. Many parking spaces free to commuters are paid for by employers, and drivers who are not employees must pay to park. Many parking spaces are also validated by businesses at the sites visited, and drivers who are not customers or clients have to pay to park. Therefore, if a particular driver parks free on a given trip, it does not mean the parking space is generally free to anyone who wants to park in it.

The finding that Americans park free for 99 percent of their vehicle trips also does *not* mean that 99 percent of travelers could park free if they drove for every trip they made. A numerical example shows how travelers' responses to parking charges will increase the share of vehicle trips with free parking. When you are aware of a parking charge at the end of a trip, you may seek an alternative to solo driving. Suppose on your next 100 trips you could park free for 50 percent of them but would have to pay for parking for the other 50 percent. Suppose also you always drive when you can park free. This means you would drive and park free for 50 trips. When you have to pay to park, however, you might drive for only 20 percent of your trips and walk for the other 80 percent; this means you would drive and pay for parking for 10 of the 50 pay-parking trips, and you would walk for the other 40. You would thus park free on 50 of 60, or 83 percent, of all your vehicle trips. But this statistic is as much a function of your own choices as it is of the amount of free parking available to you. You would have parked free for only 50 percent of your trips if you had driven for all 100 trips. Mode shifts to avoid parking charges thus increase the share of all your vehicle trips with free parking to 83 percent.

Validation also helps to explain why drivers park free for 99 percent of their trips. Although the posted price of parking often appears prohibitively high, with validation the parking is free to the driver, so the high price of parking is no disincentive to driving. High prices for parking encourage ridesharing only when the driver personally pays for the parking. I served for several years in a research group for a civic organization that met at the Bank of America tower in downtown Los Angeles, and Charles Young, UCLA's Chancellor, was our chair. At the end of every meeting, we had our parking tickets validated, and we then waited in the basement garage for the valet attendants to deliver our cars (we had, as usual, all driven alone). After one meeting, Chancellor Young pointed out with horror that the posted price of parking was $2.50 for every 20 minutes! This was news to everyone except me (because I tend to notice these things). Everyone instantly agreed how expensive it was to park downtown, although none of us had ever paid a penny. The high parking prices never prevented any of *us* from driving alone.

CARS ARE PARKED 95 PERCENT OF THE TIME

Automobiles are immobile most of the time. One simple way to calculate the percentage of time cars are parked is to estimate the percentage of time they are driven and then subtract this number from 100 percent. The *1995 NPTS* found the average time drivers spent driving on a typical day was 73 minutes (1.2 hours).[4] If a driver has one car, and drives it 5 percent of the time in a day (1.2 ÷ 24), then the car must be parked the other 95 percent of the time.[5]

Surveys in Perth, Australia, and Lyons, France, found similar results. George Brown, Richard McKellar, and Heidi Lansdell report the average private car in the Perth region spends 18.5 hours parked at home during the average day.[6] Of the other 5.5 hours away from home, the car spends only 45 minutes moving on the road system and is parked for the other 4.75 hours. The average car is thus parked 23.25 hours a day, or 97 percent of the time. Using data from household surveys in Lyons, France, J.P. Nicholas, P. Pochet, and H. Poimboeuf found that cars are moving only 4.7 percent of the time.[7]

How much of the day are trucks parked? In a survey of truck movements in Pittsburgh in 1958, Louis Keefer, Director of the Pittsburgh Area Transportation Study, found that the average truck is driven less than an hour a day and is at rest 95 percent of the time:

> The typical image is that of many trucks constantly in motion: picking up laundry and dry cleaning, delivering department store purchases, making calls to service television sets, and generally circulating among a diversity of urban activities. Stops are viewed as momentary and travel as continuing throughout the day. Actually, this impression is misleading; many stops are much more than momentary.[8]

In 1969, Wilbur Smith reported the results of a similar study of truck operations in five cities. Of trucks that made one or more trips on a given day, the trucks were in motion 12 percent of the time, and at rest 88 percent of the time. The heavier the vehicle, the higher the share of the day they were in motion; heavy trucks were moving 16 percent of the time, while light trucks were moving only 11 percent of the time.[9] These figures for trucks making at least one trip on a given day overstate the share of time all trucks are in motion because the same survey found many trucks are idle all day; in New York, for example, approximately one-third of all trucks were idle all day on a given workday.[10] The study concluded:

> In the final analysis, the time the average truck spends in motion is very small. For most of the day, it is parked, waiting to be loaded or unloaded, or waiting to be used. This finding emphasizes the importance of parking accommodations for trucks.[11]

Cars and trucks clearly create serious problems when they are moving, but they both spend most of their time at rest, creating less visible but equally serious problems.

APPENDIX B NOTES

1. These surveys are available online at http://nhts.ornl.gov/2001/index.shtml.
2. Table B-1 refers to the share of all vehicle trips with free parking (from the *1990 NPTS*).
3. United States Department of Transportation (2003, 2003a, 21).
4. Hu and Young (1999, Table 14).
5. We can calculate this figure in another way. If cars are driven 5 percent of the time, they are moving 438 hours a year. The 1995 NPTS found the average annual mileage per vehicle was 12,226 miles. The average speed for driving 12,226 miles in 438 hours is 28 miles an hour (12,226 ÷ 4388). If the average speed is above 28 miles an hour, driving 12,226 miles takes less than 5 percent of the hours in a year, and cars are parked more than 95 percent of the time.
6. Brown, McKellar, and Lansdell (2004, 7).
7. Nicholas, Pochet, and Poimboeuf (2003).
8. Keefer (1963, 30).
9. Wilbur Smith and Associates (1969, 56).
10. Wilbur Smith and Associates (1969, 54).
11. Wilbur Smith and Associates (1969, 56).

C

The Language of Parking

How are we parked and bounded in a pale.

— WILLIAM SHAKESPEARE

Shakespeare appears to be the first author to use the word "parked" when he wrote in *Henry VI*, "How are we parked and bounded in a pale." He was referring to soldiers trapped in an enclosure, but this meaning can also describe cars trapped in a crowded parking lot.

The *Oxford English Dictionary* states that the use of "parking" to refer to the practice of leaving a vehicle at the side of the road or elsewhere originated in the U.S. The *OED*'s earliest quoted use, from 1867, is "At night the wagons are parked in a circle." Another quotation, referring to Queen Victoria's Jubilee in 1887, is "The area…is reserved for parking carriages belonging to the Procession." An early quotation from the *Congressional Record* of 1900 is "No part of said street…shall be used for…parking cars." The concept of free parking is, of course, as old as parking itself. For example, another early *OED* quotation from 1932 is "I have only once, in two years, been asked to pay a parking fee."

The verb "to park" now means either to maneuver a car into a parking space or to leave a car in the parking space until returning and leaving the space. Although not often used, the noun "parker" describes someone who is parking a car, just as "driver" describes a person who is driving a car. Parker can also refer to the patron of a parking lot, but it does not seem to be a common term to describe a person whose car is parked (even though, and perhaps because, this definition fits most American adults most of the time). The *American Heritage Dictionary* includes "parker" as a noun but provides no definition, while the *Oxford English Dictionary* defines a parker as "One who parks a vehicle" and provides this example: "Smith had the luck to find a car leaving the meter. He reversed fast… cutting out another would-be parker." Throughout this book, I have used the word parker to mean either a driver who is parking a car or someone whose car is parked.[1]

Our language shows that parking is clearly important in our lives. For example, the *American Heritage Dictionary* says:

> It is difficult today to envision a world without garages or a language without the word garage. However, the word probably did not exist before the 19th century and certainly not before the 18th; possibly the thing itself did not exist before the end of the 19th century. Our word is a direct borrowing of French garage, which is first recorded in 1802 in the sense "place where one docks." The verb garer, from which garage was derived, originally meant "to put merchandise under shelter," then "to moor a boat," and then "to put a vehicle into a place for safekeeping," that is, a garage, a sense first recorded in French in 1901. English almost immediately borrowed this French word, the first instance being found in 1902.[2]

There are now many national and regional terms in English for a structure designed for parking cars on several levels. The standard term in Britain is "multi-storey" parking structure, and "parkade" is common in Canada. The terms used in various parts of the U.S. are garage, parking deck, parking ramp, parking structure, and parking terrace (a term apparently used only in Utah). And just as French donated the word garage to English, English has in turn donated the word parking to many other languages (such as *le parking* in French). To show the spread of parking into other languages, consider these translations of the title of this book, *The High Cost of Free Parking*, into 29 other languages (where the translation of "parking" is shown in italics).

Arabic	Al taklefah al mortafeaa le magganeyyet *entezar el sayyarat*
Chinese	Gao dai jia mian fei *ting che*
Croatian	Visoka cijena besplatnog *parkiranja*
Czech	Vyoská cena bezplatného *parkování*
Danish	Den høje pris af fri *parkering*
Dutch	De hoge kosten van gratis *parken*
Finnish	Vapaan *pysäköinnin* korkea hinta
French	Le prix élevé du *parking* gratuit
Gaelic	An costas ard ar *pháirceáil* saor
German	Die hohen Kosten des *Gratisparken*

Greek	To ipsilo kostos tou eleftherou *parking*
Hebrew	Hamehir hagavoha shel *hanaya* hinam
Hindi	Nishulk *parking* ke oonche dham
Indonesian	Tingginya biaya *parkir* gratis
Italian	L'alto costo del *parcheggio* gratuito
Japanese	Muryou *paakingu* no kou hiyou
Korean	Mooryo *joochaeui* nopeun sahoi biyong
Marathi	Paishay khoob lagthay *parking* karaila
Norwegian	Den høye kostnaden ved gratis *parkering*
Persian	Keemat ziyad *parkiink* majani
Polish	Wysoki koszt *parkowania* za darmo
Pilipino	Ang malaking halaga ng libreng *paradahan*
Portuguese	O custo elevado de *estacionamento* gratuito
Russian	Vysokaya tsena besplatnoy *parkovki*
Spanish	El alto costo del *estacionamiento* gratuito
Swedish	Det höga priset för fri *parkering*
Ulster Scots	Heich cost o free *pairkin*
Urdu	Muft *parking* ki bhari keemat
Zapotec	Wgyezh sac *estasyonamiend* digasy

Nineteen of these languages have adopted the English word parking directly (French, Greek, Hindi, Marathi, and Urdu) or have naturalized it (Croatian, Czech, Danish, Dutch, Finnish, German, Indonesian, Japanese, Norwegian, Persian, Polish, Russian, Swedish, and Ulster Scots). But the English word park is derived from the French *parc*, which is of Germanic origin. So rather than lending the word parking to French and German, perhaps English has simply repatriated it.

Languages are said to have many words that make fine distinctions for whatever is important to a culture. By that standard, parking is important to American culture because we have distinguished many different types of parking, as shown in Table C-1. These are not different words for different kinds of parking but are instead common phrases with different adjectives for the different kinds of parking. In addition, many other kinds of parking can also be distinguished by the land use for which the parking spaces are provided. Consider this sign at one church: "Church parking only. All others will be baptized." If the signs posted for parking at all land uses—hospital parking, library parking, restaurant parking, and so on—were added to the list, there would be hundreds more different types of parking.

Table C-1. 78 Varieties of Parking

Accessible parking	Off-site parking
All-day parking	Off-street parking
Alternate-side parking	On-street parking
Angle parking	Overflow parking
Assigned parking	Overnight parking
Authorized parking	Overtime parking
Automated parking	Paid parking
Back-in parking	Parallel parking
Carpool parking	Pay-and-display parking
Commercial parking	Peak parking
Commuter parking	Perpendicular parking
Compact parking	Permit parking
Courtesy parking	Private parking
Covered parking	Public parking
Curb parking	Random parking
Customer parking	Replacement parking
Daily parking	Required parking
Diagonal parking	Reserved parking
Disabled parking	Residential parking
Double parking	Restricted parking
Driver-paid parking	Robotic parking
Employee parking	Self parking
Employer-paid parking	Shared parking
Flexible parking	Short-term parking
Free parking	Snow-emergency parking
Guest parking	Side-by-side parking
Head-in parking	Spillover parking
Handicapped parking	Stack parking
Hourly parking	Staff parking
Illegal parking	Structured parking
In-lieu parking	Surface parking
Joint-use parking	Tandem parking
Loading-zone parking	Tenant parking
Long-term parking	Triple parking
Metered parking	Underground parking
Mobile parking	Unreserved parking
Monthly parking	Valet parking
Multistory parking	Validated parking
No parking	Visitor parking

APPENDIX C NOTES

1. Most businesses and professions have words to describe their members, such as carpenter, doctor, lawyer, planner, plumber, professor, or teacher, but members of the parking profession cannot simply call themselves "parkers." Lacking a simple term to describe themselves, people in the parking profession have adopted the clumsy phrase, "parking professional." Perhaps the members of the parking profession should follow the path of real-estate agents, who made up and trademarked the term Realtor® to describe themselves.

2. *American Heritage Dictionary of the English Language* (2000, 724).

D

The Calculus of Driving, Parking, and Walking

Extraordinary how mathematics help you to know yourself.

— SAMUEL BECKETT

Most automobile trips begin and end with a parking space and a walk. As we approach the end of an automobile trip, we have to decide where to park the car and then walk the rest of the way to the destination. Chapter 18 presented a simple model of parking choice that considered only the monetary cost of parking and the time cost of walking. We can develop this model further to take into account how parking location also affects the monetary and time costs of driving.

Suppose the price of parking is highest at your destination and declines with distance from this destination. There is no "search" cost to find a parking space because prices are set to make spaces available everywhere. To find the optimal parking location, consider the following variables (and their dimensions):

a	vehicle operating cost (\$/mile)
d	the distance from parking space to final destination (miles)
D	distance from the origin to the destination of a trip (miles)
n	number of people in the car (persons)
$p(d)$	the price of parking at distance d from the final destination (\$/hour)
s	vehicle speed from trip origin to parking space (miles/hour)
t	parking duration (hours)

w walking speed from parking space to final destination (miles/hour)

v value of time spent driving and walking (\$/hour/person).

The total cost of an automobile trip is the cost of driving, parking, and walking. At distance d from the final destination, the monetary cost of driving and parking and the (monetized) time cost of driving and walking are:

$2a(D\text{-}d)$	(1)	monetary cost of driving to and from the parking space
$\dfrac{2nv(D\text{-}d)}{s}$	(2)	monetized time cost of driving to and from the parking space
$tp(d)$	(3)	monetary cost of parking the car
$\dfrac{2nvd}{w}$	(4)	monetized time cost of walking to and from the destination.

The total cost of the automobile trip is the sum of the monetary cost of driving, the time cost of driving, the monetary cost of parking the car, and the time cost of walking.

$$2a(D\text{-}d) + \frac{2nv(D\text{-}d)}{s} + tp(d) + \frac{2nvd}{w} \qquad (5) \qquad \text{Total cost}$$

A parking space is an "intermodal facility" that allows travelers to change between two travel modes—driving and walking. The optimal distance, d^*, from your destination to park is the spot where the total time-and-money cost of driving, parking, and walking is minimized. This total cost is minimized where the total value of driving-and-walking time saved by parking closer equals the total parking and vehicle operating cost added by parking closer.[1] Differentiating the total cost of driving, parking, and walking (expression 5) with respect to d and setting the result equal to zero gives the distance from the final destination that minimizes the total cost:

$$-2a - \frac{2nv}{s} + t\frac{\partial p}{\partial d} + \frac{2nv}{w} = 0 \quad \text{and} \quad t\frac{\partial p}{\partial d} = -\frac{2nv}{w} + \frac{2nv}{s} + 2a \qquad (6)$$

Interpreting this equation, we find that the time-and-money cost of driving, parking, and walking is minimized at the distance where the added monetary cost of parking a little bit closer (the left-hand side of the equation) is equal to the net decrease in the monetary value of walking and driving time and vehicle operating cost of parking closer (the right-hand side). If vehicle operating cost, a, is low and driving speed, s, is high relative to walking speed, w, then a and s are negligible parts of the decision, and the solution for d^* reduces to:

$$t\frac{\partial p}{\partial d} = -\frac{2nv}{w} \qquad (7)$$

Equation (7) shows the changes in the monetary cost of parking ($t\partial p/\partial d$) and the time cost of walking ($2nv/w$) are equal in absolute value and opposite in sign for a small change in distance at the location that minimizes the cost of parking *and* walking (this is equivalent to the result found in Chapter 18, where the monetary and time costs of driving were not considered).

ELASTICITIES

In Chapter 18, the relationship between the price of curb parking and distance from a destination was assumed to be a negative exponential formula:

$$p(d) = \$1e^{-2d} \qquad (8)$$

When equation 7 is solved with this formula for $p(d)$, the optimal parking location is:

$$d^* = -\frac{1}{2}\log_e\left(\frac{nv}{tw}\right) \qquad (9)$$

In this case we can calculate the derivatives and elasticities of the optimal distance, d^*, with respect to the four variables determining it. Table D-1 shows that the derivative of d^* is positive with respect to t and w, which implies it pays to park farther from your destination if you park for a longer time or if you walk faster. The derivative of d^* is negative with respect to n and v, which implies it pays to park closer to your destination if you have more people in your car or if you place a higher value on your time.

The elasticities of d^* with respect to the variables determining it decrease (in absolute value) with increasing distance from the center (see Figure D-1). For example, the elasticity of d^* with respect to the parking duration, t, is $+1/2d^*$. At $d^* = 0.5$ miles from the center, the elasticity of d^* with respect to t is $+1$, so a 10 percent increase in parking duration shifts your optimal parking location 10 percent farther from your final destination.[2] In contrast, at a distance of two miles from the center, the elasticity is only 0.25, so a 10 percent increase in parking duration shifts your optimal parking location only 2.5 percent farther from your final destination.

COMPLICATIONS

A simple model cannot capture all the complex issues in choosing where to park, but more factors can be considered. For example, if the marginal disutility of walking increases for longer distances, the value of saving time also increases for longer distances. And walking time may have a higher cost than driving time if it is raining or a lower cost if it is a fine day. Therefore, different values can be specified for the times spent walk-

Table D-1. Elasticity of Optimal Walking Distance (d^*)

Variable	Partial derivative of d^*	Elasticity of d^*
t (parking duration)	$\dfrac{\partial d^*}{\partial t} = +\dfrac{1}{2t} > 0$	$\eta_t = +\dfrac{1}{2d^*} > 0$
w (walking speed)	$\dfrac{\partial d^*}{\partial w} = +\dfrac{1}{2w} > 0$	$\eta_w = +\dfrac{1}{2d^*} > 0$
n (number of persons)	$\dfrac{\partial d^*}{\partial n} = -\dfrac{1}{2n} < 0$	$\eta_n = -\dfrac{1}{2d^*} < 0$
v (value of time)	$\dfrac{\partial d^*}{\partial v} = -\dfrac{1}{2v} < 0$	$\eta_v = -\dfrac{1}{2d^*} < 0$

Notes:
The optimal walking distance (d^*) between parking space and destination is:

$$d^* = -1/2 \log_e\left(\frac{nv}{tw}\right)$$

The elasticity (η_i) of d^* with respect to variable i is:

$$\eta_i = \frac{\dfrac{\partial d^*}{\partial i}}{\dfrac{d^*}{i}}$$

Figure D-1. Elasticity as a Function of Distance

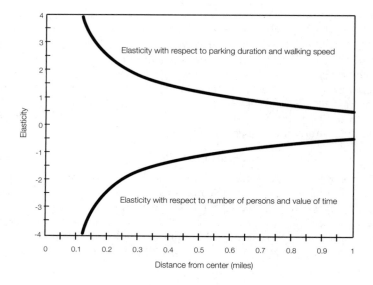

ing and driving. Using a stated-preference approach, Denvil Coombe et al. found, for example, that for drivers who parked in the center of Bristol, England, the value of saving time spent walking was 7 pence (10 cents) a minute, whereas the value of saving time spent driving was 3.6 pence (5 cents) a minute.[3] In other words, drivers appeared to be willing to pay twice as much to reduce the walking time from their parking spaces to their destinations as to reduce the driving time to the parking spaces. Using data on the parking-rent gradient in the Minneapolis Central Business District (CBD), Yong Nam Song found similar results, estimating that the value of saving walking time ranged from 1.5 to 4.6 times the value of saving driving time.[4]

Several additional factors can complicate the location decision. If parking prices decline rather than increase as you approach your destination, you may drive past your destination to find even cheaper parking and walk back. You may also choose to walk faster to save on the time spent walking. A more difficult problem is that your goal is not really to park for a certain duration but rather to visit your destination for business or pleasure. How long you want to spend at your destination depends, in part, on how much you have to pay to park and how long it takes to walk to and from your parking space. Therefore, staying a shorter time at your destination may compensate for a shorter walk from a more expensive parking space.[5] A simple model cannot capture all these factors, but basic mathematics can still help to analyze the choice.

THE PRICE OF TIME

In the parking market, time is bought and sold, and parking locations thus reveal the value travelers place on saving time. Empirical research on the trade-off between time and money in parking location has been conducted in Australia, Britain, Canada, Greece, the Netherlands, and the United States. A survey of this research shows the results are consistent with a monocentric model of parking location choice.

Thomas Lambe conducted the first research on parking location choices. Using data from a 1962 survey of 10,000 commuters who parked in 55 garages in Vancouver, British Columbia, he estimated how much they were willing to pay to park closer to their employment sites. Using data on parking prices, parking locations, and walking distances for commuters to the CBD, he found:

> [C]ommuters are willing to pay $1.00 [Canadian] per month to park 175 feet closer to their destination. On the basis of twenty trips each way per month, they pay $1.00 per 7,000 feet of walking, or $0.14 per 1,000 feet. With an observed walking speed of 270 feet per minute [about 3 miles an hour], includ-

ing delays for traffic lights, the commuters appear to value their time at $2.30 per hour.[6]

When these values are converted to U.S. dollars and adjusted for inflation to the year 2002, commuters valued savings in walking time at $12.68 an hour. They saved $4.17 a mile by walking from more remote parking spaces.[7]

With the same data from Vancouver, Lambe and S. A. Brown used a linear programming model to show how market-clearing prices for all parking spaces combine to minimize motorists' total walking time from their parking locations to their final destinations.[8] They found the market prices for off-street parking closely matched the prices that minimize total walking time, with an average error of only 20 percent. Curb parking prices were well below the level that would minimize motorists' total walking time. Because curb spaces were underpriced, drivers' curb parking locations were determined more by luck in cruising for a rare vacant space than by choosing the optimal one. Therefore, the total walking time from curb spaces to final destinations exceeded the level market prices would produce.

Again using the 1962 survey of commuters in Vancouver, but employing a more sophisticated statistical method, Lambe later reestimated the value drivers place on driving time and walking time. Using a multinomial probit model that includes driving time from the person's trip origin to the parking facility, two-way walking distance from the parking location to the person's final destination, and a parking fee that depends on the parking duration, Lambe estimated the values drivers place on walking and driving time.[9] His results indicate parkers placed a value of between $1.73 and $2.13 per kilometer on the disutility of walking between the parking space and the destination. At a walking speed of 4.5 kilometers per hour, this is equivalent to between $7.78 and $9.58 per hour. When converted to U.S. dollars and adjusted for inflation to 2002, the value of saving time spent walking was between $43 and $53 an hour.

In 1971, Gökmen Ergün analyzed a survey of drivers to downtown Chicago to estimate the value drivers placed on saving walking time. He estimated drivers who parked more than one block from their destinations saved an average of $4.50 an hour for their additional walking time ($20 an hour in 2002). For those who parked less than one block from their destinations, he estimated they passed up an average savings of $5 an hour they could have earned had they been willing to walk farther ($22 an hour in 2002).

Using a survey of commuters who worked in seven large office buildings in the Los Angeles CBD in 1973, Terence Austin estimated the value of saving time spent walking was between $10.80 and $15 an hour (between $44 and $61 an hour in 2002).[10] In a similar study of auto commuters to the Manhattan CBD, Boris Pushkarev and Jeffrey Zupan collected data on the prices drivers paid for all-day parking and the distance they walked from their parking spaces to their destinations. They found parkers in the higher-priced lots paid an average of $0.65 for the convenience of not walking an extra 1,000 feet for the round-trip, in 1969 prices. Because peak-hour driving speeds were only six to nine miles an hour, and the car-handling delays at the more central parking garages were longer, they estimated commuters saved between 2 and 2.7 minutes of walking time by parking 1,000 feet closer and the value of saving time (based on the parking price differentials) was in the range of $14.40 and $19.20 an hour (between $71 and $94 an hour in 2002 prices).[11] Pushkarev and Zupan noted these figures were well above other estimates of the value of time but explained their sample represented an atypical group: auto commuters to Manhattan were a small share of peak-hour arrivals, and their incomes were very high.

In a 1975 study of parking in the center of West Berlin, Yvo Dirickx and Peter Jennergren used a linear programming model to answer the following questions:

> If an "optimal" utilization of existing parking facilities were possible, what would it look like?... How far do drivers have to walk by foot from their vehicles to reach their final destinations? Where are there empty parking spaces on the street? What would a theoretically correct parking fee structure look like?[12]

Their model allocated cars among parking spaces to minimize the total cost of drivers' and passengers' walking time between their cars and final destinations. They found that spaces in existing facilities, if priced correctly, could satisfy the demand for parking with very little walking. To minimize walking, the price of curb parking should be at least as high as the price of the adjacent off-street parking. In practice, however, curb parking in West Berlin was greatly underpriced: it was either free or only about 20 percent of the price of off-street parking, and it was congested even though the adjacent off-street spaces were at most two-thirds full. Many long-term parkers occupied curb spaces because they arrived early in the morning when the spaces were vacant. As a result, many more short-term parkers who would have been willing to pay a premium to park in the convenient curb spaces were instead forced to walk long distances to their destinations.

In 1978, Canadian transportation economist David Gillen developed a location model similar to the one presented in this chapter, although he did not consider the number of people in a car or the length of time they parked (all motorists drove solo and the trips were all journeys to work). Using data on commuters in Toronto, Gillen found: (1) parking prices increased closer to the commuters' destinations, (2) the slope of the price gradient increased closer to these destinations, and (3) this slope was a statistically significant variable in determining parking locations. Gillen's first two findings are consistent with my assumed pattern of parking prices in equation 8, and his third finding is consistent with the optimal parking distance calculated in equation 6.

In a 1982 study of drivers to the center of Haarlem in the Netherlands, D. van der Goot estimated a model to explain drivers' choices of parking location. The walking time between the parking location and the final destination had the greatest influence on parking choices. For shopping trips, longer walking times were associated with longer parking times, which is consistent with the model presented here.[13]

In 1991, Kay Axhausen and John Polak used surveys of parkers in Birmingham, England, and Karlsruhe, Germany, to estimate the value of time associated with different components of car travel (general in-vehicle time, parking search time, and walking time to the final destination). Using a stated-preference approach to estimate the value of walking time between the parking space and the destination for work trips, they found commuters were willing to spend $11.66 to save an hour of walking time in Birmingham and $21.33 in Karlsruhe (these values are adjusted for inflation to the year 2002).[14]

Richard Arnott, Andre de Palma, and Robin Lindsey developed a theoretical model of commuters who drive solo to work in a CBD.[15] All commuters park along radial routes leading to the CBD and then walk the rest of the way from their parking spaces to the center. Commuters choose their departure time and parking location to minimize the total costs they incur from in-vehicle travel time, tolls, parking fees, walking time, and schedule delay (the cost of arriving either early or late at the destination). The model shows that if the government charges the optimum tolls to prevent traffic congestion, market-rate prices for parking will decline with distance from the center and produce a socially optimal distribution of parking location choices.

Using a 1983 survey of 1,702 commuters employed by 80 employers in the CBD of Edmonton, Alberta, John Hunt and Stan Teply estimated a model of parking behavior for work trips. They considered not only walking distance and parking cost, but also whether the parking was on or off street, the physical condition of the parking spaces (including weather protection), and several other variables such as safety and the nearby land uses. They found walking distance and parking cost were the most significant determinants of parking location, with the value commuters placed on walking time ranging between $14.04 an hour for on-street parkers and $17.49 an hour for off-street parkers (in 1983 Canadian dollars). After adjustment for inflation and conversion to U.S. dollars in 2002, the values for walking-time savings were $20 an hour for on-street parkers and $25 an hour for off-street parkers.[16]

In the 1990s the U.K. Department of Transport sponsored an extensive study of parking as a factor in travel choices. Using surveys designed to learn how drivers choose where to park, Denvil Coombe et al. found that when faced with a change in the price of parking, the most frequent response was to look for a different place to park:

> The research indicated that, given the option of changing their trip frequency, destination, time of travel, and mode of travel, respondents' most popular reaction was to try to continue to park so that they could continue with their original activity at their original destination, even if this involved changing their place and type of parking. This finding was true irrespective of journey purpose.[17]

The two most important factors in the parking location decision (far ahead of any other factors) were the price of parking and the walking distance to the destination.

In choosing their travel mode, travelers take into account both the price of parking and the time value of walking the rest of the way to a destination, so the net cost of the optimal parking location can affect the choice of whether to drive alone, carpool, ride the bus, cycle, or simply walk all the way. David Hensher and Jenny King developed a model that simultaneously considers mode choice and parking-location choice. Using the stated-preference approach, they estimated the model with data from a survey of 1,789 travelers to the CBD of Sydney, Australia. Their results indicate that increases in parking prices redistribute parking locations and shift some drivers to public transit but do not divert trips away from the CBD:

> Increases in [parking] tariffs will secure significantly greater use of public transport, a noticeable switch from parking close in to parking elsewhere in the CBD, and a small increase in relocation of parking to the fringe of the CBD and parking outside of the CBD. There is virtually no loss in travel to the CBD.[18]

This result refutes the conventional wisdom that higher parking prices will inevitably reduce employment and trade in the CBD. Using a similar stated-preference approach in Dublin, Ireland, Peter Clinch and Andrew

Kelly found a comparable result. In response to a proposed 367 percent increase in the price of curb parking in 2001, 83 percent of curb parkers indicated they would park in a different location (mainly off street), 11 percent said they would travel by another mode (mainly by bus), and only 5 percent said they would reduce the number of trips to the center of Dublin.[19]

Finally, Dimitrios Tsamboulas used interviews of drivers who parked in central Athens to estimate their willingness to pay higher prices for the opportunity to park closer to their destinations, as well as their willingness to park farther away in return for lower prices. He found most drivers preferred their current parking location, which suggests drivers do indeed attempt to optimize their parking location choices with respect to prices that decline with distance from their final destinations. He also found that commuters (who are monthly parkers) plan their trips thoroughly and are more likely to search for a parking location producing the optimum combination of walking time and parking price. He concluded:

> [Parking choices] can be explained only with a behavioural characteristic unique to Greeks: they prefer to park their cars as close as possible to their destination in order to avoid doing the exercise of walking.[20]

Perhaps even the original Olympic athletes parked their chariots as close as possible to the stadium to avoid walking. But Tsamboulas is too critical of his fellow Greeks—the desire to park close to our destinations seems to be universal.

Table D-2 summarizes the findings of these studies of the value motorists place on the time they save by parking closer to their destinations. The estimates range from $12 an hour in Birmingham to $94 an hour in Manhattan. While these estimates may seem high, they clearly indicate that when motorists choose a parking spot, they make a trade-off between paying more and walking farther. On the other hand, perhaps these estimates are not so high, especially when we think about the way many motorists (perhaps including yourself) drive around and around in

Table D-2. Estimates of the Value of Saving Walking Time ($/hour in 2002$)

Author	City	Year	Value of time
Lambe (1967)	Vancouver	1962	$13
Lambe (1996)	Vancouver	1962	$43 to $53
Pushkarev & Zupan (1975)	New York	1969	$71 to $94
Ergün (1971)	Chicago	1971	$20 to $22
Austin (1973)	Los Angeles	1973	$44 to $61
Hunt & Tepley (1993)	Edmonton	1983	$20 to $25
Axhausen & Polak (1991)	Birmingham	1988	$12
Axhausen & Polak (1991)	Karlsruhe	1988	$21

mall parking lots to find a close-in space, just so they won't have to walk a few more feet to get to the mall entrance. In any case, these estimates suggest that the most convenient curb parking spaces have the potential to earn considerable revenue at market prices. During the course of a day, curb parking spaces with a high turnover rate can save a lot of walking time for many drivers who want to park in the most convenient location for a short time during a quick trip.

The "principle of least effort" applies well to choosing a parking space. In *Human Behavior and the Principle of Least Effort*, Harvard linguist George Kinglsey Zipf proposed that, all else being equal, human behavior tends to flow into a path of minimum effort.[21] Not only does this principle help explain parking locations, but research on parking can also benefit from Zipf's recommendation about scientific methodology in general:

> We might gain considerable insight into the mainsprings of human behavior if we viewed it purely as a natural phenomenon like everything else in the universe, and if we studied it with the same dispassionate objectivity with which one is wont to study, say, the social behavior of bees, or the nestbuilding habits of birds.[22]

Likewise, we might gain considerable insight into the mainsprings of human behavior simply by observing how much drivers pay to park, how many people are in the car, how long they park, and how far they walk.

APPENDIX D NOTES

1. The values of driving time and walking time are assumed to be equal here.

2. This result follows from the assumed functional relationship between p and d. With this negative exponential relationship, the same relative increase in t, w, n, or v always produce the same absolute change in d^*.

3. Coombe et al. (1997, 67) used the Traffic Restraint Analysis Model (TRAM) to make these estimates.

4. Yong Nam Song (1995, 61).

5. In a study of commuters to downtown Toronto, David Gillen (1978) found that drivers who paid for parking by the hour substituted parking duration for walking distance: they parked for a shorter time to walk a shorter distance.

6. Lambe (1967, 411).

7. At the exchange rate of Canadian $1.08 = U.S. $1 in 1962, the value of time savings was U.S. $2.12. Adjusted for inflation to 2002, the estimated value was $12.68 an hour. Lambe noted his estimate of travel time savings of $2.30 per hour (based on commuters' choices between different parking locations) was close to Thomas Lisco's (1967) estimate of $2.60 per hour (based on commuters' choices between automobile and mass transit).

8. Brown and Lambe (1972).

9. Lambe modestly states the model is "relatively simple," but it is more sophisticated than most statistical techniques used to analyze parking data. Consider this sentence, for example: "Each relative accuracy term in Table 1 is the square root of the reciprocal of the negative of the second derivative of the natural logarithm of the likelihood function in the region of its maximum" (Lambe 1996, 211).

10. Austin (1973, 5).

11. Pushkarev and Zupan (1975, 68).

12. Dirickx and Jennergren (1975, 1).

13. Potential parkers appeared to be deterred only when the occupancy rates exceeded 120 percent, which suggests a surprising willingness to park illegally. When both legally and illegally parked cars were counted, the parking occupancy rates ranged as high as 400 percent.

14. Axhausen and Polak (1991, 78). The original values in 1988 were £4.93 and DM34.96 per hour of walking time. These values were converted to U.S. dollars using 1988 purchasing power parities (£1 = $1.66 and $1 = DM2.49), and then adjusted to 2002 by the U.S. Consumer Price Index. Axhausen and Polak estimated the value of saving walking time for shopping trips was considerably higher than for work trips. They also summarized other researchers' studies of the value of walking time.

15. Arnott, de Palma, and Lindsey (1991).

16. The exchange rate in 1983 was Canadian $1.244 = U.S. $1.

17. Coombe *et al.* (1997, 66). When asked to state the main reasons for the choice of a parking location for home-based work trips, 60 percent of respondents reported closeness to destination, 20 percent reported the charge for parking, 5 percent reported the chance of finding a space, and only 15 percent reported any other reason (see Table 1 on p. 67).

18. Hensher and King (2001, 195).

19. Clinch and Kelly (2004b).

20. Tsamboulas (2001, 120).

21. Science fiction writer Robert Heinlein paraphrased this principle as, "Progress is made by lazy men looking for easier ways to do things."

22. Zipf (1949, v).

E

The Price of Land and the Cost of Parking

Transportation is civilization.

—*RUDYARD KIPLING*

How do we decide when to build a parking structure rather than use land for surface parking? Because a parking structure displaces land that could be used for surface parking, we can estimate the cost of the parking spaces the structure adds and compare this with the cost of a surface parking lot. The cost per space added by a parking structure takes into account the opportunity cost of land by deducting the number of surface spaces lost when it is built. If the cost per space for a surface parking lot equals the cost per space added by a parking structure, surface parking and structured parking are equally cost-effective ways to increase the parking supply. The cost per space added by a parking structure therefore reveals the break-even land value at which building a parking structure becomes cost-effective. This break-even land value is an estimate of the lower-bound price of the land used as the site for the structure.

BREAK-EVEN LAND VALUES

Chapter 6 showed the construction cost per space added for each of the 15 parking structures built at UCLA between 1961 and 2002. We can use these cost estimates to calculate the break-even land values implied by the decisions to build them (see Table E-1). The break-even land value per surface space is the land value at which the cost of adding surface spaces

Table E-1. Land Value Implied by the Cost Per Parking Space Added (2002$)

Year built (1)	Structure name (2)	Break-even land value per surface space (3)	Break-even land value per square foot (4)=(3)/329
1961	5	$15,400	$47
1963	14	$11,600	$35
1964	3	$13,300	$40
1966	9	$14,800	$45
1967	8	$17,000	$52
1969	2	$14,900	$45
1977	CHS	$29,900	$91
1980	6	$23,200	$71
1983	4	$31,800	$97
1990	1	$28,900	$88
1990	RC	$30,800	$94
1991	SV	$28,300	$86
1995	3 Addition	$16,400	$50
1998	4 Addition	$29,000	$88
2002	7	$31,500	$96

Note: Surface parking lots on campus occupy an average of 329 square feet of land per parking space

equals the cost of adding structured spaces (column 3, derived from column 8 in Table 6-1). Dividing the break-even value of land per parking space by 329 square feet (the average size of a parking space at UCLA) gives the break-even value per square foot of land (column 4).

In the 1960s, the break-even land value implied by the decision to build the structures ranged from $35 to $52 a square foot (adjusted to 2002 prices). Since 1977, the break-even land value implied by the decision to build a structure ranged from $50 to $97 a square foot. It pays to build a parking structure if land values are higher than these break-even values. How do land prices near UCLA compare with the break-even land values implied by the construction costs of these parking structures? In 1988, a four-acre vacant site near the UCLA campus was sold at a price of $241 a square foot ($10.5 million an acre).[1] In comparison, the break-even land values for the two structures built in 1990 (Structures 1 and RC) were $88 and $94 a square foot. These values imply that building a parking structure was indeed much cheaper than buying land for surface parking.

If the land used for the two parking structures was also worth $241 a square foot, the land-plus-construction cost would be $32,400 per space in the larger structure and $46,800 per space in the smaller one.[2] These land-plus-construction costs per space are greater than the construction cost per space added of $28,900 for the larger structure and $30,800 for the smaller one. These figures confirm the construction cost per parking space added by a structure gives a conservative estimate of the land-plus-construction cost per parking space in the structure.[3] In short, the cost per space added by a parking structure (above and beyond the number of spaces possible with a surface lot on the structure's site) provides a lower bound on the total cost (land plus construction) for all spaces within the structure.

The cost per parking space added refers to structured parking spaces, and where the price of land is low, surface spaces cost less than structured ones. Land prices can understate the market value of surface parking spaces, however. Parking requirements tend to depress the market price of land because developers will bid less for land if the zoning code requires them to construct more parking spaces than they would otherwise provide. As explained in Chapter 5, for example, land prices fell by 33 percent when Oakland, California, introduced its parking requirement of 1 space per 1,000 square feet for apartment buildings. Where parking requirements reduce the market price of land, as in Oakland, this lower market price undervalues the opportunity cost of the land used to provide the required parking. A low market price of land therefore does not imply that providing the required parking is cheap because the requirement has itself reduced land prices.

LAND BANKS

The vast deserts of surface parking lots in many cities present a great opportunity as land banks for future redevelopment. Urban designer Jonathan Barnett explains how land can be reclaimed from surface parking by building parking structures:

> A garage can absorb five or six acres of [surface] parking while occupying less than an acre itself.... The cost of decanting the [surface] parking [into a garage] becomes the cost for the land that is made available.[4]

We can calculate the cost of recovering land from surface parking by building garages. An acre of surface parking contains about 130 parking spaces (at 330 square feet per parking space), so a six-acre lot will hold 780 spaces. If all 780 parking spaces are stacked on six levels in a garage that covers only one acre, the remaining five acres of land become available for development, without any reduction in the parking supply. If the construction cost is $10,000 per space, the total cost will be $7.8 million.[5] The cost of the five vacated acres of land formerly used for surface parking is thus $1.6 million an acre ($7,800,000 ÷ 5 acres = $1,560,000) or $36 a square foot.

This estimated cost of reclaimed land may be too high. In her book *Parking Structures*, Mary Smith, one of the nation's foremost parking structure designers, estimated structured parking is cheaper than surface parking if the price of land is more than $30 a square foot ($1.3 million an acre).[6] If Smith's estimate is accurate, the cost of converting surface parking spaces into structured ones will be about $30 per square foot of former surface parking made available for new uses. Most cites now pockmarked by parking lots may thus have an almost inexhaustible supply of vacant land available at a price of $30 a square foot even without reducing our bloated parking supply.

COST OF COMPLYING WITH PARKING REQUIREMENTS

Drivers rarely pay for parking because off-street parking requirements bundle the cost of parking into the cost of all development. We can estimate how the required parking increases the cost of development by looking at the example of office buildings (see Table E-2). Suppose aboveground parking structures cost $13,000 per space, and underground structures cost $25,000 per space.[7] The most common parking requirement for an office building is 4 spaces per 1,000 square feet of floor area.[8] The required parking thus costs $52 per square foot of office space if it is aboveground, and $100 per square foot if underground (see row 3).[9] The average cost of a Class A, steel-framed office building in Los Angeles is about $150 per square foot (including construction cost, tenant improvement costs, and "soft" costs, such as financing, insurance, and real estate taxes during construction, but excluding the cost of parking).[10] Providing four parking spaces per 1,000 square feet thus increases the construction cost of the office space by 35 percent ($52 ÷ $150) if the parking is aboveground and by 67 percent ($100 ÷ $150) if underground.[11] Because the cost of parking is bundled into the cost of office space,

Table E-2. Required Parking Increases the Cost of Office Space

	Aboveground	Underground
1. Construction cost per parking space	$13,000	$25,000
2. Parking requirement per 1,000 sq. ft.	4 spaces	4 spaces
3. Parking cost per sq. ft. of office space	$52	$100
4. Construction cost per sq. ft. of office space	$150	$150
5. Parking cost as % of cost of office space	35%	67%

Row (1) is taken from R.S. Means Co. (2001) and Table 6-1
Row (3) is Row (1) x Row (2)/1,000
Row (4) is from the Los Angeles County Assessor
Row (5) is Row (3)/Row (5)

drivers do not pay for it, so someone else must, and that someone ends up being everyone, including people without cars.

Parking requirements cause only part of the total spending for parking because most developers would supply *some* parking even if zoning did not require it. Nevertheless, in the Los Angeles example, each additional aboveground parking space per 1,000 square feet of office space adds $13 per square foot to the cost of the office space, and each additional underground parking space adds $25 per square foot.[12] If a developer wants to supply two parking spaces per 1,000 square feet of office space, and the city requires four spaces, the requirement adds between $26 and $50 per square foot to the building's cost. Even a small increase in parking requirements can significantly increase development cost and, by extension, the cost of housing and all other goods and services. Off-street parking requirements are perhaps the greatest of all unfunded mandates.[13]

APPENDIX E NOTES

1. A large R-5 residential site near campus was sold for $504 a square foot in 1989. Several small commercial sites in Westwood Village adjacent to the campus have also been sold at prices above $241 a square foot in recent years. Therefore, a price of $241 a square foot for land value seems conservative. This information was supplied by the Los Angeles County Assessor.

2. The land-plus-construction cost per space is the total construction cost of the structure plus the cost of the land valued at $241 a square foot, divided by the number of spaces in the structure.

3. The land-plus-construction cost per space in the larger structure is thus 25 percent greater than the construction cost per space added by the structure. The land-plus-construction cost per space in the smaller structure is 69 percent greater than the construction cost per space added by the structure. Including the market value of land in the cost estimate increases the cost per space more in the smaller structure in the present comparison because it is entirely aboveground and consumes more land per parking space: 121 square feet of land per parking space in the smaller structure compared with only 39 square feet of land per parking space in the larger structure. The cost per space added by a structure equals the land-plus-construction cost per space in the structure only if land is worth the break-even value at which the structure becomes cost-effective.

4. Barnett (2003, 54-55).

5. If the structure costs $7,800,000 and adds 650 spaces to the 130 spaces already on the one-acre site, the structure's cost is $12,000 per space added.

6. Smith (2001, 27).

7. Chapter 6 explains that the median cost of a parking structure in Los Angeles in 2001 was $13,000 a space. The data on underground parking structures at UCLA suggest the cost was more than $25,000 a space

8. See the results of the two surveys of parking requirements in 117 cities in Southern California in Table A-2 in Appendix A.

9. The cost of aboveground parking is 4 spaces x $13,000 per space per 1,000 square feet of office space or $52 per square foot of office space (4 x $13,000 ÷ 1,000).

10. This figure was supplied by the Los Angeles County Assessor in 1998.

11. If the office space costs less than $150 per square foot, the required parking increases the cost of the office space by an even greater percentage. The high cost of required parking is not a uniquely American phenomenon, of course. Simon Haworth and Ian Hilton (1981, 87) report that, in Scottish cities, the cost of providing all the required parking spaces increases the construction cost of retail space by up to 48 percent. The cost of the parking spaces needed to meet the highest requirement was 32.5 percent of the total development cost (including both the cost of the retail space and the required parking spaces), so the cost of providing the required parking spaces increased the cost of providing the retail space by 48 percent (32.5 ÷ 67.5).

12. If one aboveground parking space cost $13,000, one parking space per 1,000 square feet costs $13 per square foot ($13,000 ÷ 1,000). If one underground parking space cost $25,000, one parking space per 1,000 square feet costs $25 per square foot ($25,000 ÷ 1,000).

13. An unfunded mandate is usually defined as a requirement imposed by the federal, state, or local governments with no funding to pay for it. Off-street parking requirements are a requirement imposed by local governments on the private sector, with no funding to pay for the required parking spaces.

F

People, Parking, and Cities

What man had rather were true he more readily believes.

—-FRANCIS BACON

A common prejudice among academics is a willingness to believe anything bad about Los Angeles, without checking the facts. I found a perfect example of this in a 1997 book by two Berkeley professors who wrote, "In the urban United States, the automobile consumes close to half of the land area of cities; in Los Angeles the figure approaches two-thirds."[1] How did they know this? They cited a 1992 article by a Berkeley colleague who said, "In U.S. cities, close to half of all urban area goes to accommodating the automobile, while in Los Angeles the figure reaches two-thirds."[2] But how did he know this? He cited a Washington think tank's 1988 publication, which stated, "In American cities, close to half of all the urban space goes to accommodate the automobile; in Los Angeles, the figure reaches two-thirds."[3] And where did this come from? It came from a 1980 book by a New Yorker, Kirkpatrick Sale—a self-described neo-Luddite—who said, "It [the car] demands enormous amounts of space, both in the country-side, where it has so far caused 60,000 square miles of land to be paved over, and in the cities, where roughly half of all the land (in Los Angeles 62 percent) is given over to its needs."[4] It's hard to say how Kirkpatrick Sale knew this because he did not cite a source and has not responded to repeated telephone calls asking him for it. Perhaps he had seen Lewis Mumford's 1961 book, *The City in History*, which stated that more than one-third of the land in Los Angeles was consumed by the freeway system and two-thirds of its Central Business District (CBD) was devoted to streets, freeways, parking facilities, and garages. "This," he wrote, "is space eating with a vengeance."[5] Mumford likewise did not cite a source for this statement, but perhaps he had seen an article by Seymour Taylor in the July 1959 issue of *Traffic Quarterly*, which stated:

> Approximately twenty-eight percent of the land area comprising downtown Los Angeles, for example, is in street, freeways, and service ways and another thirty-eight percent is in the off-street vehicular parking and loading, so about two-thirds of the land is primarily devoted to rubber.[6]

Taylor gave no citation for this statistic, but he was the General Manager of the Los Angeles Department of Traffic, so perhaps he knew what he was talking about. If he was right, the figures are startling because more land was devoted to parking (38 percent) than to roads (28 percent) or to all other uses combined (the remaining 34 percent). The high share of land in parking might be explained in part by the city's notorious urban renewal program that had bulldozed Bunker Hill, with most of the land left as parking lots for decades before anything was built. But even if the data were accurate for downtown Los Angeles in the 1950s, it is a bit depressing to see how they floated into the middle of academic discourse referring to all Los Angeles in the 1990s.

SHARE OF LAND IN STREETS AND PARKING

In 1997, Stephen Marshall at University College London posted a message on the Internet, citing the Berkeley professors' data on the share of land consumed by cars in Los Angeles and asking for similar information about other cities. Marshall summarized the responses and made them available on the web. A planner from Australia wrote:

> The glib citing of such "data" is nonsense, of course. Many years ago, as a planning student, I tried to calculate the figure for Melbourne—and found that in older areas of Melbourne (with many wide boulevards and ninety-nine-foot local road reserves) the figure was approaching one-third—but that was largely because of the generous colonial pre-auto allocation of space to "streets." We discovered that the figure for modern suburbs was well below 25 percent, suggesting paradoxically that urban areas designed for car use in fact devoted less land to roads and streets.

This finding may seem counterintuitive, but streets existed long before cars, and the share of urban land devoted to streets is not the same as the share "consumed by cars." Perhaps cars consume only the *increase* in the share of land devoted to streets and parking since the discovery of "infernal" combustion. How then can we explain why the share of land devoted to streets in the newer parts of some cities is lower than in the parts developed before the car arrived?

In their book *Autos, Transit, and Cities*, John Meyer and José Gómez-Ibáñez used data gathered in the 1960s to examine the share of urban land in streets. Table F-1 shows the results for 15 large cities in the U.S. Columns 1 and 2 show the population density and rank order of each city. New York at the top with 24,697 persons per square mile was 10 times denser than Dallas at the bottom with 2,428 persons per square mile. Columns 3 and 4 show each city's share of land for streets, and their rank order. Somewhat surprisingly, dense New York used 30 percent of its land for streets, while sprawling Houston used only 13 percent; the denser cities typically used a larger share of their land for streets (the coefficient of correlation between population density and the share of land in streets was 0.78). But now consider columns 5 and 6, which show the area of land per person for streets in each city and their rank order. Although the denser cities used a larger *share of land* for streets, they also used less *street space per person* (the coefficient of correlation between population density and the street space per capita was -0.89). Sprawling Houston had 1,585 square feet of streets per person, while compact New York had only 345 square feet per person; that is, New York's share of land for streets was 2.4

Table F-1. Population Density and the Area of Land in Streets

	Population density		Share of land in streets		Street area per capita	
	Persons/sq. mile	Rank	Percent	Rank	Sq. feet	Rank
	(1)	(2)	(3)	(4)	(5)	(6)
New York	24,697	1	30	1	345	14
Newark	17,170	2	16	10	257	15
San Francisco	16,559	3	26	2	441	10
Chicago	15,836	4	24	4	424	11
Philadelphia	15,743	5	19	7	365	13
St. Louis	12,296	6	25	3	609	7
Pittsburgh	11,171	7	18	8	455	9
Cleveland	10,789	8	17	9	416	12
Miami	8,529	9	24	5	778	4
Milwaukee	8,137	10	20	6	724	6
Cincinnati	6,501	11	13	13	573	8
Los Angeles	5,451	12	14	12	741	5
Atlanta	3,802	13	15	11	1,120	3
Houston	2,860	14	13	15	1,585	1
Dallas	2,428	15	13	14	1,575	2

Source: Meyer and Gómez-Ibáñez (1983, 181).

times Houston's (30% ÷ 13%), but Houston's street space per person was 4.6 times New York's (1,585 ÷ 345). So which city devotes more land to streets?

Meyer and Gómez-Ibáñez explained the inverse ranking between the share of land in streets and the area of land per person in streets:

> Automobile use does *not* result in an exceptional *percentage* of land being given to transportation purposes. Rather, the automobile seems to create exceptional demands for transportation land relative to the number of people in an urban area. Specifically, cities more dependent on the automobile tend to have more street acreage per person but a smaller percentage of total land in streets.[7]

As population density decreases and people live on larger lots, the share of land in streets declines because blocks are longer and lots are deeper. In a study of suburban development patterns in the San Francisco area, for example, Michael Southworth and Peter Owens found the denser grid pattern of 1900 had 28 blocks and 26 intersections per 100 acres, while the looping streets and cul-de-sacs typical of suburbs built in the 1980s had only eight blocks and eight intersections per 100 acres.[8] A sprawling city like Houston uses a smaller share of its total land for streets, but because people live at low density they have more road space per person. A dense city like New York, with many blocks and intersections per square mile, devotes a larger share of land to streets, but because so many people live packed in close proximity on each block, they have less street area per person.

In their classic book, *The Urban Transportation Problem*, John Meyer, John Kain, and Martin Wohl calculated that in a typical downtown with 40-foot-wide streets and 12 blocks to the mile, streets take up 18 percent of the total land area. Parking, however, can take up much more land. They also calculated that if all commuters travel downtown by car and all parking is in four-level garages, parking spaces need about 38 percent of the total land area—more than twice the area taken up by streets.[9] In total, 56 percent of land would be devoted to streets and parking, although this calculation obviously depends on the downtown employment density. In practice, Meyer, Kain, and Wohl say, most cities devote at least 40 percent of the CBD land area to streets, alleys, and parking. In 1999, for example, aerial photographs of Lake Forest, Illinois, showed that off- and on-street parking occupied 39 percent of the CBD's 55 acres.[10]

Why is so much more land needed for parking than for streets, even if it is stacked in four-level garages? We tend to think of the land needed by cars as being exclusively a matter of space, but it is also a function of time. Eric Bruun and Vukan Vuchic explain the land used by a transportation vehicle is the product of the land area it occupies and the time it occupies this area (space used = area occupied x time occupied), and this equation helps explain the enormous demands of parking on the built environment.[11] Because of the distance needed between cars in traffic, each car takes up more space while it is on the road than while it is parked, but it is on the road for only a short time and is parked for a long time. In one of the first estimates of the area-hours of land occupied by vehicles for a specific trip, André Schmider calculated that for a four-kilometer round trip with an eight-hour stay at the destination, an automobile traveling 40 kilometers an hour uses 9.6 square-meter-hours for travel (the area occupied by the car in traffic multiplied by the six-minute travel time) and 64 square-meter-hours for parking (the area of a parking space multiplied by the eight-hour parking duration); the area-hours used for parking at the destination are therefore 6.7 times the area-hours used for travel to and from the destination.[12]

Using data from household travel surveys, J.P. Nicholas, P. Pochet, and H. Poimboeuf estimated that parking uses 62 percent of the total space-hours for all personal travel in Lyons, France. Moving automobiles take 34 percent of the total space-hours, while all other travel (public transport, walking, cycling, and motorcycling) take only 4 percent.[13] Parking takes up such a high proportion of space consumption for travel because cars are moving less than 5 percent of the time (4.7 percent according to the Lyons household trip survey). Cars require so much land for parking because they are parked so much of the time.

PEOPLE AND LAND: LOS ANGELES, NEW YORK, AND SAN FRANCISCO

Because cars spend about 95 percent of their lives parked, parking can consume more land than streets, and there is some truth to the notion that Los Angeles has "paved paradise to put up a parking lot." A comparison with San Francisco is apt. For a downtown concert hall, Los Angeles zoning requires, as the minimum, 50 times more parking spaces than San Francisco allows as the maximum. Does a lower population density explain why a concert hall "needs" 50 times more parking spaces in Los Angeles than in San Francisco? Here is another opportunity to explode a false notion about Los Angeles—its low density. The Census Bureau defines an "urbanized area" as a central city plus any adjacent contiguous area with a density of at least 1,000 persons per square mile.[14] The Census data for urbanized areas allow us to use the same definition of the urban boundary to compare the settled territory of different metropolitan areas. In terms of people per square mile in the urbanized area, the 2000 Census found Los Angeles has the highest population density in the United States: 7,068 people per square mile (see column 6 in Table F-2).[15] By comparison, San Francisco has 7,004 people per square mile, and New York has 5,309 people per square mile. The *city* of Los Angeles has a lower population density than do the *cities* of San Francisco and New York (column 3), but the *urbanized area* of Los Angeles has a higher population density than do the *urbanized areas* of San Francisco and New York, which have the second and third highest population densities in the U.S.

The high density of Los Angeles may seem a trick of statistics—who cares about the suburbs if we are talking about cities and downtowns—but when comparing population densities of different metropolitan areas, the Census definition of urbanized area is much more appropriate than the area of the central city alone. The City of Los Angeles is 10 times larger than the City of San Francisco (469 versus 47 square miles), but the Los Angeles urbanized area is only about four times larger than the San

Table F-2. Population Densities of Los Angeles, New York, and San Francisco

Metropolitan area	Central city			Urbanized area			Urbanized area outside central city		
	Population	Land Area	Density	Population	Land Area	Density	Population	Land Area	Density
	persons	sq. miles	pers/sq.mi.	persons	sq. miles	pers/sq.mi.	persons	sq. miles	pers/sq.mi.
	(1)	(2)	(3)=(1)/(2)	(4)	(5)	(6)=(4)/(5)	(7)=(4)-(1)	(8)=(5)-(2)	(9)=(7)/(8)
2000									
Los Angeles	3,694,820	469	7,873	11,789,487	1,668	7,068	7,708,126	1,199	6,431
New York	8,008,278	303	26,430	17,799,861	3,353	5,309	9,791,583	3,050	3,211
San Francisco	776,733	47	16,632	2,995,769	428	7,004	2,219,036	381	5,824
1990									
Los Angeles	3,485,398	469	7,427	11,402,946	1,966	5,801	7,917,548	1,496	5,291
New York	7,322,564	309	23,705	16,044,012	2,966	5,409	8,721,448	2,658	3,282
San Francisco	723,959	47	15,502	3,629,516	874	4,152	2,905,557	827	3,512
1980									
Los Angeles	2,966,850	465	6,384	9,479,436	1,827	5,189	6,512,586	1,362	4,781
New York	7,071,639	302	23,455	15,590,274	2,808	5,552	8,518,635	2,507	3,399
San Francisco	678,974	46	14,633	3,190,698	796	4,008	2,511,724	750	3,351
1970									
Los Angeles	2,816,061	464	6,073	8,351,266	1,572	5,313	5,535,205	1,108	4,995
New York	7,894,862	300	26,343	16,206,841	2,425	6,683	8,311,979	2,125	3,911
San Francisco	715,674	45	15,764	2,987,850	681	4,387	2,272,176	636	3,575
1960									
Los Angeles	2,479,015	455	5,451	6,488,791	1,370	4,736	4,009,776	915	4,381
New York	7,781,984	315	24,697	14,114,927	1,892	7,462	6,332,943	1,576	4,017
San Francisco	740,316	48	15,553	2,430,663	572	4,253	1,690,347	524	3,226

Sources: Tables P1 and GCT-PH1 of Census 2000 for 2000, and United States Census Bureau (1993) for earlier decades.

Francisco urbanized area (1,668 versus 428 square miles). And the City of Los Angeles is 50 percent larger than the City of New York (469 versus 303 square miles), but the New York urbanized area is twice as large as the Los Angeles urbanized area (3,353 versus 1,668 square miles). Using the Census definition of urbanized area allows us to compare the population densities of different metropolitan areas and of the same metropolitan area in different years without regard to the arbitrary political boundaries within these areas.

Ironically, it is the *sprawl* of the New York and San Francisco urbanized areas that reduce their population densities below that of Los Angeles (column 9). The Los Angeles urbanized area has a higher population density than New York or San Francisco because the urbanized area *outside* the city of Los Angeles has a higher density (6,431 persons per square mile) than do the urbanized areas outside the cities of New York (3,211 persons per square mile) and San Francisco (5,824 persons per square mile).

Angelenos are much more evenly spread throughout their urbanized area than are New Yorkers and San Franciscans. The suburban Los Angeles density is 82 percent of that in the central city, while the suburban New York density is only 12 percent of that in the central city, and the suburban San Francisco density is only 35 percent of that in the central city. The New York and San Francisco urbanized areas look like Hong Kong surrounded by Phoenix, while the Los Angeles urbanized area looks like Los Angeles surrounded by…well, Los Angeles.

New York's suburban population is 27 percent greater than that of Los Angeles, but New York suburbanites occupy 154 percent more land, so their population density is only half that of Los Angeles. San Francisco's suburban population is only 29 percent of Los Angeles's, but San Francisco suburbanites occupy 32 percent as much land, so their population density is only 91 percent of Los Angeles.

How long has this been going on? Table F-2 shows the data for each decennial Census since 1960, the year in which the Census Bureau established the criterion of 1,000 persons per square mile to define urbanized areas. The Census Bureau changed the definition of urbanized areas in 2000, so the 2000 results are not directly comparable with the 1960–1990 period. In 2000, urbanized areas were based on all *census tracts* with more than 1,000 persons per square mile, while in earlier years they were based on all *jurisdictions* with more than 1,000 persons per square mile. For example, San Francisco's urbanized area shrank by 51 percent between 1990 (when it was 874 square miles) and 2000 (when it was 428 square miles) because in 2000 many census tracts with fewer than 1,000 persons

Figure F-1. Population Density of Urbanized Areas

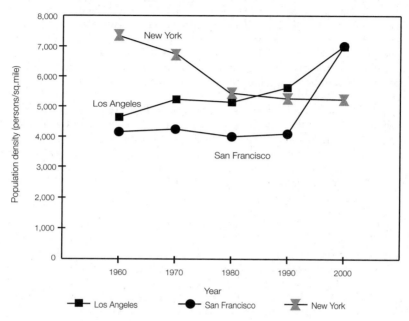

per square mile in jurisdictions with more than 1,000 persons per square mile were excluded.

Figure F-1 shows the trend in population density of the three urbanized areas from 1960 to 2000. The densities of Los Angeles and San Francisco increased because their land areas grew slower than their populations (the sharp increase in San Francisco from 1990 to 2000 was caused in part by the new definition of urbanized areas in 2000). New York's density fell by 30 percent from 1960 to 2000 because its land area grew by 77 percent while its population grew by only 26 percent. Because of their high *suburban* population density, Angelenos now occupy less land per person than do the residents of any other urbanized area in the U.S.

Many people find Los Angeles unique (both uniquely pleasing and uniquely unpleasant). So what sets Los Angeles apart if it isn't, as so many suspect, its low-density sprawl? Los Angeles may be about as dense as a city with off-street parking requirements can get, because if cities require abundant off-street parking everywhere, everyone can park free. If parking is free, most adults will own a car and use it for most trips. The cost of providing all the required parking will limit development density, and planners will also have to limit human density to control traffic congestion. In a car-oriented culture, overall population density higher than what we see in Los Angeles is difficult because the traffic congestion becomes intolerable. If people want to live at high density without being overrun by cars, high parking prices are inevitable.

So, after all this, how much of Los Angeles did cars consume in 2000? The Los Angeles Bureau of Street Services reports that it maintains 28,000 lane-miles of public streets in the city.[16] With a generous estimate that each lane is 12 feet wide, these streets cover 64 square miles. The city's total area is 469 square miles. Streets therefore occupy about 14 percent of the land in the city. Because the population was 3,695,000 persons in 2000, the 64 square miles of streets occupied about 483 square feet of land per person. No one knows how much land is devoted to parking.

APPENDIX F NOTES

1. Southworth and Ben-Joseph (1997, 4-5).

2. Hanson (1992, 66).

3. Renner (1988, 46).

4. Sale (1980, 253).

5. Mumford (1961, 510).

6. Taylor (1959, 357).

7. Meyer and Gómez-Ibáñez (1981, 180). Italics in the original. The land-use data came from Manvel (1968).

8. Southworth and Owens (1993).

9. Meyer, Kain, and Wohl (1965, 296).

10. Larsen (2000, 207).

11. Bruun and Vuchic (1995).

12. Schmider (1977). Bruun and Vuchic (1995) present a translation from French of Schmider's calculations. For the same trip, a bicycle traveling four kilometers at 12 kilometers an hour uses 6 square-meter-hours in travel and only 12 square-meter-hours when parked, so the area-hours used for parking the bicycle are only twice the area-hours used for riding it. Four kilometers is, of course, a short commute.

13. Nicholas, Pochet, and Poimboeuf (2003, 207). Their estimate of the space-hours used by parking includes only nonresidential parking; because cars are also parked many hours at home, parking actually uses much more than 62 percent of the total space-hours for personal travel.

14. An Urbanized Area "comprises one or more places ('central place') and the adjacent densely settled surrounding territory ('urban fringe') that together have a minimum of 50,000 persons. The urban fringe generally consists of contiguous territory having a density of at least 1,000 persons per square mile. The urban fringe also includes outlying territory of such density if it is connected to the core of the contiguous area by road and is within 1.5 road miles of that core, or within 5 road miles of the core but separated by water or other undevelopable territory. Other territory with a population density of fewer than 1,000 people per square mile is included in the urban fringe if it eliminates an enclave or closes an indentation in the boundary of the urbanized area. The population density is determined by (1) outside of a place, one or more contiguous census blocks with a population density of at least 1,000 persons per square mile or (2) inclusion of a place containing census blocks that have at least 50 percent of the population of the place and a density of at least 1,000 persons per square mile" (United States Census Bureau 2000c).

15. United States Census Bureau (1993).

16. The public roadway data from the Los Angeles Bureau of Street Services are available online at www.lacity.org/BOSS/StreetMaintenance/custod.htm.

G

Converting Traffic Congestion into Cash

The information needed to understand a problem depends on one's idea for solving it.

—-*MELVIN WEBBER*

A simple model can illustrate how freeway tolls will convert traffic congestion into cash. The model is roughly based on the traffic flows observed on the I-405 freeway in West Los Angeles (see Table G-1). Column 1 shows the density of cars per mile in a lane. As more cars enter the freeway and the density increases, the average speed (in column 2) declines because drivers become more cautious when cars must follow closer together. The traffic flow (in column 3) increases until it reaches a maximum of just more than 1,900 cars an hour, which occurs at a density of about 60 cars per mile and a speed of 32 miles an hour. If more cars enter the freeway and density increases further, the increasing congestion begins to reduce flow (in the "backward-bending" part of the speed-flow relationship termed "hypercongestion," as shown in the upper part of the figure beneath the table). For example, the flow can be 1,790 cars an hour with a density of 40 cars per mile and a speed of 45 miles an hour (at point C in the figure), but if more cars crowd onto the road and density increases to, say, 100 cars per mile, the speed falls to 17 miles an hour and the flow declines to 1,670 cars an hour (at point B). Hypercongestion thus reduces both speed *and* flow. The benefits of tolls are easiest to see when traffic would be hypercongested without tolls.

Table G-1. Density, Speed, Flow, Time, Cost, and the Demand for Freeway Travel

Density (cars/mile)	Speed (miles/hour)	Flow (cars/hour)	Travel time (minutes/mile)	Travel cost (cents/mile)	Travel demand (cents/mile) Low	Travel demand (cents/mile) High
(1)	(2)	(3)=(1)x(2)	(4)=60/(2)	(5)=10+15x(4)	(6)	(7)
10	73	730	0.8	22	31	76
20	62	A 1,240	1.0	25	25	70
30	53	1,580	1.1	27	20	65
40	45	C 1,790	1.3	30	18	63
50	38	1,900	1.6	34	16	61
60	32	1,930	1.9	38	16	61
70	27	1,910	2.2	43	16	61
80	23	1,850	2.6	49	17	62
90	20	1,770	3.0	56	18	63
100	17	B 1,670	3.6	64	19	64
110	14	1,560	4.2	73	21	66
120	12	1,440	5.0	85	22	67
130	10	1,330	5.9	98	23	68
140	9	1,210	6.9	114	25	70

Columns 6 and 7 show the prices that lead to the demand for the travel flow in Column 3.

Assumptions: Vehicle operating cost is $0.10 per mile and the driver's value of time is $0.15 per minute.

Travel Cost on Travel Demand

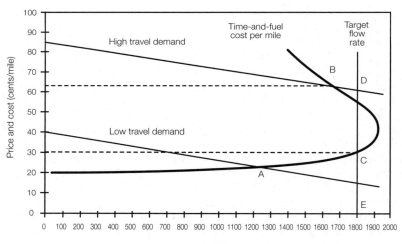

Price and cost (cents/mile)

Traffic flow (cars/hour/lane)

In our example, the uncongested flow of 1,790 cars an hour traveling at 45 miles an hour (point C) is better than the hypercongested flow of 1,670 cars an hour traveling at 17 miles an hour (point B) because more people get where they want to go, and they travel faster. With hypercongestion, fewer people get where they want to go, and they travel slower. Alas, hypercongestion with high density and low flow at low speed occurs frequently on Los Angeles freeways.[1]

The dysfunctional nature of hypercongestion can be seen by looking at the time (in column 4) it takes a car in the traffic flow to go one mile at different flow rates. In our example, with a flow of 1,790 cars an hour traveling at 45 miles an hour, it takes 1.3 minutes for each car to go one mile, while in the hypercongested flow of 1,670 cars an hour traveling at 17 miles an hour, it takes 3.6 minutes per mile. Hypercongestion slows everybody down and reduces total travel.

We can calculate a solo driver's cost of traveling a mile by assuming the vehicle's fuel cost per mile and the driver's value of time spent in travel. Column 5 shows the cost per mile of travel if we assume the vehicle's fuel cost is 10¢ a mile and the driver's value of time is 15¢ a minute ($9 an hour). At 45 miles an hour a driver's cost of travel is 30¢ a mile (10¢ + 1.3 x 15¢), while at 17 miles an hour it is 64¢ a mile (10¢ + 3.6 x 15¢). If only a few drivers want to travel on the freeway even when speeds are high, congestion is not a problem, or not much of one. Column 6 illustrates the assumed relationship between the cost of travel and the number of drivers who want to travel along the freeway when demand is low.[2] The low demand curve crosses the cost curve at point A in the figure at 1,240 cars an hour where the speed is 62 miles an hour and the cost of travel is 25¢ a mile. No need for tolls here.

Problems arise, however, if travel demand is high. Column 7 illustrates the travel demand during peak hours. The high-demand curve crosses the cost curve at point B, with a flow of 1,670 cars an hour at a speed of 17 miles an hour and a time-and-fuel travel cost of 64¢ a mile. Compare hypercongested point B with the alternative point C where the flow is 1,790 cars an hour, speed is 45 miles an hour, and the time-and-fuel cost is only 30¢ an hour. Point C is far better than point B, but if we are at point C and the demand is high, more drivers will crowd onto the road and push the speed down until the flow is hypercongested. Point B can be a stable equilibrium if 1,670 drivers are willing to travel on the road at the low speed of 17 miles an hour. Hypercongestion is a serious problem; without it, we could have both a higher flow *and* a lower time-and-fuel cost of travel.

How can we avoid hypercongestion at the time of peak travel demand? By charging a toll for driving during the peak hours. Suppose we aim to achieve a stable flow of about 1,800 cars an hour at about 45 miles an hour. Whenever flow nears 1,800 cars an hour anywhere on the freeway and the speed declines toward 45 miles an hour, introducing a toll can keep the traffic at the target flow rate without any further decline in speed. (This policy is similar to the pricing strategy on the I-15 Express Lanes in San Diego, as explained in Chapter 12.) In the figure, the vertical line ECD shows the target flow rate of 1,800 cars an hour; whenever the demand curve crosses the average cost curve to the left of point C, the toll is zero. But when demand rises and the flow approaches the target rate at point C, the toll kicks in and varies to keep the flow at a steady 1,800 cars an hour at a speed of 45 miles an hour.[3] When demand rises to the high level shown in the figure, the toll rises to 33¢ a mile (the price indicated by the line CD), the cost of fuel and time is 30¢ a mile (line CE), and the total cost to the traveler is 63¢ a mile (line DE).

A toll of 33¢ a mile may seem high, but the tolls on existing congestion-priced roads in California are even higher at the peak hours. On the I-15 Express Lanes in San Diego, for example, the peak-hour charge for an eight-mile trip on a weekday is $4, or 50¢ a mile. On the Route 91 Express Lanes in Orange County, the peak-hour charge for a 10-mile trip on Friday afternoon is $7, or 70¢ a mile. Many people are willing to pay the price for a quick trip, and keeping congestion in check makes the freeway system much more productive—more people can get where they are going in a shorter time.

In the high-demand case, we can choose between two traffic situations—without or with tolls. Table G-2 shows how the tolls affect solo drivers. *Without* the toll, a solo driver's total cost of time and fuel is 64¢ a mile. *With* the toll, the driver's total cost of time, fuel, and the toll is 63¢ a mile, so the driver saves 1¢ a mile; the flow is also 8 percent higher. The toll thus slightly reduces the driver's cost of travel and slightly increases the flow. But there is a far bigger benefit: the toll revenue. The toll is 33¢ a mile, so the public revenue is 33 times the savings to drivers. Instead of spending time stuck in traffic, drivers spend money for a faster trip, and the revenue is available to pay for public services. With a toll of 33¢ a mile and a flow of 1,800 cars an hour, one lane-mile of the freeway will generate $594 an hour in toll revenue (1,800 cars x 33¢ per mile). With 40 cars per mile, the toll is about $15 an hour per car ($594 ÷ 40). A 45-mile trip at the peak hour takes one hour at 45 miles an hour, and the toll would be $15 for the trip (45 miles x 33¢ per mile). In comparison, without the toll, the trip takes 2 hours and 40 minutes at 17 miles an hour in hypercongested traffic (45 miles ÷ 17 miles an hour). A solo driver thus pays $15 to reduce travel time by 100 minutes, or 15¢ per minute saved ($9 an hour), which is the assumed value of time savings for a solo driver.

Table G-2. Solo Driving *With* and *Without* Congestion Tolls

SOLO DRIVER

	Speed (miles/hour)	Flow (cars/hour)	Fuel cost ($/mile)	Time cost ($/mile)	Toll ($/mile)	Total cost ($/mile)
	(1)	(2)	(3)	(4)	(5)	(6)=(3)+(4)+(5)
Without tolls	17	1,670	0.10	0.54	0.00	0.64
With tolls	45	1,787	0.10	0.20	0.33	0.63
Change	+18	+117	0	-0.34	+0.33	-0.01

We can also examine how the tolls affect carpoolers. Table G-3 shows the travel cost per person in a three-person carpool. Note how little carpooling saves *without* tolls. In hypercongested traffic with a speed of 17 miles an hour, each person in a three-person carpool suffers a time cost of 54¢ a mile, and the fuel cost of 10¢ a mile is split three ways, so each person's individual cost of time and fuel is 57¢ a mile, compared with the solo driver's cost of 64¢ a mile. Carpooling thus reduces the cost of automobile travel on the untolled road by only 7¢ a mile, or by 11 percent. Now look at the case *with* tolls. At 45 miles an hour, each person in a three-person carpool incurs a time cost of 20¢ a mile, while the monetary costs of 43¢ a mile for fuel and tolls are split three ways, so each person's total cost of travel is only 34¢ a mile. Compared with the carpooler's cost of 57¢ a mile on the untolled road, carpooling thus reduces the cost of automobile travel on the tolled road by 23¢ a mile, or by 46 percent. The tolls thus strongly encourage travelers to carpool and ride public transit, so the flow of *people* along the freeway will increase even more than the flow of *cars*.

Consider how the tolls would reduce the cost of an average 30-mile round-trip commute to work in Southern California. If the tolls reduce the time-and-money cost of travel in a three-person carpool by 23¢ a mile, each person in the carpool saves $6.90 a day (23¢ x 30 miles) or $138 a

Table G-3. Carpooling *With* and *Without* Congestion Tolls

PER PERSON IN A THREE-PERSON CARPOOL

	Speed (miles/hour)	Flow (cars/hour)	Fuel cost ($/mile)	Time cost ($/mile)	Toll ($/mile)	Total cost ($/mile)
	(1)	(2)	(3)	(4)	(5)	(6)=(3)+(4)+(5)
Without tolls	17	1,670	0.03	0.54	0.00	0.57
With tolls	45	1,787	0.03	0.20	0.11	0.34
Change	+18	+117	0	-0.34	+0.11	-0.23

month after the tolls are introduced. Because each person in the carpool saves 34¢ a mile in time cost and pays only 11¢ a mile for the 33¢-a-mile toll split three ways, congestion tolls are a great bargain for carpoolers.

Traffic congestion is far more complicated than a simple model can show, but the principles of congestion pricing do not depend on the specifics of each case. The target flow rate during peak hours will depend on the circumstances, but it should always be less than the rate at which hypercongestion sets in. The tolls literally convert wasted time into real money.

USE OF THE TOLL REVENUE

Despite their obvious theoretical advantages, congestions tolls have been hard to sell to voters and therefore to politicians because drivers oppose paying for roads that are now free. As a way to generate political support for tolls on congested freeways, Chapter 19 proposed returning the revenues to the cities through which the freeways pass. Consider how this idea might work in Southern California, which has the worst traffic congestion in the U.S.[4] Los Angeles County's 882-mile freeway system passes through 66 of the county's 88 cities. Suppose California charges congestion tolls on these freeways and distributes the resulting revenue to these 66 cities on a per-capita basis to compensate them for the freeways' harmful effects. In political reality, the toll-revenue distribution formula would be much more complicated than this simple proposal, but the important point is to create a formula that will energize elected officials to demand the use of tolls to reduce traffic congestion and generate municipal income.[5] Distributing the toll revenues to cities with freeways can illustrate the proposal to create politically effective claimants for the toll revenue.

Sharing the toll revenue among cities with freeways can be justified on two grounds. First, freeways remove large swaths of land from cities' property tax rolls, and motorists pay no sales taxes as they drive through the city. The toll revenue can therefore be considered payments in lieu of the property and sales taxes the cities would otherwise receive. Second, drivers pollute the air as they pass through cities, the roar of traffic violates the surrounding neighborhoods, and the freeways themselves are often ugly. The toll revenue can therefore be justified as compensation to those who must live with this air, noise, and visual pollution. One obvious use of the revenue is to build soundwalls to protect the residents of the cities penetrated by the intrusive freeways. In thinking about congestion tolls, every mayor, council member, and interest group will know the toll revenue from the freeways within their borders will stay in their city, while most of the drivers who pay the tolls will only be passing through.

By reducing traffic congestion, the tolls will also improve air quality in these cities. Residents will therefore benefit from the tolls because their environment will improve and they will get better public services. This toll-sharing policy can thus remove a political obstacle to congestion pricing: the beneficiaries will become easier to organize.

The per capita income is only $20,100 a year in the 66 cities *with* freeways, but is $35,100 a year in the 22 cities *without* freeways, so congestion tolls will transfer money to poorer cities from richer ones (see Table G-4).

Table G-4. Per Capita Incomes of Cities in Los Angeles County ($ per person per year)

	66 Cities *with* Freeways				
City	Income/Capita	City	Income/Capita	City	Income/Capita
Agoura Hills	$39,700	El Segundo	$34,000	Norwalk	$14,000
Alhambra	$17,500	Gardena	$17,300	Palmdale	$16,400
Arcadia	$28,400	Glendale	$22,200	Paramount	$11,500
Artesia	$15,800	Glendora	$26,000	Pasadena	$28,200
Azusa	$13,400	Hawaiian Gardens	$10,700	Pico Rivera	$13,000
Baldwin Park	$11,600	Hawthorne	$15,000	Pomona	$13,300
Bell	$9,900	Industry	$9,900	Redondo Beach	$38,300
Bell Gardens	$8,400	Inglewood	$14,800	Rosemead	$12,100
Bellflower	$16,000	Irwindale	$13,100	San Dimas	$28,300
Burbank	$25,700	La Cañada Flintridge	$52,800	San Fernando	$11,500
Calabasas	$48,200	La Mirada	$22,400	San Gabriel	$16,800
Carson	$17,100	La Verne	$26,700	Santa Clarita	$26,800
Cerritos	$25,200	Lakewood	$22,100	Santa Fe Springs	$14,500
Claremont	$28,800	Lancaster	$16,900	Santa Monica	$42,900
Commerce	$11,100	Lawndale	$13,700	Signal Hill	$24,400
Compton	$10,400	Long Beach	$19,100	South El Monte	$10,100
Covina	$20,200	Los Angeles	$20,700	South Gate	$10,600
Culver City	$29,000	Lynwood	$9,500	South Pasadena	$32,600
Diamond Bar	$25,500	Maywood	$8,900	Torrance	$28,100
Downey	$18,200	Monrovia	$21,700	Vernon	$17,800
Duarte	$19,600	Montebello	$15,100	West Covina	$19,300
El Monte	$10,300	Monterey Park	$17,700	Westlake Village	$49,600
				Average	**$20,100**

	22 Cities *without* Freeways				
City	Income/Capita	City	Income/Capita	City	Income/Capita
Avalon	$21,000	La Puente	$11,300	Rolling Hills Estates	$51,800
Beverly Hills	$65,500	Lomita	$22,100	San Marino	$59,200
Bradbury	$57,700	Malibu	$74,300	Sierra Madre	$41,100
Cudahy	$8,700	Manhattan Beach	$61,100	Temple City	$20,300
Hermosa Beach	$54,200	Palos Verdes Estates	$69,000	Walnut	$25,200
Hidden Hills	$94,100	Rancho Palos Verdes	$46,300	West Hollywood	$38,300
Huntington Park	$9,300	Rolling Hills	$111,000	Whittier	$21,400
La Habra Heights	$47,300			**Average**	**$35,100**

Source: U.S. Census 2000
The two groups' average incomes are weighted by the cities' populations.

A city doesn't need to have a freeway running through it to suffer from external costs, however. The four poorest cities without freeways (Cudahy, Huntington Park, La Puente, and Temple City) could be included among the recipient cities because freeways pass close by all four, and their per-capita incomes are below the average of other recipient cities. If so, the per capita income would be $20,000 a year in the 70 "recipient" cities, and $47,000 a year in the remaining 18 "donor" cities.[6] High-income cities without freeways won't receive any toll revenue, but think of it this way: would they prefer to have freeways so they could share the revenue? Probably not. The tolls can make a big contribution to public finance in low-income cities bearing an unfair share of the freeways' costs.

Both federal and state laws will have to be changed to permit congestion tolls, and distribution of the revenue will be more complicated than simply giving it to cities with freeways.[7] Motorists will pay the tolls, after all, and using some of the revenue to improve the freeways may reduce the motorists' opposition to the tolls without significantly reducing the cities' support. The tolls may have to be high to clear congestion at specific bottlenecks, for example, and some of the revenue can be used to increase capacity at these locations.[8] But because they will reduce traffic congestion, the tolls might also substitute for other transportation investments that make sense only if the roads remain free. For example, between 2005 and 2030 the Southern California Association of Governments (SCAG) proposes spending $47 billion for transportation improvements (including $13 billion for road improvements and $29 billion for a high-speed rail system). In its bottom-line summary of the results, SCAG estimates that in 2030 the region's average vehicle occupancy rate will fall from 1.4374 persons per car without the investments to 1.4364 persons per car with them.[9] In comparison, congestion tolls can yield billions of dollars a year in revenue, immediately increase travel speeds, and significantly increase the average vehicle occupancy rate.

Because congestion tolls can eliminate the need for some astronomically expensive rail and highway projects, they can free up gasoline taxes to maintain the existing transportation system. All things considered, congestion tolls can greatly improve transportation finance even if most of the revenue is distributed to cities. The right use of the revenue is a sine qua non for congestion tolls, and it is more a matter of politics than economics.

ESTIMATES OF THE TOLL REVENUE

Using a transportation model calibrated for Southern California, Elizabeth Deakin and Greig Harvey estimated the revenue that would result from congestion tolls in the Los Angeles region: $3.2 billion in 1991, rising to $7.3 billion in 2010.[10] Kenneth Small estimated that congestion tolls in Los Angeles would have produced $3 billion, net of collection costs, in 1991.[11] These estimates are conservative compared to the Texas Transportation Institute's estimate that the total costs of traffic congestion in Los Angeles were $8.4 billion in 1991 and $12.8 billion in 2001.[12]

Congestion tolls in Los Angeles County can generate several billion dollars a year and substantially improve local public finances. Because 9.2 million people live in the 70 toll-recipient cities and the unincorporated area, each $1 billion would produce about $110 per capita in municipal revenue. If the congestion tolls yield $5 billion a year net of collection costs, for example, they will generate about $550 per capita for the recipient cities. Because the 70 toll-recipient cities' general revenues averaged $577 per capita in 2001, the tolls will almost double these cities' general revenues, and the poorest cities will gain the most in proportion to their income.[13] The toll revenue for Maywood, for example, will amount to 6 percent of the city's per-capita income ($550 ÷ $8,926), while cities with per-capita income greater than $53,000 a year will receive nothing because they have no freeways. This pattern of revenue distribution can help redress the wide disparities among rich and poor cities in parks, police protection, and other public services.

Nonresidents, such as tourists and trucks driving through the region, will also pay tolls, so the total revenues will exceed the residents' payments.[14] And because these nonresidents will save valuable time, even they will be better off if their time savings are worth more than their toll payments. The time saved will be especially valuable for goods movement on trucks to the ports of Los Angeles and Long Beach, which have the two largest volumes of container cargo in the U.S. Trucks from throughout the country converge on the overburdened freeways leading to these ports, making Southern California the nation's colon for foreign trade. In response to congestion tolls, port-bound trucks will either pay for peak-hour driving or shift to off-peak hours, and the region's residents will benefit in either case.

Will tolls on the freeways divert some drivers onto the parallel surface streets? Speed on the freeways will increase in response to the congestion tolls—that is the reason for the tolls—and the traffic flow can increase rather than decrease. If the tolls increase speed and traffic flow on the freeways, how can they also increase traffic on the parallel surface streets? Instead, shorter travel times on the faster freeways may draw traffic off the surface streets. But if traffic tolled off the freeways does crowd the parallel surface streets, congestion tolls will also be appropriate on these streets to keep them flowing freely. Residents can be exempt from paying tolls on surface streets in their own city but would pay for driving on congested streets in other cities. Just as parking spaces can provide public revenue for neighborhoods, congested surface streets can create public revenue for cities, and in both cases the revenue will be paid by nonresidents. Any spillover traffic from the tolled freeways can thus provide even more revenue for low-income cities.

INCOME DISTRIBUTION AND POLITICAL SUPPORT

Deakin and Harvey estimated that higher-income motorists will pay most of the tolls because the highest-income quintile (the top 20 percent of the income distribution) own 3.1 times more cars than the lowest-income quintile and drive 3.6 times more vehicle miles per day.[15] Because higher-income motorists also drive more during the peak hours, the highest-income quintile will pay five times more in tolls than the lowest-income quintile.[16] Thus the tolls will transfer money from high-income motorists to low-income cities. But high-income motorists will also benefit. Travel speeds will increase after tolling begins, and drivers who place a high value on saving time are better off as a result of the tolls and the time savings taken together. After all, when we are driving to work, hurrying to catch a plane, or rushing to the hospital for an emergency, do we want the freeways congested by low-value, discretionary trips easily made at off-peak hours? Most people would surely be willing to forego a few of their least essential peak-hour, single-occupant vehicle trips if they could, in exchange, drive much faster for all their other peak-hour trips, and congestion tolls offer exactly that bargain. In addition, the tolls will convert congested traffic into cash for low-income cities and turn wasted time into public services.

Distributing the toll revenue on a per-capita basis will moderate the region's income inequality. Figure G-1 shows the distribution of personal income and toll revenue in Los Angeles County. The horizontal axis measures the cities' cumulated share of the county's population, arrayed according to increasing per-capita incomes. The vertical axis measures the cities' cumulated share of the county's total income and toll revenues. The upper and lower curves show toll revenue and income as a function of population.[17] The 20 percent of the population who live in the 33 poorest cities receive 12 percent of the county's income but 21 percent of the toll revenue. In contrast, the 20 percent of the population who live in the 43 richest cities receive 30 percent of the county's income but only 17 percent of the toll revenue. The 1 percent of the population who live in the eight richest cities receive 4 percent of the county's income and no toll revenue.

These distributional results refute any objections to congestion tolls on the grounds they will harm the poor. A few poor people who live in the

Figure G-1. Cities' Shares of Population, Income, and Toll Revenue

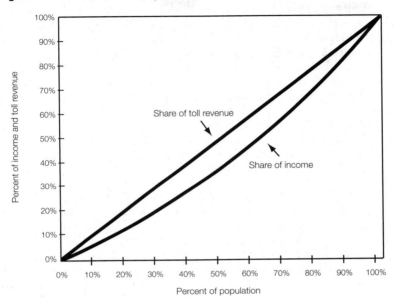

richest cities and drive during congested hours may lose a little, but the great majority will save time, breathe cleaner air, and gain better public services at a lower cost. When we consider the whole population, the congestions tolls will clearly be progressive, not regressive, because the lowest-income people don't own cars and won't pay tolls but will receive better public services. Even when we consider only drivers and ignore the better public services in low-income cities, the results can still be progressive because peak-hour driving is lowest among the poorest drivers. Almost everyone can win from congestion tolls.

University of Southern California transportation economist Genevieve Giuliano says the conventional complaint about congestion tolls—they are regressive and will harm the poor—may actually be motivated by a baser and more short-sighted reason: drivers simply oppose paying to use roads they believe should be free.[18] Returning the toll revenue to cities with freeways can turn this typical debating ploy around. Politicians can support congestion tolling on the high-minded grounds that it will reduce traffic, improve the environment, and help the poor even if another reason is more important—their cities need the money, and they deserve it!

Returning the revenue to cities with freeways will create far greater political support than would using it to reduce general taxes because any tax cut would be small and hard to perceive. Many people would also doubt that taxes would be reduced at all. And if taxes are not reduced, any increase in general public spending—regardless of its worth—would also be hard to perceive, while drivers will pay the tolls every day. In either case, the benefits of reduced taxes or increased general spending would be so indirect, distant, delayed, and diffuse that most people may disregard them entirely. In contrast, returning the toll revenue to cities with freeways will produce direct, proximate, immediate, and concentrated benefits that can embolden politicians from cities with freeways to insist on congestion charges. No one will have to organize the beneficiaries—cities—because they are already organized.

Using some of the revenue to finance transportation, if done in the right way, might further increase the political appeal of congestion tolls. For example, the Los Angeles Metropolitan Transportation Authority (MTA) funds public transportation and a wide array of transportation projects including bikeways, pedestrian facilities, and local road and highway improvements throughout the county. Most of its local tax support comes from an added 1¢ sales tax rate throughout the county, which generated $1.1 billion in 2003.[19] Thus, if $1.1 billion of congestion toll revenue were allocated to the MTA, the sales tax rate in the county could be reduced by 1¢, from the current 8.25 percent to 7.25 percent.[20] The congestion tolls, by themselves, will greatly improve transportation, and if the toll revenue were $5 billion a year, $3.9 billion a year would still be available to cities.

The 70 toll-recipient cities plus the county (representing the unincorporated territory) could become a lobby for the congestion tolls, and they already have a strong influence in the legislative process. To show the importance of this potential coalition, consider an alternative use of the toll revenue—a revenue-neutral reduction in the gasoline tax. Reducing the gasoline tax may seem reasonable because it would compensate motorists who are paying the tolls and would not take more money for the government. But those who would receive the toll revenue—motorists—are not organized as a political entity. Millions of motorists would benefit from the lower gas tax but not by enough to make a strong political demand for the congestion tolls. At best, the reduction in gasoline taxes would mollify motorists but would not create a coalition to support the tolls.[21] If the revenue is distributed to cities with freeways, however, many elected officials may buy into the congestion tolls because they have been bought off by the resulting revenue.

A purely economic analysis of congestion tolls misses the key political point. Unless the revenue provides benefits to interest groups who will support road pricing, congestion tolls will remain difficult in practice no matter how efficient and fair in theory. If the revenue goes to cities with freeways, politicians will not have to say they are going to charge everyone for driving in congested traffic and then figure out how to spend the money. Instead, they can propose a fair way to deal with three problems at once—traffic congestion, the environmental costs of freeways, and the fiscal distress of low-income cities. Drivers will pay the tolls only when they get a direct individual benefit—faster travel—and cities with freeways will get better public services—such as parks, police protection, sidewalk repairs, and soundwalls. Many people will have good reason to champion road pricing.

APPENDIX G NOTES

1. In its *2004 Regional Transportation Plan*, the Southern California Association of Governments (2004, Appendix C, Exhibit C.5) shows that large sections of the freeway system have average speeds ranging from 15 to 24 miles per hour during the PM peak (3 p.m. to 7 p.m.). Although hypercongestion is a complex phenomenon difficult to model, many people are familiar with travel on freeways at low speed in closely spaced traffic. Small and Chu (2003) and Verhoef (2003) explore the complex nature of hypercongestion.

2. Columns 6 and 7 show the marginal willingness to pay for a mile of travel on the freeway as a function of the number of cars in the flow (in column 3) during periods of low and high demand. These values are plotted as the two demand curves.

3. Small and Chu (2003, 329) say the speed-flow relationship is often quite flat until capacity is reached. The optimal flow is thus frequently near to capacity, suggesting that the marginal cost curve becomes almost vertical near capacity. If so, the line CDE can be considered the marginal cost curve after point C is reached. Lindsey and Verhoef (2000) explain that the maximum feasible flow on any road segment depends on factors such as the number and width of traffic lanes, grade, road curvature, speed limit, weather, vehicle types, and the behavior of individual drivers.

4. According to the Texas Transportation Institute's *2003 Annual Urban Mobility Study*, Los Angeles has the worst traffic congestion in the United States. In 2001, 88 percent of peak-hour VMT was in congested traffic. The TTI estimated 667 million person-hours and 1 billion gallons of gasoline were wasted in congested traffic, and these figures more than tripled since the first estimates in 1982. The estimated cost of congestion was $1,005 per person in 2001.

5. Like a city, Los Angeles County would receive toll revenue in proportion to the length of freeways in the unincorporated area.

6. Removing the four poorest cities from the "without freeways" group sharply increases the weighted-average income per capita of the 18 remaining cities because the four poorest cities have large populations while most of the richer cities have small populations. Avalon, which would be the poorest remaining city without a freeway, is on Catalina Island 26 miles off the coast, and it would be unaffected by the congestion tolls.

7. In practice, the formula for distributing the toll revenue might resemble the federal formulas for distributing gasoline tax revenues to states.

8. Just as high prices for curb parking will reveal where investment in off-street parking is justified, high congestion tolls will reveal where investments in additional road capacity are and are not justified. The tolls thus have another benefit: they will provide an excellent guide for investment decisions. If tolls reveal where investment is most productive, the existing gasoline tax revenue may be more than enough to finance it. In this case, all the congestion toll revenue can be distributed to cities.

9. Southern California Association of Governments 2004, Appendix C, p. C-29. Although one would expect the average vehicle occupancy rate to increase, not fall, as a result of these investments, the decline of 0.001 persons per car predicted 25 years in the future obviously has no statistical significance.

10. Deakin and Harvey (1996, Tables 7-14 and 7-18).

11. Small (1992, 371).

12. See the Texas Transportation Institute's *2003 Annual Urban Mobility Study*, which is available online at http://mobility.tamu.edu/ums/mobility_data/tables/los_angeles.pdf.

13. The cities' general revenues are taken from the California State Controller's Office, *Cities Annual Report, Fiscal Year 2000-2001*. General revenues are defined as revenues that cannot be associated with any particular expenditure; examples include property taxes, sales taxes, and business license fees. General revenues do not include fees and charges for direct services, such as the revenue from municipally owned electric utilities. The population of Los Angeles County is 9.5 million, of whom 990,000 live in unincorporated areas.

14. In calculating the net revenue distributed to cities, however, the toll collection costs must also be considered. If these collection costs are less than the tolls paid by nonresidents, the cities will earn more revenue than the regions' residents pay.

15. Deakin and Harvey (1996, Tables 8-1 and 8-3). At the national level, in 2002 the highest-income quintile of households owned 2.9 times more cars than the lowest-income quintile (U. S. Bureau of Labor Statistics, 2004, Table 1).

16. Deakin and Harvey (1996, 8-6). And because men are more likely then women to drive in congested conditions, men will also pay more in tolls (Deakin and Harvey 1996, 8-7).

17. The Lorenz curve for distribution of income among *individuals* would lie below the curve for the distribution of income among *cities* because the average income in the 88 cities mask the inequality of individual incomes within each city. A curve showing the distribution of toll payments among individuals would also lie below the curve for the distribution of the revenue because both VMT and the propensity to drive in congested traffic increase with income.

18. Giuliano (1992).

19. See the Los Angeles County Metropolitan Authority's financial statements on their web site at www.metro.net/about_us/finance/propositions.htm.

20. Although the congestion tolls would provide $1.1 billion a year to the MTA, note that using the toll revenue to replace the sales tax would provide a benefit to everyone in the County, not just to motorists. What might look like throwing a bone to motorists would, in reality, be a tax cut for everyone, most of whom happen to be motorists.

21. In their study of the gasoline tax in Britain and the United States, Ian Parry and Kenneth Small (2002) estimated the optimal tax rate is about $1 per gallon, or 2.5 times the current U.S. tax rate. Using the congestion toll revenue to reduce the gasoline tax would thus do nothing to remedy the undertaxation of gasoline. Because collection costs will undoubtedly be higher for congestion tolls than for gasoline taxes, the reduction in gasoline taxes would be less than the toll payments.

H

The Vehicles of Nations

If you can look into the seeds of time,
and say which grain will grow,
and which will not,
speak then to me.

—*WILLIAM SHAKESPEARE*

Table H-1 shows the human and vehicle populations of the U.S. and the world during the twentieth century. The U.S. data are shown for all years, and the world data are shown for all years in which they are available (every year since 1950, as well as a few previous years). The table allows comparisons between the U.S. and the rest of the world in their growth of vehicle ownership.

In 2000, the U.S. owned 771 vehicles per 1,000 persons, while the rest of the world owned only 89 per 1,000 persons—the same as the U.S. rate in 1920. The world outside the U.S. took 70 years (from 1930 to 2000) to increase its vehicle-ownership rate from 5 to 89 vehicles per 1,000 persons, while the U.S. ownership rate increased by that much between 1910 and 1920. The U.S. owned more than half the world's vehicles until 1965, but the rest of the world is catching up; in 2000, the U.S. owned only 30 percent.

During the 1990s, the U.S. added 29 million vehicles, while the rest of the world added 123 million; the rest of the world thus added 4.3 vehicles for every additional vehicle in the U.S. Although the vehicle population was growing faster in the rest of the world than in the U.S. in the 1990s, the U.S. added 880 vehicles for each 1,000 additional persons (29 million more vehicles for 33 million more people), while the rest of the world added

Table H-1. Vehicle Ownership Rates in the U.S. and the World, 1900–2000

	Motor vehicles (millions)			Population (millions)			Vehicles per 1,000 persons			U.S. as % of world		Equivalent U.S. year of vehicles/1,000 in rest of world
Year	United States	Rest of world	World	United States	Rest of world	World	United States	Rest of world	World	Vehicles	Population	
(1)	(2)	(3)	(4)	(5)	(6)	(7)	(8)	(9)	(10)	(11)	(12)	(13)
1900	0.01			76	1,574	1,650	0.1				4.6%	
1901	0.01			78			0.2					
1902	0.02			79			0.3					
1903	0.03			81			0.4					
1904	0.06			82			0.7					
1905	0.08			84			0.9					
1906	0.11			85			1					
1907	0.14			87			2					
1908	0.20			89			2					
1909	0.31			90			3					
1910	0.47			92	1,658	1,750	5				5.3%	
1911	0.64			94			7					
1912	0.94			95			10					
1913	1.26			97			13					
1914	1.76			99			18					
1915	2.49			101			25					
1916	3.62			102			35					
1917	5.12			103			50					
1918	6.16			103			60					
1919	7.58			105			72					
1920	9			106	1,754	1,860	87				5.7%	
1921	10			109			97					
1922	12			110			112					
1923	15			112			135					
1924	18			114			154					
1925	20			116			173					
1926	22			117			189					
1927	23			119			196					
1928	25			121			205					
1929	27			122			220					
1930	27	9	36	123	1,947	2,070	217	5	17	74%	5.9%	1910
1931	26			124			210					
1932	24			125			195					
1933	24			126			192					
1934	25			126			200					
1935	27	11	38	127	2,173	2,300	209	5	16	71%	5.5%	1910
1936	29			128			223					
1937	30	13	43	129			233			69%		
1938	30	14	44	130			230			68%		
1939	31	15	46	131			237			68%		
1940	32	14	46	132			246			70%		
1941	35			133			262					
1942	33			135			245					
1943	31			137			226					
1944	30			138			220					
1945	31			140			222					
1946	34	11	46	141			243			75%		
1947	38	15	53	144			263			71%		
1948	41	17	58	147			280			71%		
1949	45	19	64	149			300			70%		
1950	49	21	70	152	2,403	2,555	323	9	28	70%	6.0%	1911
1951	52	22	74	155	2,438	2,593	335	9	29	70%	6.0%	1911
1952	53	25	78	158	2,477	2,635	338	10	30	68%	6.0%	1912
1953	56	27	83	160	2,520	2,680	351	11	31	68%	6.0%	1912
1954	59	30	88	163	2,565	2,728	359	12	32	66%	6.0%	1912
1955	63	33	96	166	2,614	2,780	378	13	34	65%	6.0%	1913
1956	65	37	103	169	2,664	2,833	386	14	36	64%	6.0%	1913

Year	Motor vehicles (millions) United States	Motor vehicles (millions) Rest of world	Motor vehicles (millions) World	Population (millions) United States	Population (millions) Rest of world	Population (millions) World	Vehicles per 1,000 persons United States	Vehicles per 1,000 persons Rest of world	Vehicles per 1,000 persons World	U.S. as % of world Vehicles	U.S. as % of world Population	Equivalent U.S. year of vehicles/1,000 in rest of world
(1)	(2)	(3)	(4)	(5)	(6)	(7)	(8)	(9)	(10)	(11)	(12)	(13)
1957	67	41	108	172	2,716	2,888	390	15	37	62%	6.0%	1913
1958	68	44	112	175	2,770	2,945	391	16	38	61%	5.9%	1913
1959	71	48	120	178	2,819	2,997	401	17	40	60%	5.9%	1913
1960	74	53	127	181	2,859	3,039	409	19	42	58%	5.9%	1914
1961	76	59	135	184	2,896	3,080	414	20	44	56%	6.0%	1914
1962	79	67	146	187	2,950	3,136	424	23	47	54%	5.9%	1914
1963	83	72	155	189	3,016	3,206	437	24	48	53%	5.9%	1914
1964	86	80	166	192	3,085	3,277	450	26	51	52%	5.9%	1915
1965	90	88	178	194	3,152	3,346	465	28	53	51%	5.8%	1915
1966	94	96	190	197	3,220	3,416	478	30	56	49%	5.8%	1915
1967	97	106	203	199	3,287	3,486	488	32	58	48%	5.7%	1915
1968	101	116	216	201	3,357	3,558	503	34	61	47%	5.6%	1915
1969	105	127	232	203	3,430	3,632	519	37	64	45%	5.6%	1916
1970	108	138	246	205	3,503	3,708	529	39	66	44%	5.5%	1916
1971	113	149	262	208	3,578	3,785	544	42	69	43%	5.5%	1916
1972	119	161	280	210	3,652	3,862	566	44	72	43%	5.4%	1916
1973	126	173	298	212	3,727	3,939	593	46	76	42%	5.4%	1916
1974	130	184	314	214	3,801	4,015	608	49	78	41%	5.3%	1916
1975	133	195	328	216	3,872	4,088	616	50	80	41%	5.3%	1917
1976	139	203	342	218	3,942	4,160	635	52	82	41%	5.2%	1917
1977	142	219	361	220	4,013	4,233	645	55	85	39%	5.2%	1917
1978	148	231	380	223	4,083	4,305	667	57	88	39%	5.2%	1917
1979	152	242	394	225	4,156	4,381	675	58	90	39%	5.1%	1917
1980	156	255	411	227	4,229	4,457	686	60	92	38%	5.1%	1918
1981	158	269	427	229	4,303	4,533	690	62	94	37%	5.1%	1918
1982	160	279	439	232	4,382	4,613	689	64	95	36%	5.0%	1918
1983	164	292	456	234	4,460	4,694	700	66	97	36%	5.0%	1918
1984	166	307	473	236	4,538	4,774	705	68	99	35%	4.9%	1918
1985	172	316	488	238	4,617	4,855	722	68	100	35%	4.9%	1918
1986	176	324	500	240	4,697	4,938	732	69	101	35%	4.9%	1918
1987	179	336	515	242	4,781	5,024	738	70	103	35%	4.8%	1918
1988	184	355	540	244	4,866	5,110	754	73	106	34%	4.8%	1919
1989	187	370	557	247	4,950	5,196	759	75	107	34%	4.7%	1919
1990	189	394	583	250	5,034	5,284	756	78	110	32%	4.7%	1919
1991	188	407	595	253	5,114	5,367	744	80	111	32%	4.7%	1919
1992	190	423	614	257	5,193	5,450	742	81	113	31%	4.7%	1919
1993	194	423	617	260	5,271	5,531	747	80	112	31%	4.7%	1919
1994	198	431	629	263	5,348	5,611	753	81	112	31%	4.7%	1919
1995	202	445	647	266	5,425	5,691	757	82	114	31%	4.7%	1919
1996	206	465	671	269	5,499	5,769	766	85	116	31%	4.7%	1919
1997	208	475	683	273	5,572	5,845	762	85	117	30%	4.7%	1919
1998	212	484	696	276	5,648	5,924	767	86	117	30%	4.7%	1919
1999	216	497	713	279	5,723	6,002	775	87	119	30%	4.6%	1919
2000	218	517	735	282	5,797	6,079	771	89	121	30%	4.6%	1920

Sources:
Column (2): United States Department of Transportation (2000, Table MV-1) and earlier editions.
Column (3) = Column (4) - Column (2).
Column (4): American Automobile Manufacturers Association (1998); *Ward's Motor Vehicle Facts and Figures* (2002).
Column (5): United States Census Bureau (2000a).
Column (6) = Column (7) - Column (5).
Column (7): United States Census Bureau (2000b).
Column (8) = 1,000 x Column (2) / Column (5).
Column (9) = 1,000 x Column (3) / Column (6).
Column (10) = 1,000 x Column (4) / Column (7).
Column (11) = Column (2) / Column (4).
Column (12) = Column (5) / Column (7).
Column (13) is Column (9) compared with Column (8).

only 160 vehicles for each 1,000 additional persons (123 million more vehicles for 763 million more people). Population growth was therefore accompanied by five times more additional vehicles in the U.S. than in the rest of the world (880 ÷ 160).

Figure H-1 (derived from Table H-1) shows the growth of the human and vehicle populations in the U.S. since 1900. The number of humans without vehicles has slowly decreased in the U.S. since 1945, but most children still don't own cars, so humans still outnumber vehicles. Figure H-2 (also derived from Table H-1) shows the growth of the human and vehicle populations outside the U.S. since 1945. Because the vehicle stock outside the U.S. started from a very low base, the number of humans without vehicles has increased despite the higher growth rate of the vehicle stock. If the rest of the world ever does achieve the U.S. vehicle ownership rate, however, parking will be a monumental problem.

Table H-2 shows the vehicle-ownership rates in 150 countries in 2000, arranged from the lowest (Bangladesh) to the highest (the U.S.). Column 5 shows the year in which the U.S. had the same ownership rate each of the other countries had in 2000 (from column 8 in Table H-1). For example, India owned 7 vehicles per 1,000 persons in 2000, the same as the U.S. did in 1911.[1]

The rest of the world's vehicle population grew three times faster than its human population during the second half of the twentieth century (see Table H-3). Between 1950 and 2000 the vehicle population grew by 7.2 percent a year (from 21 million to 513 million vehicles) while the human population grew by 1.9 percent a year (from 2,403 to 5,797 million persons).

Twentieth-century trends in vehicle ownership will not continue through the twenty-first century, of course, and the vehicles themselves may change dramatically. To cite one example, pollution-free fuel cells may power most cars in the future. If so, parked cars may become a source of electric power. The fuel cells in cars parked at home may generate electricity that households will use or sell to the grid. Timothy Lipman speculates:

> If we suppose that half the vehicles in California's South Coast Air Basin were fuel-cell powered (say by 2020 or so), with each vehicle able to supply 50 kW of power to the grid half the time, the total generating capacity of these vehicles would be nearly double the present level of installed generating capacity in the entire state…. This arrangement would require some additional equipment where the electricity produced by the vehicle interfaces with the electrical grid. However, if "smart meters" could monitor the spot price of electricity and activate the system when the price is right, electricity generated by the fuel cell could be sold to the grid at a profit. Imagine getting a check from the utility company instead of a bill! Particularly with the early fuel-cell vehicles, which will be expensive, this arrangement could help to offset some of the

Figure H-1. People and Vehicles in the U.S.

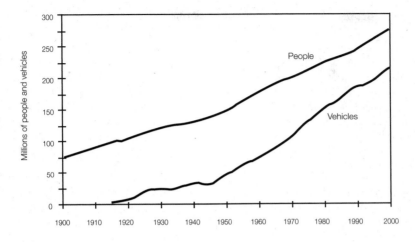

Figure H-2. People and Vehicles outside the U.S.

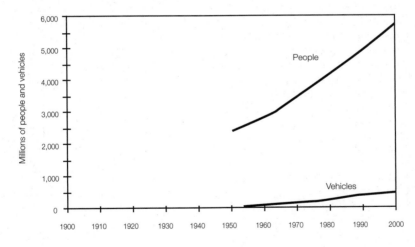

vehicle's cost. For example, a 50 kW automotive fuel-cell system producing electricity an average of twelve hours per day could see a profit of $0.02 per kWh, which would net approximately $4,380 per year for the vehicle's owner.[2]

Table H-2. National Vehicle Ownership Rates in 2000

Nation	Motor Vehicles	Population (thousands)	Vehicles per 1,000 persons	Equivalent year in U.S.
(1)	(2)	(3)	(4)=(2)/(3)	(5)
Bangladesh	129,984	131,050	1	1906
Kenya	33,000	30,092	1	1906
Mali	15,000	10,840	1	1906
Myanmar	77,000	47,749	2	1907
Ethiopia	109,546	64,298	2	1907
Tanzania	61,045	33,696	2	1907
Afghanistan	52,200	26,550	2	1907
Somalia	20,000	9,940	2	1907
Malawi	23,000	10,311	2	1907
Sudan	79,387	31,095	3	1909
Vietnam	207,000	78,523	3	1909
Mozambique	55,212	17,691	3	1909
Niger	36,800	10,832	3	1909
Benin	22,500	6,272	4	1907
Rwanda	27,800	7,738	4	1907
Uganda	87,923	22,210	4	1907
Guinea	33,000	7,405	4	1907
Pakistan	760,029	138,080	6	1910
Sierra Leone	29,400	5,031	6	1910
Mauritania	16,000	2,665	6	1910
Burkina Faso	68,100	11,274	6	1910
Congo Dem. Republic	310,000	50,948	6	1910
Burundi	42,400	6,807	6	1910
Angola	90,326	13,134	7	1911
Madagascar	108,239	15,523	7	1911
Gambia	9,000	1,248	7	1911
India	7,540,000	1,015,923	7	1911
Ghana	149,071	19,306	8	1911
Nigeria	1,050,000	126,910	8	1911
Haiti	66,500	7,959	8	1911
China	13,400,000	1,262,460	11	1912
Honduras	80,034	6,417	12	1912
Indonesia	3,023,414	210,421	14	1913
Liberia	46,000	3,130	15	1913
Cameroon	220,097	14,876	15	1913
Paraguay	81,600	5,496	15	1913
Senegal	160,000	9,404	17	1913
Zambia	175,284	10,089	17	1913
Guyana	13,800	761	18	1914
Guatemala	209,150	11,385	18	1914
Congo	55,700	3,018	18	1914
Iran	1,175,000	63,664	18	1914
El Salvador	131,700	6,276	21	1914
Papua New Guinea	119,600	5,130	23	1914
Syria	405,903	16,189	25	1915
Algeria	860,435	30,399	28	1915
Togo	129,400	4,527	29	1915
Colombia	1,255,000	42,299	30	1915
Tunisia	285,000	9,564	30	1915
Zimbabwe	378,300	12,627	30	1915
Nicaragua	156,959	5,071	31	1915
Cote d'Ivoire	498,779	16,013	31	1915
Philippines	2,464,932	75,580	33	1915
Gabon	39,500	1,190	33	1915
Sri Lanka	651,000	19,359	34	1915
Yemen	598,900	17,507	34	1915
Cuba	384,200	11,188	34	1915
Swaziland	36,755	1,032	36	1916
Iraq	845,634	23,264	36	1916
Peru	953,393	25,661	37	1916
Egypt	2,557,315	63,976	40	1916
Cape Verde	18,000	394	46	1916
Bolivia	438,282	8,329	53	1917
Jamaica	138,970	2,633	53	1917
Morocco	1,626,239	28,705	57	1917
Dominican Republic	492,000	8,373	59	1917
Ecuador	762,239	12,646	60	1918
Vanuatu	12,000	197	61	1918
Dominica	5,700	83	69	1918
St. Vincent & the Grenadines	8,200	119	69	1918
Botswana	115,187	1,602	72	1919
Namibia	129,000	1,727	75	1919
Jordan	386,098	4,887	79	1919
Trinidad & Tobago	103,827	1,301	80	1919
Hong Kong	575,843	6,797	85	1919
Turkey	5,965,300	65,293	91	1920

Nation	Motor Vehicles	Population (thousands)	Vehicles per 1,000 persons	Equivalent year in U.S.
(1)	(2)	(3)	(4)=(2)/(3)	(5)
Saudi Arabia	2,896,979	29,723	97	1921
United Arab Emirates	284,200	2,905	98	1921
Belize	24,300	240	101	1921
Mauritius	122,425	1,186	103	1921
Venezuela	2,542,249	24,170	105	1921
Lebanon	468,483	4,328	108	1921
Seychelles	8,500	78	109	1921
Thailand	7,050,000	60,728	116	1922
Ukraine	6,310,829	49,051	129	1922
Panama	369,712	2,856	129	1922
Libya	690,926	5,290	131	1922
Chile	2,053,779	15,211	135	1923
Singapore	557,203	4,018	139	1923
Costa Rica	555,875	3,811	146	1923
Fiji	121,053	812	149	1923
Oman	361,153	2,395	151	1923
South Africa	6,704,600	42,801	157	1924
Romania	3,590,417	22,435	160	1924
Brazil	28,975,309	170,406	170	1924
Samoa	11,600	65	178	1925
Argentina	6,613,500	37,032	179	1925
Mexico	18,486,835	97,966	189	1926
Uruguay	655,776	3,337	197	1927
Suriname	84,987	417	204	1927
Yugoslavia (former)	2,170,000	10,637	204	1927
Bulgaria	1,911,767	8,653	221	1929
Bahamas	67,000	303	221	1929
Antigua & Barbuda	14,673	66	222	1929
Malaysia	5,242,200	23,270	225	1936
Taiwan	5,393,103	22,191	243	1939
French Polynesia	57,200	235	243	1939
Brunei	84,743	338	251	1940
South Korea	12,040,195	47,275	255	1940
French Guiana	44,060	168	262	1941
Slovak Republic	1,435,066	5,402	266	1947
Barbados	73,172	267	274	1947
Hungary	2,749,000	10,022	274	1947
Israel	1,754,058	6,233	281	1948
Latvia	675,581	2,372	285	1948
Puerto Rico	1,155,000	3,920	295	1948
Poland	11,856,624	38,650	307	1949
Bahrain	214,504	691	310	1949
Qatar	200,900	585	343	1952
New Caledonia	77,100	213	362	1954
Czech Republic	3,732,746	10,273	363	1954
Ireland	1,536,709	3,794	405	1959
Greece	4,279,524	10,560	405	1959
Denmark	2,230,421	5,336	418	1961
Reunion	293,149	691	424	1962
Kuwait	920,915	1,984	464	1964
Netherlands Antilles	100,300	215	467	1965
Finland	2,431,600	5,177	470	1965
Netherlands	7,489,400	15,919	470	1965
Portugal	4,750,000	10,008	475	1965
Sweden	4,388,031	8,869	495	1967
Belgium	5,151,414	10,252	502	1967
Cyprus	384,119	757	507	1968
United Kingdom	30,545,600	59,739	511	1968
Norway	2,297,655	4,491	512	1968
Andorra	39,596	75	528	1969
Bermuda	33,300	63	529	1970
Australia	10,180,000	19,182	531	1970
Switzerland	3,840,034	7,180	535	1970
Spain	21,284,100	39,465	539	1970
Austria	4,433,847	8,110	547	1971
France	33,813,000	58,892	574	1972
Germany	47,306,200	82,150	576	1972
Canada	16,815,000	29,123	577	1972
Malta	233,413	390	598	1972
Italy	36,165,300	57,690	627	1975
Iceland	180,401	281	642	1976
Luxembourg	283,685	438	648	1977
Japan	82,652,926	126,870	651	1977
Monaco	21,000	32	656	1977
New Zealand	2,674,980	3,831	698	1983
United States	217,566,789	282,224	771	2000

Sources: Columns (2) and (3): *Ward's Automobile Facts and Figures 2002*; Column (5) from Table H-1.

Table H-3. Vehicle Ownership Rates in the United States and the World, 1950–2000

	Number of vehicles (millions)			Number of persons (millions)			Vehicles per 1,000 persons		
	1950	2000	Growth rate	1950	2000	Growth rate	1950	2000	Growth rate
United States	49	221	3.3%	152	282	1.4%	323	771	1.9%
Rest of world	21	513	7.2%	2,403	5,797	1.9%	9	89	5.1%
Total	70	735	5.2%	2,555	6,079	1.9%	28	121	3.3%
U.S. as % of Rest of World	70%	30%	–	6.0%	4.6%	–	3,653%	871%	–

Source: Table H-1

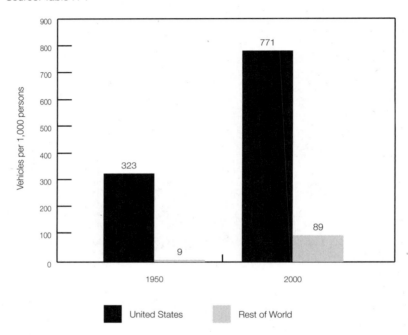

In this fuel-cell-powered future, parked cars can become a resource, not a liability, and they may earn enough money to pay for their parking (although no one knows where the fuel for the fuel cells will come from). Just as computing power moved from mainframe machines to personal computers in the late twentieth century, electricity generation might move from power plants to parked cars in the twenty-first century. But even the most optimistic speculation about future automobile technology does not justify off-street parking requirements.

APPENDIX H NOTES

1. The data on vehicle ownership rates in countries other than the United States are taken from *Ward's Motor Vehicle Facts & Figures 2002*. Because the record keeping is unreliable or inconsistent in many countries, the data for individual countries are not necessarily reliable, and in many cases the Ward's data differ from the data on the number of vehicles in use shown in the *United Nations Statistical Yearbook*. I have used the Ward's data merely to illustrate the low number of vehicles per 1,000 persons in most countries. I am grateful to Francisco Contreras and Seth Stark for their research assistance in compiling Tables H-1 and H-2.

2. Lipman (2000, 11).

Afterword

Twenty-First Century Parking Reforms

You cannot escape the responsibility of tomorrow by evading it today.

— ABRAHAM LINCOLN

The Preface highlighted some of the parking reforms that have taken place since the publication of the hardback edition of *The High Cost of Free Parking* in 2005. Other reforms have also been adopted, and this afterword gives more detail about them in relation to the three basic policies recommended in the book: (1) set the right price for curb parking, (2) return parking revenue to pay for local public services, and (3) remove minimum parking requirements.

1. SET THE RIGHT PRICE FOR CURB PARKING

Cities typically keep their meter rates constant throughout the day and let the occupancy rates vary. Instead, cities can vary the meter rates by time of day to maintain occupancy rates of about 85 percent. Several cities have begun to experiment with right-priced curb parking because of its theoretical appeal and practical feasibility. Pilot programs for curb pricing can quickly be adjusted or abandoned if they don't work well; in contrast, off-street parking requirements have major, almost irreversible, effects. To use a medical analogy, performance parking prices are like physical therapy while minimum parking requirements are like major surgery. Because physical therapy is much cheaper and does much less damage if it turns out to be the wrong choice, many physicians recommend physical therapy to see if it can resolve a problem before they resort to surgery. Performance parking policies—setting the price of curb parking to yield one or two open spaces on every block—can be called price therapy for parking problems.

Cities with Performance Parking Prices

Washington, D.C. In 2008, Washington, D.C., established a performance parking pilot project near a new ballpark that has 41,000 seats but only 1,300 off-street parking spaces.[1] The District of Columbia Department of Transportation is authorized to adjust meter rates to achieve vacancy rates between 10 percent and 20 percent for the curb spaces, to adjust the days and hours during which the meters operate, and to adjust fines to dissuade illegal parking. The city returns 75 percent of the meter revenue to the metered neighborhoods for nonautomobile transportation improvements. On game days, the meter rates are $8 an hour during events at the ballpark and $2 an hour during the rest of the day. On nongame days, the meter rates are $1 or $1.50 an hour.[2]

New York City. New York City began its PARK Smart program with a pilot project in Greenwich Village in 2008. Meter rates, which had been $1 an hour all day, were doubled to $2 an hour between noon and 4 p.m. In subsequent surveys, 61 percent of drivers and 57 percent of merchants reported that parking became easier or remained about the same compared with prepilot conditions. Only 46 percent of drivers and 34 percent of merchants said they were aware of the new rates, suggesting that raising the rates did not encounter strong opposition.[3] A second pilot began in Park Slope, Brooklyn, in 2009. The meter rates, which had been 75¢ an hour all day, were doubled to $1.50 an hour between noon and 4 p.m. Peak-period parking durations declined by 20 percent; the number of vehicles that parked at the curb increased by 18 percent; and traffic volume declined by 7 percent, probably because there was less cruising. Only 46 percent of parkers were aware they had paid the new peak-period rates, and only 15 percent of pedestrians had arrived by car.[4] A third pilot project began in 2010 on Manhattan's Upper East Side, where the meter rates are $2.50 an hour at off-peak hours and $3.75 an hour from noon to 4 p.m.

Ventura. Ventura, California, north of Los Angeles, adopted a performance parking program in 2010. The municipal code language is simple: "The City Transportation Manager may adjust pay station and meter rates up or down 50 cents per hour in twenty-five-cent increments based on average occupancy rates in order to achieve a target occupancy rate of 85 percent."[5] The code also specifies, "All moneys collected from parking pay stations . . . shall be devoted exclusively to purposes within the geographic boundaries of the parking district from which the revenue is collected."[6] Time limits were removed for all metered spaces.[7]

Seattle. The Seattle City Council voted unanimously in 2010 to establish a performance parking program. It directed the Seattle Department of Transportation (SDOT) to "set rates to achieve approximately one or two open spaces per block face throughout the day. The policy objective is to ensure that visitors to neighborhood business districts can find a parking spot near their destination. SDOT may both *raise* and *lower* rates in different areas as appropriate to meet the occupancy target."[8] After conducting the first occupancy counts in the city's 22 meter districts in 2011, SDOT increased meter rates in four districts, left them unchanged in seven districts, and reduced them in 11 districts.

The council won strong support from business groups because the city is switching from a revenue goal to an outcome goal for setting meter rates. The city will clearly continue to earn revenue, but revenue will no longer be a justification for raising meter rates. The policy goal of one or two open spaces per block is an easy way to explain that the purpose is to guarantee parking availability.[9]

Because parking demand can vary from one block to another, Seattle's goal of one or two vacant curb spaces on each block suggests that the geography of meter rates will be fine grained. The council directed SDOT to divide existing meter zones into "smaller neighborhood parking areas based on business patterns and parking occupancy. This division will result in more distinct parking areas throughout the City and will allow rates to be better tailored to neighborhood patterns."[10]

The Right Occupancy Rate for Curb Parking

A performance pricing policy requires a parking occupancy goal. Should that goal be 85 percent, or something different? The answer depends on the value of having a few more spaces occupied and on the resulting costs associated with more cruising for scarcer vacancies. Ninety-five percent occupancy, for example, would still leave a few vacant spaces, but it would increase the number of occupied spaces by only 12 percent while reducing the number of open spaces by 67 percent.[11] The higher occupancy rate would increase the difficulty of finding an open space, so drivers would have to spend more time cruising and would have to walk farther from their cars to their destinations and back.

Perhaps Seattle's goal of one empty space on each side of every block is the most sensible policy. Given the random nature of arrivals and departures, cities that adopt performance pricing will need to accept some time with two or more vacancies so there will be less time with no vacancies. Instead of aiming for an average of 85 percent occupancy over an hour, a city can aim for a target share of the hour with at least one vacancy on each block. A city will have at least three goals in setting a target for the number of minutes during an hour with an open space on the block:

(1) Ready availability. Availability is defined as the share of an hour with at least one vacant space on the block. Ready availability means that drivers can usually find a convenient open space.

(2) High occupancy. Occupancy is the average share of spaces that are occupied during the hour. High occupancy means that the curb spaces are well used and serve many customers.

(3) Revenue. Revenue depends on both the meter price and the occupancy rate. Revenue should not be the primary goal, but it should result from good management.

Cities face a trade-off between ready availability and high occupancy. These two goals conflict, because raising the meter rates to ensure at least one vacant space during a greater share of an hour will reduce the average occupancy rate. Suppose, for example, a city sets prices to ensure a vacant space on each block for at least 45 minutes during each hour. If at least one vacant space is available on that block for only 30 minutes in an hour, the availability target is not met, and the price should increase. This price increase, however, means that the average occupancy during the hour will decline.

Curb parking is a perishable good, which means its costs are fixed and it cannot be stored. (Airline seats are another example of a perishable good—an empty seat on a flight cannot be resold later.) Private operators set prices of perishable goods to maximize revenue, but a city's goal for curb parking should be different. Full occupancy of curb parking produces unwanted cruising, while low occupancy means the curb spaces are not delivering customers to the adjacent businesses. A city must balance the competing goals of reliable availability and high occupancy. The greater the random variation in demand during a time period, the greater the conflict between the two goals. Nevertheless, it seems sensible to focus on a driver's probability of finding an open space upon arrival as a key measure in setting prices.

Performance Pricing Is Not Privatization

Cities can charge performance prices for curb parking without privatizing it, and can privatize curb parking without charging performance prices for it. In 2008, Chicago privatized its parking meters and missed a great opportunity to make performance pricing a part of the deal. Chicago's primary goal for the concession contract was not to manage curb parking but "to maximize the amount of the upfront payment made for the Concession."[12]

Chicago's meter rates before the privatization were probably far too low. In 2008 they were only $3 an hour in the Loop, $1 an hour in the rest of the CBD, and from 25¢ to 75¢ an hour elsewhere. The concession contract sets caps on the meter rates in 2013 at $6.50 an hour in the Loop, $4 an hour in the rest of the CBD, and $2 an hour everywhere else in the city.[13] From 2014 to 2084, the meter rates can increase only at the rate of inflation. Chicago thus privatized its parking meters without using prices to manage the system properly.

Chicago also failed to get the highest possible upfront payment, because limiting meter rate increases after 2013 to the inflation rate must have limited what bidders were willing to pay for the 75-year concession. Even with the price caps, however, the winning bid was $1.16 billion for the 36,000 metered spaces. The parking spaces are thus worth at least $32,000 apiece.

Rather than setting caps on future meter rates, a city can set performance goals for a privatized system. For example, the contract could require the concessionaire to set meter rates so that the curb occupancy rate remains between 75 percent and 95 percent on every block for at least a certain number of hours every day, with penalty payments for failure to meet the occupancy goal. If professional operators can manage performance parking more effectively and at lower cost than the city's staff can, privatization with appropriate performance goals may turn out to be a good way for a city to charge the right prices for curb parking.

Like burning the furniture to stay warm on a cold night, selling assets to pay current expenses is a bad idea. Some cities are considering more farsighted parking concessions that share the annual revenue rather than maximize the upfront payment. A concession with a professional operator who meets performance goals and shares the resulting revenue with the city can give the city two big advantages: (1) a well-managed parking system, and (2) a perpetual stream of income.

Graduated Parking Fines

Cities cannot successfully manage curb parking without effective enforcement (see pp. 486–489). Enforcement is a difficult political issue, however, because parking citations create hostility toward the government. Fortunately, a few cities have developed a way to enforce parking regulations without costing most drivers anything. Modest fines are a sufficient deterrent for most drivers who rarely receive a parking ticket. For minor violations, such as overtime parking, cities can issue a warning for the first offense within each year and attach a brochure explaining the rules. The warnings show citizens that raising revenue is not the chief goal of enforcement.

Warnings are not an effective deterrent for repeat violators, who often account for a large share of all violations. In Los Angeles, for example, 8 percent of all the license plates that received tickets in 2009 accounted for 29 percent of all the tickets in that year. In Beverly Hills, 5 percent of license plates accounted for 24 percent of the tickets. Californians are not the only serial offenders. In Manchester, New Hampshire, 5 percent of the plates accounted for 22 percent of the tickets; and in Winnipeg, Manitoba, 14 percent of the plates accounted for 47 percent of the tickets.

The many tickets for a few repeat offenders suggest that some drivers view parking violations as an acceptable gamble or just another cost of doing business. If cities raise fines high enough to deter the few chronic violators, however, they unfairly penalize many more drivers for occasional—and often inadvertent—violations.

Graduated fines are the best way to deter chronic violators without unfairly punishing anyone else. They are lenient for the many car owners with only a few tickets but punitive for the few with many tickets. In Claremont, California, for example, the first ticket for overtime parking in a calendar year is $35, the second $70, and the third $105. For illegally using a disabled space, the first ticket is $325, the second $650, and the third $975. The graduated parking fines began in 2009, and the total number of citations fell by 22 percent between 2008 and 2010. Repeat citations fell the most, with greater declines for license plates with a greater number of citations; for example, citations for license plates with four or more violations fell by 31 percent.

Until recently, enforcement officers had no way of knowing how many tickets a car had previously received. Now, however, officers carry handheld ticket-writing devices that wirelessly connect to the city's ticket database. These devices can automatically assign the proper fine for each violation according to the number of previous tickets for the license plate.

A driver who receives many tickets for the same offense is probably either careless, unlucky, or a scofflaw who thinks risking a ticket is a rational gamble. If the price of a ticket multiplied by the probability of receiving a citation is less than the price of paying the meter, the temptation to risk a ticket is strong (see pp. 486–489). Scofflaws can do a simple cost-benefit calculation—they may get one ticket for each 10 violations, but each ticket carries the same fine. Graduated fines can therefore reduce the number of serial violations without penalizing occasional violators. Graduated fines are thus fairer and more effective than flat-rate fines.

Introducing performance prices that vary by time of day will require cities to inform drivers about the new system and enforce the new laws. A warnings-first policy for minor offenses can politely inform drivers about the rules and reduce political opposition to enforcement, while higher fines for chronic offenders will help to ensure that drivers pay for parking. Repeat offenders will pay more, but everyone else will pay less.

For graduated parking fines to be effective, cities will have to ensure that drivers pay all the citations they receive, and New York City has mounted a pilot program to increase the probability that drivers will not ignore tickets. New York will use self-release boots to immobilize cars that have accumulated more than $350 in unpaid parking tickets. Drivers who call a toll-free number and pay their fines by credit card will get a code allowing them to unlock the boot. Drivers will then have to return the boot to the city within a set time period or face another penalty. If this pilot program is effective, drivers will have a strong incentive to pay the performance parking prices rather than risk a ticket.

All May Park, All Must Pay

Many states mandate that all cars with disabled placards can park free for an unlimited time at metered on-street spaces.[14] The goal of making curb parking accessible to people with disabilities is laudable, but treating disabled placards as free parking passes has encouraged widespread abuse by drivers without disabilities who simply want to park free for an unlimited time. If many drivers with placards pay nothing at meters, performance prices cannot effectively manage parking spaces.

A survey in 2010 on a block in downtown Los Angeles shows the potential for placard abuse to obstruct a performance parking program. The block has 14 parking meters, and most of the spaces were occupied most of the time by cars with disabled placards. For five hours of the day, all 14 spaces were occupied by cars with placards. The meter rate was $4 an hour, but the meters earned an average of only 32¢ an hour. Cars parked free with placards consumed $477 worth of meter time per day, or 81 percent of the potential meter revenue on this block. If these observations represent a typical day, cars with placards account for about $8,900 in lost revenue per meter per year, or $125,000 for the 14 meters on the block.[15]

Because higher meter rates will increase the rewards for placard abuse, more of the metered spaces will probably be occupied by cars with placards. Higher meter rates will also reduce the willingness of drivers without placards to park at meters. Performance prices can thus produce an unwanted result: more placard abusers occupying the curb spaces and fewer drivers paying for parking. Increased placard abuse can even reduce the availability of curb spaces for people with genuine disabilities. If placard abusers drive out both paying parkers and legal placard users, prices will not manage curb parking properly.

Almost everyone has seen expensive cars with disabled placards and seen agile people jumping out of them (see pp. 488–490). Disabled does not mean destitute, and a placard does not guarantee a disability. If a state exempts all cars with placards from paying at meters, how can cities adopt a performance pricing program *and* preserve parking availability for people with disabilities? Virginia has a sensible policy to deal with this problem. Virginia exempts vehicles displaying disabled placards from paying at meters, but it also allows cities to set aside this exemption if they give reasonable notice that payment is required.[16] In 1998, Arlington, Virginia, opted out of the exemption for placards and posted "All May Park, All Must Pay" on every meter pole (see Figure AF-1). Because it is easier to park in and pull out of the end space on a block, Arlington reserves some of these end spaces for cars with disabled

Figure AF-1. All must pay in Arlington.

placards. The purpose is to provide parking in convenient locations for people with disabilities, not to offer a discount scheme that treats people with disabilities differently from other people and invites gross abuse. Cities can reserve the most accessible meter spaces for disabled placard holders, but accessible does not mean free.

Alexandria, Virginia, is considering a similar opt-out policy "as part of a broader strategy to properly manage on-street parking and reduce the potential for abuse by holders of handicapped permits."[17] Anticipating the ordinance, in 2010 the Alexandria Police Department conducted a study of placard use:

> During the summer, the Police staked out parked vehicles with handicapped placards or license plates in locations throughout the City. When the occupants returned to the vehicles, Police checked that the person to whom the placard or plate was issued was among the occupants of the vehicle, as man-

dated by law. Police stated that approximately 90% of the placards and license plates checked were being used illegally. This is a very labor intensive enforcement process. There have also been anecdotal statements about the ease of legally obtaining handicapped placards, which may contribute to the abuse of handicapped parking privileges.[18]

Parking with placards seems to be an almost ethics-free zone, and any placard policy should consider the potential for abuse. Raleigh, North Carolina, has pioneered an ingenious policy to make its parking meters accessible for people with disabilities without creating financial incentives for abuse. Raleigh allows cars with disabled placards to park for an unlimited time at meters, but drivers must pay for the time they use.[19] Placard users push a button on the meter allowing them to pay for time beyond the normal limit. Enforcement officers can then check to see whether the cars using this privilege display a placard. Cities can achieve this same accessibility for people with disabilities by removing the time limits for all cars, making the special technology for placard users unnecessary.

If people with disabilities must pay at meters, their difficulty of getting to and from the meters may be a barrier, especially with pay-and-display meters. If it is raining or snowing, the barrier will be even greater. To solve this problem, cities can offer placard holders the option to pay with in-vehicle meters or by cell phone (see pp. 387–390). Offering these options can forestall objections that charging placard users for curb parking will present a barrier to people with disabilities because the payment method is itself a barrier.[20]

Ending free parking for placard users will bring in new revenue that can pay for services benefiting all people with disabilities, not just drivers with placards. For example, if a city proposes to end free parking for cars with placards, it can estimate the total meter revenue currently lost because of placard use and commit some or all of the new meter revenue to pay for specialized transportation services for all people with disabilities.[21]

The data from Alexandria illustrate how the disabled community can benefit from an all-must-pay policy. The police survey found that placard abuse accounts for 90 percent of the revenue lost from the placard exemption. Alexandria has also estimated that an all-must-pay policy will raise $133,000 a year in new meter revenue.[22] If placard abusers account for 90 percent of this lost revenue, they receive $119,700 of the subsidy intended for people with disabilities, while people with disabilities receive only $13,300.

People with disabilities *who live in Alexandria* do not receive all of the $13,300 subsidy for legal placard users. A survey of the license plates on cars with placards parked at meters in Alexandria found that only 21 percent of them were from Virginia (see Table AF-1). Sixty-nine percent were from Maryland, 8 percent from the District of Columbia, and 2 percent from other states.[23] At least 79 percent of the cars with placards were therefore not from Alexandria, and many of them were probably driven by commuters who use the placards to park free at work. Resident legal users receive only 2.1 percent of the city's subsidy for free parking at meters (21% x 10%), or $2,793. If Alexandria adopts an all-must-pay policy, the new meter revenue will be about 50 times greater than the parking subsidy its residents with disabilities now receive.[24]

These survey data from Alexandria were not based on random samples, and they do not predict what will happen if Alexandria or other cities charge placard users at parking meters. The data do, however, suggest that an all-must-pay policy can prevent placard abuse and finance new services for the disabled community. Using a subsidy to provide services for everyone with disabilities seems much fairer than wasting much of it to provide free parking for placard abusers. It is easy to see why Alexandria is considering whether to adopt Arlington's policy, and not the other way around.

Beyond raising revenue to finance services for citizens with disabilities, the all-must-pay policy can also eliminate the culture of corruption that has grown up around using fake disabled placards as

Table AF-1. Revenue lost in Alexandria as result of meter exemption for disabled placards ($/year)

Lost meter revenue	100%	$133,000
Placard abusers	90%	$119,700
Legal placard users	10%	$13,300
Out-of-state plates	79%	$105,070
In-state plates	21%	$27,930
Nonresident abusers	71%	$94,563
Resident abusers	19%	$25,137
Nonresident legal users	8%	$10,507
Resident legal users	2%	$2,793

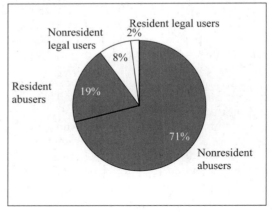

free parking passes. Cities encourage this corruption by making it so easy, so profitable, and so rarely punished.

Finally, curb parking will never be appropriately used until it is appropriately priced. If cities cease treating disabled placards as free parking passes, charging performance prices to manage curb parking will be more effective.[25]

2. RETURN PARKING REVENUE TO PAY FOR LOCAL PUBLIC SERVICES

Performance prices for curb parking may make sense in both theory and practice, but they are tough to sell politically. Paying for parking is a "grudge purchase" in marketing terminology—a purchase the buyer does not want to make, such as repairing a car after an accident. For some people, the idea of charging market prices for curb parking amounts to a thought crime. After all, taxes have already paid for the streets, so why should drivers have to pay even more to park on them? Nobody wants to pay for parking, but some cities have found strong political support for parking meters by using the meter revenue to pay for local public services the residents want.

Cities with Revenue Return

Chapter 16 explains how, in California, Pasadena and San Diego return all or a share of parking meter revenue to its source. Several more cities have begun to return meter revenue to the metered districts. Austin, Texas, uses parking meter revenue to pay for improved sidewalks, curb ramps, and street trees in its Parking Benefit District next to the University of Texas.[26] In California, Redwood City and Ventura return all the meter revenue to pay for added public services on the metered streets. In its performance parking pilot district, Washington, D.C., returns 75 percent of the meter revenue to pay for transportation improvements, including lighting, benches, and bicycle racks.

Eugene, Oregon, has pioneered an ingenious way to return benefits to a neighborhood. The University of Oregon wanted to build a new $227 million basketball arena, but residents of the nearby Fairmont neighborhood were concerned that events at the arena would attract drivers who would occupy all the on-street parking during games. But residents also did not want to pay for a permit district to solve a problem created by the new arena.

In 2010, the City of Eugene and the University of Oregon worked together to create an Event Parking District near the arena (see Figure AF-2).[27] The university can sell 500 event-day parking permits in the district for up to 22 events a year at the arena. Unlike a conventional permit district where residents pay for their permits, residents receive two free residential permits per property in the Event Permit District, and they can buy additional permits at the market price. The university charges ticket holders $8 to $10 for event parking in the permit district on game days and uses the resulting revenue to pay the city the full cost of managing the permit district. If the university does not receive enough revenue from the sale of the event parking permits, it pays the city the difference from its own funds. Parking fines double during events to ensure that the regulations are effective.

Figure AF-2. Event Parking District in Eugene

The Event Parking District creates substantial benefits for everyone. The university avoids the game-day parking crush without building an expensive parking structure that would be underused much of the year. The adjacent neighborhood gets a residential permit district at no cost to the residents. The City of Eugene gets the revenue necessary to manage the district.

Eugene's Event Parking District shows the possibility of a symbiotic relationship between residential neighborhoods and nearby traffic generators. Commercial developments with few on-site parking spaces increase demand for something the nearby neighborhoods can sell to nonresidents: curb parking. Other cities also charge nonresidents for parking in residential permit districts (see Chapter 17, especially pp. 451–465). Eugene's program demonstrates the benefits of this policy for land uses that cause short, sharp, and infrequent peaks in parking demand.

Parking Increment Finance

If a city puts all its meter money into the general fund, proposing to return this money to the metered districts will be politically difficult, because the general fund will lose what the metered districts gain. Cities can have it both ways—continuing to feed the general fund *and* earmarking revenue for the metered districts—if they return only the subsequent *increment* in meter revenue (the amount above the existing meter revenue) that arises after the city begins to charge performance prices. This arrangement can be called *parking increment finance* (see pp. 528–530). Business districts can receive the increment in meter revenue when they adopt performance parking programs. More meters, higher rates, and longer hours of operation will provide money to pay for added public services. The added revenue will provide the local incentive for business leaders to support a performance parking program.

In 2008, St. Louis created a parking increment finance arrangement for its Grand Center Arts District, a business improvement district in the downtown. Grand Center receives 75 percent of any increase in the meter revenue above the 2008 baseline revenue.[28] Grand Center pays for installing any new equipment and enforces the parking regulations. The incremental revenue can be used to pay for sidewalk repairs, increased security, additional lighting, and streetscape improvements.

Both the city and Grand Center benefit from parking increment finance. St. Louis receives all the meter revenue it would have received, plus 25 percent of the incremental revenue produced by the improved parking management. Grand Center receives 75 percent of the incremental revenue, and it also benefits from more efficient use of its curb spaces.

Parking Federalism

If cities return all parking meter revenue to the districts that earn it, inequalities will arise because some areas have much higher demand for curb parking than others. And if the demand for curb parking is higher in higher income areas, the richer areas will receive more meter revenue than the poorer ones. What can a city do to avoid this inequality and yet maintain the incentive to adopt performance parking prices?

Suppose, for example, the parking meters in a city yield an average revenue of $1,500 per meter per year ($4.10 per day) but yield $2,000 per year in rich neighborhoods and only $1,000 per year in poor neighborhoods. It seems unfair that a prosperous business district in a rich neighborhood would receive twice as much meter money as a struggling business district in a poor neighborhood, although the meter rates are adjusted to produce 85 percent occupancy in both districts.

In this case, the city might offer to return $1,000 per meter per year to pay for added public services in every district that adopts performance pricing. This revenue will offer a strong incentive to adopt performance pricing, every district will receive the same revenue per meter, and the city's general fund will get a third of the total revenue. If performance parking prices increase the city's average meter revenue above $1,500 per year, the general fund will receive even more than a third of all meter revenue. And if the general fund's spending is spread evenly throughout the city, the performance parking program will transfer money from rich to poor areas.

Returning $1,000 per meter per year to pay for added public services in each metered district is only an example, but most federal and state transportation funds are distributed to local governments by similar formulas, such as per-capita grants. The formula for sharing the meter revenue would be a social contract between a city and its neighborhoods: The city will charge performance prices for curb parking, and the metered districts will get better public services. If the formula for sharing the revenue is fair, the performance parking policy will be fair.

This system of parking federalism can work in both commercial and residential areas. In the densest residential areas with a high demand for curb parking, a city could auction resident permits (perhaps on eBay) every year and split the revenue with the permit neighborhoods (see Chapter 17). Each block could vote whether to adopt permit parking, and the blocks that opt for performance prices would receive added public services financed by a share of the added parking revenue. Most of the curb spaces on each block could be reserved for residents, and a few made available for guests in performance-priced meter spaces. In the densest residential neighborhoods where only a tiny share of the residents can park on the streets, such as in New York City and San Francisco, never before will so many pedestrians receive so many benefits paid for by so few drivers.

Performance Pricing without Revenue Return

Performance pricing will be more popular where cities can commit to spending at least some of the meter revenue on public services in the districts where it is collected. Nevertheless, the programs in New York, San Francisco, and Seattle show that cities can charge performance prices even without returning any of the resulting revenue. San Francisco is unusual, however, because the San Francisco Municipal Transportation Agency (SFMTA) is a semiautonomous body that operates both the public transit system and on-street parking, and it uses the meter revenue to subsidize public transit. The SFMTA is also responsible for the city's entire surface transportation network, so it wants to reduce cruising, which congests traffic, slows public transit, and endangers cyclists and pedestrians. Even if the meter revenue disappeared into the city's general fund, the SFMTA would still want to get the prices of curb parking right, but earmarking the meter revenue for the SFMTA surely increases its interest in performance parking.

Parking Holidays

Putting meter revenue into the general fund can make cities quite careless about charging for parking. For example, many cities wrap their parking meters during the Christmas season and offer everyone free parking at the time of peak demand, as a gift from the mayor and city council (see pp. 7–8). Consider the program in Bellingham, Washington, in 2010:

> This year, for the two weeks before Christmas the city will offer all-day free parking. . . . To help shoppers park close to businesses and keep spaces available, the city is asking that people still observe the time limits at meters. Shoppers planning to be downtown for more than a couple of hours are encouraged to park on the ground floor of the Parkade.[29]

It is not clear how free curb parking will "keep spaces available" or whether "asking that people still observe the time limits at meters" will convince many motorists to comply. Bellingham's meter holiday probably transferred public funds to commuters who park all day in metered spaces, meaning that the employees of downtown businesses got free parking where once the city got revenue, and there was less parking for customers. Meter holidays, although well meant, create a shortage of curb parking at the busiest time of year, increase the time needed to find a curb space, and make traffic congestion even worse. If a city wants to be generous during the Christmas season, it might instead post signs on the meters saying, "All parking meter revenue from December 15 to 25 will be donated to pay for food and shelter for the city's homeless population." Some shoppers might like this policy and feel better about paying to park downtown. If cities set performance prices rather than offer meter holidays during the Christmas season, they can prevent parking shortages, help businesses that depend on curb parking, and generate substantial revenue to aid the homeless.

Christmas meter holidays are not the key issue here. The point is to use parking revenue to show everyone that performance-priced parking meters can do some good for the world. Dedicating meter revenue to provide public services in the metered districts for 50 weeks a year and to provide aid for the homeless for two weeks at Christmas could increase political support for performance parking prices. Wanting free parking for Christmas would begin to look quite selfish.

If meter revenue is spent wisely, everyone can gain from performance-priced curb parking. Reduced congestion, energy savings, and cleaner air are important benefits, but they are widely distributed throughout the city. These widespread benefits probably won't motivate residents to demand performance parking programs in their own neighborhoods. If the city returns the revenue to provide tangible public improvements in a neighborhood, however, and if everyone knows the meters pay for these improvements, experience shows that performance prices can be a political success. Performance prices are popular because the revenue pays for public amenities that everyone can see, not because they improve transportation. Cities can take credit for improving transportation and the environment, but the added public services—cleaner and safer neighborhoods—will probably create the greatest political support for performance parking prices.

3. REMOVE MINIMUM PARKING REQUIREMENTS

Parking spaces are essential for automobile travel, almost as oxygen in the atmosphere is essential to life. As a result, most people seem to think that parking requirements are an essential feature of urban planning. On the other hand, nobody wants to see off-street parking spaces until they want to park. Most cities have approached this conflict between goals—ample parking for cars versus a good environment for people—by requiring ample parking. Some cities are tilting toward a better environment for people by removing or reforming their parking requirements. Setting the right price for curb parking is much easier than requiring the right amount of off-street parking.

Estimating the Economic Burden of Minimum Parking Requirements

A recent large-scale econometric study found that minimum parking requirements significantly increase the number of parking spaces in cities. Bowman Cutter, Sofia Franco, and Autumn DeWoody used data for 9,279 nonresidential properties in Los Angeles County to investigate whether parking requirements force up the parking supply.

They took two approaches to answer this question. First, they compared the number of parking spaces at office buildings with the parking requirements. They found the buildings provided, on average, only 97 percent of the spaces that cities required, showing that most developers provide only the required number of spaces.[30]

Second, they used data on the sales prices of buildings to compare the marginal cost of a parking space with the resulting increase in a building's value. For the entire nonresidential sample, the last parking space added $7,500 more to a building's cost than it added to the building's value.[31] For service retail, such as restaurants with high parking requirements, the last parking space added $14,700 more to a building's cost than it added to the building's value.[32] Minimum parking requirements thus place a heavy economic burden on development by forcing developers to provide parking spaces that lose money. In effect, minimum parking requirements are a tax on building area to subsidize parking.

A recent study in New York City also found that most developers build only the minimum number of parking spaces required by zoning. Simon McDonnell, Josiah Madar, and Vicki Been studied 38 large residential projects in Queens and compared the number of actual spaces in the buildings to the city's parking requirements. They found the number of parking spaces equaled the minimum parking requirement in 47 percent of the buildings and fell short of the required minimum in another 11 percent. The parking supply exceeded the required minimum by more than 25 percent in only 13 percent of the buildings. They concluded that the city's parking requirements probably forced most developers to provide either more parking spaces or fewer housing units than the market would have otherwise provided.

Converting Curb Parking Spaces into Outdoor Cafés

A few cities have recently discovered that curb parking spaces can be far more valuable for outdoor cafés than for storing cars. Mountain View, California, became one of the first cities to allow outdoor cafés to occupy parking lanes, and the program has become very popular.[33] In 2010, New York City and San Francisco began to allow similar cafés in curb spaces.[34]

Mountain View has sophisticated design guidelines for the cafés in curb spaces (see Figure AF-3).[35] A restaurant that wants to expand into the parking lane must obtain a license that is issued for one year and pay the city $600 per parking space per year. The city's Development Review Committee must approve the location, layout, and design of the café in accordance with the sidewalk café guidelines.

Converting a curb parking space into an outdoor café turns conventional planning requirements upside down. Most cities require restaurants to provide additional off-street parking spaces if they want to put tables on the sidewalk. Instead, Mountain View allows restaurants to use curb spaces for outdoor dining, without providing any additional off-street parking. If the city also sets performance prices for the remaining curb spaces, cafés in the parking lane will not create a parking shortage. This arrangement can create substantial new revenue for the city, because it receives sales taxes on the cafés' receipts.

An outdoor café in a curb space will employ more people, pay more taxes, and enliven a street far more than one parked car will. During the winter, when outdoor dining is infeasible, the cafés in curb spaces can quickly be converted back to parking, which is perhaps why New York City calls them "pop-up cafés." The designer of New York's first pop-up café said, "It was just barely a month from the concept to actual on-street implementation. The idea is that this is temporary, or at least seasonal, so we wanted the restaurants to have enough time to use it."[36] Janette

City of Mountain View

Figure AF-3. Curb parking space converted into an outdoor café in Mountain View

Sadik-Khan, commissioner of the New York City Department of Transportation, said, "Inventions like this help make our streets into destinations and improve the quality of life for the thousands of people who live, work, and play in Lower Manhattan."[37] European cities such as Paris and Rome have also adopted the policy of extending sidewalk cafés into the curb lanes.

If cities allow outdoor cafés in curb spaces, they should not require off-street parking spaces for the new dining areas. Especially in cold climates, where the outdoor cafés operate only during the warm months, requiring off-street parking spaces for temporary tables would make outdoor dining prohibitively expensive (see pp. 157–158). Rather than require off-street parking for outdoor dining, cities can convert on-street parking into outdoor cafés.

Preventing Poaching

If cities remove off-street parking requirements, problems will arise where most buildings now offer free parking. Some drivers who visit a new building that does not provide free parking will be tempted to poach a space in one of the many free lots at other buildings nearby. This poaching problem is one argument against removing off-street parking requirements. Most building owners with free parking do not want to begin policing their lots and chasing away drivers who are not their customers. Preventing unauthorized people from parking in a free lot sounds like a monumental hassle. Minimum parking requirements may seem justified because they avoid the poaching problem, but building owners in some cities have found a way to prevent poaching and also to produce revenue from their parking lots: They contract with private operators to manage their lots as paid public parking and split the resulting revenue.

The simplest way for a business to convert a free private lot into a paid public lot is to install multispace meters and validate parking for customers who make a minimum purchase, while charging noncustomers to park in the lot (see Figure AF-4).[38] A business will have to experiment with the parking charges and the validation threshold to optimize use of the lot, but customers will continue to park free and the formerly free-for-all lot will begin to earn revenue.

A similar practice is to reserve parking for customers during the time a store (or bank or church or any other land use) is open and to employ a private operator to manage it as a paid lot at other hours when other businesses create a demand for parking. This arrangement generates revenue from otherwise vacant land and increases the parking supply for nearby businesses.

Yet another way to convert free private parking into paid public parking is for a business to contract with the city to install meters and to enforce parking regulations on the private lot, sharing the revenue.[39] A business can still decide how much to charge for parking and whether to validate customers' charges, just as when a private operator manages the lot. Many cities already manage their own off-street public lots, and expanding this service on a contract basis to formerly free private lots can be a new public-private partnership that benefits both parties.

Figure AF-4. Customer parking lot converted into paid lot in San Diego

One big difference between free parking and paid parking is that free parking costs much more because drivers demand so many more spaces. If cities remove off-street parking requirements, large free parking lots can become smaller paid parking lots, releasing much valuable land for infill development. The market will reclaim land from cars, and people will displace parking.

Solar Parking Requirements

Solar panels have begun to find a new place in the sun—on large parking lots surrounding commercial and industrial buildings, mounted on canopies providing shade for the parked cars. Parking lots in asphalt-rich cities have great solar potential because the panels can be oriented to maximize power production during summer afternoons, when electricity is most valuable. Google, for example, has installed "solar trees" on its parking lots to provide 30 percent of its headquarters' power demand.

Solar-powered parking lots can mitigate the substantial increase in peak-hour power demand created by major developments. Nevertheless, few developers install solar canopies above their parking lots. What can cities do to increase power production from parking lots?

One solution is for cities to incorporate solar power into their parking requirements for major developments. Cities already regulate many features of required parking lots, such as the size of the spaces and their landscaping. Cities can also require that a share of these spaces be covered with solar panels to provide for the increased peak-hour electricity demand created by large new buildings. The legal basis for requiring solar power in a parking lot is similar to that for requiring the parking lot itself. If a development increases the demand for scarce energy during peak hours, the solar requirement for its parking lot will help to meet this peak-hour demand. If massive air conditioners for a new development significantly increase the risk of neighborhood power failure on hot summer days, requiring the developer to offset this risk seems reasonable.

Cities can amend their zoning codes to require solar power generation in the parking lots of large new buildings. Rather than require solar panels over a specific number of parking spaces, cities can require a solar generating capacity per parking space, giving the developer the freedom to meet the requirement in the most cost-effective way. A developer who prefers not to install the required solar capacity on a parking lot can be offered the option to put it on the roof or to pay an in-lieu fee that the city can use to install an equivalent solar capacity in another location, such as a school or other public building.

It is hard to argue that solar arrays will mar the appearance of parking lots, because most parking lots are already ugly. Solar installations can even improve the appearance of parking lots. They can also help to reduce the NIMBY problems associated with building power plants and the transmission lines needed to deliver power to where it is consumed (see Figure AF-5).

The federal government and many state governments provide generous subsidies for solar panels, so developers will not have to pay the full cost of a city's solar parking requirement. Because the parking lots for large buildings are also large and have unobstructed solar access, the solar panels can take advantage of economies of scale in construction and can capture all the available sun-light. In contrast, few houses have properly oriented roofs, unob-structed solar access, and the struc-tural capacity to support solar panels. Therefore, solar parking lots can generate more energy per dollar of government subsidy than residen-tial uses can.

Beyond their economic advantages, solar-powered parking lots will be a decentralized source of back-up elec-tricity in an emergency, such as a nat-ural disaster or terrorist attack. Reducing the demand for energy from the electric grid will also reduce power plant emissions that con-tribute to smog and acid rain. The solar parking lots can also help elec-tric utilities meet state requirements to obtain a specific share of their energy from renewable sources.[40]

Donald C. Shoup

Figure AF-5. Solar parking lot in Los Angeles

Solar panels in parking lots will start producing power and bringing in revenue a few weeks after installation begins, a far shorter start-up period than for many other power sources, such as nuclear plants, which take years to construct. Solar parking lots distributed throughout the city will also generate electricity right where it is used, reducing transmission losses on the power grid and helping to prevent power outages caused by overloaded transmission lines. Because solar panels produce the most electricity on sunny days when the demand for air-conditioning peaks, they reduce the load on conventional power plants at the most critical time.

With only a slight change to the parking requirements in their zoning ordinances, cities can lead the way toward a future powered by renew-able energy.

Other Reforms

Chapters 9 and 10 present incremental reforms of minimum parking requirements, such as giving developers the option to pay fees in lieu of providing required parking spaces. Several further incremental reforms have emerged and show promise.

Fewer land uses with individual parking requirements. High parking requirements for some uses, such as restaurants, effectively prohibit these uses in old buildings that lack the required spaces. When Redwood City, California, adopted performance prices for curb parking, it also reduced the number of land uses with parking requirements to only three in the downtown zone: residential, hotel, and commercial.[41] Because all commercial uses now have the same parking requirement, any commercial building can be changed to a new use without adding more parking spaces. As a result, there has been dramatic investment in new restaurants. Redwood City, until recently derided as Deadwood City, had free curb parking but few customers in its historic downtown. Now, with performance-priced parking meters and the same parking requirement for all commercial uses, the downtown has become a popular dining destination.

Unbundled parking requirements. Some cities require owners of residential buildings to price parking separately from housing (see Chapter 20). The ordinance in Boulder, Colorado, is one example:

> All off-street parking spaces accessory to residential uses in new structures of ten dwelling units or more, or in new conversions of nonresidential buildings to residential use of ten dwelling units or more, shall be leased or sold separately from the rental or purchase fees for dwelling units for the life of the dwelling units, such that potential renters or buyers have the option of renting or buying a residential unit at a price lower than would be the case if there were a single price for both the residential unit and the parking space.[42]

Residents who own fewer cars will thus pay less for their housing.

Bellevue, Washington, requires unbundling the prices for parking and office space in some buildings in its downtown and requires that the minimum price for monthly parking is not less than the cost of a bus pass.[43]

Bicycle parking requirements. Many cities now require developers to provide bicycle parking spaces based on the same criteria as car parking requirements, such as one bicycle parking space per 2,000 square feet of floor area in a restaurant. The bicycle parking requirements are intended to promote cycling, which suggests, of course, that car parking requirements promote driving.

Cities can go beyond requiring bicycle parking by allowing developers to substitute bicycle parking spaces for required car parking spaces. Grants Pass, Oregon, allows developers to substitute two covered bicycle parking spaces for one required car parking space, and four or more bicycle parking spaces for two required car parking spaces.[44] Developers who want to provide fewer than the required number of car parking spaces will find bicycle parking spaces an attractive option.

CONCLUSION

Minimum parking requirements increase the supply of off-street parking, regardless of the costs and heedless of the consequences. They represent the hard path to solving the parking problem with asphalt and concrete. In contrast, performance prices for curb parking are an alternative soft path to solving the parking problem through better management.[45] If cities adjust the price of curb parking to aim for one or two open spaces on every block, and use the resulting revenue to improve public services on the metered streets, this soft path can greatly improve urban life.

The many large and small reforms reported here and in the Preface suggest that planners and politicians are beginning to acknowledge that minimum parking requirements create many serious problems for cities and society. All the required parking spaces were paved with good intentions, but the result is a plague of parking lots.

Urban problems often become widely recognized only after solutions become available, and now that performance parking prices are available it is easier to recognize all the problems caused by requiring too much parking. Minimum parking requirements maximize the likelihood that everyone will own a car and drive wherever they go. They do provide the free parking we want, but we give up a lot to get it. As Little Richard once sang, "He got what he wanted, but he lost what he had."

AFTERWORD NOTES

1. "Performance Parking Pilot Zone Act of 2008." Available at http://ddot.dc.gov/DC/DDOT/On+Your+Street/Traffic+Management/Parking/Performance+Based+Parking+Pilots.

2. District Department of Transportation (2009, 7). Available at http://ddot.dc.gov/DC/DDOT/On+Your+Street/Traffic+Management/Parking/Performance+Based+Parking+Pilots.

3. "PARK Smart Greenwich Village Pilot Program – Results." Available at www.nyc.gov/html/dot/html/motorist/parksmart.shtml.

4. "Park Slope Program Update, June 17, 2010." Available at www.nyc.gov/html/dot/html/motorist/parksmart.shtml.

5. Section 16.225.010 of the San Buenaventura Municipal Code.

6. Section 16.225.050 of the San Buenaventura Municipal Code.

7. Ventura's program is explained at www.cityofventura.net/pw/transportation/parking.

8. Seattle City Council Green Sheet 11-3-A, September 12, 2010, p. 1; emphasis in the original.

9. On a typical block face with eight curb parking spaces, one vacant space corresponds to an occupancy rate of about 85 percent. See p. 355 for the estimate that the average block face has eight curb parking spaces. Because some blocks are short and have few spaces while others are long and have many spaces, the goal of one or two vacant spaces on every block cannot be applied rigidly.

10. Seattle City Council Green Sheet 11-3-A, September 12, 2010, p. 2.

11. The increase in occupancy from 85 to 95 cars per 100 spaces adds only 10 cars, or 12 percent (10 ÷ 85), to the number of parked cars, while it reduces vacant spaces from 15 to 5, or by 67 percent (10 ÷ 15).

12. City of Chicago (2009, 12–13).

13. Ibid., 14–15.

14. For example, Section 22511.5 of the California Vehicle Code states, "A disabled person or disabled veteran is allowed to park in any metered parking space without being required to pay parking meter fees."

15. Williams (2010, xiv–xv). Several drivers with disabled placards were observed carrying heavy loads between their cars and the adjacent businesses.

16. Section 46.2-1245 of the Code of Virginia.

17. City of Alexandria. 2010. Memorandum from the City Manager, November 10, 2010, p. 1. Available at http://dockets.alexandriava.gov/fy11/111310ph/di14.pdf.

18. Ibid., p. 2.

19. Dash (2011). North Carolina requires cities to provide parking without time limits for people with disabilities but does not require that the parking must be free.

20. Arlington offered the option of using in-vehicle meters to pay for parking when it adopted its all-must-pay policy in 1998.

21. As a way to make parking reform politically acceptable, the policy of ending free parking for placards and returning the revenue to pay for services for the disabled community resembles the policy returning meter revenue to pay for public services on the metered streets.

22. City of Alexandria. 2010. Memorandum from the City Manager, November 10, 2010, p. 4. Available at http://dockets.alexandriava.gov/fy11/111310ph/di14.pdf.

23. City of Alexandria, 2010. Memorandum from the City Manager, April 16, 2010, p. 7. Available at http://dockets.alexandriava.gov/fy11/111310ph/di14.pdf.

24. Most of the current parking subsidy goes to placard abusers who live outside the city. If at least 79 percent of the drivers who park with placards come from outside the city, and if 90 percent of them are placard abusers, at least $94,600 of the meter revenue the city loses each year subsidizes placard abusers who do not live in the city ($133,000 x 90% x 79%).

25. Manville and Williams (2010) analyze the fairness and efficiency of removing the parking meter exemptions for disabled placards.

26. A description of Austin's Parking Benefit District is available at www .ci.austin.tx.us/ parkingdistrict/default.htm.

27. City of Eugene Parking Services, Event Parking District Information. Available at www.eparkeugene.com.

28. The baseline is adjusted upward for any citywide parking rate increases.

29. *Bellingham Herald*, December 13, 2010. Berkeley, California, has a similar program, and the Downtown Berkeley Association happily informed its members, "There will be no pay and no time limits! And, remember that this is a gift to our customers. Please tell your employees to leave this space available for customers." Berkeley's city manager estimated that the city would lose between $20,000 and $50,000 in meter and ticket revenue for each day of the meter holiday (Klein 2010). If the City of Berkeley used the meter revenue to pay for added public services downtown, the merchants probably would not be so cavalier about recommending a meter holiday.

30. Some developers probably received variances to provide fewer than the required number of parking spaces, which may help to explain why the buildings had an average of only 97 percent of the required number of spaces.

31. Table 7 in Cutter, Franco, and DeWoody (2010) shows that for all buildings the marginal cost per square foot of land used for parking exceeds the resulting marginal increase in building value by $21.43 per square foot of land used for parking. They assume an average of 350 square feet of land per surface parking space, so the marginal parking space adds $7,500 more to the cost of the building than it adds to the value of the building ($21.43 x 350 = $7,500). If a developer is required to provide 100 parking spaces for a building, adding the last required parking space (going from 99 to 100 spaces) therefore reduces the total value of the project by $7,500.

32. Table 7 in Cutter, Franco, and DeWoody (2010) shows that for service retail buildings the marginal cost per square foot of land used for parking exceeds the resulting marginal increase in building value by $42.02 per square foot of land used for parking. The marginal parking space thus adds $14,707 more to the cost of the building than it adds to the value of the building ($42.02 x 350 = $14,707).

33. City of Mountain View, Downtown Sidewalk Café Standards. Available at www.ci.mtnview.ca.us/civica/filebank/blobdload.asp?BlobID=2487.

34. Klayko (2010) and Thoi (2010).

35. For example, planter boxes or wrought iron fencing must be placed to visually define and secure the café area; the planters must contain live plants and flowers at all times; and tables and chairs cannot be stacked outside at any time or be secured to streetlights, trees, or other street furniture. The image in Figure AF-3 of a café in a curb parking space is taken from Mountain View's design guidelines.

36. Thoi (2010, 2).

37. Thoi (2010, 2). New York City's regulations for pop-up cafés are available at www.nyc.gov/html/dot/html/sidewalks/popupcafe.shtml.

38. Converting free parking for customers into paid parking for the public is becoming a common practice in the United Kingdom. "ASDA Parking Scheme Aims to Ease Congestion," *Belfast Telegraph*, November 12, 2009.

39. Because cities can issue tickets to violators at the meters they manage, and private operators cannot, cities might be able to enforce regulations on private lots more easily than private operators can.

40. For example, California's Renewables Portfolio Standard sets a requirement to increase the percentage of renewable energy in the state's electricity mix to 20 percent by 2017.

41. Article 30.2 of the Redwood City Municipal Code. Another feature of the code is a shared parking bonus: Any shared parking space counts as two parking spaces toward fulfilling the minimum requirement.

42. Section 9-9-6(1) of the Boulder Municipal Code. San Francisco has a similar unbundling requirement.

43. Section 14.60.080(B)(1)(c) of the Bellevue City Code requires "identification of parking cost as a separate line item in such leases [between building owners and tenants] and a minimum rate for monthly long-term parking, not less than the cost of a current Metro two-zone pass."

44. Article 25.065 of the Grants Pass Development Code.

45. Amory Lovins (1976) used the terms *hard* and *soft* to describe two future paths for energy production. The hard path relies on building more coal and nuclear power plants to increase the supply of electricity, while the soft path relies on making more efficient use of electricity produced from renewable sources.

REFERENCES

Abrahams, Marc. 2000. "Nobel Thoughts—Horst Störmer." *Annals of Improbable Research (AIR)* 6, no. 2 (March/April).

Adams, Gerald. 2003. What Makes Alan Jacobs Work?" *Planning* 69, no. 11 (December): 22-27.

Adiv, Aaron, and Wenzhi Wang. 1987. "On-Street Parking Meter Behavior." *Transportation Quarterly* 41, no. 3 (July): 281-307.

Adler, Moshe. 1985. "Street Parking: the Case for Communal Property." *Logistics and Transportation Review* 21, no. 4: 375-387.

Alchian, Armen, and Harold Demsetz. 1973. "The Property Right Paradigm." *Journal of Economic History* 33, no. 1: 16-27.

Albanese, Brett, and Glenn Matlack. 1998. "Environmental Auditing: Utilization of Parking Lots in Hattiesburg, Mississippi, USA, and Impacts on Local Streams." *Environmental Management* 24, no. 2: 265-271.

Alexander, Christopher, Sara Ishikawa, and Murray Silverstein. 1977. *A Pattern Language.* New York: Oxford University Press.

Allmendinger, Philip, Alan Prior, and Jeremy Raemaekers, eds. 2000. *Introduction to Planning Practice.* New York: Wiley.

Al-Masaeid, Hashem, Bashar Al-Omari, and Ahmad Al-Harahsheh. 1999. "Vehicle Parking Demand for Different Land Uses in Jordan." *ITE Journal* 69, no. 5 (May): 79-84.

Alonso, William. 1964. *Location and Land Use.* Cambridge, Mass.: Harvard University Press.

Altshuler, Alan, and José Gómez-Ibáñez. 1993. *Regulation for Revenue.* Washington, D.C.: Brookings Institution Press.

American Public Transit Association. 1997. *1997 Transit Fact Book.* Washington, D.C.: American Public Transit Association.

Amis, Kingsley. 1958. *Lucky Jim.* New York: Viking Press.

Andelson, Robert. 1979. "Neo-Georgism." In *Critics of Henry George,* edited by Robert Andelson. London: Associated University Presses, pp. 381-393.

Andelson, Robert, and Mason Gaffney. 1979. "Seligman and His Critique from Social Utility." In *Critics of Henry George,* edited by Robert Andelson. London: Associated University Presses, pp. 273-290.

Anderson, Larz. 1995. *Guidelines for Preparing Urban Plans.* Chicago: Planners Press.

Andrews, James. 2000. "Don't Park Here." *Planning* 66, no. 10 (October): 20-23.

Apogee Research. 1994. *The Costs of Transportation: Final Report.* Boston: Conservation Law Foundation.

Arnott, Richard, Andre de Palma, and Robin Lindsey. 1991. "A Temporal and Spatial Equilibrium Analysis of Commuter Parking." *Journal of Public Economics* 45: 301-335.

Arnott, Richard, T. Rave, and Ronnie Schöb. Forthcoming. "Some Downtown Parking Arithmetic." In *Alleviating Urban Traffic Congestion.* Cambridge, Mass.: MIT Press.

Arnott, Richard, and John Rowse. 1999. "Modeling Parking." *Journal of Urban Economics* 45: 97-124.

Arnott, Richard, and Joseph Stiglitz. 1979. "Aggregate Land Rents, Expenditure on Public Goods, and Optimal City Size." *Quarterly Journal of Economics* 93, no. 4 (November): 471-500.

Arroyo Group. 1978. *A Plan for Old Pasadena.* Pasadena, Calif.: City of Pasadena.

Austin, Terence. 1973. "Allocation of Parking Demand in a CBD." *Highway Research Record* no. 444: 1-8.

Axhausen, Kay, and John Polak. 1991. "Choice of Parking: Stated Preference Approach." *Transportation* 18, no. 1: 59-81.

Babcock, Richard. 1966. *The Zoning Game.* Madison, Wisc.: University of Wisconsin Press.

Babcock, Richard, and Charles Siemon. 1985. *The Zoning Game Revisited.* Boston: Oelgeschlager, Gunn & Hain.

Bacon, Robert. 1993. "A Model of Travelling to Shop with Congestion Costs." *Journal of Transport Economics and Policy* 27, no. 3 (September): 277-289.

Baker, Laurence. 1987. "Company Cars: Their Effects on Journey to Work in Central London." *Traffic Engineering and Control* 28, no. 10 (October): 530-536.

Balchin, Paul, David Isaac, and Jean Chen. 2000. *Urban Economics*. New York: Palgrave.

Banham, Reyner, Paul Barker, Peter Hall, and Cedric Price. 1969. "Non-Plan: An Experiment in Freedom." New Society, March, pp. 435-433. Reprinted in Jonathan Hughes and Simon Sadler eds. 2000. *Non-Plan: Essays on Freedom, Participation and Change in Modern Architecture and Urbanism*, Oxford: Architectural Press.

Barnett, Jonathan. 2003. *Redesigning Cities: Principles, Practice, Implementation*. Chicago: Planners Press.

Barrett, Paul. 1983. *The Automobile and Urban Transit*. Philadelphia: Temple University Press.

Barry, Keith. 2010. "City Parking Smartens Up with Streetline." *Wired*, November 29.

Barter, Paul. 2010. "Parking Policy in Asian Cities." Asian Development Bank, November. Available at www.reinventingparking.org/2010/11/parking-policy-in-asian-cities-report.html.

Barton Aschman Associates Inc. 1986. *Los Angeles Central Business District Employee Travel Baseline Survey, Final Report*. Los Angeles: Los Angeles Community Redevelopment Agency.

Bassett, Edward. 1926. "A New Kind of Garage." *City Planning* 2, no. 1: 64.

Basu, Pritwish, and Thomas Little. 2002. "Networked Parking Spaces: Architecture and Applications." *Proceedings of the 56th IEEE Vehicular Technology Conference*. Vol. 2. Piscataway, N.J.: IEEE Service Center, pp. 1153-1157.

Baum, Lyman Frank. 1903. *The Wizard of Oz*. Indianapolis: Bobbs-Merrill.

——. 1910. *The Emerald City of Oz*. Chicago: Reilly & Lee Co.

Bayliss, David. 1999. "Parking Policies and Traffic Restraint in London." In *Parking Policy*. Brussels: UITP Documentation Centre, pp. 27-31.

Becker, Gary. 1993. "Nobel Lecture: The Economic Way of Looking at Behavior." *The Journal of Political Economy* 101, no. 3: 385-409.

Beckmann, Martin. 1968. *Location Theory*. New York: Random House.

Beebe, Richard. 2000. "Automated Parking Structures." In *The Dimensions of Parking*. 4th ed. Washington, D.C.: Urban Land Institute, pp. 39-42.

Behdad, Hamid. 2006. "Adaptive Reuse Program." Los Angeles: Mayor's Office of Housing and Economic Development, City of Los Angeles, February. Available at www.ci.la.ca.us/LAHD/AROHandbook.pdf.

Berg, John. 2003. "Listening to the Public: Assessing Public Opinion about Value Pricing." Working Paper #1, Hubert H. Humphrey Institute of Public Affairs.

Berg, Phil. 2003. *Ultimate Garages*. St. Paul, Minn.: Motorbooks International.

Bertha, Brian. 1964. "Appendix A." In *The Low-Rise Speculative Apartment*, by Wallace Smith. Berkeley: Center for Real Estate and Urban Economics, Institute of Urban and Regional Development, University of California.

Bifulco, Gennaro. 1993. "A Stochastic User Equilibrium Assignment Model for the Evaluation of Parking Policies." *European Journal of Operational Research* 71, no. 2: 269-287.

Bird, Richard. 1991. "Tax Structure and the Growth of Government." In *Retrospectives on Public Finance*, edited by Lorraine Eden. Durham, N.C.: Duke University Press, pp. 263-275.

——. 1997. "User Charges: An Old Idea Revisited." In *Tax Conversations: A Guide to the Key Issues in the Tax Reform*

Debate, Essays in Honour of John G. Head, edited by Richard Krever. London: Kluwer Law International, pp. 513-546.

Birnie, Arthur. 1939. *Single-Tax George.* London: Thomas Nelson and Sons.

Bish, Robert, and Hugh Nourse. 1975. *Urban Economics and Policy Analysis.* New York: McGraw-Hill.

Black, Ian, Kevin Cullinane, and Chris Wright. 1993. "Parking Enforcement Policy Assessment Using an Economic Approach, Part 1: Theoretical Background and the Development of an Economic Model." *Transportation Planning and Technology* 17: 249-257.

Blake, John. 1999. "Car Parking Bombshell." *Town and Country Planning* 68, no. 2 (February): 46-47.

Blaug, Mark, ed. 1992. *Henry George (1839–1897).* London: Edward Elgar.

Boarnet, Marlon, and Randall Crane. 2001. *Travel by Design: The Influence of Urban Form on Travel.* New York: Oxford University Press.

Bolton, Roger. 1985. "Three Mysteries about Henry George." In *Henry George and Contemporary Economic Development,* edited by Stephen Lewis. Williamstown, Mass.: Williams College, pp. 7-24.

Boorstin, Daniel. 1962. *The Image; or What Happened to the American Dream.* New York: Atheneum.

Boston Transportation Department. 2001. *Parking in Boston.* [Accessed October 28, 2004]. Available at www.cityofboston.gov/accessBoston/pdfs/parking.pdf.

Bottles, Scott. 1987. *Los Angeles and the Automobile.* Berkeley: University of California Press.

Box, Paul. 1970. "The Curb Parking Effect." *Traffic Digest & Review,* pp. 6-10.

Bradley, John. 1996. "Toward a Common Parking Policy: A Cross-Jurisdictional Matrix Comparison of Municipal Off-Street Parking Regulations in Metropolitan Dade County, Florida." *Transportation Research Record* 1564: 40-45.

Branch, Melville. 1985. *Comprehensive City Planning: Introduction and Explanation.* Chicago: Planners Press.

Brett, Simon. 1985. "Parking Space." In *A Box of Tricks.* London: Victor Gollancz Ltd.

Brierly, John. 1972. *Parking of Motor Vehicles.* 2nd ed. London: Applied Science Publishers.

Brilliant, Ashleigh. 1989. *The Great Car Craze.* Santa Barbara, Calif.: Woodbridge Press.

Brinkley, David. 1988. *Washington Goes to War.* New York: Alfred A. Knopf.

Brinkman, Lester. 1948. "Offstreet Parking." *Journal of the American Institute of Planners* 14, no. 4 (Fall): 26-27.

Brooks, David. 2002. "Patio Man and the Sprawl People." *The Weekly Standard* 007, no. 46: 19-29.

Brooks, Michael. 2002. *Planning Theory for Practitioners.* Chicago: Planners Press.

Brown, George, Richard McKellar, and Heidi Lansdell. 2004. "A Regional Parking Strategy for Perth." Paper presented at the World Parking Symposium, Toronto, Canada, May.

Brown, Jeffrey, Daniel Hess, and Donald Shoup. 2001. "Unlimited Access." *Transportation* 28, no. 3 (August): 233-267.

——. 2003. "Fare-Free Public Transit at Universities: An Evaluation." *Journal of Planning Education and Research* 23, no. 1 (fall): 69-82.

Brown, Leon. 1937. "Effective Control by Parking Meters." *American City,* August, 53-54.

Brown, S. A., and Thomas A. Lambe. 1972. "Parking Prices in the Central Business District." *Socio-Economic Planning Sciences* 6: 133-144.

Bruun, Eric, and Vukan Vuchic. 1995. "Time-Area Concept: Development, Meaning, and Applications." *Transportation Research Record* 1499: 95-104.

Bryson, John, and Robert Einsweiler. 1988. *Strategic Planning: Threats and Opportunities for Planners.* Chicago: Planners Press.

Buckley, Drummond. 1992. "A Garage in the House." In *The Car and the City*, edited by Martin Wachs and Margaret Crawford. Ann Arbor, Mich.: The University of Michigan Press, pp. 124-140.

Buel, Ronald. 1973. *Dead End*. Baltimore, Md.: Penguin Books.

Bunnell, Gene. 2002. *Making Places Special, Stories of Real Places Made Better by Planning*. Chicago: Planners Press.

Buttke, Carl, and Eugene Arnold. 2003. "Discussion." *Journal Transportation and Statistics* 6, no. 1: 13-14.

Button, Kenneth. 1977. *The Economics of Urban Transport*. Westmead, England: Saxon House.

Caldwell, Bruce. 1997. "Hayek and Socialism." *Journal of Economic Literature* 35. no. 4 (December): 1856-1890.

California Department of Transportation. 2002. *Statewide Transit-Oriented Development (TOD) Study, Parking and TOD: Challenges and Opportunities*. Sacramento: California Air Resources Board.

California Governor's Office of Planning and Research. 1997. *A Planner's Guide to Financing Public Improvements*. [Accessed October 28, 2004]. Available at http://ceres.ca.gov/planning/financing/index.html#contents_anchor.

Calthorpe, Peter. 1993. *The Next American Metropolis*. New York: Princeton Architectural Press.

Calthrop, Edward, and Steff Proost. 2003. "Environmental Pricing in Transport." In *Handbook of Transport and the Environment*, edited by David Hensher and Kenneth Button. Amsterdam: Elsevier.

Calthrop, Edward, Steff Proost, and Kurt Van Dender. 2000. "Parking Policies and Road Pricing." *Urban Studies* 37, no. 1: 63-76.

Cameron, Michael. 1991. *Transportation Efficiency: Tackling Southern California's Air Pollution and Congestion*. Los Angeles: Environmental Defense Fund.

_____. 1994. *Efficiency and Fairness on the Road*. Oakland, Calif.: Environmental Defense Fund.

Campoli, Julie, Elizabeth Humstone, and Alex MacLean. 2002. *Above and Beyond*. Chicago: Planners Press.

Casella, Sam. 1985. *Tax Increment Financing*. Planning Advisory Service Report No. 389. Chicago: American Planning Association.

Cassady, C. Richard, and John Kobza. 1998. "A Probabilistic Approach to Evaluate Strategies for Selecting a Parking Space." *Transportation Science* 32, no. 1 (February): 30-42.

Cassidy, John. 2000. "The Price Prophet." *The New Yorker*, February 7, 44-51.

Castells, Manuel. 1983. *The City and the Grassroots*. Berkeley: University of California Press.

Catanese, Anthony, and Alan Steiss. 1970. *Systematic Planning: Theory and Application*. Lexington, Mass.: Heath Lexington Books.

Centre for Science and Environment. 2009. "Choc-A-Block: Parking Measures to Address Mobility Crisis." New Delhi: Centre for Science and Environment. Available at www.cseindia.org/node/100.

Cervero, Robert. 1988. "America's Suburban Centers: A Study of the Land Use-Transportation Link." Report No. DOT-T-88-14, U. S. Department of Transportation.

_____. 1996. "Paradigm Shift: From Automobility to Accessibility Planning." Working Paper 677, Institute of Urban and Regional Development, University of California, Berkeley.

_____. 1998. *The Transit Metropolis*. Washington, D.C.: Island Press.

Cervero, Robert, and Yu-Hsin Tsai. 2003. "San Francisco's City CarShare: Travel-Demand Trends and Second-Year Impacts." Working Paper 2003-5, Institute of Urban and Regional Development, University of California, Berkeley.

Chapin, F. Stuart. 1957. *Urban Land Use Planning*. New York: Harper & Brothers.

_____. 1965. *Urban Land Use Planning*. 2nd ed. Urbana: University of Illinois Press.

Chapin, F. Stuart, and Edward Kaiser. 1979. *Urban Land Use Planning*, 3rd ed. Urbana: University of Illinois Press.

Cheshire, Paul, and Edwin Mills, eds. 1999. *Handbook of Regional and Urban Economics*, Vol. 3, Applied Urban Economics. Amsterdam: North-Holland.

Chicago Regional Transportation Authority. 1998. *Opportunity Costs of Municipal Parking Requirements*, Prepared by Fish & Associates, K.T. Analytics, and Vlecides-Schroeder Associates, Final Report, April.

Churchill, Anthony. 1972. *Road User Charges in Central America*. Baltimore, Md.: The Johns Hopkins University Press.

Ciriacy-Wantrup, Siegfried. 1952. *Resource Conservation: Economics and Policies*. Berkeley: University of California Press.

City of Chicago, Office of the Inspector General. 2009. "Report of the Inspector General's Findings and Recommendations: An Analysis of the Lease of the City's Parking Meters." Chicago: Office of the Inspector General, June 2. Available at www.chicagoinspector general.org/pdf/IGO-CMPS-20090602.pdf.

Clark, Peter. 1993a. *An Assessment of the Likely Impact of Changes in Short Term Metered Parking Prices on Parkers in the Central City Area*. TP 608. Cape Town, South Africa: Town Planning Branch, Cape Town City Council.

_____. 1993b. *Policies to Manage Parking in the Central City Area*. TP 608/PC. Cape Town, South Africa: Cape Town City Planning Department.

Clinch, J. Peter, and J. Andrew Kelly. 2004a. "The Influence of Parking Pricing on the Profile of On-Street Parkers," presented at the Annual Meeting of the Transportation Research Board, January 2004, and forthcoming in the *Transportation Research Record*.

_____. 2004b. "Testing the Sensitivity of Parking Behaviour and Modal Choice to the Price of On-Street Parking," presented at the Annual Meeting of the Transportation Research Board, January 2004, and forthcoming in the *Transportation Research Record*.

_____. 2004c. "Temporal Variance of Revealed Preference On-Street Parking Price Elasticity." Working Paper 04/2 , Environmental Studies Research Series (ESRS), Department of Environmental Studies, University College Dublin.

Colliers International. 2003. "North America CBD Parking Rate Survey." *The Parking Professional*, September, 27–31.

Collins, Michael, and Timothy Pharoah. 1974. *Transport Organisation in a Great City, the Case of London*. London: George Allen & Unwin Ltd.

Cook, John, Roderick Diaz, Lee Klieman, Timothy Rood, and John Wu. 1997. "Parking Policies in Bay Area Jurisdictions: A Survey of Parking Requirements, their Methodological Origins, and an Exploration of their Land Use Impacts." Research Paper for *City Planning* 217, Spring 1997, University of California, Berkeley.

Coombe, Denvil, Peter Guest, John Bates, Paul Masurier, and Colin Maclennan. 1997. "Study of Parking and Traffic Demand, 1: The Research Programme." *Traffic Engineering and Control* 38, no. 2 (February): 62-67.

Cord, Steven. 1965. *Henry George: Dreamer or Realist?* Philadelphia: University of Pennsylvania Press.

Crawford, Clan. 1969. *Strategy and Tactics in Municipal Zoning*. Englewood Cliffs, N.J.: Prentice Hall.

Creighton, Roger. 1970. *Urban Transportation Planning*. Urbana: University of Illinois Press.

Cullinane, Kevin. 1993. "An Aggregate Dynamic Model of the Parking Compliance Decision." *International Journal of Transport Economics* 20, no. 1(February): 28-50.

Cullingworth, Barry, and Vincent Nadin. 2002. *Town and Country Planning in the UK*. 13th ed. London: Routledge.

Curtler, William. 1920. *The Enclosure and Redistribution of Our Land.* Oxford: Clarendon Press.

Cutter, Bowman, Sofia Franco, and Autumn DeWoody. 2010. "Do Minimum Parking Requirements Force Developers to Provide More Parking Than Privately Optimal?" Working Paper, Pomona College Department of Economics, August.

Dagan, Hanoch, and Michael Heller. 2001. "The Liberal Commons." *Yale Law Journal* 110, no. 4 (January): 549-623.

Dahlman, Carl. 1980. *The Open Field System and Beyond: A Property Rights Analysis of an Economic Institution.* Cambridge: Cambridge University Press.

Dales, J. H. 1968. *Pollution, Property, and Prices.* Toronto: University of Toronto Press.

Daniels, Thomas, John Keller, and Mark Lapping. 1995. *The Small Town Planning Handbook.* 2nd ed. Chicago: Planners Press.

Dardia, Michael.1998. *Subsidizing Redevelopment in California.* [Accessed October 28, 2004]. Available at www.ppic.org/content/pubs/R_298MDR.pdf.

Dash, Gordon. 2011. "Enhancing Parking for the Disabled in Raleigh, NC." *The Parking Professional* 27, no. 1: 26-28.

Davis, Audrey, and Toby Appel. 1979. *Bloodletting Instruments in the National Museum of History and Technology.* Washington, D.C.: Smithsonian Institution Press.

Davis, Stacy, and Susan Diegel. 2002. *Transportation Energy Data Book: Edition 22.* Oak Ridge, Tenn.: Oak Ridge National Laboratory.

Day, Alan, and Ralph Turvey. 1954. "The Parking Problem in Central London: An Economic Appraisal." *Journal of the Institute of Transport* 25, no. 11 (July): 406-411.

Deakin, Elizabeth, and Greig Harvey. 1996. *Transportation Pricing Strategies for California: An Assessment of Congestion, Emission, Energy, and Equity Impacts.* Sacramento: California Air Resources Board.

De Alessi, Louis. 1983. "Property Rights, Transaction Costs, and X-Efficiency: An Essay in Economic Theory." *American Economic Review* 73, no. 1 (March): 64-81.

de Cerreño, Allison. 2002. "The Dynamics of On-Street Parking in Large Central Cities." New York: Rudin Center for Transportation Policy and Management, New York University, December.

DeCorla-Souza, Patrick, and Anthony Kane. 1992. "Peak Period Tolls: Precepts and Prospects." *Transportation* 19: 293-311.

Deering, Stephen, Tom Doan, Matthew Fleming, Margaret Hill, Scott Jacobs, and Lauren Larson. 1998. *Ann Arbor Parking Study.* [Accessed October 28, 2004]. Available at www.fordschool.umich.edu/academics/pdf/aps5.pdf.

de Jong, Gerald. 1997. "A Microeconomic Model of the Joint Decision on Car Ownership and Car Use." In *Understanding Travel Behaviour in an Era of Change,* edited by Peter Stopher and Martin Lee-Gosselin. Oxford: Pergamon, pp. 483-503.

Delucchi, Mark. 1997. "The Annualized Social Cost of Motor-Vehicle Use in the U.S., 1990-1991: Summary of Theory, Data, Methods, and Results." UCD-ITS-RR-96-3 (1), Institute of Transportation Studies, University of California, Davis, June.

Delucchi, Mark, and James Murphy. 1998. "Motor-Vehicle Goods and Services Bundled in the Private Sector." UCD-ITS-RR-96-3 (6), Institute of Transportation Studies, University of California, Davis, December.

Demsetz, Harold. 1964. "The Exchange and Enforcement of Property Rights." *Journal of Law and Economics* 7 (October): 11-26.

_____. 1967. "Toward a Theory of Property Rights." *American Economic Review* 57, no. 2 (May): 347-359.

Denman, Donald, and Sylvio Prodano. 1972. *Land Use*. London: George Allen & Unwin Ltd.

Dewberry, Sidney, and Phillip Champagne. 2002. *Land Development Handbook: Planning, Engineering, and Surveying*. 2nd ed. New York: McGraw Hill.

DeWitt, John, Sacha Peterson, Barb Thoman, and David Van Hattum. 2003. *The Myth of Free Parking*. St. Paul, Minn.: Transit for Livable Communities.

Dickey, J. 1983. *Metropolitan Transportation Planning*. 2nd ed. New York: McGraw-Hill Book Company.

Dickerson, Marla. 2004. "Mexico's Economy Is Vrooming." *Los Angeles Times*, December 26.

Dickson, Thomas. 1765. *A Treatise on Bloodletting with an Introduction Recommending a Review on the Materia Medica*. London.

DiPasquale, Denise, and William Wheaton. 1996. *Urban Economics and Real Estate Markets*. Englewood Cliffs, N.J.: Prentice Hall.

Dirickx, Yvo, and L. Peter Jennergren. 1975. "An Analysis of the Parking Situation in the Downtown Area of West Berlin." *Transportation Research* 9: 1-11.

District Department of Transportation. 2009. "Ward 6 Ballpark District Performance Based Parking, December 2009 Report." Washington, D.C.: District Department of Transportation.

Donahue, John. 1997. "Tiebout? Or Not Tiebout? The Market Metaphor and America's Devolution Debate." *Journal of Economic Perspectives* 11, no. 4 (fall): 73-81.

Dorsett, John. 1998. "The Price Tag of Parking." *Urban Land*, May.

Dougherty, Conor. 2007. "The Parking Fix." *Wall Street Journal*, February 3.

Downs, Anthony. 1992. *Stuck in Traffic*. Washington, D.C.: The Brookings Institution and the Lincoln Institute of Land Policy.

Drake, Leonard. 1946. "Traffic Moves in Central Philadelphia." *American City* 61, no. 3 (March): 111-112.

Drèze, Jacques. 1995. "Forty Years of Public Economics: A Personal Perspective." *Journal of Economic Perspectives* 9, no. 2 (spring): 111-130.

Dreyfuss, John. 1982. "Spring Street: On the Road to Respectability." *Los Angeles Times*, May 14.

Duany, Andres, Elizabeth Plater-Zyberk, and Jeff Speck. 2000. *Suburban Nation*. New York: North Point Press.

Dueker, Kenneth, James Strathman, and Martha Bianco. 1998. *Strategies to Attract Auto Users to Public Transportation*. [Accessed on October 28, 2004]. Available at http://gulliver.trb.org/publications/tcrp/tcrp_rpt_40.pdf.

Dunn, James. 1998. *Driving Forces: The Automobile, Its Enemies, and the Politics of Mobility*. Washington, D.C.: Brookings Institution Press.

Dunphy, Robert. 2000. "Parking Strategies." *Urban Land*, October.

———. 2003. "Big Foot." *Urban Land*, February.

Dunphy, Robert, Deborah Myerson, and Michael Pawlukiewicz. 2003. *Ten Principles for Successful Development around Transit*. Washington, D.C.: Urban Land Institute.

Eckert, Ross. 1979. *The Enclosure of Ocean Resources*. Stanford, Calif.: Hoover Institution Press.

El-Fadel, Mutasem, and Hayssam Sbayti. 2001. "Parking Facilities in Urban Areas: Air and Noise Impacts." *Journal of Urban Planning and Development* 127, no. 1 (March): 16-33.

Ellerman, A. Denny, Paul Joskow, Richard Schmalensee, Juan-Pablo Montero, and Elizabeth Bailey. 2000. *Markets for Clean Air: The U.S. Acid Rain Program*. Cambridge: Cambridge University Press.

Ellickson, Bryan. 1973. "A Generalization of the Pure Theory of Public Goods." *American Economic Review* 63, no. 3 (June): 417-432.

Ellickson, Robert. 1998. "New Institutions for Old Neighborhoods." *Duke Law Journal* 48, no. 1 (October): 75-110.

Elliott, J. R., and C. C. Wright. 1982. "The Collapse of Parking Enforcement in Large Towns: Some Causes and Solutions." *Traffic Engineering and Control*, June, 304-310.

Emerson, M. Jarvin. 1975. *Urban and Regional Economics*. Boston: Allyn and Bacon.

Eno Foundation. 1942. *The Parking Problem*. Saugatuck, Conn.: The Eno Foundation for Highway Traffic Control.

Epstein, Richard. 2001. "The Allocation of the Commons: Parking and Stopping on the Commons." [Accessed on October 28, 2004]. Available at www.law.uchicago.edu/faculty/epstein/resources/parking.pdf.

Evans, Alan. 1985. *Urban Economics*. Oxford: Basil Blackwell.

Fabian, Lawrence. 2003. "Making Cars Pay: Singapore's State-of-the-Art Congestion Management." *Transportation Planning* 33, no. 1 (winter): 1-10.

Fabos, Julius. 1985. *Land-Use Planning*. New York: Chapman and Hall.

Falcocchio, John, Jose Darsin, and Elena Prassas. 1995. "An Inquiry on the Traffic Congestion Impacts of Parking and Pricing Policies in the Manhattan CBD." New York City Department of Transportation Division of Parking, University Transportation Research Center, Region II, Polytechnic University of New York Transportation Training and Research Center. February.

Fan, Henry, and Soi Hoi Lam. 1997. "Parking Generation of Commercial Developments in Singapore." *Journal of Transportation Engineering* 123, no. 3 (May/June): 238-242.

Fang, Hanming, and Peter Norman. 2003. "To Bundle or Not To Bundle." Discussion Paper No. 1440, Cowles Foundation for Research in Economics at Yale University.

Feitelson, Eran, and Orit Rotem. 2004. "The Case for Taxing Surface Parking" *Transportation Research Part D: Transport and the Environment* 9, no. 4 (July): 319-333.

Ferling, John. 1988. *The First of Men, A Life of George Washington*. Knoxville, Tenn.: University of Tennessee Press.

Fielding, Gordon, and Daniel Klein. 1997. "Hot Lanes: Introducing Congestion Pricing One Lane at a Time." *Access* no. 11: 11-15.

Fischel, William. 1985. *The Economics of Zoning Laws*. Baltimore, Md.: The Johns Hopkins University Press.

_____. 2001a. *The Homevoter Hypothesis*. Cambridge, Mass.: Harvard University Press.

_____. 2001b. "Municipal Corporations, Homeowners and the Benefit View of the Property Tax." In *Property Taxation and Local Government Finance*, edited by Wallace Oates. Cambridge, Mass.: Lincoln Institute of Land Policy, pp. 33-77.

Fischer, LeRoy. 1970. "Gerald A. Hale: Parking Meter Reminiscences." *The Chronicles of Oklahoma* 48, no. 3 (autumn): 341-352.

Fischer, LeRoy, and Robert Smith. 1969. "Oklahoma and the Parking Meter." *The Chronicles of Oklahoma* 47, no. 2 (summer): 168-208.

Flink, James. 1970. *America Adopts the Automobile, 1895-1910*. Cambridge, Mass.: MIT Press.

_____. 1976. *The Car Culture*. Cambridge, Mass.: MIT Press.

_____. 1988. *The Automobile Age*. Cambridge, Mass.: MIT Press.

Flyvbjerg, Bent, Mette Holm, and Søren Buhl. 2002. "Underestimating Costs in Public Works Projects, Error or Lie?" *Journal of the American Planning Association* 68, no. 3: 279-295.

Fogelson, Robert. 2001. *Downtown: Its Rise and Fall, 1880-1950*. New Haven, Conn.: Yale University Press.

Foldvary, Fred. 1994. *Public Goods and Private Communities*. Aldershot, UK: Edward Elgar.

Ford, Kristina. 1990. *Planning Small Town America*. Chicago: Planners Press.

Ford, Larry. 1994. *Cities and Buildings*. Baltimore, Md.: The Johns Hopkins University Press.

_____. 2000. *The Spaces Between Buildings*. Baltimore, Md.: The Johns Hopkins University Press.

_____. 2003. *America's New Downtowns: Revitalization or Reinvention?*" Baltimore, Md.: The Johns Hopkins University Press.

Forinash, Christopher, Adam Millard-Ball, Charlotte Dougherty, and Jeffrey Tumlin. 2004. "Smart Growth Alternatives to Minimum Parking Requirements." Paper presented at the annual meeting of the Transportation Research Board, Washington, D.C., January.

Frech, H. E., and William Lee. 1987. "The Welfare Cost of Rationing-by-Queuing across Markets: Theory and Estimates from the U.S. Gasoline Crises." *Quarterly Journal of Economics* 102, no. 1: 97-108.

Frenchman, Dennis. 2000. "Planning Shapes Urban Growth and Development." In *The Profession of City Planning: Changes, Images and Challenges, 1950-2000*, edited by Lloyd Rodwin and Bishwapriya Sanyal. New Brunswick, N.J.: Center for Urban Policy Research, Rutgers, pp. 27-30.

Fujita, Masahisa. 1989. *Urban Economic Theory*. Cambridge: Cambridge University Press.

Fujita, Masahisa, Paul Krugman, and Anthony Venables. 1999. *The Spatial Economy*. Cambridge, Mass.: MIT Press.

Fulton, Arthur, and David Weimer. 1980. "Regaining a Lost Policy Option: Neighborhood Parking Stickers in San Francisco." *Policy Analysis* 6, no. 3 (summer): 335-348.

Fulton, William. 1999. *Guide to California Planning*. 2nd ed. Point Arena, Calif.: Solano Press Books.

_____. 2001. *The Reluctant Metropolis*. Baltimore, Md.: Johns Hopkins Press.

Galbraith, John Kenneth. 1958. *The Affluent Society*. Boston: Houghton Mifflin.

Garreau, Joel. 1991. *Edge City*. New York: Anchor Books.

Gause, Donald, and Gerald Weinberg. 1989. *Exploring Requirements: Quality before Design*. New York: Dorset House.

Gebhard, David. 1992. "The Suburban House and the Automobile." In *The Car and the City*, edited by Martin Wachs and Margaret Crawford. Ann Arbor: University of Michigan Press, pp. 106-123.

George, Henry. 1879 [1938]. *Progress and Poverty, an Inquiry into the Cause of Industrial Depressions and of Increase of Want with Increase of Wealth; the Remedy*. New York: Modern Library.

_____. 1898. *The Science of Political Economy*. Reprinted in *The Legacy and Works of Henry George*. 2002. Cambridge, Mass.: Lincoln Institute of Land Policy.

Gillen, David, 1977a. "Estimation and Specification of the Effects of Parking Costs on Urban Transport Mode Choice." *Journal of Urban Economics* 4, no. 2 (April): 186-199.

_____. 1977b. "Alternative Policy Variables to Influence Urban Transport Demand." *Canadian Journal of Economics* 10, no. 4 (November): 686-695.

_____. 1978. "Parking Policy, Parking Location Decisions and the Distribution of Congestion." *Transportation* 7, no. 1: 69-85.

Gingerich, Owen. 1993. *The Eye of Heaven: Ptolemy, Copernicus, Kepler*. New York: American Institute Press.

Giuliano, Genevieve. 1992. "An Assessment of the Political Acceptability of Congestion Pricing." *Transportation* 19, no. 4: 335-358.

Glaeser, Edward, and Joseph Gyourko. 2003. "The Impact of Building Restrictions on Housing Affordability." *Economic Policy Review* 9, no. 2 (June): 21-39.

Glaeser, Edward, and Erzo Luttmer. 2003. "The Misallocation of Housing under

Rent Control." *American Economic Review* 93, no. 4 (September): 1027-1046.

Glassborow, D. H. 1961. "Parking Charges and Parking Meters." *Westminster Bank Review*, November, 26-34.

Glazer, Amihai, and Esko Niskanen. 1992. "Parking Fees and Congestion." *Regional Science and Urban Economics* 22: 123-132.

Gómez-Ibáñez, José, and Gary Fauth. 1980. "Downtown Auto Restraint Policies." *Journal of Transport Economics and Policy* 14, no. 2 (May): 133-153.

Gómez-Ibáñez, José, William Tye, and Clifford Winston. 1999. *Essays in Transportation Economics and Policy, a Handbook in Honor of John R. Meyer*. Washington, D.C.: Brookings Institution Press.

Goodman, Nathan G., ed. 1945. *A Benjamin Franklin Reader*. New York: Thomas Y. Cromwell Company.

Goodwin, Philip. 1989. "The Rule of Three: A Possible Solution to the Political Problem of Competing Objectives for Road Pricing." *Traffic Engineering and Control* 30: 495-497.

_____. 1995. "Road Pricing or Transportation Pricing." In *Road Pricing: Theory, Empirical Assessment and Policy*, edited by Börje Johansson and Lars-Göran Mattsson. Boston: Kluwer Academic Publishers.

_____. 1997. "Solving Congestion: Inaugural Lecture for the Professorship of Transport Policy, University College London." [Accessed October 28, 2004]. Available at www.cts.ucl.ac.uk/tsu/pbginau.htm.

_____. 2001. "Traffic Reduction." In *Handbook of Transport Systems and Traffic Control*, edited by Kenneth Button and David Hensher. Amsterdam: Pergamon, pp. 21-32.

Gordon, H. Scott. 1954. "The Economic Theory of a Common-Property Resource: the Fishery." *Journal of Political Economy* 62, no.2 (April): 124-142.

Gordon, Peter, and Harry Richardson. 2001. "Transportation and Land Use." In *Smarter Growth: Market-Based Strategies for Land Use Planning in the 21st Century*, edited by Randall Holcombe and Sam Staley. Westport, Conn.: Greenwood Press.

Gordon, Tracy. 2004. *Planned Developments in California: Private Communities and Public Life*. San Francisco: Public Policy Institute of California.

Goulard, Thomas. 1784. *A Treatise on the Effects and Various Preparations of Lead: Particularly of the Extract of Saturn, for Different Chirurgical Disorders*. London: Elmsley in the Strand.

Gould, Carol. 2003. "Parking: When Less is More." *Transportation Planning* 27, no. 1 (winter): 3-11.

Government Institute for Economic Research (Finland). 2001. *Acceptability of Fiscal and Financial Measures and Organisational Requirements for Demand Management* (AFFORD). [Accessed October 28, 2004]. Available at http://data.vatt.fi/afford/reports/final-report2.pdf.

Gratz, Roberta, and Norman Mintz. 1998. *Cities Back from the Edge: New Life for Downtown*. New York: John Wiley & Sons.

Groth, Paul. 1990. "Parking Gardens." In *The Meaning of Gardens*, edited by Mark Francis and Randolph Hester. Cambridge, Mass.: MIT Press, pp. 130-137.

Groves, Martha. 2010. "L.A. Program Aims to Make Parking Easier." *Los Angeles Times*, August 22.

Gruen Associates. 1986. *Employment and Parking in Suburban Business Parks: A Pilot Study*. Washington, D.C.: Urban Land Institute.

Gruen, Victor. 1973. *Centers for the Urban Environment: Survival of the Cities*. New York: Van Nostrand Reinhold Co.

Gur, Yehuda, and Edward Beimborn. 1984. *Transportation Research Record* 957: 55-62.

Gutfreund, Owen. 2004. *Twentieth-Century Sprawl: Highways and the Reshaping of the American Landscape*. New York: Oxford University Press.

Haar, Charles. 1989. "Reflections on Euclid: Social Contract and Private Purpose."

In *Zoning and the American Dream*, edited by Charles Haar and Jerold Kayden. Chicago: American Planning Association, pp. 333-354.

Haar, Charles, and Jerold Kayden, eds. 1989. *Zoning and the American Dream*. Chicago: Planners Press.

Hall, Peter. 1982. *Great Planning Disasters*. Berkeley and Los Angeles: University of California Press.

_____. 2002. *Urban and Regional Planning*. London: Routledge.

Halperin, Lawrence. 1963. *Cities*. New York: Reinhold Publishing Corporation.

Hamond, M. Jeff, Stephen DeCanio, Peggy Duxbury, Alan Sanstad, and Christopher Stinson. 1997. *Tax Waste, Not Work: How Changing What We Tax Can Lead to a Stronger Economy and a Cleaner Environment*. Oakland, Calif.: Redefining Progress.

Hardin, Garrett. 1977. "The Tragedy of the Commons." In *Managing the Commons*, edited by Garrett Hardin and John Baden. San Francisco: W. H. Freeman and Company, pp. 16-30. First published in *Science* in 1968.

_____. 1991. "The Tragedy of the *Unmanaged* Commons." In *Commons without Tragedy*, edited by Robert Andelson. London: Shepheard-Walwyn, pp. 165-182.

Hardwick, M. Jeffrey. 2004. *Mall Maker: Victor Gruen, Architect of an American Dream*. Philadelphia: University of Pennsylvania Press.

Harrington, Winston, Alan Krupnick, and Anna Alberini. 1998. "Overcoming Public Aversion to Congestion Pricing, Discussion Paper 98-27." [Accessed October 28, 2004]. Available at www.rff.org/Documents/RFF-DP-98-27.pdf.

Harriss, C. Lowell. 1972. "Property Taxation." In *Modern Fiscal Issues: Essays in Honor of Carl Shoup*, edited by Richard Bird and John Head. Toronto: University of Toronto Press, pp. 292-317.

Haskell, Douglas. 1937. "Architecture on Routes U. S. 40 and 66." *Architectural Record* 81, no. 5 (May): 15-22.

Haster, Amy, Donald Fisher, and John Collura. 2002. "Drivers' Parking Decisions: Advanced Parking Management Systems." *Journal of Transportation Engineering* 128, no. 1 (January/February): 49-57.

Haworth, Simon, and Ian Hilton. 1981. "Car Parking Standards in Development Control." *Traffic Engineering and Control* 23 (February): 86-88.

_____. 1982. "Parking Elasticity—a Tool for Policy Implementation?" *Traffic Engineering and Control* 23 (July/August): 365-369.

Hayek, Friedrich. 1974. "The Pretence of Knowledge." [Accessed October 28, 2004]. Available at http://nobelprize.org/economics/laureates/1974/hayek-lecture.html.

Heilbrun, James. 1987. *Urban Economics and Public Policy*. 3rd ed. New York: St. Martin's Press.

Heller, Michael. 1998. "The Tragedy of the Anticommons: Property in the Transition from Marx to Markets." *Harvard Law Review* 111, no. 3 (January): 621-688.

Henderson, J. Vernon. 1985. *Economic Theory and the Cities*. Orlando, Fla.: Academic Press.

Henderson, William, and Larry Ledebur. 1972. *Urban Economics*. New York: Wiley.

Hennessy-Fisk, Molly, and Tami Abdollah. 2007. "Shoppers Can Spend a Lot, Save a Little." *Los Angeles Times*, November 24.

Hensher, David. 2001. "Modal Diversion." In *Handbook of Transport Systems and Traffic Control*, edited by Kenneth Button and David Hensher. Amsterdam: Pergamon, pp. 107-123.

Hensher, David, and Jenny King. 2001. "Parking Demand and Responsiveness to Supply, Pricing and Location in the Sydney Central Business District." *Transportation Research Part A* 35: 177-196.

Henstell, Bruce. 1984. *Sunshine and Wealth.* San Francisco: Chronicle Books.

Hester, Amy, Donald Fisher, and John Collura. 2002. "Drivers' Parking Decisions: Advanced Parking Management Systems." *Journal of Transportation Engineering* 128, no. 1 (January/February): 49-57.

Higgins, Richard, William Shughart, and Robert Tollison. 1988. "Free Entry and Efficient Rent Seeking." In *The Political Economy of Rent-Seeking,* edited by Charles Rowley, Robert Tollison, and Gordon Tullock. Boston: Kluwer Academic Publishers.

Higgins, Thomas. 1985. "Flexible Parking Requirements for Office Developments: New Support for Public Parking and Ridesharing." *Transportation* 12: 343-359.

_____. 1993. "Parking Requirements for Transit-Oriented Developments." Paper presented at the annual meeting of the Transportation Research Board, Washington, D.C.

Highway Research Board. 1955. *Parking Requirements in Zoning Ordinances. Bulletin 99.* Washington, D.C.: Highway Research Board.

Hirsch, Werner. 1973. *Urban Economic Analysis.* New York: McGraw-Hill.

_____. 1984. *Urban Economics.* New York: Macmillan.

Hirschman, Albert. 1970. *Exit, Voice, and Loyalty: Responses to Decline in Firms, Organizations, and States.* Cambridge, Mass.: Harvard University Press.

Hoch, Charles, Linda Dalton, and Frank So, eds. 2000. *The Practice of Local Government Planning.* Washington, D.C.: International City/County Management Association.

Hogentogler, C. A., E. A. Willis, and J. A. Kelley. 1934. "Intangible Economics of Highway Transportation." In *Proceedings of the Thirteenth Annual Meeting of the Highway Research Board* (December 7-8, 1933). Washington, D.C.: Highway Research Board, pp. 189-205.

Holland, Daniel. 1970. *The Assessment of Land Value.* Madison, Wisc.: University of Wisconsin Press.

Hoover, Edgar. 1965. "Motor Metropolis: Some Observations on Urban Transportation in America." *Journal of Industrial Economics* 13, no. 3 (June): 177-192.

_____. 1975. *An Introduction to Regional Economics.* 2nd ed. New York: Alfred A. Knopf.

Hormann, Nancy, and M. Bradley Segal. 1998. "PBIDS: A Tool for Revitalizing Business Districts." *California Planner,* November/December, 3-7.

Houstoun, Lawrence. 1997. *BIDs: Business Improvement Districts.* Washington, D.C.: Urban Land Institute in cooperation with the International Downtown Association.

Howitt, Arnold. 1980. "Downtown Auto Restraint Policies: Adopting and Implementing Urban Transport Innovations." *Journal of Transport Economics and Policy* 14, no. 2: 155-167.

Hu, Patricia and Jennifer Young. 1999. *Summary of Travel Trends, 1995 Nationwide Personal Transportation Survey.* Report No. FHWA-PL-00-006. Washington, D.C.: United States Department of Transportation.

Huber, Matthew. 1962. "Street Travel as Related to Local Parking," In *Proceedings of the 41st Annual Meeting of the Highway Research Board.* Washington, D.C.: Highway Research Board, pp. 333-352.

Hultgren, Lee, and Kim Kawada. 1999. "San Diego's Interstate 15 High-Occupancy/Toll Lane Facility Using Value Pricing." *ITE Journal* 69, no. 6 (June): 22-27.

Institute of Transportation Engineers. 1985. *Parking Generation.* Washington, D.C.: Institute of Transportation Engineers.

_____. 1987a. *Parking Generation.* 2nd ed. Washington, D.C.: Institute of Transportation Engineers.

_____. 1987b. *Trip Generation.* 4th ed. Washington, D.C.: Institute of Transportation Engineers.

_____. 1991. *Trip Generation*. 5th ed. Washington, D.C.: Institute of Transportation Engineers.

_____. 1997. *Trip Generation*. 6th ed. Washington, D.C.: Institute of Transportation Engineers.

_____. 2000. *Residential Permit Parking Informational Report*. Washington, D.C.: Institute of Transportation Engineers.

_____. 2003. *Trip Generation*. 7th ed. Washington, D.C.: Institute of Transportation Engineers.

_____. 2004. *Parking Generation*. 3rd ed. Washington, D.C.: Institute of Transportation Engineers.

Inwood, J. 1966. *Some Effects of Increased Parking Meter Charges in London*. Harmondsworth, U.K.: Road Research Laboratory.

Isard, Walter. 1956. *Location and the Space-Economy*. Cambridge, Mass.: MIT Press.

_____. 1960. *Methods of Regional Analysis: an Introduction to Regional Science*. Cambridge, Mass.: MIT Press.

Isard, Walter, Iwan Azis, Matthew Drennan, Ronald Miller, Sidney Saltzman, and Erik Thorbecke. 1998. *Methods of Interregional and Regional Analysis*. Aldershot, U.K.: Ashgate.

Jackson, John. 1980. The *Necessity for Ruins*. Amherst, Mass.: University of Massachusetts Press.

Jacobs, Allan. 1993. *Great Streets*. Cambridge, Mass.: MIT Press.

Jacobs, Jane. 1961. *The Death and Life of Great American Cities*. New York: Random House.

_____. 1962. "Downtown Planning." Reprinted in *Ideas That Matter, the Worlds of Jane Jacobs*, edited by Max Allen. 1997. Owen Sound, Ontario: The Ginger Press, pp. 17-20.

_____. 1987. "Small Improvements." Reprinted in *Ideas That Matter, the Worlds of Jane Jacobs*, edited by Max Allen. 1997. Owen Sound, Ontario: The Ginger Press, p. 27.

James, P. D. 1972. *An Unsuitable Job for a Woman*. London: Faber and Faber.

Janis, Irving. 1982. *Groupthink: Psychological Studies of Policy Decisions and Fiascoes*. Boston: Houghton Mifflin.

Jia, Wenyu, and Martin Wachs. 1998. "Parking and Affordable Housing." *Access* no. 13 (fall): 22-25.

Johnson, Craig, and Joyce Man. 2001. *Tax Increment Financing and Economic Development: Uses, Structures, and Impacts*. Albany, N.Y.: State University of New York Press.

Jones, Bernie. 1990. *Neighborhood Planning: A Guide for Citizens and Planners*. Chicago: Planners Press.

Kadesh, Eileen, and Jay Peterson. 1994. "Parking Utilization at Work Sites in King and South Snohomish Counties, Washington." *Transportation Research Record* 1459: 58-62.

Kaiser, Edward, David Godschalk, and F. Stuart Chapin. 1995. *Urban Land Use Planning*. 4th ed. Urbana: University of Illinois Press.

Kaku Associates. 1994. "Assessment of Future Parking Demand for the Broxton Triangle Development in Westwood Village." Prepared for the City of Los Angeles Department of Transportation, February.

Kanafani, Adib, and Lawrence Lan. 1988. "Development of Pricing Strategies for Airport Parking—A Case Study at San Francisco Airport." *International Journal of Transport Economics* 15, no. 1 (February) 55-76.

Karban, Richard. 1982. "Increased Reproductive Success at High Densities and Predator Satiation for Periodical Cicadas." *Ecology* 63, no. 2: 321-328.

Katz, Arnold, and Shelby Herman. 1997. "Improved Estimates of Fixed Reproducible Tangible Wealth, 1929-1995." *Survey of Current Business*, May, 69-92.

Kay, Jane Holtz. 1997. *Asphalt Nation*. New York: Crown Publishers.

Keefer, Louis. 1963. "Trucks at Rest." *Highway Research Record Number 41*. Presented at the 42nd Annual Meeting of the

Highway Research Board, Washington, D.C., January 7-11.

Kelly, Ben. 1971. *The Pavers and the Paved*. New York: Donald W. Brown.

Kenworthy, Jeffrey, and Felix Laube. 1999. *An International Sourcebook of Automobile Dependence in Cities, 1960-1990*. Boulder: University Press of Colorado.

Khattak, Asad, and John Polak. 1993. "Effect of Parking Information on Travelers' Knowledge and Behavior." *Transportation* 20: 373-393.

Kimley-Horn and Associates. 2003. "Downtown Los Angeles Parking Study for Portions of the Historic Core and Adjacent Areas." Prepared for the Community Redevelopment Agency of the City of Los Angeles, September 19.

Kipling, Rudyard. 1909. *With the Night Mail, a Story of 2000AD*. New York: Doubleday, Page & Company.

Klayko, Branden. 2010. "New York Expands Pop-Up Café Program in 2011." *The Architect's Newspaper*, November 30.

Klein, Eric. 2010. "Parking Holiday Approved for Christmas Shopping." *Berkeleyside*, December 8.

Klose, Dietrich. 1965. *Parkhäuser und Tiefgaragen* [Multi-story and Underground Garages]. Stuttgart: Verlag Gerd Hartje.

Kneafsey, James. 1975. *Transportation Economic Analysis*. Lexington, Mass.: D. C. Heath.

Kodransky, Michael, and Gabrielle Hermann. 2011. "Europe's Parking U-Turn: From Accommodation to Regulation." New York: Institute for Transportation and Development Policy. Available at www.itdp.org/documents/European_Parking_U-Turn.pdf.

Kolozsvari, Douglas. 2002. "Parking: The Way to Revitalization, A Case Study on Innovative Parking Practices in Old Pasadena." Masters thesis, University of California, Los Angeles.

Kolozsvari, Douglas, and Donald Shoup. 2003."Turning Small Change into Big Changes." *Access* no. 23 (fall): 2-7.

Komanoff, Charles, and Michael Smith. 2000. "The Only Good Cyclist." [Accessed October 28, 2004]. Available at www.panix.com/%7Ejlefevre/cars-suck/research/cyclists.pdf.

KPMG Peat Marwick. 1990. "Dimensions of Parking." Prepared for the U.S. Department of Transportation, Urban Mass Transportation Administration, Office of Budget and Policy, September 10.

Krueger, Anne. 1974. "The Political Economy of the Rent-Seeking Society." *American Economic Review* 64, no.3 (June): 291-303.

Kuhn, Thomas. 1957. *The Copernican Revolution*. Cambridge, Mass.: Harvard University Press.

_____. 1996. *The Structure of Scientific Revolutions*. 3rd ed. Chicago: University of Chicago Press.

Lambe, Thomas. 1967. "The Choice of Parking Location by Workers in the Central Business District." *Traffic Quarterly* 23, no. 3 (July): 397-411.

_____. 1996. "Driver Choice of Parking in the City." *Socio-Economic Planning Sciences* 30, no. 3: 207-219.

Lan, Lawrence, and Adib Kanafani. 1993. "Economics of Park-and-Shop Discounts, a Case of Bundled Pricing Strategy." *Journal of Transport Economics and Policy* 27, no. 3 (September): 291-303.

Lange, Oskar. 1936. "On the Economic Theory of Socialism." Reprinted in *Economic Theory and Market Socialism, Selected Essays of Oskar Lange*, edited by Tadeusz Kowalik. 1993. Aldershot, UK: Edward Elgar, pp. 252-270.

Langley, Noel, Florence Ryerson, and Edgar Woolf. 1989. *The Wizard of Oz*, the Screenplay. New York: Dell Publishing.

Larsen, Larissa. 2000. "A Classic Chicago Suburb Thought Community Character Deserved a Separate Plan." *Planning* 66, no. 11 (November): 22-23.

Lave, Charles. 1992. "Cars and Demographics." *Access*, fall, 4-10.

_____. 1995. "The Demand Curve under Road Pricing and the Problem of Political Feasibility: Author's Reply." *Transportation Research-A* 29, no. 6: 464-465.

Lawler, Amy, and Michael Powers. 1997. "Traffic Impact Fees—Survey Results." *California Planner*, July/August, 3-5.

Le Corbusier. 1967. *The Radiant City: Elements of a Doctrine of Urbanism to be Used as the Basis of our Machine-Age Civilization*. Translated from the French by Pamela Knight, Eleanor Levieux, and Derek Coltman. London: Faber.

Lee, Douglas. 1987. *"Streets as 'Private' Goods."* In *Public Streets for Public Use*, edited by Anne Vernez Moudon. New York: Van Nostrand Reinhold Company, pp. 261-266.

Lerable, Charles. 1995. *Preparing a Conventional Zoning Ordinance*. Planning Advisory Service Report No. 460. Chicago: American Planning Association.

Levine, Jonathan, and Yaakov Garb. 2002. "Congestion Pricing's Conditional Promise: Promotion of Accessibility or Mobility?" *Transport Policy* 9: 179-188.

Levinson, David. 2002. *Financing Transportation Networks*. Northampton, Mass.: Edward Elgar.

Levinson, Herbert. 1982. "Parking in a Changing Time." In *Urban Transportation; Perspectives and Prospects*, edited by Herbert Levinson and Robert Weant. Westport, Conn.: Eno Foundation for Transportation, pp. 214-219.

_____. 1984a. "Whither Parking in the City Center." *Transportation Research Record* 957: 77-79.

_____. 1984b. "Zoning for Parking—A Global Perspective." *ITE Journal* 54, no. 11 (November): 18-22.

Levy-Lambert, Hubert. 1974. "Cost Benefit Analysis and Urban Traffic Congestion: The Example of Paris." In *Transport and the Urban Environment*, edited by Jerome Rothenberg and Ian Heggie. New York: John Wiley and Sons.

_____. 1977. "Investment and Pricing in the French Public Sector." *American Economic Review* 67, no. 1 (February): 302-313.

Lewis, C. S. 1942. *The Screwtape Letters*. London: Geoffrey Bles, The Centenary Press.

Liebmann, George. 2000. *Solving Problems without Large Government*. Westport, Conn.: Praeger.

Lindsey, Robin, and Erik Verhoef. 2000. "Congestion Modeling." In *Handbook of Transport Modelling*, edited by David Hensher and Kenneth Button. New York: Pergamon, pp. 353-373.

Liebs, Chester. 1985. *Main Street to Miracle Mile: American Roadside Architecture*. Boston: Little, Brown and Company.

Lin-Fu, Jane. 1992. "Modern History of Lead Poisoning: A Century of Discovery and Rediscovery." In *Human Lead Exposure*, edited by Herbert Needleman. Boca Raton, Fla.: CRC Press.

Link, Rex. 1975. "Telephone Survey of Environmental Protection Agency's Metropolitan Los Angeles Air Quality Control Region." Rex Link and Associates.

Lipman, Timothy. 2000. "Power from the Fuel Cell." *Access*, no. 16 (spring): 8-13.

Lipp, Ronald. 2001. "Tragic, Truly Tragic: The Commons in Modern Life." In *The Commons*, edited by Tibor Machan. Stanford, Calif.: Hoover Institution Press.

Lisco, Thomas. 1967. *The Value of Commuters' Travel Time: A Study in Urban Transportation*. PhD diss., University of Chicago.

Litman, Todd. 1998. "Parking Requirement Impacts on Housing Affordability." *Transportation Planning* 23, no. 4 (winter): 7-10.

_____. 2003. "The Online TDM Encyclopedia: Mobility Management Information Gateway." *Transport Policy* 10, no. 3 (July): 245-249.

Lloyd, F. J. 1967. "Discussion of Mr. Thomson's Paper." *Journal of the Royal Statistical Society. Series A (General)* 30, no. 3: 371-373.

Longstreth, Richard. 1992. "The Perils of a Parkless Town." In *The Car and the City*, edited by Martin Wachs and Margaret

Crawford. Ann Arbor: University of Michigan Press, pp. 141-153.

———. 1997. *City Center to Regional Mall: Architecture, the Automobile, and Retailing in Los Angeles, 1920-1950*. Cambridge, Mass.: MIT Press.

———. 1999. *The Drive-In, the Supermarket, and the Transformation of Commercial Space in Los Angeles, 1914-1941*. Cambridge, Mass.: MIT Press.

Lossing, Benson. 1859. *Mount Vernon and Its Associations*. New York: W. A. Townsend & Company.

Lovins, Amory. 1976. "Energy Strategy: The Road Not Taken." *Foreign Affairs* 55, no. 1: 65–96.

Lund, Hollie, Robert Cervero, and Richard Willson. 2004. "Travel Characteristics of Transit-Oriented Development in California." [Accesssed November 4, 2004]. Available at www.csupomona.edu/~rwwillson/tod/Pictures/TOD2.pdf.

Macrae, Fiona. 2010. "Why It Takes Us Nearly a Year Just to Park the Car." *Daily Mail*, October 25.

Mansfield, Edwin. 1983. *Economics*. 4th ed. New York: Norton.

Manville, Michael. 2010. "Parking Requirements as a Barrier to Housing Development: Regulation and Reform in Los Angeles." UCLA Lewis Center Working Paper, University of California, Los Angeles. Available at www.its.ucla.edu/research/rpubs/Manville_ARO_DEC_2010.pdf.

Manville, Michael, and Jonathan Williams. 2010. "The Price Doesn't Matter If You Don't Have To Pay: Legal Exemption as a Barrier to Congestion Pricing." UCLA Lewis Center Working Paper, University of California, Los Angeles. Available at www.its.ucla.edu/research/rpubs/Manville_Williams_Placards_Dec_2010.pdf.

Manvel, Allen. 1968. "Land Use in 106 Large Cities." In *Three Land Use Studies*. Research Report 12 National Commission on Urban Problems. Washington, D.C.: United States Government Printing Office.

Martin, Russell. 2000. *Beethoven's Hair*. New York: Broadway Books.

Masello, David. 1988. "Where to Put the Car?" *Metropolis*, April, 76-79.

May, Anthony. 1975. "Parking Control: Experience and Problems in London." *Traffic Engineering and Control*, May, 227-229.

Mazumder, Taraknath. 2004. "Methodology for Assessing the Social Cost of On-Street Parking and Its Implications: Case Study of Kolkata." PhD diss. Indian Institute of Technology.

McCarthy, Patrick. 2001. *Transportation Economics*. Oxford: Blackwell Publishers Ltd.

McClintock, Miller. 1924. "Parking—When, Where, and Why?" *American City Magazine*, April, 360-361.

———. 1925. *Street Traffic Control*. New York: McGraw-Hill Book Company.

McCord, Carey. 1953. "Lead and Lead Poisoning in Early America." *Industrial Medicine and Surgery* 22, no. 9: 393-399.

McCourt, Frank. 1999. *'Tis: A Memoir*. New York: Scribner.

McDonnell, Simon, Josiah Madar, and Vicki Been. 2011. "Minimum Parking Requirements and Housing Affordability in New York City." *Housing Policy Debate* 21, no. 1: 45-68.

McFadden, Daniel. 2002. "The Path to Discrete Models." *Access* no. 20 (spring): 2-7.

McShane, Mary, and Michael Meyer. 1982. "Parking Policy and Urban Goals: Linking Strategy to Needs." *Transportation* 11: 131-152.

Means, R. S. 2001. *Building Construction Cost Data, 2001*. 59th annual ed. Kingston, Mass.: R. S. Means Co.

———. 2002. *Square Foot Costs*. 24th annual ed. Kingston, Mass.: R. S. Means Co.

Meck, Stuart, ed. 2002. *Growing Smart Legislative Guidebook: Model Statutes for Planning and the Management of Change. 2002 Edition*. Chicago: American Planning Association.

Merton, Robert. 1936. "The Unanticipated Consequences of Purposive Social Action." *American Sociological Review* 1, no. 6: 894-904.

Meyer, John, John Kain, and Martin Wohl. 1965. *The Urban Transportation Problem.* Cambridge, Mass.: Harvard University Press.

Meyer, John, and José Gómez-Ibáñez. 1981. *Autos, Transit, and Cities.* Cambridge, Mass.: Harvard University Press.

Meyer, Michael, and Eric Miller. 2001. *Urban Transportation Planning.* 2nd ed. New York: McGraw Hill.

Meyer, Mohaddes Associates. 2001. "Old Pasadena Parking Study." City of Pasadena.

Mieszkowski, Peter, and Mahlon Straszheim, eds. 1979. *Current Issues in Urban Economics.* Baltimore, Md.: Johns Hopkins University Press.

Mildner, Gerard, James Strathman, and Martha Bianco. 1997. "Parking Policies and Commuting Behavior." *Transportation Quarterly* 51, no. 1 (winter): 111-125.

Mill, John Stuart. 1965. *Principles of Political Economy.* In *Collected Works of John Stuart Mill.* Vol. 3. London: University of Toronto Press and Routledge & Kegan Paul.

Millard-Ball, Adam. 2002. "Putting on their Parking Caps." *Planning,* April, 16-21.

Mills, Edwin. 1972. *Urban Economics.* Glenview, Ill.: Scott, Foresman and Company.

Minett, John. 1994. "Parking in Downtown Tempe." Interim report, Parking Task Force of Downtown Tempe Community Inc.

Mitchell, Robert, and Chester Rapkin. 1954. *Urban Traffic: A Function of Land Use.* New York: Columbia University Press.

Mogren, Edward, and Wilbur Smith. 1952. *Zoning and Traffic.* Saugatuck, Conn.: Eno Foundation for Highway Traffic Control.

Mokhtarian, Patricia, and Ilan Salomon. 2001. "How Derived is the Demand for Travel? Some Conceptual and Measure-

ment Considerations." *Transportation Research A* 35, no. 8: 695-719.

Monissen, Hans. 1999. "Explorations of the Laffer Curve." [Accessed October 28, 2004]. Available at www.gmu.edu/jbc/fest/files/Monissen.htm#_edn1.

Morris, Marya. 1989. "Parking Standards—Problems, Solutions, Examples." *Planning Advisory Service Memo,* July.

Moudon, Anne Vernez, ed. 1987. *Public Streets for Public Use.* New York: Van Nostrand Reinhold Company.

Mowbray, A. Q. 1969. *Road to Ruin.* New York: J. B. Lippincott Company

Mukija, Vinit. 2003. *Squatters as Developers?* Aldershot, U.K.: Ashgate.

Multilevel Parking Industry Association of Japan (Rittai-Chushajou Kougyou-Kai). 1997. *Parking Annual Report, 1997.*

Mumford, Lewis. 1961. *The City in History.* New York: Harcourt.

Muth, Richard. 1969. *Cities and Housing.* Chicago: University of Chicago Press.

———. 1975. *Urban Economic Problems.* New York: Harper and Row.

———. 1983. "Energy Prices and Urban Decentralization." In *Energy Costs, Urban Development, and Housing,* edited by Anthony Downs and Katherine Bradbury. Washington, D.C.: Brookings Institution Press, pp. 85-109.

Myers, Ransom, and Boris Worm. 2003. "Rapid Worldwide Depletion of Predatory Fish Communities." *Nature* 423: 280-283.

Nagurney, Anna. 2000. *Sustainable Transportation Networks.* Northampton, Mass.: Edward Elgar.

National Multi Housing Council. 2000. "Apartments and Parking." Research notes, National Multi Housing Council, January.

Nau, Robert. 1929. "No Parking—a Year and More of It." *American City* 40, no. 3 (March): 85-88.

Nechyba, Thomas. 2001. "The Benefit View and the New View: Where Do We Stand, Twenty-Five Years into the Debate?" In *Property Taxation and Local*

Government Finance, edited by Wallace Oates. Cambridge, Mass.: Lincoln Institute of Land Policy, pp. 113-121.

Nelson, Amanda. 1997. "Fear of Parking." *Town and Country Planning* 66, no. 1: 3.

Nelson, Arthur, and James Duncan. 1995. *Growth Management Principles and Practices*. Chicago: Planners Press.

Nelson\Nygaard Consulting Associates. 2003. "Parking Zoning Ordinance Update." Technical memorandum no. 1 to the City of Palo Alto, February.

Nelson, Robert. 1980. *Zoning and Property Rights: An Analysis of the American System of Land-Use Regulation*. Cambridge, Mass.: MIT Press.

_____. 1999. "Privatizing the Neighborhood: A Proposal to Replace Zoning with Private Collective Property Rights to Existing Neighborhoods." *George Mason Law Review* 7(summer): 827-879.

Netzer, Dick. 1974. *Economics and Urban Problems*. New York: Basic Books.

New York, City of, Department of City Planning. 2002. *An Evaluation and Update of Off-Street Parking Regulations in Community Districts 1-8 in Manhattan*, July.

Newman, Oscar. 1972. *Defensible Space*. New York: Macmillan Company.

_____. 1980. *Community of Interest*. Garden City, N.Y.: Anchor Press.

_____. 1996. *Creating Defensible Space*. Washington, D.C.: U.S. Department of Housing and Urban Development.

Newman, Peter, and Jeffrey Kenworthy. 1989. *Cities and Automobile Dependence: A Sourcebook*. Aldershot U.K.: Gower Publishing Company Limited.

Nicholas, J.P., P. Pochet, and H. Poimboeuf. 2003. "Towards Sustainable Mobility Indicators: Application to the Lyons Conurbation." *Transport Policy* 10, no. 3 (July): 197-208.

Nijkamp, Peter, ed. 1996. *Handbook of Regional and Urban Economics, Vol. 1, Regional Economics*. Amsterdam: North-Holland.

Noble, John, and Mike Jenks. 1996. *Parking: Demand and Provision in Private Sector Housing Developments*. Oxford: Oxford Brookes University School of Architecture.

Nozzi, Dom. 2003. *Road to Ruin*. Westport, Conn.: Praeger.

Nriagu, Jerome. 1983. *Lead and Lead Poisoning in Antiquity*. New York: John Wiley & Sons.

Obolensky, Kira. 2001. *Garage, Reinventing the Place We Park*. Newton, Conn.: Taunton Press.

O'Donnell, Edward. 1995. "Alternate-Side-of-the-Street-Parking." In *The Encyclopedia of New York City*, edited by Kenneth Jackson. New Haven, Conn.: Yale University Press, p. 16.

Olson, Mancur. 1965. *The Logic of Collective Action*. Cambridge, Mass.: Harvard University Press.

_____. 1969. "The Principle of "Fiscal Equivalence": The Division of Responsibilities among Different Levels of Government." *American Economic Review* 59, no. 2: 479-487.

Olsson, Marie, and Gerald Miller. 1979. *The Impact on Commuters of a Residential Parking Permit Program*. Washington, D.C.: The Urban Institute.

O'Malley, Marianne. 1985. "Cruising for Parking in Harvard Square: A Model to Evaluate City Parking Policies," John F. Kennedy School of Government, Harvard University, June 17, 1985. Selected by the American Planning Association's Transportation Planning Division for the national award as Best Student Paper for 1985.

Oppewal, Harmen, and Harry Timmermans. 2001. "Discrete Choice Modelling: Basic Principles and Application to Parking Policy Assessment." In *Regional Science in Business*, edited by Graham Clarke and Moss Madden. Heidelberg: Springer, pp. 97-114.

Orbanes, Philip. 1988. *The Monopoly Companion*. Boston: Bob Adams.

Organisation for Economic Co-Operation and Development. 1980. *Evaluation of Urban Parking Systems*. Paris: Organisation for Economic Co-Operation and Development.

_____. 1988. *Cities and Transport*. Paris: Organisation for Economic Co-Operation and Development.

Orwin, Charles, and Christabel Orwin. 1967. *The Open Fields*. 3rd ed. Oxford: Oxford University Press.

Ostrom, Elinor. 1990. *Governing the Commons*. New York: Cambridge University Press.

Owen, Wilfred. 1959. *Cities in the Motor Age*. New York: Viking Press.

Ozbay, Kaan, Bekir Bartin, and Joseph Berechman. 2001. "Estimation and Evaluation of Full Marginal Costs of Highway Transportation in New Jersey." *Journal of Transportation and Statistics* 4, no. 1: 81-103.

Paben, Jared. 2010. "Bellingham to Offer Free Downtown Parking for Two Weeks before Christmas." *The Bellingham Herald*, December 13.

Palo Alto, City of, California, Planning Commission. 1995. "Application to rezone property at 725-753 Alma Street." Staff Report, May 10, 1995.

Papacostas, Constantinos, and Panos Prevedouros. 1993. *Transportation Engineering and Planning*. 2nd ed. Englewood Cliffs, N.J.: Prentice Hall.

Parker, Ian. 2002. "Traffic." In *Autopia*, edited by Peter Wollen and Joe Kerr. London: Reaktion Books.

Parking Consultants Council. 1992. *Recommended Zoning Ordinance Provisions for Parking and Off-Street Loading Spaces*. Washington, D.C.: National Parking Association.

Parry, Ian, and Kenneth Small. 2002. "Does Britain or the United States Have the Right Gasoline Tax?" Discussion Paper 02-12. Resources for the Future, Washington, D.C. March.

Parsons Transportation Group. 2002. "Parking Study for Home Depot's Southwest Division." Washington, D.C.: Parsons Transportation Group.

Patterson, Theodore. 1979. *Land Use Planning*. New York: Van Nostrand Reinhold Company.

Payton, Neal. 1993. "Architects Take a Second Look at Parking." *Parking*, May, 37-43.

Peiser, Richard, with Anne Frej. 2003. *Professional Real Estate Development: The ULI Guide to the Business*. 2nd ed. Washington, D.C.: Urban Land Institute.

Pickrell, Don. 1992. "A Desire Named Streetcar: Fantasy and Fact in Rail Transit Planning." *Journal of the American Planning Association* 58, no. 2: 158-176.

_____. 2001. "Induced Demand: Its Definition, Measurement, and Significance." Paper presented at the Eno Transportation Foundation Policy Forum, Washington, D.C., February 22-23.

Pickrell, Don, and Paul Schimek. 1999. "Growth in Motor Vehicle Ownership and Use: Evidence from the Nationwide Personal Transportation Survey." *Journal of Transportation and Statistics* 2, no. 1 (May): 1-17.

Pickrell, Don, and Donald Shoup. 1981a. "Land Use Zoning as Transportation Regulation." *Transportation Research Record* 786: 12-18.

_____. 1981b. "Employer-Subsidized Parking and Work Trip Mode Choice." *Transportation Research Record* 786: 30-39.

Pierce, Emmet. 2010. "It's Change for the Better in New Parking Meters." *San Diego Business Journal*, November 29.

Planning Advisory Service. 1964. *Off-Street Parking Requirements*. Planning Advisory Service Report No. 182. Chicago: American Planning Association.

_____. 1971. *An Approach to Determining Parking Demand*. Planning Advisory Service Report No. 270. Chicago: American Planning Association.

_____. 1983. *Flexible Parking Requirements*. Planning Advisory Service Report No. 377. Chicago: American Planning Association.

_____. 1991. *Off-Street Parking Requirements: A National Review of Standards.* Planning Advisory Service Report No. 432. Chicago: American Planning Association.

_____. 2002. *Parking Standards.* Planning Advisory Service Report No. 510/511. Chicago: American Planning Association.

Polanis, Stanley, and Keith Price. 1991. "Parking Regulations in Southeastern Cities: A Summary Report." *ITE Journal* 61, no. 6 (June): 31-34.

Pollock, Richard, and Donald Shoup. 1977. "The Effect of Shifting the Property Tax Base from Improvement Value to Land Value: An Empirical Estimate." *Land Economics* 53, no. 1 (February): 67-77.

Polzin, Steven, Xaeuho Chu, and Lavenia Toole-Holt. 2003. "The Case for Moderate Growth in Vehicle Miles of Travel: A Critical Juncture in U. S. Travel Behavior Trends." [Accessed October 28, 2004]. Available at http://nhts.ornl.gov/2001/articles/moderateGrowth/moderateGrowth.pdf.

Popper, Karl. 1985. "The Rationality Principle." In *Popper Selections*, edited by David Miller. Princeton: Princeton University Press, pp. 357-365.

Porter, Richard. 1999. *Economics at the Wheel: The Costs of Cars and Drivers.* San Diego: Academic Press.

Portland Metro Regional Transportation Planning. 1995. "Regional Parking Management Program for the Portland Metropolitan Area." Submitted to the Oregon Department of Transportation.

Portland TriMet. 2002. *Community Building Sourcebook.* [Accessed October 28, 2004]. Available at www.trimet.org/inside/publications/pdf/sourcebook.pdf.

Prest, Alan. 1981. *The Taxation of Urban Land.* Manchester, UK: Manchester University Press.

Proost, Steff, and Kurt Van Dender. 2001. "The Welfare Impacts of Alternative Policies to Address Atmospheric Pollution in Urban Road Transport." *Regional Science and Urban Economics* 31: 383-411.

Public Technology Inc. 1982. *Flexible Parking Requirements.* An Urban Consortium Information Bulletin, DOT-1-82-57, U.S. Department of Transportation.

Pucher, John. 2003. "Socioeconomics of Urban Travel: Evidence from the 2001 NHTS." *Transportation Quarterly* 57, no. 3

Puget Sound Regional Council. 2000. "Parking Inventory for Seattle and Bellevue, 1999." [Accessed October 28, 2004]. Available at www.psrc.org/datapubs/pubs/parking1999.htm.

_____. 2003. "Parking Inventory for the Central Puget Sound Region, 2002." [Accessed October 28, 2004]. Available at www.psrc.org/datapubs/pubs/parking2002.htm.

Pushkarev, Boris, and Jeffrey Zupan. 1975. *Urban Space for Pedestrians.* Cambridge, Mass.: MIT Press.

Raphael, Steven, and Michael Stoll. 2001. "Can Boosting Minority Car-Ownership Rates Narrow Inter-Racial Employment Gaps?" *Brookings-Wharton Papers on Urban Affairs* 2: 99-137.

Raskin, Andy. 2007. "The Hunter-Gatherer, Parking Division." *New York Times*, February 25.

Ready, Randy. 1998. "Public Involvement, Understanding, and Support: Lessons Learned from the City of Aspen Transportation and Parking Plan." *Journal of Parking* 1, no. 2: 7-12.

Reed, Charles. 1984. "About Retail Parking Zoning Requirements." *The Zoning Report* 2, no. 12 (October): 1-8.

Renner, Michael. 1988. *Rethinking the Role of the Automobile.* Washington, D.C.: World Watch Institute.

Richardson, Harry. 1978. *Urban Economics.* Hinsdale, Ill.: Dryden Press.

_____. 1979. *Regional Economics.* Urbana, Ill.: University of Illinois Press.

Richardson, Harry, Peter Gordon, Myung-Jin Jun, and Moon Kim. 1993. "PRIDE and Prejudice: the Economic Impacts of

Growth Controls in Pasadena." *Environment and Planning A*. 25: 987-1002.

Rittel, Horst, and Melvin Webber. 1973. "Dilemmas in a General Theory of Planning." *Policy Sciences* 4: 155–169.

Robertson, William. 1972. *National Parking Facility Study*. Washington, D.C.: National League of Cities.

Rodriguez, Daniel, David Godschalk, Richard Norton, and Semra Aytur. 2004. "The Connection between Land Use and Transportation in Land Use Plans." Final Report for Project 2003-16, prepared for the North Carolina Department of Transportation, November 1. Available at www.ncdot.org/doh/preconstruct/ tpb/research/download/2003-16 FinalReport.pdf.

Rodwin, Lloyd. 2000. "Images and Paths of Change in Economics, Political Science, Philosophy, Literature, and City Planning, 1950-2000." In *The Profession of City Planning: Changes, Images and Challenges, 1950-2000*, edited by Lloyd Rodwin and Bishwapriya Sanyal. New Brunswick, N.J.: Center for Urban Policy Research, Rutgers, pp. 3-23.

Rose, Carol. 1986. "The Comedy of the Commons: Custom, Commerce, and Inherently Public Property." *University of Chicago Law Review* 52 (summer): 771-781.

_____. 1998. "The Several Futures of Property: Of Cyberspace and Folk Tales, Emission Trades and Ecosystems." *Minnesota Law Review* 129: 129-182.

_____. 1999. "Expanding the Choices for the Global Commons: Comparing Newfangled Tradable Allowance Schemes to Old-Fashioned Common Property Regimes." *Duke Environmental Law and Policy Forum* 10 (fall): 45-72.

Roth, Gabriel. 1965a. *Paying for Parking*. London: Institute for Economic Affairs.

_____. 1965b. *Parking Space for Cars: Assessing the Demand*. London: Cambridge University Press.

Rybczynski, Witold. 1995. *City Life*. New York: Scribner.

Safdie, Moshe. 1997. *The City after the Automobile*. New York: Basic Books.

Sale, Kirkpatrick. 1980. *Human Scale*. New York: Coward, McCann, & Geohagan.

Salomon, Ilan. 1984. "Toward a Behavioural Approach to City Centre Parking: The Case of Jerusalem's CBD." *Cities* 3, no. 3 (August): 200-208.

Saltzman, Robert. 1994. "Three Proposals for Improving Short-Term On-Street Parking." *Socio-Economic Planning Sciences* 28, no. 2: 85-100.

_____. 1997. "An Animated Simulation Model for Analyzing On-Street Parking Issues." *Simulation* 69, no. 2: 79-90.

Salzman, Gerald, and Jean Keneipp. 2000. "Parking Demand." In *The Dimensions of Parking*. 4th ed. Washington, D.C.: Urban Land Institute, pp. 11-15.

Salzman, Randy. 2010. "The New Space Race." *Thinking Highways* 5, no. 3: 24-27.

Samuelson, Paul. 1983. "Thünen at Two Hundred." *Journal of Economic Literature* 21 (December): 1468-1488.

Samuelson, Paul, and William Nordhaus. 1989. *Economics*. 13th ed. New York: McGraw-Hill.

San Diego Association of Governments. 1999. "Report to the California Legislature: San Diego's Interstate 15 Congestion Pricing & Transit Development Demonstration Program." [Accessed October 28, 2004]. Available at http://argo.sandag.org/fastrak//pdfs/ leg_report.pdf.

_____. 2000. "I-15 Congestion Pricing Project, Monitoring and Evaluation Services, Phase II Year Two Overall Report."[Accessed October 28, 2004]. Available at http://argo.sandag.org/ fastrak//pdfs/yr3_overall.pdf.

San Diego, City of, California. 1995. *Parking Meter Program Survey*. San Diego: Transportation Department Street Division.

Santa Clara Valley Transportation Authority. 1997. *Eco Pass Pilot Program Survey Summary of Findings*. San Jose, Calif.: Santa Clara Valley Transportation Authority.

Scannell, Nancy. 1992. "Urban Metered Parking as a Factor in Retail Sales: an Econometric Case Study for Chicago, Illinois." PhD diss., University of Illinois at Chicago.

Schafer, Andreas. 2000. "Regularities in Travel Demand: An International Perspective." *Journal of Transportation and Statistics* 3, no. 3 (December): 1-31.

Schaller, Bruce. 2006. "Curbing Cars: Shopping, Parking and Pedestrian Space in SoHo." New York: Transportation Alternatives. Available at www.transalt.org/files/newsroom/reports/soho_curbing_cars.pdf.

Schelling, Thomas. 1978. *Micromotives and Macrobehavior.* New York: W. W. Norton and Company.

Schilling, Theodor. 1995. "Subsidiarity as a Rule and a Principle, or: Taking Subsidiarity Seriously." [Accessed October 28, 2004]. Available at www.jeanmonnetprogram.org/papers/95/9510ind.html.

Schmider, André. 1977. "L'Espace Urbain, Un Bien Public." *Metropolis*, January, 55-57.

Schneider, Kenneth. 1971. *Autokind vs. Mankind; An Analysis of Tyranny, a Proposal for Rebellion, a Plan for Reconstruction.* New York: W. W. Norton & Company.

Schön, Donald. 1983. *The Reflective Practitioner: How Professionals Think in Action.* New York: Basic Books.

_____. 2000. "Town Planning: Limits to Reflection-in-Action." In *The Profession of City Planning: Changes, Images and Challenges, 1950-2000*, edited by Lloyd Rodwin and Bishwapriya Sanyal. New Brunswick, N.J.: Center for Urban Policy Research, Rutgers, pp. 62-83.

Schultze, Charles. 1977. *The Public Use of Private Interest.* Washington, D.C.: Brookings Institution.

Schumpeter, Joseph. 1942. *Capitalism, Socialism, and Democracy.* New York: Harper and Brothers.

_____. 1954. *History of Economic Analysis,* New York: Oxford University Press.

Scott, Mel. 1995. *American City Planning since 1890: a History Commemorating the Fiftieth Anniversary of the American Institute of Planners.* Chicago: Planners Press.

Seattle, City of, Strategic Planning Office. 2000. *Seattle Comprehensive Neighborhood Parking Study-Final Report.* [Accessed October 28, 2004]. Available at www.seattle.gov/transportation/parking/parkingstudy.htm.

Seburn, Thomas. 1967. "Relationship between Curb Uses and Traffic Accidents." *Traffic Engineering*, May, 42-47.

Segal, David. 1977. *Urban Economics.* Homewood, Ill.: R. D. Irwin.

Segelhorst, Elbert, and Larry Kirkus. 1973. "Parking Bias in Transit Choice." *Journal of Transport Economics and Policy* 7, no. 1 (January).

Seligman, Edwin. 1931. *Issues in Taxation.* 10th ed. New York: Macmillan.

Shaw, John. 1997a. *Planning for Parking.* Iowa City: University of Iowa Public Policy Center.

_____. 1997b. "Parking: Legislation and Transportation Plans." *Traffic Quarterly* 51, no. 2 (spring): 105-115.

Shiftan, Yoram. 2002. "The Effects of Parking Pricing and Supply on Travel Patterns to a Major Business District." In *Travel Behaviour: Spatial Patterns, Congestion, and Modelling*, edited by Eliahu Stern, Ilan Salomon, and Piet Bovy. Cheltenham, UK: Edward Elgar, pp. 37-52.

Shoup, Donald. 1969. "Advance Land Acquisition by Local Governments: A Cost-Benefit Analysis." *Yale Economics Essays* 9, no. 2: 147-207.

_____. 1970. "The Optimal Timing of Urban Land Development." *Papers of the Regional Science Association* 25: 33-44.

_____. 1978. "The Effect of Property Taxes on the Capital Intensity of Urban Land Development." In *Metropolitan Financing and Growth management Policies: Principles and Practice*, edited by George

Break. Madison: University of Wisconsin Press, pp. 105-132.

_____. 1990. *New Funds for Old Neighborhoods: California's Deferred Special Assessments*. Berkeley: University of California, California Policy Seminar.

_____. 1995. "An Opportunity to Reduce Minimum Parking Requirements." *Journal of the American Planning Association* 61, no. 1: 14-28.

_____. 1997a. "The High Cost of Free Parking." *Journal of Planning Education and Research* 17, no. 1: 1-18.

_____. 1997b. "Evaluating the Effects of Cashing Out Employer-Paid Parking: Eight Case Studies." *Transport Policy* 4, no. 4: 201-216.

_____. 1997c. *Evaluating the Effects of Parking Cash Out: Eight Case Studies*. [Accessed on October 28, 2004]. Available at www.arb.ca.gov/research/abstracts/93-308.htm#93-308.

_____. 1998. "Congress Okays Cash Out." *Access* no. 13 (fall): 2-8.

_____. 1999a. "In Lieu of Required Parking." *Journal of Planning Education and Research* 18, no. 4: 307-320.

_____. 1999b. "The Trouble with Minimum Parking Requirements." *Transportation Research Part A: Policy and Practice* 33A, nos. 7/8 (September/November): 349-574.

_____. 2002. "Parking Cash Out," in *Managing Commuters' Behaviour, a New Role for Companies*, Report of the Hundred and Twenty-First Roundtable on Transport Economics, Paris: European Conference of Ministers of Transport, 2002, pp. 41-173. Also published in French as "Rétribution en Cas de Renoncement au Parking Gratuit," in *Gérer les Déplacements du Personnel, un Nouveau Rôle pour l'Enterprise*, Rapport de la Cent Vingt et Unième Table Ronde d'Économie des Transports, Paris: Conférence Européenne des Ministres des Transports, 2002, pp. 45-197.

_____. 2003a. "Truth in Transportation Planning." *Journal of Transportation and Statistics* 6, No. 1: 1-16.

_____. 2003b. "Buying Time at the Curb." In *The Half-Life of Policy Rationales: How New Technology Affects Old Policy Issues*, edited by Fred Foldvary and Daniel Klein. New York: New York University Press, pp. 60-85.

_____. 2004. "The Ideal Source of Local Public Revenue." *Regional Science and Urban Economics* 34, no. 6 (November): 753-784.

_____. 2005. *Parking Cash Out*. Planning Advisory Service Report No. 531. Chicago: American Planning Association. March.

Shoup, Donald, and Mary Jane Breinholt. 1997. "Employer-paid Parking: a Nationwide Survey of Employers' Parking Subsidy Policies." In *The Full Social Costs and Benefits of Transportation*, edited by David Greene, David Jones, and Mark Delucchi. Heidelberg: Springer-Verlag, pp. 371-385.

Shoup, Donald, and Don Pickrell. 1978. "Problems with Parking Requirements in Zoning Ordinances." *Traffic Quarterly* 32, No. 4 (October): 545-563.

_____. 1980. *Free Parking as a Transportation Problem*. Washington, D.C.: U.S. Department of Transportation.

Shoup, Donald, and Richard Willson. 1992. "Employer-Paid Parking: The Problem and Proposed Solutions." *Transportation Quarterly* 46, no. 2 (April): 169-192.

Simons, Henry. 1948. *Economic Policy for a Free Society*. Chicago: University of Chicago Press.

Simpson, Hawley. 1927. "Downtown Storage Garages." *The Annals* 123 (September): 82-89.

Small, Kenneth. 1992. "Using the Revenues from Congestion Pricing." *Transportation* 19: 359-381.

Small, Kenneth, and Xuehao Chu. 2003. "Hypercongestion." *Journal of Transport*

Economics and Policy 37: 319–352.

Small, Kenneth, and Camilla Kazimi. 1995. "On the Costs of Air Pollution from Motor Vehicles." *Journal of Transport Economics and Policy* 29, no. 1: 7-32.

Small, Kenneth, Clifford Winston, and Carol Evans. 1989. *Road Work*. Washington, D.C.: Brookings Institution.

Smeed, R. J., and J. G. Wardrop. 1964. "An Exploratory Comparison of the Advantages of Cars and Buses for Travel in Urban Areas." *Institute of Transport Journal* 30, no. 9 (March): 301-315.

Smith, Adam. 1776 [1937]. *An Inquiry into the Nature and Causes of the Wealth of Nations*. New York: Modern Library.

Smith, Herbert. 1993. *The Citizen's Guide to Planning*. Chicago: Planners Press.

Smith, M. J. P. 1988. "Parking Carcases." *Inland Architect*, November/December, 58-63.

Smith, Mary. 1996. "Circle Centre: How Parking Helped Make Urban Retail/Entertainment Development Work." *Parking*, September, 25-33.

_____. 1999. "Parking." In *Transportation Planning Handbook*, 2nd ed., edited by John Edwards. Washington, D.C.: Institute of Transportation Engineers.

_____. 2001. "Planning for Structured Parking." In *Parking Structures*, 3rd ed., edited by Anthony Chrest, Mary Smith, Sam Bhuyan, Donald Monahan, and Mohammad Iqbal. Boston, Mass.: Kluwer Academic Publishers, pp. 7-36.

Smith, Mary, and Thomas Butcher. 1994. "How Far Should Parkers Have to Walk." *Parking*, September, 29-32.

Smith, Steven. 1990. "Using the ITE Parking Generation Report." *ITE Journal* 60, no. 7 (July): 25-31.

Smith, Steven, and Alexander Hekimian. 1985. "Parking Requirements for Local Zoning Ordinances." *ITE Journal* 53, no. 9 (September): 35-40.

Smith, Thomas. 1988. *The Aesthetics of Parking*. Planning Advisory Service Report No. 411. Chicago: American Planning Association.

Smith, Wilbur. 1947. "Influence of Parking on Accidents." *Traffic Quarterly* 1, no. 2 (April): 162-178.

Smith, Wilbur, and Charles LeCraw. 1946. *Parking*. Saugatuck, Conn.: Eno Foundation.

Smolensky, Eugene, T. Nicholas Tideman, and Donald Nichols. 1972. "Waiting Time as a Congestion Charge." In *Public Prices for Public Products*, edited by Selma Mushkin. Washington, D.C.: The Urban Institute.

So, Frank, and Judith Getzels. 1988. *The Practice of Local Government Planning*. Washington, D.C.: International City Management Association.

Song, Yong Nam. 1995. *Inferring the Value of Walking Time from Parking Rent Data in a Diffused CBD Model*. PhD diss., University of Minnesota.

South Coast Air Quality Management District. 2000. *Best Available Control Technology Guidelines*. [Accessed October 28, 2004]. Available at www.aqmd.gov/bact/BACTGuidelines.htm.

Southern California Association of Governments. 1996. *1996 State of the Commute Report*. Los Angeles.

_____. 2004. *2004 Regional Transportation Plan*. Los Angeles.

Southern California Association of Non-Profit Housing. 2004. *Parking Requirements Guide for Affordable Housing Developers*. [Accessed November 4, 2004]. Available at www.scanph.org/publications/Pubs2004/Parking%20Requirements%20Guide_forweb.pdf.

Southworth, Michael, and Eran Ben-Joseph. 1997. *Streets and the Shaping of Towns and Cities*. New York: McGraw Hill

Southworth, Michael, and Peter Owens. 1993. "The Evolving Metropolis: Studies of Community, Neighborhood, and Street Form at the Urban Edge." *Journal of the American Planning Association* 59, no. 3 (summer): 271-287.

Sowell, Thomas. 1980. *Knowledge and Decisions*. New York: Basic Books.

Spirn, Ann Whiston. 1984. *The Granite Garden: Urban Nature and Human Design.* New York: Basic Books.

Stedman, Donald. 1994. *On-Road Remote Sensing of CO and HC Emissions in California.* [Accessed October 28, 2004]. Available at www.arb.ca.gov/research/abstracts/a032-093.htm.

Sternberg, Robert. 2001. "How Much Money Should One Put into the Cognitive Parking Meter?" *Trends in Cognitive Sciences* 5, no. 5: 190.

Stevenson, Glenn. 1991. *Common Property Economics: A General Theory and Land Use Applications.* New York: Cambridge University Press.

Stewart, Ian. 1997. "Monopoly Revisited." *Scientific American*, October, 116-119.

Stiglitz, Joseph. 1988. *Economics of the Public Sector.* 2nd ed. New York: W. W. Norton.

Still, Ben, and David Simmonds. 2000. "Parking Restraint Policy and Urban Vitality." *Transport Reviews* 20, no. 3: 291-316.

Stover, Vergil, and Frank Koepke. 2002. *Transportation and Land Development.* 2nd ed. Washington, D.C.: Institute of Transportation Engineers.

Stubbs, Michael. 2002. Car Parking and Residential Development: Sustainability, Design and Planning Policy, and Public Perceptions of Parking Provision." *Journal of Urban Design* 7, no. 2: 213-237.

Sussman, Joseph. 2000. *Introduction to Transportation Systems.* Boston: Artech House.

Sutermeister, Oscar. 1959. "Zoning Related to General Programs for Parking Relief." *Traffic Quarterly*, April, 247-259.

Swan, Herbert. 1922. "Our City Thoroughfares-Shall They Be Highways or Garages?" *American City*, December, 496-500.

Swanson, Wayne. 1989. "Parking: How Much Is Enough." *Planning* 55, no. 7 (July): 14-17.

Takesuye, David. 2001. "America's Main Street." *Urban Land* 60, no. 10 (October): 34-39.

Talen, Emily, and Gerrit Knapp. 2003. "Legalizing Smart Growth." *Journal of Planning Education and Research* 22, no. 4 (summer): 345-359.

Taylor, Brian. 2000. "When Finance Leads Planning: Urban Planning, Highway Planning, and Metropolitan Freeways in California." *Journal of Planning Education and Research* 20, no. 2: 196-214.

Taylor, Michael, William Young, and Peter Bonsall. 1996. *Understanding Traffic Systems: Data, Analysis and Presentation.* Aldershot, UK: Ashgate Publishing.

Taylor, Seymour. 1959. "Freeways Alone Are Not Enough." *Traffic Quarterly*, July, 346-365.

Teitz, Michael. 2000. "Reflection and Research on the U.S. Experience." In *The Profession of City Planning: Changes, Images and Challenges, 1950-2000*, edited by Lloyd Rodwin and Bishwapriya Sanyal. New Brunswick, N.J.: Center for Urban Policy Research, Rutgers, pp. 275-304.

Texas Transportation Institute. 2003. *2003 Annual Urban Mobility Study.* [Accessed October 28, 2004]. Available at http://mobility.tamu.edu/.

Thirsk, Joan. 1967. "Enclosing and Engrossing." In *The Agrarian History of England and Wales*, edited by Joan Thirsk. Cambridge: Cambridge University Press, pp. 200-255.

Thoi, Linh. 2010. "Sidewalk Sipping with Sadik-Khan at NYC Pop-Up Café." *The Architect's Newspaper*, August 19.

Thomas, Lewis. 1981. "Medicine without Science." *The Atlantic Monthly*, April, 40-42.

Thompson, Russell, and Anthony Richardson. 1998. "A Parking Search Model." *Transportation Research Part A: Policy and Practice* 32, no. 3 (April): 159-170.

Thomson, J. Michael. 1967. "An Evaluation of Two Proposals for Traffic Restraint in Central London." *Journal of the Royal*

Statistical Society. Series A (General) 30, no. 3: 327-377.

_____. 1977. *Great Cities and their Traffic.* Harmondsworth: Penguin Books Ltd.

Thucycides. 1998. *The Peloponnesian War.* Translated by Steven Lattimore. Indianapolis, Iowa: Hackett Publishing Company.

Thuesen, H. G. 1967. "Reminiscences of the Development of the Parking Meter." *The Chronicles of Oklahoma* 45, no. 2 (summer): 112-142.

Tiebout, Charles. 1956. "A Pure Theory of Local Public Expenditures." *Journal of Political Economy* 64 (October): 416-424.

Tollison, Robert. 1982. "Rent Seeking: A Survey." *Kyklos* 35, no. 4: 575-602.

Topp, Hartmut. 1991. "Parking Policies in Large Cities in Germany." *Transportation* 18, no. 1: 3-21.

_____. 1993. "Parking Policies to Reduce Car Traffic in German Cities." *Transport Reviews* 13, no. 1: 83-95.

Transit Cooperative Research Program. 2003a. *Strategies for Increasing the Effectiveness of Commuter Benefits Programs.* Report 87. Washington, D.C.: Transportation Research Board.

_____. 2003b. *Traveler Response to Transportation System Changes, Chapter 18 — Parking Management and Supply.* Report 95. Washington, D.C.: Transportation Research Board.

Transport for London. 2003. *Congestion Charging: Six Months On.* London: Transport for London.

Transportation Alternatives. 2007. "No Vacancy: Park Slope's Parking Problem and How to Fix It." New York: Transportation Alternatives. Available at www.transalt.org/files/newsroom/reports/novacancy.pdf.

_____. 2008. "Driven to Excess: What Under-priced Curbside Parking Costs the Upper West Side." New York: Transportation Alternatives. Available at www.transalt.org/files/newsroom/reports/driven_to_excess.pdf.

Transportation and Land Use Coalition. 2002. *Housing Shortage/Parking Surplus.* Oakland, Calif.: Transportation and Land Use Coalition.

Transportation Research Board. 1985. *Highway Capacity Manual.* Special Report 209. Washington, D.C.: Transportation Research Board, National Research Council.

Trillin, Calvin. 2001. *Tepper Isn't Going Out.* New York: Random House.

Trinkaus, John. 1984a. "Compliance with Parking for the Handicapped: An Informal Look." *Perceptual and Motor Skills* 58, no. 1: 114.

_____. 1984b. "Shopping Mall Parking Violations: An Informal Look." *Perceptual and Motor Skills* 59: 30.

Tsamboulas, Dimitrios. 2001. "Parking Fare Thresholds: A Policy Tool." *Transport Policy* 8, no. 2 (April): 115-124.

Tufte, Edward. 1978. *Political Control of the Economy.* Princeton, N.J.: Princeton University Press.

Turner, Michael. 1980. *English Parliamentary Enclosure.* Folkstone, England: Dawson.

United Kingdom Department of the Environment, Transport and the Regions. 1998a. *Planning Policy Guidance 13: Transport.* London: Department of the Environment, Transport and the Regions.

_____. 1998b. *Parking Standards in the South East.* London: Department of the Environment, Transport and the Regions.

United Kingdom Department for Transport. 1992. *Transport Statistics Report, Transport Statistics for London 1992.* London: Department of Transportation.

_____. 1998. *A New Deal for Transport: Better for Everyone.* London: Department of Transportation.

_____. 2002. *Making Travel Plans Work.* London: Department for Transport.

United Kingdom Ministry of Transport. 1964. *Road Pricing: The Economic and Technical Possibilities.* London: Her Majesty's Stationery Office.

United States Census Bureau. 1983. *Statistical Brief.* SB/93-5. Washington, D.C.: U.S. Census Bureau.

———. 1993. *1990 Census of Population and Housing, Supplementary Reports, Urbanized Areas of the United States and Puerto Rico.* 1990 CPH-S-1-2. Washington, D.C.

———. 1997. *1997 Economic Census.* [Accessed October 28, 2004]. Available at www.census.gov/epcd/www/econ97.html.

———. 1998. *1995 Property Owners and Managers Survey.* H121/98-1. Washington, D.C.

———. 2000a. National Population Estimates. "Historical National Population Estimates: July 1, 1900 to July 1, 1999." [Accessed October 28, 2004]. Available at www.census.gov/population/estimates/nation/popclockest.txt.

———. 2000b. "Total Midyear Population for the World." [Accessed October 28, 2004]. Available at www.census.gov/ftp/pub/ipc/www/worldpop.html.

———. 2000c. "Selected Historical Decennial Census Urban and Rural Definitions and Data." [Accessed October 28, 2004]. Available at www.census.gov/population/www/censusdata/ur-def.html.

———. 2000d. *Compendium of Government Finances, 1997.* GC97(4)-5. [Accessed October 28, 2004]. Available at www.census.gov/prod/gc97/gc974-5.pdf.

———. 2000e. *American Housing Survey for the United States: 1999.* [Accessed October 28, 2004]. Available at www.census.gov/prod/2000pubs/h150-99.pdf.

———. 2000f. *Census 2000.* [Accessed December 8, 2004]. Available online at www.census.gov/main/www/cen2000.html.

———. 2001a. *American Housing Survey for the United States: 2001.* [Accessed October 28, 2004]. Available at www.census.gov/hhes/www/housing/ahs/ahs01/tab1a7.html.

———. 2001b. *Current Population Survey.* [Accessed October 28, 2004]. Available at www.census.gov/population/socdemo/hh-fam/cps2001/wgt-schip-chng.pdf.

———. 2002a. *Foreign Trade Statistics, FT900, U.S. International Trade in Goods and Services.* [Accessed December 31, 2004]. Available at www.census.gov/foreign-trade/www/index.html.

———. 2002b. *National Intercensal Estimates (1900-2000).* [Accessed October 28, 2004]. Available at www.census.gov/popest/archives/EST90INTERCENSAL/US-EST90INT.html.

———. 2003. *2003 Statistical Abstract of the United States.* [Accessed on November 4, 2004]. Available at www.census.gov/prod/www/statistical-abstract-03.html.

United States Congress, House Committee on Public Works. 1959. *The Federal Role in Highway Safety,* Letter from the Secretary of Commerce, March 8.

United States Department of Commerce, Bureau of Economic Analysis. 1998. "Fixed Reproducible Tangible Wealth in the United States." *Survey of Current Business,* September, pp. 36-46.

United States Department of Energy. 1994a. *Emissions of Greenhouse Gases in the United States 1987-1992.* DOE/EIA-0573. Washington, D.C.: Energy Information Administration.

———. 1994b. *Household Vehicles Energy Consumption 1994.* [Accessed October 28, 2004]. Available at www.eia.doe.gov/emeu/rtecs/toc.html.

United States Department of Transportation. 1990. *1990 Nationwide Personal Transportation Survey.* Washington, D.C.

———. 1995a. *1995 Nationwide Personal Transportation Survey.* Washington, D.C.: U.S. Dept. of Transportation.

———. 1995b. *Highway Statistics Summary to 1995.* [Accessed October 28, 2004]. Available at www.fhwa.dot.gov/ohim/summary95/.

———. 1995c. *Highway Statistics 1995.* [Accessed October 28, 2004]. Available at www.fhwa.dot.gov/ohim/1995/index.html.

_____. 1996. *Highway Statistics 1996*. [Accessed October 28, 2004]. Available at www.fhwa.dot.gov/ohim/1996/index.html.

_____. 1997a. *Our Nation's Travel: 1995 NPTS Early Results Report*. [Accessed October 28, 2004]. Available at www.cta.ornl.gov/npts/1995/Doc/EarlyResults.shtml\.

_____. 1997b. *Highway Statistics 1997*. [Accessed October 28, 2004]. Available at www.fhwa.dot.gov/ohim/hs97/hs97page.htm.

_____. 1997c. *National Transportation Statistics, 1997*. Washington, D.C.: Bureau of Transportation Statistics.

_____. 1997d. *Federal, State, and Local Transportation Financial Statistics, Fiscal Years 1982-94*. BTS97-E-02. Washington, D.C.: Bureau of Transportation Statistics.

_____. 1998. *Highway Statistics 1998*. [Accessed October 28, 2004]. Available at www.fhwa.dot.gov/ohim/hs98/hs98page.htm.

_____. 1999. *Highway Statistics 1999*. [Accessed October 28, 2004]. Available at www.fhwa.dot.gov/ohim/hs99/index.htm.

_____. 2000. *Highway Statistics 2000*. [Accessed October 28, 2004]. Available at www.fhwa.dot.gov/ohim/hs00/mf121t.htm.

_____. 2001. *Highway Statistics 2001*. [Accessed October 28, 2004]. Available at www.fhwa.dot.gov/ohim/hs01/index.htm.

_____. 2002a. *Government Transportation Financial Statistics 2001*. [Accessed October 28, 2004]. Available at www.bts.gov/publications/government_transportation_financial_statistics/.

_____. 2002b. *Highway Statistics 2002*. [Accessed October 28, 2004]. Available at www.fhwa.dot.gov/policy/ohim/hs02/index.htm.

_____. 2003a. *NHTS Highlights Report*. [Accessed November 1, 2004.] Available at www.bts.gov/publications/national_household_travel_survey/highlights_of_the_2001_national_household_travel_survey/pdf/entire.pdf._the_2001/.

_____. 2003b. *A Guide for HOT Lane Development*. [Accessed October 28, 2004]. Available at www.itsdocs.fhwa.dot.gov/JPODOCS/REPTS_TE/13668.html.

United States Environmental Protection Agency. 1993. *The Climate Change Action Plan*. Washington, D.C.: U.S. Environmental Protection Agency.

_____. 1995. *National Air Quality and Emissions Trends Report, 1995*. 1995. [Accessed November 1, 2004]. Available at www.epa.gov/airtrends/aqtrnd95/report/index.html/.

_____. 2004. *Parking Alternatives/Community Places*. Washington, D.C.: U.S. Environmental Protection Agency.

United States Federal Transit Administration. 1998. *National Transit Summaries and Trends for the 1997 National Transit Database Report Year*. Washington, D.C.: Federal Transit Administration, U.S. Department of Transportation.

University of Washington Transportation Office. 1997. "Stadium Expansion Parking Plan and Transportation Management Program: Draft 1997 Data Collection Summary." Seattle. December 19.

Urban Land Institute. 1960. *The Community Builders' Handbook*. Washington, D.C.

_____. 1965. *Parking Requirements for Shopping Centers*. Washington, D.C.

_____. 1982a. *Parking Requirements for Shopping Centers*. Washington, D.C.:

_____. 1982b. *Office Development Handbook*. Washington, D.C.

_____. 1983. *Shared Parking*. Washington, D.C.

_____. 1999. *Parking Requirements for Shopping Centers*. Washington, D.C.

Urban Task Force. 1999. *Towards an Urban Renaissance*. London: Spon.

Van Hattum, David, Cami Zimmer, and Patty Carlson. 2000. "Implementation and Analysis of Cashing Out Employer-Paid Parking by Employers in the Minneapolis-St. Paul Metropolitan Area." Final report submitted to the Minnesota Pollution Control Agency and the U.S. Environmental Protection Agency by the Downtown Minneapolis Transportation Management Organization, June 30, 2000.

van der Goot, D. 1982. "A Model to Describe the Choice of Parking Places." *Transportation Research* 16A, no. 2: 109-115.

Van Horn, John. 1999. "Berkeley Makes the Move to Multi-Space Parking Meters." *Parking Today* 4, no. 8 (September): 42-44.

van Kooten, G. Cornelis. 1993. *Land Resource Economics and Sustainable Development: Economic Policies and the Common Good.* Vancouver: University of British Columbia Press.

Venturi, Robert, Denise Scott Brown, and Steven Izenour. 1986. *Learning from Las Vegas: the Forgotten Symbolism of Architectural Form.* Cambridge, Mass.: MIT Press.

Verhoef, Erik. 1996. *The Economics of Regulating Road Transport.* Cheltenham, UK: Edward Elgar.

_____. 2003. "Inside the Queue: Hypercongestion and Road Pricing in a Continuous Time—Continuous Place Model of Traffic Congestion." *Journal of Urban Economics* 54, no. 3: 531-565.

Verhoef, Erik, Peter Nijkamp, and Piet Rietveld. 1995. "The Economics of Regulatory Parking Policies: The (Im)possibilities of Parking Policies in Traffic Regulation." *Transportation Research A* 29A, no. 2: 141-156.

_____. 1996. "Regulatory Parking Policies at the Firm Level." *Environment and Planning C: Government and Policy* 14: 385-406.

Vickrey, William. 1954. "The Economizing of Curb Parking Space," *Traffic Engineering,* November, pp. 62-67. Later incorporated in testimony to the Joint Committee on Washington, D.C., Metropolitan Problems in 1959, and republished in the *Journal of Urban Economics* 36 (1994): 42-65.

_____. 1955. "Some Implications of Marginal Cost Pricing for Public Utilities." *American Economic Review* 45, no. 2: 605-620.

_____. 1967. "Optimization of Traffic and Facilities." *Journal of Transport Economics and Policy* 1, no. 2: 123-136.

_____. 1993. "My Innovative Failures in Economics." *Atlantic Economic Journal* 21, no. 1 (March): 1-9.

_____. 1994. "Statement to the Joint Committee on Washington, D.C., Metropolitan Problems." *Journal of Urban Economics* 36: 42-65.

Voith, Richard. 1998a. "The Downtown Parking Syndrome: Does Curing the Illness Kill the Patient?" *Federal Reserve Bank of Philadelphia Business Review,* January/February, 3-14.

_____. 1998b. "Parking, Transit, and Employment in a Central Business District." *Journal of Urban Economics* 44, no. 1: 43-58.

Vuchic, Vukan. 1999. *Transportation for Livable Cities.* New Brunswick, N.J.: Center for Urban Policy Research.

Wachs, Martin. 1989. "When Planners Lie with Numbers." *Journal of the American Planning Association* 55, no. 4 (autumn): 476-479.

_____. 1994. "Will Congestion Pricing Ever Be Adopted?" *Access* no. 4 (spring): 15-19.

Walters, Alan. 1961. "Empirical Evidence on Optimum Motor Taxes for the United Kingdom." *Applied Statistics* 10, no. 3: 157-169.

Ward's Communications. 1999. *Ward's Automotive Yearbook 1999.* 61st ed. Southfield, Mich.: Ward's Communications.

_____. 2000. *Ward's Automotive Yearbook 2000.* 62nd ed. Southfield, Mich.

_____. 2001. *Ward's Motor Vehicle Facts and Figures 2001.* Southfield, Mich.

_____. 2002a. *Ward's Automotive Yearbook 2002.* 64th ed. Southfield, Mich.

_____. 2002b. *Ward's Motor Vehicle Facts and Figures 2002.* Southfield, Mich.

_____. 2002c. *Ward's World Motor Vehicle Data 2002*. Southfield, Mich.

_____. 2003. *Ward's Automotive Yearbook 2003*. 65th ed. Southfield, Mich.

Warner, Sam. 1992. "Learning from the Past." In *The Car and the City*, edited by Martin Wachs and Margaret Crawford. Ann Arbor, Mich.: University of Michigan Press, pp. 9-15.

Washington State Department of Ecology and City of Olympia Public Works Department. 1995. *Impervious Surface Reduction Study: Final Report*. Olympia, Washington: Washington State Department of Transportation.

Washington State Department of Transportation. 1999. *Local Government Parking Policy and Commute Trip Reduction*. Olympia, Washington: Washington State Department of Transportation, Commute Trip Reduction Office.

Wasserman, Louis. 1979. "The Essential Henry George." In *Critics of Henry George*, edited by Robert Andelson. London: Associated University Presses, pp. 29-43.

Weant, Robert, and Herbert. Levinson. 1990. *Parking*. Westport, Conn.: Eno Foundation.

Weaver, Clifford, and Richard Babcock. 1979. *City Zoning: The Once and Future Frontier*. Chicago: Planners Press.

Webster, Chris. 2003. "The Nature of the Neighborhood." *Urban Studies* 40, no. 13 (December): 2591-2612.

Weinberger, Rachel, John Kaehny, and Matthew Rufo. 2010. "U.S. Parking Policies: An Overview of Management Strategies." New York: Institute for Transportation and Development Policy. Available at www.itdp.org/documents/ITDP_US_Parking_Report.pdf.

Weiner, Edward. 1999. *Urban Transportation Planning in the United States: An Historical Overview*. Westport, Conn.: Praeger Publishers.

Whitaker, John. 1997. "Enemies or Allies? Henry George and Francis Amasa Walker One Century Later." *Journal of Economic Literature* 35, no. 4: 1891-1915.

Whiteside, Clara. 1926. *Touring New England on the Trail of the Yankee*. Philadelphia: The Penn Publishing Company.

Whyte, William. 1988. *City*. New York: Doubleday.

_____. 1989. "The City: Rediscovering the Center." *Inland Architect*, July/August, 50-55.

Wigan, Marcus. 1977. "Traffic Restraint as a Transport Planning Policy 3: The Effects on Different Users." *Environment and Planning A* 9, no. 10: 1177-1188.

Wilbur Smith and Associates. 1965. *Parking in the City Center*. New Haven, Conn.

_____. 1966. *Transportation and Parking for Tomorrow's Cities*. New Haven, Conn.

_____. 1969. *Motor Trucks in the Metropolis*. New Haven, Conn.

_____. 1972. "A Peripheral Parking Program, Central City—Los Angeles." Los Angeles: City of Los Angeles Board of Parking Commissioners.

_____. 1981. "Los Angeles Central City Parking Study," Los Angeles.

Wildavsky, Aaron. 1973. "If Planning Is Everything, Maybe It's Nothing." *Policy Sciences* 4, no. 2: 127-53.

_____. 1979. *Speaking Truth to Power*. Boston: Little, Brown and Company.

Williams, Heathcote. 1991. *Autogeddon*. London: Jonathan Cape.

Williams, Jonathan. 2010. "Meter Payment Exemption for Disabled Placard Holders as a Barrier to Managing Curb Parking." Thesis submitted for the degree of Master of Arts in Urban Planning, University of California, Los Angeles. Available at http://shoup.bol.ucla.edu/MeterPaymentExemptionForDisabledPlacardHolders.pdf.

Williams, Norman and John Taylor. 1986. *American Planning Law, Land Use and the Police Power*. Wilmette, Ill.: Callaghan & Company.

Williams, P. Buxton, and Jon Ross. 2003. "Parking as an Engine of Economic Development." *The Parking Professional*, September, 20-24.

Willson, Richard. 1995. "Suburban Parking Requirements: A Tacit Policy for Automobile Use and Sprawl." *Journal of the American Planning Association* 61, no.1: 29-42.

_____. 2000. "Reading between the Regulations: Parking Requirements, Planners' Perspectives, and Transit." *Journal of Public Transportation* 3, no. 1: 111-128.

Wilson, James. 1980. "The Politics of Regulation." In *The Politics of Regulation*, edited by James Q. Wilson. New York: Basic Books, pp. 357-394.

_____. 1997. "Cars and Their Enemies." *Commentary*, July, 17-23.

Wilson, James and George Kelling. 1982. "Broken Windows." *The Atlantic* 249, no. 3 (March): 29-38.

Winston, Clifford, and Chad Shirley. 1998. *Alternate Route*. Washington, D.C.: Brookings Institution Press.

Witheford, David K., and George E. Kanaan. 1972. *Zoning, Parking, and Traf-fic*. Westport, Conn.: Eno Foundation for Transportation.

Wittenberg, Jason. 2002. "Garages: Not Just for Cars Anymore." *Zoning News*, August, 1-5.

_____. 2003. "Parking Standards in the Zoning Code." *Zoning News*, January, 1-4.

Wohl, Martin, and Brian Martin. 1967. *Traffic System Analysis for Engineers and Planners*. New York: McGraw-Hill Book Company.

Wolf, Winfried. 1996. *Car Mania, A Critical History of Transport*. London: Pluto Press.

Wormser, Lisa. 1997. "Don't Even Think of Parking Here." *Planning*, June, 10-14.

Yelling, James. 1977. *Common Field and Enclosure, 1450-1850*. London: Macmillan Press.

Young, Arthur. 1801. "An Inquiry into the Propriety of Applying Wastes to the Better Maintenance and Support of the Poor," *Annals of Agriculture* 36: 497-547.

Yousif, Saad, and Purnawan. 1999. "On-Street Parking: Effects on Traffic Congestion." *Traffic Engineering and Control*

INDEX

Donald Shoup, FAICP, is a professor of urban planning at the University of California, Los Angeles. He holds a doctorate in economics from Yale. From 1996 to 2001, Shoup directed the Institute of Transportation Studies at UCLA and, from 1999 to 2003, he chaired the university's Department of Urban Planning.